S0-AHJ-520

FIVE
FAMILIES

ALSO BY SELWYN RAAB

Mob Lawyer (with Frank Ragano)

Justice in the Back Room

FIVE FAMILIES

UPPER SADDLE RIVER LIBRARY
245 LAKE ST.
UPPER SADDLE RIVER, NJ 07458

The Rise, Decline, and Resurgence of America's Most Powerful Mafia Empires

Selwyn Raab

THOMAS DUNNE BOOKS
St. Martin's Press ❦ New York

THOMAS DUNNE BOOKS.
An imprint of St. Martin's Press.

FIVE FAMILIES. Copyright © 2005 by Selwyn Raab. All rights reserved.
Printed in the United States of America. No part of this book may be
used or reproduced in any manner whatsoever without written permission except in the case of brief quotations embodied in critical articles
or reviews. For information, address St. Martin's Press, 175 Fifth
Avenue, New York, N.Y. 10010.

www.stmartins.com

ISBN 0-312-30094-8
EAN 978-0-312-30094-4

First Edition: September 2005

10 9 8 7 6 5 4 3 2 1

For my parents, William and Berdie,
and my grandson, William Raab Goldstein:
May fortune bestow upon him his namesake's integrity
and zest for life.

Contents

Introduction

Everyone I know in the New York area has brushed up against the American Mafia at one time or another. Most were unaware of it.

Over the greater part of the twentieth century and into the new millennium, the Mafia, aka the Cosa Nostra and the Mob, generated a toxic effect on the lives of all New Yorkers and untold millions of Americans from coast to coast, surreptitiously rifling our pockets and damaging our overall quality of life. Much of the nation unwittingly subsidized in myriad ways the nation's five most powerful and traditional Cosa Nostra organized-crime gangs, all based in New York, who prefer the warmer title of "families."

From their New York headquarters, the families collectively created a vast domain, establishing outposts along the East Coast and in plum spots in Florida, California, and elsewhere. One of their sweetest financial coups was pioneering the secret acquisitions of big-time casinos in Las Vegas, converting a drowsy desert town into an international gambling mecca.

Unquestionably, the gangs known as the Bonanno, Colombo, Gambino, Genovese, and Lucchese crime families evolved into the reigning giants of the underworld. For decades, they alone possessed the authority and veto power to dominate many of the country's other Mafia organizations, reducing some to virtual satellites.

New York—the Cosa Nostra's crown jewel—supported them through indirect "Mob" taxes on the purchases of clothing and basic foods like vegetables, fruit, fish, and meat. They siphoned handsome illegal profits when drivers filled up at gasoline pumps. They controlled waterfront commerce in the country's largest port. They preyed on our garbage, inflating the cost of discarding every piece of refuse from homes and work sites. They cashed in on a billion-dollar construction industry, extracting payoffs from major government and private projects, ranging from courthouses to suburban housing tracts, apartment complexes, hospitals, museums, and skyscrapers. They even profited from their arch law-enforcement enemies by squeezing kickbacks from the builders of new FBI offices, police headquarters, and prisons.

The human cost of the Mafia's depredations and plunder is incalculable. Their chieftains were directly responsible for the widespread introduction of heroin into cities of the East and Midwest in the late 1950s and early '60s. Other less organized criminal groups, witnessing the enormous profits spawned by drug trafficking, followed in their footsteps. But it was the Cosa Nostra's greed for narcotics dollars that accelerated crime rates, law-enforcement corruption, and the erosion of inner-city neighborhoods in New York and throughout the United States.

My first journalistic collision with the Mafia arose from an unexpected quarter — New York City's public school system. That introduction, however, reflected the Mob's insidious influence in so many shadowy areas of big-city existence.

In the early 1960s, my assignment as a new reporter on a major newspaper, the old *New York World-Telegram and The Sun*, was the education beat. I normally wrote about issues like declining reading and mathematics test scores, attempts to unionize teachers, and racial integration disputes — until I was pulled away by a mini scandal concerning shoddy construction and renovations that were endangering the safety of thousands of students and teachers in their classrooms. There was stark evidence of crumbling roofs, walls, floors, electrical fire hazards, and one instance of sewage mixing with drinking water in a high school. All of these violations stemmed from inferior, substandard materials and installations provided for years by a small clique of companies.

Digging into the backgrounds of the building-trades companies unearthed an unwholesome pattern: many firms had unlisted or phantom investors who were "connected" to Mob families. Much of the low bidding competition for lucrative school jobs apparently had been rigged by the Mafia to balloon profits through a gimmick called "changed orders."

School officials responsible for construction and contract oversight were fired or abruptly quit, and negligent contractors were banned from future school work. But not a single mafioso involved in the mess was indicted. The reason: officials retreated, saying there were no clear paper trails incriminating mobsters in money skimming; and no contractor had the courage to testify about the Mob's role in the scandal. In short, the Mafia endangered thousands of children and escaped unscarred, with its loot untouched.

Later as an investigative newspaper and television reporter, I kept running across the Mafia's fingerprints on numerous aspects of government, law enforcement, unions, and everyday life.

There were stories of mobsters introducing and overseeing heroin trafficking in Harlem. Without strong police interference, blue-collar neighborhoods were destabilized and turned into drug souks.

There was the ordeal of George Whitmore, a black teenager framed for a triple murder and wrongly imprisoned for years, with the help of rulings by a judge appointed through the support of Mafia bosses.

There was the exposure of perfectly fit mafiosi obtaining "Disabled Driver" permits that allowed them to park almost anywhere in the congested city. Their redundant "friends" at police headquarters authorized the valuable permits.

There was the chronic intimidation of Fulton Fish Market merchants who were compelled to fork over "protection" payments to mobsters to avoid daily harassment of their business operations.

And, there were the uphill struggles of honest painters, carpenters, and teamsters, who were brutally assaulted when they spoke up at union meetings about mobsters taking over their locals and ripping off their welfare and pension funds.

It required little sagacity for a reporter to determine that, by the 1970s, the Mafia operated as a surrogate state in the New York metropolitan area, brazenly dominating vital businesses and imposing its farrago of invisible surcharges on everyone. In fact, the Mob's economic surge in the second half of the century was astonishing. A government analysis estimated that, in the 1960s, the illicit profit of the nation's twenty-odd Mafia families topped $7 billion annually, approximately the combined earnings of the ten largest industrial corporations in the country. The lion's share of the illicit wealth was reaped by the most powerful segment of the Cosa Nostra conglomerate—the five New York gangs.

For much of the twentieth century New York's municipal and law-enforcement authorities seemed indifferent to these criminal inroads. Questioned in the 1970s about the Mafia's sway, officials privately conceded that previous attempts to dislodge them had been largely futile and there was no public outcry for similar meaningless crackdowns. Then, too, the authorities felt that the public largely tolerated mafiosi as unthreatening to the general population, viewing them as a loosely organized group engaged largely in nonviolent crimes like bookmaking and operating popular neighborhood gambling dens.

The apologists contended that strict regulatory enforcement of the wholesale food, construction, and garbage-carting industries might produce severe economic headaches. City Hall and many law-enforcement agencies tacitly subscribed to a laissez-faire accommodation with the Mob. Almost everyone in power was content so long as food supplies reached restaurants and supermarkets, construction projects were completed, and refuse was picked up on schedule. A consensus decreed that so long as there were no incessant complaints, there was no reason to stir up trouble about mobster involvement in producing basic necessities.

Far too long, the majority of media editors were of a similar mind with officialdom. They preferred reporting on the occasional sensational homicides or internecine Mob wars in place of costly long-range inquiries to document Cosa Nostra's economic clout and its manipulation of municipal agencies. A sizable part of the media preferred glamorizing mobsters as an integral and colorful segment of New York's chaotic texture. Despite their criminal records and suspected participation in multiple murders, John Gotti, Joey Gallo, and Joe Colombo were accorded celebrity status and often portrayed not as merciless killers but as maverick, antiestablishment folk heroes.

Indeed, a commonly recycled story by newspapers and television subtly praised the Mafia, citing its formidable presence for low street-crime rates in predominantly Italian-American sections. With predatory crime soaring, two Mafia strongholds, Manhattan's Little Italy and Brooklyn's Bensonhurst, were presented as safe havens to live in. Unreported and underemphasized were the factors behind these statistics. Significantly, the gangsters relied on sympathetic neighborhood residents to alert them to the presence of probing law-enforcement agents and suspicious outsiders trying to encroach on their bastions. These watchdogs helped turn their neighborhoods into xenophobic enclaves, sometimes resulting in violence against strangers, especially African-Americans and Hispanics.

The legend about security in Mafia-tainted neighborhoods still prevails in the new century. A friend in the suburbs expressed his relief about his daughter's move to New York because she had found an apartment in a safe part of the city—Little Italy—protected by local "Mob guys."

The world of organized crime is totally unlike any other journalistic beat, Accurate, documented data about the Mafia's clandestine activities usually is difficult to verify. The five families never issue annual financial reports, nor do their bosses happily consent to incisive personality profiles. Over more than four decades, I compiled information piecemeal, combing through a variety of public and confidential records, court transcripts, real estate transactions, and files from federal and state law-enforcement agencies obtained through Freedom of Information laws.

There were also interviews with scores of active and former investigators, highlighted by the late Ralph Salerno, whose encyclopedic knowledge and documentation of the American Mafia remains unchallenged.

Then, too, there were the grim details of beleaguered workers resisting Mafia musclemen in control of their unions. Facts about labor rackets were gleaned with the aid of Herman Benson and James F. McNamara, two lifelong advocates of union reform, who could locate witnesses to mobster takeovers of their locals. Benson is a founder of the Association for Union Democracy, the principal national civic organization that aids activists battling corruption and organized-crime infiltration in the labor movement. McNamara, a former union organizer, became an expert consultant on labor racketeering for several law-enforcement agencies.

Persuading admitted mafiosi and their helpmates to talk candidly is never easy. I was fortunate in getting several to unravel the Mafia's mysterious codes and culture and to elucidate the art of surviving in a volatile criminal environment.

One breakthrough in learning about contemporary Cosa Nostra lore and traditions came about obliquely in the early 1980s from a *New York Times* style rule. A mobster named Pellegrino Masselli was a central figure in a high-profile case about alleged Mafia profiteering from a New York City subway project and a mysterious murder. Most of the press delighted in referring to him by his underworld sobriquet, "Butcher Boy." Because the *Times* prohibits the use of pejorative nicknames, my stories always referred to the gangster with an honorific: "Mr. Masselli." Obviously unaware of newspaper etiquette, Masselli, out of the blue, telephoned a compliment for exhibiting proper "respect" to him in print. He also volunteered to be interviewed in his prison cell about the subway deal and the gangland slaying of his son.

That encounter initiated a relationship that lasted until Masselli's death—from natural causes. Over five years, with the proviso that he would never be identified in new stories, Masselli offered tips on Mafia-related developments and enlightenment on ingrained Cosa Nostra customs. He was particularly revealing about the pathological mind-set of his fellow mobsters and how they judged one another's conduct. Committing murder might be a horrific act for a normal person, but Masselli explained that a committed mafioso is unperturbed by violence. Moreover, he is applauded by his bosses and colleagues as long as "the piece of work is done professionally and competently," even if a "hit" requires killing a good friend.

A lengthy on-the-record interview with another admitted mafioso, Anthony Accetturo, provided unique insight into a veteran Cosa Nostra's experiences and thinking. A longtime "capo," the head of a crew or unit in New Jersey, Accetturo, after being imprisoned for racketeering, agreed to be questioned and to reminisce freely about his Mob career and his dealings with important mafiosi.

Compelling information about the Mafia's white-collar activities on Wall Street and other financial crimes came from a Cosa Nostra "associate," or helper. Proclaiming himself "rehabilitated," he described various schemes inaugurated to fleece investors when the Mafia capitalized on the 1990s stock market mania. His explanation for coming clean was a desire to appease his conscience and to prevent future suckers from being snared in organized-crime financial traps. Whatever his reasons, the information proved to be accurate. To protect him from retaliation, his identity must remain undisclosed.

In the last years of his life, Frank Ragano, a self-described "Mob lawyer," offered an in-depth narrative of sordid legal and social relationships with prominent mobsters. Before he died, Ragano vowed to atone for ethical shortcomings that led him to defend the Cosa Nostra in court and behind the scenes. Belatedly, he acknowledged that ambition drove him to represent the Mafia as a fast track to wealth and recognition as an important attorney. He supplied unprecedented material on the personalities and machinations of his top clients, two powerful Southern bosses, Santo Trafficante and Carlos Marcello, and their contentious ally, teamsters' union chief Jimmy Hoffa. He also knew intimate details of the Mob's hatred and death wishes for President John F. Kennedy and his brother Robert.

These recent accounts by Mafia insiders and a legion of defectors, combined with a trove of intelligence reports from the FBI and other law-enforcement agencies, have contributed immensely to the history and comprehension of an underworld phenomenon. The collective goal of the five families of New York was the pillaging of the nation's richest city and region. This is the saga of how they did it.

FIVE FAMILIES

A Fiery Saint

"If I betray my friends and our family, I and my soul will burn in hell like this saint."

As Tony Accetturo recited this grave oath, the holy picture in his hand perished in flames. A cluster of nodding, stone-faced men lined up to embrace him, kiss him on the cheek, and vigorously shake his hand, a collective gesture of solemn congratulations. For Accetturo, it was the most memorable moment of his life. The ceremony burnt into his soul; his prime ambition was fulfilled. He was now the newest member of an exclusive, secret coterie: he was a "made" man in the American Mafia.

Twenty years of faithful service, first as a stern loan-shark enforcer and later as a major "earner," moneymaker, for important mobsters in New Jersey, had paid off bountifully for Accetturo. Earlier that afternoon, he intuitively grasped that this day would be significant. His orders were to rendezvous with Joe Abate, a reclusive figure who rarely met face-to-face with underlings, even though their lucrative extortion, gambling, and loan-sharking rackets enriched him. Abate, a sagacious *capo* in a *borgata* or *brugard*—Mafia slang for a criminal gang that is derived from the Sicilian word for a close-knit community or hamlet—supervised all operations in New Jersey for the Lucchese crime family.

Abate was waiting for Accetturo at a prearranged spot in the bustling Port Authority Bus Terminal in Midtown Manhattan. As a capo or captain, Abate was the impresario for more than one hundred gangsters, who illegally harvested millions of dollars every year for themselves and, as a tithe, sent a portion of their earnings to the administration, the Lucchese family leaders across the Hudson River in New York. Already in his mid-seventies, Abate bore no resemblance to a pensioner. Tall, lean, almost ramrod erect, he greeted Accetturo with a perfunctory handshake and walked briskly from the bus terminal.

On that June afternoon in 1976, there was little conversation as Accetturo, almost forty years younger than his capo, quickened his pace to keep in step with the energetic older man. Accetturo, a strapping, muscular two hundred pounds on a five-feet eight-inch frame, knew from a bitter encounter with Abate never to initiate small talk with him. Among New Jersey mafiosi, Joe Abate was a feared presence, a veteran combatant with an exalted aura. He had been a gunslinger for Al Capone in Chicago when Capone was America's most notorious gangster in the 1920s. And in Abate's presence, it was prudent to answer his questions directly and to carry out his commands without hesitation.

Several blocks from the bus terminal, at a clothing factory in Manhattan's Garment Center, Abate introduced Accetturo to a grim-faced man who would drive them to another location. He was Andimo "Tom" Pappadio, an important soldier responsible for handling the Lucchese's extensive labor extortions, bookmaking, and loan-sharking rackets in the Garment Center. Like the brief walk to the Garment District, the thirty-minute drive was a silent trip until they pulled up in front of a simple frame house. Unfamiliar with much of New York, Accetturo thought they were in the Bronx, the borough just north of Manhattan.

Inside a drab living room, several men unknown to Accetturo were waiting and one of them introduced himself as Tony Corallo. Accetturo knew that in the insular planet of the Mafia, this unsmiling, short, stocky man in his sixties was widely recognized by another name, "Tony Ducks." And he keenly understood what that name represented. Antonio Corallo, whose nickname originated from a lifetime of evading arrests and subpoenas, was the boss of the entire Lucchese family. The small group of men were gathered in the living room for one reason: a secret ceremony that would transform Accetturo into a "Man of Honor," a full-fledged "made" man.

Tony Accetturo was aware that "the books," membership rosters in New York's five Mafia families, had been closed for twenty years. Recently, whispers abounded that the rolls finally were being reopened for deserving people. Accetturo had agonized over his future, eager to end his long apprenticeship with coveted membership as a "soldier."

"Making your bones," the Mafia euphemism for passing its entrance examination, requires participating in a violent crime — often murder — or becoming a big earner for the family. Accetturo was confident that he had made his bones with high marks in both categories.

Accetturo had heard older men drop hints about the ritual of getting made. He had a vague idea that it involved incantation of ancient oaths of loyalty, sworn over a gun, a knife, a saint's picture, and validated by bloodletting through a cut trigger finger. Yet when his ceremony was over, Accetturo was surprised and slightly disappointed by its brevity.

Without preamble, Tony Ducks rose from his chair in the living room, said, "Let's get started," and then bluntly told Accetturo that he was the "boss" of the family. Accetturo was handed a picture of a saint on a square piece of paper, told to burn it with a match, and to repeat the oath Corallo somberly intoned: "If I betray my friends and our family, I and my soul will burn in hell like this saint."

Despite the abruptness and informality of the rite, Accetturo glowed inwardly with enthusiasm at its meaningfulness. "I was bursting with excitement. It was the greatest honor of my life. They set me apart from ordinary people. I was in a secret society that I was aching to be part of since I was a kid, from the time I was a teenager."

Soon afterward, returning to his haunts in New Jersey, Accetturo learned from older made men, who could now talk openly with him because he had attained prized membership, the reason for the brusque initiation. Abate and other overseers in the Lucchese family thought so highly of his accomplishments and behavior that the trappings used to inculcate ordinary recruits were deemed unnecessary. He already knew the ground rules and was considered far superior and more knowledgeable of the Mafia's code of conduct than most new soldiers. There was no question that he was suited for "the life."

Over the next two decades, Accetturo would himself witness and learn from his underworld cronies how a more typical induction was performed by the American Mafia in the late twentieth and early twenty-first centuries. The ritual, modeled on secret practices with religious undertones begun by the Mafia in Sicily as far back as the nineteenth century, was intended to mark the vital passage from "wannabe," an associate in the crime family, a mere striver without prestige, to a restricted rank with extraordinary dividends and extraordinary obligations.

While the liturgy was roughly similar throughout the country, in the New York area, the American Mafia's acknowledged capital, a rigid formula prevailed among its five long-established gangs. The candidate had to be sponsored by the capo he would work for and personally cleared by the ultimate leader, the family *representante*, or boss. The final exam was the submission of the proposed soldier's identity to the leaders of the other four borgatas for vetting to determine if there were any black marks or negative information against him. To maintain the fixed sizes and strength of the families and to prevent unauthorized expansions, a prospective member could only be added to replace a dead mafioso in his borgata.

Although probably surmising that his induction loomed, the recruit was never specifically told what was in store or the date he would be "straightened out," promoted. On short notice he was instructed to "get dressed," meaning wear a suit and tie, for an unspecified assignment. Made members picked up and escorted the initiate to the ordination. Driving to the site, a process known as "cleaning" or "dry cleaning," was often employed to evade possible law-enforcement surveillance. The passengers might switch cars in public garages. They also drove aimlessly for as long as half an hour and then "squared blocks," driving slowly with abrupt sharp turns, or reversed directions to shake investigators who might be tailing them on routine surveillance.

The special precautions were intended to conceal the meeting place from prying eyes, mainly because the family's boss and other high-ranking leaders would be in attendance and protecting them from law-enforcement snoops was a paramount consideration.

Unlike the ceremony he conducted for Accetturo, at most inductions Tony Ducks Corallo officiated with greater pomp and formality. "Do you know why you are here?" he would ask at the outset, and the candidate was expected to reply untruthfully, "No." This charade was enacted because the induction was presumed to be a closely guarded secret to prevent leaks to law-enforcement investigators and outsiders about the identities of the family's leaders and its members.

Continuing, Tony Ducks explained, "You are going to be part of this family. Do you have any objections to that?"

Another member of the group circling the ceremonial table would then use a needle, knife, or safety pin to prick the candidate's trigger finger, dropping blood over a picture of a saint. As the candidate held the bloody image aloft, someone put a match to it, and Tony Ducks directed the new member to repeat, "May I burn, may my soul burn like this paper, if I betray anyone in this family or anyone in this room."

After scattering the ashes of the saint's holy picture, Corallo or one of his lieutenants warned the newly made man that henceforth the borgata's needs — including committing murders — came before any other obligation in his life. The initiate no longer owed allegiance to God, country, wife, children, or close relatives, only to the crime family. Decrees from the boss, who ruled as the family's "father," must instantly be obeyed, even if it meant neglecting a dying child.

At the ceremony for Tommy Ricciardi, a longtime sidekick of Accetturo's, Tony Ducks and his henchmen carefully enumerated the family and the Mafia's inviolable rules and protocol. The foremost principle was *omertà*, the code of silence that forbade the slightest cooperation with law enforcement, or more ominously, informing, ratting on anyone in the underworld.

A new "button man," or soldier, remained under the direct control of the capo who recommended his membership. All illegal activities the soldier engaged in and even his legal businesses were "put on record" or "registered" with the family through his capo so that the organization could profit from these projects and utilize them for planning crimes and deals. Booty from legal and illegal activities was shared with the soldier's capo; a percentage, depending on the mood of the boss, was funneled to him as a sign of respect and was used also for the borgata's needs and overhead costs.

In business or social matters, only a made man from the Lucchese family and other borgatas could be introduced to other mafiosi as an *amico nostro*, a friend of ours. Others associated or working with the Mob were referred to simply as "a friend," or "my friend," as a cautionary signal that the third man was not made and no Mafia secrets should be discussed in his presence.

And the awesome word "Mafia" was banished from the group's vocabulary. Its use, even in private conversations, was forbidden because it could be considered incriminating evidence at trials if overheard by prosecution witnesses or detected by investigators through electronic eavesdropping. Instead, if an organizational name had to be mentioned, the more innocent sounding Cosa Nostra, Our Thing, or the initials C.N. were used.

Despite any knowledge the recruit might possess at the time of his initiation, he was nevertheless formally instructed about the composition and powers of the family hierarchy. At the summit, the boss set policies as to what crimes and rackets the family would engage in and appointed and removed capos and other high-ranking leaders.

Like an imperial caesar, the boss's most terrifying arbitrary authority was deciding who lived and died. Murders inside the family for internal reasons or the elimination of anyone outside the borgata could be sanctioned only by him.

Usually present at induction ceremonies were the "underboss," the second-in-command, who assisted in running the family's day-to-day business, and the *consigliere*, the counselor and adviser on family matters and on relations and disputes with other Mafia groups.

At Lucchese inductions, the identities of the bosses of New York's four other large Mafia families (Genovese, Gambino, Bonanno, and Colombo) and a smaller one (DeCavalcante) based in New Jersey were disclosed to the new soldier. This confidential information came with the admonition that if another family boss was encountered he should be accorded the utmost respect.

Finally, several New York families concluded their ceremony with a *ticada*, Italian for "tie-in" or a "tack-up." To demonstrate the internal solidarity of their secret organization, all witnesses and the new member clasped hands to unite in what the boss declared "the unbreakable knot of brotherhood."

Alphonso D'Arco's big day in the Lucchese family was August 23, 1982. He was instructed to "get dressed, you're going somewhere" by his capo, picked up at a street corner in Manhattan's Little Italy section, and like Tony Accetturo driven to a modest home in the Bronx. Four other candidates sat in the parlor, waiting to be summoned into another room, a kitchen. When D'Arco's turn came, he was introduced to Tony Ducks Corallo and other members of the administration seated around a table.

"Do you know why you're here?" one of the men asked, and D'Arco dutifully replied, "No."

"You're going to be part of this family," the man continued. "If you're asked to kill somebody, would you do it?"

D'Arco nodded his assent and then his trigger finger was pricked and the saint's picture burned. One of the men surrounding the table removed a towel that covered a gun and a knife lying on the table. "You live by the gun and the knife and you die by the gun and knife if you betray anyone in this room," the speaker said somberly. Finally, D'Arco repeated a version of the Mafia's holy oath: "If I betray my friends and my family, may my soul burn in hell like this saint."

Later, when the ceremony for all of the recruits was completed, Ducks Corallo rose and asked everyone to *attaccata*, to tack or tie up by holding hands. "*La fata di questa famiglia sono aperti*," Corallo announced, meaning the affairs of this family are open. He then lectured his new soldiers on basic principles, precepts etched in D'Arco's memory.

"We were told not to deal in narcotics, counterfeit money, or stolen stocks and bonds, to respect the families or other members and not to fool around with other members' wives or daughters. If any disputes arise that you and members cannot resolve, you must go to your captain. You do not put your hands on other family members. You are to maintain yourself with respect at all times. When your captain calls, no matter what time or day or night, you must respond immediately. This family comes before your own family. Above all, you do not discuss anything about this family with members of other families. If you do not abide by these rules, you will be killed."

Another unbreakable rule was imposed by Corallo: police and other law-enforcement agents could never be "whacked," killed.

"Whatever happened here tonight is never to be talked about," Corallo warned. Instructing the group to once more tack up, he finished in Italian: "*La fata di questa famiglia sono chiuso.*" ("The affairs of this family are now closed.")

The afternoon event ended on a nonalcoholic, sober note with coffee, simple snacks, and pastry offered the men before the old hands and freshly minted mobsters dispersed in small groups.

D'Arco would learn that Corallo banned involvement in narcotics and counterfeiting and stealing stocks and bonds because these were federal offenses and meant heavy prison time. Corallo, like other Mob leaders, had good reasons to prevent hits on law-enforcement personnel. Murdering a cop, an investigator, or a prosecutor would unleash the fury of the law against the Mob and make normal business hazardous. Furthermore, the rule was aimed at maintaining strict discipline and preventing rash, unauthorized acts by hot-headed troops.

The day after the induction ceremony, D'Arco was the guest of honor at a select dinner with other crew members, given by his capo. It was an occasion for him and the twenty-odd members of his crew to be introduced to one another as equals. D'Arco's new companions laughingly explained to him what would have occurred if he had refused at the Bronx ceremony to accept membership in the borgata: He would have been killed on the spot. His refusal would have been proof that he was an agent or an informer trying to infiltrate the family.

In the early days of his membership, more Cosa Nostra customs and rules were passed on to him by older soldiers. Some shibboleths were strange, particularly those concerning grooming and wardrobe. New York's Mob leaders frowned on soldiers growing mustaches or wearing fabrics containing the color red. Mustaches were considered ostentatious and red was looked upon as too flashy by the conservatively dressed hierarchs. Inexplicably, some Mob big shots also believed that red garments were favored by "rats," squealers.

Although they were always under the thumb of a capo and the administration's kingpins, there were enormous potential benefits for loyal, ambitious soldiers like Al D'Arco and Tony Accetturo. A made man automatically had greater respect, prestige, and money-making opportunities. For starters, he was entitled to a larger share of the loot from his criminal activities than had been doled out to him as a wannabe or an "associate," someone who works or cooperates with the family. And the newcomer became eligible for a cut of the profits from other family-controlled rackets.

Another gift to a soldier was the authority to organize and exploit his own wannabes in illegal activities. Most associates aspired to become made men, but only those of Sicilian or Italian ancestry were eligible. At one time, nearly all the families would induct only men whose mother and father were Italian. Eventually, the requirement was eased: as long as the father's roots were Italian an applicant was eligible. Regardless of his value to the borgata, an associate without Italian heritage—even if he served as a hit man committing murders on demand or was a major earner—could never gain admission. A non-Italian might be highly respected but would never be acknowledged as equal to the lowest-ranking mafioso.

Equally important, as long as a soldier complied with the Mafia's code of conduct, the family's financial and legal connections were available. If he got into a jam and was arrested, the family paid for expensive legal talent. If a made man wound up in prison, the borgata's family administration or his capo were expected to support his wife and children.

For loyalty and service to the family in a violent, dangerous environment, there was yet another vital bequest: a life insurance policy. A made man could be killed only on the orders of his boss and only for a serious infraction of a Mafia rule. Others who worked for a borgata or who were involved in deals with mafiosi lacked comparable protection. They could be whacked or maimed at the whim of a made man if a conflict arose between them. A soldier had the added security of knowing that other criminals who suspected or were aware of his connections feared injuring or insulting him; the lethal retaliatory power of the organization was well known in the underworld.

Joining the Mafia in the mid and late twentieth century was arduous and hazardous, but there was no shortage of applicants; and for recruits like Tony Accetturo, full membership glittered as a prize with outstanding financial rewards.

2

Tumac's Tale

Anthony Accetturo's attachment to the Mafia's code of honor was a passport to underworld glory and respect. It eventually brought him a high rank in the Mob's upper echelons and turned him into a multimillionaire.

His early life, however, did not augur success in any field. One of six children born to immigrant Sicilian parents, Accetturo grew up in the 1940s and early '50s in Orange, a scruffy blue-collar suburb of Newark, New Jersey. His father, Angelo, a butcher and the owner of Accetturo's Meat Market, tried unsuccessfully to interest Tony in his legitimate trade. The youngster preferred perfecting his talents in pool halls.

He had no interest in education, becoming a chronic truant after the sixth grade, and his parents, who placed little value on traditional education, consented to an early departure from school when he was sixteen. Barely out of his teens, the boy was sent to live with relatives in Newark, where he established himself as a fearsome scrapper in an Italian-American street gang of fifty to sixty young roughnecks. At sixteen, his reputation was enshrined when he brandished a crutch to batter an opponent unconscious, earning him the nickname "Tumac." The name, based on the rugged caveman hero played by Victor Mature in a 1940 movie, *One Million B.C.*, delighted the young Accetturo, and he adopted it as a lifelong sobriquet.

When not brawling, Accetturo largely supported himself by "popping," breaking open and stealing coins from jukeboxes and cigarette-vending machines, unleashing a small-time crime wave that disturbed neighborhood merchants, and more important, a local big shot, Anthony "Ham" Delasco. A former professional boxer, Delasco summoned the teenager for a disciplinary lecture. From street talk and from his own observations of the deep respect accorded Delasco in the neighborhood, Accetturo knew he was encountering a substantial made man. "Those machines belong to me," Delasco said menacingly. "I want this bullshit to stop."

Delasco also saw potential in the aggressive seventeen-year-old and gave him a $75-a-week job. The teenager's duties were to assist in running Delasco's "numbers," an illegal lottery gambling game, and using his brawn to collect debts and payments in his "shylocking," loan-sharking operations.

Accetturo readily signed on and the wily mobster soon curbed his acolyte's independent streak while teaching him an elementary Mafia lesson. "Go get me an ice cream," Delasco one day ordered Accetturo as the young man stood with a group of admiring friends on a street corner. The embarrassed Accetturo knew he would be demeaned in front of his pals if he acted as an errand boy. But understanding that Delasco was testing his obedience, he bought his boss the ice cream.

"I knew that if I wanted to stay with Ham and learn from him, he had to have absolute control over me," Accetturo explained. "He had to break me and I took the bit in my mouth."

Accetturo became a prize pupil for Delasco and later for other mafiosi who replaced Delasco after his death. Tumac's only slip-up as a wannabe occurred when he delivered a package stuffed with cash to Joe Abate, the austere capo. It was Abate's monthly share of the proceeds from the Lucchese family's Newark branch, and he was sitting alone in a parked car awaiting his payoff.

Eager to ingratiate himself with Abate, whom he had not previously met, young Accetturo remarked how honored he was to be in his presence. Abate icily ordered him out of the car and sped off. Three hours later, Accetturo was blisteringly reprimanded by an older mobster, Lenny Pizzolata, whom Abate had called.

"Who the fuck are you to start a conversation with Joe Abate?" Pizzolata barked. "If you want to stay alive, never mention his name and speak only when you are spoken to."

Except for that single mistake, during the 1950s and '60s Accetturo advanced smoothly in the borgata. He dramatically proved his mettle in the late '60s when Newark's African-American population increased sharply and black criminals began forcefully taking over numbers territories from white bookies. Bolstered by Accetturo and his handpicked gang of armed goons, the Lucchese faction held on to its stake in the numbers games. Police intelligence officials determined that Accetturo had smashed attempted incursions into Lucchese domains by a gang of militant Black Panthers. Although no homicide charges were brought, the police suspected that Accetturo's unit was responsible for several murders committed to maintain Mafia dominance.

In 1979 the seventy-seven-year-old Abate was slowing down and went into semiretirement. Ducks Corallo did not hesitate to anoint Accetturo as his New Jersey capo, promoting Tumac over older soldiers who earlier had been his tutors. Accetturo quickly demonstrated his administrative skills. He enlarged the family's traditional gambling, loan-sharking, and narcotics-trafficking schemes and began dabbling in labor racketeering. Through strong-arm tactics, the New Jersey crew gained control of corrupt union officials, clearing the way for the milking of employee welfare funds and threatening companies with Mob-enforced work stoppages unless payoffs were supplied for labor peace.

The new capo expanded the family's operations to Florida, where he nurtured similar criminal ventures in the Miami area and, as a sideline, fixed horse races. Accetturo's underworld successes allowed him to invest and become a partner in seemingly legitimate real estate, insurance, equipment rental, and other enterprises in New Jersey, Florida, and North Carolina. He maintained homes in each of the three states and planned to retire in North Carolina, where he posed as a respectable businessman.

His fortune grew so immense that he boasted of having stashed about $7 million in one-thousand-dollar bills, gems, gold, and rare coins as an emergency nest egg, in a safe concealed in a vault behind a bathroom vanity cabinet. While the riches flowed in, Accetturo thrived in the shadows, a relatively obscure mafioso, his name and importance largely unknown except to a handful of New Jersey law-enforcement experts on organized crime.

When sporadic problems with the law arose, Tumac could afford costly legal talent to get him suspended sentences or jail terms of only a few months for serious felonies. He had the money and the contacts for a $100,000 bribe to a juror to win acquittals for himself and twenty members of his New Jersey crew tried on racketeering charges. On another occasion, his stable of lawyers obtained a dismissal on charges against him of intimidating a vital witness in an assault case. In Florida a thorny conspiracy indictment was overcome by finding psychiatrists who classified him as mentally unfit to stand trial. The diagnosis of presenile dementia, early Alzheimer's disease, was a total fraud. "I slipped and banged my head in the shower and the Alzheimer's went away," he told friends, grinning unabashedly.

For almost four decades, the Mafia—the Cosa Nostra—with its sordid deals, violence, and murders, was an existence Accetturo accepted and cherished. He considered a Mafia life so admirable and worthwhile that he welcomed one of his two sons into the fold as a made man in his crew.

Engraved in his mind was the day he held the flaming picture of a saint in his hand, swearing eternal allegiance to the borgata that embraced him. Even before his induction, he understood that the most unforgivable transgression a made man could commit was violating *omertà*, the code of silence. The penalty for informing was usually a bullet in the back of the apostate's head, and Accetturo never doubted that such executions were deserved.

But after a lifetime of loyalty, Tumac, the renowned, dreaded capo, the quintessential Mafia success, renounced *omertà* and other principles he once lived by. He became a traitor. To prosecutors, to investigators, he disclosed criminal secrets from decades of intrigue. His words exposed dozens of mobsters who had followed and obeyed him as their trusted commander. Moreover, his defection symbolized an unprecedented malaise afflicting the Cosa Nostra. *Omertà* and the other maxims that for seventy years had shielded Accetturo and other self-appointed Men of Honor were being undermined by relentless internal and external forces.

As the twenty-first century dawned, the Cosa Nostra was imperiled as never before. During the previous century the Mafia had forged a unique and almost unassailable criminal organization in America. And much of its frightening power arose from an arcane legacy transported to urban America from provincial Sicily.

3

Roots

To the casual traveler, Sicily for centuries was an enchanted land, one of the most pleasant places on earth to live. It was comforting to be seduced by the island's inordinately gracious people, sunny weather, alluring palm trees, and the delicate fragrance of its orange and lemon blossoms.

But those intoxicating, superficial impressions were largely a mirage. For over two thousand years, most of Sicily's population endured tyranny and suppression under foreign conquerors and feudal overlords. From ancient times until the mid-nineteenth century, the nine-thousand-square-mile island was raided, invaded, and even traded—actually exchanged for other territories—by foreign rulers. Sicily's strategic and vulnerable location, almost in the center of the Mediterranean Sea, close to southern Italy and North Africa, subjected it to an endless succession of occupation and oppression by Phoenicians, Greeks, Etruscans, Carthaginians, Romans, Byzantines, Normans, Arabs, French, Spanish, Austrian, and finally hostile Italian armies.

Sicilians survived these occupations by developing a culture rooted in two basic concepts: contempt for and suspicion of governmental authorities; and tight-knit alliances with blood relatives and with fellow countrymen facing the same perils.

Analyzing the fundamental siege mentality of large numbers of Sicilians from the vantage point of the twentieth century, Luigi Barzini, in his book *The Italians*, observed: "They are taught in the cradle, or are born already knowing, that they must aid each other, side with their friends and fight the common enemy even when the friends are wrong and the enemies are right; each must defend his dignity at all costs and never allow the smallest slights and insults to go unavenged; they must keep secrets, and always beware of official authorities and laws."

Over time, these historical and cultural underpinnings spawned furtive clans, in Sicilian dialect, *cosche*, for self-preservation against perceived corrupt oppressors. Without the security of reliable public institutions to protect them or their property, the clans, which were mainly in the countryside, relied on stealth, compromise, and vendetta to extract private justice.

Eventually, the secret *cosche* became commonly labeled in Sicily by a single name: Mafia. Over hundreds of years, they evolved from guerrilla-like, disorganized bands for self-defense into greedy, terrifying gangs, whose basic concepts and guiding principles would extend, with profound influence, far across the seas to America.

Like much of the Sicilian Mafia's roots, the origin of its name is cloaked in folklore and mystique. A romantic legend maintains that the name was born in the late thirteenth century during an uprising against French Angevin forces in Palermo, Sicily's main city. According to this tale, a Sicilian woman died resisting rape by a French soldier and, in revenge, her fiancé slaughtered the attacker. The fanciful episode supposedly sparked the creation of a rebellious, acronymic slogan from the first letter of each word: "*Morte alla Francia Italia anela*" ("Death to France is Italy's cry"). A revolt against the French occupation army in 1282 was called the Sicilian Vespers, because the signal for resistance was the ringing of church bells for evening prayers.

A less romantic and more likely derivation of the name *Mafia* is a combined Sicilian-Arabic slang expression that means acting as a protector against the arrogance of the powerful. Until the nineteenth century, the appellation *mafioso*, a Mafia member, had wide currency in Sicily as a noncriminal, resolute man with congenital distrust of centralized authority.

"A mafioso did not invoke State or law in his private quarrels, but made himself respected and safe by winning a reputation for toughness and courage, and settled his differences by fighting," the English historian Eric J. Hobsbawm noted. "He recognized no obligation except those of the code of honor or *omertà* (manliness), whose chief article forbade giving information to public authorities."

To a nineteenth-century Sicilian with a cultural heritage of centuries of danger and oppression, true manhood was said to consist of an independent arrogance in which a man kept silent in the event of a crime. The Sicilian reserved the right of personal *vendetta*, vengeance, for offenses committed against himself and his relatives.

Mafia clans never functioned under a united, centralized command for the entire island. They sprung up as regional bands organized primarily to protect specific local interests from foreign aggressors and intruders from other regions of Sicily. As late as the mid-nineteenth century, mafiosi were portrayed by some writers as patriotic partisans who had defended and upheld the island's hallowed traditions. The clans were also called "families," with the leader of each referred to as *padrino*, father, or as the *capo di famiglia*, the autocratic chief of the family who arbitrated disputes and controversies in his extended group.

In 1860 Giuseppe Garibaldi, a military hero of the Risorgimento, the movement to unify Italy, landed in Sicily with a thousand volunteer fighters immortalized as "Red Shirts" for their distinctive military attire. Aided by popular support on the island, Garibaldi easily defeated the troops of the King of the Two Sicilies, and the last Spanish Bourbon monarch was deposed.

Among the rebels who rallied to Garibaldi's army and his call for social justice were about two thousand roughhewn farmers from the countryside who, as economic conditions warranted, alternated between working the fields and holing up in caves as bandits. Symbolizing the respect afforded to these part-time peasants and part-time brigands, they were glorified by Garibaldi as his "*Squadri della Mafia*," Mafia squadron.

A year after Garibaldi's landing and lightning military victory, Sicily—an area about the size of Vermont—was incorporated as a province into the newly formed state of Italy. In 1863 a play appeared in Sicily titled *I Mafiosi della Vicaria*, translated in English as "Heroes of the Penitentiary." The mafiosi in the drama were oppressed but valiant patriots and prisoners who showed their physical audacity in knife duels. The play toured Sicily and Italy and the performances were instrumental in introducing the words *Mafia* and *mafiosi* into the common language of Italy. An Italian dictionary from 1868 defined "mafia" in noncriminal terms as denoting "bravado."

Within a decade, however, liberation and the removal of the old pillars of authority brought widespread disorder and rampant crime to the island. These conditions created fertile prospects for the best-organized Mafia *cosche*, which could mobilize small private watchdog armies. They took advantage of the turmoil and the judicial and governmental vacuums by turning to subtle forms of criminal activities. During a period of little law or order, the *cosche* demanded systematic payments from wealthy landholders and businessmen to safeguard their properties from vandals and to protect them and their relatives from abductions and ransom demands.

Oddly, to restore a semblance of law and order, the new national government in the 1870s enlisted the clans to help capture the most violent non-Mafia bandits. These roving marauders were terrorizing the island and were viewed as a criminal epidemic, threatening public safety and Sicily's economic stability.

As a reward for the Mafia's aid, the nascent government in Rome secretly pledged that the *cosche* could continue without interference their own refined style of plunder and economic domination over sections of Sicily. The Rome officials, mainly from north and central Italy, were unfamiliar with the nuances of Sicilian culture and viewed the private deal as an expedient compromise. Overconfident, they believed the Mafia leaders would serve as temporary middlemen between themselves and the island's population, and would help to maintain order until the young constitutional monarchy gained the strength to impose its own will.

The arrangement, however, gave a virtual license and a new impetus to Mafia families. The strongest clans were in northwestern Sicily near Palermo; they began functioning openly and more brazenly, without any thought of relinquishing their privileged positions.

Italy's unification and new government led to the breakup of many of Sicily's feudal estates and a measure of economic freedom. These additional opportunities were seized upon by the Mafia groups. With the weak central government looking the other way, the clans, in effect, became a substitute, extra-legal government, especially in remote rural areas. Through hints of violence, the families began extorting payoffs from new and absentee landowners to insure that crops were harvested. They initiated similar shakedowns from merchants in cities and towns, promising to use their influence to ward off harassment from the government, particularly tax collectors.

The Catholic Church became a willing collaborator with various *cosche*, relying on them to safeguard its vast land holdings on the island and to stifle peasant demands for land or for larger payments as tenant farmers. Grateful for the protection, church leaders refrained from denouncing the mafiosi's strong-arm tactics.

When it suited a clan "father," he could simply authorize his mafiosi to cheaply acquire or monopolize profitable businesses the family wanted to possess. The families might pretend that they served as benefactors, protectors, and dispensers of justice to powerless peasants and small merchants, but their basic goal was self-enrichment.

Any assistance a Mafia family provided to individuals in business or in land disputes came with a price tag. Sooner or later, the recipient of the favor might be asked in a none too subtle manner to perform some deed—a legal or illegal quid pro quo—as compensation for the family's aid.

Unification gave Sicilian men the right to elect representatives to a national parliament and local offices. This democratic reform also was a boon to the clans. Through intimidation and control of blocs of voters, the mafiosi helped elect numerous politicians, who as a result were indebted to them and under their sway.

After Italy's unification, in Sicily the most prevalent image of the typical mafiosi was that of the unsparing enforcer with a *lupara*, a sawed-off shotgun, slung over his shoulder, eager to exact Mafia-style justice.

In the late nineteenth century, the strongest *cosche* sought to solidify their power and resist encroachments from rival families by adopting a new practice: the ritual of the loyalty blood oath of *omertà*. Once inducted, a new member considered himself in the select ranks of the *onorato società*, or honored society, and as a "Man of Honor" and "Man of Respect" he could mockingly boast, "The King of Italy might rule the island but men of my tradition govern it."

The ambivalent reverence and fear inspired by each clan was epitomized by the Sicilian folklore authority and supernationalist Giuseppe Pitre: "Mafia is the force of the individual, intolerance toward the arrogance of others," Pitre wrote misguidedly at the turn of the century. "Mafia unites the idea of beauty with superiority and valor in the best sense of the word, and sometimes more awareness of being a man, sureness of soul and audacity but never arrogance, never haughtiness."

Risorgimento brought a new form of government but not prosperity to millions of landless peasants and impoverished laborers in southern Italy and Sicily. The nineteenth-century and early-twentieth-century open-door immigration policies of the United States became a magnet for Italians, especially rural Sicilians seeking to escape the economic and social hardships of their native land.

Between 1890 and 1920, an estimated four million Italian and Sicilian immigrants settled in America. The vast majority were law-abiding artisans, farmers, and unskilled toilers. But, as in every large ethnic immigrant category, sprinkled in were criminals, men on the run from the law who were aware of the Mafia's traditions, and men who were minor mafiosi, seeking new opportunities or fleeing vendettas.

At the time of this immigration wave, none of the Sicilian *cosche* tried to establish beachheads or branches in the United States. After all, there was no need. In Sicily, the Mafia families were among the favored "haves," not the downtrodden "have-nots." They had no reason to relinquish their enviable, comfortable station in life for risky ventures in a foreign land.

New Orleans was one of the earliest American ports of call for Italian immigrants. They arrived on ships called "lemon boats" because the vessels carried citrus fruits as well as passengers from Sicily and southern Italy.

In the history of the American Mafia, New Orleans accidentally became the Cosa Nostra's Plymouth Rock, the setting for the first Sicilian and southern Italian gangsters in America. They were petty criminals who imitated the tactics of the original Mafia, even employing the name of the secret society. Eventually, their descendants and successors became an authentic American Mafia family.

By 1890, more than one thousand Italian immigrants lived in New Orleans, and two violent gangs fought for control of the port's stevedoring business. At the height of the feud, Chief of Police David Hennessey, who was suspected of taking bribes from one of the factions, was shot and killed. The murder infuriated a large group of vigilantes who lynched sixteen Italian men, several of whom had been charged with complicity in the police chief's slaying.

The grand jury that investigated the affair produced the first documented recognition that some form of the Mafia had arrived in the United States, and spotlighted the difficulties in unearthing information about this obscure entity. In a report, the jury in 1891 declared: "The range of our researches has developed the existence of the secret organization styled 'Mafia.' The evidence comes from several sources fully competent in themselves to attest its truth, while the fact is supported by the long record of bloodcurdling crimes, it being almost impossible to discover the perpetrators or to secure witnesses."

Although New Orleans witnessed the country's first incident of Mafia infiltration, it was to northeastern cities like New York that the masses of Sicilian and Italian immigrants gravitated. In addition, in the early 1900s mafiosi imitators and other predators also flocked there. These thugs preyed on their own apprehensive countrymen, who were adapting to a different language and different customs and who were distrustful of American law-enforcement authorities.

In the early stages of Italian immigration, the police in New York and in other large eastern cities often confused the Mafia with individuals and gangs operating under the name of "*La Mano Nero*," or the Black Hand. The Black Hand, which had no direct relationship with the Mafia, referred to a crude technique of random extortion used by individuals and small gangs. It was not an organization. The extortionists would deliver letters, mainly to businessmen and shopkeepers in Italian neighborhoods, warning them of dire injuries or death if they failed to pay bribes for their continued safety. To magnify the intimidation, a frightening symbol—the picture of a black hand, fringed by a knife and skull—was imprinted on each letter.

Faced with soaring crime and murder rates in Italian sections, the New York Police Department in 1883 recruited its first Italian-speaking officer, Giuseppe "Joe" Petrosino. A native of southern Italy, Petrosino immigrated to New York with his parents at age thirteen, and worked as a shoeshine boy and street sweeper before becoming a police officer. An assertive, solidly built individual, Petrosino was only five-feet three-inches tall, and officials had to waive the department's minimum height requirement to bring him onto the force.

Unlike ineffective English-speaking officers and detectives who were unable to glean clues, let alone solve crimes, in the Italian and Sicilian precincts, the hardworking street-smart Petrosino proved his worth in rounding up dangerous suspects. In 1895 Theodore Roosevelt, then the city's highest civilian police official, promoted Petrosino to detective. A master of disguises and able to speak several Italian and Sicilian dialects, Petrosino's work led to prison sentences for more than five hundred criminals. His exploits earned him the rank of lieutenant, and whenever a serious crime occurred involving Sicilians or Italians, commanders would cry out, "Send for the Dago."

Like many ambitious police officers in dangerous roles, Petrosino counted on good press accounts to further his career and he tipped off newspaper reporters to pending arrests in big cases. One instance was the help he provided to fabled tenor Enrico Caruso when he received a Black Hand demand for $5,000, a princely sum at the turn of the twentieth century. Caruso intended to pay until Petrosino persuaded him that he would be opening himself to more and larger extortions. The detective set a trap and personally collared the man who came to collect Caruso's payoff.

Petrosino tried to educate the police brass about the reasons Italian criminals found New York and other big cities such tempting targets. "Here there is practically no police surveillance," he reported in a memorandum. "Here it is easy to buy arms and dynamite. Here there is no penalty for using a fake name. Here it is easy to hide, thanks to our enormous territory and overcrowded cities."

By 1909, Petrosino's advice was being heeded and he was heading a twenty-five-man unit, the Italian Squad, when Police Commissioner Theodore Bingham sent him on a secret assignment to Italy and Sicily. A new American law allowed the deportation of any alien who had been convicted of a crime in another country and who had lived in the United States for less than three years. With a long list of known villains in hand, Petrosino was to seek out proof of their criminal misbehavior in Italy and return with the evidence to boot them out of America.

Unfortunately, while Petrosino was abroad, the publicity-seeking Bingham disclosed the nature of his assignment to a New York newspaper, and the Mafia in Sicily got wind of the detective's arrival there. Sicilian mafiosi, apparently alarmed over Petrosino's digging in their backyard and determined to send a deterrent message to other potential American investigators, caught up with the detective in Palermo on his first day in the city. He was gunned down in daylight in the crowded Piazza Marina, standing near a statue of Garibaldi. At close range, professional assassins shot him twice in the back of the head and once in the face.

Vito Cascio Ferro, a Mafia *padrino*, claimed afterward that he was responsible for the murder. Don Vito had lived briefly in New York and apparently was incensed by Petrosino's diligent investigation of Sicilian criminals.

At Petrosino's funeral in New York, 250,000 people lined the streets in mournful tribute as the cortege passed. To honor the fallen hero, the city dedicated a minuscule parklet in lower Manhattan as "Lieutenant Joseph Petrosino Square." Today, that bare, benchless concrete slab serves as a road divider and pedestrian-safety island near Little Italy, one block from the old police headquarters where Petrosino got his fatal final orders from Commissioner Bingham.

Petrosino achieved the distinction of being the only New York police officer murdered on an overseas assignment. His killers were never caught. Decades later, near the close of the twentieth century, New York's Mafia families were still firmly in place and as defiant as their predecessors had been earlier in Sicily. Ironically, across the street from Petrosino Square, the restaurant La Donna Rosa opened in the 1980s. Its owner was Alphonse D'Arco, then a high-ranking mobster. Within easy sight of a plaque memorializing Lieutenant Petrosino's crusade against the Mafia, the restaurant was used by D'Arco as a secure meeting site for the Lucchese crime family to map out plans for murders and other crimes.

4

The Castellammarese War

During the first two decades of the twentieth century, Italian immigrant criminals in New York were either undisciplined street gangs or individual predators. By 1920, nearly one million Italian immigrants, predominantly from Sicily and southern Italy, lived in New York. About 15 percent of the city's population, they were squeezed into three neighborhoods: Little Italy and East Harlem in Manhattan and Williamsburg in Brooklyn. Like other ethnic criminal groups, the newly arrived mafiosi and other Italian gangsters largely confined themselves to victimizing their own countrymen. Irish hoodlums carried out similar activities on Manhattan's West Side; the turf for Jewish thugs was the Lower East Side.

A political and social earthquake—Prohibition—would revolutionize crime in America for these small-time Italian, Jewish, and Irish underworld characters. Combined with another upheaval—the triumph of Fascism in Italy—the two events would significantly alter the Mafia's role in America and transform it into the nation's preeminent criminal organization.

Prohibition, the Eighteenth Amendment to the Constitution, went into effect in January 1920, making the manufacture and sale of all alcoholic beverages a federal crime. The historian Stephen Fox described the law as an "ethnic experiment in social control," an attempt to preserve the nation's Anglo-Saxon character from the influx of foreign cultures. Prohibition's supporters characterized the ban as a crusade to protect the presumed wholesome pastoral values of rural America from decadent big cities and their huge alien populations.

Indeed, in the immoral urban centers, many Italian, Jewish, and Irish gangsters quickly recognized the significance of the law and the rich opportunities it offered for a new type of crime: bootlegging, or supplying beer and booze to a clientele that was law-abiding but extremely thirsty. Overnight in apartments, in sheds, in the backrooms of stores, primitive stills or distilleries dubbed "alky cookers" sprouted in New York's ethnic ghettos.

At the same time, in Sicily, the Mafia's half century of serene growth was suddenly being challenged. The Fascist regime of Benito Mussolini took control of the Italian government in the early 1920s and moved rapidly to wipe out all opposition to the absolute supremacy of the Fascist dictatorship. A northerner, Mussolini was well aware of the Mafia's extraordinary influence in Sicily and its historical contempt for all national governments in Rome.

Mussolini's antagonism toward the Mafia was inflamed by the cool, insulting reception he received on a visit to Sicily in 1924. The head of a *cosca*, Don Ciccio Cuccia, who was the mayor of the small town Piana dei Greci, aptly demonstrated the Mafia's disrespect for *Il Duce* (the Leader). When the haughty Mussolini rose to deliver a speech, the main piazza was empty except for a collection of seedy beggars and village idiots collected by the mayor. At a reception in another town, despite the vigilance of his bodyguards, the Mafia managed to steal Mussolini's hat.

Mussolini's revenge was swift and exacting. He gave a ruthless official from the north, Cesare Mori, totalitarian police powers and an army of special agents to eradicate the Mafia. Dubbed the "Iron Prefect" and aided by landowners and businessmen who resented the Mafia's power and extortion demands, Mori brutally rounded up and imprisoned scores of clan "fathers" and their soldiers.

One of the first victims in Mussolini's war was the imprudent Don Ciccio Cuccia. A month after the insult of the piazza, Mussolini retaliated with a long jail sentence for Don Ciccio, without the formality of a trial. (The appelation "Don" is a form of honor and great respect for an individual, not an inherited or aristocratic title.)

As a method of publicly degrading those mafiosi who did come to trial, Mori constructed iron cages to exhibit them in courtrooms. Distressed at the slow pace of one of the early judicial proceedings, Mussolini issued this blunt directive: "Fascist justice must be rapid and decisive. If the trial does not go faster, the liquidation of the Mafia will not be done until the year 2000."

Before Mori's mass roundups and trials ended, more than twelve hundred suspected mafiosi were convicted and sentenced to terms ranging from a few months to life imprisonment. Palermo was the center of the crackdown and the accusations were usually "banding together for criminal purposes," and the specific crimes of murder, extortion, blackmail, robbery, and theft.

Mussolini reaped a bonus from the reign of terror against the Mafia. It was a convenient pretense to arrest and eliminate Sicilian liberals, leftists, and other political opponents, all of whom were falsely smeared as mafiosi.

The Sicilian Mafia never conceived a plan to infiltrate America or to establish branches in the United States. But the Mussolini-Mori suppression proved so severe that it led to a widespread exodus from Sicily of experienced and apprentice mafiosi fleeing certain torture and imprisonment. Unlimited entry to the United States ended in 1924 with the enactment of the National Origins Act, a law that virtually halted immigration from Italy. Undeterred by immigration restrictions and portraying themselves as political victims of Fascism, many of the routed Sicilian mobsters headed for New York. They had little difficulty sneaking into the country and linking up with entrenched Sicilian gangs.

One of these earliest illegal aliens was Joseph Bonanno, who would create a Mob empire in America. Bonanno, whose father and close relatives were sworn mafiosi, came from Castellammare del Golfo (Castle by the Sea), a hallowed Mafia bastion on Sicily's west coast. His trip to America was arranged with financial and moral support from clan members in Castellammare who had gone underground to survive Mussolini's purge, and from Castellammarese kin in America. In 1924, at age nineteen, Bonanno slipped into the United States from Cuba, and made his way to Brooklyn's Williamsburg section, where an immigrant Castellammarese borgata was already in business.

Like other mafiosi newcomers, Bonanno was astonished by the rosy prospects Prohibition offered. It was the "golden goose," he rhapsodized. His first illicit venture was opening a still in Brooklyn with other young Castellammarese immigrants. "When I first got into bootlegging, I thought it was too good to be true," Bonanno wrote in his autobiography, A Man of Honor, published sixty years later. "I didn't consider it wrong. It seemed fairly safe in that the police didn't bother you. There was plenty of business for everyone. The profits were tremendous."

Violating or ignoring the Prohibition amendment was considered a good-natured sport, not a stigma, by most Americans. After the amendment was ratified, Congress approved the National Prohibition Act (commonly called the Volstead Act) to define and strengthen the law. All beverages containing more than 0.5 percent alcohol were banned as intoxicating.

The bootleggers, rumrunners, and speakeasy owners who slaked the nation's gigantic thirst were generally looked upon by most public officials, judges, and ordinary citizens as providing an essential product and service. Except for a tiny corps of diligent, incorruptible federal agents, local and federal law-enforcement agents had blind eyes and open palms when it came to enforcing a singularly unpopular law. National enforcement was delegated largely to the newly created Prohibition Bureau in the Treasury Department. The agency soon became a laughing stock, ridiculed for its huge conglomeration of politically appointed corrupt and incompetent hacks, masquerading as investigators.

Little enthusiasm was expended by most local law-enforcement units to disturb bootlegging operations. Indeed, many states and communities where political sentiment was pro "wet" (anti-Prohibition) passed laws that seemingly benefited bootleggers. New York State may have gone the farthest to protect the illegal industry. In 1923 the New York legislature repealed a weak state Prohibition law, thereby eliminating any requirement by local police to initiate or assist federal agents in arresting violators.

Encouraged by the lax enforcement in New York, the Sicilian gangs and the Jewish and Irish bootleggers abandoned the primitive, rot-gut alky cookers. They developed more sophisticated and profitable techniques, smuggling quality liquor from Britain and Canada and opening their own covert breweries. In addition to the Castellammarese overseas clan, several other loosely organized Sicilian gangs, some with southern Italian members from the Naples region, were thriving in New York by the late 1920s, mainly due to bootlegging.

Profits from breweries were enormous. Each barrel of beer cost less than five dollars to produce and netted about $36 upon delivery to a speakeasy. The illegal, untaxed income from supplying whiskey and other hard spirits was even greater.

In the competition between ethnic rivals, the Sicilian-Italian bootleggers lacked the political influence of the Irish underworld; the largely Irish police force gave them an advantage in corrupting cops. And the Jewish gangsters were almost equal in numbers to the Italians. But the Italian mobsters had a distinct asset: they were recognized by their rivals as better disciplined, more vicious, and more deadly whenever fights erupted over territorial control and customers.

New York's largest Italian gang in the mid-1920s was based in East Harlem and headed by Giuseppe "Joe" Masseria, a middle-aged Sicilian immigrant. Short and corpulent, Masseria's puffy cheeks and small, narrow eyes earned him the nickname "the Chinese." Masseria, however, dubbed himself "Joe the Boss" and was the first to use that designation for the head of an American Mafia family instead of the traditional Sicilian title "father."

Masseria's ascension rested on a violent, blood-soaked record. He led a gang that killed more than thirty opponents in battles over bootlegging territories and illegal gambling operations. His favorite expression for ordering the execution of a rival was instructing an underling to "Take that stone from my shoe."

Despite his unathletic portly physique, Masseria possessed an uncanny agility when dodging bullets and outrunning and escaping assassins in street ambushes and gunfights. His carnal appetite was as gross as his quest for power. He would sit down several times a day to huge meals, wolfing down three plates of pasta just as a side dish. Masseria's trencherman habits and atrocious table manners—food often splattered from his mouth as he harangued dining companions—gave rise to another nickname from his detractors: "Joe the Glutton."

Masseria's success stemmed partly from a keen eye for talent to run and protect his rackets. Three of his brightest young recruits, who had emigrated as boys to America, were Salvatore Lucania, Francesco Castiglia, and Gaetano Lucchese. Lucania would become Charles "Lucky" Luciano; Castiglia would change his baptismal name to Frank Costello; and Lucchese would be better known as Tommy "Three-Finger Brown." Later the trio would attain eminence in the American Mafia's pantheon.

In 1925 the Castellammarese clan was rejuvenated by the arrival of Salvatore Maranzano, another illegal immigrant driven out of Sicily by the Mussolini-Mori juggernaut. A well-established mafioso with the honorific title Don Turriddu, Maranzano, then in his early forties, was a devoted defender of Mafia tradition. One of the clan's best warriors in the old country, he came to America with a small fortune and quickly branched out into bootlegging.

No small-time operator, Maranzano built quality whiskey stills in Pennsylvania and upstate New York, and took the twenty-year-old Joe Bonanno under his wing. Bonanno handpicked a squad of armed marksmen to safeguard Maranzano's whiskey trucks, often camouflaged as milk tankers, from rival hijackers.

Unlike Joe the Boss Masseria, Maranzano fancied himself a sophisticated, educated European. Although he had sparse command of English, Maranzano bragged about being literate in Latin and Greek and, in his basso profundo

Sicilian dialect, delighted in lecturing his unschooled, barely literate minions on classical literature and the virtues of his idol, Julius Caesar. As a cover to conduct his bootlegging business, Maranzano set up a company in Little Italy that supposedly was involved in export and import trade.

There was a harsher side to Maranzano's business and personality that he revealed in a monologue to young Bonanno. He cautioned his protégé that hunting animals was relatively simple, but taking the life of another man demanded courage and caution. "When you aim at a man, your hands shake, your eyes twitch, your heart flutters, your mind interferes," Bonanno recalled Maranzano advising him. "If possible you should always touch the body with your gun to make sure the man is dead. Man is the hardest animal to kill. If he gets away he will come back to kill you."

Those words soon proved to be prophetic. In 1930 other members of the Castellammarese borgata turned to Maranzano for guidance and leadership when Masseria demanded $10,000 payoffs as tributes recognizing his assumed position as "Joe the Boss" of all New York mafiosi. Masseria also began dispatching hit men against recalcitrant Castellammarese soldiers. The firebrand Maranzano refused to submit to Masseria or acknowledge his supremacy, thereby igniting an unprecedented large-scale conflict between the area's two largest borgatas. As casualties mounted, each side sought reinforcements from the other New York gangs and from mafiosi in other cities. In the Sicilian-Italian underworld, the Mob carnage was spoken of as "The Castellammarese War."

Aware that they were prime ambush targets, Masseria and Maranzano surrounded themselves with bodyguards, traveling around town in convoys of armored-plated cars. Maranzano relied on a custom-built Cadillac with metal-plated sides and bulletproof windows. He shared the rear seat with a machine gun mounted on a swivel to fire out the windows; for backup weapons in close combat, he carried two large-caliber handguns and a dagger.

Although he worked as a top lieutenant for Masseria, twenty-nine-year-old Lucky Luciano worried that the shoot-outs, with cadavers and wounded men sprawled on streets, attracted unwelcome notoriety to the borgata gangs. Even worse, the fighting compelled the police to launch investigations that could endanger the smooth stream of loot flowing to him and his pals.

From the start, Luciano had opposed the tyrannical thrust for absolute control and power by Joe the Boss, fearing that it would end in death and chaos for the main participants. Before the war broke out, Luciano had become increasingly frustrated by Masseria's refusal to adopt his ideas for modernizing and expanding their rackets. Content with the easy money from bootlegging and protection shakedowns, Masseria brushed off Luciano's proposals to cash in on new ventures.

Luciano's business ideas included streamlining international bootlegging by cooperating with other Italian and with non-Italian gangs to bring in greater quantities of booze and eliminate hijackings. He knew that such cooperation would also prevent interference from the law by guaranteeing that more law-enforcement personnel would be adequately bribed.

Additionally, Luciano wanted to expand the areas of labor racketeering, gambling, and prostitution. Many of these activities would require temporary or permanent partnerships with Jewish and Irish gangsters. The distrustful Masseria, reluctant to accept alliances even with rival Sicilian and Italian mobsters whom he knew, vetoed any deals with Jewish or Irish hoods.

Representing an emerging generation of English-speaking mafiosi who had been raised in America, Luciano grew increasingly contemptuous of the erratic, archaic methods of Masseria and his older immigrant counterparts. Luciano and his closest confederates referred disparagingly to Masseria and his ilk as "Mustache Petes" and "greasers."

After eighteen months of combat and with no end in sight to the Castellammarese War, Luciano intervened by double-crossing Masseria. According to Joe Bonanno, who served as Maranzano's wartime chief of staff, at a clandestine meeting with Maranzano, Luciano offered to halt the hostilities by eliminating Masseria and assuming control of the dead boss's gang. In exchange, Maranzano would call off his hit men, recognize Luciano as an equivalent boss, and peace would reign between the two factions.

Armed with the secret pact, Luciano moved swiftly. He set up Masseria, inviting him to Coney Island for a lavish lobster lunch, a card game, and a conference at one of Joe the Boss's favorite trattorias, the Nuovo Villa Tammaro, where he would feel safe.

The meeting on April 15, 1931, was ostensibly to find a way to ambush Maranzano. Masseria drove to the luncheon date in his personal armored car with one-inch-thick bulletproof windows, and with three bodyguards. Before dessert arrived, Luciano left for the toilet. Mysteriously, Masseria's bodyguards vanished from the restaurant as four of Luciano's killers suddenly appeared and riddled Joe the Boss with a volley of gunfire. The *New York Daily News* reported (with melodramatic exaggeration) that Masseria died "with the ace of spades, the death card, clutched in a bejeweled paw."

Picked up for questioning by detectives, Luciano could offer no theory about a motive for the murder. Unfortunately, he added, he had no clue about the gunmen because he was washing his hands and had seen nothing.

With Masseria out of the way, Maranzano was hailed as a conquering hero by the surviving Castellammarese clan. Luciano got his reward by taking over Masseria's large gang and Maranzano gave his blessings to new leaders of three smaller borgatas whom he considered trustworthy allies.

Maranzano, however, had a surprise in store for Luciano. Signaling his presumed dominance, Maranzano summoned Chicago's Al Capone and Mafia leaders from the rest of the country to a meeting in a resort hotel in tiny Wappingers Falls, seventy-five miles from Times Square, to inform them of New York's new power lineup. The major implication of the meeting was clear: Maranzano had crowned himself as the highest-ranked leader in New York, and because of the city's prominence as the Mafia's emerging American polestar, he expected to be recognized as superior to all other bosses in the country.

Maranzano, in effect, had declared himself "*capo di tutti capi*," boss of bosses.

In New York he began issuing organizational decrees to the Castellammarese mafiosi and to the other borgatas. Recalling his admiration for Caesar, he wanted the families modeled loosely on the military chain of command of a Roman legion. Towering above all others, a father, or boss, or *representante*, would govern with unquestioned authority. His main assistant or executive officer was the *sottocapo*, underboss. Crews or street units, *decini*, would be formed, consisting of ten or more inducted soldiers or button men. Each crew would be led by a *capodecina, capo*, or captain, appointed by the boss, and the units would be the family's workhorses for all illegal operations.

Maranzano further mandated that Mafia rules, which were inviolable in Sicily, be imposed on all the New York clans. His fundamental precepts, all carrying the death penalty if ignored, were unquestioned obedience to the father, or boss, and his designated officers; no physical assaults or insults against a fellow mafioso; a ban on desiring or courting the wife or sweetheart of another mafioso, and, most important, obeying *omertà*, the code of secrecy.

Maranzano's high-handed moves provoked Luciano, who now reassessed him as more backward in his thinking than Masseria had been. Not only had Maranzano reneged on their deal for equality in New York, but he was thirsting for power throughout the country.

From his trusted crony Tommy Three-Finger Brown Lucchese, Luciano got wind of more alarming news. The duplicitous Lucchese had cozied up to Maranzano and his top lieutenants and learned that Maranzano had marked Luciano for a machine-gun assassination by the Irish cutthroat Vincent "Mad Dog" Coll.

Befitting his new grandeur, Maranzano had moved his headquarters from Little Italy to an elegant suite of offices in the building atop Grand Central Terminal. Lucchese's spies tipped off Luciano that Maranzano was having tax troubles and expected that his phony export-import business records would be scrutinized by the Internal Revenue Service. In anticipation of an audit, Maranzano had instructed his bodyguards to be unarmed while in his office to insure there would be no arrests for gun violations.

Acting quickly to catch Maranzano off guard, Luciano decided that the Grand Central office would be his best chance. On September 10, 1931, Lucchese showed up unannounced at the office for a courtesy call on Maranzano. Minutes later, a group of men swept in, announcing they were IRS agents. None appeared to be Sicilian or Italian, and neither Maranzano nor his bodyguards suspected they were hired killers. Before the bodyguards could react, the hit men got the drop on them, and at gunpoint lined them up along with Lucchese and a female secretary, with their faces pressed to the wall.

Lucchese identified Maranzano with a head movement and a gunman nudged Maranzano into his private office. There were sounds of a struggle followed by a barrage of gunfire. Five months after his arch foe Joe the Boss had been annihilated, Maranzano lay dead, his body torn by bullets and knife wounds.

Organized-crime historians are uncertain if Luciano had schemed from the start to remove both Masseria and Maranzano as dinosaurs, antiquated obstacles to the Mafia's progress and realignment. A thin, slightly built, dark-haired man with an impassive, pockmarked face, Luciano came to New York as a boy of nine from a village near Palermo. A school dropout at fourteen, within a decade he compiled an arrest record for armed robbery, gun possession, assault, grand larceny, gambling, and possession of narcotics. Remarkably, most of the charges were dropped, and except for an eight-month sentence, Luciano avoided any long jail time. A prison psychiatrist aptly analyzed him as highly intelligent but "an aggressive, egocentric, antisocial type."

As a teenager, Luciano held only one honest job as a five-dollar-a-week shipping clerk in a hat factory. He quit the day after he won $244 in a dice game, but used his experience at the factory to hide heroin that he transported and sold in hat boxes. At age eighteen, he admitted to a probation officer that he found regular work unsuitable for his personality. "I never was a crumb and if I had to be a crumb, I would rather be dead," he told the interviewing officer. In Lucky's lexicon, "a crumb" was an average person who slaved at a dull or laborious job, squirreled away money, and never indulged in extravagant pleasures.

By the time he was in his twenties, Luciano had been tagged with the nickname Lucky, but it is unclear whether he acquired it for his gambling exploits, for surviving gun and knife attacks, or from American mispronunciations of his Italian surname. His closest call came in 1929 when he was abducted, beaten, and strung up by his hands from a beam in a Staten Island warehouse. True to his calling, Luciano refused to tell the police who had taken him for a ride and the reason for it. The episode left a jagged scar on his chin.

On the Lower East Side, as a wild teenager before joining Masseria's gang, Luciano cemented alliances with Jewish gangsters that would endure for a lifetime. Charlie Lucky's closest Jewish criminal companions were the shrewd Meyer Lansky and Lansky's volatile colleague, Benjamin "Bugsy" Siegel.

There was little doubt among New York's mafiosi that Luciano had engineered Maranzano's murder and that the hit team had been mustered by his Jewish confederates. Luciano, however, circulated the message that he had indisputable evidence that the power-mad Maranzano, without cause, had been preparing to kill him, and therefore the hit was justifiable under Mafia rules.

The Castellammarese clan presented the only danger to Luciano of a new war or an assassination attempt to avenge their chief's death. But Luciano's self-defense claim was readily accepted, even by Maranzano's staunchest protégé, Joe Bonanno. Reflecting on Maranzano's imperious behavior after winning a brutal struggle, Bonanno decided that his patron had been an astute warlord but unable to adapt to the culture and tactics of the new, Americanized breed. Despite six years in America, Maranzano spoke little English and was unable to communicate with younger criminals or comprehend their street talk and slang.

"Maranzano was old-world Sicilian in temperament and style," Bonanno explained in his autobiography. "But he didn't live in Sicily anymore. In New York he was adviser not only to Sicilians but to American-Italians."

Set for anointment as head of the Castellammarese borgata, Bonanno saw the wisdom of Luciano's new look for the Mafia and accepted what he characterized as the "path of peace." With the war between them over, Luciano and Bonanno held a conclave with the heads of three other substantial borgatas in New York whom Luciano considered agreeable to his plans. The other bosses were Gaetano Gagliano, Vincent Mangano, and Joe Profaci. Without any specific blueprint, in 1931 five Mafia families had evolved from a convulsive decade.

The five families would survive, under various names and leaders, into the next century. No other American city would have more than one Mafia family, nor would any other borgata come close to matching the size, wealth, power, and influence of any of the New York families.

Before the year ended, the New York bosses traveled to Chicago for a national conference with Al Capone, Chicago's Italian Mob titan, and the leaders of more than twenty other Mafia factions in the country. The great innovator, Luciano, explained his concepts for avoiding intra-family and interfamily Mob wars and for establishing lasting prosperity. He accepted as pragmatic Maranzano's organizational structure of crews performing the bulk of the work for the families but added a wrinkle for the hierarchies. Besides a *sottocapo*, an underboss, each family regime or administration would have a consigliere, a skilled counselor or diplomat, to iron out problems inside the family and to resolve feuds with other borgatas.

Luciano saw the practical wisdom of the Sicilian traditional reliance on *omertà*, absolute loyalty to the family, and many of the other rules and security measures that Maranzano had suggested to prevent penetration by law-enforcement agents. These behavioral standards would serve as the Mafia's sacred code, its Ten Commandments.

Without discussion or debate, it was universally understood by the bosses that membership throughout the country would be open only to men whose parents were both from Sicily or southern Italy. Italian heritage of only one parent would be insufficient for acceptance into a family. Bloodlines were critical factors for determining trustworthiness and for acceptance as a Man of Honor. The size of each family was fixed at the number of made men it had at that time, with replacements allowed only for dead members. Freezing the strength of each borgata was intended to prevent surreptitious expansions to dominate other families and possibly ignite territorial conflicts. Limiting membership also was seen as a business-like means of selecting the best and most competent candidates.

Luciano made it clear that Mafia membership was a lifetime obligation; there were no provisions for resignation or early retirement. "The only way out is in a box," Lucky emphasized.

While not a written document, the code illuminated the Mafia's fundamental guiding principle: the survival of each family and the combined national Mafia overshadowed the needs and safety of the individual mafioso.

Every family was therefore obligated to maintain the organizational viability that would withstand any assault by law enforcement. The purpose of the code was to enable the family to continue functioning efficiently, even if the boss or other hierarchs were removed.

The organization would be supreme; its parts, replaceable.

Luciano unveiled one more idea, his most striking innovation, without precedent in the Sicilian Mafia or among Americanized gangsters. It was the creation of the Commission, the equivalent of a national board of directors that would establish general policies and regulations for all families in the country and would settle territorial and other disputes that might arise. The Commission would be the vital link between families throughout the nation, ensuring cooperation and harmony on joint criminal ventures. It would be analogous to an underworld Supreme Court, whose primary function was to prevent warfare while recognizing the sovereignty of the individual groups.

Luciano and Bonanno originally wanted to name the new body, the "Committee for Peace," after its main purpose. But younger, American-reared mafiosi found the name too difficult to pronounce in Italian or Sicilian.

Clearly defining New York's keystone position in the Mafia's national pecking order, Luciano gave representation on the Commission to all five New York families. Other members of the new body would come from Chicago and Buffalo, with the proviso that more families could be added if necessary.

Chicago's selection was an obvious recognition of Capone and his gang's strength, wealth, and domination of numerous rackets in the Midwest. The boss of the Buffalo family was Stefano Magaddino, another immigrant from Castellammare del Golfo. Magaddino was highly respected and feared because he was a cousin of Joe Bonanno and had business ties to Mafia organizations in the Midwest and in Canada.

Luciano surprised the underworld convention by insisting that each family on the Commission have a single vote, with all decisions determined by the majority. His successes in New York had elevated him into a position of unrivaled national importance, and there was little doubt that among the nation's Mafia bosses he was first among equals.

There would have been no opposition if Charlie Lucky had nominated himself as the first *capo di tutti capi*, boss of bosses. But Luciano realized that the bloodshed in the previous decade as families fought for dominance and underworld monopolies, climaxed by the Castellammarese War, had demonstrated the futility of attempts to impose a supreme leader.

Martin A. Gosch, a Hollywood movie producer, claimed that thirty years after the Chicago conclave, Luciano reminisced about it with him in preparation for a proposed film version of Luciano's life. Gosch asserted that Luciano summarized his main purpose for the meeting with this colorful quote: "I explained to 'em that all the war horseshit was out. I explained to 'em we was in a business that hadda keep movin' without explosions every two minutes; knockin' guys off just because they come from a different part of Sicily, that kind of crap was given' us a bad name, and we couldn't operate until it stopped." Although the substance of Gosch's conversations with Luciano was never documented elsewhere, the quotation matched accounts that investigators dug up of Luciano's goals at the session in Chicago.

Cosa Nostra experts agree that all of Luciano's remodeling proposals were accepted by the nation's Mob families. Luciano's game plan clearly established that the American borgatas would never be subsidiaries or satellites of the Sicilian Mafia. Although drawing on Sicilian traditions, especially omertà, America's independent mafiosi were adapting themselves to the unique social and cultural forces that existed on their continent.

The Chicago secret meeting reportedly ended at the Blackstone Hotel, with Al Capone hosting a feast where the delegates, acting as if they were at a jazz era orgy, made merry, enjoying the favors of a plethora of prostitutes.

Without the awareness of the nation's vast law-enforcement apparatus, in 1931 an American Mafia had been custom-designed for efficient plunder. And New York was its epicenter.

5

Dirty Thirties

For millions of Americans, the 1930s was the paradigm of hard times, the decade of the Great Depression. Justifiably known as "the Dirty Thirties," it was an era clouded by unprecedented economic impoverishment, bank failures, shuttered factories, violent strikes, abandoned farms, homeless wanderers, bread lines, and soup kitchens. At the nadir of crisis in 1931, about fifteen million people, almost 25 percent of the nation's workforce, were unemployed.

The newly hatched Mafia families, however, had no financial worries. The decade was the onset of unparalleled prosperity and cooperation that would extend far into the century. At the 1931 Chicago conclave of top mobsters, Lucky Luciano, the Mafia's visionary criminal genius, installed the organizational foundations that each of the score of existing borgatas used to construct networks of illicit enterprises.

Joe Bonanno, one of the bosses present at the creation of the modern American Mafia, was gratified by the long period of serenity that Luciano's grand scheme inaugurated. "For nearly a thirty-year period after the Castellammarese War no internal squabbles marred the unity of our Family and no outside interference threatened the Family or me," Bonanno marveled in his autobiography.

Luciano's managerial revolution was intended to build bulwarks that would protect and insulate himself and the other bosses from implication in the transgressions committed by their families. Thereby, each chieftain or godfather would reap the profits from his family's criminal activities without risking indictment or imprisonment.

Ironically, while Luciano's blueprint safeguarded most of his fellow bosses, he was the only New York mobster of his era to suffer a long prison sentence.

Prohibition had been the catalyst for transforming the neighborhood gangs of the 1920s into smoothly run regional and national criminal corporations. Men like Luciano, Bonanno, and Lucchese began as small-time hoodlums and graduated as underworld leviathans. Bootlegging gave them on-the-job executive training in a dangerous environment. It taught them how to plan and run the intricate machinery necessary for producing and supplying huge quantities of beer and whiskey. Still in their twenties and thirties, this new breed of mafiosi became expert in marshaling small armies of smugglers, truckers, cargo handlers, and gunmen. The young millionaire mobsters also became adept at laundering money to dodge tax-evasion problems, and learned how to bribe and manipulate political and police contacts to forestall law-enforcement headaches.

The Chicago meeting was a success. A power structure was in place. The nation's Mafia leaders tacitly agreed to assemble every five years at a national crime forum—much like a political party convention or a religious synod—to fraternize and review mutual concerns.

Within the new Luciano and Bonanno families, their ranks had enlarged as a by-product of the Castellammarese War and the need for reinforcements in a costly campaign. While the Luciano plan and the Commission united all of the country's borgatas in generally recognized rules and concepts, there were regional distinctions about membership. Joe Bonanno refused to subscribe to the idea of his borgata as a melting pot for all Italians. Only men of full Sicilian heritage, he insisted, could be faithful to Cosa Nostra culture and obligations.

None of the families would permit the utterance of the name *Mafia* to identify their organizations. The New York families adopted Cosa Nostra (the Mafia code name in Sicily), Chicago called itself "the Outfit," Buffalo chose, "the Arm." Others, especially in New England, preferred the neutral sounding "the Office."

Eventually, among mafiosi the most popular mode for identifying a "made man" was the simple expression, "He's connected."

As the gangsters dispersed from Chicago, most of them realized that Prohibition—the lush money machine—was on its deathbed. A majority of the public and most politicians wanted to rescind the law as unenforceable, unpopular, and a corruptive influence on law-enforcement agencies. The worsening Depression provided another anti-Prohibition argument for the new administration in 1933 of President Franklin D. Roosevelt; supporters of "Repeal" contended that it would revive the legitimate alcohol industry and generate thousands of new jobs.

In December 1933, the Twenty-first Amendment to the Constitution was adopted, repealing the Eighteenth Amendment that had outlawed the production and sale of alcoholic beverages. On the first night that the thirteen-year dry spell ended, in New York tens of thousands of revelers poured into Times Square in a spontaneous celebration. The huge throngs required the emergency mustering of almost the entire city police force of 20,000 officers for crowd control.

The five New York Mafia families were prepared for the cosmic change. Prohibition had enriched them so handsomely that they had sufficient startup money and muscle to bankroll new rackets and crimes or to simply take over existing ones from rival ethnic Irish and Jewish gangsters. As an example of the Mafia's financial resources, movie producer Martin Gosch said that Luciano told him that his gross take from bootlegging alone in 1925 was at least $12 million, and that after expenses, mainly for a small army of truck drivers and guards and bribes to law-enforcement officials and agents, he cleared $4 million in profits.

Prohibition was barely in its grave before the New York Mafia was feasting from a smorgasbord of new and expanded traditional crimes: bookmaking, loan-sharking, prostitution, narcotics trafficking, robberies, cargo hijackings, and the numbers game. "Racket" became the popular term for these new Mafia endeavors. The use of "racket" as slang to describe an underworld activity can be traced back to eighteenth-century England. Its exact derivation is unclear, though it might be related to alternate definitions of racket: a clamor, a social excitement, dissipation, or gaiety. In the mid- and late nineteenth century, the term came into use as a raucous private party held by Irish-American gangs in New York. To subsidize their "rackets," the gang members demanded or extorted contributions from merchants and individuals whose property and lives would otherwise be endangered.

"Racketeer" is a totally American invention, probably coined by a newspaper reporter to describe the innovative 1930s breed of mobsters.

One shake-down the post-Prohibition mafiosi borrowed from the defunct

Black Hand was setting up phony "security" companies to protect businesses from arsonists and vandals who might damage their properties. Merchants and restaurateurs who declined to sign up with these spurious watchguard services often found their windows smashed or their premises ravaged by suspicious fires.

Jewish gangsters in New York had invented the art of industrial racketeering in the Garment Center, which had a large percentage of Jewish workers and sweatshop proprietors. The Jewish thugs had been invited into the industry by both sides during fierce strikes in the 1920s. They worked as strikebreakers for manufacturers and were employed by some unions as gorillas to intimidate factory owners and scabs during organizational drives. When the confrontations ended, the gangsters who had worked illegally for both sides stayed on, gaining influence in the unions and in management associations. Their alliances with union leaders gave the Jewish racketeers the power to extract payoffs from owners by threatening work stoppages and unionization drives. Alternately, the unions paid them off by allowing Mob-owned companies to operate nonunion shops. Some mobsters muscled into companies as secret partners, getting payoffs from the principal owners in exchange for allowing them to operate nonunion shops or for guaranteeing sweetheart labor contracts if they were unionized.

Lucky Luciano, the only godfather with close ties to top Jewish gangsters during Prohibition, had little difficulty in absorbing Jewish Garment Center rackets into his own dominion. Jewish hoods became junior partners and vassals of Luciano in one of the city's largest and most profitable industries. According to Joe Bonanno, who shunned mergers and deals with the Jewish underworld, Luciano in the mid-1930s was the dominant Mob figure in the garment industry. "Luciano had extensive interests in the clothing industry, especially in the Amalgamated Clothing Workers Union," Bonanno wrote later. Charlie Lucky offered to place Bonanno's men in important positions in the Amalgamated, which was the principal union involved in manufacturing men's and boys' clothing. Once empowered in the union, Bonanno, like Luciano, could control vital jobs, set union contractual terms, and share in kickbacks from the manufacturers.

Luciano's offer was politely turned down because Bonanno did not want to be obligated to another family. The independent-minded Bonanno had another good reason to go it alone: he had his own connections to the other vital clothing industry union, the International Ladies Garment Workers Union.

Like the other New York bosses, Bonanno had numerous traditional criminal activities and new "front" enterprises to keep him busy and affluent. He had taken over a variety of legitimate businesses: three coat manufacturing companies, a trucking company, laundries, and cheese suppliers. There was also a Joe Bonanno funeral parlor in Brooklyn that was suspected of being used to secretly dispose of victims murdered by the family. The ingenious Bonanno was said to have used specially built two-tiered or double-decker coffins with a secret compartment under the recorded corpse that allowed two bodies to be buried simultaneously. Income from these fronts was a handy means for warding off tax audits and justifying his above-average lifestyle.

Bonanno's underlying capitalist philosophy rested on a basic theory that guided him and other bosses: eliminate all competition. "One must remember that in the economic sphere one of the objectives of a Family was to set up monopolies as far as it was possible," he explained in *A Man of Honor*.

In addition to the garment industry, the five Mafia families used strong-arm tactics and their influence in unions to control and obtain kickbacks from stevedore companies on the Brooklyn waterfront, the Fulton Fish Market, the wholesale meat and produce markets in Manhattan and Brooklyn, construction and trucking companies, and hotels and restaurants.

The Sicilian-Italian gangs even forced out Jewish racketeers from their pioneering roles in the $50-million-a-year kosher chicken business. New York's large Jewish population and its Orthodox dietary rules guaranteed a steady demand for the interrelated poultry industry. The Jewish hoods were content with simple, old-fashioned protection tactics. They engaged in small shake-downs of frightened and defenseless businessmen trying to keep their companies and their bodies intact. Inspired by Tommy "Three-Finger Brown" Lucchese, the Mafia had more grandiose plans. Lucchese's gunmen pushed aside their Jewish counterparts and, in what would become a classic model for industrial racketeering, established a cartel among live-chicken suppliers, wholesalers, and slaughtering companies. Lucchese formed a supposed trade group, the New York Live Poultry Chamber of Commerce, and through a combination of subtle intimidation and promises of ample profits, forced most kosher-chicken businesses to join. Prices were fixed to put an end to normal competition and each company was assigned a share of the market. In return, the company paid a fee depending on gross sales to the Mafia-front poultry association. Lucchese and his helpmates, of course, took a hefty cut for establishing the cartel and preventing new companies from competing in New York. The companies that kicked back part of their profits to Lucchese simply passed along the "crime tax" through higher prices to their customers.

Within the industries they controlled, from the garment center to the waterfront, the mafiosi profited further from illegal gambling and loan-sharking rings that fleeced wage earners.

No competition was allowed by the five families. Jewish and Irish gangsters, who had run their own powerful Prohibition-era gangs, offered little resistance to the Mafia's drive for absolute control. Even Meyer Lansky, the most influential Jewish gangster of his time in the 1930s and '40s, needed the approval of his Mafia partners for most of his projects. Lansky accompanied Luciano to Mafia conventions but was never allowed to sit in on discussions.

Before the Mafia takeover, the undisputed Jewish criminal virtuoso of the 1920s was Arnold Rothstein. His omnibus activities included international bootlegging, labor racketeering, stock frauds, fencing stolen diamonds and bonds, narcotics trafficking, and gambling schemes.

Rothstein's legendary coup was engineering "the Black Sox Scandal," by fixing the 1919 baseball World Series in which the heavily favored Chicago White Sox were defeated by the Cincinnati Reds. Known along Broadway as "the Brain" and "the Big Bankroll," Rothstein was an unthreatening-looking figure, soft-spoken, and a spiffy dresser. His authority was enforced by an entourage of brutal henchman, and he tutored a crop of future Jewish and Italian underworld stars, including Lansky and Luciano. The charismatic Rothstein is believed to have been the inspiration for F. Scott Fitzgerald's gangster Meyer Wolfsheim in *The Great Gatsby*.

Whatever obstacles Rothstein might have created to the Mafia's takeover of New York rackets were eliminated before Prohibition ended. On the night of November 4, 1928, he was found staggering on a sidewalk in Midtown Manhattan, shot in the stomach. Rothstein survived two days but, true to his own code of *omertà*, refused to identify the shooter or the motive. "I'm not talking to you," a detective quoted him as saying from his hospital deathbed. "You stick to your trade. I'll stick to mine." He was dead at age forty-six.

George Wolf, a Jewish lawyer in New York who represented Cosa Nostra and Jewish gangsters in the 1930s and '40s, had a close-up view of the new ethnic underworld relationships. "The two groups have always worked in surprisingly good harmony," Wolf commented. "The Italians respecting the Jews for their financial brains, and the Jews preferring to stay quietly behind the scenes and let the Italians use the muscle needed."

Mafia strength stemmed partly from the ultimate organized-crime weapon—murder. At the 1931 Chicago meeting, the bosses figuratively set in concrete the rule that only mafiosi could kill mafiosi. And while they could kill outsiders, other criminals would face death for even threatening a made man.

A Jewish racketeer, Michael Hellerman, warned of the danger in challenging Mafia authority in matters of money. "Jews, outsiders, wind up on the short end of any sit-down chaired and run by the Mafia," he grumbled. "Somehow, we always wound up paying, even when we were right."

During Prohibition, Irish gangsters dominated many sections of New York. Their most powerful and ruthless icon was Owney Madden. Madden began his career as a predatory gunman-hijacker in the Hell's Kitchen neighborhood on Manhattan's rough West Side. His Prohibition-era escapades glamorized him as a celebrity millionaire with stakes in two-dozen night clubs, including the acclaimed Cotton Club in Harlem. Madden's reputation for revenge and craftiness and his political influence at City Hall were so potent that even the Italian gangs stayed out of his territory.

But the death of Prohibition and the rise of the Mafia persuaded Madden that he could no longer survive or compete in any sphere with the Italian gangs. In 1933 the forty-year-old Madden announced that he was retiring from New York, relocating south to Hot Springs, Arkansas. At that time, Hot Springs, a city famed for its compliant and corrupt police and public officials, was a refuge for nonviolent criminals. After his fierce battles in New York, Madden found the ambiance in Hot Springs easy pickings; he became that city's illegal gambling monarch.

The Mafia had similar post-Prohibition successes against their former Irish and Jewish rivals in other cities. Sizable Irish crews in Chicago and Boston and Jewish contingents in Detroit (the Purple Gang) and Philadelphia faced two choices. They were either whacked or induced to become hired hands for specific crimes, or allowed to work as compliant bookies paying the Mafia protection money.

While the New York families were solidifying their organizations in the early 1930s, law-enforcement efforts against them were at best haphazard. The insulated bosses, however, took careful note of the legal trap that ensnared Alphonse Capone—a tax-evasion case.

———

Al Capone's birthplace and date of birth are uncertain; various records indicate that he was born in the late 1890s, either in southern Italy or, more likely, in Brooklyn, where he grew up. Like many of his era's gangsters, Capone was an early school dropout and got his basic training as a battler in street gangs. Working as a bouncer in a combination bar and brothel, Capone was slashed on the left side of his face, providing him with the sinister nickname "Scarface."

He arrived in Chicago as an enforcer and gun-toting bodyguard just as Prohibition and the beer wars were raging. By the mid-1920s, Capone had shot his way to the top of Chicago's gangland and was running multimillion-dollar bootlegging, prostitution, and gambling enterprises. The raucous climate generated by Prohibition turned gangsters into press celebrities and rogue heroes. Capone basked in the limelight. His favorite interview statements were: "I am just a businessman, giving the people what they want," and, "All I do is satisfy a public demand."

The stout, balding Capone made no attempt to avoid cameras and attention. He relished front-row box seats at baseball games, where players queued to sign autographs for him, and he hosted lavish parties at Chicago hotels and in his fourteen-room mansion on exclusive Palm Island in Florida.

His conspicuousness and violence finally backfired. On St. Valentine's Day in 1929, six members of the gang of his archenemy, George "Bugs" Moran, and an innocent optometrist who had stopped by to visit, were lined up against a garage wall and machine-gunned to death. Chicago's law-enforcement authorities were in Capone's pocket and made no serious effort to investigate the slaughter or any of Capone's activities. But the horrendous St. Valentine's Day Massacre provoked the administration of President Herbert Hoover to pin something on the haughty Capone. Furthermore, the administration was committed to enforcing Prohibition, and Capone's open defiance and his striking visibility were embarrassing and mocking.

An extensive paper chase by a special Treasury Department unit barely scratched the surface of Capone's actual illicit spoils. But the squad of auditors and investigators unearthed records linking payments to him from 1924 to 1929 totaling $1,038,654, income never declared for tax purposes. (Capone was defeated by diligent accountants, not by the Federal Bureau of Investigation, nor by the intrepid G-Man Eliot Ness, and his band of incorruptible sleuths featured in popular Hollywood and television versions of the story.)

Found guilty of tax evasion, Capone began serving his sentence in 1932. Suffering from advanced syphilis, he was imprisoned for seven years in the dreaded Alcatraz Penitentiary and other stringent federal prisons. Released in 1939, the once invincible Capone was a broken, pitiful invalid. He never returned to Chicago, dying in 1947 at his Florida mansion.

His downfall had no impact on the New York bosses except as a warning about tax-evasion investigations. Capone's authority had been confined to the Chicago area, and his Commission seat could easily be filled by one of his lieutenants. The New Yorkers also viewed Capone as a questionable believer in the Mafia's culture and its structure. They had doubts about him because he declined to comply with the ritual induction of made men into his gang, and failed to appoint capos or a consigliere. In essence, they were uncertain that he even considered himself a mafioso. To Cosa Nostra purists, Capone's Outfit functioned more like a partnership than a traditional borgata, and he violated a cardinal tradition by delegating responsibilities to non-Italians.

Capone made a fortune from his rackets, but his reputation among the shadowy New York godfathers was diminished by his penchant for publicity. His fame was greater than his actual influence and power. At the end, Capone's exaggerated underworld importance became a fatal liability for him.

6

Runaway Jury

Al Capone's misfortunes in the early 1930s had no immediate counterpart in New York, where local and federal law-enforcement authorities were either too corrupt, too indifferent, or too ignorant to disturb Mafia families.

The city's newspapers, then the principal source of news and information, were equally passive about investigating and reporting the emergence of the new organized-crime phenomenon. Gangsters, murders, and kidnappings made good copy during Prohibition, almost a welcome relief from the grim economic news of the Depression. For the most part, reporters and editors portrayed individual racketeers sympathetically, and Damon Runyon's colorful *Guys and Dolls* yarns about lovable rogues became the accepted universal myth about mobsters and criminals. Instead of exposing the Mob's almost wide-open gambling, labor-industrial racketeering, extortion-protection, and prostitution activities, some influential editors and columnists hobnobbed, gambled, and drank with the underworld characters. Herbert Bayard Swope, the editor of the prestigious *New York World*, at one point owed his Mob bookies $700,000. Walter Winchell and other nationally syndicated Broadway columnists cultivated relationships with gangsters for gossipy tips and scoops.

Law-enforcement authorities were even more negligent than the sycophantic press. A string of elected district attorneys in Manhattan (New York County), the center of the city's vice industry, never probed any of the blatant rackets. The district attorneys were usually hand-picked incompetents designated by the Democratic Party's Tammany Hall Club, a group of party leaders who controlled nominations and elections in Manhattan, a Democratic stronghold. Since the early days of Prohibition, Tammany's leaders were on the slush-fund payrolls of Italian and Jewish gang leaders to protect them from potential reform crusaders and police interference.

The routine impaneling of a Manhattan grand jury in March 1935 unexpectedly provoked a law-enforcement earthquake. Following his customary interest in easily solved crimes, the ineffectual Manhattan district attorney, William Copeland Dodge, instructed the jurors to concentrate on indicting his regular agenda of suspects arrested for minor felonies. Dodge's only other priority target was the absurd threat of the "Red Menace," and he suggested that the jurors focus on the Communist Party newspaper, *The Worker*, which he felt was using the Depression to foment insurrection.

A grand jury's task is to weigh evidence and to vote whether or not there is sufficient evidence to hold a defendant for trial. Normally, grand juries are easily manipulated by prosecutors, and after hearing only the prosecution's version, churn out felony indictments in assembly-line fashion. But the twenty-three Manhattan grand jurors, led by a strong-minded member, revolted, demanding an independent investigation into the spreading rackets in the city. Their outcry was endorsed by the city's bar association, and by several ministers and civic associations. The runaway jury was a hot newspaper story, and its pressure forced Governor Herbert Lehman to appoint a special prosecutor to examine the reformers' allegations.

Lehman, a Democrat, selected a thirty-three-year-old former federal prosecutor, the Republican Thomas E. Dewey. Raised in the small town of Owosso, Michigan, Dewey stayed in New York after getting a law degree at Columbia University. A three-year stint in the U.S. Attorney's Office in Manhattan turned him into a formidable prosecutor. Most of his federal cases involved bootlegging and income-tax charges, and Dewey quickly exhibited a trademark courtroom talent: an uncanny memory for the tiniest detail of a crime that would trip up a hostile witness in cross-examination. Giving up a successful Wall Street practice, Dewey leaped at the prosecutorial opportunity offered by Lehman, even though it meant a huge salary cut.

Unlike the apathetic Tammany Hall DAs, the aggressive Dewey didn't sit back waiting for cases to come to him. He understood how to gather evidence and had the foresight to make his objective the destruction of criminal organizations, rather than convicting low-level hoodlums. At the time of his appointment, there were virtually no restrictions on the use of telephone taps by state prosecutors in New York, and Dewey made maximum use of that tool to dig up evidence and leads.

Dewey lacked precise insight into the existence of the Mafia borgatas or their organizational structures, but he instinctively understood that he was being challenged by a new kind of criminal, the racketeer who never personally committed a murder or a hijacking or extorted a penny from a victim. The dirty work was left to henchmen who were the ones risking arrest.

To prosecute Mob bosses effectively, Dewey had to overhaul a cumbersome criminal-procedure law. Under an existing New York rule, a defendant could be tried only on each specific count. That meant multiple trials, even if the culprit had been indicted for one hundred separate acts. With the help of lobbying by reform politicians and organizations, Dewey persuaded the legislature to authorize "joinder" indictments, a procedure used in federal courts that permitted a single trial on combined charges. It was a legal weapon that Dewey could employ in court to try leading gangsters on multiple counts and link them to the crimes actually committed by their flunkies.

The first prominent racketeer targeted by Dewey was Dutch Schultz. Born Arthur Flegenheimer, Schultz was another ragtag criminal who cashed in on the floodgates opened by Prohibition. He formed a bootlegging gang, mainly of Jewish strongmen, and took over distribution of beer in the Bronx. Through terror tactics, murders, kidnappings, and torture, Schultz rivaled the Mafia in the scope of his operations and in the enmity he aroused. When Dewey became the Special State Prosecutor, Schultz's gang was the only non-Italian organization left in New York that was not subservient to the Mafia. Underworld cognoscenti referred to the five Cosa Nostra families and Schultz's outfit as "the Big Six."

Schultz also had sound business sense. As bootlegging waned, he acquired control of a restaurant workers' union and used it to extort labor-peace bribes from restaurants. Renowned spots, including Broadway's Lindy's and the Brass Rail, were compelled to bribe him in order to remain open. In his search for easy money to replace the lost bootlegging revenue, Schultz and his ferocious leg breakers took over the numbers or policy racket in Harlem from African-American and Hispanic "bankers."

During Prohibition, bootlegging was so extraordinarily profitable that the various gangs looked askance at the income from numbers as chump change and had little interest in operating in primarily black neighborhoods. The racist gangsters derisively regarded numbers as "the nigger pool." But tens of thousands of New Yorkers played the numbers games that paid 600-to-1 for picking three digits chosen daily from the wagering "handle," the last three numbers of the total pari-mutuel betting at a horse-racing track. For a Depression-racked population, winning the numbers was a popular fantasy, even if the wager was just a few pennies.

Dutch envisioned the numbers game as an essential substitute for his vanished income from bootlegging. He consolidated scores of small-time independent numbers operators in Harlem and the Bronx. The old-timers had the choice of working and paying a generous percentage of their take to Schultz or winding up in the morgue. Schultz quickly found that his plunge into numbers was the right move. The games grossed an estimated $20 million a year in bets, and there were few lucky winners to cut into Schultz's profits.

Schultz's incendiary temperament probably helped eliminate opposition to his new acquisitions. If enraged, Schultz, dubbed "the Dutchman" in the New York underworld, would kill, even in front of witnesses. J. Richard "Dixie" Davis, Schultz's lawyer, once remarked that the Dutchman murdered friends and enemies "just as casually as if he were picking his teeth." He once ended an argument over money with one of his underlings by shoving a gun into the man's mouth and blasting his head off. When he suspected that one of his long-time trusted lieutenants, Bo Weinberg, was plotting against him with Italian mobsters, Schultz personally encased Weinberg's legs in cement and dumped him into the Hudson River while still alive. (Half a century later, the barbaric slaying of Weinberg became a riveting scene in E. L. Doctorow's novel, *Billy Bathgate*, and in the film version.)

Tax indictments were seemingly the government's only strategy for convicting high-profile gangsters like Schultz, but he beat two attempts by federal prosecutors to snare him on tax-evasion charges. For one trial, Schultz obtained a change of venue to the rural town of Malone, New York, where he endeared himself to the jury by bribing almost the entire community with personal gifts and charitable contributions.

Once the tax problems were resolved, Schultz became aware that Dewey's first major move as special prosecutor was to cast a spotlight on him through the impaneling of a special grand jury. The investigation further unhinged him and made him more bloodthirsty. Seeking to ingratiate himself with Lucky

Luciano and gain the support of the most respected Mafia leader, Schultz converted to Roman Catholicism. He apparently believed that religion would bond him with Italian bosses and make him more acceptable to them as a coequal. One of the underworld dignitaries invited to the convert's baptism was Charlie Lucky himself.

More ominously, Schultz began scheming to assassinate Dewey. His men shadowed Dewey and discovered that every morning, after leaving his Manhattan East Side apartment, the prosecutor stopped to make telephone calls from a nearby pharmacy before heading to his downtown office. To avoid disturbing his sleeping wife, Dewey used the pharmacy's public pay phone to confer with his staff on overnight developments. One or two bodyguards accompanying Dewey remained outside the drugstore. Schultz decided that the store was an ideal trap. A lone hit man, using a gun equipped with a silencer, could drill Dewey while he was seated in the booth, and then knock off the pharmacist. The early-morning sidewalk and traffic noise, Schultz reckoned, would drown out the gunfire and cover the hit man's escape.

With his plan worked out, Schultz offered the job to Albert Anastasia, one of the Mafia's most efficient triggermen, who had Lucky Luciano's ear. Schultz rationalized that Dewey was a menace to all the bosses, not just him, and his elimination was a priority. Anastasia lost no time in relaying the news to Luciano, who summoned an emergency meeting of the Commission.

The Mafia's supreme council unanimously vetoed Schultz's scheme. According to Joe Bonanno, the bosses considered the plot insane. They feared that slaying a prosecutor with Dewey's prestige would spark enormous public outcry against the rackets. Among the American Mafia's original leaders, there was unanimous accord that incorruptible law-enforcement officials and investigators—straight arrows—were immune from underworld revenge and violence. Murdering Dewey, the bosses reasoned, would only unleash more Thomas E. Deweys and law-enforcement fury against all of them.

The Commission session did end with approval of a hit—but the target would be the Dutchman. Schultz had become a serious liability to the Mafia godfathers; his irrational ravings about Dewey and his unquenchable thirst for violence attracted too much attention to their own rackets. The Mafia preferred a quiet style of business.

Trying to evade Dewey's scrutiny, Schultz holed up in a three-room suite at the best hotel in Newark, New Jersey. To eradicate Schultz, the Commission selected the Mob's star executioner, Albert Anastasia, whom Schultz had wanted to hire for the hit on Dewey. Anastasia is believed to have assigned the Commission's contract to Jewish professional executioners working for the Mafia. Three armed men cornered Schultz as he was having dinner on October 23, 1935, at the Palace Chop House and Tavern in downtown Newark. In the men's room, one gunman mortally wounded Schultz. A fusillade by the trio finished off two of his bodyguards and Otto Berman, better known along Broadway as "Abbadabba," the mathematical genius and accountant in charge of Dutch's financial ledgers.

Schultz's death eliminated the last big-time non-Mafia gang and automatically expanded Lucky Luciano's empire. Without opposition, Lucky appropriated Schultz's numbers banks and took charge of the Dutchman's restaurant shake-downs. Schultz's warnings, however, about the danger of Dewey's long reach were prescient.

7

Unlucky Lucky

The Mob's murder of Dutch Schultz cleared the way for Dewey's vigorous team of prosecutors and investigators to home in on another inviting quarry: Charles "Lucky" Luciano.

Charlie Lucky, although the strongest Mob dictator in 1936, was relatively unknown to the public. His last arrest and prison stretch occurred when he was a teenager and, like other New York Mafia notables, he preferred operating behind the scenes and keeping his name out of headlines. He was less discreet about his alliances with Tammany Hall leaders and socialized openly with them at major political gatherings.

At the 1932 Democratic Party convention in Chicago, which nominated Franklin D. Roosevelt for the presidency, Luciano and his politically farsighted adjutant, Frank Costello, accompanied the Tammany delegation. Of course, the mafiosi could not cast votes at the convention, but they were treated like royalty by the powerful Tammany leaders. Lucky shared a suite with James J. Hines, a West Side district leader who would later be convicted of taking underworld bribes to fix police and judges in gambling cases. Costello's roommate was one of their close friends and a high-powered political connection, Albert Marinelli. Affectionately nicknamed "Uncle Al" by mobsters, Marinelli was the first Italian Democratic district leader in New York and held the pivotal post of city clerk. His job included supervising inspectors who tabulated votes in city elections. Besides having the ability to stuff ballot boxes, Marinelli was of particular help to the Mafia and other criminals because he oversaw the selection of grand jurors.

Despite Luciano's attempts to keep a low profile, Dewey's squad was aware of his high underworld rank and his political ties to the Democratic machine. The investigators were not deceived by his pretense that he made a substantial living from shooting craps, sports gambling, and bookmaking. Dewey's examiners discovered that Luciano's luxurious lifestyle could never be financed solely through bookmaking and gambling. For starters, Luciano maintained his own private plane for jaunts to Saratoga Springs, Miami, and other resorts. Dewey's detectives theorized that Luciano also kept the plane as an emergency getaway vehicle in the event of trouble. A stylish dresser, bachelor, and party animal, Lucky registered under the assumed name Charles Ross at the elegant Waldorf-Astoria Hotel, where he lived year-round in 36C, a posh three-room suite. The apartment rented for $7,600 a year, the equivalent of more than $100,000 in today's money.

The governor's executive order establishing Dewey's temporary office as special prosecutor specified that his main mandate was the eradication of the numbers rackets in the city. Dewey, whose stern visage and bristling black mustache were frequently pictured in newspaper stories, wasted no time in broadening his prosecutorial horizons. Trying to rally support for his gang-busting campaign, he announced through newspapers and radio broadcasts that his objectives went far beyond wiping out numbers banks. His goal, he declared, was to rid the city of what he termed "industrial rackets," the Mob's violent exploitation of businesses and unions that inflated prices for a hard-pressed Depression-era population. On the radio, in his mellow baritone, he appealed to the public to supply him with leads and tips.

Dewey's first stabs at surveillance and background investigations of Luciano failed to turn up damaging racketeering evidence against him. Detectives and lawyers discovered that Luciano, obviously wary of wiretaps, was circumspect in his telephone conversations. Moreover, he apparently kept no records on paper; all incriminating financial details were in his head.

But Dewey's agents unexpectedly came upon a lead that entangled Luciano in a vice crime. The path to Luciano began when Dewey's only woman staff member, Eunice Carter, badgered him into examining corruption inside the city's Women's Court. Carter suspected that there was unrestrained fixing of cases and flouting of the law among judges, lawyers, and bondsmen when prostitutes were brought before that special court. Dewey reluctantly gave tentative approval for a limited inquiry, insisting that he was more interested in industrial rackets and did not want to be portrayed as a puritanical prosecutor of fallen women and madams.

To Dewey's amazement, the Women's Court investigation went far beyond corrupt court personnel. It led directly to Lucky's gangsters. Unlike federal statutes and court rulings that, in the 1930s, virtually prohibited government agents from installing wiretaps and bugs, New York State law permitted court-approved telephone interceptions. Mainly through wiretaps of brothels, investigators uncovered clues that an organization referred to in the wiretapped conversations as "the Combine" and "the Combination" was in control of about three hundred whorehouses in Manhattan and Brooklyn, which employed two thousand working girls. More crucial to Dewey was the discovery that a top Luciano henchman, often seen with him, David "Little Davie" Betillo, was overseeing bordello operations and siphoning a huge hunk of the $12 million-a-year gross from organized prostitution. The investigation revealed that Italians had largely replaced Jewish gangsters as the dominant force in the brothel business, a pattern similar to the Mafia's takeover of other rackets in the city from Jewish and Irish hoodlums.

In January 1936, Dewey's men simultaneously raided eighty bordellos, arresting hundreds of prostitutes, madams, and "bookers," men who helped manage the houses, recruit women, and assign them to different locations as needed. Using threats of high bail and long pretrial imprisonment unless the suspects cooperated, Dewey's staff convinced a good number of prostitutes, madams, bookers, and pimps caught in the sweeps to testify and dramatize the magnitude of the huge network. In addition to witnesses who implicated Luciano's lieutenants, three prostitutes claimed that they had direct knowledge of Charlie Lucky's involvement in the ring.

Aware that Dewey was closing in, Luciano fled to Hot Springs, the Arkansas refuge for Owney Madden and other privileged gangsters. Dewey obtained an extradition order to bring him back on ninety counts of "aiding and abetting compulsory prostitution." An Arkansas state judge complied by jailing Luciano for a hearing. Luciano, however, had well-placed friends in the easily corrupted Hot Springs government and, after barely four hours in the lockup, he was released. His $5,000 bail had been provided by no less an official than the chief detective of Hot Springs.

"I may not be the most moral and upright man that lives," an indignant Luciano told reporters after learning of the charges. "But I have not at any time stooped so low as to become involved in aiding prostitution."

Luciano's lawyers were busy finding reasons to rescind the extradition order when Dewey's men swooped down on Hot Springs and, with the help of state troopers, rearrested the celebrity fugitive. Before Luciano's attorneys and Hot Springs officials could react, Dewey's detectives kidnapped Luciano and spirited him out of the Razorback State.

The trial of Luciano and twelve codefendants in May and June 1936 marked the first time that Dewey used his new legal weapon, joinder indictments, to link a group of defendants in a single case. Luciano, of course, was the central target. In his opening statement Dewey gave him star billing as New York's "czar of organized crime" and the headman of "the Combine," the prostitution racket.

Dewey lined up sixty-eight witnesses, almost all hookers, pimps, madams, bookers, and jailbirds who admitted they had been promised lenient sentences, immunity, or probation for aiding the prosecution. Dewey's main strategy was to depict the prostitutes as desperate victims of the Depression, exploited and terrorized by the Combine's ruthless sentries.

"I tell you, I was afraid," a former prostitute testified. "I know what the Combination does to girls who talk. Plenty of girls who talked too much had their feet burned and their stomachs burned with cigarette butts and their tongues cut."

Only three erstwhile prostitutes from Dewey's large clutch of witnesses provided testimony directly linking Luciano to the accusations. The most damaging allegations came from an admitted heroin addict named Cokey Flo Brown, who said she had accompanied her pimp to late-night meetings with Lucky at which business matters were discussed. According to Cokey Flo, she heard Lucky propose a plan to franchise whorehouses, "the same as the A and P." She further recalled that Luciano once pondered the idea of placing the madams on salary, instead of allowing them to take a cut from the gross proceeds.

Another prostitute said she had sex several times with Lucky in his Waldorf-Astoria Towers apartment, and after some sessions overheard snatches of his conversations with codefendants. She claimed to have listened in as Luciano gave instructions to punish an uncooperative madam by wrecking her establishment. On another occasion, she testified, Luciano had ordered a hike in prices to increase profits. A Waldorf chambermaid and a waiter identified other defendants as having often been seen visiting Lucky in his suite. Their testimony hardened Dewey's case against Luciano by implicating him through association with men against whom there was more concrete evidence.

Defense lawyers attacked the prosecution witnesses as a collection of unreliable drug addicts and felons pressured by Dewey into lying to save themselves from prison sentences. Luciano was the victim of "the distorted imaginations of broken-down prostitutes," the defense team argued. The attorneys characterized Dewey as a headline-hunting, ruthlessly ambitious prosecutor—"a boy scout" and "a boy prosecutor"—who manufactured a sensational case against Lucky as a catapult for his own political career.

A questionable defense ploy was an attempt to portray Luciano as a successful gambler and bookie, too wealthy and virtuous to taint himself in the sordid demimonde of prostitution. Lucky took the dangerous step of testifying and matching wits with Dewey. Under gentle questioning by his lawyer, the overconfident witness denied ever meeting the former whores who testified against him, maintained he only knew one of his dozen codefendants, and had no knowledge of the so-called Combine or Combination.

"I give to 'em," Lucky quipped when asked if had ever profited from or was involved in organized prostitution. "I never took."

Cross-examination proved more hazardous. Having culled confidential police files and gathered from informers every tidbit about Luciano's past, Dewey coolly lacerated Lucky. Pounded by Dewey about contradictions in his testimony, a squirming and perspiring Luciano acknowledged that he might have lied or omitted details in direct examination. He could only weakly muster, "I don't know" or "I can't remember," to a spate of Dewey's questions about his falsehoods on the witness stand.

The prosecutor further undermined Luciano's denials of acquaintance with many of his codefendants by producing records of telephone calls from his Waldorf Astoria suite to their numbers. Luciano's explanation that someone else probably used his private phone for personal calls must have sounded lame to the jury. Dewey also produced hotel records that phone calls were made to Al Capone and to a veritable "Who's Who" list of reputed major criminals in the country.

Dewey dug up Luciano's tax returns from 1929 to 1935, which showed his highest declared gross annual income was $22,500. Stammering and mumbling, Luciano was unable to explain how he lived like a sultan on his reported income.

Probably the most embarrassing moment for the proud Mafia don was Dewey's disclosure that in 1923, when he was twenty-five, Luciano had evaded a narcotics arrest by informing on a dealer with a larger cache of drugs.

"You're just a stool pigeon," Dewey belittled him. "Isn't that it?"

"I told them what I knew," a downcast Luciano replied, in effect conceding to his peers that he had once violated the code of *omertà*.

The jury needed only nine hours to deliberate. Luciano listened stolidly as the foreman intoned guilty verdicts on all counts against him and his main co-defendants. For Lucky it meant a prison sentence of thirty to fifty years. The next year, his appeal was rejected despite recantations by the three principal witnesses against him. Dewey rebutted the appeal with evidence that the recantations were perjuries, obtained from intimidated or drug-addicted witnesses by Luciano's troops.

Overnight Dewey's triumph magnified him into a national hero. He lectured on the radio and in movie newsreels (the 1930s equivalent of network television) about the dangers of syndicated crime.

Hollywood noticed his exploits. The popular movie *Marked Woman*, based on the Luciano case, opened in 1937 with Humphrey Bogart playing the lead male role, a dynamic DA modeled on Dewey. Bette Davis starred as the courageous heroine who risked her life to expose vicious racketeers and their abuse of women. In the movie the women were portrayed as naive nightclub hostesses, not prostitutes.

The courtroom contest with Luciano was undoubtedly a boon to Dewey's political career, almost sending him to the White House. He went on to win elections as DA of Manhattan and governor of New York State, but was unsuccessful as the Republican candidate for the presidency in 1944 and 1948.

Lucky Luciano was the only major New York Mafia leader of his era that Dewey or any other prosecutor convicted of a serious felony. The evidence by the three witnesses that tied him directly to the prostitution enterprise was astonishingly thin. Defense lawyers made a monumental blunder by allowing Luciano to testify, thereby opening the door to Dewey's hammering cross-examination about issues that were extraneous to the charges: his criminal past, his lifestyle, and his links to the well-known Al Capone.

Most Mafia and legal scholars who have reviewed the trial record agree that Luciano as the family boss profited from the prostitution racket; yet, in retrospect, they suspect there is a strong possibility that he may have been framed by compliant witnesses with false accusations. These experts believe that as the nation's supreme Mafia godfather, he was too important and busy to micro-manage the bordello business and allow himself to become implicated in the specific counts leveled against him, "aiding and abetting compulsory prostitution." It would have been out of character for the leader of the nation's largest Mafia borgata to bother with the minutiae of running brothels, as the prosecution asserted. There is, however, indisputable evidence that members of Luciano's crime family established a protection racket, compelling the independent madams and brothel operators to pay a franchise fee to stay open. The correct accusation against Luciano should have been extortion, but Dewey lacked sufficient evidence to pin that more complicated charge on him.

Another contemporary big-time boss, Joe Bonanno, who was well versed in the magnitude of the Mafia's 1930s rackets, was dubious about Dewey's contention that Luciano was a prostitution profiteer. Lucky's "earners" most likely dropped his name to intimidate whorehouse owners into paying for protection, Bonanno recounted in *A Man of Honor*. "Lastly, Dewey built up a case not so much against Luciano as against Luciano's name," Bonanno pointed out.

Another naysayer with credentials was Polly Adler, New York's best-known madam of high-class brothels, and an authority on the underworld society of the 1930s and '40s. "Certainly," she bragged in her memoirs, "I believe that in the many years I was associated with prostitution if there had even been even a hint of a rumor of a tie-up between Charlie and 'the Combination' I would have heard of it."

Far from his luxury surroundings in Manhattan, Lucky was imprisoned in the Siberia of the state penal system, the maximum-security Clinton Penitentiary in Dannemora, New York, near the Canadian border. As inmate 92168, Luciano was assigned to work in the steaming prison laundry. But just as on the outside, Lucky found a comfortable niche inside prison walls. In return for gifts of food and money and as homage to his godfather status, prisoners substituted for him in the laundry, cleaned his cell, and took care of all his odious prison chores. Little Davie Betillo, a codefendant convicted in the prostitution case, became Luciano's personal valet and chef, preparing Lucky's favorite delicacies in a cellblock kitchen that the authorities set aside for his private use.

Guards, aware of Luciano's criminal stature, never disturbed him. He spent most of his time playing cards, strolling around the prison, and watching handball and baseball games. Inmates lined up in the recreation yard for the opportunity to talk with him.

"He practically ran the place," a guard observed. "He used to stand there in the yard like he was the warden."

8

Prime Minister

Lucky Luciano was gone but his crime family was intact, functioning just as smoothly as when he had been at the helm.

In accordance with Mafia tradition, a boss's crown can be relinquished only by death or by abdication. Thus, even behind prison walls five hundred miles from New York, Charlie Lucky remained as titular leader of his family, with the authority, if it pleased him, to transmit commands to the city through reliable messengers who visited him in Dannemora.

But the gang's day-to-day operations and urgent decisions had to be in the hands of someone on the scene. Before departing for prison, Luciano turned over the administrative reins of the borgata to a regent, Frank Costello, appointing him as acting boss. At the start of Luciano's imprisonment, there was still a faint hope that his conviction would be overturned on appeal and he would return to the throne before long. When the appeal failed in 1937, Luciano was seemingly doomed to spend the rest of his life in prison. Costello, by default, assumed the title of boss of America's largest Mob family, with more than three hundred soldiers under his command.

Dewey's conviction of Luciano paradoxically proved the wisdom of Lucky's managerial strategy for Mafia survival. Costello easily filled Luciano's shoes, and the rest of the borgata's structure—the capos, the crews, the soldiers, the associates—remained secure. The law-enforcement establishment may have rejoiced at the victories over Luciano and Capone, but they failed to understand a seismic change had occurred in the families of organized crime: the viability of Mafia families was not endangered by the imprisonment of a top man. Unlike the loosely organized Jewish and Irish ethnic gangs fashioned haphazardly by the likes of Dutch Schultz and Owney Madden, a cohesive borgata did not disintegrate at the sudden absence of its head man.

Dewey and his successors for decades after the 1930s successfully prosecuted dozens of mid- and low-level Italian-American and other ethnic mobsters. Under the prevailing laws, Dewey focused on individuals, not on their organizations. It is doubtful that Dewey—the most distinguished and respected rackets prosecutor of his era—and other leading law-enforcement authorities visualized the dimensions of the Mafia's makeup and power.

In 1937 Frank Costello was a highly regarded and well-known figure in New York's underworld and in the nation's Mafia legions. Yet he took control of the Luciano family without exciting the faintest interest or concern within New York and federal law-enforcement agencies.

Christened Francesco Castiglia in 1891, he was the youngest of six children in a family from Cosenza, a mountain village in Calabria, a province in the toe of Italy. The family emigrated when Costello was four; space in steerage was so tight, he said, that he slept in a large cooking pot. The journey ended in East Harlem, and like so many of his future Mafia partners, he exchanged rustic poverty for an urban slum.

At seventeen and twenty-one, Costello was arrested for robbing women in the streets, but alibis provided by relatives and friends won him acquittals. He was less fortunate at twenty-three, when he was picked up for carrying a concealed gun and served ten months in prison. He later claimed that he never again packed a gun and that his prison stretch taught him to get results by using his head instead of violence.

Out of prison, Francesco Castiglia legally changed his name to Frank Costello, apparently because he felt an Irish name sounded more American, and teamed up with Lucky Luciano in Joe the Boss Masseria's gang. Financed partly by Arnold Rothstein, Costello became a premier bootlegger. He was particularly successful in running vast hauls of expensive Scotch whiskey from Canada to the New York area. Influenced by Luciano's open-door ethnic policy,

Costello had no compunctions about forging temporary partnerships and making deals with Jewish and Irish rumrunners. Costello's underworld pals said he would later boast that one of his prohibition collaborators in the 1920s was Joseph Kennedy, the father of President John F. Kennedy.

Preparing for the end of Prohibition, Costello concentrated on upgrading his gambling and bookmaking rings. One of his brilliant strokes was arranging "layoff" pools. For a fee, Costello allowed smaller bookies to transfer or spread bets to his organization. When they were overloaded with wagers on one team or a horse and faced huge losses if their customers collectively picked one big winner, they could "lay off" part of their bets to Costello's pools.

Even before the death of Prohibition, New York's gangland recognized Costello's robust success as "King of the Slots," in a sure-thing gambling gimmick. One of his fronts, the aptly named True Mint Novelty Company, ostensibly a candy-vending-machine outfit, was the biggest supplier of illegal slot machines to mom-and-pop groceries, small soda fountains, and other neighborhood shops. At the height of the slots craze in the early 1930s, Costello's 25,000 one-armed bandits grossed about $500,000 a day. Profits were enormous, even though he had to share some of it with Luciano and others in the borgata. Naturally, there were protection payoffs to Tammany Hall and police officials to encourage them to ignore the gambling laws.

Conditions got sticky for Costello in 1934 when the reform administration of Republican and Fusion Party mayor Fiorello H. LaGuardia ousted the Tammany Democrats from City Hall. LaGuardia's police raids on slots suppliers uncovered records revealing that in 1932 alone, Costello's machines brought in $37 million. Vowing to cleanse the city of "tinhorn" gamblers and racketeers, the feisty LaGuardia got immense publicity mileage by personally wielding an ax to destroy confiscated machines and dumping them into the river.

While LaGuardia's campaign did rid the city of slots, Costello found an alternate site for his arsenal of machines. Going into partnership with a southern Mafia family and the corrupt Huey Long political machine in Louisiana, he flooded bars and clubs in New Orleans and suburban towns with his one-armed moneymakers. At the time, New Orleans was so openly hospitable to bookies, roulette wheels, and high-stake card games that visitors were genuinely unaware that gambling was illegal in the state.

The LaGuardia administration's anti-slots crusade was a minor inconvenience hardly interfering with Costello's overall operations or those of the other Mafia families. As a new boss Costello faced a larger threat from a resentful rival in his own family, Vito Genovese, who believed he was Luciano's rightful heir.

Genovese's ambitions could not be easily dismissed by Costello. He ran one of the toughest crews in the family; his crew had been Luciano's main hit men. A glare from Genovese's dark eyes from beneath bushy eyebrows intimidated the bravest mafioso.

Six years younger than Costello, Genovese had emigrated as a teenager from Rosiglino, a town near Naples, had little schooling, spoke passable but broken English, and made his headquarters in the Little Italy section of Manhattan. Despite his reputation as a thief, thug, and killer, the burly Genovese was only arrested once, when he was twenty, on a gun charge, and served sixty days in jail. His penchant for solving problems—even romantic ones—through violence became Mafia lore. Vito's first wife died in 1931 of tuberculosis, and he fell in love with a married cousin, Anna Vernitico. Associates believed Vito had her husband strangled to death so that he could marry her.

When Costello took over from Luciano, Genovese was branching out into drugs and was the family's leading narcotics trafficker. A murder case, however, relieved Costello of immediate worries about Genovese's jealousy. In 1937 Vito was implicated in the killing three years earlier of a partner who had helped him in a swindle. The slaying occurred after the partner had the temerity to complain about not getting his share of the loot. Learning that prosecutors had a witness ready to testify against him, Genovese fled to Italy. The penniless boy immigrant returned to his native land in comfortable circumstances, reportedly with $750,000 in ready cash. Additionally, Anna Genovese made frequent visits as a courier to Vito, each time carrying $50,000 to $100,000 in cash from Genovese's brother, Michael, who was looking after Vito's racket interests in the United States.

Genovese's departure removed internal hostility to Costello's reign from other factions in the family and quelled resentment of his large slice of the family's spoils from gambling, loan-sharking, Garment Center shakedowns, and the routine thefts and hijackings. The good times enabled Costello to establish himself in legitimate businesses, using relatives as screens for investments in liquor importing, real estate, and oil companies.

Unquestionably, the most dangerous of Costello's activities was his subtle infiltration of important government institutions through his influence in the city's Democratic Party. He was the shadowy broker who undermined justice in the courts and corrupted major officials to protect mobsters and their rackets.

Picking up from Luciano's liaisons with Democratic politicians, Costello used outright bribes and secret contributions to cultivate unprecedented criminal control over Tammany Hall.

Dating back to 1789, Tammany Hall (or its official title, the Executive Committee of the New York County Democratic Committee) was the prototypical big-city political machine by the 1930s. The name Tammany Hall was synonymous with rigging elections, awarding municipal contracts, and handing out patronage jobs. Except for an occasional and short-lived victory by reformers uniting with the Republican Party to elect an independent mayor, Tammany had dominated the city's government for more than one hundred years.

William Marcy Tweed (Boss Tweed), Tammany's chairman in the 1850s and 1860s, became an unparalled symbol of corruption. His most outrageous plundering was the construction of a courthouse behind City Hall that should have cost $250,000. Under Tweed's guidance and sticky fingers, the price tag soared to $12 million.

Tweed's excesses finally landed him in jail, where he died in 1878, but his scandals failed to end Tammany's influence. He was the last Protestant head of Tammany, and his demise led to a takeover by a succession of Irish-American politicians who were in charge when Costello moved in.

Fiorello LaGuardia's election in 1933 and his bashing of Tammany unexpectedly made the Democratic machine politicians more subservient than previously to Mob money. Under the benevolent administration of the playboy Mayor Jimmy Walker from 1926 to 1933, Tammany had filled thousands of municipal posts and got kickbacks from job holders. LaGuardia stripped Tammany of its patronage, its horde of civil service jobs, and its ability to obtain graft by fixing municipal contracts. Bereft of its normal flow of funds to ensure elections to scores of vital city posts, including judgeships and district attorneys, Tammany turned to Frank Costello. The Mob boss gladly opened the money spigots and, in return, became the de facto head of Tammany Hall.

"Costello ran Tammany for decades," noted Ralph F. Salerno, a New York City detective and an expert on organized crime. "A lot of politicians and judges owed their elections and positions to him."

Until Costello came along, the city's Democratic Party was largely in the grip of Irish ward heelers. The Mafia boss thought it was time to install more Italian-American district leaders in Tammany's hierarchy, many of whom were on his payroll, and he did so. The changes in effect placed a Mafia leader in charge of the Democratic Party's most important branch in the city, with the power to nominate candidates for the highest elected offices. Thomas Kessner, a biographer of LaGuardia, found that Costello reversed the relationship that had existed between the Mob and Democratic leaders. "In its heyday Tammany had sold organized crime protection, but by the 1940s the gangster Frank Costello called the shots, and before he was through Tammany spoke with an Italian accent," Kessner wrote.

Other Mafia bosses became indebted to Costello for exerting his sway when their soldiers and associates needed a favor from a judge, a prosecutor, or a well-placed city official. Costello's ability to pull political and judicial strings enhanced his standing in the Mafia's Commission and his bargaining strength with other bosses. Among mafiosi, his political savvy earned him a proud nickname: "the Prime Minister."

Judges, important politicians, congressmen, authors, and New York society and café figures had no qualms about attending soirees that Costello frequently hosted in his penthouse at the Majestic Apartments overlooking Central Park. Tastefully decorated in art deco style, the only ostentatious notes in the apartment were a gold-plated piano and several slot machines. The affable Costello made no attempt to conceal his fascination with gambling, urging his guests to take a whirl at the slots. Unfailingly, every player won a small jackpot of clanking coins. When a guest tried to return the quarters, Costello admonished him, "What do you think I am, a punk? Nobody loses in my house."

Costello successfully camouflaged his political muscle and his criminal background from the public until 1943, when he was tripped up by a legal wiretap on his home phone installed by rackets investigators working for Frank S. Hogan, the Manhattan DA who succeeded Tom Dewey. The inquiry failed to implicate Costello in any rackets charge, but the wires caught him talking unabashedly about his involvement in election campaigns. A conversation with Thomas Aurelio, who had just gotten Tammany Hall's nomination for a state supreme court judgeship, clearly exposed Costello's ability to put judicial robes on obliging candidates.

"Good morning, Francesco, how are you, and thanks for everything," Aurelio said as an opener.

"Congratulations," Costello replied. "It went over perfect. When I tell you something is in the bag, you can rest assured."

"Right now," the grateful Aurelio continued, "I want to assure you of my loyalty for all you have done. It's undying."

At a hearing concerning the nomination, Costello readily admitted that he had obtained Tammany's blessings for Aurelio, which assured his election. An imperturbable Costello acknowledged that he had put in office the current Tammany Hall leader, Michael Kennedy, by persuading four district leaders to swing their support to him. Costello had a simple explanation as to why the district leaders followed his advice: they were "old friends."

The DA released the telephone tapes to the press in an attempt to derail Aurelio's judgeship. Nevertheless, with Tammany's backing, Aurelio was elected to a fourteen-year term. The disclosures of Costello's behind-the-scenes political strength brought him widespread notoriety but failed to loosen his grip on Tammany Hall.

Years later, revelations about a Costello meeting with William O'Dwyer spotlighted how his authority extended to City Hall when the Democrats regained the city's mayoralty in 1946. A former policeman, lawyer, and judge, the Democrat Bill O'Dwyer was elected in 1940 as the Brooklyn District Attorney. The next year, as the Democratic candidate he was defeated for mayor by Fiorello LaGuardia, who won a third term. In World War II, O'Dwyer, now an army brigadier general, attended a December 1942 cocktail party in Costello's penthouse. Three top Tammany Hall leaders were also there, and witnesses observed O'Dwyer and Costello having a long, private tête-à-tête in a corner.

It is inconceivable that as a district attorney and an experienced politician O'Dwyer would have been unaware of Costello's underworld eminence. Political insiders believe that O'Dwyer most likely was looking ahead and courting Costello's good will and endorsement for the 1945 Democratic mayoral nomination. He did get Tammany's support and was elected.

The meeting with Costello became public knowledge after O'Dwyer left office. The former mayor contended that he had sought out Costello as part of a military investigation into reports that a business partner of Costello's was cheating the army in a uniform-manufacturing contract. O'Dwyer, however, admitted that he never filed an official report about contacting Costello or on his presumed inquiry into the uniform contract.

Twice elected mayor in the 1940s, O'Dwyer conceded when he was out of office that he had owed political favors to Costello. Part of the debt was repaid, O'Dwyer acknowledged, by appointing friends of Costello and other Mafia big shots to important municipal positions, including the Fire Department commissioner and the second-highest official in the city's law department. "There are things you have to do politically if you want cooperation," O'Dwyer replied cryptically when questioned about the appointments and his relationship with

Costello. The import of O'Dwyer's admissions was clear: the Mob had been an unseen power in the political governing of America's largest city for decades.

In the rare interviews that Frank Costello gave, he never admitted any involvement with the Mafia or any attempt to corrupt New York's government. But it was obvious that he craved the same acceptance in the sophisticated upperworld that he had achieved in the underworld. "Other kids are brought up nice and sent to Harvard and Yale," he said, lamenting his meager education and his "dees and dose" street-talk diction. "Me? I was brought up like a mushroom."

Searching for inner peace while hovering between criminal affiliates and respected society, Costello tried psychoanalysis. His analyst suggested that the successful mobster was ashamed of his past and recommended that he ditch his old pals and develop new relationships by spending more time with cultured friends. It was an impossible solution for a borgata boss, and Costello dropped the analyst instead of the gangsters.

Despite an outburst of headlines about Costello's unsavory background, his importance and influence was recognized by philanthropic groups that sought his support. The Salvation Army named him vice chairman of a charity drive in 1949. Costello gladly turned over the popular Copacabana nightclub, in which he was a secret owner, for a Salvation Army fund-raising dinner. Besides Costello's mafiosi brethren, the dinner was dutifully attended by scores of judges, city officials, and politicians, all apparently unconcerned by published reports tarnishing Costello as an underworld and political power broker. About the same time, in an interview with the journalist Bob Considine, Costello tried to justify his life. He groped for an explanation defining his chosen career. "For a long time I've been trying to figure just what a racketeer is," Costello said—and then proceeded to give a terse Mafia apologia for the sociological reasons that compelled him to become a criminal. "I never went to school past the third grade, but I've graduated from ten universities of hard knocks, and I've decided that a racketeer is a fellow who tries to get power, prestige, or money at the expense of entrenched power, prestige, or money."

Murder Inc.

With his conservative, smartly tailored appearance and genial smile. Frank Costello reinvented himself to his society friends as a successful gambler-investor—an average nonviolent businessman. Like much of his life, Costello's public persona was a fraud. Staying on top required all Mafia bosses to maintain death squads that guarded their flanks and guaranteed that their edicts would be enforced. The Prime Minister was no exception.

Whenever violence or threats were required to protect his assets, Costello often counted on Willie Moretti, a longtime hoodlum buddy from Prohibition days and the Masseria gang. Moretti lived in northern New Jersey and headed a rugged crew of cutthroats who could roam anywhere. Another private deadly resource available to Costello and other Mafia hierarchs was a band of professional contract killers that a newspaper reporter would one day dub "Murder Incorporated."

Spawned by Jewish gangsters, this murderous arm of the Mafia was mainly the brainchild of Louis Buchalter, better known by his shorter nickname, "Lepke." He was one of four sons brought up in New York's Lower East Side. In his boyhood, the storied neighborhood was a densely populated, turbulent warren of tenements, sweatshops, peddlers, pushcarts, and immigrants striving to survive. It was also a swirling carnival for every species of criminal.

Buchhalter's nickname stemmed from the Yiddish diminutive "Lepkele," Little Louis, his mother's favorite name for him. Despite the family's poverty, his three brothers were well educated and became, respectively, a rabbi, a dentist, and a pharmacist. In contrast, by the time Lepke Buchalter finished the eighth grade he was a well-schooled mugger and an accomplished pickpocket. Sent as a juvenile to reformatories and prison for robberies and thefts, in 1920, at age twenty-three, he was released just in time for the advent of Prohibition. Slightly built and physically unimposing, Lepke signed on as a strong-arm enforcer for Arnold Rothstein and other Jewish gangsters, mainly for strikebreaking duties in the Garment Center.

By 1927, Lepke had shot his way to the top of a predominantly Jewish gang, the Gorilla Boys, and learned it was more profitable to take over union locals than to work solely as a strikebreaker. That way he could cash in from both sides, terrorizing and shaking down both owners and unions in the garment, fur, trucking, and bakery industries.

The Gorilla Boys' murderous record was known and appreciated by the Mafia's high command. Albert Anastasia gave the contract to assassinate Dutch Schultz to Lepke, who dispatched three of his accomplices to finish off the Dutchman.

In the 1930s, many garment manufacturers operated factories and shops in Brownsville, a largely Jewish neighborhood in Brooklyn. Lepke hired a local gang of young killers and loan sharks to handle his garment-industry rackets there. The Brownsville gang had earlier committed murders on request and come under the hegemony of a major Mafia figure in Brooklyn, Albert Anastasia. Known by the honorific "Don Umberto," Anastasia, a notable in the Vincent Mangano borgata, hit upon a novel plan for carrying out Mafia murders, which was endorsed by Costello and the other Commission members. With Anastasia relaying orders through Lepke, the "Boys from Brooklyn" would be paid to track down and slaughter victims the Mob wanted eliminated. Thus Jewish killers, rather than Italians, would take all the risks but would be ignorant about the motive for the murders. Even if the hit went awry and the assassins were arrested, they would have no information or evidence to implicate the Mafia in their crimes.

A standard formula was used for most freelance contract murders in New York and out of town. An assassin would meet someone who would "finger," point out, the intended target, who would then be whacked at an opportune moment and place. The hit man would leave the area immediately, and the local associates of the victim would have ironclad alibis.

Long before he took over Murder Inc., Anastasia, a native of southern Italy, had made his mark in New York's Mafia by his psychopathic enjoyment of watching suffering victims die. He relished the private honorific his mates bestowed on him, "the Executioner," which the press later transformed into "Lord High Executioner," borrowing the title from Gilbert and Sullivan's *The Mikado*. Anastasia and his brother Anthony "Tough Tony" Anastasio (a made man who spelled his surname differently) dominated Brooklyn's waterfront for the Mangano borgata through Anthony's position as the head of Local 1814 of the International Longshoremen's Association (ILA) and Albert's squad of bruisers and gunmen.

Even in hard times, the Brooklyn piers were a treasure chest for the two brothers and the Mangano family. Most longshoremen were not steadily employed by stevedoring companies, and jobs were parceled out by ILA foremen at shape-ups when ships docked. Kickbacks to foremen from workers needing jobs were routine, with a large portion of the payments funneled to Tough Tony, who appointed the foremen. All of the Mob's bread-and-butter gambling and loan-sharking rackets on the waterfront were monopolized by Albert the Executioner. And inside knowledge about valuable cargo entering and leaving the harbor provided ripe opportunities for big-time hijackings and thefts.

For about five years, the contract-murder plan operated smoothly for the Mafia and Lepke. By the late 1930s, Lepke had about 250 musclemen working for him in labor rackets and loan-sharking, and in a drug-trafficking ring dealing in heroin brought in from Asia and distributed throughout the country. About a dozen Boys from Brooklyn, proficient with guns, ice picks, and ropes to shoot, stab, and strangle their prey, carried out the bulk of Murder Inc.'s assignments.

Murder Inc.'s corporate name was invented by Harry Feeney, a reporter on the old *New York World-Telegram*. Among the Jewish contingent of savage-tempered slayers were Harry "Pittsburgh Phil" Strauss, who, upset by slow restaurant service, pierced the eye of a waiter with a fork; Charles "the Bug" or "Handsome Charlie" Workman, who finished off Dutch Schultz with one blast from his .45 caliber pistol; Philip "Farvel" Cohen; Abe "Pretty" Levine; Samuel "Tootsie" Feinstein; and Seymour "Red" Levine, whose religious piety compelled him to decline assignments if they fell on the Jewish High Holy Days.

The killing machine of Murder Inc. was partly integrated, and Anastasia sometimes called upon a corps of Italian-American assassins, including Harry "Happy" Maione, Frank "Dasher" Abbandando and Vito "Chicken Head" Gurino, who sharpened his skills by shooting off the heads of live chickens.

Unlike the frightening Albert Anastasia, his partner in murder, Lepke appeared unintimidating, with soft brown eyes and a mild voice. His passion for reading, spending nights at home with his wife and young son, and playing golf, instead of carousing with boisterous flunkies, brought him a collegial nickname that he liked, "the Judge." This outward demeanor was totally deceptive. Ordering murders was part of his routine agenda, and he seemingly enjoyed participating in the gruesome ones.

Homicide detectives were never able to pinpoint the precise number of slayings committed by Murder Inc., but prosecutors estimated that the contract killers left a trail of at least sixty bodies. Some law-enforcement officials believe the total was far above one hundred, with most of the slayings in the New York area. There was also disagreement over how many were ordered by the Mafia and how many were killed solely for Lepke's benefit or for other clients.

The efficiency of Murder Inc., and rumors of the Mob's matchless death platoon reinforced in America's underworld the terrifying effect of a Sicilian proverb: "Between the law and the Mafia, the law is not the most to be feared."

Various techniques were used for Cosa Nostra rubouts, often depending on the motive for the slaying. An informer would have a canary or a rodent placed in his mouth as a warning of the harsh penalty meted out to "squealers" and "rats" for helping the police. Witnesses to crimes who had agreed to testify would have their eyes shot or carved out. And men who coveted or molested a female relative of a mafioso were killed and castrated.

Murder Inc. devised another technique to escape detection, patterned slightly on the death of Hamlet's sleeping father, who was murdered by poison poured into his ear. The Boys from Brooklyn sometimes dispatched a victim by stabbing him with an ice pick deep enough in an ear to strike the brain, in the belief that a careless autopsy might attribute the death to a cerebral hemorrhage.

Santo Trafficante, the Mafia's standard bearer in Florida from the early 1950s until his death in 1987, once explained to his lawyer, Frank Ragano, the reason why many corpses in Mob executions vanished. Ragano knew that Trafficante was allied with several New York families and that he and the northern mobsters used similar murder methods.

"First of all, if there's no body, the police have a harder time finding out who did it," Ragano recalled Trafficante saying to him in a candid moment. "And number two, some guys do things so bad, you have to punish their families after they're gone." By punishing the families, Trafficante meant that there could be no church mass or burial for the victim; and under most state laws, the relatives would be unable to collect life insurance for at least seven years, when the missing man could finally be declared legally dead.

Lepke's success was unhindered until, at the height of his power in 1938, he discovered that Thomas Dewey's hound dogs were hot on his trail. The DA's detectives and accountants uncovered leads indicating that through industrial rackets Lepke was extorting $5 million to $10 million a year from companies and unions. Dewey suspected that a percentage of Lepke's take in Manhattan and Brooklyn was going to the Costello and Mangano families.

Deciding to employ Murder Inc. for his own personal use, Lepke went into hiding and gave Anastasia a list of potential "rats" that he wanted killed before Dewey reached them. At least seven possible witnesses against Lepke were wiped out. With federal authorities hunting Lepke on separate narcotics charges, the Commission decided the manhunts were creating too much law-enforcement pressure and it was time to sacrifice the fugitive before he endangered them. Like Dutch Schultz, Lepke had become a liability and a threat to the Mafia.

For some enigmatic reason, the Commission spared Lepke's life. With the assistance of an intermediary, the newspaper columnist Walter Winchell, on August 24, 1939, Lepke surrendered to J. Edgar Hoover, the director of the Federal Bureau of Investigation. Winchell on his weekly radio broadcasts had urged the gangster to give up peacefully before he was gunned down in a shoot-out with the police or federal agents. Albert Anastasia drove Lepke from a hide-out in Brooklyn to the rendezvous with Hoover and Winchell on a midtown Manhattan street, near Madison Square Park. Before Lepke agreed to come out of his safe house, Anastasia reportedly assured him that with the Mafia's help, a deal had been negotiated that he would be tried only on federal charges, not by Dewey. The next year, Lepke was convicted on federal drug-trafficking violations and sentenced to fourteen years. But Anastasia had deceived him. Of course there was no Mafia pact with Dewey, who prosecuted him on a state indictment for extortion and tacked on a separate sentence of thirty years.

Lepke's involvement with the Brownsville gang also surfaced; he was hit with an additional charge in Brooklyn that he had ordered the murder of an independent trucker before the man could inform on Lepke's violent takeover of garment-industry trucking routes. One of the brutal cogs in Murder Inc., Abraham "Kid Twist" Reles, was arrested for homicide in 1940 and, to save his neck, agreed to testify against Lepke and other members of the gang in cases brought by the Brooklyn DA's office. (Reles obtained the Kid Twist moniker from his ability to deftly strangle an unsuspecting victim with one artful turn of a rope.)

Investigative leads from Reles, who possessed a photographic memory about dozens of contract slayings, were crucial in constructing a homicide case against Lepke in 1941 and condemning him to execution in the electric chair. Desperate to save himself, Lepke played his last card, reportedly offering to testify about organized-crime ties to one of the nation's most prestigious labor icons, Sidney Hillman, the founder of the Amalgamated Clothing Workers Union. Lepke asserted that from 1932 to 1937, he got a weekly retainer from Hillman that was normally passed along to him through henchmen. A portion of the payment, Lepke indicated, went to Luciano and other mafiosi who also had their hooks into the union and garment-industry rackets.

The payoffs were mainly for slugging or enforcement work against union and management troublemakers who were causing problems for Hillman. Lepke claimed that he occasionally met privately with Hillman, and that the labor leader once gave him a $25,000 bonus for helping his union win a tough strike. Lepke's most serious accusation implicated Hillman in the 1931 murder of a garment manufacturer who had fiercely resisted a unionizing drive by the Amalgamated.

Lepke's accounts were passed on to Manhattan District Attorney's Office, the FBI, and the Federal Bureau of Narcotics. Two of Lepke's butchers, Paul Berger and Albert Tannenbaum, who were under arrest on murder and other accusations, added substance to Lepke's allegations by declaring that they could verify segments of his stories about Hillman.

Dewey had long been distrustful of Hillman and the city's other powerful clothing industry union head, David Dubinsky, the president of the International Ladies Garment Workers Union. Soon after his appointment as a special prosecutor, Dewey invited the two union dignitaries to his home for dinner, seeking their help in combating the industry's gangsters. Both adamantly denied the slightest knowledge of any racketeering or union corruption.

Years later, after his retirement, Dewey, in an oral history of his life given to Columbia University, scoffed at Dubinsky's and Hillman's assumed ignorance. "They both dealt with these gangsters and knew all about them," Dewey stated. "But they wouldn't give me the slightest bit of help of any kind."

None of the law-enforcement officials and prosecutors who reviewed

Lepke's claims launched a deep investigation into the assertions of Hillman's Mob connections. Dewey's office and the other agencies said they lacked independent corroborating evidence of corruption and other grave felonies described by Lepke and his cronies. Federal and state prosecutors were wary of undertaking an intensive investigation of the politically prominent Hillman in the early 1940s, based on testimony from Lepke, an arch villain on death row, as their prime witness. At that time, Hillman was a supporter of and adviser to President Franklin D. Roosevelt, and any hint that he was linked to organized crime would have ignited a monumental scandal at the White House.

With the allegations against Hillman buried, Lepke's last hope to escape the electric chair was a 1944 appeal for clemency to the governor of New York State. The governor at that time happened to be Thomas E. Dewey, serving his first term, and he declined to commute the death sentence to life imprisonment.

Thus, Louis Lepke Buchalter, at age forty-seven became the only significant American organized-crime leader to be executed for murder.

In addition to Lepke, Abe Reles's testimony sent six other Murder Inc. assassins to the electric chair and three others to long prison sentences. On the witness stand, Reles detailed the structure of the gang, identified Don Umberto Anastasia as "our boss" and as the Mob boss of Brooklyn. Don Umberto, however, was never accused of homicide or of any charge involving the lethal Boys from Brooklyn and Murder Inc.

Three days before he was scheduled to testify at Lepke's murder trial, Kid Twist Reles met a mysterious and puzzling death. He and three other prosecution witnesses were under twenty-four-hour police protection in a ten-room suite at Coney Island's Half Moon Hotel. Of the four material witnesses in protective custody, Reles was the only one permitted to sleep alone in a private room. Just before dawn on November 12, 1941, Reles plunged to his death from a window in his room.

According to the police, the thirty-seven-year-old Reles used knotted bedsheet strips, strengthened with a length of copper wire, which he attached to a radiator to lower himself from his sixth-floor window. The makeshift rope snapped, dropping him at least four stories to his death. Three of the five police officers guarding him claimed they were asleep, and two who supposedly were on duty said they had dozed off. Neither the guards nor the three other material witnesses in the suite heard Reles clamber out the window. Seeking explanations for the suspicious death of a vital witness, police officials maintained that Reles had attempted a harebrained escape, or that, as a prank, he had intended to reenter the building from the floor about ten feet below his room and then return to surprise the police officers with his daredevil stunt.

A skeptical press, wondering if Reles might have been shoved out the window, immortalized his death in news stories such as "The canary who could sing but not fly."

The publicity over the episode turned the Half Moon, an undistinguished hotel in a fading beach resort, into one of New York's Mafia landmarks and a tourist curiosity for decades.

At the time of the Murder Inc. trials and Reles's death, William O'Dwyer, the future mayor and the acquaintance of Frank Costello, was the Brooklyn DA. Several years later, an investigation under another district attorney, Miles F. McDonald, turned up a surprising angle. During Reles's testimony at four Brooklyn trials, Albert Anastasia had gone into hiding and O'Dwyer's office had put out a "Wanted" notice to all police precincts that he was being sought for questioning. But after Reles's death, the "Wanted" notices were withdrawn by O'Dwyer's office, and the Mafia despot again was visible on the streets of New York and Brooklyn.

Organized-crime insiders said there were persistent rumors that Frank Costello and other Cosa Nostra bosses raised $100,000 for a contract to kill Reles before he could implicate Anastasia. None of the policemen assigned to guard the celebrated canary was ever brought up on charges of bribery or complicity in Reles's strange finale. Nevertheless, Reles's plunge effectively ended the Murder Inc. investigation and any possibility of connecting that killing machine to Anastasia and the Mafia in a courtroom. O'Dwyer, in fact, defended the police guards at departmental trials for misconduct, and he promoted the officer in charge of the witness-protection unit.

Ten years later, McDonald impaneled a special grand jury to reinvestigate Reles's end. It concluded that the guards were inexplicably lax and the original investigation was slipshod. But the jury believed that Reles "met his death while trying to escape."

The biggest winners from the demise of Lepke, Reles, and Murder Inc. were the five New York borgatas. Whenever necessary, Anastasia and other mafiosi could still muster hit men for important assignments, so the loss of Murder Inc. was not a hardship. And, as a financial windfall, Lepke's most desirable rackets fell into the laps of the Cosa Nostra families run by Frank Costello and Vincent Mangano.

10

A Profitable War

On Sunday, December 7, 1941, the Japanese attacked Pearl Harbor and other U.S. military bases in Hawaii, and America was at war. No further combat occurred in the American homeland and there were no severe civilian privations, but for most of the nation the four-year duration of the war was a time of rationing of scarce goods and personal sacrifice.

The American Mafia sacrificed nothing. As calculating predators, many mafiosi seized upon wartime conditions as a rare opportunity to make substantial profits. The war would also unexpectedly benefit the Mafia's only imprisoned leader, Lucky Luciano.

Before Pearl Harbor, except for Dewey's efforts as special prosecutor and as Manhattan DA, law enforcement in the rest of the New York area and in the country generally had been lax, corrupt, or incompetent in coping with the Cosa Nostra. Wartime put additional strains on federal and state police agencies, many of which lost their best personnel to the military services. Confronting new priorities of protecting the country from spies and saboteurs, law enforcement became even less vigilant and less interested in the difficult task of investigating organized crime.

For the first time since the onset of the Great Depression, the war and the huge defense industry created a roaring economy, full employment, and an abundance of loose money looking to be spent. The New York Mob's gambling mills in sports betting, horse racing, and numbers expanded mightily during the war as economic worries vanished and other recreational and travel opportunities declined.

But it was wartime rationing and the black market that generated the biggest gains for aspiring mafiosi. The government placed strict curbs on obtaining gasoline, tires, clothes, shoes, meat, butter, canned goods, sugar, and other staples, issuing special stamps, coupons, and permits necessary for purchasing the items. Mobsters became instant abusers, mainly by counterfeiting coupons or by getting corrupt government employees to supply them illegally with the scarce federal stamps and selling them for huge profits.

"Wartime rationing of gasoline, meat, and groceries opened a nationwide black market that the American public patronized as eagerly as it had once bought booze," Paul Meskill, a journalist and expert on the Mafia in the 1940s, observed.

Overnight, an obscure capo in Brooklyn, Carlo Gambino, become a millionaire by exploiting the rationing system. A refugee from the Mussolini campaign against the Sicilian Mafia, Gambino in 1921 stowed away on an Italian ship, and sneaked into the United States as an illegal alien at age nineteen. He settled in Brooklyn, where he had numerous relatives, and soon brought over two younger brothers—budding mafiosi from Sicily. At the start of the Castellammarese War, he was attached to "Joe the Boss" Masseria's camp. Before the battle ended in 1931, Gambino switched to the winning Maranzano faction but actually stayed on the sidelines, dodging involvement in any dangerous scrapes.

A bootlegger, closely associated with Albert Anastasia and Vincent Mangano, one of the founding five New York godfathers, Gambino remained in the illegal booze business even after Prohibition ended and, in 1939, was convicted for conspiracy to defraud the government of liquor taxes. The conviction was overturned because of an illegal federal wiretap, and Gambino sidestepped a two-year prison sentence. When the nation went to war in 1941, Gambino, an economic dynamo in the Mangano family, became an entrepreneur in the black market.

Joseph Valachi, a Mob defector who become a government informer, admitted that he, too, had been a black marketeer. Valachi identified Gambino as the Mafia's black-market magnate who pocketed millions of dollars from ration stamps. Gambino, he said, resorted to theft and to bribery to acquire huge supplies of the ration stamps from the Office of Price Administration (OPA), the government agency that oversaw rationing.

"Him and his brother Paul . . . made over a million from ration stamps during the war," Valachi later testified before a Senate committee. "The stamps came out of the OPA's offices. First Carlo's boys would steal them. Then, when the government started hiding them in banks, Carlo made contact and the OPA men sold him the stamps. He really got rich on that." Even Valachi, a low-level soldier, cleaned up on the black market, netting about $150,000 a year by bribing OPA workers to hand over valuable stamps. "There were so many legitimate stamps around, I didn't think it was wise going around with counterfeit stamps," he said.

Through a twist of fate, the war proved immensely useful to Lucky Luciano, languishing in a maximum security prison in upstate New York, far from the city. At the outbreak of the war with Japan, Germany, and Italy, American and Allied ships were being torpedoed and sunk by Nazi submarines (U-boats) off the East Coast at a horrific rate. More than one hundred twenty vessels and hundreds of lives were lost in the first three months of 1942; no U-boats were sunk.

Fear of sabotage on the New York waterfront, America's largest port, heightened in February 1942 when the French luxury liner Normandie, while being converted into a troop ship, caught fire, capsizing in the Hudson River. Much later, it was determined that the fire was apparently caused by workers using acetylene torches, but in early 1942 Naval Intelligence suspected that the ship had been sabotaged by Axis sympathizers. In June 1942, anxiety about harbor security intensified after eight German spies and saboteurs, who had made it to Long Island and Florida from U-boats, were captured.

Concerned that some of the hundreds of Italian-American longshoremen on the docks and fishermen operating small boats might be Mussolini supporters, secretly aiding the U-boats and saboteurs, a Naval Intelligence unit, B-3, assigned more than one hundred agents to ferret out information. The efforts to unearth leads about possible disloyalty were fruitless. Agents quickly discovered that on the Mob-controlled waterfront, strangers were kept at bay by suspicious, tight-lipped stevedores and commercial fishermen.

Looking for help to protect the port of New York, B-3 officials contacted Frank Hogan, the Manhattan DA. Hogan's racket investigators set up a meeting for the intelligence officers with Joseph "Socks" Lanza, the head of a

Seafood Workers' Union local in the Fulton Fish Market and widely recognized as the market's crime commissar. Lanza's underworld nickname "Socks" had no relationship to hosiery; it stemmed from his reputation as a vicious Mafia enforcer.

In 1942 Lanza was a capo in the Costello-Luciano family, and at the Fulton Fish Market—the nation's largest wholesale seafood distribution center—a tyrannical union racketeer. His main stock in trade was double-crossing his union members by extorting bribes from the market's employers for sweetheart contracts. As a sideline show, suppliers and merchants had to pay off Lanza's minions for unloading and loading services; otherwise their perishable products would rot before being sold and transported from the market.

Lanza was willing to cooperate with the federal counterspies, but his power was limited to the Fulton market on the East River in lower Manhattan. His authority did not extend to the vital West Side and Brooklyn piers, all dominated by mafiosi through alliances with the International Longshoremen's Association. Lanza advised the federal agents to reach out to the imprisoned Lucky Luciano, the only man, he said, who could "snap the whip in the entire underworld."

Following up on Lanza's tip, Murray I. Gurfein, a top aide to Hogan, relayed the Navy's request for Luciano's cooperation to his lawyer, Moses Polakoff, and to Meyer Lansky, Luciano's Jewish confederate. Through government intervention, Luciano was transferred from Dannemora to Great Meadow Prison in Comstock, New York, sixty miles north of Albany, a more convenient site for visits by Polakoff and Lansky. To convince Luciano of their good intentions and his importance to their plan, the government also allowed Frank Costello and Socks Lanza to meet with him in prison.

Before his conviction on prostitution charges, Luciano had few racketeering interests in the harbor. But members of his crime family and other Mafia borgatas, and Irish hoodlums who operated on the waterfront, owed him favors. He instructed Meyer Lansky to act as his middleman and to spread the message that he wanted everyone to cooperate and comply with Naval Intelligence requests. Because of Lansky's long relationship with Luciano, none of the Mob controllers of the unions and other activities on the docks questioned the authenticity of his instructions.

Luciano had been in prison for six years and was ineligible for parole for another twenty-four years when the navy request came. He made it clear to his lawyer that he expected his aid to the government to lead to a sentence reduction.

But there was another thought in the back of his mind, and he stressed to Polakoff and Lansky that he wanted his cooperation kept secret. Never naturalized as a citizen, Lucky realized that he could be deported and feared that Mussolini loyalists in Italy might kill or assault him if his wartime assistance to the Allies was disclosed and the Fascists were still in power.

Before the July 1943 Allied invasion of Sicily, Luciano's Mob helpers found several Sicilians who aided Naval Intelligence in preparing maps of Sicilian harbors, and digging up old snapshots of the island's coastline. Press reports after the war that Luciano had managed to contact and instruct Sicilian Mafia leaders to assist in the invasion were absurd fabrications. Luciano was out of touch with the Sicilian Mafia, and neither they nor the American Cosa Nostra made any significant contributions to the Allied victory in Italy. Luciano's influence provided limited help to the war effort. Mobsters obtained ILA union cards that allowed intelligence agents to work and mingle on the waterfront, and none of the unions called strikes or work stoppages that would have crippled the port. There were no acts of sabotage—but there had been none before Luciano's intervention, and there is no evidence that any were ever planned by German agents or Nazi sympathizers.

Even before the war ended, Luciano tried to capitalize on his cooperation with Naval Intelligence. His 1943 appeal for a sentence reduction was rejected, but in the summer of 1945, as the war was ending, he again petitioned the governor for executive clemency, this time citing his assistance to the navy. Naval authorities, belatedly embarrassed that they needed and had recruited organized-crime assistance, refused to confirm Luciano's claim. But the Manhattan DA's office authenticated the facts, and the state parole board unanimously recommended to the governor that Luciano be released and immediately deported. That governor was Thomas E. Dewey, the former prosecutor who had sent Luciano to prison for a minimum of thirty years. In January 1946, Dewey granted Luciano executive clemency, with provisions that he be deported, and—if he reentered the country—that he be treated as an escaped prisoner and forced to complete his maximum sentence of fifty years.

"Upon the entry of the United States into the war," Dewey said in a brief explanation for the release, "Luciano's aid was sought by the Armed Services in inducing others to provide information concerning possible enemy attack. It appears that he cooperated in such effort, although the actual value of the information procured is not clear."

Charles "Lucky" Luciano (center), the visionary godfather and designer of the modern Mafia, escorted by two detectives at a New York City court on June 18, 1936, where he was sentenced on compulsory-prostitution charges. Some experts believe Lucky was framed on the prostitution counts. Deported to Italy when his prison sentence was commuted, Lucky helped mastermind the Mafia's flooding of heroin into America's big cities. *(AP/Wide World Photos)*

Debonair Mafia kingpin Frank Costello, who strived to pass as a legitimate businessman and liked to match wits with Congressional interrogators, smokes a cigarette while testifying before a Senate committee in 1950. Asked about his illegal gambling empire, Costello shrugged: "Maybe I don't know about it." He retired abruptly in 1957 as the boss of a major Mafia family after feared rival Vito Genovese put a contract out on his life. *(AP/Wide World Photos)*

A rare photo of a smiling Vito Genovese taken shortly after he usurped the crown in 1957 from Frank Costello and became boss of a crime family that still bears his name. Vito had a reputation for treachery, including whacking his wife's first husband to clear the way to marry the widow, and for escaping prison sentences. He was finally convicted in 1959 of narcotics trafficking and died in prison a decade later. *(Photo courtesy of Frederick Martens archive)*

One of the original five godfathers, Joe Profaci, appears displeased at having his picture taken after being detained by state troopers at the Mafia's aborted 1957 summit meeting in Apalachin, New York. Celebrated as the "Olive Oil King," he was the largest importer of olive oil and tomato paste in the country and founded the Mafia gang in 1931 known today as the Colombo family. A mob boss for thirty years, Profaci never spent a day in an American jail, amassing a fortune from bootlegging, prostitution, and the numbers and loansharking rackets. *(Photo courtesy of Frederick Martens archive)*

A dour Paul Castellano, then forty-five, also was picked up in the police raid at the Apalachin convention, along with more than fifty Mafia leaders from throughout the country. Nicknamed "Big Paul" when he became boss of the Gambino family, Castellano was at the 1957 conclave as an aide to his godfather and brother-in-law, Carlo Gambino. *(Photo courtesy of Frederick Martens archive)*

One of the biggest catches at Apalachin was Carlo Gambino, shown in a 1934 Rogues' Gallery photo. After engineering the 1957 barbershop assassination of an incumbent boss, Albert "Lord High Executioner" Anastasia, Don Carlo created the nation's most powerful borgata, which still bears his name—the Gambino family. *(Photo courtesy of the New York City Police Department)*

A ramrod-straight Big Paul Castellano, aka "the Pope," appears unperturbed after his arrest by the FBI in February 1985 as lead defendant in the watershed Commission Case. He was accused of being the boss of the Gambino family and a major figure on the Mafia's Commission, or national board of directors. *(Photo courtesy of the Federal Bureau of Investigation)*

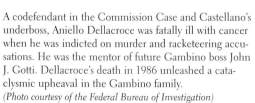

A codefendant in the Commission Case and Castellano's underboss, Aniello Dellacroce was fatally ill with cancer when he was indicted on murder and racketeering accusations. He was the mentor of future Gambino boss John J. Gotti. Dellacroce's death in 1986 unleashed a cataclysmic upheaval in the Gambino family. *(Photo courtesy of the Federal Bureau of Investigation)*

Free on a $2 million bond, Big Paul Castellano was killed by gunmen as he arrived for dinner with capos at a Manhattan restaurant on December 18, 1985. Even as the Gambino godfather's body was being removed, investigators focused on John Gotti as the new Gambino emperor and prime suspect behind the rubout. *(Crime Scene Photo)*

Anthony Salerno, a prominent figure in the Commission Case, sent fellow mafiosi Christmas cards in the early 1980s. "Fat Tony" posed in pajamas, a bathrobe, a baseball cap on backwards, and his trademark cigar. The FBI and prosecutors branded him the notorious head of the Genovese family but later discovered that he had never been a godfather or boss. *(Author's archive)*

The gangland murder of Carmine "Lilo" Galante at a Brooklyn restaurant in July 1979 was a controversial issue at the Commission trial. Prosecutors claimed that the Commission authorized the hit to prevent Galante from taking over the Bonanno family and dominating the Mafia's narcotics trafficking. Galante's body is on the right of the table with a cigar clenched in his mouth. *(Photo courtesy of the New York City Police Department)*

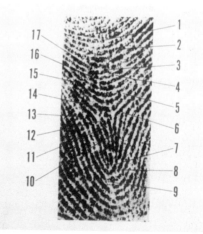

Six years after Galante's murder, Pat Marshall, the FBI case agent for the Commission investigation, used a new technology to obtain a latent palm print from the getaway car. The print enabled the prosecution to indict Anthony Bruno Indelicato, a Bonanno soldier, as a member of the hit team. *(Photo courtesy of the Federal Bureau of Investigation)*

G. Robert Blakey, law professor and former Justice Department prosecutor, was the chief architect in 1970 of RICO—the Racketeer Influenced Corrupt Organizations Act. For almost ten years Blakey tried vainly to persuade federal prosecutors to use the law to attack entrenched Mafia families. *(Photo courtesy of G. Robert Blakey)*

Rudolph Giuliani (right), the United States Attorney in Manhattan, who utililized the RICO law, and Judge William Webster, the FBI Director, provide details of the Commission indictment at a news conference in February 1985. Although it is unclear who first proposed using RICO against the Commission, Giuliani is credited with being the catalyst for developing the case. *(Photo courtesy of United States Department of Justice)*

Carmine Persico (left), the boss of the Colombo family, on a walk-talk in Brooklyn, with bodyguard and ace partner in crime, Hugh "Apples" McIntosh, in the early 1970s. The moody Persico elicited contradictory nicknames. To his admirers he was "Junior;" to his detractors, "the Snake." *(Surveillance photo courtesy of the Waterfront Commission of New York Harbor)*

CTIVE BUREAU
OGRAPHIC UNIT

BROOKLYN DISTRICT ATTORNEY SQUAD
VIA 34¾ POST NEW YORK

PLEASE POST IN A
CONSPICUOUS PLACE

WANTED

FOR
RIBERY AND RACKETEERING

INE PERSICO AKA "THE SNAKE", AKA "JUNIOR", MALE, WHITE, 5'5",
LBS., BROWN EYES, BLACK HAIR, 51 YEARS OF AGE, DOB 8-8-33.
DENCE 84-20 11 AVE., BROOKLYN, N.Y. ALT. RESIDENCE BLUE
TAIN ROAD, SAUGHERTIES, N.Y. FREQUENTS SOUTH BROOKLYN AREA &
EN ISLAND.

ED FOR BRIBERY AND RACKETEERING ON ARREST WARRANT ISSUED ON
3-84 IN THE SOUTHERN DISTRICT OF NEW YORK. SUBJECT IS THE
S* OF THE COLOMBO ORGANIZED CRIME FAMILY AND IS TO BE CONSID-
ARMED AND DANGEROUS.

INFORMATION CONTACT THE JOINT ORGANIZED CRIME TASK FORCE DET.
IAM VORMITTAG OR SPECIAL AGENT RICHARD SUTER AT #553-2828.

R NO. 64/197
EPARED 11/14

POLICE DEPARTMENT
CITY OF NEW YORK

LIMITED TO
DEPARTMENT
CIRCULATION

Eluding an FBI dragnet for four months, Persico was
betrayed by a relative in whose Long Island home he was
hiding. Handcuffed and covering his face, Persico later
autographed his Most Wanted posters for arresting agents.
(Photo courtesy of the Federal Bureau of Investigation)

Facing two RICO trials, Persico hid
out as a fugitive in 1984 and became
the only Mafia boss ever included in
the FBI's list of Ten Most Wanted
Criminals. *(Photo courtesy of the
Federal Bureau of Investigation)*

Normally well groomed and a natty dresser,
Gennaro Langella, the Colombo underboss, sprouted a beard and dressed less fashionably to escape
arrest as a codefendant with Persico. The disguise
failed when an informer tipped the FBI to "Jerry
Lang's" hideout. *(Photo courtesy of the Federal Bureau
of Investigation)*

Ralph Scopo's bugged conversations
alerted the FBI to evidence for the
Commission Case. A Colombo soldier,
and laborers' union president, Scopo was
the bagman for shaking down concrete
contractors at major construction projects. *(FBI Surveillance Photo)*

Alphonse Persico, Carmine's eldest son, talked about becoming a lawyer but became a Colombo capo. Carmine's attempt to install "Little Allie Boy" as boss ignited an internal mob war. Allie Boy grew a beard while imprisoned for racketeering in the early 1990s and was indicted in 2004 for ordering the murder of a Colombo rival. *(Photos courtesy of the Federal Bureau of Investigation)*

Surrounded by bodyguards and loyal followers, Victor "Little Vic" Orena enters his car during the Colombo War. Orena's plan to seize power crumbled when he was convicted on RICO and murder charges and sentenced to life imprisonment. *(Photos courtesy of the Federal Bureau of Investigation)*

A warlord for the Persico faction, Gregory Scarpa was shot in the eye during the Colombo War when a narcotics deal went awry. After Scarpa died in prison of AIDS, the government disclosed that he had committed crimes while secretly a high-level FBI informer for thirty years. *(Photo courtesy of NYC Department of Correction)*

Luciano sailed into exile on a cargo ship from a navy yard in Brooklyn on February 10, 1946. The night before, Frank Costello and several other mafiosi, using their ILA connections, slipped past guards to board the ship for a farewell dinner of lobster, pasta, and wine with their erstwhile boss. Lucky was shipped back to his native Sicilian village of Lercara Friddi, where he was given a royal welcome as a poor boy who had come back fantastically wealthy. Hundreds of villagers, unconcerned about his Mafia ties, cheered and waved American flags as he was driven to the town square in a police car. But Luciano had no nostalgic or pleasant memories of the primitive village; he soon left for Palermo and then Naples.

Luciano's release created a damaging legacy for Dewey. Soon after the mobster's departure, news stories were published exaggerating his wartime assistance to the government. The syndicated columnist and radio broadcaster Walter Winchell reported in 1947 that Luciano would receive the Congressional Medal of Honor, the nation's highest military award, for his secret services. Winchell was suspected of getting that hot tip from an acquaintance and neighbor in his apartment building—none other than Frank Costello.

Almost from the start, press allegations circulated that Dewey had sold Luciano his pardon. Finally, in 1953, while still governor, Dewey ordered a confidential inquiry by the state's commissioner of investigation. In 1954 a 2,600-page report documented Luciano's involvement with the navy without finding any wrongdoing by Dewey or the parole board in granting clemency.

Naval officials in Washington reviewed the report and once again were chagrined that their reliance on the Mafia would be exposed. Offering feeble excuses that the report would be a public-relations disaster for the navy and might damage similar intelligence operations in the future, the navy brass pleaded with Dewey to suppress the findings. Despite the harm to his reputation, Dewey complied with the navy's request and buried the report in his personal papers. The essential facts about the Luciano episode remained confidential until they were made public by Dewey's estate in 1977.

Before his death, Dewey confided to friends that Luciano's thirty-year minimum sentence was excessive and that ten years—exactly what he served before clemency was granted—would have been sufficient for the crime of aiding and abetting prostitution. The former prosecutor was confident that Luciano had been an organized-crime mastermind. But Dewey's odd comment about the harshness of the sentence buttressed the view of many independent observers that the trial evidence against Luciano had been flimsy, and that the main witnesses against him, who later recanted, had been cajoled and pressured by Dewey's insistent investigators.

Perhaps, in commuting the sentence, there was a tinge of a troubled conscience in Dewey's concession that the sentence was overly severe. Was the former prosecutor acknowledging that he got the right man for the wrong crime?

11

Serene Times

When it came to using World War II for personal benefit, Vito Genovese was a master. Moreover, before the fighting ended, he managed the tricky feat of aiding both the Axis and the Allied sides and enriching himself immensely.

Forced to flee the United States in 1937 to escape an impending indictment on an old Brooklyn murder case, Genovese, still an Italian citizen, planted himself in Naples. To keep in the good graces of Mussolini's regime, he became an avid supporter of Il Duce and, as a demonstration of his loyalty, contributed $250,000 for the construction of a Fascist Party headquarters near Naples. He further aided the dictator in wartime by using his American Mob connections to arrange a contract in New York: the assassination in January 1943 of Mussolini's old foe Carlo Tresca, the antifascist refugee editor of *Il Martello* (the Hammer).

For service rendered, Mussolini, the intransigent enemy of the Sicilian Mafia, awarded the American-trained gangster the title *Commendatore del Re*, a high civilian honor, an Italian Knighthood.

When the tide of war turned and the Allies invaded Italy in the summer of 1943, Genovese disavowed his fascist sympathies. Capitalizing on his literacy in English and his knowledge of American customs, he became an interpreter and adviser to the U.S. army's military government in the Naples area. Don Vito quickly resorted to doing what he knew best: conceiving criminal opportunities in any environment. Working out deals with corrupt military officers, Genovese became a black market innovator in southern Italy. Officers supplied him at military depots with sugar, flour, and other scarce items, which he transported in U.S. army trucks to his distribution centers. It was later learned that he laundered large sums of money through confidential Swiss bank accounts that he had established when he returned to Italy before the war.

In war-wracked and starving Italy, Don Vito was living in high style when Army Intelligence investigators dismantled the black market ring and arrested him in August 1944. Genovese tried to bribe his way out of trouble by dangling $250,000 in cash before an intelligence agent, Orange C. Dickey. The upright agent rejected the offer and in a background check learned of the Brooklyn warrant for Genovese's arrest on a homicide indictment.

Genovese was extradited in June 1945. By the time he arrived in the United States, however, the homicide case against him had collapsed because of the strange death of a material witness in protective custody in Brooklyn. Prosecutors were counting on eyewitness evidence from an innocent cigar salesman named Peter LaTempa to corroborate the murder accusations against Genovese. Understandably worried about LaTempa's safety on the streets before the trial, the DA's office had him locked up in the Raymond Street jail. While behind bars, presumably for his own safety, LaTempa suffered a gallstone attack and was given what should have been prescription painkilling tablets. Several hours later, he was dead. The city medical examiner reported that the pills LaTempa swallowed were not the prescribed drugs and contained enough poison "to kill eight horses." Although a witness in protective custody was murdered inside a city prison, no one was arrested for the crime or for involvement in an obvious conspiracy to silence the cigar salesman.

Burton Turkus, the lead prosecutor in the Murder Inc. cases, expressed the frustration of trying to solve Mob-ordered slayings and overcoming *omertà*. "There is only one way organized crime can be cracked," he said. "Unless someone on the inside talks, you can investigate forever and get nowhere."

A free man as a result of LaTempa's death, Genovese was back in the top rung of the Mafia, ostentatiously flashing the wealth acquired in the New York rackets and the Italian black market. To signal his importance, he built an elaborately furnished mansion on the New Jersey shore in Atlantic Highlands, where he and his wife, Anna, dined on gold and platinum dishes.

Genovese's return in 1946 was an unsettling event for Frank Costello.

Lucky Luciano was quarantined in Italy, and apparently had abdicated the title of boss of the borgata that he had founded. Now, after a decade of running the crime family, Costello faced a dangerous challenge from Genovese, who had considered himself the gang's underboss and heir apparent to the throne when he abruptly hightailed it out of the country.

Like other members of his family, Costello was familiar with Genovese's Machiavellian intrigues and savage inclinations. "If you went to Vito," Joe Valachi noted, "and told him about some guy who was doing wrong, he would have this guy killed, and then he would have you killed for telling on this guy."

Genovese spread the word that during his temporary exile, his crew had not been treated favorably by Costello and had not prospered as much as the rest of the family. Ever the diplomat, Costello arranged a truce with Genovese and his revived faction that left Costello as boss of the family. "Costello treated him with great respect," recalled Ralph Salerno, the New York organized-crime expert. "Genovese was resentful because he had been ahead of Costello when he left the country and believed he should have been the boss. Instead Costello remained on top and he was just a capo."

War had helped the Mafia; peace was even better. For the nation, victory in 1945 over Germany in May and Japan in September ushered in a round of national prosperity and a pent-up spending binge. Good times and the lifting of wartime restrictions on wages and traveling was a boon for the five New York borgatas' biggest racket and money producer—illegal gambling. Bookmaking on sports and the numbers games were certain winners for all mafiosi. Costello and other New York big shots also had extensive interests in illegal casinos near Miami and New Orleans. The largest expansion in underworld wealth, however, would arise from a new concept: exploiting legalized gambling in Las Vegas.

Various types of gambling had been sanctioned in Nevada since its frontier days in the 1870s, and in 1931 almost every conceivable form of gaming was authorized by the legislature in the misconceived hope it would help the state overcome the Depression. At the end of the war, Nevada was the only state with wide-open gambling, but it was a minuscule industry in a hard-to-reach area that was unappealing to the high rollers. The handful of tiny casinos in Reno and Las Vegas resembled desert dude ranches with poker as the main attraction for their gambling clientele.

Transforming Las Vegas from a dreary desert rest stop for drivers on the way to Los Angeles into a gambling mecca was the inspiration of Benjamin "Bugsy" Siegel, a garish Jewish gangster-racketeer from the East Coast. Siegel was born in New York and as a teenager teamed up with another ambitious Jewish hoodlum, Meyer Lansky. Both of them would provide valuable services for Luciano, Costello, and other Mafia bosses.

Lansky, whose birth name was Maier Suchowljansky, emigrated in 1911 as a young boy with his family from Grodno in Byelorussia, or White Russia, part of the Pale of Settlement, the area where Jews were compelled to live under the czars. Street brawls between Italian, Jewish, and Irish teenagers were common on the Lower East Side, and, according to Lansky's biographer, Robert Lacey, Lansky and Luciano first met during one of these encounters. Lansky, scrawny and slightly built at five-feet three-inches, impressed Luciano with his pluckiness and sharp back talk when outnumbered by a group of Italian toughs.

On the Lower East Side, Siegel and Lansky's pack of hoodlums were called *schtarkers*, Yiddish for strongmen or tough guys, and became recognized as the "Bug and Meyer Gang." The gang protected crap games run by Lansky and Siegel, and rode shotgun to prevent hijackings of shipments of beer and liquor for Luciano during Prohibition.

Siegel supposedly acquired his nickname when a judge reviewing charges of a savage street fight, commented, "You boys have bugs in your head." Throughout their alliance, Lansky was viewed as the inventive idea man and the combustible-tempered Siegel was feared for his reckless violence. Anyone who dared call him "Bugsy" to his face might get punched out and kicked in the ribs, often with the warning: "The name is Ben Siegel. Don't you ever forget it." He reportedly admitted participating in twelve murders. Most organized-crime historians believe that Lansky, as a favor to Luciano, drafted Jewish hit men for the murders of Joe Masseria and Salvatore Maranzano, and that Siegel was a triggerman in the two slayings that resolved the Castellammarese War.

By 1936, Siegel was operating mainly out of Los Angeles, where Luciano sent him to revamp a Mafia outpost of his empire that was headed by Jack Dragna. Luciano and other members of his borgata considered Dragna an unproductive remnant of the Mustache Pete generation, lax in developing prostitution and gambling rings, and unable to exploit labor-racketeering opportunities at Hollywood movie studios.

A natty dresser, suave if not handsome, and with inexplicable charm for women, Siegel was the perfect Mafia steward for Los Angeles and Hollywood.

He installed discipline into the disorganized Los Angeles gang, expanded its illegal gambling interests, and added a new wrinkle by launching an offshore casino—on a boat. Looking to cash in on Hollywood's main industry, he rigged elections in the stagehands' union, thereby gaining the muscle to extort the studios for labor peace.

Enjoying Hollywood glamour, Siegel palled around with actor George Raft, who was the movie's stereotypical Italian-American gangster, and toyed with the idea of taking a screen test himself. Besides the social high life, Siegel funneled millions streaming in from gambling and shake-downs before and during the war to Costello's East Coast borgata. He kept enough to build a thirty-five-room mansion for his wife and two daughters, and to put on a respectable front that enabled him to join some of the area's exclusive country clubs. On the West Coast, Siegel showed the mafiosi back in the East that he had organizational brains as well as a killer's instincts. Burton Turkus, the Brooklyn Murder Inc. prosecutor, credited him with opening up and exploiting Southern California for the Mafia.

After the war, Las Vegas became Siegel's obsession. He had previously been there to look after minor Mob bookmaking matters at the existing shabby casinos, and became convinced that the desert town was ideal for a unique casino-hotel concept. With travel restrictions lifted, Las Vegas was in easy reach by car for Southern California's exploding population, and air travel could bring in well-heeled suckers from the Midwest and East to the only legal luxury casino in the country.

In 1946 Siegel raised $3 million from Costello, Lansky, and a consortium of Mafia and Jewish underworld investors. Siegel was hardly a novice in the gambling business, having been a longtime partner with Costello and Lansky in an illegal gambling club in Hallandale, Florida, near Miami, that was run by Lansky. By most estimates, Siegel's dream casino-hotel, the Flamingo, should have cost about $1 million to build, but he spent three times over the original budget and still needed more. The Flamingo's rushed opening on December 26, 1946, was a disaster. In its first weeks the casino had an incredible run of bad luck, actually losing money; and there was no income from the hotel because its rooms were unready for occupancy.

Siegel closed the Flamingo for two months to straighten out the kinks and to gather more investments and loans from his backers. The casino reopened in March 1947, but continued to lose money.

On June 20, 1947, Siegel was alone in the Los Angeles home of his mistress,

Virginia Hill, who had stormed out after a spat. Besides her liaison with Siegel, Virginia had earlier been a companion to several other gangsters and reputedly was an underworld courier employed to transfer money and messages.

Siegel sat reading a newspaper on a living-room couch when, shortly before midnight, he was killed by a barrage of nine .30 caliber bullets from an army carbine, fired through a window, that riddled his head and upper body.

There was no shortage of suspects but, like almost all gangland murders of that era, the crime was unsolved. The financial losses at the Flamingo had antagonized and alienated many of Siegel's backers, who believed he was cheating them. Though there were press rumors that Jewish underworld investors ordered and arranged the execution, the Mob grapevine attributed the slaying to East Coast mafiosi upset by Siegel's independence and incessant demands for more of their money.

"The Jews don't fuck with the Italians," observed Jimmy "the Weasel" Fratianno, a Los Angeles-based mobster from the Siegel era. "They learned that lesson a long time ago."

Eventually, the Flamingo, under new Mob management, became a resounding success, the forerunner of a building surge of casinos that were controlled by the Mafia for decades. The Flamingo brought Las Vegas into the modern era and it was the original centerpiece of Las Vegas's famous Strip. Las Vegas was a new resource and territory for the Cosa Nostra and, to avoid jurisdictional conflicts, the Commission declared it an open city, which meant that any crime family could operate there.

In the late 1940s, Nevada's casino regulators welcomed with open arms the Italian and Jewish gambling specialists who flocked to Las Vegas. Protecting and encouraging the growth of an infant industry that promised to become the state's largest revenue gusher, state officials discreetly ignored the underworld links of these casino investors. The officials pretended that the newcomers were professional gamblers, not professional criminals.

At several of the Mob-run Las Vegas casinos, Meyer Lansky, an experienced major domo of illegal clubs in Florida, New York, and Texas, and of legal ones in Havana, Cuba, was brought in as a trusted behind-the-scenes manager. Lansky's illegal gambling clubs, commonly known as "carpet joints," were more upscale, with fine food and drinks, and better furnished than the ordinary grimy parlors run by the Mob in New York and other big cities. He was unequaled at the bookkeeping art of "skimming," diverting cash before it was counted as a casino's winnings, to avoid paying the state of Nevada its share of the earnings.

Despite his affiliations with Luciano and Costello, Lansky was at best a junior partner who knew his subservient status in the Mafia universe. Among his unschooled criminal companions, he was admired as a financial wizard, a deep thinker who was a member of the Book-of-the-Month Club. More important to his underworld survival was his reputation as a trusted big earner for important mafiosi who profited from his gambling deals. Yet because he was not of Italian heritage, Lansky could never become a made man or be admitted into the Cosa Nostra's inner councils, where policies were set and life and death decisions were made. He took orders and never gave them.

The inspiration for the Mafia's bonanza in Las Vegas must be attributed to the pioneering efforts of Bugsy Siegel. He was "the first important criminal to recognize the potential of legalized gambling in Nevada," Howard Abadinsky, an organized-crime historian, says. Lansky biographer Lacey points out that Siegel's murder put his new gambling palace on the front pages of most newspapers in America. Ironically, it was the enormous coverage of Bugsy's death that publicized the Flamingo and helped make the entire Las Vegas Strip famous.

Expanding into Las Vegas was another Mafia success that met no concentrated resistance from the authorities. Even when not corrupted by Mob money, federal and local law-enforcement efforts against the high and low ranks were woeful and uncoordinated. Federal agencies and police departments around the country operated independently, rarely sharing intelligence information, and sometimes stumbling over each other in their infrequent investigations of a mobster or a Cosa Nostra racket.

The Federal Bureau of Investigation, the nation's largest crime-fighting force, had the interstate jurisdiction to delve into almost any crime that occurred from coast to coast. J. (John) Edgar Hoover, the FBI's director since its inception in 1924, dismissed as fantasy suggestions that an American Mafia or any interrelated national crime organization existed. As a result, there were no FBI authorities on organized crime; through the 1940s not a single agent, even in Mob-infested cities like New York and Chicago, was assigned exclusively to organized-crime work.

An unsurpassed manipulator of the press, movies, television, and radio, Hoover crafted the spurious image of the omnipotent, incorruptible "G-Man" overcoming the nation's most dangerous criminals and foreign enemies. His main targets in the 1930s were kidnappers and bank robbers, and he reaped enormous acclaim from his agents' stalking and gunning down John Dillinger, the much-publicized bank bandit. During World War II, the FBI's emphasis shifted to enemy spies and saboteurs. With the beginning of the Cold War in the late 1940s, the bureau focused on Soviet espionage and suspected Communist and leftist traitors.

Hoover's standard rebuttal to questions about the possible existence of an interstate "crime syndicate" and sophisticated organized-crime gangs was to label them as mere hoodlums and regional police problems outside the FBI's jurisdiction. "The federal government can never be a satisfactory substitute for local government in the enforcement field," Hoover once chided a congressional committee that raised the question.

Even the use of the word "Mafia" in internal bureau communiqués and reports was banned by Hoover. He prohibited agents from working undercover to infiltrate and expose illicit complex enterprises, fearing that associating in any manner with criminals might someday taint or compromise the FBI's integrity.

Playing it safe, Hoover compiled glowing statistics by concentrating on easily solved federal crimes, especially interstate shipments of stolen cars and bank robberies. Stolen cars could be traced through tips on where they were stored and vehicle identification numbers. Bank holdups were often committed by inept amateurs who could be traced down easily through witness identifications and license-plate numbers of getaway cars.

A consummate bureaucrat and power broker, Hoover maintained confidential, unflattering dossiers on congressmen and government officials, "greymail," to discourage critics who might have the courage to challenge his views. Typically, he would use messengers to subtly inform a legislator or an official that the bureau was aware of an ethical or romantic lapse, and that Hoover—as a friendly gesture—would do his best to suppress the embarrassing information.

The FBI director serves at the pleasure of the president, and Hoover held on to the post for forty-eight years, even though Presidents Harry Truman and John F. Kennedy despised him. He ran the bureau as his private kingdom, and his idiosyncrasies became enshrined. Agents were supposed to represent his vision of the ideal white American male. Until the final years of his reign, Hoover personally vetted each trainee at a brief meeting in his office, and a damp or limp handshake automatically disqualified the prospective agent. He instituted a rigid dress code, known as "Hoover Blue," requiring all agents on duty to wear dark business suits with a white breast-pocket handkerchief, white shirts, gleamingly polished black shoes, and hats. Ties, of course, were de rigueur, but rookies in training school were informed that red ones were banned because Hoover considered the color "insincere." For almost half a century, the dressed-alike agents (during Hoover's tenure they were also forbidden to grow mustaches and beards) were easily recognizable at crime scenes, and their "Hoover Blue" outfits often compromised them on surveillance and other investigative assignments.

Hoover's reluctance to seriously challenge the Mafia stemmed from three main factors, according to former FBI agents and criminal-justice researchers. First was his distaste for long, frustrating investigations that more often than not would end with limited success. Second was his concern that mobsters had the money to corrupt agents and undermine the bureau's impeccable reputation. And third, Hoover was aware that the Mob's growing financial and political strength could buy off susceptible congressmen and senators who might trim his budget.

Armed with the FBI's glowing public reputation and with his bureaucratic skills, Hoover had a free hand in choosing his investigative priorities. The only official who challenged his assertion that a dangerous Italian-American crime organization did not exist was rival law-enforcement expert Harry J. Anslinger, the director of the Federal Bureau of Narcotics. As head of the agency since its formation in 1930, Anslinger's mission was to deter and uproot drug trafficking. Unlike Hoover, Anslinger's investigative tactics were dynamically original, unorthodox, and far ahead of his time. He dispatched numerous agents masquerading as criminals to penetrate narcotics rings, promised immunity from prosecution to criminals who switched sides, and recruited paid informers. Justifying payments to squealers, Anslinger said that informing was a dangerous occupation and that several of his snitches were murdered by suspicious drug dealers. He also authorized harsh third-degree interrogation methods that were commonplace among police units in the 1930s and 1940s but were unconstitutional. Disregarding civil rights, in gathering information his agents battered uncooperative suspects, sometimes working them over with rubber hoses. And Anslinger resorted to illegal wiretaps without court approval to gather intelligence and arrest drug dealers. "The world belongs to the strong," the dour, huskily built Anslinger said, justifying his methods to another government official. "It always has, it always will."

Lacking Hoover's bureaucratic clout and gift for political intrigue, Anslinger, in thirty-two years as head of the Narcotics Bureau, never got the substantial government support and media attention that the FBI obtained. Hoover won the headline war as the government's unrivaled crime fighter while Anslinger labored in relative obscurity. With a maximum of three hunderd agents, Anslinger's agency was a third the size of the FBI, and its agents were paid far less than Hoover's men. Nevertheless, Anslinger assembled a band of hard-boiled agents, including former cops, who were familiar with the culture and nuances of the drug trade.

When Anslinger organized his agency in 1930, he found that the illegal drug business was diversified with Jewish gangsters predominating, although Chinese tongs and Irish and Italian groups operated in many big cities. By the late 1930s, however, through undercover work and arrests, his agents discovered a major shift in the nation's narcotics networks: all were virtually controlled by Italian-American gangs. "They seemed to have an extraordinary cohesion," Anslinger later said of the Mafia gangs, in an interview with the writer Frederick Sondern Jr. "But none of us were aware that they were predominantly Sicilian or what that meant. It took us a while to find that out."

Aware of the Mob's rising strength, Anslinger hired Italian-American agents because they might better understand its mores and practices than other investigators. Anslinger's strategy turned up a trove of intelligence about Mafia activities that went far beyond narcotics. He compiled files on some 800 mafiosi that he called "The Black Book." Hoover, in a typical sign of contempt for other law-enforcement agencies, declined Anslinger's offer of a copy of his invaluable records.

Anslinger's operatives in the 1940s obtained enough intelligence information to work on narcotics cases involving the Gagliano, Bonanno, and Costello-Genovese borgatas in New York, and other major Mafia families, especially those headed by Santo Trafficante in Tampa and Carlos Marcello in Louisiana. The vigilant Anslinger kept his eagle eye on Lucky Luciano when he was deported, and assigned agents to bird-dog the exiled boss in Italy. "That dirty son-of-a-bitch Asslinger," Luciano said, deliberately mangling the name when he was told that narcotics investigators suspected he might try to open new drug routes to America.

In late 1946, Anslinger discovered that Luciano was in Havana, apparently testing the waters to determine if he could resume control of his crime family from Cuba. Luciano summoned Costello, Genovese, other high ranking members of the family, and Meyer Lansky for a meeting in Havana. Anslinger got wind of Lucky's machinations and, based on his discovery, the American government pressured the Cubans to kick Luciano out of the country, effectively ruining his comeback plan.

Narcotics in the 1930s and '40s was not the scourge it was later to become in the United States. The narcotics bureau estimated that 95 percent of the drugs entering the United States immediately after World War II was smuggled by Mafia traffickers. Alarmed by its intelligence reports, the bureau in a March 1947 memorandum issued a clear warning to other federal agencies concerning the larger menace it had perceived after more than a decade of narcotics investigations.

"For many years," the report declared, "there has been in existence in this country a criminal organization, well-defined at some times and places, and at other periods rather loosely set up. This is composed of persons of Sicilian birth or extraction, often related by blood and marriage, who are engaged in the types of criminal specialties in which a code of terror and reprisal is valuable. These people are sometimes referred to as the MAFIA."

Anslinger and the narcotics bureau recognized the general outlines, if not the totality and magnitude of the Mafia's framework. But the FBI and all other competing federal law-enforcement units ridiculed the intelligence analysis as unsubstantiated rumors and hypotheses by an agency seeking undeserved glory and praise. No attention was paid to Anslinger's incisive findings.

At mid-century, almost two decades after their formation, the five New York families were prospering, with four of the original godfathers still in place, controlling huge criminal conglomerates. The borgatas run by Joseph Bonanno, Joseph Profaci, Vincent Mangano, and Gaetano "Tommy" Gagliano were secure and under no pressure from the law. These four men were powerful crime figures; yet their names and their organizations were invisible to the public and to most law-enforcement investigators. The only Mafia boss with a widely recognized name was Frank Costello, Lucky Luciano's successor. Costello became a public figure because of his scandalous political influence in Tammany Hall and his gambling and slot machine interests. But the full extent of his domain as the boss of the nation's largest organized-crime family was unknown, and the word Mafia was never publicly linked in government reports and the media to the name Frank Costello.

Overall, about two thousand made men, assisted by thousands of wannabes and associates, operated in New York City and nearby suburbs. The five bor-gatas constituted almost half of the total five thousand mafiosi in the country's twenty-four crime families. The combined strength of the New York families dwarfed the second-largest Mob group of roughly three hundred soldiers in Chicago.

A postwar bonus for the New York gangsters was the departure in 1945 of Mayor Fiorello LaGuardia, who did not seek a fourth term after twelve years in City Hall. LaGuardia's gadfly administration and scrupulously honest police brass had not disrupted any major racket except for Costello's slots. The reform mayor, however, had at least driven gambling and other traditional Mafia money-making franchises underground, and had forced mafiosi and their helpers to worry about police raids.

Conditions changed radically in the new administration of former Brooklyn DA William O'Dwyer, the candidate of Tammany Hall and Frank Costello. Soon after Mayor O'Dwyer took office, the police department seemingly adopted a laissez-faire policy toward gambling, a supposedly nonviolent crime. The changeover was most visible in low- and middle-income neighborhoods. For years, bookmakers and numbers operators had conducted their businesses furtively, in back rooms of stores and pool rooms. Now, under the new adminis-tration, police pressure was relaxed. In sections like the Lower East Side, Harlem, Williamsburg, Brownsville, and the South Bronx, bookies and num-bers runners worked freely on the streets, some using clipboards to openly record wagers. The relaxed crime-fighting atmosphere suggested that "the pad," police talk for systemic corruption in local precincts and districts, was back.

Police laxity became so outrageously flagrant that the FBI took note. Begin-ning in LaGuardia's administration, some precinct commanders failed to list all reports of unresolved thefts and robberies so as to burnish their crime-solving statistics. Inside the department, the practice of discarding crime complaints in waste cans became a common joke: "Assign the case to 'Detective McCann.'" Under O'Dwyer's police commissioners, the "Detective McCann" case load became so excessive that the FBI in 1949 refused to publish New York City crime statistics, citing them as unreliable and discredited.

All Mafia families continued to rely heavily on proven garden-variety rack-ets: sports gambling, numbers, loan-sharking, and hijackings. Each also devel-oped separate criminal niches, sometimes jointly with another borgata. Costello's gang dominated the Manhattan waterfront and the Fulton Fish Market, and together with other families controlled trucking and other interests in the garment industry.

Vincent "Don Vincenzo" Mangano, the boss of a Brooklyn-based borgata, had a stranglehold on the Brooklyn docks and, with Costello's organization, had begun to take over private garbage-carting companies in the city.

Another Brooklyn-based boss, Joe Profaci, had entered the country illegally with Vincent Mangano. They were boyhood friends and fellow refugees from Mussolini's Mafia shackles in the 1920s in Sicily, where Profaci had served a year in prison for theft. In the New York region, Profaci used Mob money from bootlegging, prostitution, and the numbers and loan-sharking rackets to acquire twenty legitimate businesses. The gross take from his numbers or lottery action was a staggering $5 million a week, according to a confidential FBI analysis. Famous in the grocery industry as "the Olive Oil King," he was the largest importer of olive oil and tomato paste in the country through the Mama-Mia Olive Oil Company. Anslinger's investigators suspected it was used as a cover to smuggle narcotics. Despite convictions for violating the Food and Drug Act and for income-tax evasion, Profaci never served a day in an American jail, getting off leniently with fines or probation. He lived modestly in Brooklyn but owned a hunting lodge, a private airport, and a 328-acre estate in rural Hightstown, New Jersey.

The godfather in the Bronx was Tommy Gagliano, a low-profile, secretive figure, unknown outside of the Mafia's select ranks. Gagliano's longtime right arm and underboss, Tommy Three-Finger Brown Lucchese, was his front man in setting up a variety of cash cow garment industry and union rackets. Lucchese also oversaw the family's narcotics trafficking interests and its protection kickbacks from garbage haulers and construction contractors in Long Island.

Joe "Don Peppino" Bonanno's family equaled Costello's in overall illicit wealth, with extensive sports gambling, loan-sharking, numbers, and narcotics deals. There were also Bonanno Mob-engineered monopolies providing restaurants with laundry services and supplying mozzarella cheese in the New York area. He remedied a problem stemming from his illegal entry into the country by briefly staying in Canada and returning legally to the United States through Detroit; that ploy cleared the way for his naturalization in 1945, ruling out potential deportation proceedings that plagued Luciano, Genovese, and other top-echelon mafiosi. For relaxation from his hectic activities in the city, Bonanno retreated to a fourteen-room colonial-style house he built on a 280-acre estate and dairy farm in upstate New York.

Impressed by the organizational strength and wealth of the New York families, some Cosa Nostra leaders in the country sent young mafiosi there for training in the 1940s. A notable prodigy was Santo Trafficante Jr., son and heir of the Mafia boss in Tampa. Junior got special tutoring from Tommy Lucchese and other members of the Gagliano family. Later, after becoming Tampa's Mafia boss, Trafficante told his lawyer, Frank Ragano, that he picked up invaluable lessons in New York about illegal business ventures, Mafia lifestyles, and a code of behavior concerning women.

From the New Yorkers, Trafficante learned that mafiosi were expected to maintain a higher regard for "the sanctity of their women" than the rest of male society. "Their rigid code prohibited an affair with the wife or girlfriend of another mobster under penalty of death," Ragano noted. "And they were obligated to protect the wife or mistress of a fellow mobster if he was not around." Trafficante explained to Ragano that the Mafia had no objection to married soldiers having affairs, but there was a caveat. "Santo had a mistress but conducted the affair with discretion to spare his wife and daughters embarrassment," Ragano added. "That was expected of all Mafia members."

By the late 1940s, the Prohibition era of bloodshed and rivalries between the New York families was a distant memory. Bonanno and Profaci further secured their relationship through the marriage of Bonanno's son Salvatore "Bill" to Rosalie Profaci, Joe Profaci's niece. Uniting two Mafia royal houses, the wedding was attended by all the aristocracy of La Cosa Nostra, with the singer Tony Bennett serenading three thousand guests. The opulent reception at New York's Hotel Astor was the social event of the year for the American Mob and it became the model for the opening wedding scene in the movie *The Godfather.*

Except for Frank Costello, who delighted in mixing with political and café society, the other godfathers shunned ostentatious lifestyles. Joe Bonanno, however, made one exception. He started a flashy trend among mobsters by wearing huge ruby, sapphire, jade, and onyx pinkie rings.

As a respite from serious mobster meetings and Commission business, Bonanno, Mangano, Profaci, and Gagliano enjoyed one another's company at purely social events, each hosting parties featuring gargantuan home-cooked meals. Frequent rendezvous took place at Mangano's horse farm on Long Island, where he personally prepared multicourse dinners of fish, veal, filet mignon, and pasta, which were washed down with numerous bottles of wine.

Bonanno wrote that a typical meal with Mangano and Profaci was highlighted by the Sicilian custom of toasting each other in rhyming couplets.

Bonanno cited a "witty" example of one of his favorite toasts:

Friends, if after this meal I die in Brookulino,
I ask to be buried with my mandolino.

These fraternal meals symbolized the serene prosperity that prevailed midway through the twentieth century for the bosses within their own families and with their fellow godfathers. The next decades, however, would not be so carefree.

12

"Wake Up, America!"

Two freshman senators wanted the prize. It would be an enviable plum: investigating organized crime.

The competitors were Estes Kefauver of Tennessee and Joseph R. McCarthy of Wisconsin. Both were groping in 1950 for the politically hot issue that would get them national headlines. Simultaneously they struck upon the idea of a coast-to-coast examination of the strength and political influence of organized crime. The impetus came largely from complaints by civic crime commissions and mayors that illegal gambling and interstate crime were soaring without interference from the federal government. Since Kefauver's party, the Democrats, controlled the Senate, he outmaneuvered the Republican McCarthy for appointment as chairman of a special subcommittee to investigate interstate "gambling and racketeering activities."

As a consolation, McCarthy found another provocative subject: probing Communist influence in the government. McCarthy's unscrupulous investigative methods and exaggerated claims of Communist infiltration brought him worldwide attention, far greater than Kefauver received. His ruthless distortions, unethical tactics, and browbeating of witnesses earned his methods an eternal unflattering eponym, "McCarthyism."

At the outset, little was expected of an organized-crime inquiry led by Estes

Kefauver, an unlikely provincial crusader from Tennessee. He was a relatively inexperienced legislator, best known for campaigning in his home state with a massive grin and wearing a coonskin cap perched absurdly on his head. Nevertheless, the investigation and Kefauver's decision to concentrate on gambling was opposed by the Democratic administration of President Harry Truman. Northern Democratic leaders feared that the committee's conservative Southern Democrats and Republicans would focus mainly on big-city Democratic machines, the party's bedrock.

Kefauver's staff got no help from the administration or from Hoover's FBI. Echoing Hoover's sentiments, Attorney General J. Howard McGrath thundered that federal investigation would be wasteful because there was no evidence that a "national crime syndicate" existed. Local remedies were the best solution for combating illegal gambling, the attorney general declared, signifying the White House's animosity.

On the local level, most police departments offered little help to Kefauver's congressional investigation. Undaunted, Kefauver and his staff pressed on, aided by Anslinger's narcotics bureau, Manhattan District Attorney Frank Hogan, several other state prosecutors, and private municipal crime commissions in Chicago and New Orleans. Ralph Salerno, who became a New York Police Department Mafia expert, and ten other New York detectives were ordered to quickly assemble the sparse intelligence files they possessed on the city's mafiosi. "The Police Commissioner knew that Kefauver was coming to town and he wanted to be prepared to answer questions and not look foolish," Salerno recalled. "It turned out that no other city police department kept any files on mobsters. These cities would get some old-timer cop to talk with Kefauver's people but they had no records, no solid information."

From May 1950 to May 1951, the subcommittee, formally titled the "Special Committee to Investigate Organized Crime in Interstate Commerce," held public hearings in fourteen cities. Overall, the committee called more than six hundred witnesses but its proceedings got generally lackluster attention until it arrived in New York for nine days of climatic sessions in March 1951.

In New York, the subcommittee and the Mafia discovered the power of the new television medium. The three major networks then in existence, ABC, CBS, and NBC, televised the hearings live in a rare coast-to-coast hookup. The parade of shady characters, bookies, pimps, politicians, and slippery lawyers on TV screens captivated the nation, becoming television's first live spectacular public event, drawing an unprecedented audience of between 20 and 30 million viewers daily.

The highlight of the event was the appearance of Frank Costello. Other important Mafia leaders—Tommy Lucchese, Vito Genovese, Albert Anastasia—and lesser lights subpoenaed by the committee relied on the Fifth Amendment protection against self-incrimination to clam up and get out of the TV glare quickly. Not Costello. Even though he was the nation's most important underworld figure and his ties to Tammany Hall had been previously exposed, Costello agreed to enter the lion's den and testify. He apparently wanted to escape the onus of being automatically tarred as an underworld generalissimo like the witnesses who used the Fifth Amendment as a refuge. And he believed he had the wits to deflect harsh questioning and maintain for his reputable friends the myth that he was a businessman.

Costello made one demand that the committee accepted: the TV cameras could not show his face. During his three grueling days of testimony, the cameras focused on his hands, with close-ups of his cuticles, his fingers drumming on the table, and his hands clasping and unclasping. The eerie combination of Costello's hands and his accented, gravel-crunching voice cast him in a more sinister and mysterious role than showing his face on television. His hands became the frightening symbol of an otherwise unseen criminal empire. One television comedian devised a skit in which Costello's unattached hands ran the gamut of emotions—surprise, innocence, anguish—and finally, in fury, they strangled Estes Kefauver.

The television audience was unaware of the medical reason for the intimidating sounds that emerged from their sets. Costello's vocal chords had been damaged in an unsuccessful operation to remove throat polyps, resulting in a hard-edged, unnatural timbre. In the movie *The Godfather*, Marlon Brando, who played the title role of a first-generation Mafia autocrat, is said to have imitated Costello's voice and cadence from his televised jousting with the committee.

Although he testified, Costello refused to answer hostile questions and skirted others. The only light moment and spectator laughter came when a senator, noting Costello's reputed illegal gambling operations, asked what he had done for America in return for the riches he had accumulated. "Paid my tax," Costello countered.

The committee hearings wrote finus to William O'Dwyer's political career by reexamining Costello's political influence with Democrats in New York's

Tammany Hall and City Hall. O'Dwyer, the candidate who had solicited Costello's support at the infamous 1942 cocktail party, had already resigned as mayor in 1950 and had been appointed by President Truman as ambassador to Mexico. "My country needs me," said O'Dwyer, disingenuously explaining his abrupt departure. The actual reason was a brewing graft scandal involving his administration and widespread police protection for bookies and other gamblers.

In a tense exchange with committee curmudgeon Senator Charles W. Tobey, O'Dwyer conceded that he had coveted Costello's endorsement and financial contributions.

"What has he got?" Tobey, a New Hampshire Republican, asked, referring to Costello's political influence. "What kind of appeal does he have? What is it?"

O'Dwyer, after a long pause, replied, "It doesn't matter whether it is a banker, a businessman, or a gangster, his pocketbook is always attractive."

Before the public hearings ended, several senators saw interrelated threats from "the syndicates," and the nation's Cold War with the Soviet Union and the ongoing Korean War. "The two great enemies within our ranks, the criminals and the Communists, often work hand in hand," Senator Tobey warned. "Wake up, America!"

Based on its whirlwind investigation, the committee concluded that the Mafia was a reality, that it was aided by widespread political and police corruption, and that its two major territories were New York and Chicago. More ominously, according to the senators, the gangsters' strength stemmed from an alien conspiracy.

"There is a sinister criminal organization known as the Mafia operating throughout the country with ties in other nations in the opinion of the committee," the panel summarized in a final report. "The Mafia is a loose-knit organization specializing in the sale and distribution of narcotics, the conduct of various gambling enterprises, prostitution, and other rackets based on extortion and violence."

The findings marked a breakthrough in that a federal body for the first time publicly identified the Mafia as a group alive and flourishing in America. But since the committee lacked specific evidence of crimes, the FBI and most law-enforcement agencies minimized the committee's declarations as unsubstantiated generalities, and failed to pursue the leads that surfaced at the hearings. Congress also disregarded the committee's work, declining to pass any meaningful legislation that might hamper organized crime.

Despite its efforts, in retrospect the committee unmasked little of the Mob's vast holdings, was less than half right about its size and influence, and over-looked numerous Mafia bosses. In New York, its investigators failed to pinpoint or call as witnesses three major godfathers: Joe Bonanno, Joe Profaci, and Gaetano Gagliano.

The biggest casualty of the Congressional investigation was Frank Costello, the only don intrepid enough to testify. His sidestepping answers about his net worth resulted in a Contempt of Congress conviction and a fifteen-month prison sentence.

Costello's TV appearance and revived notoriety galvanized the Internal Revenue Service, the Mafia's chronic nemesis, to form a task force to scrutinize his tax returns. Remembering Al Capone's downfall, Costello had been careful about concealing his actual wealth. But he was trapped by his wife's jealousy. Whenever she discovered her husband's dalliance with a mistress, Mrs. Costello went on a spending binge. An IRS audit found that over a six-year span, she had spent $570,000, a spree that was unjustified by Costello's reported income for those years or by withdrawals from his legitimate holdings and investments. He was convicted of tax evasion and was imprisoned for eleven months before the conviction was overturned on appeal.

Even behind bars, Costello had little difficulty running his crime family and transmitting orders from prison through trusted intermediaries.

While the Kefauver committee was unaware of many authentic Mafia barons, it plopped Meyer Lansky in the center ring and magnified his importance. Lansky used the Fifth Amendment as a shield when called to testify but, along with Costello, he was severely damaged. Lansky had largely avoided scrutiny before the hearings, but he became one of the committee's prime targets. Disclosures about his gambling background and criminal pals forced disgraced local authorities to close his illegal "carpet joint" casinos in Florida's Broward County and in Saratoga Springs, in upstate New York. He pleaded guilty to gambling charges in Saratoga, where he was jailed for three months and fined $2,500.

Describing Lansky erroneously as one of the principal organized-crime leaders in New York and on the East Coast, an unrestrained Kefauver denounced him as one of the "rats" and the "scum behind a national crime syndicate." The committee's limelight mistakenly elevated Lansky from his true role as a wealthy but junior partner with the Cosa Nostra into the position of a

Mafia financial Goliath. Until his death at age eighty in 1983, Lansky was relentlessly pursued by law-enforcement agencies, although never convicted of a federal felony.

As he had hoped, Kefauver emerged from the hearings a political somebody. The national exposure also brought him rebukes and criticism. Questions were raised as to why he had steered away from underworld gambling fiefs in Memphis in his home state, in Hot Springs, Arkansas, in Nevada, and in states whose senators were on the subcommittee. Reporters digging into Kefauver's personal life pounced on a seemingly hypocritical element: the sanctimonious, anti-gambling reformer got free passes and other perks on his frequent visits to racetracks.

Kefauver's sudden national fame enabled him to throw his coonskin into the 1952 contest for the Democratic Party's presidential nomination. His investigation, however, had antagonized Harry Truman and the big-city political bosses, who gave the nomination to Adlai E. Stevenson. Four years later, Kefauver, on better terms with the party's bigwigs, ran unsuccessfully for vice president when Stevenson lost for a second time to incumbent Dwight D. Eisenhower.

As Kefauver's investigators searched for evidence of Mob activities, a vital power shift occurred right under their noses. In 1951 Vincent Mangano, an original Commission member, disappeared; he had headed his Brooklyn-based borgata for twenty years. His body was never found, but there was no doubt among other Commission members that Mangano had been eliminated by his nefarious underboss, a founding partner in Murder Inc., Albert Anastasia.

Anastasia boldly appeared at a Commission meeting to announce his presence as the new godfather of Mangano's family. The other dons considered Anastasia a hothead, but accepted the fait accompli and, in effect, violated a cardinal Commission rule by overlooking an unsanctioned slaying of one of their own elite untouchables. Without explicitly admitting that he had killed Mangano, Anastasia relied on a flimsy Mafia excuse: he indicated that he had struck first in self-defense because Mangano resented him and was plotting his assassination. Even Joe Bonanno, who had been close to Mangano for twenty years, exonerated Anastasia, declaring that he wished to avoid a war between families. Although Anastasia came from the Italian mainland, Bonanno reasoned that since he admired ancient Sicilian traditions, he deserved a boss's crown and should be honored and distinguished as "Don Umberto."

Celebrating his new rank, Anastasia built a mansion in Fort Lee, New Jersey, near the George Washington Bridge. Anastasia, "the Executioner," was vigilant about his own safety. He surrounded himself with bodyguards, and at his new home erected seven-foot-high barbed-wire fences and unleashed ferocious Doberman pinschers to patrol the grounds.

Anastasia's malevolence as "the Executioner" extended beyond the Mafia itself. In February 1952, Willie "the Actor" Sutton, an elusive bank robber and prison escape artist, was captured in Brooklyn. A reward for the arrest was given to twenty-one-year-old ex–Coast Guardsman Arnold Schuster, who trailed Sutton and alerted the police after spotting the bank thief in the subway. Watching Schuster being interviewed on television, an incensed Anastasia reportedly blurted out, "I can't stand squealers. Hit him." Joe Valachi later disclosed that the Mafia grapevine resonated with news that Schuster was gunned down near his Brooklyn home by Anastasia's hirelings.

Another significant Mafia development overlooked by the Kefauver inquiry and law enforcement was the changing of the guard in the borgata founded by Gaetano Gagliano in the early 1930s. Fatally ill from a heart aliment, Gagliano relinquished control to Gaetano Tommy "Three-Finger Brown" Lucchese, his longtime number-two powerhouse. The borgata became known as the Lucchese family.

Born in Palermo in 1900, at age eleven Lucchese emigrated with his parents to the overcrowded tenements of East Harlem. A disobedient teenager and a petty thief, Lucchese's juvenile escapades dishonored his parents, and when he was sixteen his father threw him out of their apartment. He briefly worked in a machine shop—the only legitimate job he ever held—where his right index finger was mangled in an accident. The injury soured him on a workman's life, and he launched a full-time career in crime. A policeman who fingerprinted Lucchese, arrested for car theft when he was twenty-one, jokingly bestowed on him the alias "Three-Finger Brown." (The officer was a fan of the Chicago Cubs pitcher Mordechai "Three-Finger" Brown.) The nickname stuck.

During Prohibition, Lucchese enlisted in the Masseria gang and formed partnerships with Lucky Luciano. A Luciano confidant, his duplicity set up the murder of Salvatore Maranzano, enabling Luciano to create the five families and the Commission in 1931. Luciano rewarded him by landing him the number-two position in Tommy Gagliano's new family, and Lucchese's underworld business acumen enriched Gagliano and himself.

Thin, fidgety, and hyperactive, Lucchese over two decades became a Mafia trailblazer, inventing money-making schemes and refining conventional Mob rackets. Using muscle and brain power, he acquired control of New York's kosher-chicken cartel; a protection shakedown that masqueraded as a window-cleaning company; garment-industry trucking companies; and a narcotics-trafficking ring.

Lucchese's masterstroke was replacing Lepke Buchalter as the garment industry's most feared Shylock and introducing a new loan-sharking gimmick. A perennial headache for clothing manufacturers was raising capital to stay in business while awaiting sales receipts for their new lines of seasonal coats, suits, and dresses. Unable to get legitimate loans, the owners' last resort was Lucchese. He supplied cash but only on terms known as a "knockdown loan." This meant that the borrower paid usurious interest of five points (5 percent) weekly for at least twenty weeks before the principal could be whittled down. Thus, for a $10,000 loan, the borrower paid $500 a week or $10,000 over twenty weeks. At the end of the twenty-week period, the manufacturer still owed the mobster the complete principal. Under threat of physical harm, the victim had to continue paying $500 a week indefinitely until the full original sum of $10,000 was paid separately. At a minimum, Lucchese doubled the profit on each illegal loan. The scheme is said to have generated more than $5 million a year even during the darkest days of the Depression.

As a cover and for income-tax purposes, Lucchese kept an office in the Garment Center and listed his occupation as "dress manufacturer." He did own or had publicly registered interests in more than a dozen dress factories in New York and in Scranton, Pennsylvania. The garment-industry unions, obviously aware of his Mafia importance, made no attempt to unionize his sweatshops.

Boss of more than one hundred Men of Honor, Lucchese was sufficiently wealthy and confident to give his capos and soldiers wide latitude in their own numbers, gambling, and hijacking operations. Under his leadership, a sphere of influence that became increasingly important was the rough-and-tumble business of professional boxing.

Since the early days of Prohibition, Irish, Jewish, and Italian gangsters were deeply involved in managing fighters and promoting matches. Owney Madden, Dutch Schultz, Al Capone, Lucky Luciano, and other racketeers had all been secret owners of popular boxers and champions. It was a violent sport—similar to their own risky occupations—that mafiosi and other gangsters understood and identified with. Authentic fans, they enjoyed the ambiance and macho electricity of arenas and training gyms. Just as owning nightclubs gave mobsters a demimonde status, there was a similar underworld prestige in possessing and controlling champions and contenders.

Many bouts were actually on the level, but others were predetermined, and there was almost good-natured internal competition among mafiosi to fix fights and pull off betting coups. In the 1940s, a Lucchese hit man began a gradual takeover that made his borgata dominant in the fight game and squeezed out the other families. The soldier who acted in Lucchese's behalf was best known as Frankie Carbo, although his real given names were Paul John. Reared in the Bronx, starting at age eighteen Carbo chalked up a lengthy police record for homicides and assaults. Arrested on four murder charges and suspected in the assassination of Bugsy Siegel, Carbo was convicted of only one killing, serving five years for manslaughter in the 1920s.

After an acquittal in 1942 for a slaying involving an assignment from Murder Inc., Carbo turned most of his attention to boxing. By that time his monikers included "Frank Tucker" and "Mr. Fury," but his alias in arranging rigged fights was "Mr. Gray." A keen student of boxing, Carbo actively managed several fighters. His main influence was exerted through violence and threats against managers, promoters, and trainers. Those who balked at Carbo's suggestions were visited by lead-pipe-carrying sluggers. His control of fighters and managers forced promoters to do Carbo's bidding if they wanted to stage top-rated bouts and remain healthy.

From the 1940s until the early 1960s, Carbo was the undisputed Mob linchpin and underworld commissioner of the boxing game. It was "Mr. Gray" who determined the contestants in many lightweight, middleweight, welterweight, and heavyweight division championship titles. He often had a hand in deciding the results. Carbo cashed in by getting a thick cut of fighters' purses and a share of the promoters' profits, and by always placing the right bets.

Carbo's boss, Tommy Lucchese, impressed his neighbors in the upscale Long Island town of Lido Beach with his knowledge of boxing and urged them to wager on big fights; they said he always gave them tips on the winners.

Long after his retirement, Jake LaMotta admitted that Carbo ordered him to take a dive in a 1947 bout with Billy Fox. LaMotta dumped the fight and, in return, Carbo gave him a crack at legitimately winning the middleweight championship from Marcel Cerdan two years later.

"When the man known as 'Mr. Carbo' wanted to see somebody it was a command performance," "Sugar Ray" Robinson, a middleweight and welterweight champion of the 1940s and '50s, said. One of the stellar boxers of his era, Robinson wrote in a biography coauthored by Dave Anderson that he rejected Carbo's order to fix a series of fights with LaMotta. Robinson's popularity and drawing-power apparently allowed him to politely defy Carbo and survive unharmed.

Nat Fleischer, the editor and publisher of the boxing industry's bible, *Ring Magazine*, at a congressional hearing in 1960 tersely summed up the terror exerted by Carbo. "Everybody was scared of him," Fleischer said of the pudgy gangster with owlish horned-rimmed glasses.

The mobster's reign was finally shattered by law-enforcement investigations begun in the late 1950s. The Manhattan DA's office obtained an indictment, accusing him of "illegal matchmaking." The prosecutor in charge of the case, Alfred J. Scotti, labeled Carbo "the most powerful figure in boxing." In Los Angeles in the early 1960s, Carbo was convicted on federal charges of extortion and threatening managers and promoters. The sentence was twenty-five years in prison. Before his imprisonment, Carbo's final accomplishment for Lucchese was gaining control of Sonny Liston and a huge slice of the million-dollar purses earned by him as the heavyweight champion from 1962 to 1964. Liston was KO'd by Muhammad Ali, the first heavyweight champ in three decades believed to be totally free of gangster influence.

Carbo's misfortunes barely affected Lucchese's illicit income in New York and elsewhere. Outside his home territory, he forged narcotics trafficking and other deals, principally with Santo Trafficante Jr., the boss of the Tampa borgata. Lucchese had been close to Trafficante's father in the 1940s, and he had helped train the son. The younger Trafficante met frequently in New York with Lucchese, and on one jaunt he brought along his lawyer, Frank Ragano, and Ragano's future wife, Nancy Young.

The two Mafia emperors treated each other regally on visits, sparing no expense. One night Lucchese invited Trafficante and his other Florida guests to an expensive restaurant, Mercurio's, near Rockefeller Center. The Mob bosses spent most of the dinner talking with each other in Sicilian until Lucchese suddenly turned to Nancy Young, a vivacious blond, addressing her in English. Upon learning in the conversation that the young woman did not own a fur coat, Lucchese insisted upon making her a gift of one. Ragano was impressed by the generosity but, reluctant to become indebted to Lucchese, tried to decline. Trafficante frowned and whispered to the lawyer that he should accept, warning him that he was violating a Mafia rule by crossing a godfather. "Don't embarrass me," Trafficante ordered. "You'll insult him by refusing." The next day, Lucchese escorted the wide-eyed Nancy through a fur salon filled with racks of hundreds of fur coats, stoles, jackets, and pelts. With Lucchese's guidance she chose a full-length black mink that Ragano estimated cost at least $5,000, a year's salary for a factory worker at that time.

Ragano characterized Lucchese as Trafficante's most trusted ally in the New York families. The Florida boss particularly admired Lucchese's liaisons with corrupt government officials. "This guy has connections everywhere in New York," Trafficante told Ragano with a touch of envy. "He's got politicians and judges in his pocket."

In the political sphere, Lucchese maintained a close alliance with Frank Costello and, like the Prime Minister, became a power broker in New York's Democratic Party machine and in the appointments of corrupt judges, assistant district attorneys, and city officials. But unlike Costello, Lucchese's interests remained hidden, never attracting public attention. Lucchese also cultivated Republican officials and extended his range to the radical wing of politics. He successfully lobbied Vito Marcantonio, the congressman representing his old East Harlem neighborhood, the only member of the House of Representatives repeatedly elected by the leftist American Labor Party, to nominate his son for appointment to West Point. (One of Meyer Lansky's sons was also a West Pointer.) Lucchese's suburban home was far removed from the railroad flats of East Harlem, but the Mob still swayed votes in the then heavily Italian section.

Tommy Lucchese's discreet influence with legislators and politicos was further demonstrated when he was naturalized as a citizen in 1943 through a private bill approved by Congress. About the same time, several legislators persuaded the New York State Parole Board to grant Lucchese a "Certificate of Good Conduct," expunging his arrests and convictions in the 1920s for auto theft and bookmaking.

In 1945, probably in a back-room deal with Frank Costello and Tammany Hall, Lucchese chose a minor clubhouse politician and fellow Sicilian-American, Vincent R. Impellitteri, as O'Dwyer's running mate on the Democratic ticket. O'Dwyer was elected mayor, and Impellitteri, whose only job experience was as a law clerk to a Democratic judge, became City Council president, a mainly ceremonial office. When O'Dwyer resigned in 1950, Impellitteri ("Impy" in tabloid headlines) succeeded him as acting mayor. Tammany leaders, however, considered Impellitteri too incompetent, too inarticulate, and too lightweight even by their modest standards. They endorsed Judge Ferdinand Pecora in the 1951 election for mayor.

Impellitteri, who had grown accustomed to the pomp, power, and perks of City Hall, refused to drop out of the race, running as the sole candidate of a newly created "Experience Party." The election put the Mafia in the enviable position of having a stake in both candidates, as Lucchese secretly supported Impy while Costello backed Pecora.

With revelations from the Kefauver hearings still fresh in voters' minds, Impellitteri centered his campaign against Tammany Hall, the Mafia, and Costello, the very group that had raised him up from law clerk to mayor. He highlighted every stump speech by declaring, "If Pecora is elected, Frank Costello will be your mayor." With the help of a slick public-relations campaign, Impellitteri won a startling upset, becoming the only independent party candidate ever elected mayor of New York. Soon after taking office, Impellitteri was spotted dining in a restaurant with Lucchese and a former federal prosecutor. Questioned by reporters, the mayor innocently claimed he barely knew Lucchese and that the gangster had been introduced to him as a clothing manufacturer. A floundering blunderer, Impellitteri was turned out of office in 1954, after one abbreviated term. In that mayoralty contest, the tables were turned on him: he was accused by reformers of being in league with organized crime. Impelliteri's political and Mafia friends did not forsake him. They eased him into a comfortable judgeship. With Impy's defeat, however, the Mob's invaluable pipeline to City Hall was essentially severed.

13

Heroin and Apalachin

His brief prison sentences and the Kefauver Committee hearings behind him, Frank Costello in the spring of 1957 was confidently going about his usual business. Shunning bodyguards and bullet-proof limousines, the sixty-six-year-old godfather met with his Mafia associates in restaurants and traveled about Manhattan in taxis like any ordinary businessman.

On May 2, 1957, Costello had a late dinner date with Anthony "Tony Bender" Strollo, one of his capos, at Chandler's, a theater-district restaurant. As usual he took a taxi back to his luxury Central Park West apartment. As Costello walked toward the building's elevator, a man wearing a dark fedora brushed past a doorman and shouted, "This is for you, Frank." Turning, Costello heard what sounded like a "firecracker," as a bullet grazed the right side of his forehead, knocking him to the ground. The gunman fled in a waiting black Cadillac.

Wounded slightly, his head bandaged in a hospital emergency room, a dour Costello provided no information to the police about his being shot at almost point-blank range. "I didn't see nothing," he told detectives. A search of his pockets produced an interesting item: a slip of paper with the notation "Gross casino win as of 4-27-57—$651,284." That figure, detectives later discovered, matched the precise "house take" or gross winnings that day at Las Vegas's new Tropicana casino, in which Costello was a major secret partner.

Although Costello professed ignorance as to why anyone would want to kill him, detectives had a strong theory that Vito Genovese had the most likely motive to place a contract on the Prime Minister. Released from the hospital, Costello informed the police that he had no fear for his life and would continue his normal rounds without a single bodyguard. The police brass, however, assigned two detectives to keep an eye on the wounded boss. When the detectives showed up in the vestibule outside of his apartment, the urbane Costello insisted that they come in for breakfast with him and his wife. One of the investigators was an Italian-American and he told fellow detective Ralph Salerno that the unruffled Costello bantered with him. "What's an Italian boy like you doing with all these Irish cops?" Costello asked. "They pay you peanuts. Come along with us. We pay bananas and they come in big bunches."

On the first day of their assignment, the plainclothesmen followed Costello's taxi to the Waldorf-Astoria Hotel in an unmarked car. He went there almost daily for a manicure, a hair trim, and a massage, and for conferences in the hotel's bar and restaurant. Irritated by the prospect of being shadowed constantly, Costello proposed a compromise. "Let's be gentlemen," he said to the detectives. "I'm going to see my girlfriend and I don't want you guys behind me." Advising the detectives that he could easily slip $100 to a cabbie to shake them, making them look bad, he promised to return to the Waldorf in about two and a half hours, and they could then resume their watch over him. For the next several days, until the police canceled their protection, the "gentlemen's agreement" existed between the detectives and Costello whenever he had an assignation.

Manhattan DA Frank Hogan was not so obliging as the police. He subpoenaed Costello before a grand jury, demanding answers about the shooting and $651,284 in casino winnings. This time citing his Fifth Amendment rights, Costello refused to talk about the attempt on his life and the slip of paper found in his pocket. As a result, before anyone was arrested for creasing his brow with a bullet, it was the victim Costello who served sixty days in the "workhouse," the municipal jail, for contempt of court.

Costello might have been reluctant to cooperate, but the doorman of his building, Norval Keith, picked out a suspect from the rogue's gallery files. He identified Vincent "Chin" Gigante, a chauffeur and muscleman for Vito Genovese, and holder of an arrest record for bookmaking, auto theft, and other petty crimes. A former light heavyweight prize fighter, the twenty-nine-year-old Gigante vanished after the shooting for three months before voluntarily surrendering. At Gigante's trial in 1958 for attempted murder, Frank Costello was a reluctant prosecution witness. Under oath, Costello admitted having been a bootlegger, a bookie, a slot machine operator, and the owner of a gambling club in New Orleans. But, he added, he was now retired.

Smiling during most of his testimony, Costello grew serious when for the first time he gave his version of the attack that nearly cost him his life. "I walked through the front door into the foyer. I heard a shot; it sounded like a firecracker to me at the time. I paid little attention to it for the moment. Then I felt something wet on the side of my face. It was blood and I realized I was shot."

Under cross-examination, Costello complied with the oath of *omertà*. He testified that he had not seen the gunman even though he had briefly faced him, did not know Gigante, and knew of no reason why Gigante would want to shoot him. As Costello walked from the well of the courtroom, newspaper reporters heard Gigante whisper, "Thanks a lot, Frank."

Even though the doorman stuck to his story that Gigante was the assailant, after six hours of deliberations the jury brought in a verdict of not guilty. The jury foreman told reporters that the doorman's identification was questionable, and that the entire case against Gigante was weak.

His close call changed Costello's belief in his invulnerability. Vito Genovese, he knew, was trying to settle an old score. "He went around without bodyguards because he never suspected that Genovese or anyone else would try to kill him," Salerno said. "Ten years had gone by since Genovese had come back from Italy and Costello thought everything was okay." Soon after the bullet nicked Costello's skull, Salerno and other detectives learned that he had assured Genovese that he was taking early retirement. "That shot from Gigante was just as effective as if it had killed him," Salerno added.

True to his word, Costello relinquished all of his Mob holdings to the new boss, Don Vito Genovese. For the rest of his days, Costello lived peacefully in Manhattan, rarely going out at night, and tending to the garden at his country home in Sands Point, Long Island. His few public appearances were at flower shows to display his own prized entries. His continual notoriety contributed to the revocation of his citizenship in 1961, because he had lied about his occupation and criminal record at his naturalization hearing in 1925. In 1973

Costello, former Prime Minister of the underworld, died of a heart attack, almost a forgotten figure. He was eighty-two.

Although Costello surrendered unconditionally to Genovese in 1957, his ally Albert Anastasia was infuriated by the assault on a fellow godfather with whom he had sponsored mutually profitable deals. Six years earlier, Anastasia, "the Executioner," remorselessly eradicated Vincent Mangano and took over his family without first seeking approval from a majority of the Commission members. Now, he asked the Commission to allow him to wage war against Vito Genovese for taking over a family without permission, just as he had done. Joe Bonanno, the secure leader of his own family, took congratulations for preventing a ruinous battle between the Genovese and Anastasia factions by bringing the two rival killers together at "a select dinner," where they kissed each other on the cheek and presumably made peace. Recounting his intervention, Bonanno demeaned Anastasia and Genovese as "impetuous" ruffians, while heaping praise upon himself as "debonair," "articulate," and "prepossessing." Commission rules might bar a *capo di tutti capi*, but Bonanno immodestly considered himself first among equals: a *capo consigliere*, chief counselor, to whom other bosses looked for diplomatic guidance on thorny issues. He pompously christened the results of his mediation on the Commission between Anastasia and Genovese as the "Pax Bonanno."

Five months after resolving the Anastasia-Genovese dispute, in October 1957, Don Peppino Bonanno flew to Italy on a mission that would have momentous consequences for the Mafia and for the United States. He was accompanied by ranking members of his borgata and business associates from New York. Bonanno and his party were greeted like royalty by government officials in Italy and Sicily. Red carpets were actually rolled out for the group at airport ramps. In Rome, a minister of the ruling Christian Democratic Party—strongly and openly supported in Sicily by the Mafia—was on hand to welcome the visitors.

Writing almost thirty years later, Bonanno, in his self-serving autobiography, described his first trip back to Sicily as a nostalgic sightseeing journey to his native land, an opportunity to become reacquainted with relatives and boyhood friends, and to visit his parents' graves in Castellammare del Golfo. There is a casual reference in his book to conversations in Palermo with some men of honor, without further amplification.

The primary reason for his trip to Sicily was omitted in Bonanno's book. He was heading an American Mob delegation negotiating a pact with the Sicilian Mafia for the importing of huge quantities of heroin to the United States.

The Grand Hotel et des Palmes, an upscale but fading belle epoque relic in the 1950s, was a favorite meeting spot for Sicilian *cosca* nabobs and their retainers. When in Palermo, Charlie Lucky Luciano, the exiled American don, made the hotel his second home; his favorite conference nook always was reserved for him in the bar-lounge.

Unbeknownst to Italian and American law-enforcement agencies, more than thirty Sicilian and American Mafia leaders assembled at the hotel for a fateful parley from October 10 through October 14, 1957. Each day they met in the Sala Wagner, an ornate suite named after Richard Wagner, the nineteenth-century German composer, who had orchestrated works while staying at the hotel. With a Renoir portrait of Wagner staring at them from the wall, the Sicilians and Americans used the room to map out details for an explosive expansion of the heroin trade in America.

Illustrating how little American investigators knew about the Mafia at mid-century, the major U.S. law-enforcement agencies remained unaware of the meeting and its significance for twenty-five years. These agencies and their Italian counterparts finally learned about the Grand Hotel sit-down in the 1980s, when it was revealed by Sicilian and American Mafia defectors.

Luciano had narcotics interests and vital Mob connections on both sides of the Atlantic, and he brought the two groups together. Shortly before the meeting, Luciano had even persuaded the main Sicilian Mafia chiefs to adopt one of his American innovations by establishing a Commission-like body to resolve their disputes. In Sicily it was called "the Cupola."

Indicating the gravity of the deliberations, at Bonanno's side in the sessions in Palermo were his underboss, John Bonventre, and his consigliere, Carmine Galante, who was also his principal drug trafficker and narcotics adviser. At the hotel conclave, the new Cupola leaders heard about the American priorities. Bonanno explained that the United States bosses were worried about potential danger from the recent passage by Congress of a tough narcotics-control law, the Boggs-Daniels Act of 1956, which imposed sentences of up to forty years for drug convictions. The Americans feared that mandatory penalties could induce mafiosi nailed on drug charges to save themselves by breaking the oath of *omertà*, becoming informers and possibly compromising and implicating bosses and other hierarchs. Narcotics was far from the top moneymaker for the Americans, but drug arrests were a threat because the five New York families and their satellite associates imported and supplied more than 90 percent of the heroin in the nation.

Since the formation of the Commission in 1931, the Sicilian Mafia clans had not operated in America. The centerpiece of the Grand Hotel et des Palmes plan was the Americans permitting the Sicilians to take over the risky task of distributing heroin in the states. With ample supplies of heroin from re-fineries run by Corsicans in France, and later by themselves in Italy, the Sicil-ian bosses would obtain a captive market in America.

The American mobsters would benefit because there would be less danger of their soldiers being caught smuggling and distributing drugs, especially by Harry Anslinger's narcotics investigators. Profits for the Americans would come from "franchise fees"—a share of the income—for allowing the Sicilians to sell large amounts of heroin to wholesale drug dealers on United States territory. Until the 1950s, heroin and cocaine use in America had largely been limited to a tiny segment of the population, mainly musicians, prostitutes, criminals, gamblers, and affluent thrill seekers. A sinister innovation in the Sicilian-American plan was the scheme to develop vast heroin sales and usage by reduc-ing the price of the drug and pushing it in working-class black and white neighborhoods.

American and Sicilian mafiosi had long slipped into each other's countries undetected by local law-enforcement units. The American police had no rec-ords or mug shots of the Sicilians, and the Italian authorities were equally igno-rant of the American gangsters. By operating far from home, the Sicilian drug runners would be reasonably safe in America, and the Italian police would nei-ther know nor care what the Sicilians were up to in a foreign land. Another cover for the new heroin channel was the fact that the American and Italian law-enforcement agencies went their separate ways, never sharing information.

To mark the heroin accord, most of the mafiosi concluded the international conference at a twelve-hour banquet in a closed-off seafood restaurant on the Palermo waterfront. Only one incident marred the prolonged celebration for the normally cool-tempered Bonanno. A waiter, apparently unaware of Bo-nanno's prominence and his knowledge of the Sicilian dialect, mumbled an in-sult about Bonanno being a haughty, demanding American tourist. Overhearing the remark, Bonanno hurled a pitcher of ice water at him. The waiter suddenly realized his extraordinary mistake and pleaded for forgiveness.

The Cosa Nostra's variegated crimes—its murders, loan-sharking, extortions, gambling, brutal beatings, prostitution, political fixes, police corruption, and union and industrial racketeering—created immeasurable costs and pain for America. None of these illicit activities, however, inflicted more lasting distress on American society and damaged its quality of life more than the Mafia's large-scale introduction of heroin. In the decades following the Palermo agreement, the Sicilian Mafia and its American helpers inundated the United States with the drug. An estimated 50,000 Americans were addicts in the late 1950s. By the mid-1970's, according to studies by government and private groups, at least 500,000 were hooked.

The Mob carved out a boundless market for itself and future ethnic crime groups that wanted a share of the gigantic profit from heroin, cocaine, and the drugs that followed. Violent ripple effects from narcotics trafficking, especially in New York and other big cities, were staggering. Crime rates skyrocketed as thousands of junkies turned to muggings and burglaries to support their addictions. Rival drug gangs staged gun battles on the streets, killing and wounding innocent victims. Large swathes of inner-city neighborhoods were ravaged, making life there almost unbearable for its beleaguered residents and merchants. And the credibility and reliability of police forces were undermined by massive bribes from drug dealers.

About the same time in 1957 that Luciano helped the American Mafia create the world's largest heroin-exporting venture, he sat for an interview with the writer Claire Sterling for a magazine profile. When she raised the subject of narcotics, Charlie Lucky dismissed as nonsense rumors of his involvement in large-scale international smuggling. Instead, he complained about police surveillance and their ceaseless efforts to pin a drug charge on him. "They been watchin' a long time; let 'em watch," he groused.

Luciano died in 1962, in exile in Naples, of a heart attack. He was sixty-five. Shortly after his death, American and Italian officials announced that he had been targeted for arrest as an alleged member of a ring that smuggled $150 million worth of heroin into the United States.

Two weeks after the Palermo conclave, on the bright Manhattan morning of October 25, 1957, Albert Anastasia eased himself into a barber's chair at the Park Sheraton Hotel, near Central Park, for his daily shave and trim. Seated in the next chair was his nephew, Vincent Squillante, who took care of the family's private garbage-carting shakedown rackets. As they chatted, two men sauntered into Grasso's Barber Shop and fired a fusillade of five shots into Anastasia's head and chest. The professional hit men knew their grisly business. Anastasia toppled to the floor, killed instantly. The gunmen walked briskly into the hotel lobby and disappeared in the crowd. Shouting, "Let me out of here," Squillante bolted unscathed from the shop. As so often happens in well-planned Mob executions, Anastasia's bodyguard was conveniently absent when the assassins appeared. The bodyguard, Anthony Coppola, had driven Anastasia to the hotel but was inexplicably missing from his boss's side when the shooting occurred.

There were several touches of ironic justice to the slaying of Anastasia, a killer who prided himself on his preoccupation with security. Dreaded mainly for his homicidal ingenuity as one of the founders of Murder Inc, he was caught completely off guard at the peak of his power. Crime historians also noted that he was murdered in the same hotel where Arnold Rothstein had lived and into which he staggered after being fatally shot on the sidewalk twenty-nine years earlier. Anastasia had the distinction of being the first Mob boss since the 1931 peace pact to have been rubbed out in old-fashioned gangland style in a public area; when he had eliminated his chief and rival, Vincent Mangano, Anastasia had performed the murder discreetly, and the body was never found.

The Mafia's wise men quickly realized that the execution was sponsored by two leaders who had the most to gain from Anastasia's death: Vito Genovese and Carlo Gambino. Despite Bonanno's intervention, Genovese feared that Anastasia was gunning for him to avenge the attempt on Frank Costello's life and for forcing his ally on the Commission into retirement. Gambino, although Anastasia's consigliere, suspected that his erratic, seething boss had grown resentful of his wealth and influence in their borgata and intended to ensure his position by whacking him.

With a mutual interest in eliminating Anastasia, Gambino and Genovese put their heads together and found byzantine reasons to plot Anastasia's extermination. Gambino, the former black marketeer, would be enthroned as the head of one of the nation's largest Mob families and automatically become a member of the ruling Commission. Genovese, a boss for only four months, would solidify his position by acquiring Gambino as an ally. And there would be a third boss in the new alliance, Tommy "Three-Finger Brown" Lucchese. Lucchese had become close to Gambino through his daughter Frances's marriage to Gambino's son Tommy. The two in-laws and Genovese would form a young troika on the Commission, effective opposition to the two old-time, more conventional bosses, Joe Bonanno and Joe Profaci.

Of all the Mafia hits in New York, the shooting of Anastasia in a busy, midtown location, before eyewitnesses, was one of the most audacious. The memorable murder was frequently reenacted in movies (most notably the Italian film *Mafioso*) and in fiction. The vivid image of a helpless victim swathed in white towels was stamped in the public memory.

The police's hottest first lead and suspicion centered on Santo Trafficante Jr., the Tampa godfather, who was in town for sit-downs with Anastasia. Registered at a hotel under the name B. Hill, Trafficante had checked out just two hours before Anastasia's final haircut and then disappeared for several weeks. Detectives learned that Anastasia was trying to get a share of the manna flowing from Havana, where Trafficante was a major Mob player with large interests in three casinos. One deal on the table was an offer from Trafficante to become partners with Anastasia in the casino concession for the Hilton Hotel being built in Havana. A minor sticking point was a demand by Cuban dictator Fulgencio Batista for a yearly bribe of $1 million. It was unclear if the fiery New York don was trying to strong-arm his way into Havana or work out a peaceful compromise with Trafficante.

The theory implicating Trafficante fizzled out, even though he was untraceable for weeks. Eventually detectives concluded that Gambino and Genovese were the conspirators behind the murder and most likely had given the contract to a thug in Joe Profaci's family, Joseph "Crazy Joey" Gallo. Shortly after the hit, Gallo proudly hinted to close friends that his crew was responsible. "You can call the five of us the barbershop quintet," a police informer quoted the smirking Gallo.

These "intelligence" nuggets concerning "the three G's"—Gambino, Genovese, and Gallo—could only be interred in the confidential dossiers of the police department's Detective Bureau. They were tidbits adding to the fascinating folklore of gangland violence and intrigue but worthless as evidence that could stand up in a courtroom. Detectives in robot fashion went through the motions of seeking Anastasia's killers, knowing in their hearts that Mob homicides were destined to be classified as unsolved. They rationalized the futility of working on Mafia hits by reciting a popular police maxim: "It's only vermin killing other vermin."

The hubbub over Anastasia's murder was of little interest to the police in a rustic slice of New York called the Southern Tier, near the Pennsylvania border,
150 miles west of Manhattan. Three weeks after the slaying, on November 13,
1957, a state police sergeant, Edgar D. Croswell, was investigating a bad check
complaint at the Parkway Motel in the region's main town, Binghamton, when
his interest was aroused by a young man booking three rooms, and informing
the desk clerk that his father would pay for them. The young man was the son
of Joseph Barbera Sr., a wealthy local resident and soft-drink and beer distributor, who Croswell knew had been a bootlegger with an arrest record in his
younger days for murder and assaults.

That afternoon, Croswell and Trooper Vincent Vasisko drove out to Barbera's home, a secluded hilltop English manor house nestled in a 130-acre estate in a hamlet called Apalachin (pronounced by the locals as Apple-*ay*kin).
Observing more than a dozen cars, many with out-of-state license plates,
Croswell realized something was afoot and surveillance was warranted. His interest was further piqued when a local food supplier told him that Barbera had
ordered 207 pounds of steak, 20 pounds of veal cutlets, and 15 pounds of cold
cuts to be delivered that day.

Suspecting that a conspiratorial meeting at Barbera's place was under way
to plan the violation of liquor laws, Croswell asked for help from a local unit of
the Federal Bureau of Alcohol, Tobacco, and Firearms. The next afternoon,
November 14, Croswell and Vasisko, with two ATF agents, drove to Barbera's
house and spotted more than thirty large autos and limousines parked on the
grounds. As the investigators backed out of the driveway to set up a barricade on
the public road leading from the estate, about a dozen men scampered pell-
mell from the house. "One of the guys looked up at the road and hollered, 'It's
the staties,' and they all started running into the fields and woods," Vasisko said.

Croswell radioed for more troopers. Ultimately, the police picked up for
questioning forty-six men leaving hurriedly in cars, and twelve others slogging
through the woods and fields. Those struggling on foot on the raw, rainy day
looked bedraggled and unfit for country hikes; they were middle-aged and elderly, dressed in pointy wing-tipped shoes and business suits. Most of the men
offered the same explanation as to why they had gathered at the manor house in
sleepy Apalachin: it was a coincidence that they all came for a mass sick call on
Barbera, an ailing friend recovering from a cardiac problem.

The investigators knew the story was ridiculous. Quick identification checks
turned up a star-studded cast of underworld figures from New York, New Jersey,

California, Florida, Texas, Pennsylvania, New England, and the Midwest. The New Yorkers taken for questioning to a state police barracks included Vito Genovese, Carlo Gambino, Gambino's brother-in-law, Paul Castellano, Joe Profaci, and Joe Bonanno.

An unknown number of Barbera's guests slipped past the hastily formed police roadblocks, and several who were en route turned back after hearing radio reports about the roundup. Tommy Lucchese was the only borgata boss from New York who evaded the cordon; along with Sam Giancana, the Chicago godfather, he got to a road and hitchhiked out of the area.

All who were picked up carried wads of money, between $2,000 and $3,000 in cash, an extraordinary amount of pocket money. But without evidence of a crime and finding no unlicensed weapons, the police released everyone without photographing or fingerprinting them. The press immediately identified the organization that linked the men and their prominence. "Seize 62 Mafia Chieftains in Upstate Raid," blared the front-page headline in the *New York Daily News*. (The actual number, according to police records, was fifty-eight.)

From electronic eavesdropping, from tips from informers, and from Joe Bonanno's autobiographical admissions, the reasons for the Apalachin get-together were gradually pieced together. Since 1931, the Commission and Mafia leaders from other parts of the country had met every five years. The regular 1956 meeting had been held safely and comfortably at Barbera's estate. Another refugee from Sicily's Castellammare del Golfo, Barbera was the boss of a borgata that operated mainly in the Scranton, Pennsylvania, area and he gave assurances that the sparse, unsophisticated police detachments in Apalachin posed no threat to a mobster convention.

The brainstorm for the unscheduled 1957 meeting came from Vito Genovese. Following Anastasia's murder and Costello's resignation, he decided that the rest of the country's Mob families should be reassured that all was well and stable in New York. A national conference, Don Vito thought, was the best forum to introduce himself and Carlo Gambino as new bosses to the rest of the Cosa Nostra elite.

Another important emergency item on the agenda was setting policy on coping with the stricter new federal drug law—the Boggs-Daniels Act—and dealing with the Sicilian heroin importers. Before Sergeant Croswell broke up their session, the godfathers gave lip service to a total ban on drug deals by declaring that the penalty for made men involved in narcotics trafficking could be Mafia capital punishment. As time went by, the prohibition was selectively, if ever, enforced because drug profits were immense. Some of the bosses, re-calling Frank Costello's frequent cautions about the dangers of deep involve-ment in narcotics, were ambivalent about how to resolve the question. Narcotics money was too tempting for avaricious dons and their henchmen to forsake. What they feared most was that the new law's harsh prison penalties could induce soldiers facing certain conviction to save their skins by becoming informers. There was also the possibility that traffickers could themselves be-come addicted and undermine discipline and secrecy. And last, there was a public-relations issue. Most Mafia operations, especially gambling, were tacitly approved by an indifferent public, but widespread involvement in drugs could provoke public outrage and demands for more vigilant enforcement.

"They knew the new law would be trouble and it was an accurate progno-sis," said detective Ralph Salerno. "What the edict against narcotics really meant was that if you're involved, don't compromise any other made guys by being seen with them when you are making drug deals. That was the main mes-sage to the troops—work alone without endangering the family."

The godfathers' final act before the state police interruption was to "close the books," put a temporary halt on adding new members, and leaders were ad-vised to prune unqualified mafiosi from their lists. They knew that one of Anas-tasia's cronies had been selling memberships in his borgata for as much as $40,000, thereby enrolling untested and undeserving people. The new mem-bership ban, with only a few nepotistic exceptions for close relatives of leaders, lasted twenty years in many families.

Joe Bonanno was out of the country, returning from his trip to Italy, when Vito Genovese set up the second Apalachin conference. Bonanno had presided at the undisturbed national meeting the year before in Barbera's home. In his memoirs Bonanno claimed that he opposed the 1957 rendezvous because it vi-olated established protocol of a mass meeting every five years, and it was too risky to congregate one year later at the same site. Other bosses believed Bo-nanno was chagrined because he had not been consulted about the second meeting, and that his influential position in New York and in the country was being challenged by the upstart Genovese.

In his autobiography, Bonanno maintained that he was near Apalachin for private sit-downs but boycotted the big powwow at Barbera's home. The state police, he insisted, mistakenly identified him because one of his gofers, who was stopped, was using Bonanno's driver's license. His explanation was contra-dicted in a confidential report on the police raid prepared for then New York governor Averrill Harriman. The report specified that troopers found an embarrassed Bonanno thrashing through a corn field adjoining Barbera's property and that he told them he was "visiting" a sick friend.

The 1957 attempted murder of Frank Costello, the slaying of Albert Anastasia, the Apalachin disaster—all in a six-month period—put the Mob squarely back in the public eye for the first time since the Kefauver hearings six years earlier. There was renewed pressure on law-enforcement officials for explanations about the mystifying sequence of events culminating in Apalachin. The obvious, disquieting questions were: Who summoned all these reputed gangsters to a mass meeting? What was its purpose? And how powerful is this group?

A federal grand jury indicted twenty-seven of the Apalachin participants and twenty were convicted of conspiracy to commit perjury and to obstruct justice. The verdicts were overturned unanimously by an appeals court on grounds of insufficient evidence of a conspiracy or of perjury. A principal reason cited in the judicial decision exposed the widespread naïveté that prevailed at the time in the criminal-justice system about the existence of the Commission and the Mafia's methodology. Although noting the "bizarre nature" of the Apalachin gathering, the three-judge panel reasoned that "common experience" precluded the notion that a criminal plot would be hatched in such a large, seemingly nonsecretive assemblage. The judges may have ruled correctly about the lack of evidence in the case, but like most jurists at that time they were clearly clueless about the Mafia's operations and its motive for the meeting. The only reason for the Apalachin deliberations was to plot and plan criminal activities.

Even after Apalachin, J. Edgar Hoover, the nation's most prominent law-enforcement expert, was still publicly in denial about the existence of the Mafia. The FBI viceroy, however, was privately humiliated after Apalachin by the kudos given to his knowledgeable arch rival, Harry Anslinger, the Narcotics Bureau head. Overnight, Anslinger was recognized by the press as law enforcement's best authority on organized crime. Hoover had to respond. Characteristically, without acknowledging previous misjudgments or mentioning the forbidden word "Mafia," he ordered a crash catch-up program modeled on one of his public-relations successes, the FBI's "Ten Most Wanted List." Every FBI bureau would identify and seek prosecutions of the "Ten Top Hoodlums" in their jurisdictions. "Hoodlums" in Hoover's terminology was a code name for mafiosi. Coming up with ten targets was simple for agents in New York, Chicago, Philadelphia, and other big cities. But bureaus in states where the Cosa Nostra had never ventured—Wyoming, Idaho, Montana, Iowa, Utah,

Nebraska, and many others—complied with Hoover's command by apprehending petty criminals and juvenile delinquents. The program nabbed dozens of small-time bookies and gamblers but the overall impact of the arrests was meaningless.

Hoover's other step was clandestine and more effective in gleaning intelligence information—but it was illegal. He issued confidential instructions for "black-bag jobs," FBI argot for planting bugs without court authorization, in suspected mafiosi hangouts. In a directive to SACs, Special Agents in Charge, of regional offices, he told them to employ "unusual investigative techniques," a euphemism for electronic surveillance.

It was a difficult assignment since most agents and bureau supervisors were almost totally ignorant of Mafia ways or where its leaders talked business. As in the top-hoodlum campaign, little intelligence was gained except for a lucky break in Chicago where aggressive agents bugged a room above a tailor shop used by Sam "Momo" Giancana, that city's godfather. They picked up one conversation that conclusively demonstrated the importance of the Apalachin meeting and the humiliation caused by the police roundup. Agents heard Giancana on the telephone chastising Stefano Magaddino, the Buffalo boss, for helping to organize the meeting. The illicit eavesdropping could never be used as evidence in a court, but parts of it were leaked by FBI agents to the press seven years later.

"Well, I hope you're satisfied," a sarcastic Giancana complained to Magaddino. "Sixty-three of our top guys made by the cops."

"I gotta admit you were right, Sam," replied Magaddino. "It never would have happened in your place."

"You're fucking right it wouldn't," Giancana exploded. "This is the safest territory in the world for a big meet. We could have scattered you guys in my motels. We could've given you guys different cars from my auto agencies, and then we could have had the meet in one of my big restaurants. The cops don't bother us here."

Hoover had one more secret ace up his sleeve. Under the direction of a top aide, William C. Sullivan, a monograph or special report was researched for him on whether or not the Mafia actually existed. Completed in July 1958, it declared: "The truth of the matter is, the available evidence makes it impossible to deny logically the existence of a criminal organization known as the Mafia, which for generations has plagued the law-abiding citizens of Sicily, Italy and the United States."

Pulling no punches, the report found that many law-enforcement officials were "unable to comprehend the Mafia," and "it is easy to rationalize and conclude there is no formal organization called the Mafia." Finally, Sullivan's analysis warned: "In this sense, it is the American counterpart of the old Sicilian-Italian Mafia. It exists not as a distinctly outlined, conventional organization, but as a criminal movement and a mode or way of life no less harmful to the United States."

The monograph was essentially a historical account of the origins and nature of the Mafia in Sicily and its transplantation to America. Only a handful of the director's most trusted lieutenants were permitted to read the report, which totally discredited his infallibility on the contentious subject. After receiving it, Hoover buried it in an FBI vault as a classified document.

Regardless of Hoover's obstinacy, the fallout from Apalachin reached Congress in 1957 in the form of a new committee with a jaw-breaking title: "The Senate Select Committee on Improper Activities in the Labor or Management Field." Its chairman, Senator John L. McClellan, an Arkansas Democrat, was attached to the party's southern, conservative, states'-rights, anti-integration wing; they were known as the Dixiecrats. Reared in a small town near Hot Springs, the crusty senator was not beholden to union and Mob-backed big-city Democratic machines. He also was a crafty negotiator for getting legislation that he wanted approved by Congress.

Noting that twenty-two of the identified Apalachin visitors were employed by unions or in labor-relations jobs, the committee convened a special hearing on the mobster conference. Except for stating their names and official legal occupations, the subpoenaed bosses and their assistants took refuge in the Fifth Amendment. Carlo Gambino listed himself as a labor consultant and counselor. One of his prized accounts was a $36,000-a-year fee for advice on union matters to the developers of the Levittowns on Long Island and in Pennsylvania. William J. Levitt, the giant company's chief executive, denied that the payments for Gambino's unspecified services were a "shakedown" to avoid labor disruptions, but Levitt executives were unable to provide background material to support Gambino's dubious claim of being an expert in construction or union relations.

There was also little information forthcoming from Tommy Lucchese and Vito Genovese. All the senators learned from Lucchese was that he was "a dress contractor"; Genovese said his income derived from investments in trash-handling and package-delivery businesses. Genovese set an unofficial record by invoking the Fifth Amendment more than 150 times. At one point in the hearings, a scowling McClellan, incensed by the parade of uncooperative gangster witnesses, many of them immigrants, lashed out with nationalistic fervor: "They do not belong to our land, and they ought to be sent somewhere else. In my book, they are human parasites of society and they violate every law of decency and humanity."

Testimony before the committee about Mob intrigues in unions and evidence from a previous hearing about corruption in the International Brotherhood of Teamsters led to significant labor legislation: the passage of the Landrum-Griffin Act in 1959, a law regulating union elections and requiring the submission of annual union financial reports to the Department of Labor.

"The testimony we have heard," McClellan summed up at the hearings, "can leave no doubt that there has been a concerted effort by members of the American criminal syndicate to achieve legitimacy through association and control of labor unions and business firms. The extent of the infiltration poses a serious threat to the very economy of our country."

Apalachin and the Senate hearings were particularly embarrassing to Vito Genovese. His fellow bosses blamed him and his imperial ambitions for having the unprecedented meeting in the first place, and the hearings unveiled fissures in his personal life. To spotlight Genovese's bulging wealth, the chief counsel for the McClellan Committee, young Robert F. Kennedy, presented evidence from a separation suit by Genovese's wife. As part of a property settlement, Mrs. Genovese gave details of Don Vito's illegal income from gambling, racetracks, nightclubs, union shakedowns, extortions, and other rackets. By her calculations he netted more than $40,000 a week and had secret caches in numerous safe-deposit boxes in America and Europe. Kennedy's exposure of the separation settlement notified every mafiosi in the country that Anna Genovese had left the Mob boss. Genovese's murderous temperament was feared in the Mafia, and his wife's departure and financial revelations were inordinate insults to the godfather's prestige. Don Vito, who had wed Anna after arranging her first husband's slaying, had a soft spot for his "bride by murder" and never made a move to harm her.

Genovese's marital problems were overshadowed by a small-time drug pusher in East Harlem named Nelson Cantellops. During the Apalachin uproar, the Puerto Rican Cantellops was serving time for a drug conviction. Seeking a deal for early prison release, he told federal narcotics investigators that he had worked directly for Vito in drug trafficking. The authorities said he passed lie-detector tests and volunteered firsthand information that corroborated Genovese's complicity in a heroin operation.

Mainly on Cantellops's testimony, Genovese was convicted on narcotics charges in 1959 and sentenced to fifteen years in prison. "All I can say, Your Honor, is I am innocent" were Genovese's only remarks at the sentencing. He may have been telling the truth about this specific narcotics charge. In a parallel to Lucky Luciano's trial, the validity of the guilty verdict in Genovese's case was later questioned by many experienced detectives and lawyers. They believed the government got a kingpin mobster for the wrong crime. Ralph Salerno emphasized in his book, *The Crime Confederation*, that the most incriminating witness against Genovese was the low-level courier Cantellops, who swore in court that he had personally met and talked with the boss of a Mafia family about details of the drug network. Salerno found this relationship totally contrary to traditional Mob practices. "To anyone who understands the protocol and insulation procedures of Cosa Nostra, this testimony is almost unbelievable," he wrote.

Vito Genovese's imprisonment culminated the most tumultuous decade of leadership shifts in the Mafia since the five families had been organized. In one gang, Vincent Mangano and Albert Anastasia were murdered, leaving Carlo Gambino in charge. Frank Costello, the successor in his family to Lucky Luciano, retired after being wounded; and that borgata's new godfather, Vito Genovese, was imprisoned. In a third gang, Tommy Lucchese had replaced Gaetano Gagliano after his death. The five families had endured the humiliation of the Apalachin mess, the scrutiny of the Kefauver and McClellan hearings, and three major family power shifts. Yet they remained as vibrant as ever.

But confrontations with unyielding, defiant mafiosi had whetted the fervor of Senator McClellan and his investigative committee's counsel, Robert Kennedy. Their implacable commitment to dig deeper into the fabric of organized crime would alter the future of the Mafia.

14

Death of a President

"For a hundred years of health and to John Kennedy's death."

With unrestrained elation, the two men dining in Tampa's ritziest restaurant clinked their glasses of Scotch. They were celebrating the assassination only a few hours earlier of John Fitzgerald Kennedy. It was the evening of November 22, 1963, and Santo Trafficante Jr., the Mafia boss of Tampa, and his lawyer and confidant, Frank Ragano, knocked back several more joyful toasts with loud introductory *salutes*, and with gusto enjoyed an expensive dinner and several bottles of wine at Tampa's International Inn. "Isn't that something, they killed the son-of-a-bitch," Trafficante repeated several times during the meal. "The son-of-a-bitch is dead."

Trafficante and Ragano's merriment was vividly noticeable in the restaurant, but the two men were unconcerned about the reactions of the other subdued and mournful diners and the staff, who were stunned by the murder that day of a young, popular president. Among Mob leaders, Trafficante's behavior was probably the most conspicuous public display that evening of the relief that swept through the Mafia after the death of Kennedy. "This is like lifting a load of stones off my shoulders," Trafficante confided to Ragano. The mobster meant, and his lawyer clearly understood, that Kennedy's elimination would ease and perhaps abruptly end an unprecedented law-enforcement threat to himself and his Mafia cohorts throughout the country.

The genesis of the Mafia's enmity for Kennedy stemmed from the 1960 presidential election and the Mob's entanglement in it. Joseph Kennedy, father of the president and patriarch of the Kennedy clan, secretly sought financial and political aid from northern Mob bosses in both the Democratic primary campaign and in the general election. The elder Kennedy was a multimillionaire, a financial tycoon, the regulatory official chosen by Franklin D. Roosevelt to reform Wall Street after the 1929 crash, and a former ambassador to Great Britain. Despite those super-respectable credentials, Joe Kennedy maintained loose ties to organized crime that dated from Prohibition, when he engaged in bootlegging partnerships with Frank Costello. Joe Kennedy was never owned and was never a flunky for a Mob boss, but he knew how to reach out to mafiosi for clandestine help in business and political matters.

Long after the 1960 presidential election, investigators and Congressional committees would learn of claims by mobsters that in the spring of 1960, at Joe Kennedy's urging, they pumped money into an early primary won by John Kennedy in West Virginia. Kennedy needed a smashing victory there against his main opponent, fellow Senator Hubert Humphrey, to prove that a Catholic could carry a heavily Protestant state. Even more important in the general election that year, the northern mafiosi, again reportedly solicited by Joe Kennedy, used their influence with big-city northern Democratic machines to produce votes for his son. Chicago's Outfit members, led by their boss, Sam Giancana, boasted that they had helped Chicago Mayor Richard J. Daley steal enough votes for Kennedy to squeak by in Illinois and provide the vital electoral votes to defeat Richard M. Nixon, the Republican candidate. It was the closest presidential election since 1916, and Mafia bosses were convinced they had a role in Kennedy's razor-thin victory.

Frank Sinatra, the singer and actor, played a role in the Kennedy Mafia drama. He helped initiate a delicate love-sex triangle between Sam Giancana, President Kennedy, and Judith Campbell Exner, an alluring young woman who moved in the show-business circles of Hollywood and Las Vegas. Sinatra, a friend of Kennedy's and of his brother-in-law, the actor Peter Lawford, was a longtime buddy of Giancana's and was on friendly terms with other mobsters. In 1960, before Kennedy's election, Sinatra introduced Ms. Campbell to Kennedy and Giancana and both men had sexual affairs with her while Kennedy was president.

Giancana, according to Ms. Exner, delighted in crediting organized crime for swinging the election to Kennedy. "Listen, honey," she quoted the mobster in a kiss-and-tell book, "if it wasn't for me your boyfriend wouldn't even be in the White House."

Because of their support, the Mob bosses expected a comfortable, relaxed relationship with the new administration. Instead, they got Robert F. Kennedy, President Kennedy's younger brother, as his attorney general.

The thirty-five-year-old Robert Kennedy assumed the job of the nation's top law-enforcement official in January 1961, unaware of his father's election requests of the Mafia. On the contrary, his most incisive memories of mobsters arose from his encounters with arrogant gangsters when he was a counsel with Senator McClellan's investigative committee. Two of Robert Kennedy's immediate priorities were destroying the backbone of organized crime—the Mafia—and dissolving the Mob's corrupt affiliations with labor unions.

A review of operations at the Justice Department and at the FBI left the new attorney general livid at the apathy he found. He was appalled to discover that America's highest law-enforcement officials not only had no strategy for combating mobsters but, even more disturbing, refused to recognize the existence of powerful Italian-American gangs.

After the publicity uproar from the Apalachin raid in 1957, the Eisenhower administration's Justice Department had created a unit of prosecutors to specialize in organized-crime investigations. The unit's major effort in three years was obtaining convictions against some of the Apalachin participants for conspiracy to obstruct justice and commit perjury. The verdicts, however, were overturned and Kennedy found that the unit had drifted into a soporific state without a single major accomplishment. Undertaking a quick shakeup, he beefed up the department's organized-crime section of prosecutors from seventeen to sixty, replacing most of the ineffective old hands with gung-ho recruits. Kennedy's impatience with placid indifference spread quickly among the newcomers, especially one of his rebukes when career administrators cited legal hurdles in launching prosecutions of mobsters. "Don't tell me what I can't do," he insisted. "Tell me what I can do."

An energetic new prosecutor, G. Robert Blakey, encountered the widespread indifference in the department to tackling the Mafia. He was greeted by blanket denials from department veterans that organized crime was a severe problem.

"They told me that the Mob does not exist. It was just a loose association of gangs. They are not organized."

One of Kennedy's first moves to overcome the lethargy was the creation of a team to zero in on labor racketeering in the nation's largest union, the International Brotherhood of Teamsters (IBT). At Senator McClellan's committee hearings, Kennedy had squared off with the union's truculent president, James R. Hoffa, over allegations that the union was beset with corrupt organized-crime connections. Kennedy hired Walter Sheridan, an investigator from the McClellan Committee and an implacable antagonist of Jimmy Hoffa, to head the unit. Sheridan's dedication was so intense that his staff pinned a hand-made valentine on his door with a photograph of a grinning Hoffa in the center and the inscription, "Always Thinking of You." Sheridan's investigators and lawyers, with the blessing of Kennedy, became known as "The Get Hoffa Squad."

At the FBI, Hoover, after completing his gimmicky but ineffective "Top Hoodlum" program in the late 1950s, had again closed his mind to the Mob. Hoover's investigative commitments were most evident in New York where a grand total of four agents were assigned full-time to keep an eye on the nation's largest and most active mafiosi detachment of more than two thousand soldiers and thousands of wannabe associates. In contrast, Hoover, chronically fearful of the espionage threat of the Communist Party, assigned more than four hundred agents to maintain surveillance in the New York area of the party's dwindling and aging members, most of whom had long ceased to be a political or a subversive threat.

The bureau's intelligence records on organized crime in 1961 consisted mainly of newspaper clippings, and Robert Kennedy eagerly accepted Harry Anslinger's long-ignored "Black Book" dossiers on Mafia suspects and turned them over to his reinforced phalanxes of prosecutors and investigators for action. At first, Hoover appeared unimpressed by Kennedy's campaign. "No single individual or coalition of racketeers dominates organized crime across the nation," he pronounced publicly, almost a year after Kennedy began moving against the Mob.

Although the bureau was structurally under the administration of the Justice Department and the attorney general, the dogmatic Hoover had always set his own agenda. But in the Kennedy administration he was unable to outflank the attorney general by maneuvering over his head to the president. This attorney general had the ear of the president and they were brothers, an affiliation too solid for Hoover to fracture.

For three decades, whenever possible, Hoover had ignored the Mafia. He had reasons for doing so. These investigations were tricky, difficult, and often unproductive. Moreover, Hoover realized that his agents, predominantly from small midwestern and southern towns, lacked the know-how and street smarts to infiltrate the borgatas or quickly make significant headway in producing cases that would stand up in court. And like all law-enforcement bureaucrats, he knew that investigations into organized crime were corruption minefields, hazardous for ordinary police officers as well as for federal agents. Mobsters, many of whom were harvesting fortunes from gambling and loan-sharking, would bribe anyone, possibly even tempting wholesome FBI agents and thereby tarnishing Hoover's reputation.

But with Robert Kennedy cracking the whip and the president supporting him, Hoover was forced to undertake an intensive investigation of the Mob. Kennedy urged him to scrutinize organized crime as fervently as he had two of his favorite targets: domestic Communists and Soviet bloc espionage. Hoover responded with his customary bureaucratic ploys, creating a new FBI Special Division for Organized Crime and developing another of his "Most Wanted" lists. After decades of disputing the Mafia's existence, he suddenly compiled a roster of forty suspects who were ripe for immediate probing. The top forty were mainly bosses and their lieutenants who had been spotlighted earlier by other law-enforcement authorities and by the press after Apalachin. New York's prominent godfathers, Carlo Gambino, Joe Bonanno, Joe Profaci, and Tommy Lucchese were high on Hoover's target list.

Ignorance was the main obstacle for agents in the FBI's new platoon of Mafia hunters. Under Hoover's aegis, agents generally had avoided cooperating closely with other federal agencies and with state and local police forces. Hoover was disdainful of the ability and the corruptibility of big-city police departments and distrusted other federal organizations as rivals. He rarely permitted joint undertakings, primarily because he had no intention of sharing recognition with any law-enforcement official. When asked to turn over their own data on criminal cases to the bureau, detectives in New York and other cities usually did so grudgingly. The bureau had a legal right to inspect police intelligence dossiers on the Mafia without having to reciprocate. Remo Franceschini, a New York organized-crime detective, was incensed at the bureau's highhanded "rape of our files." FBI agents, however, often refused to turn over information they might posses to local investigators, citing federal law restrictions. On one rare occasion, Franceschini said the bureau did give him its confidential research material on a mobster, but it was worthless. The entire FBI file consisted of intelligence reports that the city's police department had given to the bureau. Most big-city detectives resented the FBI's propaganda apparatus and its unearned reputation for excellence. As a sign of contempt for Hoover's agents, New York detectives sarcastically referred to the bureau's initials as standing for "Famous But Incompetent." Because of the FBI's zeal in generating meaningless anticrime statistics through the recovery of stolen cars, other wags labeled FBI agents "Fan Belt Inspectors."

Now Robert Kennedy's demands for results compelled Hoover's sleuths to seek help from outsiders with firsthand knowledge about the Mafia. One veteran they turned to was Ralph Salerno, the New York detective, who willingly shared his hard-earned files with them. "They had a lot of catching up to do," Salerno said. "It was the first time they came and said, 'What have you got on these guys?'" He tutored agents on fundamental tactics of gathering intelligence information about Mafia families through diligent surveillance at Mob social events: wakes, funerals, weddings, christenings, and restaurant meals. "Pecking orders" in families, the detective instructed, often could be traced through the respect shown to individuals at these occasions, which also were used for meetings to discuss family matters. The Mafia's rigid code of behavior required elaborate demonstrations of homage to leaders, and the treatment accorded to mobsters in public rituals often disclosed recent promotions, power shifts, and alliances.

The detective's practical tips included secretly photographing mobsters at the gatherings for identification purposes and slipping into wedding receptions of Mafia sons and daughters to obtain lists of guests as a means of identifying known and new members. He advocated filching lists of cash gifts that brides sometimes recorded; the amounts would indicate the importance and rank of mobster guests because, under Mafia protocol, wedding gifts were made according to status with the largest sums coming from the highest in rank. From a wiretap, Salerno once got a risible peek into Mob matrimonial etiquette. He heard an anxious Lucchese soldier's wife sounding out the wife of a family higher-up on the amount her husband was planning to give at a coming wedding. The soldier's wife said her husband wanted to be generous but was fearful of showing up his immediate superior as a cheapskate.

Hoover's other major step against the Mafia was resorting once again to illegal bugs as he had after the Apalachin embarrassment. He directed field supervisors and agents to employ "Highly confidential sources," bureau-speak for planting listening devices and eavesdropping in scores of mobsters' homes and hangouts—without court authorization. In this avenue of investigation, the FBI, with decades of experience from espionage surveillance, was unrivaled. The bureau's electronic technicians even impressed Ralph Salerno. "I saw them install a bug in thirty seconds. They were real good, masters at their trade."

In 1962, under confusing existing laws and court rulings, federal agencies were prohibited from "interception and disclosure" of telephone conversations. In 1954, during the Eisenhower administration, Attorney General Herbert Brownell gave Hoover the discretion to use bugs—concealed microphones or transmitting apparatus—in "internal security" cases. The authority was intended for use by the FBI against Soviet bloc nations and the Communist Party. Hoover now dynamically interpreted and expanded that authorization to include organized-crime investigations. The FBI's theory was that it could secretly "intercept," listen in, on bugs and telephone or wire taps, so long as the contents were not "disclosed." The information from the eavesdropping could never be used as evidence in a court, but it would provide the bureau with invaluable intelligence and clues about Mafia activities.

The electronic spying was a carefully guarded secret and Hoover never officially told Robert Kennedy that he had launched the illegal project, which some agents referred to by another coded name: "the June Files." For the record, the bureau maintained that its sudden cornucopia of information and insight on the Mob came from informers, turncoats, and intensive leg work by agents. Only one official in the Justice Department, William G. Hundley, the head of Bobby Kennedy's Organized Crime Section, was discreetly informed that agents might be resorting to illegal and unconstitutional eavesdropping. "Hoover never asked for authorization," Hundley said. "Occasionally, my counterparts in the FBI would hint in a roundabout way that they had some information from a bug but they were never specific." Hundley believed that the agents informed him unofficially of the eavesdropping as a bureaucratic cover, which would allow the FBI to claim that the Justice Department was aware of the legally questionable program, should it blow up into a scandal. It was apparent to Hundley that some prosecutors in the department, from careful reading of FBI reports, could deduce that the confidential information could have come only from surreptitious bugs, known as "black-bag jobs."

When Kennedy learned belatedly about the bureau's electronic tactics, he asked Hundley why he had kept the sensitive information to himself. "Kennedy

said to me in effect, 'You knew about it? Why didn't you say something to me?' "
Because of the legally questionable nature of the bugs and wiretaps, Hundley
had kept his mouth shut to protect Kennedy from personal damage if the surveillance program became a political hot potato. "It was one of those things you
don't talk about," Hundley conceded. "Hoover had never done anything on organized crime. His game plan was to catch up in a hurry with the bugs. Later
he could use the information from the bugs to develop informers, make cases
and nobody would ever know."

Technically, the electronic spying techniques were near perfect. Nevertheless, it took time for agents unfamiliar with Mafia slang expressions and its puzzling protocol and culture to figure out what they were hearing. They were sent
to language schools to learn Italian, especially the Sicilian dialects that were often spoken or interjected into profanity-laced conversations by gangsters. A
naive FBI squad in Las Vegas, oblivious to mobster schedules, at first routinely
worked on surveillance and electronic eavesdropping from 8:00 A.M. to 5:00
P.M. Eventually the agents discovered that mafiosi and their gambling coteries
conducted most of their business well past midnight, when the agents were off
duty and asleep.

In less than a year, the FBI had surmounted the learning curve, and bugs
were flooding the bureau and the Justice Department with leads. "They had to
learn from scratch," Bob Blakey, one of Kennedy's lawyer-prosecutors, said of
the FBI's efforts. "But by mid-1962, they got it all down."

Robert Kennedy opened another front by trying to isolate mobsters from the
lawyers and accountants who willingly or unwillingly abetted them. Defense
lawyers traditionally considered themselves and prosecutors equal members of
the same professional fraternity—the legal bar—and therefore immune from
investigation of their association with dubious clients. To cripple the Mob,
Bobby Kennedy broke that unwritten, seemingly sacrosanct rule. Without evidence of possible illegal acts, the FBI began investigating lawyers, accountants,
and businessmen who provided support services for Mob families. A long-range
goal was to discourage or intimidate these specialists from sheltering the vital
interests of mobsters and protecting them from indictments and convictions.
Isolated from their skilled hired hands, mafiosi might be more vulnerable to
prosecutions and imprisonment. A secondary goal of the plan was to "turn" or
persuade these noncriminal supporters to inform or cooperate with the government in cases against the Mob. Since the professionals were well aware of the
fate that awaited squealers, this part of the program got few results.

Kennedy also implemented the deportation power of the Immigration and Naturalization Service against high-ranking mobsters who had entered the country illegally or had questionable immigration status. His first big-shot quarry was Carlos Marcello, the undisputed Mob boss of New Orleans. Marcello, whose baptismal name was Calogero Minacore, was born in 1910 in Tunisia, then a French colony with a sizable Sicilian population. At the age of eight months, he and his mother arrived in New Orleans to be reunited with his father. His crime career was similar to other mafiosi of his generation: an early school dropout, petty crimes followed by robbery and narcotics trafficking convictions. Marcello's big break came when he connected with Frank Costello's gambling operations in the late 1930s and '40s in Louisiana, eventually becoming a partner with Costello and Meyer Lansky in illegal casinos. In 1947, at age thirty-seven, Marcello became one of the nation's youngest Mafia godfathers when he took control of the New Orleans family. Because he was only five feet, four inches tall, the new don was commonly known in the New Orleans underworld as "the Little Man," a sobriquet that was totally misleading in terms of his influence and assets.

Marcello's legal covers were pinball and jukebox companies, real estate developments, and a shrimp-boat fleet. The Mob boss's pride and joy was a 3,000-acre plantation, Churchill Farms, that he bought and restored in a New Orleans suburb. On immigration and other government forms where he had to list his occupation, Marcello modestly described himself as a "tomato salesman and real estate investor." Illegally, he ran casinos, bookmaking rings, slot machines, brothels, and a horse-racing wire service to bookie parlors in the South and Midwest. Federal narcotics agents long suspected that Marcello's shrimp business was a cover for smuggling heroin and cocaine from Central America and Mexico by boat, but they could never cobble together a case against him.

Because of his wealth and political influence, gained through widespread bribery, Marcello had extraordinary status within the American Mafia. He was the most respected and autonomous godfather outside of New York and Chicago, and had the unique privilege of shaping major crime policies and admitting members to his family without clearing his decisions with the Commission.

The Kefauver hearings, however, had exposed Marcello's immigration Achilles' heel: neither he nor his parents had applied for citizenship. After 1952 he had to report every three months to the immigration inspectors for a check on his legal right to remain in the country as an alien. It was a nuisance for the crime boss, but he showed up for the routine quarterly examination for eight years without trepidation.

Singling out Carlos Marcello as one of his first pet projects, Robert Kennedy moved decisively against him. On April 4, 1961, just three months after the new attorney general was sworn in, Marcello dutifully appeared at the New Orleans office of the Immigration and Naturalization Service. This time, Kennedy's immigration agents clasped handcuffs on him and suddenly accused him of holding a passport from Guatemala that had been obtained through a forged birth certificate. Despite the protests of a lawyer who had accompanied Marcello, he was ordered deported immediately. Without a court hearing, the infuriated Mafia boss was hustled onto a government plane and flown to Guatemala City.

For two months, as lawyers scrambled to get the suddenly stateless Marcello readmitted to the United States, he was booted out of one country after another. Guatemala deported him to neighboring El Salvador, where he was locked up in military barracks before being driven to the Honduran border and forced to cross on foot. The paunchy, fifty-one-year-old godfather, dressed in a business suit and tie, trekked seventeen miles under a torrid sun before reaching a peasant village. Finally, Marcello and an American lawyer who was with him got a ride to the Honduran capital, Tegucigalpa, where investigators lost track of him until he suddenly emerged in New Orleans. How he managed to reenter the country without being stopped by immigration officials is unclear. A prevalent theory is that Marcello got to Mexico and from there sneaked into the country on one of his own shrimp boats, which brought him to a secluded bayou in Louisiana. Rediscovered in New Orleans, Marcello was socked by the government with charges of evading $835,396 in federal taxes, illegal reentry to the country, and perjury. The seething don privately vowed revenge against the young attorney general who had disrupted his life.

While Kennedy spurred his prosecutors and the FBI to harass and dismantle the Mafia, his biggest intelligence and public-relations success arrived serendipitously in the form of a semiliterate criminal named Joseph Valachi. A seasoned "button man," soldier, and small-time narcotics dealer, Valachi's career in 1962 was effectively over. Although he had never been convicted of a homicide, Valachi was suspected of being the hit man or wheel man in more than twenty slayings. He was fifty-nine and serving a twenty-year narcotics sentence in Atlanta Federal Penitentiary, the same maximum-security prison where his family boss, Don Vito Genovese, was imprisoned for a separate drug conviction. Valachi's claims to fame were that he had survived the Castellammarese War and that Genovese had been the best man at his wedding.

A combination of convoluted events involving Genovese suddenly made prison life dangerous for Valachi. Rumors spread that he was an informer, and Genovese wanted him to kill another inmate who had supposedly insulted Valachi by calling him a rat. Convinced that the devious Genovese actually distrusted him and had bestowed on him "the kiss of death," Valachi became semi-paranoid and constantly watchful. On June 22, 1963, walking in the prison yard, he believed that an approaching inmate was an enforcer, Joseph "Joe Beck" DiPalermo, sent by Don Vito to kill him. Grabbing an iron pipe from a construction site in the yard, Valachi battered the other inmate to death. He had killed an innocent man, mistaking his victim for DiPalermo.

From solitary confinement, Valachi sent a message to federal narcotics agents that he was ready to tell all he knew about his thirty years as a mafioso. Valachi and the agents were aware that Genovese's hatred guaranteed that he would be killed once he was convicted and returned to the general prison population. A deal was cut with the Justice Department: Valachi pleaded guilty to second-degree manslaughter and, in exchange for disclosing what he knew about the Mafia, was promised a lifetime of protection as a pampered prisoner.

Although Valachi's information was limited to his experiences in the New York area as a lowly soldier in the trenches, he painted the first clear canvas of life inside the Mafia. He confirmed the existence of the five families; he outlined their organizational structure; he exposed the secret "blood" induction ceremony; he explained the effectiveness of the *omertà* vow; and he identified the leaders of each family, thereby for the first time attaching a name tag to each borgata. From Valachi's debriefings, myths and vague theories about the Mafia were punctured or proven. Hoover's confidential bugs and wiretaps were a great intelligence victory for the FBI; yet the meaning of segments of conversations and arcane references eluded agents. Valachi, however, with a little prodding, supplied the Rosetta Stone for one mystery: the common identifying name used by all families.

Agents had picked up frequent references beginning with a word in Italian that sounded to them like *cosa*, the Italian for thing, or *casa*, house, or *causa*, cause. At times the phrase was translated by agents as *casa nostra*, our house, or *causa nostra*, our cause. *Nostra* means our. A skilled FBI interrogator, James P. Flynn, raised the subject of the puzzling expression with Valachi, demanding to know if the families used the name Mafia.

"No," Valachi replied. "It's not Mafia. That's the expression the outsiders uses [sic]."

Fencing with Valachi, Flynn bluffed, saying he knew that the real name began with *cosa* and waited for an answer. The agent recalled that Valachi blanched then said, "*Cosa Nostra*. So you know about it."

Cosa Nostra. Our Thing. It became part of the American idiom. Uncovering the confidential organizational name was a delicious bureaucratic triumph for Hoover over Harry Anslinger, the head of the Narcotics Bureau, who for twenty years had championed the name Mafia. Forgetting his past disclaimers that a crime organization with national links existed, Hoover took total credit for having unearthed the name of the dreaded crime syndicate. Continuing the FBI ban on the title Mafia, Hoover, adding an unnecessary article to the name, adopted "La Cosa Nostra (inaccurately, The Our Thing)" and the abbreviation, LCN, as the crime organization's only proper appellation in FBI official documents and statements. Other law-enforcement agencies, officials, and the media, however, continued to use Mafia as an equally accurate designation for the families and the Commission.

Robert Kennedy seized upon Joe Valachi's defection as the ideal prop to garner support from Congress and the public for his assault on the newly minted LCN or Mafia. Reminiscent of the publicity engendered by the Kefauver Committee hearings, in the fall of 1963, Valachi was presented through television at hearings before Senator McClellan's investigations committee as the nation's first reliable witness on the inner workings of the Mafia. Unlike the faceless Frank Costello at the Kefauver hearings, Valachi appeared in full view before the cameras, and under gentle questioning from the senators, described his initiation as a mafioso, the murders that he knew about, and his other sordid experiences as a soldier.

The FBI displayed photographs, charts, and graphs for the committee and the TV audience, seeking to present an image of the families as rigidly organized military units, with strictly defined duties for each rank. While it was a generally accurate outline of each family's framework, the portrait missed the essential point that each member was an individual entrepreneur who had to be an earner and a producer to survive, prosper, and advance. Valachi stressed the necessity of illegal business skills when asked by Senator Karl Mundt of South Dakota if he got a regular paycheck from the family's boss. "You don't get any salary, Senator," Valachi explained, adding that part of his loot had to be given to the hierarchs.

"Well, you get a cut then," Mundt continued.

"You get nothing," Valachi said. "Only what you earn yourself. Do you understand?"

Questioned by senators from rural and agricultural states about the large number of Italian-Americans from big cities in the rackets, Valachi countered with a valid explanation. "I'm not talking about Italians. I'm talking about criminals."

Before his public appearance, Valachi had been coached by agents, spoon-fed information about other families that the bureau had picked up through electronic surveillance. Subtly brainwashed, Valachi believed his disclosures before the committee emanated from his own experiences and intimate under-standing of the American Mafia. Hoover had used him as a transmittor to pub-licize facts the FBI wanted Congress and the public to know about the Mob, without revealing that the data had been obtained through unconstitutional methods.

Valachi's Cosa Nostra knowledge was primarily limited to his activities in one crew or subgroup of a family, and he lacked evidence and leads that could generate a single indictment. Comparatively ignorant of details about other New York families and borgatas in the rest of the country, Valachi was even un-aware that Chicago's Mob called itself "the Outfit," New England's was "the Office," and Buffalo's was "the Arm." He also harped on second-hand historical stories, misleading the FBI and the senators into accepting the gory tale of "The Night of the Sicilian Vespers."

When Lucky Luciano arranged the September 1931 murder of Salvatore Maranzano, Valachi told the spellbound senators, a wave of gangland slayings eliminated Luciano's enemies throughout the country. Valachi wrongly veri-fied long-persisting rumors that the death toll ranged from a dozen to more than one hundred, with forty knocked off in one day of mass executions. Be-lievers of the supposed massacre named it "The Sicilian Vespers" purge, a refer-ence to the thirteenth-century violent uprising against the French. As late as 1987, the FBI gave credence to the 1931 "Vespers" yarn by citing it in an offi-cial report on the history of La Cosa Nostra.

But a study in 1976 by historian Humbert S. Nelli of the gangland hits two weeks before and two weeks after Maranzano's murder, discounted Valachi's "Vespers" concoction. Nelli found that on the day of the killing and in the fol-lowing three months, three Mob-style slayings were reported in the New York area and one in Denver. It was even unclear if those four hits were related to Maranzano's assassination and they certainly did not constitute a bloodbath.

Despite Valachi's shortcomings, his testimony gave investigators a rough sketch of the dimensions of the Mafia's strength and its operational methods. So little had been known about the Mob's inner workings that his revelations engrossed the public. Valachi may have been a low-ranking hoodlum, but he was the first "made" man to shatter the oath of *omertà* and provide accurate details about the Mafia's customs and codes of behavior. And with Hoover and the attorney general endorsing Valachi's accounts, all of the nation's law-enforcement agencies—even previous naysayers—had to jump on the bandwagon to acknowledge the existence of the Mafia or LCN, even if they disagreed with the magnitude of its threat.

For his cooperation, Valachi obtained the most comfortable treatment and lavish furnishings the Federal Bureau of Prisons could provide. A two-room air-cooled prison suite with couches and a kitchenette, isolated from the general inmate population, was built for him at the La Tuna Penitentiary near El Paso, Texas. The FBI and the Bureau of Prisons had sound reasons to quarantine their celebrity inmate and fear for his safety. At the time that Valachi testified, an FBI bug on Stefano Magaddino, the Buffalo boss and a Commission member, heard his views on Valachi. "We passed laws that this guy has got to die," Magaddino said to his underlings. William Hundley, the Justice Department official, who served as Valachi's counsel at the Senate hearings, said a plan by Robert Kennedy to provide Valachi with a new identity and "put him and a girlfriend on a desert island fell through." Valachi's solitary existence, always alone except for guards, was not a bed of roses; he once tried to commit suicide by hanging. In 1971, at age sixty-eight, Joe Valachi died in prison of natural causes.

On Friday, November 22, 1963—a month after Valachi's groundbreaking testimony before a Senate committee—President John F. Kennedy was assassinated riding in an open limousine in a motorcade in Dallas's Dealey Plaza. Barely an hour later, in another section of Dallas, Lee Harvey Oswald, a twenty-four-year-old ex-Marine and a supporter of left-wing causes, was arrested and accused of murdering President Kennedy and gunning down a police officer who tried to apprehend him. Two days later, as Oswald was being escorted from the basement of the Dallas police headquarters to a county jail, a stubby middle-aged man jumped out of a crowd of news reporters and photographers and fatally shot Oswald; live television captured the scene.

The gunman was Jack Ruby, a raunchy local nightclub owner, with longtime ties to organized-crime figures. By audaciously killing Oswald, Ruby would emerge as an enigmatic segment of a larger vexing puzzle: Did the Mafia plot the assassination of a president?

15

"The Ring of Truth"

Vice President Lyndon Baines Johnson, riding in another limousine in the motorcade on that fateful Friday in Dallas, was uninjured, and that day took the oath of office as president. With the prime goal of determining if Kennedy had been the victim of a foreign or a domestic conspiracy, Johnson appointed a commission headed by the highly respected Earl Warren, Chief Justice of the United States, to issue a conclusive report on the assassination. The Warren Commission relied on the FBI as its main investigative arm after Hoover craftily usurped jurisdiction from the Secret Service, the agency responsible for protecting the president. Hoover spearheaded the investigation through an obscure jurisdictional technicality that federal property had been destroyed when the assassin's bullet struck the windshield of the president's limousine.

Dependent essentially on the bureau's detective work, the commission issued its findings in September 1964. The main conclusions ratified Hoover's analysis: there had been no conspiracy; Oswald, a disgruntled loner with a history of erratic behavior, was the sole shooter, firing a cheap mail-order rifle from a sixth-floor window in the Texas School Book Depository, where he worked. The bulk of the FBI investigation was hastily completed in less than a month. Under Hoover's orders, many investigative areas and clues were ignored.

Almost from the moment the commission's 888-page report was released, its essential judgments came under withering fire as being inaccurate, misleading, and undermined by glaring omissions. A large crop of critics disputed the commission's verdict that Oswald was the lone gunman. These challenges— centering on the number of bullets fired and the direction they came from— generated a large variety of conspiracy theories.

The first suspects were the Mafia and Fidel Castro.

Leads about the Mob's possible complicity trickled out gradually over the years and much of it was compiled and revealed in 1979. That year, a select committee of the House of Representatives completed a two-year reevaluation of the Warren Commission's investigation. A principal area that the committee explored was the possibility of a Mafia scheme to murder the president as the most effective method of halting his brother's crusade against them. Another as- sassination theory stemmed from the Central Intelligence Agency's recruitment of influential mafiosi in the early 1960s to help kill Castro, thereby inciting the Cubans to retaliate by murdering President Kennedy.

Evidence that many Cosa Nostra leaders feared Robert Kennedy's offensive against them and of their rising hatred of the attorney general and the president were found by the committee in previously secret FBI files. The intriguing in- formation came from bugs installed before the assassination, during Hoover's clandestine electronic surveillance catch-up program against the Mob.

Hoover had withheld important information from the Warren Commission. He did not reveal the existence of the bugs and the valuable evidence and in- sight derived from them. The commission was never aware that the FBI had recorded the rampant hostility expressed by important mafiosi toward the Kennedys. In another odd twist, Hoover had assigned the assassination probe in 1963 to the FBI division that handled bank robbery and destruction of federal property investigations. The two most qualified FBI units for looking into do- mestic or foreign conspiracies, the organized-crime and national security divi- sions, were largely sidetracked from participating in the investigation. Congressional investigators later speculated that Hoover's unorthodox assign- ment was deliberate. They said he might have feared that a more wide-ranging examination by qualified agents and hard-nosed prosecutors would have ex- posed the illegal bugging and blighted his reputation.

By the time the congressional committee began its work in the late 1970s, the FBI tapes had been erased or destroyed. The new investigators were forced to fall back on incomplete summaries and partial transcripts of the recorded conversations. Most of the suggestive threats made by mobsters were plucked from fragments of longer conversations. The covert FBI bugs revealed outright loathing of the Kennedy brothers, particularly Robert. In the taped conversations, many mobsters reviled individual FBI agents, but there were surprisingly few threats or malicious comments aimed at J. Edgar Hoover.

On May 2, 1962, agents heard Michelino "Mike" Clemente, an important captain in New York's Genovese family, express his views to several soldiers. "Bob Kennedy," Clemente warned, "won't stop today until he puts us all in jail all over the country. Until the Commission meets and puts its foot down, things will be at a standstill." Stressing the need for increased secrecy to thwart Kennedy, he added, "When we meet, we all got to shake hands, and sit down and talk, and, if there is any trouble with a particular regime [family], it's got to be kept secret, and only the heads are to know about it, otherwise some broad finds out, and finally the newspapers."

A year later in May 23, 1963, Stefano Magaddino, Joe Bonanno's cousin, the boss of the Buffalo borgata, and a member of the Commission, was apprehensive about the government's inroads, lamenting to lieutenants, "We are in a bad situation in Cosa Nostra. They know everything under the sun. They know who's back of it, they know *amici*, they know *capodecina*, they know there is a Commission. We got to watch right now, this thing, where it goes and stay as quiet as possible."

Magaddino was unaware that he was being bugged and that most FBI intelligence about the Mob was coming from unguarded conversations. On June 6, 1963, Magaddino was at it again, cautioning several of his men about the difficulties created by the Kennedys. "Here we are situated with this administration. We got from the president down against us. But we got to resist." There was then a sound like a fist slamming a table.

That same month, the godfather admitted to one of his soldiers, Anthony DeStefano, that after a visit from FBI agents he was perplexed by the bureau's ability to gather intelligence. "You see, the Cosa Nostra. The other day they made me become frightened. They know our business better than us. They know the heads of the families, the *capodecina*, the FBI does. Therefore, that's why, the other day, I say be careful before you open your mouth. Because sometime, somebody could be a spy and you might think he is an *amico nostro*."

A month before the assassination, on October 31, 1963, Magaddino's son, Peter, a made man, heatedly told his father that the president "should drop dead." The son added, "They should kill the whole family—the mother and father too."

Early on in the Mob investigation, on February 9, 1962, FBI agents listened to inflammatory remarks in a gripe session between Angelo Bruno, the boss of the Philadelphia family, and Willie Weisberg, a trusted business associate. "See what Kennedy done," Weisberg said. "With Kennedy, a guy should take a knife, like one of them other guys, and stab and then kill the fuck, where he is now . . . I'll kill. Right in the fucking White House. Somebody's got to get rid of this fuck."

On the subject of Mob revenge, the congressional committee took a hard look at Carlos Marcello, the New Orleans potentate, and his malice toward the Kennedys. Robert Kennedy acknowledged responsibility for Marcello's tempo-rary deportation to Central America in 1961, maintaining the expulsion had been done in accordance with immigration laws. Before the assassination, the mobster repeatedly had vented his outrage against the attorney general for his humiliation. A troublesome issue that concerned the committee was a reported conversation in September 1962 between Marcello and Edward Becker, a wheeler-dealer with known business ties to underworld figures. Becker had var-ious occupations: investigator for a private-eye firm headed by a former FBI agent; public-relations man; show business manager; television producer. He claimed that he heard Marcello pledge that he would get his revenge against Robert Kennedy for deporting him. "Don't worry about that little Bobby son-of-a-bitch," Becker quoted Marcello. "He's going to be taken care of."

In 1967 the FBI looked into the story of Marcello's purported threat af-ter learning that Becker had provided an account of it to Ed Reid, a writer on organized-crime subjects. An internal bureau memorandum based on an inter-view with Reid, said that Becker had recalled Marcello telling him that "in order to get Bobby Kennedy they would have to get the president and they could not kill Bobby because the president would use the Army and the Marines to get them." Marcello allegedly told Becker that killing President Kennedy "would cause Bobby to lose his power as attorney general because of the new president." Becker was dismissed by the FBI as disreputable and unreliable, so no effort was made by the bureau to interview him, or to adequately verify or refute his information.

A decade after the FBI turned a cold shoulder to Becker, he was questioned by House Assassination Committee investigators. He recounted that he had met three or four times in New Orleans with Marcello between September 1962 and January 1963, regarding a fuel-oil additive business that Becker and an associate of the Mob boss wanted Marcello to invest in. During the course of one meeting at Marcello's Churchill Farms estate in September 1962, Becker asked Marcello about pressure from Robert Kennedy's investigation, and it was then that the Mob boss exploded in rage. Becker could not recall Marcello's exact words, but said he "clearly stated that he was going to arrange to have President Kennedy murdered in some way," and that someone outside of the Mafia would be manipulated to carry out the actual crime. Becker also asserted to committee investigators that Marcello made a reference to President Kennedy's being a dog and Robert Kennedy the dog's tail. Becker paraphrased Marcello as saying ominously, "The dog will keep biting you if you cut off its tail, but that if the dog's head is cut off, the dog would die." The shrill comments occurred during a minute or two of a business meeting that lasted more than an hour, Becker told investigators.

Marcello's harangue disturbed Becker, but he was accustomed to hearing mobsters and other criminals routinely threaten adversaries, and he did not take them seriously. His fear of Mob retribution if he reported Marcello's remarks to the authorities before or immediately after President Kennedy's assassination had kept him silent for years.

The House committee's staff substantiated the objective facts of Becker's story concerning dates and places that he met with Marcello, and found that the FBI had unjustifiably disparaged Becker and his information. "They made no attempt to impartially investigate what he had to say," a committee lawyer reported. "All they did was shoot the messenger and discredit him."

Called before the special House committee in executive session, Marcello became enraged when he retold how he had been "snatched" by Bobby Kennedy's agents and dumped summarily in Guatemala. But he vigorously denied making the threatening statements attributed to him against President Kennedy. "No, sir, I never said anything like that. Positively not, never said anything like that." With only Becker's word to go on, the committee's inquiry into Marcello's possible involvement in the assassination came to a dead end. Ironically, on November 22, 1963, the day that President Kennedy was shot, Marcello was acquitted by a New Orleans jury of conspiracy to falsify his Guatemalan passport, one of the charges brought against him by Robert Kennedy's prosecutors. He was never again deported.

A second Mafia luminary, Florida's Santo Trafficante Jr., also was of particular interest to the committee. Trafficante, who had Mob rackets on both Florida coasts in Tampa and in Miami, worked closely with Marcello; their provinces comprised the Mob's southern citadels. Before Castro's revolution in 1959,

Trafficante was the dominant American mafioso in Cuba; he had investments in three casinos and was heavily involved in shipping narcotics to the United States. While most mobsters dashed back to America when Castro seized power, Trafficante, who spoke fluent Spanish, remained in Cuba, confident he could retain his lucrative casinos by bribing the new regime. He soon learned that he was mistaken. Castro's government did not cooperate with gamblers or drug traffickers; it appropriated Trafficante's holdings, imprisoned him, and threatened to execute him. There are two versions of how Trafficante escaped Castro's revolutionary justice: he was kicked out after all his property was confiscated; or he bribed a prison official who released him without the knowledge of higher-ups.

Incensed by his losses in Cuba, Trafficante returned to Florida where he cultivated ties with the anti-Castro exile movement. His hatred of Castro and his links to the émigrés attracted the secret attention of U.S. spymasters. A year before the House committee began its work on Kennedy's assassination, the Senate Select Committee on Intelligence in 1975 disclosed an embarrassing intrigue by the Central Intelligence Agency; it employed Trafficante and other mafiosi in a ludicrous scheme to kill Castro.

An alliance with the Mafia was one of the eight conspiracies hatched by the CIA from 1960 to 1965 to eliminate Castro and topple his leftist government. In the summer of 1960, the CIA asked Robert Maheu, a former FBI agent with Mob contacts, to find mafiosi who could pull off a hit on the Cuban dictator. Maheu enlisted John Roselli, a Los Angeles hood, who brought in Chicago's Sam Giancana and Tampa's Santo Trafficante Jr. Of the trio, only Trafficante had intimate knowledge of Cuba and had close ties to anti-Castro exiles.

CIA operatives gave Maheu $150,000 to pass along to the putative assassins. During the planning stage, an internal agency review accurately described the Mafia participants as untrustworthy racketeers and emphasized that they were interested mainly in reacquiring "gambling, prostitution and dope monopolies" if Castro was overthrown. The cautionary red flag was ignored, and in late 1960 or early 1961, at a meeting in a room at Miami's elegant Fontainebleau Hotel, Maheu gave Trafficante a briefcase crammed with CIA money. He also handed over lethal capsules to be used by the plotters to poison Castro when he dined at a favorite restaurant in Havana. The poison-pill comic-opera caper never materialized. A confidential CIA review was unable to pinpoint why the plan failed or whether it was even attempted. Neither the CIA nor the Senate committee could trace what happened to the $150,000 earmarked for the operation.

Of the hit team trio recruited by the CIA, only Santo Trafficante was alive to testify before the Kennedy assassination committee. Subpoenaed before the committee in 1978, Trafficante sketched a portrait of himself as an insignificant bit player and translator in the CIA attempt to murder Castro. CIA money? Poison pills? His memory was a total blank.

Sam Giancana was murdered in his home the night before he was scheduled to be questioned in 1975 by the Senate committee investigators looking into the CIA's ventures in Cuba. He was shot at close range in the back of the head and in his mouth and throat. For Mafia analysts, the method of execution imparted a clear message. In a traditional Mob hit, bullets in the mouth or throat signify that the victim has been "talking" and that he will never "rat" again.

John Roselli vanished in 1976, shortly after secretly testifying before the Senate committee and two days after a dinner date with Trafficante in Fort Lauderdale. Two weeks later, Roselli's legless corpse was fished out of a 55-gallon oil drum floating in Dumfoundling Bay in North Miami. The manner of Roselli's murder also fit a Mafia pattern. Mutilation and torture before he was strangled meant that he had already violated the oath of *omertà* or that he was about to.

Trafficante, of course, maintained that he knew nothing about the slayings of his collaborators in the CIA-Castro escapade. Concerning knowledge of Kennedy's slaying, Trafficante was equally evasive before the House committee. The panel had evidence that he knew Jack Ruby, and that Ruby had worked for the Mob before Castro's takeover, apparently smuggling money out of Cuba for Trafficante and other mobsters involved in Havana casino and prostitution rackets. The Florida godfather's memory again failed him when it came to his dealings with Ruby. Asked about meetings or associations with Ruby, the mobster's answers were "I don't remember," or "I don't recall."

Before the public hearings began, the committee came across another tantalizing Mob threat against John Kennedy, this one presumably uttered by Trafficante. A prominent Cuban exile leader, José Alemán, informed investigators in a private interrogation that in 1962 Trafficante had told him that President Kennedy was "going to be hit." But called before the committee in a public session, Alemán was a reluctant witness, indicating that he feared for his life and requesting government protection. On the intriguing issue of Trafficante's "hit" statement, Alemán radically altered his original version. He testified that he had understood Trafficante to mean that if Kennedy sought reelection, he was going to be "hit by a lot of votes" and that there had been no implied threat on the president's life. Alemán's 180-degree turn led to another blind alley for committee investigators searching for clues to an old mystery.

The committee's final report in 1979 raised doubts about the Warren Commission's most consequential conclusion fifteen years earlier—that only one shooter, Oswald, had been responsible for President Kennedy's death. The congressmen did agree with the commission that there had been no conspiracy involving Cuba, the Soviet Union, the CIA, or any other federal agency. They nevertheless gave great weight to compelling circumstantial evidence that more than one gunman fired at Kennedy in Dealey Plaza. But the committee conceded that its two-year investigation had failed to turn up sufficient evidence to implicate anyone except Oswald.

G. Robert Blakey, a former aide to Robert Kennedy and the committee's chief counsel and principal drafter of the report, asserted that "organized crime had a hand" in the assassination. There was ample evidence from the bugs, he believed, that Mafia leaders were at least thinking about removing President Kennedy and his brother. Blakey's analysis specified a powerful motive for the murder of the president: his death would derail Robert Kennedy's sustained and comprehensive assault on organized crime.

In its report, the committee suggested that the Mafia leaders most likely to have conspired against Kennedy were Carlos Marcello and Santo Trafficante Jr. The committee explored another enticing angle: Oswald's move to New Orleans in the spring and summer of 1963. Shortly before the assassination he lived for a time with his uncle, Charles "Dutz" Murret, a bookmaker in Marcello's organization. The committee questioned whether Oswald might have been inveigled into being used as a hapless fall-guy shooter by Marcello or someone in his borgata. But it reached no definite conclusion. There was also a tangential Marcello linkage to Dallas, part of his Mafia empire. There, Jack Ruby's Carousel Club had been a watering hole for local mafiosi, many of them working for Joe Civillo, Marcello's underboss and guardian of his interests in Texas.

An essential part of the committee's investigation was its independent combing of FBI records of the electronic surveillance of mobsters before and after the assassination. The tapes produced no smoking gun, no concrete evidence, of a Mafia plan to kill the president. But after reviewing the FBI's overall conspiracy investigation, the congressmen and their investigation staff branded it as "seriously flawed." They rebuked the bureau for having concentrated narrowly on Oswald as the only suspect; for failing to pursue fresh and worthwhile leads about organized-crime involvement; for disregarding Becker's allegations about Marcello's threats; and for withholding from the Warren Commission vital information, including evidence from the secret bugs reflecting the Mafia's animosity to the Kennedy administration.

The findings obliquely pointed out the FBI's inability in the early 1960s to penetrate the criminal webs of Marcello and Trafficante as effectively as it had the borgatas of northern Mob leaders. The bureau had neglected to bug Marcello even once, and it had electronically eavesdropped on Trafficante only four times, without meaningful results. An unidentified FBI official conceded to the committee that Trafficante's organization in Tampa and Marcello's in Louisiana were "blind spots" for the FBI in the 1960s. Summing up the failure to investigate and eavesdrop on Marcello, the official said crisply, "He was too smart." Congressional staffers privately evaluated the bureau's agents in New Orleans as either incompetent or corrupt for ignoring Marcello's Mob empire.

Sixteen years after the committee finished its work, more indirect evidence surfaced to buttress the belief that major mafiosi had roles in an assassination conspiracy. The new information came from Frank Ragano, a lawyer for Trafficante, Marcello, and Jimmy Hoffa, the teamsters' union president, when Kennedy was killed. In an autobiography, *Mob Lawyer*, written with this author, Ragano shed light on the Mafia's loathing of the Kennedys. Of greater importance, Ragano said that Trafficante, shortly before he died, made statements to him that amounted to confirmation that mobsters were involved in the assassination.

A Florida-based attorney, Ragano represented Trafficante over a thirty-year period, and for much of that time he was a close friend and confidant of the don. Their relationship was so warm that Ragano considered Trafficante his guiding star and the equivalent of an older brother. Ragano admitted that until late in his life he had struck a Faustian bargain with Trafficante that brought him financial riches. As a quid pro quo, he had forsaken his ethics and had become "house counsel" and "Mob lawyer" for a ruthless criminal boss and his organization. Through his intimate relationship with Trafficante, Ragano met and partied with numerous southern and northern Mafia godfathers, capos, and soldiers. The experience gave him firsthand exposure to their twisted morals.

When northern Mob dignitaries vacationed in Florida, Trafficante entertained them at Capra's, a favorite restaurant in Miami, and often invited Ragano. In the months before the assassination, Ragano said he heard Sam Giancana, the Chicago boss, lash out at Robert Kennedy and the FBI for harassing him and Phyllis McGuire, a popular singer with whom he had a highly publicized affair. At one dinner, Ragano recalled Giancana blustering that his organization won—or stole—the 1960 election for Kennedy by fixing votes in Cook County. "That rat bastard, son-of-a-bitch," Giancana said. "We broke our balls for him and gave him the election and he gets his brother to hound us to death."

Shortly after the assassination, Ragano was dining with Tommy Lucchese and other New York mobsters and their women friends when the topic of Kennedy's murder came up. "It couldn't have happened to a nicer guy," Lucchese commented acidly.

Ragano was at the celebratory dinner with Trafficante in Tampa on the night of the assassination when the mobster was in a radiant mood. He was buoyant, Ragano said, convinced that the president's death would end investigations of himself and Marcello, and of Hoffa, with whom both southern bosses had crooked deals. Previously, Trafficante had ranted repeatedly against President Kennedy for allowing Castro to remain in power, thereby blocking him from regaining his profitable casinos in Havana. He despised President Kennedy for withholding American air support from the anti-Castro forces in the 1961 Bay of Pigs invasion and, in his view, dooming the operation. "We'll make money out of this and maybe go back to Cuba," Ragano remembered Trafficante saying happily the night John Kennedy was killed.

One of Ragano's confidential roles for Trafficante and Marcello was acting as their conduit to Hoffa, camouflaging their relationship to the teamsters' union head from the FBI's prying eyes. They used Ragano to arrange Hoffa's blessings for multimillion-dollar loans from the teamsters' pension fund for projects in which they were behind-the-scenes partners or brokers.

It was through Trafficante's intervention that Ragano joined Hoffa's legal team. The lawyer said that he was never paid directly for his services to Hoffa. Instead, like the Mafia bosses, he was richly rewarded through Hoffa's misuse of the teamsters' pension fund for real estate development deals. Ragano was paid off in brokerage fees and in direct profits for arranging union loans on favorable terms for himself, mobsters, and legitimate business people, which Hoffa speedily authorized. Lavish loans from the billion-dollar fund—at the time the largest union welfare pool in the country—promoted the development of Mob-backed casinos in Las Vegas. Although the pension fund was jointly administered by union and management representatives, Hoffa virtually controlled the authorization of loans that were intended to produce guaranteed profits.

Hoffa was candid with Ragano about the teamsters' compacts with mobsters. In frank conversations, Hoffa rationalized that he and earlier IBT leaders had been compelled to use Mafia muscle in the 1930s and '40s to counterbalance brutal strikebreakers hired by companies fighting the union. Mob support was the keystone of Hoffa's success. New York families created "paper" or nonexistent locals in New York that were vital to his election as IBT president. Defending the underworld alliance, Hoffa said that mobster influence had helped the union grow and obtain unparalleled wages, fringe benefits, and working conditions for its blue-collar workers. Hoffa was confident he could swing pragmatic deals with Mafia leaders without surrendering his or the union's independence. Under his vigorous command, the teamsters' membership swelled from 800,000 in 1957 to nearly two million by 1963, making it America's largest union.

But the teamsters' corruption scandals tarnished the entire American labor movement, and in 1957 the AFL-CIO expelled the Hoffa-led union on charges that it was widely infiltrated by gangsters. The Kennedy administration was also concerned; it feared that Hoffa and his Mafia bedfellows had the power to cripple the country's economy through a nationwide trucking strike. In the summer of 1963, shortly before the assassination, Ragano claimed that Hoffa was consumed by Robert Kennedy's intensive investigations of his activities and his organized-crime affiliations. Ragano met frequently with Hoffa at his headquarters near the Capitol in Washington, to discuss legal matters.

At a private session on July 23, 1963, Hoffa brushed aside Ragano's questions about legal issues in a pending criminal trial that was prosecuted by Robert Kennedy's staff. Instead, the union leader, with the authority of a drill sergeant, had orders for Ragano. Hoffa commanded him to relay an urgent demand to Santo Trafficante and Carlos Marcello. He wanted them to engineer the president's assassination. "Something has to be done," Ragano said Hoffa instructed him. "The time has come for your friend and Carlos to get rid of him, kill that son-of-a-bitch John Kennedy."

Ragano said that he believed Hoffa was venting his spleen over criminal charges launched against him by Robert Kennedy and did not take the outburst seriously. The next day, however, Ragano had a prearranged meeting with Trafficante and Marcello at the Royal Orleans Hotel in New Orleans, to discuss an illicit loan contract they were working out with Hoffa. Although Ragano regarded Hoffa's request for a hit on Kennedy as a bad joke, he dutifully relayed it to the Mafia godfathers. "You won't believe this," Ragano told them, "but he wants you to kill John Kennedy." The two mobsters stared back in icy silence. Aware that he might have stepped into a minefield, Ragano quickly changed the subject.

On November 22, 1963, minutes after Kennedy was fatally shot in Dallas, Ragano said, Hoffa telephoned him in his office. "Did you hear the good news?" the union president said exuberantly. "Yeah, he's dead. I heard over the news that Lyndon Johnson is going to be sworn in as president. You know he'll get rid of Booby." ("Booby" was Hoffa's derisive name for Robert Kennedy.)

Three days after the assassination, Ragano attended a meeting in Hoffa's office in Washington with other lawyers to discuss his criminal cases. Declaring that the Kennedys had hounded him, Hoffa refused to allow the American flag on the building's roof to be lowered to half-staff in mourning and respect for the slain president. After the legal strategy meeting, Hoffa pulled Ragano aside. "I told you they could do it," Hoffa whispered. "I'll never forget what Carlos and Santo did for me."

For Ragano an epiphany about the assassination came almost a quarter of a century after Kennedy's death. On a Friday morning, March 13, 1987, he said that he picked up Trafficante at his home in Tampa and, following the mobster's wishes, took him for a drive in his own car. At seventy-two, Trafficante was seriously ill: his hands trembled continuously; dialysis kept his kidneys functioning, and he was about to undergo a second open-heart surgery. On the drive along Tampa's scenic Bayshore Boulevard, Trafficante at first reminisced about their mutual friends and experiences before veering back to the subject of the Kennedys' long-ago campaign against the Mafia.

Speaking to Ragano in Sicilian as he often did, Trafficante grumbled: "God-damn Bobby. I think Carlos fucked up in getting rid of Giovanni—maybe it should have been Bobby." To Ragano's astonishment, Trafficante added: "We shouldn't have killed Giovanni. We should have killed Bobby." Ragano knew that "Giovanni" was John Kennedy.

Moments later, Ragano said that Trafficante talked to him about another fateful event in their lives: Jimmy Hoffa's disappearance in 1975. Ragano had been on Hoffa's defense team in 1964, at two trials when Robert Kennedy's "Get Hoffa Squad" succeeded in winning convictions on jury-tampering, fraud, and conspiracy charges. Hoffa was serving a thirteen-year prison term when his sentence was commuted in 1971 by President Richard M. Nixon. Later, Ragano asserted that Hoffa and one of his top aides admitted to him that the commutation was obtained through a million-dollar contribution secretly funneled to Nixon supporters, presumably as a contribution to the Republican Party's reelection campaign for Nixon in 1972.

But after Hoffa's release from prison, Trafficante told Ragano that the belligerent union leader had alarmed the New York families by announcing that he was writing a book that would expose the Mob and that he wanted to regain control of the teamsters' union. Trafficante related to Ragano that he had warned Hoffa that the northern Mafia believed he had become an uncontrollable, disruptive force who could endanger their financial interests in the union.

On their ride in Tampa, Trafficante gave Ragano his version of Hoffa's abduction and slaying in 1975. He was lured to a garage in the Detroit suburbs, supposedly for a peaceful sit-down meeting to discuss his attempt to regain power in the union with Anthony "Tony Jack" Giacalone, a high-ranking Detroit mafioso. In the garage, Hoffa was knocked unconscious and strangled by a hit team assembled by Anthony "Tony Pro" Provenzano, a teamsters' union head in New Jersey and a Genovese capo, who had a long-festering feud with Hoffa. Trafficante added that Hoffa's body probably would never be found.

Under guidelines established when he first represented Trafficante, Ragano said he was obligated to listen to whatever Don Santo wanted to divulge to him but he was prohibited from ever asking incisive questions. Under those rules, he was unable during that talk with Trafficante to get him to amplify his revelations about the murders of President Kennedy and of Hoffa—and the disposition of Hoffa's body. Four days later, on March 17, 1987, Trafficante died while undergoing heart surgery.

From his earliest days as a lawyer, Ragano kept detailed notes and diary descriptions of meetings and conversations with clients. The yellowed, sometimes crumpled records, combined with hotel receipts substantiating Ragano's whereabouts, tend to support his accounts of business and social sessions with mafiosi and with Hoffa. His records included a note that he said he jotted down a day after his farewell conversation with Trafficante. In it Ragano wrote about the mobster's alleged knowledge of the murders of President Kennedy and Jimmy Hoffa.

Afterward, Ragano came to believe that Trafficante, an amateur student of history and a voracious reader of biographies of important men, had confessed to him out of perverse pride. Trafficante, he speculated, may have wanted the world to know that he and his Mob partners had masterminded the elimination of a president, outwitted the government's top law-enforcement agencies, and escaped punishment.

To stay alive during three decades as a Mob attorney and as a confidant to Trafficante, Ragano maintained his own strict oath of *omertà*. His legal and social affiliations with Trafficante and other mobsters, however, put him in the thick of Robert Kennedy's campaign targeting professional aides of major mobsters. The intense scrutiny of Ragano by the FBI and by the IRS led to two convictions on relatively minor income-tax-evasion complaints. He served ten months in prison in 1993 on the second conviction.

Through his book Ragano broke his long vow of silence. All of the disreputable Mafia clients he had served were dead and his lawyer-client obligation of silence had ended. Moreover, he was ill and realized that his own end was approaching. To many of Ragano's relatives and friends, his public confessions about his checkered past and his aggressive ambition and quest for wealth were signs of Catholic remorse, repentance, and atonement for a misspent career. At age seventy-five in 1998, Ragano died in his sleep, apparently suffering a heart attack.

Although not categorically conclusive, Ragano's assertions are among the starkest signs implicating Mafia bosses in the death of President Kennedy. G. Robert Blakey, an unsurpassed authority on the assassination and on organized crime, characterized Ragano's information as plausible. "It has the ring of truth," he added.

The Cosa Nostra's own warped moral code rejects violence against honest officials, and John and Robert Kennedy should have been immune from Mob retaliation. But the FBI's electronic spy tapes and Ragano's testimony show that Mob bosses believed that Joseph Kennedy had made a commitment for his sons, and, wittingly or unwittingly, the sons had violated it. The bosses felt they had been double-crossed. By reneging on what the Mafia considered an iron-clad bargain, the Kennedys might have been viewed as fair game for their savage vindictiveness.

The Mafia-LCN lords had good reason to fear Robert Kennedy. In 1960, the last year of the Eisenhower administration, a scant thirty-five low-level gangsters were convicted, mainly on petty gambling charges. During Kennedy's blitz against higher-ranking mobsters, which lasted less than four years, 116 made mafiosi and associates were indicted, including Jimmy Hoffa. To the nation's Mafia VIPs those statistics were alarming, and they knew the attorney general was committed to destroying them.

On the legislative front, Robert Kennedy's warnings about the Mob's uncontested power, combined with the political strength of the president; created a groundswell for easy passage in Congress of the first package of bills aimed at a national crime organization. Four new laws broadened the federal government's jurisdictional power to indict mobsters. The main statutes prohibited traveling across state lines for racketeering purposes and the interstate shipment of gambling equipment. Although the laws were difficult to enforce, they marked the first concentrated effort by Congress to impede the Mob.

Within the Johnson administration, Robert Kennedy had a troubled political and personal relationship with his brother's successor. He stuck it out for nine months, resigning one month after Hoffa's conviction in 1964. Elected to the Senate from New York, Kennedy in 1968 met the same fate as his brother—an assassin's bullet—while campaigning in Los Angeles for the Democratic presidential nomination that almost assuredly was his. The assassin, Sirhan Sirhan, had no connection with the Mob.

Clearly, President Kennedy's murder halted the federal government's first diligent drive against the Mafia. The steam went out of the Justice Department's campaign after Robert Kennedy's departure. His successor, Attorney General Ramsey Clark, concerned about the warrantless electronic surveillance program, pulled the plug on the bugs that were providing the FBI with essential intelligence. Mafia investigations were effectively shelved. Keenly aware of the administration's indifference, Hoover dropped the Mafia-LCN as an investigative priority.

With the FBI and the government once more quiescent, Mob dons could relax. The pressure was off. Whether or not they had a part in it, the Mafia had triumphed as a big winner after the assassination of President John F. Kennedy.

16

A Splendid Band: The Mob

"We're bigger than U.S. Steel."

The catchy phrase sounded like a clever advertising slogan, touting the strength and prominence of a multinational corporation. It was actually an offhanded remark about the Cosa Nostra in an unguarded, totally candid moment, from the lips of the Mob's financial guru, Meyer Lansky.

During Robert Kennedy's clamp down, and as part of Hoover's orders to employ "Highly confidential sources," agents arranged with several New York hotel detectives to listen in on mobsters who favored their hotels. Mafiosi and their important associates were assigned rooms or suites that had been turned into secret recording studios. Lansky, the last of the big-league Jewish gangsters, and an economic asset for Cosa Nostra, checked into one of these suites at the Volney Hotel on Manhattan's East Side in May 1962.

Lansky had become a disreputable national figure after his appearance a decade earlier before the Kefauver Committee. With Kennedy on the warpath, Hoover placed Lansky high up on his list of organized-crime targets. The FBI director described the aging, bantam-sized racketeer as an exceptionally important individual in the national crime picture, and he instructed agents to employ "extraordinary investigative techniques" — Hoover's euphemism for illegal electronic surveillance.

Recuperating from a recent heart attack, Lansky spent most of his time in his suite, chatting idly about personal matters with relatives and friends. The FBI listened to every word. On the evening of Sunday, May 27, 1962, Lansky and his wife were alone, watching David Susskind's television program *Open End*, a talk show. The Justice Department's campaign against the Mafia was spawning headlines and Susskind's topic that night was organized crime. An agent's report on the bugging, leaked years later to reporters, stated that Lansky was silent until one of the panelists on the TV show referred to organized crime as being second in size only to the government itself. It was then that Lansky flippantly remarked to his wife, "We're bigger than U.S. Steel."

Although excluded from the Mafia's ruling class, Lansky was enmeshed in many deals with Mob leaders and reflected their self-confidence at mid-century. Despite the damage done by Bobby Kennedy's assault, the bosses were not raising a white flag of surrender. Hoover knew this. The Lansky tapes were part of the rich intelligence information secretly gathered through bugs that provided Hoover and his top aides with data on the Mafia's enormous vitality.

Astonishingly, government statisticians believed that Lansky had vastly undervalued the Mafia's overall resources in his sardonic U.S. Steel quip. A confidential Justice Department analysis in the mid-1960s conservatively estimated that organized crime's profits were equaled by those of the *ten* largest industrial corporations combined. The big ten companies cited were General Motors, Standard Oil, Ford, General Electric, Chrysler, IBM, Mobile Oil, Texaco, Gulf, and U.S. Steel. (It was an unscientific analysis based largely on assumptions that the Mob's profits came mainly from illegal gambling, loan-sharking, hijackings, and narcotics sales. Factoring in the Mafia's huge markups, low overhead, and avoidance of taxes, the government's rough estimate was that, nationwide, the mafiosi and their accomplices netted $7 billion to $10 billion a year.)

At the end of 1964, however, Hoover was again free to use his own judgment in determining FBI agendas. There was no interference from Lyndon Johnson's administration, which was absorbed in the pressing issues of an expanding guerrilla conflict in Vietnam, the War on Poverty, the civil-rights movement, and riots and disorders in some inner cities. Despite the huge number of cases developed in the Kennedy years, the bureau's director rapidly downgraded the Mafia as a vital priority. Complying with a directive from Attorney General

Ramsey Clark to use electronic surveillance only for "national security" matters, Hoover retired his most effective weapon: the bugs in Mob hangouts.

The Johnson administration's political concerns dovetailed with Hoover's own conservative, Cold War priorities. He accelerated investigations of groups that he personally classified as un-American or subversive; these included opponents of the Vietnam War and organizations championing civil rights for African-Americans. (The only hate-filled organization on the other side of the political spectrum that Hoover tried to repress was the rabidly antiblack and anti-Semitic Ku Klux Klan.) A new tactic, Cointelpro, FBI-speak for Counter Intelligence Program, was established to monitor and disrupt groups Hoover looked upon unfavorably, and to infiltrate them with agent provocateurs eager to manufacture criminal cases.

An internal letter distributed to all FBI field offices laid bare Hoover's goals and his divide-and-conquer strategy concerning legitimate civil-rights and political organizations. "The purpose of this program [Coiutel] is to expose, disrupt, and otherwise neutralize the activities of the various New Left organizations, their leadership and adherents. In every instance, consideration should be given to disrupting the organized activity of these groups and no opportunity should be missed to capitalize on organizational and personal conflicts of their leadership."

By the mid-1960s, Hoover's force of almost 8,000 agents did occasionally arrest blundering minor mobsters whose mistakes could not be ignored. However, with Robert Kennedy gone, there was no longer encouragement from FBI headquarters in Washington to put in exhaustive hours on Mafia-LCN cases. Some dedicated agents continued to be vigilant, but in most regional bureaus the incentive was missing; it was easier to win promotions by capturing amateur bank bandits or concentrating on political dissidents—Hoover's perennial targets— than through the tedious and unrewarding pursuit of insulated Mob generals.

So the bureau removed the electronic bugs from the Mob's hangouts and installed them in the gathering places of persons and groups Hoover deemed as subversive or leftist. Investigations of violent radical fringe groups like the underground, bomb-planting Weathermen were unquestionably justified. But the FBI resorted to illegal, unconstitutional methods to bug, wiretap, and place under surveillance prominent political and civil-rights figures who Hoover by his own fiat determined were threats to America's fundamental values. These included Adlai E. Stevenson, Democratic presidential candidate in 1952 and 1956; civil-rights leader Dr. Martin Luther King Jr., considered a "communist tool"; British writer Graham Greene, producer of "anti-American" works; and anti–Vietnam War activists from show business, including John Lennon and Jane Fonda.

The federal cutbacks were matched by a similar slackening-off in the few big-city police departments that had special units investigating organized crime. Robert Kennedy's drive, combined with Joe Valachi's compelling testimony, had temporarily persuaded high-ranking police officials in New York of the Mafia's extensive threat. With Kennedy gone from Washington, New York detectives Ralph Salerno and Remo Franceschini saw interest in the Mafia at the top police department echelons—the brass—gradually diminish in New York. Franceschini's investigations and wiretaps of gambling activities in the Bronx convinced him that sophisticated organized-crime elements were running multimillion-dollar networks. A chief in the Central Intelligence Bureau, the CIB, rejected Franceschini's request to expand his investigation, insisting that the Mafia was a fictional delusion. "The chief thought Italian hoods were just a couple of guys rubbing two fifty-cent pieces together," Franceschini recalled. "He told me, 'It's not formalized, it's not a bureaucracy, it's not Wall Street.' "

The consensus among the department's brass was that Jewish bookmakers were raking in the big bucks as organized crime's most productive moneymakers. Franceschini got nowhere trying to convince officials that major bookies were not independent and could operate only with the acquiescence of one of the five families.

Many CIB cases and intelligence tidbits stemmed from illegal gambling. It was one of the easiest crimes to investigate even though those arrested were usually petty runners, collectors of bets, and bookkeepers who got off easy with fines or light sentences. One method of unearthing tips about gambling operations was bugging and wiretapping social clubs, mafiosi gathering spots in predominantly Italian-American neighborhoods. The clubs were storefronts converted into private dens where made men and wannabes could drink espresso, play cards, gossip with their pals, and plan their activities before heading out for the day's illicit work. In many respects, the clubs were American mobsters' versions of cafés in Sicilian village squares.

CIB investigators in the summer of 1964 were listening to a bug and a wiretap in Salvatore "Big Sam" Cavalieri's club, a Lucchese family rendezvous in East Harlem. Cavalieri was a Lucchese soldier overseeing a large-scale numbers and sports-betting complex of more than fifty bookies. Like the FBI, the CIB used bugs primarily for intelligence purposes, though New York State law allowed tapes to be used as court evidence under restricted conditions. Seemingly unconcerned about electronic eavesdropping, the leading lights in Big Sam's place talked openly, and their conversations often allowed the police to puff up arrest statistics by raiding several of Cavalieri's gambling parlors. More useful to CIB detectives than the low-level collars were the insights they picked up through secret microphones about the Lucchese family's culture and connections.

One day Carmine Tramunti, a top capo, showed up at Cavalieri's club and telephoned a soldier about an assignment for his crew from none other than Tommy Lucchese, the boss. Tramunti did not specify details about the job but said gravely, "He wants us to do it." Franceschini, at a "plant," a listening post a few blocks away, heard the exchange. "Tramunti's tone clearly overflowed with reverence and pride at being selected for the job. It was like Lucchese just elevated them to sainthood," Franceschini said.

That same summer, the detective heard Tramunti telephone Jilly Rizzo, the proprietor of Jilly's, a trendy Midtown restaurant, and a friend of Frank Sinatra. "Hey," Tramunti said to Rizzo, "the feast is on. Back at the social club we're gonna have some steaks, we're gonna have some sausage. Why don't you come on up? Bring the ballplayers up too." Franceschini was aware that some New York Yankee players often stopped by Jilly's. "Oh yeah?" Rizzo replied. "Frank's in town. Maybe I'll bring Frank up."

Several hours later, according to police surveillance logs, Sinatra showed up with Rizzo at the social club for an impromptu meal with leading members of the Lucchese family. Wiseguys from all over town streamed into the club to shake hands and speak with Sinatra. After Sinatra left, one of the neighborhood wannabes who served him drinks called his grandmother with the exciting news of the singer's visit. "Frank Sinatra gave me a fifty-buck tip," he exclaimed.

New York's police headquarters simply disregarded the intelligence that investigators were compiling of the Mafia's growing affluence and its indifference to law enforcement. A wave of frustration and cutbacks hit the CIB, the only group responsible for keeping an eye on the borgatas, as officials turned to new commitments. Duplicating the FBI's fear of political and civil unrest by opponents of the Vietnam War, the department organized a handpicked unit, the Bureau of Special Services Investigations. Many officers assigned to the ominous sounding BOSSI (also known as the "Red Squad") believed their main tasks were to destroy terrorist radical organizations, prevent riots in black and Hispanic neighborhoods, and investigate groups supposedly dedicated to assassinating cops. Franceschini and other Mafia specialists were transferred to BOSSI in the mid- and late 1960s. The department's shift in emphasis, Franceschini observed, gave the Mob "pretty much of a free ride during those years."

Even the lowliest wannabes in New York, the Mafia's capital, sensed the relaxation of law enforcement. Enjoying the balmy atmosphere, mafiosi and their legion of associates coined a popular slang name for themselves, "wiseguys." The new generation of wiseguys felt they had carte blanche for every imaginable violent crime and financial scheme.

"Everyone I knew was into money schemes and almost nobody ever got caught," Henry Hill, a Lucchese associate in that era, recounted to the writer Nicholas Pileggi. "That's what people from the outside don't understand. When you're doing different schemes, and everyone you know is doing these things, and nobody is getting caught, except by accident, you begin to get the message that maybe it's not so dangerous. And there were a million different schemes."

Corruption also was an underlying factor in providing New York's wiseguys a comfortable environment. Investigations later revealed that through most of the 1960s a sizable portion of the 30,000-member police department was paid off for protection by Mob-affiliated bookies and gamblers. The routine graft was known as "the pad," in which bribes were distributed regularly to officers in units primarily responsible for enforcing gambling and vice laws, the amounts depending on their rank and status. Officers and supervisors who accepted occasional or systemic bribes, Ralph Salerno said, did not want to be told by members of his anti-Mafia squad that the bribers were organized-crime "ogres and monsters" with blood on their hands. "Very few people in the department wanted to believe they [the Mafia] existed and were as powerful as they were. They simply wanted to picture them as bookies and gamblers, not as murderers and drug dealers."

Nevertheless, Salerno's understaffed unit kept a watchful eye on the Mob and its digging and surveillance work was tolerated, if not encouraged, by the police brass. "Why didn't they squash us? You got to have some guys who are honest and breaking balls. It allows the dishonest ones to say to the bad guys, 'We will protect you from the ball breakers.' The more balls I broke, the more money I made for them," Salerno commented wryly.

More than one mafioso racketeer chastised Salerno for investigating fellow Italian-Americans. They complained, "Why does it have to be one of your own kind that hurts you?" Salerno would snap back, "I'm not your kind and you're not my kind. My manners, morals, and mores are not yours. The only thing we have in common is that we sprang from an Italian heritage and culture—and you are the traitor to that heritage and culture which I am proud to be part of."

A native New Yorker, Salerno's first knowledge of the Mob's terrifying aura came from frightening events in the lives of his immigrant parents. Before his birth, they lived in Mafia-dominated East Harlem. One summer day, his mother, while buying ices for her four older children from a street vendor, witnessed the shooting murder of a hood known as "Charlie the Dude" by another neighborhood gangster called "Mickey Icebox."

"That night," Salerno said, "a guy, a *paisano*, from my father's hometown in Italy, came to their apartment with a message for my father. 'Tell your wife to keep her mouth shut. Otherwise your kids could get thrown in the East River.'" Salerno said his mother was consumed by anxiety for months, fearful that Mickey Icebox would be arrested, and that she would be tagged as an informer and her children killed. "She was able to breathe again after eighteen months when someone killed Mickey Icebox and the threat to her family was over," said Salerno.

About that same time, Salerno's parents and their children were sitting down to dinner when several men burst into their apartment through an open fire-escape window. On the run from the police, they told the family to remain silent until they felt it was safe to leave. A week later, Salerno's father stopped at a barber shop that served as a center for news about the neighborhood and the old country. A parcel was waiting for him from the men who had escaped the police through the Salernos' apartment. Attached was a note: "You did the right thing." The package contained a gift of a straight-edged razor and a shaving mug engraved in gilt letters with his father's name.

Those episodes inspired Salerno to detest the Mafia and to devote his twenty-year police career to uprooting gangsters. "I kept that shaving cup on my desk for decades as a reminder how those bastards intimidated my parents. I didn't want my children and grandchildren or anyone's children to grow up in that kind of atmosphere."

In 1967 Salerno, a sergeant in charge of the CIB's detectives, left the police department, convinced he would be more effective working as a consultant on organized crime for congressional investigation committees. "Unfortunately, when I was on the police force the Mafia was probably twenty times more powerful than they had been in my parents' time."

Joe Bonanno's private 1960s sobriquet for the New York Mafia was "the Volcano." Although outside pressure from federal and local investigators had receded, internal disturbances were seething beneath the Volcano's surface. Running a borgata in New York was beginning to have drawbacks as each of the five money-hungry families competed for greater wealth and importance. In cities that had only one family, godfathers enjoyed long careers and died of natural causes, Bonanno later wrote about that era. "In New York City, however, where strife was almost routine, fathers led precarious lives."

The death from cancer on June 11, 1962, of Joe Profaci, Bonanno's fellow godfather and closest ally, suddenly undermined his position as a commanding force on the Commission and in New York's unpredictable underworld. Bonanno was the last of the 1931 bosses still alive and active, and Profaci's death abruptly and decisively shifted the balance of power on the Commission to the tandem of Carlo Gambino and Tommy Lucchese. The imprisoned Vito Genovese maintained de facto control of his family, and Bonanno expected that his delegates in a showdown would side with the Genovese-Lucchese alliance. In another setback for Bonanno, his powerful cousin Stefano Magaddino, the Buffalo godfather, a permanent Commission member, had grown increasingly estranged and opposed to Bonanno's views because of a festering territorial dispute in Canada. Bonanno was maneuvering to expand his criminal empire into Magaddino's backyard in Toronto. "He's planting flags all over the world," Magaddino was heard on an FBI bug, fuming about his cousin's attempts to muscle into areas in California and Canada deemed "open" by the Commission.

Magaddino was right. After thirty years as a boss and still a relatively young fifty-eight, Bonanno had lost none of his cunning or ambition to remain on top of the Mafia pyramid. His first move was to support Joe Magliocco, Profaci's brother-in-law and underboss, as the new head of Profaci's borgata, although Magliocco's claim to the title was shaky. Profaci's last years had been troubled by a revolt led by "Crazy Joey" Gallo and his brothers, Albert "Kid Blast" and Larry, contract killers for Profaci. They considered Profaci a voracious despot and wanted a larger share of the family's spoils for carrying out the family's essential work of murders and beatings. The Gallos were believed to have been the core of the barbershop hit team that assassinated Albert Anastasia in 1957.

Headlined as "the Gallo Wars," the brothers' insurrection was the first serious breach of discipline in a New York family since the bloody struggles in 1930 and 1931. The conflict was unresolved at the time of Profaci's death, and the Gallos' refusal to accept Magliocco as their boss encouraged Gambino and Lucchese to deny Magliocco—Bonanno's candidate and ally—a seat on the Commission.

Bonanno's solution to his and Magliocco's roadblocks, according to most Mafia investigators at the time, was to eliminate by murder his main rivals: Gambino and Lucchese. The experts speculated that he also wanted his cousin Magaddino executed. Grateful for Bonanno's support, Magliocco went along with the plan and gave the multiple-hit contracts to Joseph Colombo, a loyal Profaci capo with a deserved reputation for violence. By deviously using Magliocco and Colombo as fronts for removing his enemies, Bonanno thought the bloodbath would not be traced to him.

Joe Colombo was forty years old, experienced and wise enough to comprehend the futility of devising a double or a triple execution of godfathers; and he sensed which bosses had the upper hand in the internal struggle for dominance in New York. He reached out to Gambino—not to kill him but to warn him of Bonanno and Magliocco's machinations.

Armed with Colombo's evidence, Gambino, Lucchese, and the rest of the Commission summoned Bonanno and Magliocco for a Mob trial. Magliocco, physically ailing and betrayed by one of his own capos, readily confessed and pleaded for mercy. Instead of a bullet in the back of his head, he was banished from the Mafia for his lifetime. Acting as if the Commission were subject to audits, the godfathers fined Magliocco $43,000 to cover the costs incurred in investigating the complaints against him and Bonanno. The disgraced Magliocco assembled his loyal capos in September 1963 to announce a cease-fire in the war with the Gallos and to tell them that the Commission had deposed him as Profaci's heir. Within a year he was dead of a heart attack. Gambino and the remaining bosses rewarded Colombo for being an ace stool pigeon, and perhaps saving some of their skins, by anointing him boss of the old Profaci family with a seat on the Commission.

Joe Bonanno never showed up for a confrontation with other Commission godfathers. He went on the lam, hiding out in California and in Canada, while exploring opportunities for poaching on rackets in those areas. He left his New York operations to trusted aides and appointed his eldest son, Salvatore "Bill" as the family's consigliere. California loomed large in Bonanno's plans. Tremendous wealth was being generated in Southern California, and Bonanno felt that

Frank DeSimone, the boss of the Los Angeles family, had failed to exploit it. Bonanno plotted to replace DeSimone and his crew with Bill, who would provide better leadership, and forty soldiers who would generate larger profits. As a Commission member, Bonanno already had some oversight responsibilities in California of small families operating in San Francisco and San Jose. By seizing control over Los Angeles, Bonanno believed he would dominate Mafia activities on both coasts.

Some FBI tapes were still spinning, and agents got an earful about Bonanno's conflict with the Commission from a bug installed in the headquarters of Simone "Sam the Plumber" DeCavalcante, the boss of a New Jersey family based in Elizabeth. Talking with a capo in his family, Joseph Sferra, on August 31, 1964, DeCavalcante mentioned Bonanno's difficulties. "It's about Joe Bonanno's borgata. The Commission don't like the way he's comporting himself." DeCavalcante added that Bonanno had promoted Bill to consigliere, and that the son also had angered the Commission by refusing to appear before it when summoned for questioning. "Well, he made his son consigliere—and it's been reported, the son, that he don't show up," DeCavalcante explained.

On September 21, 1964, DeCavalcante outlined to Joseph Zicarelli, a Bonanno soldier, why the all-powerful Commission balked at Magliocco's attempt, with Bonanno's backing, to become a boss. "The Commission went in there and took the family over. When Profaci died, Joe Magliocco took over as boss. They threw him right out. 'Who the hell are you to take over a borgata?' And Signor Bonanno knows this. When we had trouble in our outfit, they came right in. 'You people belong to the Commission until this is straightened out.'"

Bonanno's rival godfathers relied on the Commission as the foundation of the Mafia's strength and structure and resented his defiance and newly spun expansionist schemes. Magaddino, speaking with one of his soldiers in Buffalo about Bonanno's plots, without Commission approval, to control California and Canada, said, "Not even the Holy Ghost could come into my territory without authorization."

The Genovese family hierarchy also lined up against Bonanno. On an FBI bug in September 1964, Thomas "Tommy Ryan" Eboli, a capo, told Vito Genovese's brother Michael that Bonanno was creating a rift that could destroy the Mafia or make it as divisive as other ethnic gangs. "If one member can dispute a Commission order you can say good-bye to Cosa Nostra, because the Commission is the backbone of Cosa Nostra. It will be like the Irish mobs who fight among themselves and they [the Italians] will be having gang wars like they had years ago." In Chicago, an FBI bug heard Sam Giancana's solution to Bonanno's refusal to appear before the Commission. "Don't send him another message. Kill him!"

Don Peppino Bonanno had another problem. He was the only major Mafia leader endangered by the antiracketeering organized-crime bills steered through Congress by Robert Kennedy before he resigned as attorney general. A grand jury impaneled by Robert M. Morgenthau, the aggressive U.S. Attorney in Manhattan, subpoenaed Bonanno for a round of questioning. On the night of October 20, 1964, the day before he was to testify or face possible imprisonment for contempt, Bonanno had dinner with three of his lawyers in Manhattan. Afterward, he and attorney William Power Maloney taxied to Maloney's apartment building on Park Avenue and 36th Street, where he was going to spend the night. It was close to midnight and raining. Bonanno stepped out of the cab to pay the fare when, he later claimed, he was grabbed by two strong-arm men who warned, "Come on, Joe, my boss wants you," and shoved him into the rear of a waiting car. Maloney told the police that when he ran over to intervene, shouting at the two men, one of them fired a warning shot to scare him off. In his autobiography, published two decades later, Bonanno asserted that his kidnapping was carried out by men who worked for his cousin Stefano Magaddino. Forced to crouch on the car's floor, he was driven to a farmhouse in a rural area in upstate New York, where his cousin warned him that he had fallen into disfavor because the Commission considered him power hungry. Bonanno's account was vague. He said his captors held him for six weeks, then drove him at his request to Texas and released him unharmed. Free again, he grew a beard to disguise his appearance and spent the ensuing nineteen months in hideaways in Tucson and in New York.

What really happened to Bonanno during his disappearance is a mystery. What is clear is that without notice, he surfaced in May 1966, with his lawyer, at the federal courthouse in Manhattan's Foley Square, with the terse explanation that he had been abducted two years previously. His long delay in complying with the subpoena led to an indictment for failing to appear before a grand jury. He challenged the legality of the indictment for five years until the accusation was dropped.

From the night Bonanno's lawyer reported him missing, New York and federal investigators doubted that he had been abducted. The police were unable to verify Maloney's account that a warning shot had been fired; no shell casing was found at the scene. Moreover, since Bonanno was engaged in a brewing mortal confrontation with Gambino and Lucchese, it was uncharacteristic and foolhardy for him, an endangered boss, to roam around unescorted by body-guards. Detective Salerno learned that after the vanishing act, it was quickly ap-parent from electronic eavesdropping that he was alive. "When someone of importance is killed, Mob guys refer to him as *la bon anima*, the good soul," Salerno pointed out. "No one close to Bonanno spoke about him that way; rather, they were saying, 'That son-of-a-bitch took off and left us here alone.'"

Two days after the Park Avenue incident, FBI agents bugging New Jersey's Sam the Plumber DeCavalcante, obtained a clue that Bonanno had staged the kidnapping. Discussing Bonanno with one of his lieutenants, Frank Majuri, DeCavalcante said that the New York bosses were mystified and knew nothing about the disappearance. "Then he must have done it," Majuri replied, rein-forcing the suggestion that the abduction was a fake.

Most investigators theorized that Bonanno had two compelling reasons to get away from New York: he wanted time to work out a truce or a peace pact with his enemies on the Commission; and he feared an indictment by Morgen-thau's grand jury. During his absence, Gambino and Lucchese happily incited turmoil in the Bonanno family by encouraging dissidents to oppose the surro-gate leadership of Bill Bonanno. The son was resented by old-timers in the fam-ily, who believed he had not earned his spurs as a proven leader. While Bonanno was missing, there were several casualties in the conflict for control of the borgata. The battles were headlined as "the Bananas War." The elder Bo-nanno's surprise reappearance in May 1966 was probably propelled by an at-tempted ambush of his son five months earlier. Showing up for a nighttime meeting in Brooklyn, Bill and his bodyguards were greeted by a hail of gunfire. No one was hit, but at least twenty shots were fired, and the police recovered seven handguns tossed onto the pavement.

Soon after his return to New York, Bonanno, after thirty-five years as an in-domitable boss, conceded defeat. Even one of his closest lieutenants, Gaspar "Gasparino" DiGregorio, the best man at his wedding and Bill Bonanno's reli-gious godfather, had defected to lead the internal opposition against him. Bo-nanno had overreached in his clash with the Commission, and it crushed him, retaining its prerogative to confirm the selection of bosses and its power to de-termine expansion rights. In a deal with the Commission, the chastened Bo-nanno was allowed to abdicate and retire peacefully as the head of the gang that once was the nation's most powerful Mob organization. He sold his regal house in Hempstead, Long Island, and a fourteen-room farmhouse near Middletown,

New York. Severing all ties to New York, he exiled himself to Tucson where he had maintained a home for health reasons since the early 1940s. Although he was finished as a majestic godfather in the East, Don Peppino continued to dabble in lesser rackets in Arizona and California with his sons. The last of the original Commission members, he began planning his memoirs, a document that would lead to far-reaching complications for himself and other mafiosi.

Bonanno's lust for power almost cost him his life. Years after the episode, Ralph Salerno learned that the Commission, after much debate, gave Bonanno "a pass" because he was one of the Mafia's founding fathers and because he pledged never to meddle again in Mob affairs in New York or other Cosa Nostra centers of power. If he dared to return to New York, he would have faced an automatic death sentence. Salerno and other investigators believed that the Commission godfathers also realized that killing one of their own would be a precedent that endangered themselves.

In the late 1960s, with the brief and minor Bananas War over and with barely any concern about law-enforcement interference, Mafia leaders could conduct their businesses with equanimity. They might be followed and badgered occasionally by FBI agents or local detectives, but there was no longer a concerted effort to destroy their organizations. For public-relations reasons, police departments in major Mob cities like New York, Chicago, and Philadelphia periodically sprang into action against them—usually before elections for a district attorney or sheriff, or after an outrageous murder or internecine war that left too many corpses on the streets to go unnoticed. These were temporary interruptions.

Sometimes, however, there was a slipup, an unforeseen, careless Mafia blunder. For example, on the Thursday afternoon of September 22, 1966, thirteen men gathered around a banquet-size table in a private dining area of La Stella, a modest Italian restaurant in the New York borough of Queens. The middle-aged and elderly men joked and talked, sipping cocktails, awaiting the first course. Before they could taste the robust meal, plainclothes policemen trooped in and arrested the lot of them. All the diners were Mob bosses and hierarchy officials.

The arrests resulted from a routine tail of the high-ranking Genovese consigliere Mike Miranda by detectives from Salerno's police intelligence squad. They followed Miranda to La Stella, and while staked out there, the sharp-eyed cops were astonished to see the pride of the American Mafia arriving separately and entering the restaurant. The startled police notified their supervisors that they had stumbled onto something big and needed help. When reinforcements arrived, the plainclothesmen marched into the restaurant. None of the mobsters was in sight. Noticing a stairway, the cops descended to a secluded downstairs dining room where the group was settling in for lunch. "Don't move," a detective commanded. "Keep your seats." Plainclothesmen then collected the names of the chagrined diners. They included Carlo Gambino, his underboss, Aniello Dellacroce, Joe Colombo, Tommy Eboli, the acting boss for Vito Genovese, Carlos Marcello of New Orleans, Santo Trafficante of Florida, assorted top henchmen, and the apparent host, Mike Miranda.

Uncertain what charges to lodge against the baker's dozen of mafiosi, a supervising detective came up with an old standard harassment complaint: consorting with known criminals—each another. Hauled away in handcuffs from their aborted lunch for booking at a police station house, the thirteen prisoners were compelled, like all criminal suspects, to strip ignominiously to their underwear for a body search. Like ordinary thieves and robbers, they were fingerprinted and photographed for the rogue's gallery mug files.

When Queens District Attorney Nat Hentel learned of the arrests, he rushed to the station house. A Republican, Hentel had been appointed as an interim district attorney by Governor Nelson A. Rockefeller, and he was an underdog candidate for election as a full-term prosecutor in a heavily Democratic borough. The bagging of celebrity mobsters in his jurisdiction was an unexpected publicity windfall. Hentel quickly rescinded the "consorting" charges. He convened a grand jury for the stated purpose of investigating organized crime in Queens and thought it wiser to hold the thirteen as material witnesses. The consorting charge was vague and judges were increasingly dismissing it as unconstitutional.

Hentel was right about the publicity bonus. The arrests were played as a major story in New York and elsewhere. Faces of the arrested mobsters were splashed on Page One and the meeting was headlined as "Little Apalachin." Hentel milked the affair for publicity and name recognition for himself. Basking in television, radio, and newspaper attention, the prosecutor—without the slightest evidence—issued hyperbolic statements that the gangsters had assembled to chart the future course for the Mob in the entire country. He melodramatically termed the curtailed luncheon a historic gathering, more important than the Apalachin meeting nine years earlier.

Showing their disdain for the DA and the police who arrested them, the southern bosses Carlos Marcello and Santo Trafficante, accompanied by a retinue of bodyguards and lawyers, returned a week after the raid to the same table at La Stella. This time they invited the press and posed for photographs, lifting wine glasses in merry toasts, shouting *salute*. "Why don't they arrest us now?" Marcello asked contemptuously as reporters took notes. The dons then ordered the same banquet they had been denied by the raid: escarole in brodo, linguine in white clam sauce, and baked clams, topped off with several bottles of wine, and ending with fruit and espresso.

All of the Little Apalachin Thirteen invoked the Fifth Amendment when called before a grand jury. Hentel's investigation fizzled into obscurity without producing a single indictment or sliver of information. Unfortunately for Hentel, the publicity generated by the arrests failed to help his election bid; he was overwhelmingly defeated. For the big-shot mobsters the arrests were a trivial inconvenience. For law-enforcement officials, the restaurant raid displayed both their ineffectiveness in combating the Mob and their ravenous appetite for publicity.

Trafficante told his attorney, Frank Ragano, that the luncheon-meeting was a sit-down to resolve a complaint by Marcello that New York mobsters were intruding on his territory in New Orleans without permission. New York detectives had different ideas. Some believed that the La Stella gathering was a "sidebar" event for several of the families, following the regular meeting of the nation's Mafia bosses, which was then held every five years. That year, it had been conducted in the New York region, without a hitch and undetected. Other detectives theorized that the main topic for the small group at La Stella concerned enlarging the size of Marcello's family in Louisiana. Another theory was that the principal discussion dealt with Tommy "Three-Finger Brown" Lucchese, who was incurably ill, and the question of who would succeed him.

Little Apalachin was a bigger mystery than Apalachin and another glaring example of the decline in law-enforcement's knowledge of the Mob's business plans and motives.

Lucchese, suffering from a brain tumor, died a few months later at age sixty-seven. His funeral was a revealing underworld and upperworld event. Despite the unconcealed surveillance cameras wielded by local detectives and federal agents, the rites were attended by hundreds of mafiosi as well as judges, politicians, and businessmen. The mobsters showed their respect for a distinguished idol while simultaneously exhibiting their scorn for the impotent lawmen. Even more disturbing was the appearance of eminent "civilians" who felt indebted to the criminal chieftain, and who had reasons to remain on good terms with his successors.

Two years after Lucchese's death, Vito Genovese, who had retained the title of boss during his narcotics-trafficking imprisonment, died of a heart attack in a prison hospital on Valentine's Day in 1969. He was seventy-one. Bonanno's forced exile and the deaths of Lucchese and Genovese catapulted Carlo Gambino to the Mafia's Olympian heights. He emerged as the supreme figure on the Commission and exalted leader of the Mob's largest and most influential family. While the Mafia never acknowledged the rank of "boss of bosses," Gambino in effect assumed the power that went with it.

For New York's unchallenged borgatas, success seemed boundless, and the decade was ending with an inexhaustible supply of wannabes competing to enlist as wiseguys in the enterprise bigger than U.S. Steel. At the time, few police commanders were knowledgeable or concerned about the Mafia's inroads. An exception, Assistant Chief Raymond V. Martin, bluntly assessed Cosa Nostra's alluring appeal in Italian-American neighborhoods in Brooklyn and other parts of New York:

"On so many street corners in Bath Beach, in so many luncheonettes and candy stores in Bensonhurst, boys see the Mob-affiliated bookies operate. They meet the young toughs, the Mob enforcers. They hear the tales of glory recounted—who robbed what, who worked over whom, which showgirl shared which gangster's bed, who got hit by whom, the techniques of the rackets and how easy it all is, how the money rolls in. What wonder is it that some boys look forward to being initiated into these practices with the eagerness of a college freshman hoping to be pledged by the smoothest fraternity on campus. With a little luck and guts, they feel, even they may someday belong to that splendid, high-living band, the Mob."

17

The Birth of RICO

Asked about his ethnicity, George Robert Blakey, as a boy and as an adult always had one answer: "I'm an American."

The reply was not based on inflated patriotism. In his formative years the question of Blakey's ancestral roots was never raised by his parents and relatives. He was born and reared in Burlington, North Carolina, in the 1930s and '40s—in the South an era of intractable Jim Crow racial laws and oppressive segregation of blacks. The prevailing distinctions between families in Burlington, a textile-manufacturing town of about 20,000 in the northern part of the state, was whether they were black or white, whether they were country-club gentry or hardscrabble mill hands. People in the Piedmont region never identified themselves in hyphenated terms as being Irish-American, German-American, or Polish-American. If Italian- or Sicilian-Americans lived in Burlington, young Blakey, who preferred to be called Bob, never met any of them. As for the Mafia—the subject that would dominate Blakey's career—it was a foreign-sounding term that totally escaped his attention until adulthood.

Blakey's father was a Texan who became the president of the First National Bank of Burlington, after working as a bank examiner. Of English stock, the Blakeys were staunch Baptists who had fought for the Confederacy in the Civil War. Bob Blakey's mother was of Irish descent, and she raised him as a devout

Roman Catholic. His father died of a heart attack in 1945, when Blakey was nine, but providently left him, an older brother, and his mother in reasonably comfortable financial circumstances. Blakey went north for his higher education, graduating with honors from Notre Dame University in South Bend, Indiana. He majored in philosophy, intending to lead a sedate life as a teacher, until he learned of the meager earnings a philosophy professor could command in academia. Hoping to have a large family (he would have eight children), Blakey switched to law as his best bet for a livable income and won a scholarship to Notre Dame's law school. To support himself during these years, he worked in the summers as a bakery-truck driver, and his on-the-job contacts sharpened his interest in labor law. There were practical lessons to be learned outside the classroom by working side by side with flinty unionized teamsters at the bakery. Blakey found these blue-collar workers proud of the economic gains they had won by signing on with a scrappy union; at the same time they felt helpless to reform its undemocratic structure, which limited their right to choose national and regional leaders.

Blakey made the nuances of collective bargaining and union statutes his prime areas of study, and in 1960 he graduated second in his class. Instead of concentrating on labor law as he had planned, Blakey was selected in a national honors program for a modest-salaried $6,500-a year job as a Special Attorney with the Justice Department in Washington, assigned to the Organized Crime and Racketeering Section.

Joining the department at the tail end of the Eisenhower administration, Blakey spent his first year reading memos and pushing paper through bureaucratic mazes. It was the period when the Justice Department accepted Hoover's views that the big-city Italian-American gangs were an inconsequential, loose collection of criminals. In rare instances, when an informer or a witness tried to volunteer information about the Mafia to Justice Department prosecutors, he was discouraged. "If anyone started talking about the Mafia or using the word, he was told to shut up," Blakey discovered. "The Mafia was not relevant to the case and we only wanted to hear about the specific crime being investigated."

Those conditions and taboos changed dramatically when Robert Kennedy became attorney general in 1961, breathing life into a drive against the Mob and labor racketeering. In law school, Blakey had taken only one course in criminal law, but he had a solid background in applying labor-law statutes to union-corruption cases. As the workload intensified, he quickly cut his teeth on the intricacies of criminal prosecution. He got an eye-opening primer in the

Mafia's pervasive power from the torrent of electronic-spying information that the FBI was suddenly providing the department's organized-crime section. The intelligence was passed on to Blakey and other lawyer-prosecutors by agents who withheld the fact that the evidence originated from illegal bugs.

"There was nothing in my background to prepare me for this rush of information about induction ceremonies, blood rites, *omertà*," he said of the newly opened window into the Mafia. "I was incredulous; it was not part of my consciousness."

Robert Kennedy's resignation as attorney general in 1964 was a signal for Blakey's leave-taking. Inspired by Kennedy, he had committed himself for three years to the unprecedented campaign against mobsters and their infiltration of major labor unions. But it was clear to Blakey that the old lackadaisical thinking had reinfected the Justice Department and that the new administrators would minimize the Mob as a priority. "I was there at the heights with Kennedy and I didn't want to be there at the bottom," Blakey told friends.

Returning to Notre Dame, he spent the next two years as an assistant professor, teaching law and mulling over his exhilarating Justice Department hitch. At the law school, he initiated a popular course on organized crime, which his students irreverently called "the gangbusters class." In retrospect, he wondered about the lasting accomplishments of Robert Kennedy's strategy. "We were a bunch of bright guys working hard but we had minimal impact," he concluded pessimistically to himself. Even the crowning prosecution of Robert Kennedy's campaign—the conviction of Jimmy Hoffa—failed to cleanse the teamsters' union of Mafia control and corruption. Hoffa's imprisonment simply opened opportunities for similarly tainted teamster officials to replace him in illicit deals. "Convicting Hoffa," Blakey reflected, "what difference did it make for the union? Zip."

The Mafia reentered Blakey's life indirectly through Lyndon Johnson's landslide victory as a full-term president over Arizona's Republican Senator Barry Goldwater in 1964. Goldwater touched upon a sensitive area in the campaign by lacerating Johnson and the Democrats for being soft on crime. After the election, violent felony rates soared and arrests dropped, bolstering the Republicans and jeopardizing the Democrats' prospects in future national elections. To blunt the GOP's damaging attacks on his crime-control policies, and perhaps to divert attention from the accelerating war in Vietnam, Johnson did what most politicians do to douse political fires: he formed a study group. Titled the President's Commission on Law Enforcement and Administration of

Justice and headed by Attorney General Nicholas de B. Katzenbach, the commission's stated goal was developing new crime-prevention strategies.

In 1966 nine task forces were established to search for answers, and Blakey signed on as a consultant to one that analyzed organized crime. After two years of research and hard thinking with other commission members, Blakey hit upon a legislative and law-enforcement plan to cripple the Mafia. His theories did not arise from any stunning epiphany but grew during a lengthy analytical process of osmosis in brainstorming sessions with two other consultants, Donald R. Cressey, a sociologist, and Thomas C. Schelling, an economics professor.

Cressey provided him with insight on the organizational composition of each Mob family—the blueprint in place since Lucky Luciano's 1931 revisions. That structure insulated the Mafia's leadership from arrests and virtually ensured each borgata's longevity through steady hierarchical replacements. Blakey saw that the blood and cultural ties of Mafia members enhanced bonding and loyalty, transforming criminal associations into true extended families. These were defining factors that distinguished the Mafia from the Jewish and Irish ragtag ethnic gangs that had been extinguished by divisive internal disputes and by law-enforcement efforts. The Mafia's unique attributes enabled it to resist traditional police tactics and encroachment and destruction.

From Schelling's research, Blakey obtained a clearer understanding of the Mob's diversified system of plunder and profits that also set it apart from other criminal bands. The Mafia families, Blakey decided, were comparable to well-managed, complex industrial corporations. "They were the mirror image of American capitalism. They were aping it." Meyer Lansky, who proudly estimated that the Mob's revenues were larger than U.S. Steel's, would have agreed with him.

Like all lawyers of his generation, Blakey had been trained to focus on an individual prosecution for a specific act or crime—not in large organizational terms. "It blew my mind," Blakey said of Cressey and Schelling's analysis of the Mob's organizational and financial underpinnings. "I started seeing things I had not seen before."

Instead of prosecutions that focused on an individual mobster and one criminal violation, Blakey began thinking in a spectacularly larger dimension: a law or series of statutes that could destroy in a mass conviction an entire organization—a Mafia crime family. Before his ideas could gel, the Katzenbach commission disbanded in 1967, issuing a list of suggestions and legislative proposals for solving the nation's crime woes. The task-force pundits on organized crime, fully recognizing the menace posed by the Mafia, recommended more federal funds and manpower to uproot mobsters in big cities. They also endorsed one of Blakey's pet proposals: legalizing electronic surveillance as a basic tool for properly investigating mobsters.

Blakey considered himself a liberal Democrat, but in 1968 he became an adviser on crime issues to Richard M. Nixon, the Republican candidate who won the presidency that year. A Republican administration, Blakey thought, would be harder on crime than the Democrats and more receptive to his innovative views on the Mob. Offered a high post in the Justice Department, Blakey turned it down for the chance of working with Senator John McClellan and getting his radical concepts on assaulting the Mafia written into law. In the decade after the Apalachin raid, McClellan, a conservative southern Democrat from Arkansas, had been Congress's most persistent advocate for harsher laws against organized crime and labor racketeering.

Following his work on the Katzenbach commission, Blakey had helped McClellan draft a groundbreaking law in 1968 on wiretapping and bugging. Known as Title III, the statute for the first time gave Congressional authorization to electronic eavesdropping. Previously under ambiguous laws and court rulings, federal agents could intercept but not disclose or use as evidence information obtained through wiretaps. Because of these restraints, the clandestine electronic spying of the FBI and federal narcotics agents was probably unconstitutional and illegal. The ban on wiretaps and bugs undoubtedly handicapped federal investigations of many crimes, not just those committed by the Mafia.

Under Title III, a provision in the broader Omnibus Crime Control and Safe Streets Act, a bill endorsed by President Johnson, federal and state prosecutors could seek court approval to wiretap and plant listening devices under strict guidelines. To install the equipment, prosecutors and agents first must get authorization from a judge by presenting evidence that there is probable cause, or sufficient facts, to believe that a crime has been committed or is being planned. The judge has to be further persuaded that electronic surveillance is indispensable and that other investigative methods are unlikely to succeed or are too dangerous. Additionally, the judicial order for intercepting conversations terminates after thirty days unless prosecutors can show incriminating results from the first order and prove that its continuance is vital for an ongoing investigation.

Title III was opposed by the American Civil Liberties Union as a violation of the Bill of Rights and portrayed as an Orwellian Big Brother expansion of the government's police powers. Blakey, an ACLU member, considered the organization's unbending position illogical. He argued that the legislation did not infringe on the civil liberties of the law-abiding public and was a long-overdue weapon for dealing with organized crime. "Our objective was to take illegal wiretaps and bugs out of the back alleys and let the courts decide if there were lawful and sufficient reasons for the surveillance. We imposed severe restrictions on the government and that is pro-civil liberties."

Championing electronic surveillance, Blakey emphasized another telling point: evidence from a defendant's own lips obtained through a bug or a wiretap was infinitely more reliable and accurate than testimony from informers who might lie to get lenient sentences for their own crimes.

The thirty-two-year-old Blakey was bristling in 1968 to enact a legislative blockbuster against the Mob when McClellan, as chairman, appointed him as chief counsel of the Senate Subcommittee on Criminal Laws and Procedures. Earlier, as a consultant to McClellan on Title III, Blakey had urged the senator to sponsor a larger package of anti-Mafia statutes. With Congress wrestling that year with the Omnibus Crime Control act and the electronic-surveillance controversy, McClellan felt the timing was unfavorable for debate and passage of a larger package of laws to disrupt the Mafia. "Half a loaf now is better than none," he said after the Title III victory.

John McClellan was seventy-three, Blakey's senior by more than forty years, when they began molding the latter's proposals into legislative language. For fifteen years, since the mid-1950's, McClellan had firsthand exposure to mobsters, presiding as he did over numerous inquiries into union corruption, rackets, and other Mafia misdeeds. At these hearings, the senator's face was usually an impassive mask. Inwardly he seethed, exasperated at the uncooperative, brazen mobsters who openly defied the government and considered themselves a law unto themselves. A rock-hard Christian fundamentalist, McClellan possessed an Old Testament sense of righteousness and was generally portrayed as a kind and considerate man, but one who truly believed in right and wrong and punishment for evildoers.

Shepherding the first specific anti-Mafia measure presented to Congress, McClellan expressed to other legislators his view that its passage was an absolute moral necessity. Anticipating a fierce civil-liberties fight over expanding the government's investigative powers, McClellan had a ready rebuttal: "The public is demanding that we recognize that the right of society to be safe transcends the right of the criminal to be free. When the forces of right and peace clash against the forces of evil and violence, something has to give."

An adroit lawmaker, McClellan tucked the measures aimed squarely at the Mafia into one statute or section of a larger, widely supported anticrime bill. It was a tactic intended to increase the survival chances of the organized-crime statute in the whipsaw process of amendments and political compromise in both houses of Congress. The overall legislation was titled the Organized Crime Control Act of 1970. For McClellan and Blakey, the essence of the act, the heart of their game plan, were provisions labeled the Racketeer Influenced and Corrupt Organizations section. The law's abbreviated title was RICO and its strange name was intentional. Blakey refuses to explain the reason for the RICO acronym. But he is a crime-film buff and admits that one of his favorite movies is *Little Caesar*, a 1931 production loosely modeled on Al Capone's life. Edward G. Robinson portrayed the central character, a merciless mobster, whose fictional nickname—serendipitously for Blakey—was Rico. Robinson's snarling characterization of the rise and fall of Rico became the prototype for movie gangsters. Dying in an alley after a gun battle with the police, Little Caesar gasps one of Hollywood's famous closing lines—also Blakey's implied message to the Mob: "Mother of Mercy—is this the end of Rico?"

Before RICO was conceived, the vast majority of Mafia bosses, underbosses, consiglieri, and capos were effectively insulated from arrest. Once in command positions, they gave orders but never personally committed crimes. Proving in court that these leaders were implicated in acts carried out by their underlings was virtually impossible under existing federal and state conspiracy statutes. It was the subordinates—the soldiers, the associates, the wannabes—who did the dirty work, and they were the ones who occasionally got caught on murder raps, dealing in drugs, shaking down loan-shark victims, bookmaking, hijacking, and other crimes. With the code of *omertà* inviolable, successful prosecutions of high-ranking mafiosi was a daunting if not impossible undertaking.

McClellan and Blakey wanted to change the equation and simplify the task of piercing the protective walls surrounding Mafia rulers. The thrust of the RICO law centered on two words: pattern and enterprise. Prosecutors could indict and convict large groups of mobsters by proving they were engaged in a "pattern" of crimes conducted in behalf of an organization, an "enterprise." A "pattern" was defined as two or more specified federal or state offenses related to the "enterprise" and committed over a substantial period of time. "Enterprise" was broadly defined to include illicit associations, like Mafia families or crews, as well as corrupt unions and corporations.

Thus, RICO empowered prosecutors to dismantle the hierarchy of a family with one sweeping indictment, instead of concentrating on low-level strays picked up on relatively minor charges. More important, under RICO for the first time a boss could be convicted if it was proved that he was linked to the criminal enterprise. Evidence that a boss or capo got a cut of the loot or was heard arranging the enterprise's activities was sufficient for conviction. Anyone planning or receiving a report about a crime involving the enterprise was as guilty as the perpetrator.

In effect, the statute outlawed the Mafia's fundamental and ingrained operating procedures. RICO mandated that committing or being an accomplice in any two of twenty itemized felonies, even over a period longer than ten years, could convict a defendant of participating as a member of an enterprise, a rackets organization. The crime categories covered involvement in almost every conceivable illegal infraction or conspiracy: murder, kidnapping, drug trafficking, robbery, loan-sharking, gambling, bribery, extortion, embezzlement from union funds, fraud, arson, and counterfeiting.

There were other groundbreaking provisions for prosecutors. Normally, except for the crime of murder, a suspect must be charged within a five-year time period after the commission of most federal crimes. RICO expanded the five-year statute of limitations almost indefinitely, depending on when the last—not the first—crimes were committed for the enterprise. Another boost for prosecutors was authorization to use previous convictions in state courts as part of federal charges against a defendant. This weapon was applied under the theory that the old crime was now being punished under the "enterprise" and "pattern of racketeering" elements of the federal law and was exempt from double jeopardy, being tried twice for the same crime. And RICO imposed draconian punishment, essentially up to forty years for bosses and others in leadership positions, and a maximum of life without parole where murder was committed to aid the enterprise.

To destroy the Mob's economic foundations, RICO's long arm extended into civil and antitrust areas. The law allowed the government to seize loot and assets squirreled away by gangsters and, through forfeitures, obtain their homes, property, and bank accounts if they were the fruit of crimes. In short, the objective was to take the profits out of organized crime. In a revolutionary step toward breaking the Mob's control or influence in unions, RICO contained an antitrust provision for civil suits by the government. Without the necessity of a criminal trial, the Justice Department could file a petition in federal court seeking to have an entire national union or a local (a branch of the union) placed under federal supervision and its leaders ousted. In order to clean up racket-plagued unions, the government would first have to prove to a judge that the unions or locals were linked to organized-crime figures.

Finally, as a means of cracking the code of *omertà*, McClellan and Blakey designed a trailblazing witness-protection program that offered immunity from prosecution for cooperating witnesses. Blakey believed that mafiosi and Mob associates, facing RICO's long prison sentences, could be converted into witnesses and informers. Potential defectors would be more likely to change sides, aid, and testify for the prosecution once the threat of Mob retaliation was removed or at least diminished. Through a witness-protection program, the government could encourage turncoats by safeguarding them and their close relatives and helping them start new lives, far from their old environment.

To overcome vigorous opposition to the proposals as anti-labor, anti–civil rights, and excessively punitive, McClellan garnered widespread support from both conservative and moderate Republicans and Democrats. A selling point to them was that RICO's main goals were expelling the Mob from legitimate businesses and unions. Senate approval of the entire bill, including RICO, was relatively easy. The biggest obstacle was Representative Emanuel Celler, a liberal Democrat from New York City, who was chairman of the House of Representatives Judiciary Committee, and leading the fight against RICO. Celler expected to weaken and emasculate the RICO section of the omnibus legislation through the parliamentary device of conference sessions. When different versions of a bill are passed by the House and by the Senate, representatives of both bodies meet in "conference" to iron out disagreements by agreeing on identical language and a single version.

Before presenting his bill to the Senate, the canny McClellan allowed Celler to introduce amendments in the House's bill modifying controversial parts of the act unrelated to RICO. The disputes over other aspects of the legislation served as lightening rods, distracting Cellar's attention from substantially altering RICO in his proposed House bill. Celler anticipated that his non-RICO objections would force McClellan to call for a conference, which would give him the opportunity to block or substantially modify RICO to his satisfaction. But McClellan surprised him by accepting the amended House version. Since the approved Senate and House bills were identical, there was no need for the conference that Celler had counted on. He had been outwitted by the senator from Arkansas.

In 1970 the entire Organized Crime Control Act was enacted without further amendments. After two years of public hearings, deft negotiations, and fine tuning, RICO was intact and became the law of the land.

"I was the draftsman but McClellan was the architect," Blakey recalled. "Without his finesse, political understanding, and zeal, it never would have happened."

Blakey had his law but he found himself in confounding limbo. No one in federal law enforcement wanted to use RICO. Cautious prosecutors were hesitant to be the first to apply an untested statute, fearing that it would be declared unconstitutional and their convictions reversed. No prosecutor wanted to give up easy cases and almost certain guilty verdicts under existing laws by experimenting with RICO's criminal provisions. The civil portions of RICO were equally unpalatable to prosecutors and FBI agents. "They were all gunslingers; for them civil litigation was for sissies," Blakey realized. "They wanted to make arrests, not serve subpoenas." Like an itinerant, optimistic evangelist of a new religion, Blakey brought the promise of RICO to FBI agents and officials and to prosecutors in U.S. Attorney's offices throughout the country. Everywhere, the reception was the same: he was looked upon as a fuzzy-minded college professor, an out-of-touch Washington-style bureaucrat peddling an impractical panacea. "We passed the bill and thought it would be implemented," Blakey complained. "But when I explain how to lawfully use it, they look at me as if I'm crazy."

His most disappointing rejection and most embarrassing encounter came at the prestigious U.S. Attorney's office in Manhattan. At least there he anticipated support because every alert prosecutor understood that the New York metropolitan area had long been the bedrock of the Mafia. On the morning of November 1, 1972, he was in the midst of his pep talk about the virtues of RICO when Whitney North Seymour Jr., the U.S. Attorney for the region, rose to his feet. A descendant of a New York patrician family, and the area's highest federal law-enforcement official, Seymour summarily ordered Blakey to leave the conference room. "You don't know what you're talking about," Blakey recalled Seymour belittling him. "You're wasting my time and my assistants'. Get out."

Years later, Seymour conceded that he and many of his senior prosecutors were dubious about the value and constitutionality of RICO. "In hindsight we were one hundred percent wrong," he acknowledged. "This is what happens when you're confronted with something new, I guess." But Seymour insisted that while disagreeing with the law professor, he had treated him courteously.

Blakey attributed those bitter experiences partly to the fact that RICO was the brainchild of advisers outside the Justice Department. "It was elitist thinking in New York and elsewhere in the Justice Department that they were the best and the brightest when it came to law-enforcement innovations, and superior to outsiders. Most of them felt they knew everything."

To his further dismay, Blakey, still the chief counsel of McClellan's subcommittee, found that neither prosecutors nor the FBI were effectively using Title III, their new electronic-surveillance powers enacted by Congress. After ceasing its legally questionable bugging program in the mid-1960s, the FBI in the early 1970s resumed using wiretaps and listening devices with judicial authorization, but it was on a limited basis, mainly confined to quickie gambling cases. Bookie investigations were easy, resulting in multiple arrests and meaningless conviction statistics; but everyone knowledgeable in law enforcement knew that convicting low-level gamblers had minimal effect on weakening the Mafia.

Obsessed with arrest numbers, FBI officialdom objected to lengthy electronic surveillance of mobsters as costly, time-consuming and statistically unproductive. Running a wire or a bug could tie up six agents on three shifts daily for thirty or more days, without guaranteed results. Taking the easy road, supervisors encouraged agents to concentrate on bank robbers. The efforts sometimes bordered on absurd parodies of the Keystone Kops. In New York and other cities, FBI agents would race the local police to bank holdups to establish jurisdictional rights in cases that usually were easy to solve.

In stump speeches about RICO to agents and supervisors in training sessions at the FBI's academy in Quantico, Virginia, Blakey's pitch that Title III was intended as a tool for long, penetrative investigations went unheeded. "They thought simplistically like cops solving individual crimes, not about systemically destroying Mob families."

The FBI's atrophied mind-set regarding investigative priorities irritated many federal prosecutors in the 1970s, but none was willing to challenge the publicly esteemed and potentially vindictive agency. A lone dissenter appeared in July 1976, when a high federal official in New York, David G. Trager, described the bureau as "suffering from arteriosclerosis" and of being "out of step" with the major goals of federal prosecutors. Trager was the U.S. Attorney for the

Eastern District of New York State, which comprises Brooklyn, Queens, Staten Island, and Long Island. His views largely echoed Blakey's critiques of the bureau's overall competence although organized crime was not one of Trager's top concerns. "Most of the cases they [the FBI] bring us are insignificant," he told the *New York Times*. "They are wasting resources on trivia, and I don't think they have the ability or the people to do the job in the areas we consider priorities—official corruption and white-collar crime."

As for the Cosa Nostra, Trager contended that the government was doing a poor job. He laid the blame on special independent units, the Organized Crime Strike Forces that had been established in major cities by the Justice Department to coordinate and spearhead Mob prosecutions. These strike forces, Trager claimed, were staffed largely with inexperienced attorneys and were "dying" without making a dent in combating the Mafia.

The government's own statistics clearly illuminated the ineffectiveness of the early strike forces. In the late 1970s, after a decade of existence, strike force prosecutors had yet to indict or convict a high-ranking Mob figure. Who were the strike forces and the FBI going after? Mainly small-time gamblers and loan sharks. Here, too, the results were pitiful. A congressional review found that 52 percent of the convictions resulted in no jail time. And, almost 60 percent of those convicted—overwhelmingly minor soldiers and associates—got soft sentences of less than two years.

Blakey had a similar low opinion of most of the heads of these new strike forces whose stated priority and goal was to prosecute the Mafia. He lectured, cajoled, and implored strike force attorneys to employ RICO as their main weapon. The responses to him were uniformly negative. "Sounds good," prosecutors would say. "but I don't want to take a chance by trying something new and blowing a good case."

As the Eastern District's U.S. Attorney, Trager supervised one of the Justice Department's largest jurisdictions, an area of New York that was teeming with mafiosi. Yet he too declined to use his prosecutorial powers to crack down on mobsters by experimenting with RICO. Nevertheless, Trager, a maverick prosecutor, tried through the country's most influential newspaper, the *New York Times*, to sound off about the FBI's outdated anticrime and anti-Mafia strategies. Like Blakey's, Trager's warnings were totally ignored by the decision-makers at the Justice Department and the FBI.

Before Bob Blakey set out on his frustrating road trips to sell RICO, he had an immensely proud moment on October 15, 1970. On that date, he was at the

White House when President Nixon signed the Organized Crime Control Act and RICO into law. Years later, Blakey grasped the surrealistic consequences of that ceremonial signing. An obscure clause of the bill enlarged the scope and type of immunity from prosecution Congress could give witnesses testifying at Senate and House of Representative hearings. Because of that uncontroversial, barely noticed provision, John W. Dean III, the former counsel to President Nixon, agreed to testify before a Senate committee in 1973 that was investigating the president. Dean disclosed that Nixon had been aware of efforts to conceal the White House's involvement in the 1972 break-in at Democratic party headquarters at the Watergate complex in Washington. Enjoying only limited immunity, Dean later was convicted of obstruction of justice for his part in the coverup. But his revelations to the Senate committee were instrumental in compelling Nixon to resign as president in 1974, rather than face impeachment by Congress over the Watergate scandal.

The irony of RICO's first triumph was not lost on Blakey.

"When Nixon signed the bill, he handed the document to John Mitchell, the attorney general, and said, 'Go get the crooks,'" Blakey remembered. "And who were the most prominent people brought down by the act—Richard Nixon and John Mitchell."

18

Unity Day

Monday, June 28, 1971, was tailormade for Joseph Anthony Colombo. Joe Colombo was in an ebullient mood and the clear, relatively cool weather was ideal for his plan—a massive Italian-American Unity Rally in the center of New York City. The pleasant temperatures that afternoon would insure a huge audience that would generate enthusiastic applause for what Colombo considered the high point of the festivities, his televised speech.

As Colombo prepared for his big day, RICO, the get-tough-with-the-Mafia law, had been on the books for almost one year and had been ignored by law-enforcement agencies. For Colombo, RICO was equally unimportant, and the law's acronym probably represented nothing more to him than a male nick-name. Major mobsters and their attentive lawyers were unconcerned about a statute that had attracted sparse attention and was not being enforced. Like Joe Bonanno, the New York bosses and their lieutenants knew they operated inside an unstable volcano, and the greatest life-threatening dangers to themselves were from internal eruptions by envious, revengeful rivals, not from external assaults by the FBI or the police.

None of the bosses was cowering in his lair, fearful of RICO's bite. On the contrary, in 1970, while RICO was being passed in Congress, Joe Colombo was organizing a national campaign—an unsubtle counterattack—to protect the

Mafia. Unlike conventional mobsters who avoided the exposure of publicity, Colombo began courting the media, contending that he and countless other Italian-Americans were being falsely vilified because of their ethnic background. At forty-eight, Colombo was cresting on a wave of unparalleled career success and widespread public popularity. He was the godfather of one of New York's five Mafia families and, simultaneously, the founder and leader of the Italian-American Civil Rights League, an organization championed by public officials, corporate executives, and show business personalities.

It was an unheard-of triumph to simultaneously run a borgata and to be acclaimed a civic leader and civil-rights pioneer. Joe Colombo had managed to accomplish it.

Shortly before noon, ten thousand people were streaming into Columbus Circle at the entrance to Central Park for the second annual Italian Unity Day rally. From eighty feet overhead, atop a distinctive column, the giant statue of Christopher Columbus gazed downward as bodyguards cleared a path for Colombo to reach the speakers' stage. Smiling and waving, Colombo ambled slowly past admirers wishing him well, striving to touch him or shake his hand, past the plastic red, white, and green buntings and streamers, the colors of the Italian flag.

In the din of the huge, noisy crowd and the band music pulsating from loudspeakers, witnesses heard three muffled pops that sounded like faint firecrackers. They were gun shots from an ancient .32 caliber pistol. The bullets ripped into Colombo's head and neck. He plummeted to the ground. As blood gushed from his mouth and ears, Colombo lay motionless, irreversibly paralyzed, his dreams of underworld supremacy, national respectability, and political influence shattered.

Joe Colombo was no stranger to violence. Growing up in South Brooklyn, one of the Mafia's spawning grounds, he knew from an early age the spectre of gangster-imposed justice. When he was sixteen, his father, Tony, a made man, met an early and brutal death over some Mob misdeed. Signifying a Sicilian-style revenge slaying, the bodies of his father and a girlfriend were found trussed and garroted in the back seat of a car.

Drafted into the Coast Guard in World War II, Colombo served three years before being discharged early, suffering from "psycho neurosis." It was a malady that cronies attributed to his theatrical skills since he later never exhibited the slightest sign of mental distress. Briefly working as a longshoreman on the gangster-saturated Brooklyn docks, he switched to running crap games, and then found his calling as a proficient hit man for the Joe Profaci gang. Mob insiders credited Colombo with being in a squad that whacked at least fifteen victims to resolve Profaci's most troublesome problems.

The Gallo brothers' war against Joe Profaci in the early 1960s proved to be a stepping-stone for Colombo's advancement. He remained loyal to Profaci against the insurgent Gallos and, after the old boss's death, seemingly supported Joe Magliocco in his aborted quest for leadership of the borgata. Stellar service as a killer for the Profaci-Magliocco faction earned Colombo a promotion to run a crew as a capo. But in the power struggle between New York's family bosses, he switched sides. Rather than obeying Magliocco, he engineered a double-cross, warning Carlo Gambino of the assassination plot hatched by Joe Bonanno with Magliocco's assistance to murder Gambino and Tommy Lucchese. Gambino outmaneuvered Bonanno to triumph as the reigning personality on the Mob's Commission. Impressed by Colombo's chicanery, Gambino, the aging leader of the largest New York family, adopted him as a protégé. Don Carlo's unqualified endorsement in 1964 eliminated any opposition to Colombo's ascending the throne as boss of the old Profaci gang. The borgata of two hundred soldiers and more than one thousand associates was swiftly renamed in Mob circles. It became the Colombo family.

Colombo's installation as a family godfather with a vote on the Commission at the comparatively young age of forty-one rankled Mafia old-timers. An FBI wiretap in the office of Sam The Plumber DeCavalcante, the boss of a small New Jersey family named after him, heard him grousing to an unidentified caller about Colombo's undistinguished qualifications and Gambino's judgment. "He was nothing but a bust-out man," Sam the Plumber said of Colombo, referring to him disparagingly in Mob slang as a small-time operator of card and dice games. "Yeah, he was always hanging on Carlo's shoulder," replied the unhappy voice on the other end of the telephone line.

Older bosses might envy Colombo's rapid ascension, but he knew how to fulfill the role of an established family Caesar. Upgrading his appearance, he outfitted his stocky frame in conservative suits, muted ties, and customed-tailored shirts, trying to pose as a prosperous businessman. As another emblem of middle-class respectability, he took up golf instead of shooting pool with the boys. Colombo's real income poured in from illicit million-dollar gambling, loan-sharking, hijacking, and shakedown rackets, but to appear legitimate, he became a "salesman" for a Brooklyn real estate company owned by an associate in his crime family. Overnight, the new venture capitalist was a partner in a funeral parlor and a florist shop. Those were popular "front" occupations for mobsters, and both of them were run by hirelings. The fictitious income from the salesman's job and investments that could be justified to the IRS allowed Colombo to adopt a lifestyle befitting his Mob title. He moved his wife and their five children into a spacious split-level house in the Italian-American neighborhood of Bensonhurst, Brooklyn's middle-class version of Little Italy. For a more elegant and bucolic retreat, he acquired a five-acre estate near the Hudson River, one hundred miles from the city.

A second-generation American, Colombo was far more articulate in English than Don Carlo Gambino and other immigrant bosses whose speech was heavily accented and grammatically mangled. And, Colombo had no fear of going *mano a mano* with law-enforcement officials and speaking his mind.

In 1964, after a soldier in Colombo's family was gunned down, Albert Seedman, then a New York detective inspector, asked Colombo to appear voluntarily at a Brooklyn station house. To Seedman's surprise, the new Mob boss showed up alone, without a lawyer, and unabashedly tore into Seedman. "If I was a Jewish businessman, you'd never dream of calling me down here on a murder," Seedman recalled Colombo railing at him. "But because my name is Italian, that's different. I'm a *goombah* mobster, not good people like you."

Before departing and without providing any information about the homicide, Colombo fired another verbal barrage at Seedman. "You lean back at that big desk, and you're thinking. 'This guy is sitting here, feeding me a line. He's nothing but a two-bit greaser trying to look respectable.' Well, you're wrong. I am an American citizen, first class. I don't have a badge that makes me an official good guy like you, but I work just as honest for a living. I am a salesman in real estate. I have a family to support."

Six years later, Colombo pulled off an even more daring surprise. His son, Joseph Jr., was indicted in April 1970 on a rare federal complaint: a $300,000 conspiracy to melt down nickel coins and sell them as silver ingots. Instead of the customary Mob tactic of retaining high-priced lawyers to win a courtroom acquittal, Colombo responded by staging demonstrations and picket lines outside of the FBI's Manhattan offices. The picket lines were manned mainly by Colombo borgata members, wannabes, and their relatives, handing out leaflets assailing the bureau for being anti-Italian and for persecuting Italian-Americans on fictitious charges.

The almost daily protests orchestrated by Colombo coincided with widespread national unrest over the Vietnam War and a rising clamor by African-Americans, Hispanics, and feminist groups for civil rights and equality. With New York as the vortex of the national and international media, the novelty of a reputed Mafia boss giving extensive television, radio, and print interviews catapulted Colombo into a media celebrity. He began appearing frequently on news and talk shows, expounding his views that "the Mafia was a myth" manufactured by law enforcement and the press, and that Italian-Americans—like black Americans and other minorities—were victims of FBI and police bias and brutality. The viewpoint, glibly expressed by Colombo and echoed to some degree by earnest, prominent Italian-Americans, struck a chord in the Italian community. Distrust of authority and government agencies, fanned by opposition to the Vietnam War, was on the rise, and the public was acutely aware of the government's abysmal record of violations of, and indifference to, the civil rights of many groups.

Colombo's son was acquitted in the silver conspiracy case, benefiting from a standard development in Mob-related trials. The key witness against twenty-six-year-old Joe Jr., a former wannabe named Richard Salomone, had an abrupt change of heart in the witness chair, recanting earlier incriminating statements by suddenly stating that young Colombo knew nothing of the scheme. After the court victory, Colombo senior revved up his personal crusade. In less than a year, he formed and become the head of the Italian-American Civil Rights League, with a claimed dues-paying membership of 45,000 and 52 chapters in the nation. Harangues by Colombo and his followers against the FBI, law enforcement in general, and the press convinced thousands of decent Italian-Americans that their community was being unfairly stigmatized as the Mafia.

"The president is knocking us down; the attorney general hates our guts," was Colombo's provocative sound bite on late-night TV talk shows. Interviewed in a thoughtful article in *Harper's Magazine*, Colombo, posing as an abused defender of his community, asked, "Is it possible in New York that only Italians have committed crimes?" Arrested thirteen times, Colombo had a police record for minor gambling misdemeanors. Having escaped major felony convictions, he could reasonably contend that he was being smeared, without proof, by the authorities as an organized-crime gangster. "I wasn't born free of sin," he thundered, "but I sure couldn't be all the things that people have said—I got torture chambers in my cellar, I'm a murderer, I'm the head of every shylock ring, of every bookmakin' ring, I press buttons and I have enterprises in London, at the airport I get seven, eight million dollars a year revenue out of there. Who are they kiddin' and how far will they go to kid the public?"

Colombo's pitch that his mistreatment typified frequent abuses suffered by law-abiding Italian-Americans was an instant success. Almost overnight the league—in effect Colombo—became an electoral weapon, recognized and respected by politicians. At the first Unity Day Rally in June 1970, the theme was "restoring dignity, pride and recognition to every Italian-American." An estimated fifty thousand people cheered Colombo and other speakers in Columbus Circle as they pounded home that message. Mindful of the league's rapid growth, elected officials quickly responded to its potential voting power. New York's Governor Nelson Rockefeller and scores of lesser politicians rushed to accept honorary league membership. At the rally, four congressmen and a New York City deputy mayor rose on the speaker's platform alongside Colombo to support the league's goals of preventing discrimination against and slander of Italian-Americans. The league's lobbying efforts intimidated Governor Rockefeller and Nixon's Attorney General John Mitchell into officially banning the use of the word "Mafia" by all law-enforcement agencies under their jurisdiction.

Hollywood also felt the sting of Colombo's wrath. Before Paramount could begin filming the first of its *The Godfather* movies, Colombo fired off a threatening press release. Characterizing Mario Puzo's novel, on which the film was based, as a "spurious and slanderous" account of Italian-Americans, he warned the producers against using the words "Mafia" and "Cosa Nostra" and depicting Italians as immoral criminals. For additional pressure, Colombo persuaded a dozen elected officials to caution the studio to portray Italians more positively than they had been characterized in the novel. Aware that the Mob's union goons could sabotage location shooting schedules, Paramount mollified Colombo; for "Mafia" and "Cosa Nostra," it substituted "family" and "syndicate" in the script. And perhaps seeking authenticity and Joe Colombo's good will, the producers hired several of the Mob boss's gofers as extras. The actor James Caan, who played Sonny Corleone, son of the godfather portrayed by Marlon Brando, spent a good deal of time cavorting with one of Colombo's capos, Carmine "the Snake" Persico, a feared killer. Caan's movie performance drew rave reviews.

Financially, Colombo's unique league seemed to be on the road to success. Frank Sinatra, who had a penchant for socializing with mafiosi, sang as the star headliner at an event in Madison Square Garden that raised $500,000 for the organization. A benefit dinner in Long Island netted $100,000. But Colombo's astonishing achievement with the league began to draw unfavorable notices among his Mafia brethren. For some mafiosi, the dissatisfaction was inspired by both the lurking green-eyed monster of jealousy and by ubiquitous greed. They were sure that a goodly portion of the funds and dues collected by the league was diverted into Colombo's private treasury and they were offended by not being cut in on a new racket. The omnipotent Don Carlo Gambino had a different concern: the league's success and Colombo's drumfire of denunciations and picket lines were embittering the somnolent FBI and police departments. Shortly before the second rally, Colombo spat out more venom at the FBI. He accused the bureau of deliberately encouraging the use the of the words "Mafia" and "Cosa Nostra" to excuse its investigative inadequacies. "When they don't solve something, it's because there's this secret organization they still haven't penetrated," he said mockingly. "You can't solve it so you blame somebody. You make up labels."

Colombo's ceaseless attacks were becoming imprudent, attracting the kind of attention that could create a backlash, Carlo Gambino told confidants. The end result, he feared, would incite investigators to strike at all the families. Gambino clearly was behind his protégé in 1970 at the first Unity Day Rally, sending out word that all longshoremen in New York's waterfront were to have the day off to attend the rally. At the approach of the second rally, Gambino issued a directive: keep the cargoes moving and no time off on the docks. Moreover, Paul Vario, a Lucchese capo and Gambino ally, abruptly resigned as the league's membership director, a clear indicator that the Luccheses had withdrawn their support. A final sign of displeasure from Don Carlo came when his army removed the 1971 Unity Day notices and placards from stores in Bensonhurst and other South Brooklyn neighborhoods. He was delivering a candid rebuke that Colombo's ego was getting too large and his boldness was endangering other families. Without Gambino's blessing, attendance at the second annual rally was expected to dip to 10,000 from the previous year's 50,000.

There was never any doubt as to who shot Joe Colombo. Despite a ring of Mob bodyguards and phalanxes of uniformed and plainclothes officers, a lone gunman had slithered through the protective shield in Columbus Circle. As Colombo sank to the ground, from fifteen feet away a horde of policemen and bodyguards pounced on the shooter, covering him like a besieged quarterback sacked in a football pileup. When the mound of bodies was peeled off, the gunman, a twenty-four-year-old black man, Jerome A. Johnson, lay dead, fatally shot three times, presumably by one of the Colombo soldiers who had failed to safeguard his boss. Embarrassed police brass assigned a special detective unit to figure out who Johnson was and who was behind the assassination attempt.

From the outset, detectives leaned toward the theory that Johnson had been a "patsy," a tool used by a Cosa Nostra enemy of Colombo to undertake a suicide contract. Four hours after the assassination attempt, a caller to the Associated Press, identifying himself as a spokesman for the "Black Revolutionary Attack Team" (BRAT), said Colombo had been shot in retaliation for violent acts committed by the white power structure against African-Americans. Detectives soon determined that the group was fictitious. They were dubious that an authentic underground black group would see any political purpose in knocking off a Mafia leader. No connection could be found between Jerome Johnson and any radical black political activists. In fact, Johnson mixed mainly with whites, and detectives were unable to find a single close black friend of his. The fake claim by BRAT, detectives speculated, might be a red herring to lead them on a false trail.

Investigators did piece together a portrait of Jerome Johnson as a petty con man, check forger, burglar, and lothario who drifted around college campuses trying to seduce women students. Somehow, Johnson, without experience as a news photographer, had wangled press credentials to cover the Columbus Circle rally from the league's chapter in New Brunswick, New Jersey. With an expensive $1,200 Bolex camera slung over his shoulder and a statuesque black woman assistant by his side, who also displayed a press card, Johnson threaded his way toward Colombo. As they approached Colombo, detectives believed, the woman passed a pistol to Johnson, an untraceable .32 caliber Menta automatic manufactured in Germany during World War I. At the opportune moment, the woman maneuvered alongside Colombo, shouting, "Hello, Joe." Halting, Colombo, turned to look through his horn-rimmed spectacles at the woman. Smiling, he responded to her with a "Hi ya." It was Johnson's opportunity. Almost at pointblank range, he fired three rounds before being knocked to the ground by a swarm of bodyguards and policemen. In the melee, Johnson's killer pumped three .38 caliber slugs into his back; the weapon, also untraceable, was found near the assassin's body.

Johnson's female accomplice darted away in the pandemonium that engulfed the crowd. Despite months-long, intensive searches, and running down scores of tips, detectives failed to identify or locate the mystery woman. Sifting through clues and intelligence reports, Albert Seedman, now chief of detectives, catalogued Johnson as a fall guy "whose head was somewhere in outer space." Johnson's lackluster criminal record led the city's sharpest detectives to conjecture that he had been inveigled, probably by the prospect of a large pot of money and false promises of an escape route, to mow down Colombo. He seemed too gullible and motiveless to have conceived and carried out the assignment without sophisticated outside guidance. Seedman's investigators reasoned that conspirators who knew how to acquire press credentials and how to determine when Colombo would be most vulnerable, must have choreographed the job for Johnson. Seedman and his detectives concluded that the plotters most likely were highly motivated mafiosi. Though lacking clear proof, Seedman firmly believed that circumstantial and logical evidence pointed in only one direction: the pilot behind Johnson's kamikaze attack was Joseph "Crazy Joey" Gallo.

19

Ubazze and Lilo

razy Joey" Gallo's underworld nickname was appropriate. As a young recruit, he epitomized the predatory hoodlum who carried out the Mob's routine scut work, a thug without the brains for complex rackets, whose specialty was extorting victims through terror. Along with his brothers, Albert and Larry, he got his start as an enforcer and hit man for Joe Profaci's gambling and loan-sharking capos in Brooklyn. With Joey as their honcho, the brothers established their headquarters in a building on President Street, near the waterfront in Red Hook. A blue-collar neighborhood, the area was later gentrified by realtors, and became the more pleasant-sounding and higher-rent district of Carroll Gardens.

Gallo's reputation soared when the Mob grapevine credited him with being the lead gunsel in the barbershop execution of Albert Anastasia in 1957. Modeling himself after the 1940s George Raft film version of a suave gangster, Gallo took to wearing dark suits, dark shirts, and white or bright-colored ties. To impress his foes and underlings with his courage, he once quartered a chained pet lion in the basement of his President Street hangout.

But after a decade of loyal service to Profaci, the ambitious Gallo boys began griping that their ungrateful boss was skimming the cream from their plunder and refusing to reward them with some of the gang's gambling and loan-sharking monopolies. Open rebellion was their solution. The Gallos, in one day in February 1961, kidnapped Profaci's brother-in-law and underboss, Joe Magliocco, and four Profaci capos. Their ransom demand was a heftier share of the borgata's multimillion-dollar take. Profaci responded in a meek manner, agreeing to be more generous. The concession was a ruse. As soon as the captives were released, Profaci gathered his forces, lured away several Gallo supporters, and began bumping off Gallo's troops. The rebellion flared on and off for more than a year, and most of the twelve slain casualties were from Crazy Joey's outgunned crew. On the day in 1961 that Larry Gallo barely escaped being murdered, Gallo's crew got a crude message that one of their ablest killers, Joseph "Joe Jelly" Gioiello, was "sleeping with the fishes." Gioiello's clothing, stuffed with fish, was tossed from an auto in front of a restaurant where the Gallos frequently dined.

While the conflict raged, Gallo's movements were limited, but Joey still had to earn money to pay his minions and to feed his lion. One gambit was enlarging a primitive extortion scheme he had cooked up. Before battling Profaci, Gallo had established on paper a phantom union of bartenders and used it to shake down tavern owners in Brooklyn. To avoid violence and vandalism, the victims had to pay $30 a week as dues for each employee, none of whom knew they belonged to Gallo's sham labor organization. Looking for more easy shakedowns, Gallo's crew branched out to Manhattan, using the same terror tactic there by suggesting to proprietors of small bars that they might meet with "unfortunate accidents" or their places might be wrecked if they failed to pay bartender "dues." One defiant owner resisted, cooperated with detectives, and secretly tape-recorded an incriminating meeting with Gallo in Luna's, a Little Italy restaurant. The evidence pinned Crazy Joey to an extortion conviction in 1962 and a maximum ten-year prison sentence. With his departure and Profaci's natural death that same year, a truce was soon arranged, and the Gallo Wars ended with Joe Colombo's enthronement as boss.

Eight years in state prison coated Joey Gallo's personality with a new patina—at least on the surface. Like many unschooled convicts, he discovered books as an antidote to the numbing boredom of confinement and became an avid reader of literature and philosophy. Upon his return to Brooklyn in 1971, Gallo could quote and discuss the nuances of Balzac, Kafka, Sartre, Camus, and Flaubert, and having taken up painting while behind bars, he began visiting museums. His pseudo-intellectual trappings were a con man's camouflage.

Brother Larry Gallo had died of cancer, but Albert Kid Blast Gallo and remnants of the old crew knew that Joey was as ambitious and determined as ever to carve himself a large slice of Mafia pie. While in prison, Gallo had planned for his comeback. He cultivated African-American inmates as potential muscle to secretly reinforce his depleted Brooklyn brigade when the time came for a showdown. He arranged for selected black recruits released from the penitentiary to link up with his brother and other crew wiseguys, who helped them with money and jobs.

Soon after his parole, Gallo made a move, demanding from Colombo $100,000 and a sizable portion of the borgata's rackets. The payments, he contended, were reasonable because he had been in prison and had never signed on with his brothers to the family's peace pact. It was an implied threat that Gallo could launch another violent campaign. Fully in control of the crime family and riding high with his civil-rights league, Colombo contemptuously brushed off Gallo as an insignificant has-been.

Exhibiting his new highbrow persona—and perhaps to lull Colombo and other old enemies—Gallo moved from dingy Red Hook to Greenwich Village, began attending the theater, and struck up relationship with the actor Jerry Orbach and his wife, Marta. Orbach had played a gangster in the movie adaptation of Jimmy Breslin's *The Gang that Couldn't Shoot Straight,* a comic novel about an incompetent Mafia crew that resembled Gallo's own second-rate outfit. Boasting that he had reformed and was writing his memoirs, the former Crazy Joey of the police blotter was lionized as a celebrity guest at show business and New York café society dinner parties.

Gallo's supposed transformation from violent reprobate to misunderstood adventurer was encouraged by mounting feeling in the country and among the intelligentsia that widespread bigotry had hobbled and forced many Italian-Americans into crime. Sympathy ran high for the Italian-Americans. This concept stemmed partly from the success of Joe Colombo's anti-discrimination league, and from the universal popularity of Mario Puzo's bestseller *The Godfather* novel and the Academy Award–winning movie version.

Mario Puzo's youth was spent in the crime-ridden Hell's Kitchen neighborhood on Manhattan's West Side. Although he never associated with or knew an authentic mobster, he drew upon his knowledge of the area, research, and his imagination to fashion a compelling tale of Mafia life and death, centering around the fictional Don Vito Corleone, played memorably in the movie by Marlon Brando, and his "family."

Although the book and the movie are rife with murders, brutality, betrayals, and mayhem, an underlying subtext appears to rationalize the virtues of Mafia or "family" loyalty. Criminal acts, including murder, can be interpreted in the story line as necessary expedients to enable early Italian immigrants and their descendants to obtain a measure of equal justice, financial success, and dignity in a hostile American culture and environment. Michael Corleone, the returning World War II hero and central figure, is compelled by fate and through belated realization of the honorable values of ethnic tradition and blood ties to commit and authorize murders. Finally, he accepts the role of Mob boss as his inherited duty to protect himself and to enlarge the criminal corporation created by his father.

A conspicuous theme of the novel and the movie revolves around Puzo's characterizations: the scrupulous, well-intentioned mafiosi (the Corleones) versus their nefarious adversaries, the devious drug-trafficking villains. In the end, like an old-fashioned Western, the anti-drug, white-hat mafiosi good guys conquer the cruel and wicked Mob desperadoes. In reality, the Mafia was chiefly responsible for flooding America's inner cities with heroin in the 1960s, and every family was enriched by drugs.

No group was more fascinated, appreciative, or proud of *The Godfather* theme than the Mafia. It mythologized mafiosi as men of honor and, perhaps unwittingly, preached that even in a criminal society loyalty and dedication to principles would triumph. Many wiseguys rejoiced in viewing the original film multiple times. Federal and local investigators on surveillance duty saw and heard made men and wannabes imitating the mannerisms and language of the screen gangsters. They endlessly played the movie's captivating musical score, as if it were their private national anthem, at parties and weddings. The film validated their lifestyles and decisions to join the Mob and accept its credo. Moreover, it apparently justified a warped belief that mafiosi were members of a respected, benevolent society of deserving superior people.

After seeing the picture in 1972, a young wannabe, Salvatore "Sammy the Bull" Gravano, who one day would acquire Mafia fame, was exultant. "I left that movie stunned," Gravano reminisced. "I mean, I floated out of the theater. Maybe it was fiction, but for me then, that was our life. It was incredible. I remember talking to a multitude of guys, made guys, everybody, who felt exactly the same way. And not only the Mob end, not just the mobsters and the killing and all that bullshit, but that wedding in the beginning, the music and the dancing, it was us, the Italian people!"

Joey Gallo blended easily into this newly spun, naive cocoon of tolerance and admiration of the Mafia. Dinner party acquaintances might easily misjudge mobsters like Gallo as posing no threat to ordinary citizens, viewing him as an entertaining anti-establishment buccaneer. Chief of Detectives Albert Seedman thought otherwise. The yearlong investigation into the shooting of Joe Colombo unearthed information about Gallo's friendly relationships with black prison inmates, and his dispatching them upon their release to his Brooklyn crew. Detectives were unable to establish a clear bridge between the dead gunman Jerome Johnson and Joey Gallo or any of his associates, but Seedman was convinced that Gallo had used an African-American prison chum to enlist the penniless Johnson, probably enticing him with the prospect of a huge payoff. The hit on Colombo, detectives theorized, was intended to clear the way for Gallo's comeback. A pariah in the Colombo family, Gallo had much to gain from the boss's elimination, and Seedman believed that the assassination attempt bore Crazy Joey's peculiar trademark. "Gallo had earned his nickname by striking when his victims least expected," Seedman stressed. "He was also right in character by going for the top of the same family he had attacked in 1960, when Joe Profaci was the don."

For added confirmation, detectives knew from informers and from unguarded remarks by Joe Colombo's soldiers that the family was thinking along the same lines. They also had Gallo in their sights as the secret hand behind the trigger that paralyzed their boss. Stopped for traffic violations or interrogations, Colombo soldiers would angrily demand, "Why don't you pat down and get that scum bag Gallo?" Called in for police questioning, Gallo maintained he had no knowledge about Johnson or about the shooting, insisting that he had straightened out his life. While appearing carefree, Gallo nevertheless kept a bodyguard close by, usually the burly Peter "Pete the Greek" Diapoulas, a crony since their schoolboy days.

Ten months after Colombo was shot, on April 7, 1972, Gallo threw a forty-third birthday party for himself at the Copacabana nightclub, always a chic watering place for mobsters. Besides his relatives, Gallo invited Marta and Jerry Orbach, other entertainers, and the *New York Post*'s Broadway columnist Earl Wilson, for champagne toasts. When the Copa closed at 4:00 A.M., a restless and hungry Gallo drove downtown in his Cadillac for a late snack. Accompanying him were his bride of three weeks, Sina; her ten-year-old daughter, Lisa; his sister, Carmella Fiorello; Pete the Greek; and Pete's girlfriend, Edith Russo. Unable to find an open restaurant in Chinatown, the party meandered a few blocks south to Little Italy's Mulberry Street. At the corner of Hester Street, they found a brightly lit, Italian-style restaurant, Umberto's Clam House.

Without realizing it, Gallo had stumbled into a recently opened restaurant run by relatives of Matthew "Matty the Horse" Ianniello, a barrel-chested capo in the Genovese family, and a Little Italy Mob enforcer. (Umberto's was a minor diversion and cover for Ianniello; his main duties were extorting kickbacks from topless bars in Times Square and gay bars on the West Side and in Greenwich Village.) Gallo's party seated itself at one of the butcher-block tables in the otherwise empty restaurant, and Gallo ordered huge helpings for all of them of conch, clams and shrimps. The carefree group was eating and laughing when a balding man in a sports jacket flung open the restaurant's side door on Mulberry Street and blasted away at the party with an automatic revolver. As the women screamed and dishes clattered to the floor, Gallo bolted for the main door on Hester Street. The gunman pegged at least five shots at Gallo; two missed, one hit him in the buttocks, another in an elbow, and the last smashed through an artery in his back. Staggering outside, he collapsed a few feet from the door.

The shooter, with a slight smile of satisfaction, backed out of the side door to a waiting car. Gallo's bodyguard, Pete the Greek, who had also been shot in the buttocks, finally managed to draw his pistol, firing a volley at the getaway car as it sped north on Mulberry Street. Within minutes, a police patrol car arrived and rushed Gallo to a hospital five minutes away. It was too late. He died in the emergency room from loss of blood before surgery could begin.

Suspicion immediately fell on Matty the Horse, the Genovese capo, who was in the restaurant when the bullets began flying. "I don't know nothing," Matty told detectives. "You think I'm crazy to let this happen in this place?" Ianniello's story that he dived to the floor in the kitchen, kept his head down, and was uninvolved in the gangland execution was true. Two weeks later, detectives had a vivid picture of Gallo's end—an unplanned, spur-of-the-moment hit, triggered by a wannabe's hankering for a bowl of Manhattan clam chowder.

The details came from an eyewitness and an admitted participant in the killing, Joseph Luparelli. A seedy, bottom-level Colombo flunky from Brooklyn's Bath Beach section, Luparelli never applied for a Social Security number because he had never held a legitimate job. An aging wannabe in his late thirties, he supported himself as a gofer and small-time fence of stolen property for Colombo soldiers, sycophantically performing menial chores.

On that fateful morning, Luparelli had been in Little Italy, trying to ingratiate himself with several made Colombo men, playing cards and making small talk with them at one of the gang's storefront hangouts. Shortly before 5:00 A.M., requiring a pre-breakfast snack, he stopped in at Umberto's, the only Italian restaurant in the neighborhood still open at that hour, for a bowl of red clam chowder. Refreshed, he was chatting outside the restaurant with Matty the Horse when the jubilant Gallo party pulled up.

Sensing a golden opportunity, Luparelli hurried along Mulberry Street until he found four Colombo soldiers in a Chinese restaurant. "The *ubazze* is eating over at Umberto's right now," he excitedly informed them; the Italian word *ubazze* means "crazy person," an obvious reference to Gallo. One of the men went to a phone booth and came back with orders from Joe "Yak" Yacovelli, the capo of their crew, to get Gallo. According to Luparelli, he drove with one of the men to a spot outside of Umberto's, stationing themselves in the "crash car" to block any police or other vehicles from pursuing the getaway car. The three other Colombo hoods parked on Mulberry Street near the restaurant's side door. Luparelli said he saw the shooter slip into Umberto's, heard the gunfire, and watched as Gallo fell mortally wounded onto the sidewalk.

After the shooting, the three men in the getaway car ditched the auto and all five drove uptown in Luparelli's car to Yacovelli's East Side apartment, where the capo congratulated them for a well-done job. The five then drove to an apartment in suburban Nyack, where Yacovelli told them to hide out until it was safe to surface. Luparelli emphasized to detectives that his motive for fingering Gallo was his hope that it would help him become a made man and make the kind of money that he craved. "They got books just like unions, you know," he said enviously. "They don't let you in for nothing. They don't care if they never let you in. They got to keep it exclusive or it gets loose."

But Luparelli's close contact in the safe house with the four Colombo soldiers made him increasingly jittery and paranoid. Their awkward behavior toward him — mainly cold stares and hushed conversations — convinced him they had decided he was untrustworthy and planned to whack him. After five days in the hideout, he lit out, drove his car to Newark Airport, and caught the first available flight to Southern California. Holed up in California with relatives, Luparelli became even more wildly paranoid. Certain that the Mob would track him down as a suspected rat, he turned himself in to the FBI, and was flown back to New York protected by detectives. Luparelli's account of the Nyack hideaway was verified, and detectives trailed and tried unsuccessfully to wiretap the four Colombo soldiers who were still encamped there. Seedman and other detectives on the case found Luparelli's story of the Gallo ambush credible. Without corroborative evidence, however, under New York State law prosecutors had no murder or conspiracy case against the four soldiers or Yacovelli. With Luparelli's sleazy background, his testimony alone was too thin for an indictment, let alone a conviction. Rewarded and aided by the authorities for his snitching, Luparelli disappeared into a witness-protection program, never to be heard from again.

Seedman was certain that his detectives had solved or found the answers to two important Mafia crimes: the shootings of Joe Colombo and Joey Gallo. The slaying of Gallo in front of innocent women relatives and a child violated Mafia protocol, but Mob rules justified it as retaliation for dishonoring Colombo and for committing the most grievous of Cosa Nostra sins: a hit on a boss without authorization by the Commission.

The shooting of Joe Colombo, and the murders of the assassin Jerome Johnson and Joey Gallo, are listed as unsolved. The only person involved in the incidents who was arrested and went on trial was Gallo's wounded bodyguard, Pete the Greek Diapoulas. He was convicted of the relatively minor charge of possession of an illegal firearm. By receiving a suspended one-year sentence, he avoided spending a single day in jail. Diapolas's six shots, which missed the fleeing killer and the escape car, became part of Mafia history. The errant bullets pockmarked the masonry of an apartment building across the street from Umberto's Clam House. The restaurant and the bullet holes became enshrined as Little Italy landmarks for Mob cognoscenti.

Joe Colombo's injuries were eventually fatal. Lingering on for seven years, unable to speak and only capable of moving two fingers of his right hand, he died in May 1978, a month short of his fifty-fifth birthday. Upon retiring as the head of New York's detective bureau, Albert Seedman reflected that a singularly colorful and audacious mobster was responsible for issuing Colombo's death warrant and, unintentionally, one for himself. "That little guy with steel balls," Seedman added with a touch of admiration, was Joey Gallo.

Gallo's ability to intrigue show business luminaries continued after his death. In 1975, the iconoclastic Bob Dylan composed and recorded the music and lyrics for a paean to the slain mobster. In Dylan's hit song, "Joey," Gallo was a misunderstood, unappreciated nonconformist who died too soon.

Two other deaths in the 1970s significantly altered Mafia history: Carlo Gambino and Carmine Galante.

The first to go was the venerated Don Carlo Gambino, who came closer than any other member of the Commission to being recognized as Boss of Bosses. Although the title of *capo di tutti capi* was a media invention, Gambino was the Mob's most potent and revered godfather in the decade stretching from the mid-1960s to the mid-1970s. He was unquestionably first among equals. In 1957, he seized control of the borgata that would bear his name by arranging the treacherous murder of the erratic Albert Anastasia, and then proceeded to unify and enlarge the racketeering scope of the family. Under Gambino's firm command, the borgata became the nation's largest with about five hundred made men and more than two thousand associates. The family's size and its wealth alone would have put him on the highest rungs of the Mafia. In addition, Don Carlo was an innovator, encouraging his capos and soldiers to expand the family's fortunes by infiltrating unions and legitimate business where the booty was larger and the risks fewer than in violent crimes. Control of teamster, construction industry, waterfront, and garbage-carting union locals created a steady cash flow from union welfare fund frauds. Their power in the unions gave the mobsters the clout to demand kickbacks from companies in exchange for labor peace and sweetheart collective-bargaining contracts. The under-the-table union deals allowed Gambino and his capos to become partners in semi-legitimate companies and to benefit extensively from inflated rigged bidding on public and private contracts.

By outwitting his main rival, Joe Bonanno, who was forced into retirement in the mid-1960's, Gambino became the senior don on the Commission. His word became dogma for the national Commission and the policies it set for the country's other crime families.

Life in the Mafia had been bountiful for Gambino. For half a century, from soldier to godfather, he was seemingly immune from law-enforcement pressure, avoiding prison terms as charges against him were dismissed or overturned on appeal. On the surface, he lived unpretentiously, renting an ordinary apartment in a middle-class section of Sheepshead Bay in Brooklyn and owning a more posh home in Massapequa on Long Island's North Shore. To tax collectors, he pretended that his income was derived from partnerships in a labor consulting firm and in trucking companies. Experience taught him to rely on caution, and he moved around in the company of select bruisers. A slightly built man, with a beaklike nose and an elfish smile, his appearance belied the deadly power he exerted on his own and other Mafia families. Once Carlo Gambino assumed the mantle of boss, except for Joe Bonanno's misconceived plot there was never an attempt on his life or a conspiracy to damage him.

Gambino adapted easily to the role of patriarch. To young mafiosi to whom he took a liking he volunteered the philosophy that inspired his success. "You have to be like a lion and a fox," he lectured attentive recruits. "The lion frightens away the wolves. The fox recognizes traps. If you are like a lion and a fox, nothing will defeat you." It is doubtful that any of the boss's untutored disciples realized that Gambino's parable was plagiarized from Niccolò Machiavelli, the sixteenth-century Italian political realist and cynic, who advocated that princes should rely on deception to seize and retain power.

Time ran out for the lion-fox on May 15, 1976. Don Carlo died at age seventy-four in his bed in Massapequa, after suffering from a heart ailment for several years. A consensus builder, always thinking about his borgata's future, Gambino selected an heir before his death. His choice was his brother-in-law and second cousin, Paul "Big Paul" Castellano. Traditionally, in the Gambino family, as in most American borgatas, a new boss must be ratified by a majority of the capos. This odd parallel to a democratic selection is usually honored in the breach, since the formal vote is predetermined in each family by the faction that has seized control.

During the last months of Don Carlo's failing health, Paul Castellano had been in training as acting boss of the family. He became Gambino's dependable right hand, channeling the family's activities into the white-collar areas of union and industrial corruption. At the time of Gambino's death, the longtime underboss, Aniello Dellacroce, was serving the final months of a prison sentence, convicted by that old Mafia bugaboo the IRS for evading $123,000 in income taxes from stock he obtained in an extortion plot. Dellacroce's ideas about the family's operations were in sharp contrast with Castellano's. A ruggedly built, cigar-chomping mobster from the tenements of Little Italy, Dellacroce relied for revenue on old-fashioned practices: loan-sharking, truck hijackings, robberies, numbers, and gambling. He had a rich assortment of Mob nicknames, "Neil," "Mr. Neil," "Tall Guy," and "Polack." His adherents in the family were chiefly recognized for their abilities as hit men and bone-breakers. Released from prison shortly after Carlo Gambino's death, Dellacroce had the heavy-duty fire power to challenge Castellano for the top spot. But, ever the good soldier, he respected Gambino's deathbed wish. Rather than unleashing an internal war, he accepted Castellano's coronation in late 1976 and agreed to continue as underboss. According to Mob folklore, "Big Paul" won over "Mr. Neil," with a practical proposal: "Anything you had with Carlo, you keep. Anything more you want, we talk." By compromising instead of selecting a new underboss committed to him, Castellano had divided Gambino's unified kingdom into two domains. But through appeasement he had avoided internecine combat, and with plenty of spoils for himself and for Dellacroce, there was little to worry about. Moreover, Big Paul was now the family's acknowledged head and his triumph made him the first American-born boss of the Gambinos, the nation's most important borgata.

A year earlier, in 1975, another native-born American, Carmine Galante, tried to assume control of New York's strife-torn Bonanno gang. Balding, bespectacled, and with a bent walk, Galante was another don whose demeanor contradicted the popular image of a Mob narcotics predator and assassin. To passersby, the chunky, five-feet four-inch tall Galante looked like a relaxed, retired grandfather as he selected fruit and vegetables at Balducci's market in Greenwich Village, or stopped for espresso and cannoli at the De Robertis Pasticceria on the Lower East Side. Yet he was a man who had been in serious trouble with the law since childhood, a man with an unsurpassed underworld resume of viciousness. Suspected by New York police of being a participant or a conspirator in more than eighty murders, Galante had deftly eluded indictment for all of them. Mafia associates said he was the actual gunman in the shocking and politically motivated 1943 murder in New York of Carlo Tresca, the exiled Italian anarchist editor and opponent of Benito Mussolini. It was a homicide to benefit Vito Genovese, who was in Italy during World War II; in courting favors from Mussolini, Don Vito wanted Tresca's pen and voice silenced.

Galante was born in 1910, and reared in the mafiosi enclave of East Harlem. His parents had emigrated from Castellammare del Golfo, the fishing village and ancient breeding-ground for the Sicilian Mafia, the incubator for Joe Bonanno and numerous Bonanno family members in America. At age ten, Galante was sent briefly to reform school as an "incorrigible juvenile defendant" for truancy and a string of street robberies. Seven years later, he was convicted of assault and sentenced to Sing Sing prison. Back on the streets, with the aid of well-connected Castellammarese relatives, Galante was an apt recruit for the Bonanno gang. By the time Galante was in his forties, Joe Bonanno promoted him to consigliere and put him in charge of the family's narcotics network. Nicknamed "Lilo" by his mobster companions, after the Italian slang word for a stubby little cigar, Galante was at Bonanno's side and his main adviser when the 1957 compact was made in Palermo with the Sicilian clans to plague America with heroin. Fluent in Italian, French, and Spanish, Galante was the Mafia's principal emissary in Europe for their multimillion-dollar drug deals. Harry Anslinger's narcotics agents caught up with him in 1960, and he was indicted on federal charges of being the "chief executive" of a gang that imported vast amounts of drugs into the country from Canada. On the eve of summations, the first trial ended when the jury foreman broke his back in a mysterious fall down a flight of stairs in an abandoned building in the middle of the night, and a mistrial was declared. Federal prosecutors believed the foreman had been assaulted to halt the trial and to terrorize and intimidate jurors, but lacked proof.

At Galante's second trial two years later, with thirteen codefendants, there were calculated attempts to bedevil the judge and jury and cause another mistrial. One of Galante's soldiers, Salvatore Panico, climbed into the jurors' section, pushing them aside and screaming vilifications. Another codefendant pitched a chair at a prosecutor that shattered against the railing of the jury box. Presiding judge Lloyd F. MacMahon awoke one morning at his suburban home to find a severed dog's head on his porch, an ancient and crude Mafia intimidation tactic. For months afterward, the judge had round-the-clock protection. MacMahon ordered several defendants gagged and shackled after frequent profane and vile outbursts directed at the jurors and prosecutors. Despite the outrageous attempts to disrupt the trial, Galante was found guilty on multiple narcotics charges. Prison psychiatrists diagnosed him as having a psychopathic personality, unable to tolerate losing arguments or being contradicted or humiliated. His piercing eyes made prison guards quiver. "Galante's stare was so dreadful that people would shrivel in their chairs," according to Detective Ralph Salerno. In his many encounters with icy Mafia killers, Salerno admitted that only two of them rattled him with their terrifying eyes: Neil Dellacroce and Carmine Galante.

Inside prison, Galante maintained his status; a small stable of other Bonanno inmates attended to his mundane needs. Disdainful of penitentiary grub, Galante shelled out $250 a month in bribes for choice cuts of meat to be served to himself and his flunkies. At the time, prison authorities gave Mafia inmates virtually a free hand to run their own sections of cell blocks. The mobsters were tolerated because they created no disciplinary or violence problems. Snitches later told investigators that the arrogant Galante vowed to prison buddies that he would restore the former glory of the splintered family, which had been in flux and without a Commission-approved boss since Joe Bonanno's forced retirement in the mid-1960s. Paroled in 1974 after serving twelve years, Galante's lust for power and his murderous instincts soon prevailed. Philip "Rusty" Rastelli, a rival for the top post and interim boss, balked at stepping aside in Galante's favor. But convicted of extortion, Rastelli began serving a six-year sentence that left the road open for Galante to become the most decisive and potent capo in the faction-riven borgata. As the former consigliere and virtual underboss to Joe Bonanno, Lilo considered himself the rightful heir to the throne, even officiating at inductions of wiseguys, a power normally reserved for the boss.

On parole, Galante masqueraded as a legitimate businessman, opening a dry-cleaning store on Elizabeth Street in Little Italy. His personal life was equally duplicitous. He had three children with his wife, but after his narcotics prison stretch he lived with another woman who had borne him two children. Galante confided in friends that as a "good Catholic" he would never seek a divorce.

Refusing to recognize Rastelli as boss, Galante made two bold moves to raise money and to reinforce his contingent. Increasing his cash flow, he stepped up narcotics deals with Sicilian exporters, designating himself "rent collector," the sole Mob magnate entitled to franchise fees from Sicilians operating in the United States. The loot would not be shared with other borgatas. And, adding muscle to his ranks, Galante imported from Sicily additional manpower known as Zips. The origin of the term "Zips" is fuzzy. Remo Franceschini, the New York detective and Mafia expert, attributes the expression to a contraction of a Sicilian slang word for "hicks" or "primitives."

Galante's undisguised attempt to dominate the Mob's narcotics market alarmed New York's reigning godfathers, who declared him persona non grata. Unconcerned by the animosity he was engendering, Galante was confident that his Zips retained the traditional Mafia virtues of loyalty and ferocity that would reinvigorate the Bonanno gang. He began using Sicilians for the toughest jobs, often relying on them as his personal guards. Two of his favorites were Baldassare Amato and Cesare Bonventre, rugged twenty-seven-year-olds and close friends from Castellammare del Golfo, whom Galante had personally inducted as made men. He had total confidence in their fealty.

On the steamy Thursday afternoon of July 12, 1979, Galante was dropped off for a luncheon date in the fading Bushwick section of Brooklyn by his nephew James Galante, a soldier and his chauffeur for that day. In earlier times when Bushwick was more prosperous, it had been a Bonanno family stronghold. Zips still liked the area for its remaining Mob storefront clubs and pizzeria hangouts where the Sicilian dialect dominated and undercover agents and narcs were as easily spotted as a herd of pink elephants. Galante's distant cousin Giuseppe Turano and his wife owned Joe and Mary Italian-American Restaurant, where Galante often dropped in for home-style Sicilian dishes and a chat with Giuseppe. The Knickerbocker Avenue restaurant retained a nostalgic image of an old-fashioned, unpretentious gathering place, with lemon-colored, floral-patterned oilcloths on the tables, and photographs of Frank Sinatra and other Italian-American celebrities bedecking the walls. Above the entrance was a large painting of the Last Supper.

The reason for Galante's visit was a bon voyage luncheon for Turano, who was leaving the next day for a vacation in Sicily. A rectangular table in a private patio was prepared for the honored guest, Lilo Galante, his cousin, and Angelo Presanzano, an elderly soldier and devoted adjutant of Lilo. Before the first course was served, Presanzano excused himself, saying he had pressing business to attend to, and left.

But soon there were unexpected Bonanno mobsters at the restaurant. The Zips, Baldo Amato and Cesare Bonventre, accompanied by Leonardo Coppola, a drug dealer in Lilo's faction, showed up and Galante invited them to his table. Giuseppe Turano was surprised that Coppola would patronize his place because the two men disliked each other. Acting as peacemaker, Galante told them he hoped a convivial luncheon would end their feuding.

The five men at the outdoor table finished their meal of salad, fish, and wine, and Galante lit up a cigar while waiting for dessert and coffee. Just then, at 2:45 in the afternoon, three ski-masked men strode into the restaurant. John Turano, the seventeen-year-old son of the owners, shouted a warning toward the open courtyard as he scrambled away. One of the trio pegged a shot at the teenager, wounding him in the buttocks. His sister, Constanza, heard her father cry out, "What are you doing?" before gunfire rang out. In the patio, the intruders—apparently joined by the Zips Amato and Bonventre—opened up with a shotgun and automatic handguns. Galante, Coppola, and Turano died instantly. Hit at close range, Galante was hurled backward, a shotgun hole in his left eye and his cigar clenched between his teeth in a death grip.

Witnesses on the street saw the masked shooters leave Joe and Mary's with Amato and Bonventre on their heels. There was no attempt by the Zip "bodyguards" for Galante to retaliate against the killers, easy targets whose backs were turned as they entered a getaway car in front of the restaurant; nor did the gunmen demonstrate any apprehension of the Zips walking calmly in another direction. It was clear that Amato and Bonventre conspired in the assassination, but there was no immediate evidence or witness's testimony to arrest or indict them.

Motives for Galante's execution buzzed through the Mafia rumor mill and were relayed by informers to detectives and FBI agents. From prison, Rastelli had dispatched a supporter to petition the Commission for approval to kill Galante as an illegitimate usurper. The Mafia's board of directors was receptive. The putative Bonanno boss had committed two unforgivable offenses that threatened the leaders of New York's four other borgatas. He had attempted to injure their interests, especially the Gambinos', by cornering the American end of the Sicilian heroin market. Possibly even more grievous, after Carlo Gambino's death he had openly predicted that he would be crowned boss of bosses. With the Gambino's Paul Castellano in the lead, the Commission sentenced Lilo Galante to death. Amato and Bonventre, two of the stalwart Sicilians he had brought over from the mother country as his praetorian guard, were reached and persuaded to betray him. Investigators concluded that they had deliberately steered Coppola to Joe and Mary's because the plotters wanted him—a fervent Galante supporter—out of the way to prevent retaliatory raids to avenge his "boss's" slaying.

Another intended victim, Angelo Presanzano, narrowly avoided a gory execution by leaving the luncheon table early. The seventy-year-old Mafia veteran, however, survived only a few more days. Hiding out in the Catskills and terrified that he was a marked man, Presanzano suffered a fatal heart attack before any gunman could track him down.

"He must have stepped on someone's toes," James T. Sullivan, New York's chief of detectives, commented after reviewing the intelligence findings about Galante. In fact, the brutal sixty-nine-year-old gangster had trampled on many.

Galante's murder once again plunged the fractious Bonannos into disarray, without a strong hierarchy to negotiate disputes or agreements with their Mob counterparts. The basic structure of the other four New York Mafia borgatas remained in solid shape, with their bosses all too eager to take advantage of the Bonanno decline.

The natural death of Carlo Gambino and the gangland shootings of Joe Colombo, Joey Gallo, and Carmine Galante had resulted in a changing of the guard in the Gambino, Colombo, and Bonanno borgatas in the 1970s. These developments in three major families were the result of internal rivalries and gangster power plays; none had been caused by pressure from law-enforcement agencies, the Title III electronic surveillance act, or the RICO law. J. Edgar Hoover died in 1972, and his three immediate successors as FBI director, L. Patrick Gray, William D. Ruckelshaus, and Clarence M. Kelley, continued the same ineffectual and indifferent policies Hoover had instituted for pursuing mafiosi.

On assignment in America in the 1970s, Frank Pulley, an organized-crime detective from Britain's Scotland Yard, was appalled by the widespread indifference in the higher ranks of most American police agencies to the Mafia's awesome threat. An intelligence specialist, Pulley was gathering evidence about attempts by American mobsters to take over London's posh legal casinos. He singled out the New Jersey State Police for its anti-Mafia efforts but thought the New York Police Department and many federal and other local units were asleep at the wheel. "Many good cops who knew what was going on were kicking against the bricks and getting no support from their superiors," Pulley recalled.

Their comfort zones seemingly secure from outside pressure, the leaders of the Commission in the mid-1970s reopened the books, permitting all of the nation's Mafia families to induct qualified members to replace mobsters who had died. New blood was needed, and there appeared to be no danger that the next generation of mafiosi would be compromised or infiltrated by the lackadaisical federal and local law-enforcement agencies.

The Mob bosses' unconcern about law-enforcement efforts and zeal was well founded. Struggling alone, Bob Blakey pleaded with prosecutors and investigators to use RICO to attack the nerve centers—Cosa Nostra hierarchies. Almost a decade had gone by since the passage of the law and the analytically minded law professor was still searching fruitlessly for allies in his combat with the Mob.

20

The FBI Wises Up

For two hardened FBI agents it was a novel assignment in unorthodox surroundings: a pastoral college town some two hundred miles from the clamor surrounding their offices overlooking the courthouses lining Foley Square, in downtown Manhattan. Driving along the campus heights at Cornell University, agents James Kossler and Jules Bonavolonta were engulfed in a picturesque landscape. On that placid Saturday afternoon in August 1979, sails fluttered from drifting boats on Cayuga Lake, the Cascadilla Gorge and waterfall were framed by velvety green hills, carefree students tossed Frisbees, and melodic chimes echoed from the clock tower. It was an idyllic picture-postcard scene. Nevertheless, Kossler and Bonavolonta groused to each other, uncertain why they had been ordered to spend a week on a remote campus in Ithaca, New York, far removed from their life's work of hunting criminals and racketeers.

Both men were new mid-level supervisors in New York, having been recently appointed by the district's highest official, Neil Welch. While welcoming the promotions, Kossler and Bonavolonta understood they were working for an iconoclastic reformer. Welch had abruptly ordered them to spend a week at Cornell. His instructions were crisp: attend a seminar and listen to certain lectures. Laconic directives were the hallmark of Welch's maverick style; the FBI official abhorred long memos and time-consuming staff meetings.

With a complement of one thousand agents—about 10 percent of the FBIs entire strength—New York was the bureau's flagship station, and overseeing it was the most coveted field assignment in the agency. In other cities, the head of an FBI office was designated Special Agent in Charge, "SAC" in bureau talk. Signifying New York's prominence, the head job there carried the prestigious title of assistant director of the FBI.

Under Hoover's autocratic reign, Neil Welch would never have advanced to New York. But after Hoover's death in 1972 and the appointment in 1978 of William Webster, a former federal judge, as FBI director, the bureaucratic reins at headquarters in Washington gradually loosened. Dedicated to changing the organization's archaic policies and to ending the Constitutional abuses winked at by Hoover, Webster gave Welch a free hand in shaking up the New York staff. Welch had chafed at Hoover's downgrading of the Mafia's importance, and he was determined to overhaul the organized-crime units under his control. The Mob, he told everyone who would listen, was an everyday reality to field agents, but a forgotten factor at FBI headquarters. "We were not trained about the Mafia or how it operated," Welch later admitted. As a tyro agent in New York, during one of Hoover's on-again, off-again forays against the Cosa Nostra, he learned that the best method for obtaining accurate leads on mobsters was to get his hands surreptitiously on the Narcotics Bureau's Black Book, the intelligence files compiled by Hoover's rival, Harry Anslinger. Hoover had banned distribution of the dossiers to his agents, an absurd consequence of his animosity toward Anslinger.

A lawyer and talented administrator, Welch in the 1960s had succeeded in landing SAC appointments in Buffalo and in Detroit, despite Hoover's coolness toward him. Both assignments were in Mafia territories, and Welch, disregarding Hoover's admonitions, launched investigations into Mob operations. His efforts generated stinging rebukes from Hoover. "He accused me of running lopsided offices, and I was in serious political trouble for years," Welch said, chuckling. "He complained that I wasn't doing anything about Communist cases and his worn-out priorities."

The post-Hoover era saw Welch move up to SAC in Philadelphia, where his disdain for red tape and headquarters' interference became the stuff of FBI legend. Outraged that a holdover supervisor called Washington for clearance on a directive that he had issued, Welch stomped into the milquetoast supervisor's office and with a pair of scissors snipped all of his telephone lines.

"It was an excellent lesson that no one was going to question my orders and call headquarters for permission on any damn thing," Welch said of the incident. "I wanted to teach everyone that we have to depend upon ourselves and we don't need anything from headquarters."

Welch viewed the New York area as the Mafia's "world headquarters" and his appointment there as his most daunting challenge. "I was pretty well advanced in my career, and I didn't want to go out with a record of meaningless statistics. I wanted to achieve something important by knocking off the country's biggest crooks."

An appraisal after settling into the new job convinced him that New York's agents were floundering in quixotic efforts against the area's five sizable borgatas. His first policy decision was to "turn the office over on its head" by raising the Cosa Nostra to the highest priority level. Previously, agents working Mob cases did a decent job in developing informers, but these liaisons produced few arrests. Welch was dismayed at the methods used by some agents to handle snitches. Informers usually became turncoats for money or as an insurance policy for leniency if they got jammed up in criminal cases. Under tacit agreements with New York agents, the informers were providing the bureau with seemingly inside information about the crime families. Welch, however, evaluated most of these tips as trivial gossip. It was a lamentable strategy that generated few concrete facts or evidence about important crimes and internal Mob developments. "We were getting general information, sort of a 'Who's Who' on relations in the families," Welch fumed. "And if something happened, we'd get a version of the event. It was the Mob's version of what they wanted us to know and we weren't going out there, investigating, doing any real work to find out if it was fact or fiction."

Welch gradually brought in a new cadre of assistants to devise strategies for a fresh campaign against the Mob. "I want you to play two ball games at the same time," he instructed the newcomers. "Continue the intelligence gathering but go after the top people. Lock somebody up!"

Many agents considered New York City a hardship post, mainly because of its expensive real estate. Almost all agents lived in the more affordable distant suburbs, but that entailed long commutes of up to three hours each way on clogged highways. Greater effort, longer hours, and tighter surveillance of mobsters were demanded by Welch. The fatiguing drives and home-life stress were disincentives for agents to put in extra hours trailing mobsters or ferreting out reluctant witnesses.

"The best thing to do for these agents is work them until their tongues hang out," Welch advised. "Make them forget they're in New York. Keep telling them they're doing significant work, that they are going to bring about important changes, and have a real effect on organized crime."

Kossler and Bonavolonta were two of Welch's first replacements. Both were in their thirties with records of adopting unusual tactics and the nerve to cast aside the bureau's petrified operational rules. With smoke plumes constantly lofting from his pipe and a contemplative mien, the red-haired Kossler could pass for a tweedy college professor rather than the rugged investigator that he had proved to be for over a decade. Unlike most agents, who had military or legal training, he had entered the bureau with a pedagogical background. A Pittsburgh native with a degree in education, Kossler specialized in teaching mentally retarded children before signing on with the bureau. A casual conversation with an FBI agent at a party whetted Kossler's interest in a career change that offered more thrills, more money, and more travel in a year than he would experience in a lifetime in a classroom.

Joining the FBI in 1970 at the tail end of Hoover's administration, Kossler was taught by sophisticated agents that the quickest escalator to success was churning out arrests of small-time criminals and hoodlums. The prevailing bureau success style was: compile a fat statistical portfolio of stolen cars, gambling, and other easily solved cases. "Your job performance was rated strictly on statistics, not the quality of arrests," Kossler said. "The word from older agents was to think about our work as being like a fireman's. We put out routine blazes every day, chalking up numbers until something big happens, like a kidnapping or a major bank robbery. Then we stop what we're doing and jump into the one big, high-profile case."

When Jimmy Hoffa vanished in 1975, Kossler was assigned to the New Jersey aspect of the investigation. He was on a squad dogging Anthony Tony Pro Provenzano, a northern-New Jersey teamster union official and Genovese family capo, suspected of a central role in arranging the abduction and presumed murder of Hoffa. The Hoffa mystery was a decisive juncture for Kossler, illustrating to him the Mafia's defiant contempt of law enforcement. By slaying a prominent labor leader and disposing of his body, the Mob blatantly demonstrated its power to maintain control of a union vital to its interests without fear of reprisal or government intervention. Kossler's probing into Tony Pro's bailiwick sharpened his understanding of the Mafia's covert and menacing ties to teamster locals. His prowess in digging up evidence for a New Jersey labor-racketeering squad brought Kossler to Welch's attention and earned him the job of organizing a similar unit in New York.

Welch understood that much of the Mafia's strength and wealth in New York was linked to the control of unions. As a partner for Kossler, Welch nominated an agent who thought along those same lines. He was Jules Bonavolonta. Lithe, a karate enthusiast, with boundless energy and a tart-tongued wit, Bonavolonta's inexorable hatred of mobsters stemmed from his childhood. Raised in Mafia-tainted Newark, New Jersey, he heard his father, an immigrant tailor from southern Italy, recount how hardworking Italian-Americans were harassed and threatened by neighborhood wiseguys. A boy in the 1950s, he witnessed crude shakedown attempts in his father's modest tailor shop. Years later, he proudly reflected on the courage his hard-pressed father had exhibited by never yielding a dime to mobsters.

Graduating from Seton Hall University, Bonavolonta was commissioned as a second lieutenant in the army and fought in Vietnam with the Special Forces, the Green Berets. The prospect of new adventures and meaningful accomplishments against mafiosi and other criminals brought him into the FBI in 1968. From the start he rebelled against the fossilized investigative system. With his street-smart Newark background, he sought undercover roles, believing them to be the most effective tool for gathering incriminating evidence against mobsters. In Bonavolonta's early years as an agent, the bureau frowned on such exploits. Even after his death and into the mid-1970s, Hoover's entrenched disciples in Washington opposed long-term undercover assignments as unproductive, costly ploys.

When organized-crime investigations did come his way, Bonavolonta usually disregarded official policy. He scraped up leads and evidence by hanging around Mafia bars, posing as a made guy and wiseguy. His main armament was the ability to imitate a swaggering mafioso style and an unflinching gaze through jet black eyes. His barroom bravado act in Brooklyn once almost erupted into a brawl and potential shoot-out with real wannabes. To Bonavolonta's dismay, he often was pulled off the streets for undesired duties. Before Welch rescued him, Bonavolonta's dreariest period was a desk job at headquarters in the J. Edgar Hoover building on Pennsylvania Avenue in Washington. Writing about his FBI days, he described that two-year stint as being trapped with "timeservers, ticket-punchers, and fat-assed desk jockeys sitting around doing not a hell of a lot of anything useful."

Neil Welch had a valid reason for dispatching Kossler, his labor-rackets specialist, and Bonavolonta, his organized-crime expert, upstate to Cornell. A lawyer as well as a masterful investigator, Welch kept abreast of criminal-law developments. He read law school reviews, sought out prosecutors and trial lawyers, and discussed legal conundrums with law professors. One professor who intrigued him was Bob Blakey, and he knew of Blakey's lament that for a decade the FBI had failed to grasp the significance of his pet project, RICO, the Racketeer Influenced and Corrupt Organizations Act.

Blakey had left Senator McClellan's committee in 1973 and moved to Cornell as a professor of criminal law and procedures. At the university, still searching for methods to counterattack the Mafia, he established a unique think tank, the Cornell Institute on Organized Crime. Starting in 1977, for two and a half years, Blakey took a break from teaching for an investigative job. He became chief counsel for the House of Representatives' thorny reinvestigation of President Kennedy's assassination, the inquiry that revealed how the Mafia profited from Kennedy's elimination, and that suggested that mobsters might have had a role in the murder.

Returning full-time to Cornell's law school afterward, Blakey cut back on cross-country stump speeches. His new approach was to sell RICO at summer seminars at Cornell. Through the prestige of the university's law school and the Institute on Organized Crime, he enticed state prosecutors into concentrating on his message in a relaxed, distraction-free campus setting. Another goal was to bypass the indifferent federal law-enforcement system by urging state officials to create "little RICO laws" modeled on the Congressional statute. This maneuver, he believed, could unleash a second legal front against the Mob.

Before Welch's arrival in New York, FBI officials there and in the rest of the country spurned Blakey's invitations for agents to attend the seminars. Typically going his own way, Welch ignored a mandate from headquarters that agents could attend training sessions only under official auspices at the FBI academy in Quantico, Virginia. He eagerly accepted Blakey's offer, and in the summer of 1979 sent the first FBI agents to participate in the RICO educational program.

In selecting Kossler and Bonavolonta, Welch knew he had two investigators with mind-sets similar to his own, committed to developing new strategies and tactics for grappling with New York's Mafia. Blakey's opening sessions on the RICO law, however, disappointed both agents. Before the trip, Bonavolonta was dimly aware of the statute; and while Kossler knew about its broad outlines, he was uncertain of its possible value to FBI investigators. Most of the hundred people at Cornell were state prosecutors, leading both agents to feel as if they were fish out of water, oddities to the other participants, who apparently understood the thrust of Blakey's lectures and his hypothetical case discussions. "It was mainly theoretical and the local prosecutors were interested in state systems that were not applicable to us," Kossler complained. "Jules and I kept asking, 'What are we doing here? We're not part of this fraternity.'" The seminar was a blend of college tutorials and an evangelical revival meeting. Articulate, with sparse graying hair, Blakey fulfilled the role of the prototypical professor clarifying the nuances of a groundbreaking law. But when drama was needed, Blakey would transform himself into a rousing circuit preacher. Reviewing a sixty-one-page history of labor racketeering in America that he had written for the program, Blakey railed, "The Mafia is a dread disease that is threatening to destroy the American labor movement. We need a comprehensive preemptive strike aimed directly at the heart of the Mafia. That is the only strategy for dealing with this cancer that has existed in America for more than half a century."

Suddenly, Kossler felt that the sermon's main message was aimed directly at him. He listened attentively as Blakey hammered away on two points. First: RICO must be twinned with Title III bugs and wiretaps as the only effective tactic for gleaning evidence. Second: investigators and prosecutors must stop wasting time on two-bit gangsters and focus entirely on royalty, the Mob bosses and their skilled ministers. "Work on the families, the enterprises, not low-level individuals," Blakey implored.

One of Blakey's favorite old movies, *Little Caesar*, which may have influenced the choice of a name that yielded the acronym RICO, was another device that the law professor used at the seminar. The movie was entertaining but he selected it to reinforce his notion that the dons should be the prime objective of investigators and prosecutors. In the film, Edward G. Robinson is cast as a ferocious thug named Caesar Enrico "Rico" Bandello, a killer clawing his way to the top of a big-city gang. Rico, however, is subservient to the city's real gangland colossus, a polished, tuxedo-wearing upper-class figure dubbed "Big Boy." A 1930s Hollywood stereotype of the crude, Italian immigrant gangster, Rico is ultimately gunned down by the police after murdering a prosecutor.

"Yes, Rico gets shot and killed in an alley," Blakey intoned to his audience of prosecutors and two FBI agents when the lights came on. "But what about Big Boy? He escapes punishment because he wasn't investigated." With elongated, dramatic pauses, Blakey then delivered the underlying motif of the weeklong seminar. "Nothing happens to Big Boy. He's still in charge. Nothing has really changed. That's the overwhelming value of RICO. It is designed to change the end of that movie."

Back in New York, Kossler and Bonavolonta were fervid converts to RICO. Their enthusiasm was endorsed by Welch but they needed more intricate explanations from Blakey on employing the law against the Mafia. Four months later, shortly before Christmas 1979, Welch authorized Kossler, Bonavolonta, and three other supervisors to meet with Blakey for a private tête-à-tête in Ithaca. At marathon sessions over two days, with meals sent into their small conference room at a Holiday Inn, Blakey amplified RICO's potential applications.

The professor outlined on a blackboard how RICO should be used to combat the Mafia. He told them that the statute included provisions on investigating, prosecuting, and obtaining long prison sentences. "You have to use all three theories, not just one," he said, pacing before the blackboard. "And you've got to attack their economic foundations through asset seizures and by bringing civil RICO cases."

Embalmed methods by federal prosecutors was another barrier the agents would have to surmount. "They want to make it simple and easy for themselves," Blakey said, critiquing federal attorneys. "They become scalp collectors, making a case against an individual and putting him in prison. That's nothing more than a merry-go-round and you've got to get off that ride. Force the prosecutors to do more. Show them that while individuals commit organized crimes, it's the organizations that make organized crime possible."

Another vital strategy was Blakey's "tip of the iceberg and dynamic probable cause theory" for installing bugs and wiretaps. Prosecutors, he cautioned, misunderstood the amount of evidence required to establish "probable cause" for obtaining court authorization for Title III electronic surveillance in RICO cases. The main thrust was to focus the investigation on an "enterprise" as outlined in the law, not a specific individual or crime like loan-sharking, extortion or gambling. The essential factor was "enterprise." Agents, he pointed out, could use informers, their own observations of mobsters gathering for obvious meetings, and records of a Mafia family's criminal history as evidence of an ongoing enterprise. Those facts would be sufficient to obtain authorization from a judge for an initial bug or wiretap applicable to RICO.

"Use what you get on the first wiretap or bug to get another," Blakey continued. "Then use the evidence from the first two bugs and taps to bug another meeting place or mobster's home."

Omertà—the Mafia code of silence and secrecy—could be outflanked by persistent electronic eavesdropping. "Don't pull a bug after you get confirmation and evidence for one easy conviction," Blakey added. "Climb the ladder until you get to the top of the organization. There's no defense against wiretaps and bugs."

Finally, he urged the agents always to think systemically and not about prosecuting specific crimes. "If you uncover evidence of a homicide, make the fact of the murder an item of evidence. Show a series of homicides and other crimes and you've proven the acts of racketeering. Demonstrate the existence and pattern of an enterprise and connect the murders and other crimes, and you've got a RICO indictment and almost certain conviction."

Because New York was the Mafia's largest regional fortress, Blakey stressed the implications of their war against the five families to his new acolytes. He envisioned that RICO victories in New York—with its media prominence and guaranteed nationwide publicity—would encourage FBI agents and U.S. Attorneys in the rest of the country to undertake similar campaigns.

As the agents settled into their car for the trip back to the city, Blakey stuck his head in the window and gave them his parting shot. "Right now, law enforcement is like a wolf to a herd of deer. You and prosecutors look for single cases, you pick off the sick and wounded, and only make the herd—organized crime—stronger."

Blakey's explanations at the private eight-hour meetings were an "epiphany" and an "adrenaline rush" for Kossler. "He unlocked my mind. He gave us a clear road map for investigating and making RICO cases. Before leaving Ithaca, I told him that the next time he writes a law he has to include a handbook so we'll know how to use it."

In New York, Kossler and Bonavolonta extolled Blakey's concepts, bending the ears of fellow agents and receptive higher-ranking personnel. Despite their zeal, the two agents were low on the FBI's bureaucratic totem pole, and they lacked the influential connections in Washington that would authorize a radical and expensive plan for challenging the Mafia.

Their first order of business in 1980 was to help Welch rectify the organizational mess that plagued New York's Mob investigations. Kossler pinpointed the worst problems as the secrecy, infighting, and internal rivalries for resources that afflicted the office's competing wings. Unlike other cities that had a single, unified FBI command, New York's immense size had spawned three jurisdictional divisions. The Manhattan office was the de facto headquarters for the entire metropolitan area, but there was a branch covering Brooklyn, Queens, and Long Island, and another in New Rochelle that was responsible for the vast northern suburbs and for the Bronx. Each of the three offices had a SAC, a Special Agent in Charge, who supervised all investigations and other criminal matters they felt to be in their province. Over time, the two outlying districts had evolved into semi-independent branches, often undertaking investigations without notifying anyone at headquarters in Manhattan.

The decentralization led to fragmented, uncoordinated efforts with embarrassing consequences. Kossler and Bonavolonta discovered that probes of Genovese family rackets had been compromised by overlapping chaos. One vivid example concerned Matty the Horse Ianniello, the Genovese capo who had been at the scene of Joey Gallo's murder at Umberto's Clam House. Ianniello was being separately investigated and trailed by four squads engaged in six different inquiries. There were ample reasons to home in on the Horse, the borgata's supervisor of protection kickbacks from topless bars and pornography shops in Times Square. Matty even profited from religion by exploiting Little Italy's annual San Gennaro Feast. Seated in an office atop Umberto's on Mulberry Street, the husky capo collected bribes from vendors seeking permission to operate food, gambling, and merchandise booths at the street festival from a front neighborhood civic group that was under the thumb of the Genovese family.

Trying to implicate Ianniello, competing surveillance teams were stumbling over each other and duplicating investigations. Even more depressing, the farcical probes had prematurely alerted Ianniello that he was a target.

Another mix-up involved a Genovese associate and big earner named Pellegrino Masselli, more popularly known in the underworld as "Butcher Boy." While one FBI jurisdiction was looking into Masselli's activities as a drug trafficker, hijacker, and hit man, another branch was trying to indict him for bribing politicians to obtain a multimillion-dollar subway construction contract. In a laughable episode, one group of agents was baffled as to the identity of a frequent confederate of Masselli's. The mystery hood turned out to be an informer sent to infiltrate Masselli's operations by another FBI unit that was working on a different case.

After several years of scrambled investigations, Matty the Horse was ultimately convicted of racketeering. The Masselli case, however, petered out in a confused jumble many years later on minor federal charges, and in acquittals and plea deals on state indictments. Masselli and former Secretary of Labor Raymond Donovan were among those cleared in 1987 of fraud and larceny charges arising from the subway corruption case.

"It is a total disaster entangled in miles of red tape," Kossler reported after reviewing the efforts of the three jurisdictions against the Mafia. "It's catch as catch can, with everyone going their own way depending on what cases they feel like opening. Then it's like a horse race to see who can come in first with an indictment."

Neil Welch's tenure in New York office ended abruptly, before all of his reforms were in place. A severe back ailment forced him into early retirement in 1980. His successor, Lee Laster, supported the moves begun by Welch, and he had Kossler draw up a blueprint for a drastic reorganization of Mob investigations. Bursting with ideas, Kossler produced a streamlined battle plan of 25 points. His proposals included: stripping the powers of the three regional SACs; centralizing operations by appointing one organized-crime supervisor in Manhattan; and extensive reliance on the RICO law and on Title III bugs and wiretaps to dislodge the leaders of New York's five Mob families.

The overall plan hinged on a drastic realignment of personnel. Kossler recommended the creation of five separate organized-crime squads, each with exclusive responsibility to investigate one of the powerful borgatas. No longer would squads in the three jurisdictions go their own rivalrous ways, investigating cases or families at will. In effect, the new units—the Gambino, Genovese, Lucchese, Colombo, and Bonanno squads—would parallel the Mafia's own organizational structure in the metropolitan area.

And, each squad would be weaned off small potatoes, inconsequential investigations. Their primary purpose would be to buttress high-level RICO inquiries and to concentrate on the Mafia's inexhaustible and gigantic gold mine—union and industry rackets. The long-range objective was the destruction of the family kingpins and the dismantling of their economic underpinnings.

"The bottom line is that the LCN is better organized than we are and we have to match them," Kossler reasoned. "We have to go after the hierarchies, seize their assets, change their culture. We can't allow these guys to endlessly pass the reins on to the next guy. In the past if we did convict a reasonably big player, all we accomplished was to create a vacancy—a career opportunity—for a younger guy to get a promotion."

Kossler's entire plan—his 25 points—was reviewed and approved in less than a month by Judge William Webster. The FBI director's alacrity astonished Kossler. It was a signal that along with Cold War espionage, the Mafia now was a high priority for the bureau. Webster gave another invaluable asset to New York by allowing it to use super-secret cameras and listening devices to spy on the Mafia. Previously, the sensitive equipment had been restricted to counterespionage cases. The equipment would reinforce a "special operations" group established solely to penetrate the five borgatas through extraordinary electronic and surveillance projects. The group was led by an imaginative ex-Marine officer and Vietnam veteran, James Kallstrom, an avid supporter of employing new RICO stratagems.

In the revamped organizational setup, Jim Kossler was promoted from "staff program manager" to Coordinating Supervisor for Organized Crime. He became the point man for overseeing Mob investigations. The consolidated five family-based squads were soon in place, but agents had to be reeducated about new goals and tactics, particularly the emphasis on labor racketeering. Before 1980, bread-and-butter work for mafiosi investigators consisted of standard extortion, gambling, and loan-sharking arrests and convictions. Normally, these cases were wrapped up with testimony from a victim, a recorded conversation of a shake-down, or a raid at a bookmaker's wire room. Labor rackets, however, were a different undertaking. These investigations were complex, requiring interpretations of recondite union rules, and uncovering secret deals between mobsters and corrupt union and management officials. Finally, to clinch guilty verdicts, paper chases were almost always required to trace tangled payoff schemes and the illegal flow of money.

The sudden shift in directions was a difficult adaptation for many mature agents. "They have a lot to learn about how Mob guys, their union counterparts, and industries operate," Kossler said wearily after he and Bonavolonta began briefing the new squads. "These are long, complicated cases and it makes their hairs hurt. But we have to reorient them into understanding that labor rackets is the highest priority."

Nineteen eighty—the radical transitional year for the New York office—ended with Jim Kossler's partner, Jules Bonavolonta, transferred to FBI headquarters in Washington. Both believed the move would benefit the long-range crackdown in New York. Bonavolonta was posted as second-in-command of the agency's new national organized-crime squad section. The job placed him in a prime position to get quick clearance from headquarters for any daring and wild escapades dreamed up in New York by Kossler and his troops.

Bonavolonta could also assist by reducing the crippling effects of a bureaucratic legacy inherited from the Hoover era. Every eighteen months, fruitful work was interrupted when an inspection team from headquarters descended on the field office. Nitpicking auditors had to certify that all regulations were being followed, that the expenditure of every penny and the use of every paper clip had been properly authorized. Additionally, inspectors compiled reports on the number of arrests produced by each unit and each agent. It was a carryover from the Hoover days when IGB (Illegal Gambling Business) arrest quotas were used to dress up the FBIs image at budget-crunching time in Congress. Agents mockingly referred to the inspections as the "invasion of the bean counters," and Bonavolonta kidded sarcastically that the inspectors would be unsatisfied until they succeeded in changing the FBI's name to the "Federal Bureau of Accountancy." The inspections had to be endured, but now Bonavolonta was strategically located to deflect and discard nuisance complaints forwarded to Washington. Almost certainly the myopic snoopers would recoil at New York's expensive, time-consuming, organized-crime operations that failed to produce immediate measurable results. It would be up to Bonavolonta to smooth out the problems.

As the five Mafia squads swung into action, Kossler invited Bob Blakey to speak to the agents and refine their thinking about compiling evidence for RICO cases. Kossler and FBI higher-ups knew they were confronting a foe with extraordinary resources. Confidential bureau reports in 1980 grimly acknowledged that the Cosa Nostra was one of the nation's most successful growth industries. Nationwide, it was raking in about $25 billion a year in illicit receipts—a conservative estimate. The "gross take" in the New York region before overhead expenses was estimated at between $12 billion and $15 billion, according to FBI and police department Mafia analysts.

Aware of the Mob's robustness, Blakey never ceased telling the agents that RICO was the ideal weapon for overcoming the Cosa Nostra. "What I'd love to see you guys do is bring a case against all the bosses in one courtroom," he told Jim Kossler over dinner one February night in 1980 at the Downtown Athletic Club in Manhattan. "I dream of indicting every boss in New York—the entire Commission."

As Kossler picked at his food, he thought to himself that it was easy for Blakey to fantasize about massive investigations of the Mafia's supreme leaders. The FBI was just beginning its first concentrated campaign and there was no guarantee of even small-scale victories. Kossler was a relatively low-ranking supervisory agent in a conservative, hidebound agency. How could he sell these risky, unprecedented concepts? How could he get the resources, the money, the manpower? He realized that if he catalogued all of Blakey's utopian proposals in an official memorandum, top officials at the FBI and the Justice Department would believe he had gone off the rails.

Yet without anyone specifically pushing a start button, a law school professor and the handful of FBI agents he inspired set in motion the machinery for a watershed event: the Commission case, an attack at the Mafia's heart.

21

The Big Boys

ive miles north of FBI headquarters, in a dingy storefront in East Harlem, a Genovese family leader was talking about the Commission. Indeed, he was demonstrating that body's dictatorial reach across the country.

"Tell him it's the Commission from New York. Tell him he's dealing with the big boys now."

Anthony "Fat Tony" Salerno delivered the commanding message to two envoys from Cleveland as he held court in his favorite redoubt, the Palma Boys Social Club, one morning in October 1984. The club was never a gathering site for boys or an adolescent recreational center. It was the business office and favorite meeting place of Tony Salerno, whose portly, genial demeanor belied his actual vocation. Salerno was recognized by the FBI and many mobsters throughout the nation as the boss of the Genovese crime family. Sipping coffee with his guests, Fat Tony was haranguing them to warn an upstart member of their group that New York bosses would make the ultimate decision on a leadership change in their Cleveland borgata. In effect, the New York Commission's sphere of influence extended as far west as Chicago. If a dispute involved a borgata further west, it was resolved jointly by the Commission and Chicago's Outfit.

Unlike other Mafia dons in New York, who were remote and reluctant to meet with outsiders, Salerno was accessible. Mafiosi from Cleveland, Philadelphia, New England, Buffalo, and other cities considered him a conduit for relaying important information to New York's other godfathers. They often consulted with him at the Palma Boys about internal problems that they wanted the Commission to consider and to resolve. Out-of-town emissaries always knew where to find Salerno.

The session with the Cleveland mobsters came at a time when the New York bosses were oblivious to the assaults the FBI was preparing against them, and Salerno had no qualms about invoking the supreme authority of the Commission, the Mafia's politburo. He felt particularly safe in East Harlem, which had been the center of his cosmos as boy and man. Salerno grew up in the neighborhood when it was exclusively Italian, remaining there as it gradually metamorphosed into Spanish Harlem, a predominately Puerto Rican barrio. In the 1980s, only a tiny pocket of elderly Italians and a scattering of Italian restaurants survived along a three-block stretch on First Avenue and the incongruously named urban avenue called Pleasant. It was an old-fashioned patch that suited Salerno's business needs. The compactness of the Italian zone was an asset, providing protection for his illicit undertakings. Prying strangers, undoubtedly cops or agents, were easily quarantined and their presence swiftly reported to Salerno's sidekicks.

Born in 1911, Salerno came of age as a gangster in the 1930s at the dawn of the Cosa Nostra's creation. Making his bones as a young man in the original and newly constituted Lucky Luciano family, he rose in the customary Mafia way, graduating from a loan-shark enforcer to a foreman of bookmaking, numbers, and loan-sharking activities for the family. East Harlem and adjacent Harlem were lush gambling territories and Salerno cashed in at an early age.

Luciano's gang eventually became known as the Genovese borgata, and Salerno was a lieutenant to Michael "Trigger Mike" Coppola, the top capo in East Harlem, who got into serious trouble in 1946. According to detectives, Coppola performed a favor for Vito Marcantonio, the neighborhood congressman. Trigger Mike assigned three of his boys to rough up a political ally who, Marcantonio suspected, had betrayed him in an election campaign. Coppola's sluggers went too far, killing the man by cracking his skull. The outrageous murder created headlines suggesting Mob involvement and a political motive for the homicide, factors compelling the normally obliging police to pressure Coppola. To escape the heat, Coppola fled to Florida. It was Tony Salerno's big break. Only in his mid-thirties, he assumed the reins of the Genovese capo in East Harlem and his fortune was assured.

As a soldier or button man, and later as a capo, Salerno endured several arrests on minor gambling charges that culminated in petty fines or quick dismissals. These brief interruptions of business were little more than expected, routine harassment in the charade performed by the police to meet arrest quotas and to demonstrate to the public that they were incorruptible. Salerno used an assortment of fictitious names, usually "Tony Palermo" or "Tony Russo" for these nuisance pinches in his younger years.

By middle age, Salerno's expanding girth of 230 pounds on his stocky five-feet seven-inch body earned him the underworld nickname Fat Tony. But once he established himself as a powerful figure in the Genovese family, no one dared utter that name in his presence. The Manhattan DA's office became acutely aware of his nickname and his importance in 1959, while investigating charges that he and other mobsters had a piece of a heavyweight title fight between Floyd Patterson and Ingemar Johansson at Yankee Stadium. Suspicions that Salerno and the Genovese family secretly financed the bout for a cut of the profits failed to pan out for the DA. No charges were filed, chalking up another legal victory for Fat Tony.

Preferring a low-key existence in East Harlem, Salerno was never spotted by investigators at gaudy Mob parties or nightclubbing at the Copacabana and other favorite Mafia bistros. His unpretentious, grubby lifestyle was accurately reflected in the Christmas card that he sent to cronies. Standing alone before a tree, the plump Mafia leader gazed dourly into the camera lens, attired in pajamas, a bathrobe, a cigar in his mouth, and sporting a baseball cap worn backwards.

Salerno's only major arrest came in 1977, at the age of sixty-six. The FBI roped him in on accusations that he was one of the city's biggest bookies and loan sharks, the head of a network with more than two hundred underground employees that grossed $10 million annually. At that time, gambling and loan-sharking arrests were FBI priorities and the bureau's main targets in its limited Mob investigations. Another favorite weapon against the Mafia was aimed at him, an income-tax evasion complaint. The indictment asserted that he reported an annual income of about $40,000 when he was actually pocketing more than $1 million a year from his rackets.

For his defense, Salerno hired Roy Cohn, an attorney known for his right-wing politics and power-broker connections, who could conjure up soft plea bargains for criminal clients. Cohn's high-profile status stemmed from his 1950s roles as an intemperate federal prosecutor in the controversial espionage convictions and executions of Julius and Ethel Rosenberg, charged with stealing atom bomb secrets for the Soviet Union. Later, he was Republican Senator Joseph McCarthy's main counsel during his erratic hunt for Communist subversives in the government and in the army. In private practice, Cohn became a favorite of indicted mobsters and was whispered to have influence as a deal maker with judges and prosecutors, thanks to his political liaisons.

Two trials on the income-tax accusations ended indecisively, with deadlocked juries. Cohn then worked out a bargain with federal prosecutors. Salerno pled guilty to reduced charges on one felony count of illegal gambling and two tax misdemeanors in exchange for a promise of leniency. Before sentencing, Fat Tony appeared in federal court in a wheelchair, claiming he was beset by life-threatening illnesses. Denying that his client was a gangster, Cohn characterized him merely as an avid "sports gambler," imploring the judge to consider Salerno's advanced age, frail health, and his unblemished record.

The tactic worked. Instead of a minimum sentence of two years, Salerno received a light term of six months and was fined $25,000. As part of the deal, Cohn got gambling charges dropped against six codefendants, including Salerno's brother Cirino. Upon hearing the judge's decision, Fat Tony said softly, "Thank you." He had good reasons to be grateful. The abbreviated sentence allowed him to be jailed in a minimal-security lockup in downtown Manhattan from which he could easily communicate with his underlings, instead of serving time in a harsher, distant penitentiary.

His legal difficulties resolved, Salerno was back on the streets in late 1978, following a predictable schedule. Mondays through Thursdays he spent most mornings and afternoons at the Palma Boys Social Club, his headquarters on East 115th Street between Pleasant and First Avenues. The club—a largely bare, single room—was decorated in standard mid-twentieth-century mafiosi fashion: there was a bar with an espresso machine, and a sprinkling of card tables and hard-backed wooden chairs. The rear section, about a third of the entire space, was reserved as Salerno's makeshift private office, where his most trusted courtiers and invited guests were allowed to confer with him around a worn table. A few steps from his club, above a fruit and vegetable store, Salerno maintained a first-floor railroad flat in a tenement building. A private street entrance leading only to his apartment door guaranteed privacy and enhanced security.

Every Thursday or Friday, Salerno changed his environment. From the ghetto tenement, he was driven two hours to rural Rhinebeck in the Hudson River Valley, site of his one-hundred-acre estate, the Spruce Bar Ranch, its entrance flanked by two massive white stone stallions. Here he raised thoroughbred horses. His lackeys were under instructions never to trouble him with Mob business on the long weekends spent with his wife and son in the unspoiled countryside. Whatever problems that arose in his enterprises waited until the carefree weekend was over, and no business meetings were held at the ranch.

Like clockwork, by 10:00 A.M. every Monday, Salerno was ensconced at the Palma Boys. When the skies brightened, Salerno, using a cane after a slight stroke in 1981, ventured outside to sun himself on a sidewalk chair in front of the club, surrounded by his faithful coterie. Puffing on a cigar, dressed in a fedora and crumpled clothes, Salerno appeared to passersby as a nondescript, aged pensioner, whiling away serene days, laughing at innocent small talk.

In the early 1980s there seemed to be no end to the pleasant times for Salerno and most Mafia leaders in New York. Fat Tony and his Cosa Nostra colleagues blithely conducted their businesses as they and their predecessors had for decades. They envisioned no reason to alter their lifestyles or customs. Secure in their privileged castles—their social clubs, homes, restaurants, cars— they talked freely about Mafia affairs. In these sanctuaries, they felt invulnerable and immune from electronic spying by lawmen. If serious external danger loomed, they apparently took no notice—even though there were abundant warning signs.

None of the bosses paid much heed to internal events within law enforcement in 1981. Eleven years earlier, in 1970, with much fanfare, New York Governor Nelson Rockefeller and the state legislature had created the state's Organized Crime Task Force. State politicians were belatedly responding to the embarrassing series of U.S. Senate hearings in the 1950s and 1960s that focused on the Mob's operations and its union rackets in the New York City metropolitan region. The task force's assignment was to investigate and coordinate cases that overlapped different counties and district attorney jurisdictions. Once established, however, it became a political boondoggle, achieving little more than providing patronage employment for lawyers pretending to be prosecutors and for former police officers looking for unchallenging retirement jobs as investigators. During its first eleven years, the unit was a monumental flop, failing to produce one significant investigation, indictment, or conviction under Republican administrations.

Deciding to breathe life into the moribund task force, in 1981 two Democratic officials, New York Governor Hugh Carey and Attorney General Robert Abrams, jointly appointed a new director to lead the agency. He was Ronald Goldstock, a lanky, six-foot-tall lawyer with a lengthy résumé of prosecuting rackets cases in the Manhattan DA's office and uncovering corruption as the acting inspector general for the U.S. Labor Department. A native New Yorker, a Harvard Law School graduate, Goldstock was well versed in the history of the New York Mafia. More significantly, he had helped run Bob Blakey's Institute on Organized Crime at Cornell and was impatient to apply Blakey's untested prosecutorial theories: attack the Mob's hold on legitimate industries and labor unions, and rely on Title III wiretaps and bugs to dig up vital evidence and intelligence.

When Goldstock explained his operational plans, Governor Carey replied, "Go do it. You have a free hand." On his first day at the task force's main office north of the city in suburban White Plains, Goldstock walked into a stagnant scene. Lawyer-prosecutors were reading newspapers and concentrating on crossword puzzles, many with their feet on their desks, oblivious to the presence of their new leader. "Not only do they have nothing to do but they don't care," a stunned Goldstock thought to himself. Even more shocking, he discovered that the agency's intelligence files were virtually worthless and that its records revealed no previous interest in going after the Mob in New York City and in Long Island, its two largest bastions in the state.

In short order, Goldstock chopped off the office's dead-wood do-nothing personnel. With a beefed-up annual budget of almost $3 million, he tripled his staff to 140, bringing in prosecutors and investigators, most with experience in handling complex criminal cases. Leaving no doubt about his intentions, Goldstock announced in July 1981 that he was targeting the Mafia's domination of key industries and unions, and its narcotics trafficking. "This is a critical time," the enthusiastic gangbuster warned in press interviews, specifying that his sights were on high-echelon mobsters—the bosses.

As the state was revving up its drive, there was more grievous news for the Bonanno family and the Commission. The FBI jubilantly disclosed—also in 1981—that an agent for the first time had infiltrated a Mafia family—a Bonanno crew—and that indictments of Bonanno members were imminent. Agent Joseph Pistone, under the name "Donnie Brasco," had successfully posed as a wannabe for almost six years. Assigned to a hijacking squad, Pistone's original objective was to identify and destroy big-time fences. But he wormed his way into a Mob crew in New York, as an earner and associate, and his mission expanded to an unimaginable extent: a Bonanno capo was ready to sponsor him for induction into the borgata. Besides the wealth of solid criminal evidence Pistone had unearthed, his exploit provided a rare peek into the mind-set of New York's rank and file mafiosi. During idle banter, Benjamin "Lefty Guns" Ruggiero, an undistinguished Bonanno soldier, gave "Donnie Brasco" and another undercover agent named "Tony," a crash course on the advantages of enlisting in the Mob. "What the fuck, Donnie, don't you tell this guy nothing?" Lefty Guns said. "Tony, as a wiseguy you can lie, you can cheat, you can steal, you can kill people—legitimately. You can do any goddamn thing you want, and nobody can say anything about it. Who wouldn't want to be a wiseguy?"

Beyond the possible damage inflicted by Pistone's embarrassing penetration of the Bonanno family, Commission members had cause for even greater alarm. Lefty Guns had used Pistone on cooperative ventures with other families in New York, Florida, and Milwaukee, thereby implicating members of several borgatas and possibly compromising the Commission itself.

Mafia reaction to Pistone's emergence as an FBI spy came quickly. Tipsters informed agents that Mob big shots were offering a $500,000 reward to the hit men who got Pistone or his wife and children before he could testify. The agent and his relatives were relocated with twenty-four-hour protection. Assuming that the murder contract had been authorized by the Mafia's highest authorities, agents Brian Taylor and Pat Marshall paid a nighttime call on Fat Tony Salerno, one of the suspected members of the Commission. They found him in his East Harlem apartment retreat with his most trusted lieutenant, Vincent "Fish" Cafaro. The agents made their point sharply: massive retaliation would befall the Mafia if Pistone and his relatives were harmed or threatened. "Get the word out, Tony; leave Pistone alone," Taylor said. "We don't hurt cops, we don't hurt agents," an unruffled Salerno replied. "Hey, you boys have a job to do, you got my guarantee." Walking out of the apartment, Marshall who had often encountered arrogant, foul-mouthed mafiosi, made a mental note to himself about Salerno's behavior. "Whatever else he was, to us he acted like a gentleman."

No harm came to Pistone and his family.

There were immediate consequences inside the Bonanno family from Pistone's masquerade and infiltration. Soldiers held responsible for Pistone's triumph were killed or ousted. Other families and the Commission shunned the already distrusted Bonannos as unreliable pariahs, cutting them out of any joint rackets. Pistone's evidence convicted Lefty Guns Ruggiero and several other minor Bonanno soldiers and associates on racketeering charges, but the other New York families and their bosses for the moment appeared to have escaped unscathed.

Yet throughout 1982 and 1983, there were clear signs that the Mafia and its widespread illicit businesses were under intensive scrutiny. The *New York Times* in April 1982 detailed the Mob's incredible hammerlock on the city's billion-dollar construction industry. A series of articles, headlined "Tainted Industry," described how rigged bids and combined union-mobster corruption were siphoning millions of dollars and inflating building costs on major public and private projects. The centerpiece story revealed that a cartel of suppliers and contractors with links to the Mafia had saddled the city with the highest concrete costs in the country—70 percent greater than in comparable parts of the Northeast. High-ranking mobsters who split kickbacks from the arranged deals called the select contractors "the club." And the group was concerned mainly with the city's most expensive undertakings, resulting in owners raising commercial and residential rents to make up for the excessive construction bills.

Every Manhattan multimillion-dollar project in the late 1970s and early 1980s was victimized by "the club," the *Times* reported. Among the well-known places hit with invisible Mob taxes were the huge Battery Park City development, the Helmsley Palace Hotel, the IBM Building, and Trump Tower. Also affected was a public showplace, the state's Jacob Javits Convention Center, where state auditors had estimated that the concrete work should cost no more than $18 million, including a healthy profit for the contractors. The Mob game plan, however, permitted only two controlled contractors to bid and their prices were $30 million and $40 million. Shocked officials negotiated the low bidder down to $26.5 million, still $8 million above their own evaluation. Several years later these concrete companies—an entity known as Nasso-S&A—that were awarded the excessive contract dissolved after disclosures that they had a secret partner—Fat Tony Salerno.

Even President Ronald Reagan sounded alarm bells about the Mafia's growth. "Today, the power of organized crime reaches into every segment of our society," Reagan dramatically announced in a televised speech on October 14, 1982, from the Great Hall of the Justice Department. Citing information that Attorney General William French Smith had presented at a special cabinet meeting, Reagan said that the Justice Department was taking a new tack. Henceforth it would "more vigorously prosecute the Mob, including use of the

RICO statute to confiscate more of its financial assets." He ordered federal agencies, essentially the FBI, to forge closer ties with state and local law-enforcement units in a combined campaign against the Mafia. Reagan was in effect officially abolishing J. Edgar Hoover's decades-old noncooperation policy of refusing to share information. Indicating that his administration would be far more aggressive than previous ones in confronting the Cosa Nostra, Reagan added that he was appointing a special presidential commission to recommend further steps against organized crime.

Gratified by the encouragement from Washington, FBI officials in New York began proclaiming that serious blows would soon befall the chieftains of the five families. They spoke publicly and confidentially about their work against the Mob as no other lawmen had in the past. Scores of indictments were in the offing, Thomas L. Sheer, the head of the bureau's criminal division in New York, boldly forecast in August 1983. "Our main focus is the hierarchy of the five families and these indictments will be significant and in large numbers," Sheer was quoted in news stories. "We are not going after fringe players." Sheer revealed that the New York office had adopted Jim Kossler's plan for tackling the Mob: almost two hundred agents were deployed on investigations, and five FBI squads had been formed to concentrate on each of the crime families.

Another self-proclaimed Mafia opponent arrived in July 1983. It was the new U.S. Attorney for the Southern District of New York, the jurisdiction that covered Manhattan, the region's hub for developing major criminal and civil cases. The appointee to the prestigious office was thirty-nine years old and his name was Rudolph William Giuliani.

After graduating from New York University Law School, Giuliani proved himself a fierce prosecutor and masterful cross-examiner as an assistant U.S. Attorney in Manhattan from 1970 to 1975. A Democrat in his earlier years who had voted for the party's liberal presidential candidate George McGovern in 1972, Giuliani by the 1980s had become a devoted Republican. Reagan's Republican administration chose him for the number-three post in the Justice Department as the associate attorney general in charge of the criminal section. When the U.S. Attorney's post in Manhattan became vacant, Giuliani opted for it, even though it was technically a lower rank than the Justice Department job he held in Washington. Explaining his decision, Giuliani said that heading the Southern District was the most challenging law-enforcement position in the country, and he had coveted the job since his apprentice days as a prosecutor. What Giuliani kept to himself was precious inside knowledge known only to a select handfull of FBI and Justice Department officials. He had been briefed about the full extent of the investigative nets being spun to ensnare New York's Mafia bosses.

A self-confessed workaholic, bordering on the chubby side, Giuliani's behavior ranged from unrelenting, steely-eyed litigator in the courtroom to convivial companion when discussing his favorite pastimes, attending the opera and rooting for the New York Yankees. The new U.S. Attorney knew how to turn a phrase, and newspaper and television reporters found him highly quotable. On taking over the Southern District, he was asked how he would use his 130 prosecutors. His ready reply: undermining the Mafia and narcotics trafficking were the highest priorities on his agenda. "The attack on the families is an excellent approach," he told interviewers, endorsing the FBI's new strategy and tactics while simultaneously warning that missiles were being prepared for the godfathers.

Citing his personal history, Giuliani emphasized to reporters the shame that the vast majority of Italian-Americans felt because of the depravities of the American Mafia. A native New Yorker and fourth-generation Italian-American, he said that his hatred of mobsters arose at a young age from listening to relatives relate the injuries inflicted on his own family. At the turn of the century, Black Hand extortionists demanded payoffs from one of his immigrant great-grandfathers, who had opened a cigar store. Another relative, a baker, committed suicide because he had been unable to meet the tribute demands of the Mafia. Frequently, Giuliani mentioned in interviews and speeches his pride in the law-enforcement achievements of his immediate family. Five uncles had been on the New York police force and a policeman cousin had been killed interrupting a holdup.

Giuliani's incentive against the Mafia might also have been motivated by a need to erase shadows that clouded his family's past and of which he never spoke publicly. Long after Giuliani's prosecutorial days were over, after his second election as mayor of New York, the criminal records of his father, an uncle, and a cousin were exposed. In a biography published in 2000, *Rudy*, investigative journalist Wayne Barrett wrote that in 1934 Giuliani's father, Harold, at age twenty-six, jobless in the Depression, had been arrested for holding up a milkman making his collection rounds in a Manhattan apartment building. Harold pleaded guilty to robbery in the third degree and served a prison sentence of sixteen months. Barrett also asserted, without providing court documentation, that Harold Giuliani collected payments in the 1950s and 1960s for his brother-in-law, Rudy's uncle, who was a reputed Brooklyn loan shark and a business partner of a made man. Barrett alleged that the uncle's son, Lewis D'Avanzo, a cousin and schoolmate of Rudy's, had worked with the Colombo and Gambino families in the 1960s and 1970s. Court records show that D'Avanzo served a prison sentence in 1969 for truck hijacking. Out on parole, he was shot and killed in 1977 by FBI agents investigating a stolen-car ring.

Whatever factors motivated Giuliani, there was no question within law-enforcement circles about his fervor to demolish the Mafia. Six months into the job as U.S. Attorney, in January 1984, his dark eyes turned grave when he related the victimization of his great-grandfather in an interview. He underlined what a great joy it would be to personally conduct a courtroom prosecution of Cosa Nostra bosses. "There are a couple of cases that I'm thinking about," he said, an obvious indication that indictments were imminent.

Regardless of the headlines about the government's determination to get tough with New York's Mafia legions, some politicians apparently were willing to lobby on behalf of convicted mafiosi. Early in Giuliani's tenure, New York Senator Alfonse D'Amato, a Republican, telephoned him about the imposition of a prison sentence on Mario Gigante, whom the government had identified as a Genovese capo. Found guilty of loan-sharking and extortion, Gigante was seeking a reduction of an eight-year term. D'Amato, the sponsor of Giuliani's appointment as a U.S. Attorney, apparently indicated that the sentence appeared severe.

Giuliani said that he had rebuked D'Amato for making the suggestion and opposed reducing Gigante's imprisonment. Two years, however, were cut from Gigante's original term after a motion was filed by Roy Cohn. Fish Cafaro, a Genovese soldier, later claimed that he had delivered $175,000 in cash to Cohn for securing the shortened term and he assumed the money was used for a "reach" or payoff.

About that same time in the early 1980s, a similar intervention was initiated by a group of New York politicians for another Genovese mobster and big earner, Vincent DiNapoli, who had pleaded guilty to labor-racketeering charges. His codefendant, Theodore Maritas, the head of the city's carpenters' union, had disappeared after his indictment, and prosecutors believed that the Mob killed him because it feared he might become a rat. Coming to DiNapoli's aid were Congressman Mario Biaggi, a Bronx Democrat, and a bipartisan group of four state legislators. They urged a federal judge to suspend DiNapoli's five-year sentence. Three of the five elected officials said they knew DiNapoli personally and recommended that he be freed to help underprivileged youths find work in the construction industry, the same industry that he had been convicted of corrupting. After a strong protest from federal prosecutors in Brooklyn, the judge refused to modify the sentence. (Congressman Biaggi was convicted by Giuliani's office in 1988 of accepting bribes to steer government defense contracts to a Bronx manufacturer, the Wedtech Corporation.)

Well-placed New York politicians might appear to be oblivious to the Cosa Nostra's activities, but suddenly there was a hardening of attitudes in high law-enforcement ranks. And, if New York's dons needed more ominous clues in 1984 that dangerous times were ahead, they simply had to ponder the words of the FBI. "We are going to make a hell of a dent in the five families," Sheer, the FBI official, pledged. In a page-one *New York Times* interview, he dropped a strong hint of why the bureau was so confident that the bosses were dead-center in its crosshairs. A large part of the evidence was flowing freely from "electronic eavesdropping and telephone taps." Sheer was telling the truth.

22

Operation Jaguar

Pelting rain shrouded Jack Breheny and two partners as they scrambled over the rattling chain-link fence. It was ideal weather for the trio's commando-style operation: breaking into a new XJ-6 Jaguar and planting a bug in the stylish sports car of a prime Mafia capo.

An electronics crackerjack for New York's Organized Crime Task Force, Breheny dropped to the ground from the five-feet-high barrier. Now he was safely inside the huge parking lot of the catering hall. Seconds later, technician Jim Stroh and investigator Richard Tennien pitched themselves over the fence. Not a person was in sight as they moved silently, crouching, some one hundred feet to the black Jaguar. "Thank God for the storm," Breheny thought. "Perfect cover. Who would wander around in a parking lot or keep a head up in this monsoon?" Breheny had a key ready for the Jag's door but, in another piece of good luck, it had been left unlocked. Tennien was the first inside the car, squatting in the rear, aiming his searchlight at the dashboard. Using ordinary screwdrivers, Breheny and Stroh dismantled the front instrument panels. The brawny six-feet-three-inch-tall Breheny left the delicate work of wriggling under the open compartment of the dashboard to the smaller, wirier Stroh. Without exchanging a word with his companions, Stroh used strips of electrical tape to attach a half-inch microphone and a three-inch transmitter to the inside of the dashboard's instrument panel cover. When the miniature devices were in place, he connected them with a spidery-thin cable to the car's fuse panel, which was already wired to the battery. The battery would provide "the juice," the power for operating the bug and the transmitter.

Together, as they had rehearsed in practice sessions, Breheny and Stroh replaced the front section of the dashboard cover. Their job done, both men trotted to the fence and scaled it. Tennien remained behind another minute or two. Removing the plastic covers that he had tossed over the front and rear seats and floors, Tennien mopped up several damp spots with a towel. This was insurance against leaving incriminating puddles, watery traces that the car had been secretly entered. His cleanup completed, Dick Tennien climbed over the fence, rejoining his teammates. Their astonishing exploit of bugging the mobile headquarters of the head of the Lucchese crime family had taken less than ten minutes. But more than a year of exhaustive surveillance and patient analytical groundwork had prepared the way for their smooth success in 1983.

The Jaguar project stemmed from the reorganization of the state's anti-Mafia task force begun in 1981 by its director, Ronald Goldstock. His objective was to cast aside reactive, catch-as-catch-can techniques of investigating Mob-related crimes after they had been committed. Goldstock divided his newly recruited staff into teams, directing them to find "nontraditional" solutions for cleansing industries known to be under Cosa Nostra control or influence. Each team had a complement of investigators and prosecutors to dig up the necessary criminal evidence for potential indictments and civil proceedings. And Goldstock added another element to the mixture. He brought in sociologists, economists, union reformers, and historians as consultants. Their role as analysts was to propose oversight legislation, regulations, and other solutions that would permanently reform Mob-contaminated industries. Goldstock wanted to end the frustrating cycle of criminal trials that sometimes removed one stratum of mobsters only to see them replaced by a new tier of predators.

In the early 1980s, every law-enforcement agency knew that garbage pickups, carting, and dumping in the New York metropolitan area were manipulated to a large degree by the Mob. Federal and local intelligence files were replete with informers' tips and confidential complaints from intimidated refuse carters about gangsters skimming money from their businesses. Yet the illicit practices flourished without meaningful intervention by the government. The convenient excuse for inaction was that honest carters were too frightened of retaliation to cooperate with the authorities, let alone dare to testify openly in court. Despite the known obstacles, Goldstock decided that the waste-disposal industry was one area to set his sights on. Early in 1982, six months after he assumed command of the task force, a team began to explore the Mafia's hold over carting companies in Long Island's two heavily populated counties, Nassau and Suffolk.

Almost every carter and detective on the island knew which Cosa Nostra group had turned Long Island's tons of trash into gold. The Lucchese family was the culprit. Years earlier, Mob informers had pinpointed for the FBI and local detectives the identity of the Lucchese leader who had concocted the basic scheme of monopolizing refuse removal on Long Island. His name was Antonio "Tony Ducks" Corallo.

Another Mafia success story from East Harlem, Corallo in his teens worked briefly as a tile setter before discovering his true calling. In the 1930s, he came under the tutelage of a future godfather, Tommy Three-finger Brown Lucchese. A dedicated Lucchese student, Corallo learned from his master the basic urban Mafia arts. The curriculum included loan-sharking, hijackings, and the more refined practices of teaming up with corrupt union stooges to shake down Garment Center companies by threatening unionization drives and work stoppages. Narcotics trafficking was another advanced course in Corallo's studies, but Harry Anslinger's indomitable drug agents captured him in 1941 with a cache of heroin worth about $150,000 wholesale, and hundreds of thousands of dollars after being "cut" for retail street sales. Corallo got a light term of six months, leading mafiosi to speculate that Lucchese thought so highly of Corallo as his main liege man in the Garment Center that he used his Democratic political pull and a payoff to sway the sentence.

From 1941 to 1960, Corallo was picked up a dozen times as a suspect in murder, robbery, hijacking, and extortion cases. All of the charges were dismissed before trial. Lucchese found Corallo's finesse with the law and ability to dissuade prosecution witnesses so amusing that he manufactured the enduring nickname for his assistant by remarking, "Tony ducks again." Corallo's elusiveness also earned a backhanded compliment from Senator John McClellan at one of his labor-racket hearings. "He is one of the scariest and worst gangsters we ever dealt with."

His luck with the law dimmed slightly in the 1960s. In 1962 he was convicted together with a federal judge, and a former U.S. Attorney, of attempting to fix a bankruptcy case. Ducks got a two-year sentence, but the charges demonstrated his and the Mafia's inordinate ability to reach important figures in the criminal justice system. Another example of Corallo's political agility surfaced in 1968 when he was enmeshed in a bribery scheme involving a close aide to New York Mayor John Lindsay. Along with former Tammany Hall leader Carmine DeSapio, Corallo was convicted of bribing a Lindsay administration commissioner, James L. Marcus, to rig a multimillion-dollar maintenance contract for a Mob company to clean city reservoirs. The conviction resulted in another stretch of two years for Corallo in a federal prison.

Before the two prison interludes, Tony Ducks's attention in the 1960s had turned to trash. Shortly after World War II, the prescient Corallo observed the population boom in the suburbs and planted the Lucchese family flag on Long Island. He moved there as the Lucchese's reigning capo, to exploit postwar suburban expansion. Long Island, a semirural suburb before the war, experienced a population boom that soared to two million by the 1960s. Corallo's initial rackets there in the 1950s were gambling, loan-sharking, and, through Jimmy Hoffa and other corrupt officials in the teamsters' union, extorting the army of developers and contractors building homes and businesses in vast tracts on the island. By the mid-1960s the construction industry had waned, but Long Island's rapid growth had transformed garbage-carting from a minor legal moneymaker into a perennial multimillion-dollar conglomerate. Corallo recognized its potential.

Tommy Lucchese died in 1967. Tony Ducks was his natural heir, and even though he was in prison on the reservoir-contract graft rap, the leadership was reserved for him. A capo specializing in narcotics, Carmine "Gribbs" Tramunti, held the fort temporarily as interim boss until he was indicted on narcotics charges. Released in 1970, Tony Ducks, at age fifty-seven, was installed as the Lucchese borgata's undisputed godfather, with a seat on the Commission. Bribes and Mob influence with guards for gourmet food and soft prison work details had allowed Corallo to lead a relatively comfortable penitentiary life. He emerged in good health with a potbelly. Befitting his elevated rank and prominence, Corallo built a $900,000 house in a posh section of Oyster Bay Cove on Long Island's affluent North Shore. Looking respectable and owlish behind horn-rimmed glasses, the graying Mob mandarin maintained to the IRS that his wealth came from the dress factories he owned. His coffers were actually overflowing from his entitlements to a percentage of all of the family's plunder and the new cash cow—Long Island's garbage.

The linchpin to controlling the industry was a so-called trade association, Private Sanitation Industry, Inc., formed by Corallo and his brethren. Ostensibly, the group's purpose was to handle collective-bargaining negotiations and to promote the growth of the carting business in Suffolk and Nassau Counties. In fact, the association was run by Corallo's vassals as a cartel to carve up collection routes, rig bids on public trash-removal contracts, suppress competition, and punish and rough up dissenters. Each carter paid $5,000 a year for the privilege of membership in the association, plus whatever secret shake-downs Corallo's minions imposed. The benefits for compliant association members were plentiful. They were guaranteed business at rates that ensured sizable profits since all extra costs or kickbacks to the Mob were passed along through higher prices to their helpless customers. Another blessing was labor peace through Corallo's alliance with the Gambino-run Teamsters' Local 813, which represented most of the carters' employees. Without Tony Ducks lifting a finger, the trade association deals lined his pockets every year with $200,000 to $400,000, and a similar payoff went to Gambino big shots for their help in controlling the teamsters.

The Organized Crime Task Force's quest was to find a gap in Corallo's armor, pry open a case on him and prove his criminality in the carting industry. The unit had no informers within the Lucchese family or in the carters' association who could substantiate probable cause for a court-authorized wiretap on Corallo's home phone. Two prison terms had increased Tony Ducks bent for secrecy and insulation. He never visited any of his family's neighborhood social clubs, although he made rare nostalgic trips to his boyhood haunts in East Harlem for a restaurant meal and a conversation with Fat Tony Salerno. Surveillance squads reported that Corallo met regularly only with a tiny corps of lieutenants. Those sessions were often conducted in parking lot "walk-talks," in which the boss strolled, spoke, and listened out of earshot of any investigators. When he dined with aides, Corallo used a wide variety of restaurants and diners, randomly chosen by him at the last moment or at a whim. Lacking advance notice where he might talk and compromise himself on a bug, the task force's investigation of Corallo seemed stymied until the appearance of an independent rebel carter. He was Robert Kubecka, a feisty volunteer willing to work under cover against a dangerous crime family.

Kubecka's father, Jerry, had started a small garbage-hauling business in Suffolk County in the 1950s before Corallo developed an acute interest in sanitation. The arrival of Lucchese wiseguys inaugurated chronic threats and vandalism that plagued the elder Kubecka. Nevertheless he kept his company going and refused to join the phony carters' trade association. In 1977, a weary Kubecka turned over daily supervision of the company to his son, Robert, and a son-in-law, Donald Barstow. Robert Kubecka, who had a degree in business management and a master's in environmental engineering, was immediately greeted with undisguised warnings. Like his father before him, he was cautioned by other carters and Lucchese leg breakers of the perils of being a maverick. But he resisted cooperating with gangsters and the carters' group. The Kubeckas provided an efficient, less costly service than the association's members offered, and a loyal clientele enabled their family business to survive. Equipped with only eight trucks, the Kubeckas were unable to compete with the association for large contracts. The smallness of the company was its salvation. The Lucchese hoodlums viewed the Kubeckas company as a minor nuisance that could be crushed if it ever challenged the cartel for highly profitable work.

Long before the state Organized Crime Task Force came on the scene, Jerry and Robert Kubecka had complained to the Suffolk County police authorities about the harassment and abuses they endured. Their reports were filed away without substantive results or redress for the embattled Kubeckas. Finally, in late 1981, Robert Kubecka found a receptive ear at the reinvigorated task force. One of the unit's new investigators, Dick Tennien, a former Suffolk County police detective, was aware of the Kubeckas' plight and their resistance to the rigged-bidding setup. Once a carter in the association signed a customer, called "a stop," no other company could compete for it, even if a new commercial or residential client took over the site. Kubecka's information about the system, known as perpetual "property rights," was added to the task force's intelligence dossiers. But it was "hearsay," supposition, inadmissible evidence in a criminal trial.

Mulling over a request from Tennien, Kubecka agreed in 1982 to participate actively in the investigation. He would wear a wire—a hidden mike. Although he was a thirty-two-year-old married man, the father of two young children, Kubecka willingly undertook the perilous, unsalaried undercover role. Investigators wanted him to seek out evidence and clues by chatting up carters in the association believed to be close to a central Lucchese player, Salvatore Avellino. Avellino, the owner of the Salem Carting Company, was more than an ordinary garbage hauler. Investigators were certain that he was the Lucchese capo who supervised Long Island's garbage money-making machine for Ducks Corallo. Kubecka wore a recording instrument strapped to his body underneath his shirt and was urged to turn it on when talking with carters trying to entice him into joining the corrupt group.

Kubecka never got close to the wary Avellino, but his efforts helped jump-start the case. Incriminating remarks and implied threats by association carters in the secretly transcribed conversations provided the task force with justification for a court-authorized wiretap on Avellino's home telephone. Avellino's telephone talks with Corallo advanced the investigation by allowing the task force to tap Tony Ducks' home phone—the cumulative tactic advocated by G. Robert Blakey. But the results were disappointing. Both mafiosi, cognizant of law-enforcement's ability to eavesdrop on telephone lines, used their home phones only for routine domestic matters. Not the slightest glimmer of Mob or garbage-industry corruption emanated from their conversations.

The telephone taps, however, did reveal a seemingly innocent routine. Most mornings, Avellino left his upscale suburban home in Nissequogue, slid behind the wheel of his glistening $100,000, 1982 Jaguar, and drove 25 miles to Oyster Bay to pick up Corallo. For much of the day the capo was Tony Ducks's chauffeur as the boss attended to business and personal chores on Long Island and in the city.

With the wiretaps proving to be barren, Goldstock, Tennien, and other task force investigators focused on the Jaguar as an alternative hot prospect. Because Corallo spent hours being driven around—often with members of his Mob cabinet—the car had to be his nerve center for discussing vital family issues. But getting a court order to bug the car was tricky. The legal foundation—or probable cause—for electronic eavesdropping normally rests on information from an informer, an agent, or from another bug, indicating that criminal activities were being planned in a specific site. While task force prosecutors could identify the Jaguar as the location used by two worthy suspects—Corallo and Avellino—they lacked proof that carting scams or other crimes were blocked out in the car.

For weeks Goldstock searched for a legal strategy that would justify a court order. One morning in March 1983, he awoke with an inspiration—"a message from God" is how he described it to his staff. The basis for the bug, he reasoned, could be built on a novel "probable cause" concept: "the relationship of parties." His eavesdropping application would contend that sufficient evidence indicated that Avellino was more important than a mere chauffeur. The task force could demonstrate that Avellino was presumed to be the Lucchese family's carting specialist, a "sounding board" and "liaison" for passing on orders issued by Corallo, the Mob family's boss.

Relying on affidavits from his state investigators and from FBI agents attesting to Corallo's lofty status and Avellino's reputed role in controlling Long

Island's carting industry, Goldstock's plan worked. But he got court permission to bug the Jaguar only after surmounting another quirky legal barrier. Avellino's Jaguar roamed through two counties on Long Island and five in New York City. A federal court order would cover a wide jurisdictional area, but Goldstock needed state court authorization to record conversations in seven different jurisdictions or counties. Rather than petioning a bevy of judges in a time-consuming process for identical orders, Goldstock devised a simpler approach. He found an appeals court judge whose jurisdiction included all of Long Island and the city boroughs of Brooklyn, Queens, and Staten Island. Another judge with authority to grant jurisdiction in the city's two remaining counties, Manhattan and the Bronx, completed the complicated process.

The legal underbrush cleared away, Goldstock's investigators and technicians still needed a plan to outwit Avellino and surreptitiously invade his Jaguar. Jack Breheny, the head of the task force's break-in and technical artists, knew from bitter experience as a New York City detective the abysmal record of car bugs. He had hidden several electronic devices in the interiors of auto seats used by mobsters, and the results had been miserable. Noise from car radios overwhelmed the conversations and the bugs' transmission ranges had been too limited to be picked up clearly in trailing vehicles. This time, however, the task force had new, state-of-the-art equipment that might succeed. In a fortuitous break, a state trooper who worked with the task force had a friend who owned an XJ-6 Jaguar model identical to Avellino's. Examining the car at a state police barracks, Breheny and his fellow technician, Jim Stroh, determined that there was only one place to secrete a bug that could be hooked easily to a power supply: a vacant space in the middle of the interior of the Jaguar's dashboard.

For three days, the two technicians and Dick Tennien, the lead investigator, experimented and rehearsed techniques for installing the bug. Finally they had it down pat. Once inside the vehicle, all they needed was four or five uninterrupted minutes. To save precious seconds, the task force obtained from the Jaguar company a key that would unlock Avellino's car door. The remaining obstacle was finding the right place and time to get at the Jaguar. Breaking in overnight while Avellino was asleep was ruled out. He parked the car in his own garage, and the interior of the garage, the house, and the approaches to the buildings were ringed with elaborate alarms.

Tennien came up with a long-shot possibility. From telephone taps, he learned that Avellino would attend the annual dinner-dance on March 23,

1983, of the Private Sanitation Industry, the carters' association dominated by the Lucchese family. Because no important mobster's car had ever been successfully bugged, Avellino might drop his guard at the dinner-dance and be temporarily careless about the Jaguar's security.

Accompanied by his wife, Avellino arrived at the dinner-dance in the Huntington Town House during a rain squall. Besides Breheny, Stroh, and Tennien in one car, nine other task-force investigators were trailing Avellino in unmarked cars as backup support for the commando unit. Handing his keys to a parking valet, Avellino was overheard saying he wanted the Jaguar parked far from the front entrance and away from other cars to avoid anyone accidentally scratching or damaging his precious vehicle. The Lucchese capo spent the rest of the evening dining and talking with other tuxedo-clad carters and politicians, while the rain-soaked investigators fulfilled their mission.

"We planned for everything to go wrong and instead everything went in our favor," Breheny said, rejoicing with his teammates that night after the bug had been installed. "It was amazing; it was meant to happen."

The next morning, in his customary manner Avellino eased the Jaguar out of the driveway of his home on Frog Hollow Road, ready for another day with Tony Ducks. An intricate surveillance system was in place to shadow the car and its occupants. The task force knew how vigilant Avellino and Corallo were on their trips together, counting on complex "dry cleaning" tricks to evade tails. Riding in the front passenger seat, Corallo always slanted the rearview mirror to keep his eyes on vehicles behind the Jaguar. Frequently, Corallo instructed Avellino to exit a highway precipitously and cut through back roads before reentering it. At other times, Avellino would pull onto the shoulder of an expressway for three or four minutes to lose any following vehicle. On city and suburban streets, Avellino would abruptly spin into a swift U-turn, to shake anyone who might be tracking him.

To outflank Corallo's defenses, the task force assigned five or six unmarked cars each day to alternate as the lead auto following the Jaguar. The drivers were positioned by a supervisor who told them on a radio hookup when to drop in and out of the pack pursuing Avellino. Each car, equipped with a transmission receiver, had to be directly behind and in sight of the Jaguar to pick up the signal from the bug. The task-force drivers could not hear the conversations in the Jaguar. Their cars were equipped with a high-tech "repeater system" that amplified and boosted the volume and the range of the transmission from the Jaguar, and relayed it to a van a mile or more behind. The van's huge antenna could not be spotted from the Jaguar, and the vehicle contained recording equipment that preserved every word uttered in Avellino's auto.

Delighted by their Jaguar success, Goldstock's investigators and prosecutors tuned in expectantly to Tony Ducks's conversations. Unfortunately, several weeks after the bugging began, Avellino and his wife left for a week's vacation in Florida. In their absence, the Jaguar stood idle in the garage and its battery was drained by the bug which continuously extracted power from it. Returning home, a chagrined Avellino could not start the car. Listening in on the telephone tap at the Avellino home, task force members heard his incensed wife call the dealer, demanding that he immediately repair the recently bought auto. Hearing that a tow truck was on the way to transport the Jaguar to the dealer's repair shop, investigators had to act quickly. Any half-bright mechanic would find the "hot wire" in the fuse box, sabotaging the eavesdropping project.

A hasty plan was whipped up by Fred Rayano, the task force's chief of investigators. He enlisted the aid of the local Suffolk County police who stopped the truck driver before he reached the garage with the Jaguar in tow. Police officers escorted the driver on foot to one of their vehicles, parked out of sight of the Jaguar. Making sure the driver's back was turned away from the Jaguar, the officers questioned him minutely about his towing permit and his special-driver's license. Confident the besieged driver was sufficiently distracted, a task force technician slipped into the Jaguar and pulled out the hot wire from the fuse panel that was connected to the bug. If the wire had been left inside, the dealers' mechanics would have traced the battery failure to the concealed microphone and transmitter. As the task force technicians hoped, the dealer was unable to explain the battery failure and simply installed a new one.

Two days later, his car running smoothly, Avellino stopped for a snack at a diner in Queens, parking in a crowded lot. It was the opportunity the task force needed. Using the skeleton key obtained by Jack Breheny, a technician entered the car, opened the fuse panel underneath the dashboard, and reconnected the "hot wire." In a few seconds, the Jaguar bug was again alive.

That spring and summer of 1983, Goldstock and other prosecutors in his office listened in wonderment to the unfettered conversations in Avellino's car. From their own mouths Tony Corallo and Sal Avellino implicated themselves and their cohorts in the garbage cartel and other Lucchese-borgata crimes. The tapes were also unearthing evidence more startling and important than the Mob rackets on Long Island. Decades before the Apalachin conclave in 1957 and Joe Valachi's defection in 1963, law-enforcement officials had heard rumors from informers about the Commission. Yet not a single tangible piece of evidence had ever been produced to convince a jury that the mysterious Cosa Nostra board of directors was a reality. As Goldstock studied the transcripts of the Jaguar conversations, he realized that the long-sought proof might be at hand. On the tapes, Corallo, Avellino, and other mafiosi were talking about an electrifying subject and discussing at length how it functioned. They were referring to it by a name—the Commission. It was an unimaginable windfall. The repercussions were beyond the most optimistic expectations of Goldstock and his staff.

23

Planting Season

While the state task force's electronic ears kept tabs on Salvatore Avellino's Jaguar, FBI equipment was similarly utilized in New York. With the zeal of Iowa farmers sowing fields in springtime, the bureau's eavesdropping virtuosos were planting a crop of bugging devices in the homes and hangouts of New York's highest-ranking Mafia potentates. From late 1982 into 1983, the intimate sanctuaries of leaders in the Colombo, Gambino, and Genovese families were penetrated by agent James Kallstrom's Special Operations division.

During the autumn of 1982, the FBI's Colombo Squad maintained a constant vigil on Gennaro Langella, better known by his street name, "Gerry Lang." The Colombo boss, Carmine the Snake Persico was in prison for violating parole on a hijacking conviction, and Langella, his underboss, was running the borgata as street boss. Known and feared for his ruthless arrogance as a loan shark and drug trafficker, Langella rarely made a statement that did not include a cascade of invectives. If he had a weakness, it was playing the gangster dandy among his roughly dressed associates. He was a vain clotheshorse. Unlike conservatively dressed Mafia royalty, Gerry Lang, favored the more contemporary Hollywood Gangster look: double-breasted blazers, sporty open-collar shirts, topped off with wraparound sunglasses.

Agents noticed that on most evenings Langella showed up at the Casa

Storta, a simple restaurant in Brooklyn's Bensonhurst section. Pretending to be couples on dates, female and male agents began dining at the Casa Storta. Langella always sat at a reserved table at the far end of the dining room, distant from other customers. At 9:00 P.M., the owner began closing up, imperiously shooing out patrons, refusing to serve them even a first cup of coffee. Gerry Lang and the wiseguys with him remained, and heaping plates of pasta, seafood, and veal were brought to their table. It was easy to see that the Colombo mafiosi considered the restaurant a snug, safe harbor to conduct their business, regardless of the chef's cuisine. Further confirmation of the place's importance came through an analysis of Persico's telephone calls from the federal prison in Danbury, Connecticut. Most of the Colombo boss's calls were to the Casa Storta.

The week before Christmas 1982, Kallstrom's tech specialists struck at 3:00 A.M. The tactics used to enter and bug the restaurant were similar to most "black bag" raids under Kallstrom's tight management. Lock men—deft-fingered artisans—led the assault. They neutralized alarm systems and entered buildings by swiftly manipulating with tiny metal instruments the most intricate burglar-resistant tumblers. Extreme care had to be exercised in picking a lock to avoid damaging or clogging it, thereby leaving evidence of a covert entry. At the Casa Storta, the lock men easily opened the padlocks on a sidewalk metal gate and on the restaurant's plate-glass front door. Inside, a second group of technicians moved in, installing mikes and transmission cables in the ceiling panels above Langella's favorite table. While the legal break-in was underway, case agents from the Colombo Squad ringed the area to alert the lock men and the technicians by radio if an intruder was in sight. The case agents were responsible for heading off anyone who might endanger or expose the technicians.

On the Casa Storta job, the tech men encountered one adversary—a watch dog inside the front door. Snarling Rottweilers and Dobermans were the favorite breeds used by New York mobsters to deter lawmen and other snoops. Black-bag agents were prepared to humanely subdue mean-tempered canines, and a resourceful agent quieted the Casa Storta's barking dog with several blasts of foam from a fire extinguisher he had brought along for just that purpose. When the hidden microphones and transmitters were in place at the Casa Storta, the agents stationed in a listening post in a nearby apartment were ready to tune in and record Gerry Lang and his soldiers while they gorged themselves and talked freely.

An extra dividend from the Casa Storta expedition was the frequent appearance at Langella's table of a short, stout, fast-talking individual. He was identified as a made man named Ralph Scopo. Agents wondered why the acting boss hobnobbed almost every night with a lowly soldier. A check on Scopo's occupation provided the answer: he was president of the New York Concrete District Workers Council, the union whose members were a vital cog in every significant construction development in the city. To their surprise, the FBI agents had uncovered a tantalizing lead. The union leader representing thousands of laborers needed for constructing foundations, walls, and floors—the sinews of every high-rise commercial and residential building in Manhattan—was a Colombo mafioso. The dinnertime chats between Langella and Scopo piqued the FBI's interest in a new investigative avenue: the fixing of multimillion-dollar concrete jobs by the Colombos in concert with other Mafia families.

Based on the Casa Storta evidence, more Title III wiretaps and bugs were authorized by judges and were concealed in Scopo's union office and in his car, and his conversations with contractors unveiled his main value to Mafia bosses. Scopo was their "bagman," the collector of payoffs from concrete companies in a Mob-controlled and Mob-named "Concrete Club" that allocated contracts and fixed prices on all large-scale construction work in New York.

Next on the FBI's eavesdropping list was Paul Castellano, the boss of the Gambino family. He was number one on the FBI's private roster of most-wanted Mafia godfathers. Big Paul had inherited the leadership of the nation's largest Mafia family upon the natural death of his blood relative Don Carlo Gambino in 1976. The succession was in keeping with Castellano's charmed gangster-racketeer odyssey.

Born in Bensonhurst in 1915, Castellano's immigrant parents baptized him Constantino Paul. Paul's father, a butcher, supplemented his income by organizing an illegal lottery game known as the "La Rosa Wheel" in a section of their Brooklyn neighborhood. A mediocre student, Paul dropped out of school in the eighth grade and became an apprentice to his father in two trades, working both as a meat cutter and a lottery runner or seller.

His recorded criminal career began inauspiciously on the July 4th weekend in 1934 when he and two neighborhood companions held up a haberdasher in Hartford, Connecticut, at gunpoint. Their total loot was $51. Unfortunately for Castellano, a witness jotted down the license plate number of the getaway car, Castellano's own. Arrested and identified as one of the amateurish gunmen, the nineteen-year-old Castellano was not yet a made soldier, but he understood the fundamental Mafia principle of *omertà*. A firm refusal to finger his accomplices in exchange for a lighter sentence established his reputation as a standup guy. Pleading guilty to robbery, Castellano served three months of a one-year prison term.

Marriage and an actual family relationship to Carlo Gambino were stepping stones in Castellano's climb to the pinnacle of the crime family. In addition to being a cousin, Gambino had married Castellano's sister, Katherine. As Carlo advanced, Paul rose with him, serving in Carlo's glory years as his most trusted capo. When Gambino's health declined in the mid 1970s, Castellano materialized as Don Carlo's alter ego and the family's acting boss before being officially crowned a full-fledged godfather. His dominant stature in the Mafia and his imposing height of six-feet two-inches ennobled him with the complimentary nickname "Big Paul."

A reader of the *Wall Street Journal* and financial magazines, Castellano pictured himself as a businessman and the conciliator of the family, equivalent to the CEO of a diversified corporation. His legal income for IRS purposes came from "investments" in meat-packing and poultry firms, and in construction companies that were incorporated in the names of his sons and other relatives. The cosmetic efforts to masquerade as an erudite businessman impressed one of his underworld equals, "Fat Tony" Salerno. At a meeting with Genovese and Gambino members present, Salvatore "Sammy the Bull" Gravano heard Salerno deliver a rare Mafia compliment: "Paul, you talk so beautiful. I wish I could talk like that."

Castellano's invisible power clearly extended into the legitimate business world, where executives were discreetly aware of the Gambino family's hold over unions and its secret interests in the Key and Waldbaum supermarket chains in the New York area. Pasquale "Pat" or "Patsy" Conte, a Gambino capo adept in narcotics trafficking, sat on the board of directors of Key Foods, and had an overbearing voice in deciding which products were stocked in the cooperative chain. Asked by agents from a presidential commission why he favored products from Castellano's companies, Ira Waldbaum, the principal owner of Waldbaum's, replied that it was the responsibility of law enforcement, not businessmen, to "take action" against organized crime. "Don't forget I have a wife and children," Waldbaum said.

Dial Meat Purveyors, a company headed by Castellano's sons, Paul Junior and Joseph, was the main supplier in New York of poultry and meat to more than three hundred independent retail butchers and many supermarkets. Through secret accords with officials in the United Food and Commercial Workers Union, Big Paul could interrupt deliveries and ignite labor problems in stores that did not accept his wares at the prices he dictated.

The clearest sign of the respect accorded Castellano by big business came from a national poultry supplier, Frank Perdue. Perdue, whose television commercials for his company brought him national recognition, acknowledged to the FBI in 1981 that he had directly solicited Castellano's aid at least twice. The first occasion was to ask if Castellano could derail attempts by the Mob-tainted United Food and Commercial Workers Union to organize his main processing plant in Accomac, Virginia. A second difficulty Perdue thought Castellano could resolve was his inability to get his chickens into many of the chain supermarkets in the huge New York region.

Perdue never clarified to the FBI what help Castellano offered or provided. At first, he said, he contacted Castellano because of his expertise as an investor in beef, poultry, and wholesale food companies in the city. Pressed by Gambino Squad agent Joseph F. O'Brien as to why he had singled out Castellano rather than supermarket and meat business officials, Perdue, with a high-pitched cackle, replied, "Why? Because he's the godfather."

The chicken-producer later amplified to investigators from a presidential fact-finding commission that he sought Castellano's intervention because he was known to have "long tentacles as an organized-crime figure. Yeah, the Mafia and the Mob."

From day one as Gambino boss, Castellano gloried in his executive skills. In 1976 he had negotiated with his own underboss, Aniello Dellacroce, the control and division of the gang's income. All white-collar crimes—bid-rigging, union corruption, political bribes, financial frauds—remained in Big Paul's sphere. Dellacroce retained the more traditional and violent rackets of loan-sharking, gambling, and hijackings. But Castellano, as supreme boss, greedily demanded his cut from the loot collected by Dellacroce's crews.

There was a brutal, blood-drenched side to Castellano's glowing self-portrait of himself. Before expanding into white-collar ventures, Castellano had organized hugely profitable gambling, loan-sharking, car theft, and extortion activities. And, of course, as boss he collected the largest share from these enterprises, even if he no longer had a significant role in running them. He also handpicked accomplished killers inside and outside the family for necessary dirty work, contract hits, to maintain his control. Probably his most feared hit man was Roy DeMeo, who in the 1970s and early '80s captained a squad that federal and city authorities said killed at least seventy-five people. Gene Mustain and Jerry Capeci in their book, *Murder Machine*, placed the body count at more than two hundred.

Most of DeMeo's victims were never found. His crew's grizzly style, according to informants, was to use a Brooklyn apartment as an abattoir where the bodies were bled dry in a bathtub, disemboweled in the living room, and packaged in cardboard boxes. Private garbage trucks then dumped the body parts in landfills. Similar to the Cosa Nostra's earlier use of Jewish executioners in Murder Inc., Castellano saw the camouflage value in hiring killers who would not be identified as mafiosi. One death squad that he recruited was a gang of ethnic Irish psychopaths from the Hell's Kitchen area. Labeled "the Westies" by a detective, these sadists specialized in hacking victims to death and disposing of them through a sewage-treatment plant on Wards Island in the East River.

Castellano sealed a coldhearted business deal with the Westies leader, Jimmy Coonan, in February 1978, in a private dining room at Tommaso's Restaurant, in Brooklyn's Bay Ridge section. The get-together was arranged by DeMeo, a friend of Coonan's and an admirer of his homicidal skills. Francis "Mickey" Featherstone, a Westie who accompanied Coonan to the meeting, later disclosed to investigators and T. J. English, a writer, that Castellano was disturbed that the Westies murder wave in Manhattan had included two important loan sharks working for the Mafia.

English befriended Featherstone after he defected and entered the Federal Witness Protection Program, and Featherstone gave him an account of Castellano's pact with the Westies. "All right, Jimmy, this is our position," Featherstone recalled Castellano saying. "From now on, you boys are going to be with us. Which means you got to stop acting like cowboys, like wild men. If anybody is to be removed, you have to clear it with my people. *Capish?*" The quid pro quo for the Westies was Castellano's permission for them to use the Gambino name as an intimidating weapon in extortions, loan-sharking, and labor racketeering on Manhattan's West Side. "But whatever monies you make, you will cut us in 10 percent," Featherstone quoted Big Paul.

Among the well-informed in New York's crime families, the tale of Castellano's son-in-law, Frank Amato, was a reminder of his unremitting wrath. A two-bit hoodlum and hijacker, Amato stepped up in the world by marrying Castellano's only daughter, Connie. The generous Big Paul handed the bridegroom a well-paid job at Dial Poultry, the wholesale company operated by

Castellano's relatives. Amato repaid Castellano by proving himself to be a reckless philander and a wife beater; the couple divorced in 1973. Soon afterward, the former son-in-law vanished without a trace. The Mob gossip mill provided a rational explanation for his disappearance. He was "clipped" on orders from Castellano, who was outraged at his physical and mental abuse of Connie.

The ability to handle both the savage and sophisticated elements of the Gambino empire made Castellano a multimillionaire and he lived like one. He built a seventeen-room mansion on one of the highest points in New York, the wooded crest of a hill in the ritzy Todt Hill section of Staten Island, offering a panoramic view of the Verrazano-Narrows Bridge arching over New York's Upper Bay. Castellano's neo-Federal creation dwarfed all others along Benedict Road, where homes were valued at a minimum of $1 million. The interior featured beautifully paneled walls and floors laid with Carrara marble. There were four master suites, eight baths, guest apartments, a wine cellar, staff quarters, and a solarium. Even the simplest meals were served on porcelain plates and Waterford crystal. For outdoor amusement Big Paul, the lord of the manor, constructed an Olympic-sized swimming pool, an English garden, and a manicured bocci court. A long circular driveway led to its white-colonnaded portico entrance. Befitting his assumed status as a national Mafia leader, Castellano thought it proper to model the exterior of the mansion on that of the nation's president and to call his home "the White House." Completed in 1981, the house was valued at $3 million, although Castellano probably got generous discounts from obliging building contractors.

By the early 1980s, Castellano grew aloof, a sovereign remote in his mansion, seeing only a coterie of confidants, rarely visiting his battalions in their neighborhood clubs. Capos were expected to pay him homage by delivering or sending his portion of their booty to the White House. Conferences were on a by-appointment-only basis, and Big Paul scheduled the meetings. His demands for larger and larger percentages of the borgata's income and his disdainful attitude toward most soldiers brought Castellano a new, and derogatory, nickname, "the Pope."

Ever since the formation of the Gambino Squad in 1981, FBI agents had searched for a vulnerability that would allow them to listen in on Castellano's secrets. One possibility was exploiting a shuttle service employed by Castellano to receive mafiosi visitors. For security reasons, most mobsters, even when summoned to the Hill, were barred from driving directly to the White House front door. They parked their cars on nearby Benedict Road and were picked up by a member of Castellano's palace guard, who chauffeured them into the gated compound. Frank DeCicco, a Staten Island capo, frequently took care of the shuttle chores, ferrying visitors to the White House and back to their autos. Several agents believed they would get "dynamite leads" bugging DeCicco's car and eavesdropping on his passengers' conversations minutes after the talks with Castellano were concluded.

G. Bruce Mouw, the supervisor of the Gambino Squad, toyed with the idea but decided it was a tangential approach. "Let's go for the big guy," he instructed his squad, meaning, "Let's bug Castellano's home."

From their surveillance and from tips from paid informers, Gambino Squad agents knew that there was no social club, no favorite restaurant that would serve their needs. A home-telephone wiretap was installed under a court order but it proved to be unproductive. Like all cautious mafiosi, Castellano had for decades avoided compromising himself on phone calls. The most reliable reports from informers indicated that the one place where Castellano routinely received reports and issued orders was a makeshift den, a dining alcove near the kitchen in his home.

Obtaining court authorization to wire Castellano's privileged sanctum was relatively easy. Previous bugs and telephone taps of Gambino soldiers gave the FBI abundant "probable causes" that Castellano was using his home for Mafia conferences. The difficult chore was penetrating the Castellano White House itself. The home was never empty; when Castellano and his minions were away, his wife, Nina, or their housekeeper and Big Paul's mistress, Gloria Olarte, were always there. The challenge of breaking into the house was herculean. Guarding against government intruders and the possibility of assassins, Castellano was prepared to thwart all invaders. An eight-foot-high brick fence encircled the grounds, and the main building was laced with electronic sensors and interior and rooftop burglar alarms. A private security company monitored the alarm system and closed-circuit video cameras around the clock. At night, floodlights illuminated the approaches to the house and its exterior. Two Doberman pinschers prowled night and day to intercept uninvited strangers.

Rather than a tricky high-tech scheme to overcome Castellano's barriers, the FBI's Special Operations Unit decided on a simpler course. Someone would walk right through his front door. Even if Castellano were present, a bug would be placed in his private quarters by a lone agent.

FBI officials, citing the need for security in future black-bag operations, never fully reveal specific details of any bugging operation. But it is known that the daring plan to penetrate the mansion worked to perfection. In March 1983, two creative FBI black-bag practitioners, John Kravec and Joseph Cantamesa, tinkered with the television cable lines leading to Castellano's set near his den. Instead of a cable company repairman, agent Cantamesa showed up in mufti to restore service while Kravec, on the outside, made sure the TV problem was not corrected until Cantamesa had figured out where to install his bugs and transmission lines. The affable Cantamesa established a rapport with members of the household and volunteered to return and repair a malfunctioning telephone near the kitchen. Accustomed to perquisites everywhere he went, Castellano gladly accepted the free services, which would prove costly in the end. After several invited visits to the house, Cantamesa solved all of the household's television and phone-line snafus, and completed his own special assignment. The obliging "repairman" used the opportunity to install miniature microphones and hard wires in the baseboards that would transmit conversations from the alcove to an FBI listening plant.

Nearby, in a rented apartment in a Staten Island two-family house, Gambino Squad agents instantly began recording-Don Paul's chats with his mafiosi subordinates. Castellano's lifestyle at first created havoc with the new bug. He constantly played the television set or a radio, and the broadcast audio drowned out clear transmission of voices; it was impossible to understand what was being said by Castellano and his guests. The frustrated head of Special Operations, James Kallstrom, sent a distress signal to the bureau's Merlins who solve electronic eavesdropping headaches for foreign counterintelligence units. At the Staten Island listening post, the technical shamans, using exotic gear and antennas, exorcised the TV and radio interference. The bug now transmitted the voices agents were eager to hear: Big Paul's intimate conversations with his confidants.

At the end of 1983, one mandatory black-bag job remained: Fat Tony Salerno's Palma Boys Club in East Harlem. Employing their customary tactics, the Special Operations magicians struck on an icy December night at 2:00 A.M. The toughest challenge was suppressing noise while they worked on an exterior brick wall to temporarily disable the club's burglar alarms. Kallstrom's sound-suppression solution was to imitate a familiar nuisance tolerated by the city's hardened citizens. He borrowed two garbage-removal trucks from a private company, dressed agents in uniforms, and instructed them to freely toss trash cans onto the pavements and to operate the truck's garbage grinders at maximum power. The sidewalk clatter at the Palma Boys nevertheless attracted someone's attention, and a fleet of police patrol cars screeched into the street in front of the club.

"We're on the job," Kallstrom imperiously announced to a sergeant, flashing his FBI credentials. "Get the fuck out of here." And the police did.

Before dawn, agents entered Salerno's headquarters and hid several mini-mikes near Fat Tony's conference table. In the cellar, the technicians drilled into the floorboards below Salerno's favorite table to hook up a transmission line for the microphones. In the dank basement, instead of threatening dogs, agents were confronted by foot-long feral rats. One of them bit John Kravec on the ankle before the wiring job was completed.

A few hours later, from underneath Salerno's feet, his throaty comments were relayed crystal-clear to an FBI listening post five blocks away. The last targeted Mafia boss had been bugged.

24

"This Is It!"

It was a dynamite concept. That's what Ronald Goldstock, a Mafia authority and scholar, knew when he came calling on Rudolph Giuliani, the new U.S. Attorney for the Southern District.

Goldstock's proposal was unprecedented: a full frontal attack on the Cosa Nostra's governing body, the Commission. And the weapon for destroying it would be the RICO law.

In August 1983, two months after Giuliani moved into his office in St. Andrew's Plaza in downtown Manhattan, Goldstock, the director of the state's Organized Crime Task Force, appeared for an exchange of ideas between prosecutors. Accompanied by his chief of investigators, Fred Rayano, Goldstock proudly summarized the successes achieved through his agency's Jaguar bug before offering his grandiose proposal. "You came in just at the right time. We have the Corallo tapes and the FBI has tapes on the Colombos, Gambinos, and Genovese. You can bring a RICO case against the entire Commission — the Commission is the enterprise."

Rayano had no idea what his boss was going to spring and he sat in suspense as Giuliani summoned several aides to listen to Goldstock's spiel. Doffing his suit jacket and rolling up his shirt sleeves, Goldstock began sketching excitedly on a flip chart the main elements and evidence gathered by his staff and the

FBI, implicating four bosses and their mainstay aides in the Lucchese, Gambino, Colombo, and Genovese families. He mapped out the felonies—predicate offenses—the specific criminal acts that he was certain showed a pattern of collective crimes that could be blended into a massive RICO indictment of all Commission members as participants in an illegal enterprise.

That same day, in a private one-on-one conversation with Goldstock, Giuliani wondered about jurisdictional conflicts with another U.S. Attorney. He was in charge of the government's Southern District in New York State, commonly shortened to SDNY, which included Manhattan, the Bronx, and the city's northern suburbs. Many aspects of the Lucchese, Colombo, and Gambino family investigations, however, centered on Long Island, Brooklyn, Queens, and Staten Island, the jurisdiction of the U.S. Attorney in the state's Eastern District. In fact, the adjoining territories were so close that Giuliani could gaze out his office window and see the Eastern District's main office building across the East River in downtown Brooklyn. Feuds over high-voltage cases flared frequently between the prosecutorial neighbors. FBI officials could settle these jurisdictional rivalries unilaterally by picking the office they wanted to handle a prosecution and submitting their evidence to it. A jurisdictional decision over a colossal Mafia case—and the prosecution of the Commission promised to be one—was out of the bureau's hands. Giuliani and Goldstock, two politically attuned prosecutors, knew the verdict could only be handed down in Washington by the attorney general and his advisers.

Before ending their meeting, Goldstock promised to support Giuliani in a showdown battle with the Eastern District. As an assistant district attorney in Manhattan, Goldstock had worked on cases with Giuliani when he was a young federal prosecutor in Manhattan. He admired Giuliani's fervid style and the loyalty that he engendered from his staff; and he believed Giuliani would be more cooperative and generous in sharing evidence and plaudits with the state task force than Eastern District prosecutors.

Giuliani moved swiftly to get a jurisdictional lock on the case. "If Bonanno can write about a Commission, I can indict it," the prosecutor confided to assistants, referring to Joe Bonnano's, A Man of Honor, published earlier that year. His staff sifted through hundreds of tapes and investigative reports, hunting for the essential components of an indictment, and prepared charts delineating RICO accusations that could be brought against the bosses and their lieutenants. A month after meeting with Goldstock, Giuliani sat down in Washington with Attorney General William French Smith and FBI Director

William Webster. He displayed the informational charts, outlined his prosecution plan, and asked both officials to support him even if it meant intruding on the Eastern District's territory. A jubilant Giuliani returned to New York in September 1983 with a green light to proceed with a "Commission case." For added incentive, he had guarantees that the attorney general and the FBI director would supply him with all the attorneys and agents he needed to expedite the investigations.

"Rudy is the 800-pound gorilla in this case," Goldstock observed upon learning of the jurisdictional victory. Political muscle in Washington and gargantuan ambition, Goldstock realized, had easily won the day for Giuliani.

Giuliani's zeal for Commission indictments ignited a debate in his own office. Walter Mack, the assistant in charge of organized-crime prosecutions when Giuliani arrived, argued that a Commission trial would "eviscerate" and skim off the best evidence from substantial work under way in the Southern and Eastern Districts to indict higher-ups in all five families. He warned that the borrowed materials for Commission indictments would hobble, if not jeopardize, important cases aimed at individual Mob hierarchies. And, suddenly shifting priorities, Mack believed, would dishearten prosecutors and agents who had labored for months on those tough investigations. "The Commission case seemed intended more for publicity than for impact on the Mafia," Mack asserted. "I thought the more effective strategy was taking out the families as quickly as possible, not the Commission: Rudy was much more bullish on the Commission as a priority and he was the boss who made the decision."

A much-praised prosecutor, Mack, in March 1984, with Giuliani's approval, did obtain an indictment in a non-Commission case against twenty-four Gambino members and associates on homicide and racketeering charges. The investigation by several law-enforcement agencies had been in progress long before Giuliani became U.S. Attorney. Soon afterward, Giuliani demoted Mack, bringing in his own appointee to oversee the organized-crime unit. "Rudy at times had problems with me," Mack conceded. "I'm strong-willed and outspoken and Rudy's management style was, 'Do things my way.'"

Once shunned at the SDNY, Bob Blakey, RICO's principal author, was welcomed back as an honored prophet by Giuliani. Since the acceptance of his theories two years earlier by the FBI brass in New York, he had been a kitchen-cabinet adviser to them. Agents jokingly dubbed him "the consigliere," and he encouraged them to seek a mammoth indictment of the entire Commission, sweeping up all of the area's bosses in a combined trial. Meeting with Giuliani,

Blakey urged him to launch that plan. "Giuliani's mind was running full speed," Blakey said. "He had the moxie to know how to use RICO; he ate it up."

The idea of undermining the bosses in a single indictment, Giuliani later insisted, had come to him alone, months before he moved to New York as a U.S. Attorney, and had been inspired by one of the Cosa Nostra's original caesars, Joe Bonanno. In early 1983, while still the number-three official at the Justice Department, Giuliani avidly watched Bonanno promote his self-glorifying memoirs on the television program *60 Minutes*. Reading *A Man of Honor*, Giuliani concluded that Bonanno had catalogued the entire structure of the Commission. In *Leadership*, a book published by Giuliani in 2002, he said that he "dreamed up the tactic" of using RICO "to prosecute the Mafia leadership for being itself a 'corrupt enterprise.'"

"I realized that Bonanno's description of how the families were organized provided a road map of precisely what the RICO statute was designed to combat. As soon as I became the U.S. Attorney I was able to hoist Bonanno by his literary petard," Giuliani wrote. He pointed out that most criminal cases were initiated by federal agents or the police. The Commission investigation was different because of his personal involvement, he claimed. Emphasizing that prosecuting borgata bosses was exceptionally meaningful to him because of his "animus" to Italian-American gangsters, he added, "I was part of the team that had developed the case from the start."

The genesis of the Commission investigation, however, remains hazy.

"I can't tell you what was in Rudy's mind the first time I spoke to him about a Commission enterprise indictment," Goldstock recalls about his meeting with Giuliani in 1983. "But he gave no indication that he was thinking about it. He said, 'It sounds very interesting and how would you put it together?'"

More than a year before Giuliani's arrival, industrious FBI officials had already recognized the possibility of a breakthrough case against the Commission. Starting in December 1982 with the bugging of the Colombo gang at the Casa Storta Restaurant, federal and state lawmen for the first time were recording frank, uninhibited conversations of several mafia hierarchs: Paul Castellano, Tony Salerno, and Tony Corallo; an acting boss, Gerry Langella; and their assorted Cosa Nostra comrades. Agents and investigators pored over compelling evidence, usable intelligence, and rewarding gossip. The bugs clarified nitty-gritty details of the confidential practices of Mafia leaders never before understood by law enforcement. Salvatore Avellino's curiosity was especially helpful. He had attended college for several years, and on the Jaguar drives he behaved like an inquisitive freshman, peppering Tony Ducks Corallo and other Lucchese old pros with incisive questions. Avellino delved into the family's history, its internal operations, and its relationships with other families.

Revelations streamed from the Jaguar about extortions and loan-sharking crimes, about the Concrete Club run in partnership with other borgatas, about compliant union leaders, and about the bosses' conflicting views on narcotics trafficking. There were personal issues, soul-searching dialogues about the wisdom of encouraging sons to follow their fathers' career paths into the Cosa Nostra, and backbiting blasts over Paul Castellano's insatiable thirst for larger shares of plunder.

At the start of the Mafia investigations, FBI officials had wide latitude on shaping the objectives of the family cases. Their original game plan was to prosecute the hierarchies of each of the five New York families separately and to destroy their spheres of influence. As the individual investigations progressed, Jim Kossler, the bureau's organized crime supervisor in New York, grew increasingly absorbed in the interlocking interests of the five families and the Commission. Every Thursday morning, Kossler met in a windowless conference room at the bureau's downtown headquarters with members of the anti-Mafia squads and city police detectives working with them in a joint task force. The purpose was to exchange information, compare notes, and try to clear up cryptic clues. "It's becoming clearer and clearer as we expand the attacks on the various families that there is a commonality about much of what they're up to," Kossler told agents. "Different squads have different pieces of the jigsaw puzzles."

A striking commonality from the FBI and the state's bugs were numerous references to the mysterious Commission. The tapes from the Palma Boys Club, the Jaguar, and other intercepted conversations were replete with references to the ruling body. Different bosses were talking about the same high-level meetings, payoff splits, and the unions and construction companies that were in their grip. Piecing together segments from hundreds of hours of electronic eavesdropping, the FBI began to comprehend the magnitude of the power of Commission members: they authorized murder contracts, carried out joint ventures, regulated relationships between the families, and blackballed the induction of soldiers in other borgatas.

Electronic eavesdropping further clarified the Mafia's impact on one of the nation's largest and most powerful unions. Kossler, a labor-racketeering expert, deciphered the importance of Tony Salerno's discussion one afternoon with representatives of the Cleveland Mob. The men were casually dropping names while selecting new leaders of a union unidentified in their discussion. Kossler was familiar with the names they mentioned. "Do you realize what these bastards up there on 115th Street are talking about?" he asked fellow agents. "They're picking the next president of the teamsters' union."

The tapes fleshed out rumors that the strife-ridden Bonanno family had been ousted at least temporarily from the Commission, and that the board of directors now consisted essentially of the four remaining big-time New York gangs. Families from Chicago and other cities no longer had automatic Commission seats. The bugs also revealed that Mafia families is Cleveland, Philadelphia, New England, Milwaukee, Buffalo, and New Jersey often acted like satellites, seeking advice or permission from New York on leadership and other grave internal decisions.

As far back as 1981, state and federal officials and prosecutors at different stages in various investigations had recognized the framework of the Commission as a viable RICO target. "We had been looking at developing a case against the Commission as early as 1981," said Thomas Sheer, the head of the FBI's New York office in 1986 and 1987. "That was one of our original and ultimate goals."

While Giuliani may not have been the first law-enforcement official to envision a Commission indictment, he assembled the disparate parts of several independent investigations into a single cohesive case. He was the undeniable catalyst. Almost from the day he took over New York's Southern District, he talked about zeroing in on the Commission. "Rudy read excerpts of Bonanno's book to us and said, 'Wouldn't that be a wonderful case?'" Walter Mack noted.

Backed by the attorney general and the FBI director, Giuliani had the authority to access all of the bureau's resources on his pet priority. In the late summer of 1983, the FBI's New York office came on board. Responding to directives from Giuliani and the Justice Department, the bureau officially opened a Commission file by assigning a case agent for the investigation — one of its brightest and most energetic investigators, Pat Marshall.

As lead agent, Marshall was the FBI liaison to Giuliani and his team of prosecutors exclusively assigned to a Commission indictment. He was responsible for reviewing and culling the many tapes to piece together incriminating segments from bugged conversations, examining thousands of old and current reports on the principal suspects, and plugging gaps in evidence required by prosecutors. The bureau's coordinating supervisor, Jim Kossler, chose Marshall for his extensive background in Mafia investigations and also for his diplomatic prowess. Acrimony, resentment, and internal jealousies were certain to erupt when agents would be asked to abruptly subordinate and perhaps abort their cases by transferring hard-earned evidence to help out another agent—in this case, Marshall. "We need someone well respected who can deal smoothly with everyone," Kossler told other supervisors. "Pat doesn't have an enemy in the world. Everyone knows he's not a poacher only out for glory for himself."

The lean, sandy-haired thirty-three-year-old Marshall had dreamed of joining the FBI while a teenager. His first job out of high school was as a clerk in the bureau's office in Baltimore, his hometown. After college he qualified for admission to the bureau, and in the early 1980s was working exclusively on organized-crime matters in New York.

The Commission assignment was the most complex and sensitive of Marshall's career. An unwritten code of conduct prohibited an agent from balking at an order. Nevertheless, the scope of the project and having to coax fellow agents to cooperate, preyed on him. Soon enough, he encountered numerous naysayers. The common refrain he heard was: "Sure, we all know the Commission exists but you're never going to prove it." Marshall soothed those objecting to the expropriation of their tapes and their witnesses with reassuring words: "I know you're pissed off. But you can still have your case and the tapes can be used again in other indictments and trials."

Besides the internal FBI rivalries, the complicated Commission case sometimes whipped up storms with the state's Organized Crime Task Force. Separate and uncoordinated investigations of the same suspects by two units thwarted at least one golden opportunity to turn up valuable evidence. In June 1983 state investigators obtained the rarest of intelligence breaks from the Jaguar bug: advance news of a scheduled Commission meeting. The task force learned that Sal Avellino would drive Ducks Corallo and other Lucchese leaders to a Commission sit-down with other bosses and Mob leaders on June 14.

It loomed as an important assembly where the bosses would review the qualifications of proposed new members into the five Mafia clans, among other items. Investigators heard Corallo proclaim to Avellino that he planned to veto the induction of a Gambino candidate because the wannabe had once testified in a civil suit. The Lucchese boss viewed taking the witness stand—even in a noncriminal matter—as cooperation with law enforcement and a disqualifying character blemish for Mafia membership.

There was no advance hint, however, of where or at what time the meeting would take place. Law-enforcement agents had never before gotten advance word on a sacrosanct Commission gathering. The task force had been handed the unique opportunity of capturing on videotape the Mafia's upper crust departing the premises and identifying a specific meeting place. Pictures of them leaving could be used as corroborative courtroom exhibits to bolster the theory that the Commission existed and to implicate its members. Aware that FBI agents often shadowed major Mob targets, Fred Rayano, the state task force investigator, notified bureau officials that on the day of the Commission gathering his men would track Ducks Corallo to the hush-hush session and attempt to photograph the participants entering and leaving. "If you are going to cover Castellano or anyone else, let's make sure we don't fall all over each other and mess it up," Rayano told his FBI counterparts.

On the afternoon of June 14, the task force relied on a helicopter and a huge posse of state investigators to pursue Avellino's Jaguar. Locating the Jaguar in Long Island was easy and, despite Avellino's normal dry-cleaning tactics to shake tails, the task force never lost sight of the car cruising on highways and wending through dense city traffic. The trail ended in a dingy section of the Bowery in Lower Manhattan. Corallo and his lieutenants were spotted entering the Bari Restaurant and Pizzeria Equipment Company near Prince Street, obviously the site of the meeting. Rayano expected the bosses to confer for several hours and he began getting his units in place to photograph and document the Mafia big shots when they exited. But only minutes after Corallo's arrival, and before the cameras were ready, Corallo, Paul Castellano, Fat Tony Salerno, and other exasperated-looking mafiosi bolted from the building, scattering in different directions, searching for their cars and hailing taxis to get out of the neighborhood. A hard-breathing Salerno escaped by squeezing through a rear window, pushed by younger mobsters.

A disappointed Rayano found out later that day from the Jaguar bug the cause of the pandemonium. Corallo explained to Avellino that the meeting was aborted by Paul Castellano's sounding an alarm that the godfathers were under the watchdog eyes of the FBI. The Gambino boss was certain he had seen agent Joseph O'Brien on the street, peering through the plate-glass front window of the Bari Pizzeria Equipment building. The Mob boss recognized O'Brien, who had been bird-dogging and trying to pry information from him for more than a year.

O'Brien denied having been near the meeting place or even tailing Castellano that afternoon. "It wasn't me. It might have been some other big guy that

Castellano saw," the six-foot-five O'Brien protested. "If I had been there, I would have admitted it." FBI supervisors backed him up, insisting that none of their agents had interfered with the state's surveillance. Nevertheless, the incident created ill feeling between the state and federal agencies. Rayano conjectured that O'Brien "out of curiosity went down on his own to get a look at what was going on." FBI meddling, he griped, spoiled a well-planned operation. Other task force investigators were convinced that deliberate snooping by O'Brien or another agent had occurred. They assumed that elitist bureau agents had tried to demonstrate their investigative superiority in unearthing the meeting, rather than allowing state investigators to claim full credit for an exceptional accomplishment.

By late 1984, an unprecedented number of FBI agents, 350, were working full- or part-time on Mob cases in the New York region. Reinforcing them were about one hundred city detectives and investigators assigned to the FBI's joint task force. It was a large complement of anti-Mafia lawmen for an enormous job. They had to maintain a watch on over more than one thousand made men and at least five thousand associates in a region stretching over New York, New Jersey, and Connecticut, and into other states. (Mafia investigators estimate that the families can count on between five to ten associates and wannabes for each inducted soldier.) Besides the continuous investigation of the five families, agents and investigators were pulled off their regular schedules for essential duty on the super-priority Commission probe. To help Pat Marshall with his mounting burdens, a second agent, Charlotte Lang, was assigned full-time as a case agent for prosecutors.

A baffling part of the pending Commission indictment centered on the 1979 luncheon murder of Carmine Lilo Galante and his two dining companions. Giuliani and his prosecutors were confident there was sufficient evidence to prove the Commission had ordered the execution of Galante, who at the time of his assassination had been identified as the Bonanno boss by most FBI and local Mafia investigators. (It turned out that the authorities were mistaken about Galante's actual rank. Twenty-five years later, the FBI would conclusively determine that he had never been the "official" head of the Bonanno family but, rather, a haughty capo intent on seizing control of the splintered borgata and being recognized as its supreme dictator.) For a motive, the prosecution counted on the theory that Galante's rival godfathers had wanted him dead, fearing that he was attempting a power move to become the boss of bosses. The big hole in the Commission case was finding enough evidence to bring a murder charge against an actual assassin with a direct relationship to the Commission. Agents had a strong suspicion that one of the three gunmen was Anthony Bruno Indelicato, a cocaine-snorting Bonanno button man. About forty-five minutes after the Galante contract had been fulfilled in a Brooklyn restaurant, a surveillance team from the Manhattan DA's squad videotaped Indelicato being hugged, kissed, and congratulated by high-ranking Bonanno and Gambino mobsters on the sidewalk outside a Gambino club in Little Italy known as the Ravenite. The DA's men were concentrating on Neil Dellacroce, the Gambino underboss, in an unrelated Mob matter, when Indelicato arrived, apparently to report the successful result of the hit on Galante. It was a warm summer day and the videotape showed the outline of the butt of a handgun, covered by a loose-fitting white T-shirt, in Indelicato's waistband. At best, the videotape could be used as circumstantial evidence, but prosecutors lacked direct proof that Indelicato was one of Galante's executioners.

The getaway car in Galante's murder, a Mercury Montego, had been found by the police shortly after the slayings, but their forensic tests had been unable to match partial palm prints—the only evidence lifted from the car—to any suspect. In the intervening years, the FBI had developed a system for identifying segments of handprints, and Pat Marshall, playing a long shot five years after the assassination, got Indelicato's complete hand prints and ran them through the bureau's forensic system. "Bingo, we have him," Marshall proudly reported to Jim Kossler and the prosecutors. "We nailed him from a left palm print on the inside of one of the doors." They had a shooter, Bruno Indelicato, and on the day of the assassination, they could link him to Dellacroce, the Gambino underboss, who often sat in on Commission meetings. The FBI and prosecutors could now pin the murder on Commission members, accusing them of having issued Galante's death warrant.

If Giuliani's interest in the Commission was sparked by Joe Bonanno's revelations, the Jaguar tapes doubled his enthusiasm about the exiled boss's literary confessions. On two tapes, Ducks Corallo and his underboss, Salvatore "Tom Mix" Santoro, derisively reviewed with Sal Avellino Bonanno's appearance on 60 Minutes to promote his book. The Lucchese mobsters reviled him as an apostate for violating the code of omertà, specifically for confirming details of the American Cosa Nostra's birth in exchange for a big-bucks book contract and a movie deal.

By bashing Bonanno, the mobsters unwittingly contributed to the accumulating evidence proving the existence of the Commission and its historical record.

Chauffeuring Santoro, Avellino several times brought up the subject of Bonanno's reminiscences and his relations with earlier godfathers Tommy Lucchese, Carlo Gambino, and Joe Profaci. On March 28, 1983, Bonnano's public disclosures dominated the thoughts of Santoro and Avellino as they talked in the Jaguar.

AVELLINO: "I was shocked. What is he tryin' to prove, that he's a Man of Honor? But he's admitting—he, he actually admitted that he has a fam, that he was the boss of a family."

SANTORO: "Right. Right. Right. Right."

AVELLINO: "Even though he says, 'This was my family. I was like the father.'"

SANTORO: "He's trying to get away from the image of a gangster. He's trying to go back to, ahh, like in Italy. See, when he says, 'My father taught me.'"

In *A Man of Honor*, Bonanno denied involvement in narcotics, a contention mocked by Santoro in these choice words: "He's full of shit, 'cause I knew he was a phony. . . . You know like he says he ain't never been in narcotics, he's full of shit. His own fucking rule, he was makin' piles of money. . . ."

The two mafiosi railed at Bonnano's apparent intent to capitalize on his former life as a Mafia don.

SANTORO: "This cocksucker, you know what he's gonna make, this cocksucker? You know much money he's gonna make now, his book. . . . Make a movie and this guy's gonna be like the technical director, forget about it, this cocksucker will make a fortune."

AVELLINO: "This will be like, the ahh, now they'll say we have the original godfather."

Two weeks later on April 6, Bonanno was the popular topic again as Avellino talked in the Jaguar with his boss, Tony Ducks. Avellino was particularly interested in Bonanno's insistence that he had been kidnapped by other mobsters in 1964. A snickering Corallo ridiculed the claim, saying that Bonanno had disappeared in fear of Mob retaliation for his unsuccessful plot to kill rival bosses Tommy Lucchese and Carlo Gambino.

CORALLO: "Bonanno. He's been squawking for years, the cocksucker. What are you, kidding?"

AVELLINO: "So what is he going to tell them about this kidnapping when he disappeared now? He's going to tell them the story that. . . ."

CORALLO: "What kidnapping?"

AVELLINO: "When he ran away."

CORALLO: "He ran away that phony cocksucker, what kidnapping? . . . He's got to make that legitimate. He's got to make it a kidnapping. I wonder if he's going to say on the windup that when they got together they wanted to kill Gambino, Tommy Brown [Lucchese]."

Avellino informed Corallo that in an interview Bonanno had maintained that a "father," or "boss," "operates a family however he wants."

CORALLO: "He said that? . . . They could call him in and lock you up and under this act over here."

AVELLINO: "This RICO Act. He admitted that he was in charge of a family. . . ."

CORALLO: "Now they could call him in. . . . They call him as a witness. . . . What are you going to do then?"

Corallo might have been reading Rudolph Giuliani's mind. The prosecutor and his staff had been working fifteen-hour days to produce the counts for the Commission indictment, and one of the final witnesses to be questioned for firsthand knowledge of the Commission's history and powers was Joe Bonanno. In November 1984, Bonanno was served with a subpoena to testify before a grand jury in New York. The seventy-nine-year-old Bonanno responded by checking into St. Mary's Hospital in his hometown of Tucson. He claimed that a weak heart and other debilitating ailments prevented him from traveling, and that the stress of testifying could be fatal. His personal physicians attested that he was suffering from a severe cardiac ailment. When government doctors diagnosed Bonanno as being in good health and fit to answer questions, Giuliani flew to Arizona in an attempt to persuade him to testify at the coming trial with an offer of immunity from prosecution.

Lying in a hospital bed with his lawyers standing by, Bonanno was cordial to Giuliani. "You're doing a good job," he congratulated the prosecutor. But he declined to cooperate, dodging questions regarding his published and television statements about the origins of the Commission and his life in the Mafia. Each question for the deposition was met with an evasive reply or an invocation of his Fifth Amendment rights against self-incrimination.

Bonanno's recalcitrance cost him fourteen months in prison for obstruction of justice. Appealing his sentence, Bonanno admitted he had been "mistaken" in writing his biography. Testifying for the government, he insisted, would "compound the problems" and violate his "principles." (After Bonnano's release from jail, he spent most of the remainder of his retirement years in Arizona, where he died in 2002 at the age of ninety-seven. Clearly, his heart had been healthier than he and his doctors contended sixteen years earlier.)

Bonnano's deposition was one of the last stages in Giuliani's preparations. He, his staff of prosecutors, Pat Marshall and Charlotte Lang, and dozens of conscripted agents spent eighteen months trying to construct an error-proof RICO "enterprise" indictment. The final product was reviewed by Giuliani, his closest aides, and Justice Department executives. It was a blockbuster assault against the reputed sovereigns of four of New York's five families, asserting that they constituted the supreme council that ruled America's Mafia. For good measure, several henchmen of the presumed bosses were named as accomplices, creating a total of nine defendants. The Mob's entire ruling class would be put in the dock.

A fifteen-count indictment specifying the accusations was approved, or handed up, in a formal vote by a grand jury in February 1985 at the Federal District Court in Manhattan. The FBI planned to arrest the mobsters early in the morning of Tuesday, February 26, the day the indictment would be unsealed and made public. But a week before the scheduled arrests, news of the gigantic case leaked to the press. "Indictments Taking Aim At Crime Family Big Shots," blazed a headline in New York's *Daily News* on Sunday, February 24. The next day, taking no chances that any of their quarry would go on the lam, agents rounded up the major targets, Paul Castellano, Antonio Corallo, Anthony Salerno, and their codefendants, at their homes. Fat Tony Salerno was the most chagrined at the timing. He was nabbed in his East Harlem apartment when FBI agents arrived simultaneously with the delivery of a huge takeout order from the neighborhood's Andy's Colonial Tavern. The agents refused Salerno's request to allow him to partake of the meal he was sitting down to enjoy with his personal physician, Bernard Wechsler, and four Genovese underlings.

The next morning in a federal courtroom, the FBI supervisor Jim Kossler sat alongside Pat Marshall, watching the spectacle of Mafia dignitaries being escorted en masse for arraignment on RICO charges. "This is it," Kossler thought to himself. "This is great. We finally did what Blakey always told us to do." Afterward, Kossler telephoned Bob Blakey at his office at Notre Dame with news of the indictment. "It's the most exciting moment of my life in the Bureau," he told the law professor.

That same day, at a packed news conference, an ebullient Rudolph Giuliani, flanked by Justice Department and FBI officials, complimented a long list of federal and state law-enforcement officials. Every investigator and prosecutor remotely involved in the preliminaries to the indictment was praised for a contribution. Talking to reporters, FBI Director William Webster briefly mentioned the anti-Mafia statute used to prosecute the bosses. "We had RICO for almost ten years before we knew what to do with it," Webster remarked. In the give-and-take of a noisy, hectic news conference, his tribute to RICO's anonymous creators passed largely unnoticed and unreported.

25

The Curtain Rises

Paul Castellano, the Gambino boss, looked buoyant. It was the week before Christmas 1985, and seemingly without a care he was handing out gifts to clerical staff at the office of his lawyer, James LaRossa. Big Paul was in the midst of one federal racketeering trial and facing another, but to LaRossa he appeared unconcerned and relaxed that late Monday afternoon. After distributing his presents, Castellano sat down for small talk with his lawyer.

Free on a $2 million bond, Castellano did not raise questions about his pressing legal headaches. He spoke only of his taking advantage of the Christmas-New Year's adjournment in the trial for a Florida vacation in Pompano Beach. Before the Commission indictment, the government had accused him of other crimes: conspiracy and profiting from a murderous car-theft crew led by one of the Gambino family's most savage hit men, Roy DeMeo. The indictment in Manhattan charged that the ring stole and shipped hundreds of luxury model cars to Kuwait, clearing $5,000 on every sedan. Castellano was said to have received $20,000 in a wad of one-hundred-dollar bills every week as his share of the profits, though it was unlikely that he had a direct hand in the crew's operation and the twenty-five murders linked to it.

DeMeo, a leading player in the international car-theft scheme, who reveled in chopping up the corpses of murder victims, had met a contract killer's ironic fate. In 1983, he was found shot to death in the trunk of his Cadillac. On the street, the word passed along was that he had become a heavy cocaine user and was considered unstable and unreliable as a codefendant of Big Paul.

A former federal prosecutor and stellar trial lawyer, LaRossa was confident the prosecution's case against Castellano in the stolen-car trial was collapsing, and cheered him by saying that the outlook was good. There were no witnesses to directly tie Castellano to the auto ring and no tape recordings implicating him. Agents in the FBI's Gambino squad, many of whom had opposed citing Castellano in the indictment, privately agreed among themselves that the evidence against him — consisting mainly of testimony from low-level turncoats — was flimsy. They believed Castellano was headed for an acquittal or at most a hung jury in this round with the government.

(Giuliani later told aides that before the trial began he received a second intervention call about a Mob investigation from Senator Alfonse D'Amato, this time concerning Castellano's case. According to published reports, Giuliani believed the senator "seemed naive," and he cautioned him never to broach such matters with him again.)

Once the stolen-cars case was completed, LaRossa planned to plunge into the broader Commission case accusations and prepare for that separate trial. The government had not as yet turned over its incriminating evidence, in legal parlance "discovery materials," to defense lawyers, so LaRossa was unaware of the contents of the tapes that the FBI had obtained from bugs planted in Castellano's house and in the sanctuaries of the other Commission defendants.

At LaRossa's office, Castellano was accompanied by his prime bodyguard and protégé, Thomas Bilotti. The two men presented contrasting versions of contemporary mafiosi. The tall seventy-year-old Castellano cultivated the image of a soft-spoken efficient executive who would be welcomed at the toniest clubs, restaurants, and homes. A man of studied dignity, bedecked in richly tailored suits on his business rounds, and at home in satin and silk dressing gowns and velvet slippers, Castellano's manners and style apparently had failed to influence Bilotti's persona. Short, stubby — built like a fireplug — Bilotti at age forty-five made no outward attempt to imitate his overlord. He wore wrinkled suits and the colors of his jackets and trousers usually clashed. His appearance was further marred by a toupee that always seemed to be on the brink of sliding over his eyes; his detractors used the ill-fitting hairpiece to deride him behind his back as "the Rug." Bilotti's reputation in the Gambino family rested on his rock-solid loyalty to Castellano and a penchant for violence rather than the sophisticated white-collar crimes that Big Paul advocated. There was little sub-terfuge in Bilotti's style: he looked like a goon and he was a goon. A major loan shark in Staten Island, his favorite means of disciplining late-paying customers was slamming them with a baseball bat.

Bilotti's legitimate-occupation cover was a partnership in a Staten Island concrete supplier, Scara-Mix Inc. He was listed as vice president; Castellano's son, Philip, was the president. Much of Scara-Mix's income, at that time in ex-cess of $1 million a year, came from subcontracts on city and state projects.

Before leaving LaRossa's office on Madison Avenue in the late afternoon, Castellano asked the lawyer for the address of a perfume shop on Fifth Avenue, where he wanted to pick up more Christmas gifts. As they walked to the office exit, Castellano whispered to LaRossa that he was pleased with his work in the auto-theft trial. "I'm very happy, Jimmy."

That evening, December 18, 1985, Castellano had a dinner date on Man-hattan's East Side with three capos, Frank DeCicco, James Failla, and Thomas Gambino (Carlo's son). At about 5:45 P.M., with Bilotti at the wheel and Castel-lano sitting alongside him, the Lincoln sedan pulled up in front of Sparks Steak House, an expensive restaurant on East 46th Street where he often dined with his lieutenants. A former butcher and meat purveyor, Castellano fancied him-self a steak connoisseur, and he particularly enjoyed the sirloin cuts at Sparks. Although stopping in an illegal parking zone, Bilotti ignored the prohibition, placing a Patrolmen's Benevolent Association placard inside the windshield.

A fusillade of fatal gunfire engulfed the two men alighting from the car. Three assassins, dressed similarly in conspicuous long, off-white trench coats and Russian-style fur hats, opened fire at close range with pistols. Castellano was hit six times in the head and torso, and Bilotti was struck four times. The triggermen escaped on foot, walking calmly past pedestrians eastward toward Second Avenue. Having reigned unchallenged as the Gambino boss for nine years, and despite the heavy security precautions taken at his home, Castellano had felt safe enough to travel around the city without a screen of guards. Tom Bilotti, his lone protector, was unarmed that evening, another indication of Castellano's confidence.

Even before the autopsy on Castellano was completed the next morning, agents and police investigators on the FBI's Gambino Squad were reasonably certain they knew who had engineered the double murder. All outward signs pointed to John Gotti, the capo of one of the most violent Gambino crews and the family's most devoted adherent of Aniello Dellacroce, Castellano's underboss. Secret FBI bugs had picked up conversations among Gambino members about chronic discord between Gotti's crew and Castellano, especially the latter's demands for information about a botched narcotics deal involving Gotti's brother Gene. Two weeks before Castellano's assassination, Dellacroce had died of cancer, and FBI agents knew that for some time he had been a buffer shielding John Gotti and his crew from Castellano's wrath.

FBI mafiologists theorized that Dellacroce's death also removed the final restraints that prevented Gotti from launching a preemptory strike, before Castellano could move against him. The speculation sounded even more credible when informers reported that soon after the double murder, Gotti had usurped Castellano's crown. John Gotti was the new boss of the Gambino borgata. But investigators were unable to find an atom of evidence attaching Gotti to the Sparks Steak House ambush.

A final indignity for Paul Castellano came when the Roman Catholic Archdiocese of New York announced that after "prayer and consultation," it had banned a public mass for Castellano because of the "notoriety" of his background. Even in death Big Paul appeared inferior to his idol and instructor, Carlo Gambino. Don Carlo had indisputably been the paradigm of a Cosa Nostra titan of his generation, but he died of natural causes, and the church, apparently oblivious to press reports about his disreputable past, accorded him the full rites of a requiem mass.

Paul Castellano and Neil Dellacroce's deaths substantially reshaped the prosecution strategy and the topography of the Commission trial. At the time of the indictments, Giuliani and the FBI had branded Big Paul as the nation's most powerful and important Cosa Nostra figure and had cast him as the star defendant. With Castellano gone, several of the bugged conversations in his Staten Island home had to be excluded as evidence because they were relevant only to him. Although the Castellano tapes would have lent support to the overall charges, the prosecution team doubted that the lost evidence endangered the substance of their case against the remaining bosses. Therefore, the trial would proceed without any direct Gambino family involvement in the case.

For tactical reasons, the prosecution eliminated another original defendant, Philip "Rusty" Rastelli, who had been installed as the Bonanno boss after Carmine Galante's murder. The evidence against him was skimpy. His voice had not been recorded on any of the bugs, although other accused Commission members and mobsters referred to him by name. Rastelli was instead indicted and convicted in the Eastern District jurisdiction on different RICO charges—that he led a Bonanno conspiracy to extort millions of dollars from New York's moving-and-storage industry.

While the Gambino and Bonanno godfathers were removed from the trial, Giuliani's prosecutors brought another boss into the Commission lineup: Carmine the Snake Persico, the alleged head of the Colombo family, was added as a defendant in a superseding set of charges. The nine mafiosi in the first indictment were reduced to eight, and Fat Tony Salerno became the lead defendant in a trial docket titled, *United States* v. *Anthony Salerno, et al.*

The revised indictment covered Commission representatives of only three of the five dominant Mob families. Anthony Salerno, identified as a boss, was the lone Genovese leader on trial. Carmine Persico and his underboss, Gennaro Gerry Lang Langella, were the reputed Colombo big shots. The largest contingent were the Luccheses: Antonio Ducks Corrallo as boss; Salvatore Tom Mix Santoro, the purported underboss; and Christopher "Christie Tick" Furnari, the suspected consigliere.

Ralph Scopo, the concrete-workers' union leader, who dined frequently at the Casa Storta with Gerry Lang, was indicted as the alleged collector of payoffs for the bosses in the Concrete Club. Identified as a Colombo soldier, he was too low-level to participate in Commission deliberations. Scopo was accused of being a Commission gofer, arranging and implementing schemes for the Mob leviathans.

The final defendant, Anthony Bruno Indelicato, a Bonanno hit man, also was not charged with being a Commission member. He was on trial for carrying out a Commission order in 1979 to assassinate Carmine Galante, who prosecutors and the FBI believed at that time was the Bonanno godfather. Indelicato's role in the murder had boosted his underworld career, leading to his promotion to capo in the Bonanno family.

U.S. Attorneys rarely serve as front-line, courtroom prosecutors, leaving those tasks to their corps of assistants. A U.S. Attorney's primary role in a major post like New York is administrative, overseeing scores of cases streaming through his office. He is not expected to spend months in a grinding courtroom battle and simultaneously fulfill—or neglect—supervisory duties. Rudolph Giuliani, however, was confident that he could handle his administrative responsibilities *and* conduct the prosecution in the most important organized-crime trial of the century, the Commission case. But events in 1986 altered his plan. A political corruption scandal erupted over the awarding of more than $20 million in equipment and maintenance contracts by New York City's parking-meters agency, the Parking Violations Bureau. The investigation culminated in an indictment against one of the city's most influential political figures, Stanley J. Friedman, the head of the Bronx Democratic Party organization, a leading lobbyist at City Hall. Here, too, Giuliani resorted to an innovative use of RICO, expanding its scope by employing it against public corruption as well as the Mafia. He charged Friedman and three city officials with fixing contracts and converting the Parking Violations Bureau into a racketeering "enterprise" covered by the RICO statute.

Torn between leading the prosecution at the Commission trial or at the equally high-profile case against Friedman, Giuliani chose the politically sensitive one. He told aides that the evidence appeared overwhelming against the Mafia bosses, and that other bright prosecutors could convict the lot. The parking bureau trial would be a closer call, he reasoned, and an acquittal would diminish his and the office's reputation. Perhaps an added ego incentive for Giuliani was the prospect of squaring off against a renowned rival and former federal prosecutor in Brooklyn, Thomas Puccio. Before becoming a defense lawyer for Stanley Friedman, Puccio had been acclaimed as one of the nation's most tenacious prosecutors against corrupt politicians and the mob—the image of invincibility that Giuliani had coveted for himself.

As his substitute for lead prosecutor in the Commission case, Giuliani tapped a relatively inexperienced assistant, Michael Chertoff. Tall, balding with a bushy black mustache, the thirty-two-year-old Chertoff had worked with Giuliani from the start of the investigation two and half years earlier, in 1983, and was immersed in every detail of the case. The son of a rabbi of the Conservative branch of Judaism, he came from the blue-collar town of Elizabeth, New Jersey. He was a graduate of Harvard Law School and had obtained a prestigious clerkship with Supreme Court Justice William Brennan before joining Giuliani's staff as an assistant U.S. Attorney. Although Chertoff had been a prosecutor only three years and had never before conducted a Mafia trial or a knotty one that hinged on electronic surveillance, Giuliani considered him a brilliant, lightening-quick litigator, who would not be fazed by the legal howitzers that would be lined up on behalf of the bosses. Hearing the news and realizing that he had been given a golden opportunity to direct a heavyweight case, Chertoff had only one thought: "I'd better win or it will be very, very embarrassing." He began putting in eighteen-hour sessions, seven days a week, preparing for the expected courtroom hostilities.

A chief judge of New York State's courts once said that a resourceful prosecutor, if it struck his fancy, could indict "a ham sandwich." An indictment might appear overwhelming on paper, but trial lawyers know how easy it is for prosecutors to persuade a grand jury composed of ordinary citizens to generate criminal accusations. Normally, a grand jury is presented with only one version of evidence—the prosecution's. The real battles are in the courtrooms and the appeals courts. Chertoff and two other young prosecutors, John F. Savarese and J. Gilmore Childres, would be confronting a battery of artful lawyers skilled in organized-crime defense maneuvers. And with deep pockets, the bosses had the money to call on expert witnesses and other resources to contest the prosecution's evidence and testimony.

There was one immediate surprise for the defense side. In an extraordinary move, claiming he had more actual courtroom experience than most lawyers, the quixotic Carmine the Snake Persico had elected to represent himself.

Hovering over both sides, even before the trial began, were the unresolved questions of the effectiveness and legality of the RICO statute. The Commission case loomed as a landmark event in the history of the American Mafia. It was the first significant courtroom test of RICO. Even if guilty verdicts against the nation's highest-ranking mafiosi were obtained, the conflict would continue. There would be hard-fought appeals to determine if convictions under the newly applied law were constitutional and sustained by the higher courts, ultimately the U.S. Supreme Court.

The three federal attorneys trying the Commission case faced another subtle handicap. The jury's decision might be affected by widespread doubts in the country that the Mafia or Cosa Nostra actually existed. Important officials were continuing to question whether the Mob was a myth invented and exaggerated by arrogant, publicity-thirty law-enforcement officials. After Castellano's slaying, New York Governor Mario Cuomo brought this issue to the forefront. He spoke out at a news conference against ethnic stereotypes and slurs that he said had been inflicted on himself and other Italian-Americans by frequent law-enforcement and press references to the Mafia. In part it somewhat echoed Joe Colombo's screed against the FBI fifteen years earlier. Cuomo lamented the frequent use of "Mafia" to describe organized crime. Since Mafia is an Italian word, Cuomo told reporters, "every time you say it, you suggest to people that organized crime is Italian—it's an ugly stereotype." Asked if the Mafia existed, the governor replied, "You're telling me that Mafia is an organization, and I'm telling you that's a lot of baloney."

To succeed at trial, the prosecution would have to convince all twelve jurors of four basic facts: the Mafia and its presumably all-powerful ruling body, the Commission, existed; the defendants were Commission members or carried out its orders; through the so-called Concrete Club, the Commission controlled a major building-trades industry; and the Commission was responsible for Carmine Galante's execution.

In September 1986, in the austere Federal District Courthouse in Foley Square, the trial began. The dramatic tone was set on the first day when presiding Judge Richard Owen agreed to a prosecution motion for an anonymous jury. Withholding the juror's identities and addresses to protect them from possible intimidation and tampering was a blow to the defense; in 1986 juror anonymity was rarely imposed. The ruling suggested to the jurors that they had to be protected from these defendants.

As its vital witness to lay out the origins and customs of the American Mafia and the Commission, the prosecution presented Angelo Lonardo, the self-described former acting boss and underboss of Cleveland's mobster family. Serving as an on-the-scene historian, Lonardo, seventy-five-years old, recalled ancient Mafia events, the formation of the Commission, and gangland killings dating back to the 1920s. He had "flipped," turned government witness, in the hope of having a life sentence reduced for a racketeering and narcotics-trafficking conviction. Besides his vivid testimony about the Mob's organizational structure, traditions, and codes of conduct, Lonardo described the rank and status of each of the defendants. He singled out "Fat Tony" Salerno as the Cleveland Mob's contact for dealing with the Commission.

On the witness stand, Lonardo was asked by prosecutor Michael Chertoff, "What are the Commission's functions within La Cosa Nostra?"

LONARDO: "Well, if there is a dispute about anything they get together and iron it out."

CHERTOFF: "Are there any other functions the Commission performs?"

LONARDO: "They make all the rules and regulations, what you can do, what you can't do."

Outlining the Commission's authority over all borgatas, Lonardo said, "Well, the rules are that they can't kill a boss in other cities or in New York City without them knowing anything about it."

Joe Bonanno's self-aggrandizement and published tales of his past glories were turned into Mafia gospel and evidence harmful to the defense. The former Bonanno boss refused to testify, but the prosecution played his TV interview on *60 Minutes* in which he boasted about his role in the birth of the Cosa Nostra and the origin and evolution of the Commission.

Colorful and more recent insight came from a former Colombo family associate, Joseph Cantalupo. An FBI informer, he said that like all members of the gang, he was apprised that Persico was anointed the borgata's boss after Joe Colombo was shot and paralyzed in 1972. Cantalupo even provided coffee-klatch details of a Commission gathering in the late 1960s, the height of Colombo's power. Claiming a cordial relationship with Colombo, Cantalupo said he gave the Mob boss a phantom job in his Brooklyn real estate firm, which Colombo used as a front for his illegal activities.

"One day, Mr. Colombo asked me if he can use my apartment for a meeting," Cantalupo recalled. "I said, 'Of course,'" Colombo then gave him culinary instructions: "Tomorrow night have your wife make a large pot of black coffee, go out and buy a couple of pounds of Italian cookies, and set the table for five. We'll be over as soon as it gets dark."

The next day, Cantalupo sat on the stoop of his building and observed Colombo, Carlo Gambino, other bosses, and their bodyguards arrive in their cars and climb the stairs to his apartment. None of them acted furtively or attempted to disguise himself. Several hours later, they came down one at a time and drove off.

Lonardo and Cantalupo's testimony about life among gangsters was garishly interesting, but both had made deals for softer sentences, and their accounts were therefore suspect—and insufficient to confirm the existence and potency of the Commission. Their tales became important only because they added flesh and meaningfulness to the prosecution's essential body of evidence: the tapes from the secret bugs.

Lonardo's version of the Commission's supremacy within the Mafia was buttressed by a recording of a meeting in the Palma Boys Social Club on the morning of October 8, 1984. Two men identified as members of the Cleveland family, John Tronolone and Joe Pieri, were heard requesting help from the Genovese's "Fat Tony" Salerno to resolve a leadership dispute in their borgata. It was at that session that Salerno told the two Cleveland emissaries that he would pass along their reports to other Commission members. His tone became more lordly when he warned them to instruct a maverick mafioso to end a feud on installing a new Cleveland boss. "Let the Commission decide," Salerno was heard saying, adding, "Tell him it's the Commission from New York. Tell him he's dealing with the big boys now."

Salerno's recorded conversations about denying Rusty Rastelli, the New Bonanno boss, a seat on the Commission, reinforced prosecution charges of how the Mafia operated. On February 29, 1984, Fat Tony explained to Mickey Generoso, a Genovese capo, his views on Rastelli. "I told the Commission," Salerno confided, "'Ah, ah, hey, listen, this guy wants to be the boss. He can be the boss as far as I'm concerned.' I said, 'but he cannot be on the Commission. One vote is enough to throw it out. Cause, the Commission thing, it's supposed to be such a sacred thing.'"

Rastelli's efforts to gain admission to the Commission came up again at the Palma Boys Social Club on May 22, 1984, when Salerno met with James Ida, a Genovese soldier, and Matty the Horse Ianniello, the Genovese capo of Umberto's Clam House fame. Ianniello told Salerno that Rastelli had given him the names of men he wanted to induct into his family, which would have to be vetted by Genovese family higher-ups.

The report provoked a tirade from Salerno about Rastelli's reliance on "junk guys," narcotics traffickers, in the Bonanno family. "Listen," he railed, "we don't recognize him down there. . . . I didn't want to meet [with Rastelli], Paul [Castellano] didn't want to meet. Tony Ducks told Rusty, he said, 'Listen,' he said, 'take care of your family first. Straighten out your family and when you straighten them out, then we talk about the Commission.'"

Concealed microphones at the Palma Boys also picked up incriminating remarks from Ducks Corallo's two closest subordinates in the Lucchese family, Salvatore Tom Mix Santoro, the underboss, and Christopher Christie Tick Furnari, the consigliere. They met with Salerno to review the question of barring Rusty Rastelli from the Commission. Fat Tony further worried that Rastelli's excessive drug deals could endanger other New York families.

The conversation about the Bonanno family's exclusion from the Commission and narcotics politics was a major piece of prosecution evidence compromising Santoro and Furnari in the RICO "enterprise." Santoro, in his seventies, was no stranger to drug deals. Like Corallo he was an alumnus of an East Harlem gang that was mixed up in drug sales before and after World War II. The biggest blot on his record was a four-year prison sentence in the 1950s for narcotics sales. Furnari had an arrest record for assault and loan-sharking, and like most mafiosi of his generation had evaded felony convictions and long prison interludes.

The Jaguar bug was indispensable for the prosecution, contributing numerous insights about the powers of a boss, including the death sentence for those ignoring a godfather's edict, the scheduling of Commission meetings, and the induction of members into families. It even revealed the contempt mobsters had for law-enforcement campaigns against them.

Two weeks after Giuliani was sworn in as U.S. Attorney in July 1983, Sal Avellino, the Lucchese capo, was filling in his boss, Ducks Corallo, on Giuliani's pronouncements that he was dedicated to uprooting the Mafia. While driving, Avellino mentioned that Giuliani and other officials believed that stepped-up government repression would rout the Mob. Mocking Giuliani, Avellino paraphrased the prosecutor's objectives.

AVELLINO: "The Italians are traditional gangsters and they [the officials] feel that within the next ten to twenty years they can completely eliminate it [the Mafia] because they've been getting more and more information on them."

CORALLO: "Yeah, they'll eliminate themselves."

AVELLINO: "Well and that was the day he [Giuliani] says, 'We have to hire more prosecutors because if we hire more we can eliminate it [the Mafia].' So I says to myself, 'Well you better go and hire six right away because we just added six last night.'"

Later in July, riding in the Jaguar, Ducks Corallo became disturbed when Avellino told him that an article in *The New York Times* had identified him, Santoro, and Furnari as the hierarchy of the Lucchese family. Both men were upset that the story reported that the gang dealt in narcotics, and it triggered a discussion about the Mafia's fluctuating attitude about drugs. Narcotics deals were profitable but attracted more police attention than their other illicit activities. Tony Ducks said he wanted his soldiers cautioned that he would order them slain if they engaged in extensive trafficking. In his Mafia code, he was imparting to Avellino the Mafia's basic theme that it was permissible to furtively peddle drugs but not to get caught.

CORALLO: "Now I couldn't be any fucking plainer than I was with some of these guys 'cause I don't want anybody fucking with junk, they gotta be killed. That's all. Fuck this shit."

AVELLINO: "Sure, this is the whole fuckin' problem. Is the junk. They [law enforcement] don't care about the gambling and all that other bullshit. They never did . . ."

A few minutes later, Corallo returned to his concern over narcotics trafficking by his troops. ". . . You can't be in the junk business without goin' in the fuckin' streets and selling this cocksucking shit. We should kill them. We should have some examples. See, other people [Mob families] ain't like us. . . . Well, anybody with us, anybody comes near us, you know, we'll kill 'em. Don't worry, that gets to their fucking ears. See?"

Several days later, Avellino and Corallo again talked in the Jaguar about the news reports identifying the family's leaders and the gang's illegal pursuits. Tony Ducks reiterated how he tried to stay out of the spotlight to evade attention from law-enforcement agencies and reporters.

At one point, Corallo and Avellino proudly confirmed Tony Ducks's underworld position.

AVELLINO: "It said in that, in that article, it says about Tony, Tony Ducks, about he controls the Garment Center, he controls waste foliage [sic] disposal business. And the construction."

CORALLO: "Yeah sure, didn't you know that?"

AVELLINO: "'Course I know that. I know it because I'm with you, but not everybody else knows."

CORALLO: "Yeah, well, they ain't supposed to know."

Both men broke into gales of laughter.

On another Jaguar excursion, Avellino and Richard DeLuca, a Lucchese soldier involved in Garment Center rackets, were surprised at the ignorance of a new "straightened out," inducted, Lucchese member concerning payoffs to the boss.

AVELLINO: "Before he was straightened out, he's telling me that the union is his, you know? So, I'm saying, 'What, what do you mean the union is yours?' He believes the fuckin' union is his. And what am I gonna say, union? Nothing is yours. Everything is the boss."

DELUCA: "Yeah."

AVELLINO: "Wait, and we, we only got the privilege of working it, or running it. Unless you got a something that is a legitimate thing, that you know, that it's yours, then they say, 'Well, that's yours.' But anything that's got to do . . ."

DELUCA: "You operate at his pleasure."

AVELLINO: "You do what he wants. I mean, and even, even if, with a legitimate thing, you operate at his pleasure ninety percent of the time."

More indirect proof that the Mafia was a secret society and that membership was a preoccupying concern came from the Jaguar tapes. A decision on whether to groom his own son for induction occupied Avellino's thoughts in the spring of 1983, and he sought advice from Corallo and Santoro in separate conversations. He raised the subject with Corallo, referring to a Colombo capo, Andrew "the Fat Man" Russo.

AVELLINO: "Andy Russo just made his other son, the youngest one."

CORALLO: "They [the Colombos] make all their kids, huh."

AVELLINO: "Yeah, he made his two sons."

CORALLO: "Would you make your kids?"

AVELLINO: "No, not now. I mean my thinking right now is no. It might change five years from now, ten years from now, but right now my thinking is no."

On another drive alone with Avellino, Santoro, the underboss, without offering reasons, said he and Corallo had never encouraged their sons to become mafiosi. Noting that other Lucchese members "feel we have to think about it," a conflicted Avellino expressed his thoughts.

"If this life was good enough for you and the life was good enough for me. If we really believe in it, why wouldn't we want our sons [to join]. If I were a doctor, I would be saying to my son, since he was a little kid, you're going to be a doctor or if I was a lawyer I would be looking for my son to be a lawyer, so they must feel that if this life was good enough for me, I want it for my son also. Otherwise we're really saying that this fucking life is no fucking good. It's for the birds. Right? Because we always want for our kids what's good for them. Right?"

Testimony about the Commission's tight supervision of the fractious Bonanno borgata came from Joseph Pistone, the FBI agent who had been a mole in the Bonanno family. Posing as a mobster named Donnie Brasco, Pistone secretly recorded conversations supporting the prosecution's contentions that the Commission possessed unquestioned authority within the Mafia.

On April 2, 1981, Benjamin "Lefty Guns" Ruggiero, a Bonanno soldier, notified Brasco that the Commission had decreed a truce among warring groups in the borgata following the murder of Carmine Galante. Ruggiero said he expected that Rusty Rastelli, the leader of his faction, would be ratified by the Commission as a boss when he was released from prison and the family became autonomous again. "So," the jury heard Ruggiero's recorded voice say, "we'll just see 'til Rusty comes home, but whether we can survive these fucking sixteen fucking months, which them bosses says no war. First guy fucks with a pistol they'll break up the whole crew."

Pistone-Brasco accompanied Ruggiero to a June 1981 meeting with Dominick "Sonny Black" Napolitano, a Bonanno capo, the head of Ruggiero's crew. The jury listened as Ruggiero promised that Brasco, the undercover agent, would be inducted into the Mafia as soon as possible. "Now you're going to get straightened out, Donnie," Lefty Guns vowed. A few seconds later, the volatile Ruggiero urged Napolitano to break the truce and wipe out the main opposition to their control of the Bonanno family, the Zips, the Sicilian-immigrant crew.

Napolitano cut him short. "I can't do that. It's Commission rules," the capo declared.

There was no shortage of tapes disclosing various views of Commission decrees. The secret microphones above table one at the Casa Storta Restaurant in Bensonhurst, Brooklyn, exposed another chapter on the Commission's authority over financial disputes between Mob families. On January 26, 1983, the acting Colombo boss, Gerry Lang Langella, dined with Dominic "Donnie Shacks" Montemarano, a Colombo capo, and Angelo "Fat Angie" Ruggiero, a friend and Gambino soldier. (Fat Angie was not related to the Bonanno's Lefty Guns Ruggiero.) Langella and Montemarano summarized for Ruggiero their displeasure at a Commission ruling that cost the Colombo family $25,000.

The clatter of dishes and silverware could not mask the anger in their voices over a failed shake-down. They told Ruggiero how one of their soldiers had squeezed $50,000 from a construction company for labor peace. The owner of the company solicited a relative, a Lucchese soldier, to intervene in the shake-down. Because of the contractor's blood ties to a Lucchese member, Ducks Corallo persuaded the Commission to reduce the Colombo's extortion fee to $25,000. At a sit-down, Langella, a mere acting boss, was outvoted and outranked three to one by Corallo, Castellano, and Salerno.

A chagrined Langella indicated to Ruggiero that a $25,000 loss was relatively small change for him, but he was incensed by the other families meddling in a Colombo scheme, a sign of disrespect. He had held his tongue at the sit-down with the bosses. Now he spoke more candidly in his typical obscene style. "'Cause I asked three guys [the bosses] if I was entitled to it [the $50,000]. 'Maybe I'm wrong,' I said. 'Maybe I'm not entitled to it.' When three people tell me I'm not entitled to it, I waive. What's the big deal? I'll make these fuckin' bosses eat shit. I'll blow their ass off."

Commiserating, Ruggiero said his uncle Neil Dellacroce, the Gambino underboss who was then alive, agreed with the Colombos. "Neil told me," Ruggiero said, "he wanted to give it [the $50,000] to youse."

Ruggiero assured Langella that Dellacroce, an old-fashioned, violence-loving gangster, was equally dismayed at the Commission's preoccupation with construction-industry rackets at the expense of other Mafia matters. "He's disgusted with construction," said Ruggiero. "He said, 'They [the Commission] meet for construction.' He said, 'I can't believe it. That's all they talk about is money. Money, money, money.'"

26

The Concrete Club

The most compelling evidence of the Commission's money-making prowess centered on the Concrete Club. At the trial, the jury got a clear picture of how the governors of three families and the slain Paul Castellano had ripped off at least $1.27 million from thirteen major building projects over a four-year period.

Prosecutors trotted out as witnesses two contractors who testified that they had been compelled to participate in the extortion scheme as the price for staying in business. "I don't think I had much of a choice," James Costigan, president of the XLO Concrete Corporation, said. He related that Ralph Scopo, the Colombo soldier and president of the concrete-workers' union, approached him in 1981 with news that he would have to kick back to mobsters 2 percent of each gross contract that he was allowed to obtain. If Costigan defied the system, Scopo threatened him with unparalleled union miseries.

Asked by prosecutor John Savarese what the effect of the labor problems would have been on his company, Costigan answered, "Cost a lot of money, you know, to the point where you may as well not be in business."

Scopo told the contractor that payoffs to the Cosa Nostra would be collected on all contracts over $2 million. "He said it was going into a pot and would be divided among the families."

Seven companies were in the club, Costigan testified: "The people who controlled it made a decision on who got what job." Costigan clarified that none of the companies suffered financially from the Mob's scheme. Indeed, they profited from the plot. Like other concrete subcontractors, he added 4 percent to his bids and simply passed along the inflated costs to the developer or general contractor in charge of the overall project. (Analysts ultimately determined that the Mafia's collaboration with corrupt contractors elevated actual overall concrete costs in the city from between 15 percent to 70 percent because all of the prearranged bids were grossly inflated.)

Scopo directed Costigan not to compete for contracts below $2 million, implying that the Mob bosses were not overly greedy. "Well, there was a lot of small contractors and he said they had to eat too."

Backing up Costigan's testimony, the prosecution played a recording made by a bug in Scopo's Lincoln sedan. On the tape Scopo was heard rejecting a request by an insistent contractor, Sal D'Ambrosi, whose company was not in the Concrete Club.

SCOPO: "The concrete's gotta be twelve million."

D'AMBROSI: "Yeah. Why can't I do the concrete?"

SCOPO: "You can't do it. Over two million you can't do it. It's under two million, hey, me, I tell you go ahead and do it."

D'AMBROSI: "Who do I gotta see? Tell me who I gotta go see?"

SCOPO: "You gotta see every family. And they're gonna tell you, no. So don't even bother."

D'Ambrosi persisted in determining what price he would have to pay if he were fortunate enough to be included in the club.

SCOPO: "First of all the job costs you two points."

D'AMBROSI: "Why two points?"

SCOPO: "That's what they pay. Anything over two million. All the guys in the club, got so much out, pay two points."

D'AMBROSI: "Uh huh. Put two points into the job."

SCOPO: "That's what I say, you gotta put it in ahead of time."

Digging a deeper hole for himself in the taped conversation, Scopo informed D'Ambrosi that, on a project not covered by the club, he would have to cough up separate bribes to him for labor peace. It was a lesson for the jury on the fundamentals of corruption and exorbitant construction costs in New York.

SCOPO: "You know, if I bring you a customer [a general contractor], twenty yards [a concrete measurement], and I tell you, Sally, the concrete is $60 a yard, the guy's gonna give you $63."

D'AMBROSI: "Three's yours."

SCOPO: "Three you gotta give me. What do you give a fuck?"

D'AMBROSI: "What do I give a fuck for."

SCOPO: "You're getting your 60."

D'AMBROSI: "That's it. What the fuck is the problem?"

SCOPO: "And meantime, I'm bringing you the customer."

The FBI tapes illuminated the Commission's power of life and death. Scopo admitted that he feared for his life should the Concrete Club come under investigation. Talking with Costigan, the XLO contractor, Scopo's mind was on the fate of Roy DeMeo, the Gambino soldier and sadistic killer who was murdered after he was implicated in the Gambino family's stolen-car network. Scopo described DeMeo as a strict enforcer with "cast-iron balls." Nevertheless, he was whacked because one boss, Paul Castellano, decided without proof that DeMeo was no longer reliable. DeMeo's fate alarmed Scopo, the Commission's bagman.

SCOPO: "Now I get indicted and they're [the bosses] afraid. 'Oh geez, we never knew that guy Jimmy Costigan.' The only guy they got to worry about is me. If I open my mouth, they're dead. So to kill the case—bango!"

COSTIGAN: "Really?"

SCOPO: "Yeah. Here I am all my life makin' them make money. I'm takin' the fuckin' chances in the street. I'm willing to go to jail, never gonna open my mouth, but they're not sure of that, see?"

Sounding grave, Scopo said that a corrupt carpenters' union leader, Theodore Maritas, recently had been murdered after his involvement with the Mob was exposed and he was about to go on trial with Mafia codefendants. He reminded Costigan of Roy DeMeo's frightening end.

SCOPO: "And I mean, he was a tough guy, all right? Bein' he got picked up, they figure, 'Maybe this guy under pressure, he'll rat.' That's bullshit. But not to take the chance, not knowin' whether he would or not, they went and killed him. It's just like what I'm doin' now. Say this thing kinda blows up. I'll be one of the first guys to get arrested."

COSTIGAN: "Why?"

SCOPO: "Because of this club shit. Now when that happens, no matter how much faith they got in you, there's always that little bit. They say, 'Oh, geez, maybe he'll open his fuckin' mouth.' And then you don't see the guy no more."

From the grave Paul Castellano contributed to the evidence against the live bosses. A Genovese soldier, Louis Giardina, a laborers' union official, had visited Castellano's Staten Island home in June 1983 to discuss interfamily business in the construction industry. Castellano dropped the names of several of the city's largest general contractors who, he said, had personally promised him they would give lucrative subcontracting jobs to Mafia-controlled companies.

The FBI bug then recorded Castellano complaining that the Century-Maxim Company, a contractor in the Concrete Club, was bidding for contracts without the bosses' permission.

CASTELLANO: "You know the Century-Maxim outfit, Century-Maxim?"

GIARDINA: "The concrete?"

CASTELLANO: "Yeah. Been acting a little funny and so far, they're not acting right. And they're supposed to be with Gerry Lang [the Colombo acting boss] and so forth. They're part of the club, part of it. They're raiding everybody."

GIARDINA: "You never want that. It don't make sense."

CASTELLANO: "It's a pain in the ass. Isn't it?"

GIARDINA: "You would think they'd be big boys. Go according to some rules like, right?"

CASTELLANO: "Well, we don't know who the hell is causing it. You know, they can't expect to do too much of the jobs. Too much work. There's work to go around and then everybody can get a piece of it."

GIARDINA: "And if they cooperate, it's gonna be good for everybody, you know, rather than creating confusion and everything else."

CASTELLANO: "Sure."

Castellano's concrete deals sometimes confused other gangsters. Fat Tony Salerno was concerned that he was getting cheated in December 1983 in a secret, three-way partnership with Castellano and Nicholas Auletta, the owner of record of a company that had been sold to Century-Maxim. Louis DiNapoli, a Genovese soldier who handled construction rackets for the family, tried vainly to chart for Salerno how a $200,000 illicit profit would be shared. Their talk was recorded in Salerno's East Harlem headquarters.

DINAPOLI: "But it's in other words like a payoff."

SALERNO: "Nah. But they still gotta give it. They give, they paying us off 200,000 down, at 20,000 a month."

DINAPOLI: "Nicky [Auletta] only was entitled to a hundred."

SALERNO: "So where's the hundred?"

DINAPOLI: "Of that money. Yeah. Now out of the hundred, he gives fifty back to Paul. And fifty back to you. Credit to what he owes you."

Still perplexed, Salerno asked why he was not getting more cash. DiNapoli's explanation that Auletta's corporation had lost money in part of the transaction left Salerno even more confused.

DINAPOLI: "It's the corporation that lost it, not just Nicky. The corporation. You own 25 percent of the corporation. And Paul owns 25 percent of the corporation, and Nicky owns 50 percent. So you split it up that way. You're under the impression that you knock a hundred off."

SALERNO: "What he owes us."

DINAPOLI: "No, it's only fifty comes off what he owes. That's why I, that's why I had to give you another twenty."

While the high-finance economics lesson might have been abstruse to Salerno—and to the jury—the conversation nevertheless clearly showed his and Castellano's complicity in illegal Concrete Club payoffs.

Some interfamily concrete transactions were far from harmonious. The Jaguar bugs bared the resentment in the top ranks of the Genovese and Lucchese families of Castellano's schemes to produce money from construction companies and unions for himself.

The Luccheses' Tony Ducks Corallo was eager to learn about new Mafia machinations he had not tried. On a Jaguar trip, Duck's underboss, Tom Mix Santoro, outlined a $500,000 score by Castellano. Santoro described a meeting with "Fat Tony" Salerno and Vincent DiNapoli, another DiNapoli brother who specialized in construction extortions for the Genovese family. In discussing shake-downs with Salerno, Santoro had deliberately roiled Salerno by telling him about Castellano's pocketing a huge amount from a concrete manufacturer, Certified Ready Mix. Santoro seemed pleased with himself as he described the conversation.

SANTORO: "Now I went and steamed Fat Tony up. I says, 'Hey, do you know Paul got one-half million for selling Certified?' He looked at me, 'What are you kidding?' 'Yeah,' I says, 'he got a half a million.'"

Santoro said that the irate "Fat Tony" Salerno called Vincent DiNapoli to his side, demanding to know, with "daggers in his eyes," why he had not been clued in to the Certified sale. More important, why had he been excluded from a slice of the profit?

Then Santoro, instructing Sal Avellino on the finer points of Mafia protocol, said Vincent DiNapoli had committed a grievous error by replying that he had thought Castellano's plot had nothing to do with Salerno, his immediate over-seer. "It's not your fucking business to think," Santoro said of DiNapoli's re-sponse. "You tell him [Salerno]. And then it's business for him to think, not you."

Avellino had his own story to tell Ducks Corallo about Castellano's acquisi-tive nature. He had accompanied Santoro to a rendezvous with Castellano and had overheard the Gambino boss whining that the leaders of a teamsters' local had reduced his yearly payment from their labor-peace shakedowns with Gam-bino muscle support to $25,000 from $200,000.

"They used to send me a bone every year, about 200,000 a year," Avellino quoted Castellano, astonished at his minimizing the payoff. "That's 'a bone,' he says."

Indicating that the incident was typical of Castellano's grasping for the largest portions of Mafia loot, Corallo said, "I got to listen to him bullshit. A bone, two hundred thousand dollars? . . . Imagine that, he didn't get enough. I don't understand this for the fucking hell of me, he didn't get enough. Imagine that, he didn't get enough money?"

The only defendants' voices missing from the electronic surveillance were those of Carmine Persico, the accused Colombo boss, and Anthony Bruno In-delicato, the Bonanno soldier on trial for Carmine Galante's murder.

During much of the time in the early 1980s when the secret tapes were pro-ducing evidence, Persico was tucked away in prison, completing a hijacking sentence. The prosecution attempted to tie him to the Commission and the Concrete Club through recorded comments about him by Gerry Langella, the family's acting boss, and the other defendants. But the most devastating evi-dence against Persico came from a witness, a cousin by marriage, Fred DeChristopher, an insurance salesman.

Before his arrest on the Commission indictment, Persico was on the run, and had used DeChristopher's home in Wantagh, Long Island, as a safe house for three months. DeChristopher tipped the FBI to Persico's hideout and re-ceived a $50,000 reward for turning in the gangster.

Questioned by Michael Chertoff, the lead prosecutor, DeChristopher told how through marriage he had become an unwitting aide to Colombo leaders and a recipient of the crime family's secrets. While Persico was hiding out in his home, DeChristopher said, he talked freely about his illegal activities, boasting that from prison he had used visitors and telephone calls to Langella and other loyalists to relay orders about criminal operations. "His business was running a crime family," DeChristopher said matter-of-factly.

DeChristopher looped two other defendants, Gerry Langella and Ralph Scopo, into Persico's crime regime. Persico frequently referred to Langella as trustworthy and characterized him as one of his key men. DeChristopher testified, "He said Ralph Scopo was his front man in the cement and concrete workers' union and that not a yard of concrete was poured in the city of New York where he and his friends didn't get a piece of it."

Through DeChristopher, Chertoff elicited evidence not only against Persico but indirectly against the entire Commission. According to DeChristopher, Persico reminisced about sharing a federal prison cell with Carmine Galante in the 1970s. Galante was serving time for narcotics trafficking and Persico, a comparatively young boss, was beginning his hijacking sentence. The two mafiosi had a good relationship, DeChristopher testified, and Persico said Galante "was a friend and the top man in the Bonanno family."

DeChristopher remembered Persico saying, "And quite frankly, I voted against him getting hurt." The quote was used by the prosecution to strengthen the charge that although Persico opposed it, the Commission took a poll and a majority sanctioned the killing of Galante.

The most substantial evidence against Bruno Indelicato in the 1979 Galante murder was the palm print lifted from the gunmen's getaway car in Brooklyn. His appearance at Neil Dellacroce's Ravenite Club in Little Italy shortly after the murder was, at best, circumstantial. But the prosecution played the surveillance videotape to the jury, showing a perspiring Indelicato being hugged and kissed on the cheeks by Dellacroce, then the Gambino underboss, and Stefano Cannone, the Bonanno consigliere. Chertoff strung together the palm print, the welcome that Indelicato got from two Mob leaders, and Persico's telling DeChristopher about voting against Galante's execution. He argued that the three elements, plus historical testimony that only the Commission could authorize the murder of high-ranking mafiosi, was sufficient proof of a conspiracy. In the prosecution's scenario, the Commission bosses ordered Galante's murder. Dellacroce was assigned to supervise the hit; Indelicato helped commit it, and then rushed to Little Italy to report his successful accomplishment to Gambino and Bonanno big shots. Chertoff also pointed out that Indelicato, previously an insignificant foot soldier in the Bonanno family, was promoted to capo after the Galante hit—a sure sign that he had been rewarded for meritorious service.

Before the trial, the battery of seven defense lawyers and an attorney serving as a legal adviser to Persico searched for a unified strategy. Five of them were former federal or state prosecutors; all were battle-tested trial attorneys. From pretrial examination of discovery materials, they could plumb the soundness of the prosecution's evidence and the prospect of acquitals.

A central point was clear: their clients' hopes were dismal. There was no possibility that these Mob kings and their steadfast subordinates could wangle plea bargains and soft sentences. Giuliani would give no quarter except for guilty pleas to the highest counts, which for most of the defendants meant life sentences without the possibility of parole, and dying in prison of old age.

The lawyers agreed that their one faint hope was an unorthodox ploy: they would tacitly acknowledge that the Commission and the Mafia existed. Their counterpoint was to convince the jury that involvement and association with these specific groups was not proof of a crime. But this strategy contravened the sacred principles of committed and tradition-minded mafiosi. By accepting their lawyers' advice, the mobsters would forsake their most cherished commandment and admit the existence of their secret organization. Fat Tony Salerno, Ducks Corallo, and their codefendants recoiled at the thought of breaking the oath of *omertà*, even if was done circuitously for them by their lawyers.

At pretrial meetings, the defense attorneys stated bluntly that they had run out of options. If they tried to contradict and deny their clients' numerous taped references to Cosa Nostra and the Commission, the lawyers would surrender all trace of credibility and logic.

"We are not going to say directly to the jury that there is a Mafia and our clients belong to it," Jim LaRossa, one of the lawyers, preached to the chagrined bosses and lieutenants. "What we will say to the jury is, 'Let me make this case easy for you. Part of the indictment charges that there was such an organization and our clients were members of that organization. Let's assume it's true for the sake of your determinations. But we contend that our clients did not commit any of the criminal acts that they are being charged with in this indictment.'" LaRossa, Castellano's lawyer, had remained on the defense team as Christie Furnari's counsel after the gangland hit on Big Paul.

Initially hesitant, the defendants grudgingly accepted the tactic so long as they were not required to admit personally the essential truth about the Mafia.

This way their consciences were clear because they had maintained *omertà*. The unenviable task of minimizing the issue fell on an articulate defense lawyer, Samuel Dawson. Through his opening speech to the jury, he tried to bury the problem by casually referring to the Cosa Nostra as an insignificant footnote in the trial. "The Mafia exists and has members," Dawson conceded, adding: "Just because someone is a Mafia member, it doesn't mean that he committed the crimes in this case."

Nevertheless, the cat was out of the bag. After a half century of denials, for the first time in an American court, accused mafiosi admitted that the Mafia was a reality by allowing their lawyers to state it as a fact.

Another dilemma was created by Carmine Persico. His decision to represent himself troubled several of his codefendants and their attorneys, who feared that his courtroom mistakes could damage the overall defense posture. But Persico was a boss, and there was no power that could override his obstinacy. In fact, some lawyers harbored the frail hope that his courtroom blunders could create a mistrial or technical grounds for a successful appeal. Unfortunately for the defense, Judge Richard Owen had scrupulously warned Persico that if he insisted on being his own lawyer, he and the other defendants would be unable to appeal a guilty verdict on grounds of "incompetent counsel."

The prosecution put on eighty-five witnesses and played more than one hundred audio- and videotapes. There was additional photographic evidence. Although the attempt by state investigators to photograph the Commission meeting in the Bowery in 1983 had gone awry, FBI agents later succeeded. Acting on a tip from an informer, on May 15, 1984, agents used a camouflaged van to snap still pictures of the bosses departing from a session in Staten Island. The meeting was in a house in the middle-class neighborhood known as South Beach, the home of a longshoreman cousin of Tom Bilotti. Except for the pariah Bonannos, all Mafia families sent representatives. Photographed leaving were Castellano, Bilotti, Salerno, Santoro, Furnari, Langella, and Scopo. The reason for the gathering was unknown, but the photographic display was a valid, persuasive suggestion that this was a full-blown Commission conference, attended by five of the men on trial.

Prosecution witnesses like Angelo Lonardo, the aged Cleveland mobster, and Joe Cantalupo, the small-time Colombo wannabe, might be discredited through cross-examination. They were men with checkered criminal pasts. On the witness stand they conceded having lied in previous trials, agreeing to testify in this one only after making deals with the government to get lighter sentences for their own crimes. The defense lawyers' nimble questions suggested that they were untrustworthy witnesses with incentives to perjure and to tailor their accounts. But there was no rebuttal to the tapes, which comprised 95 percent of the prosecution's salient evidence. They were the government's flies on the wall, providing indisputable evidence of the Mafia at work.

During nine weeks of listening to the demoralizing tapes, the defense lawyers sensed the increasing defeatism of their clients. Fat Tony Salerno became the most stoical, seemingly closing his mind to the impending doom. Held without bail as a potential danger to the community, Salerno seemed more concerned with his stomach than the outcome of the trial. He munched constantly on an inexhaustible supply of cookies and candy. At the conclusion of one session, he rose from the crowded defense table to ask Judge Owen for a favor. Displeased with the cold sandwiches provided prisoners at the midday break, he inquired plaintively of the judge, "What about a hot lunch, judge? Can't we have a hot lunch?"

Taking pity on him, codefendant Anthony Indelicato tried one day to smuggle a veal sandwich into the courtroom and pass it furtively to the ravenous Fat Tony. Unfortunately, a guard spotted the transfer and seized the sandwich as contraband.

Carmine Persico's debut as mouthpiece for himself provided the somber trial's one whiff of comedy. A stranger at first glance might have mistaken him for a respectable lawyer when he rose to cross-examine a witness or to address the jury. He dressed like many courtroom attorneys, in dark and gray suits, solid-colored shirts, and conservative striped ties. His gold-rimmed glasses and lugubrious bloodhound's eyes added to the illusion. But the facade shattered when he tried to score legal points in a folksy Brooklyn accent with phrases such as, "I sez," "you seen," and "dem kids." At times, he fumbled with his notes, asking the judge and jury, "Bear with me, please. I'm a little nervous." As a combination lawyer and defendant, he referred to himself in cross-examinations and motions as "me" and "Mr. Persico."

The brassy don, in his opening remarks, tried to garner sympathy as an oppressed underdog. "Don't be blinded by labels," he implored the jury. Pointing to the prosecutors, he said, "They are powerful, not me." From his questions to hostile prosecution witnesses, it was clear that Persico was trying to score points without endangering himself by testifying. His courtroom mannerisms and reputation attracted the attention of professional actors James Caan and Robert Duvall, who showed up in the public gallery to observe a real mafioso play a lawyer. Caan had met Persico before the filming of the original *Godfather* movie, and Duvall had played the consigliere in the same production and its sequel.

As his codefendants feared, Persico's performance weakened the defense's overall strategy. Cross-examining Joe Cantalupo, who had identified him as the Colombo boss, Persico brought out that Cantalupo had been beaten up by Persico's brother. His intent may have been to show that Cantalupo despised him and was testifying to obtain revenge. "You was angry because you was beat up, and you was beat up because you didn't pay back the money," Persico lashed out at Cantalupo. His argumentative question was a costly gaffe. The beating was over a loan-sharking debt, further illuminating Persico and his underlings as ruthless gangsters.

A similar Persico mistake occurred in his cross-examination of a Concrete Club contractor, Stanley Sternchos. Trying to illustrate the witness's unreliability, Persico got an admission from Sternchos that he had missed making required payments to Ralph Scopo, the Mob's bagman. Persico's line of questioning solidified the evidence of extortion against all of the defendants by confirming the routine system of kickbacks. Only an amateur lawyer would have made such a slip-up.

Persico might have thought he was charming the jury and getting his points across without subjecting himself to fierce cross-examination. Watching Persico, Michael Chertoff was convinced his antics had unintentionally aided the prosecution. The prosecutor was certain from reading the juror's facial reactions that Persico's testy duels with witnesses only further exposed his personality as a vindictive hoodlum.

Only one witness appeared for the defense: Fred DeChristopher's estranged wife, Catherine, Persico's cousin. She tried to refute her husband's testimony that Carmine made incriminating remarks to them about his Mafia position, but she was a marginal witness of little impact. All the defense lawyers could count on was their combined summations as the best hope of picking apart the testimony and discrediting the tapes. Persico's address to the jury, however, proved to be more riveting than any of the professional attorney's speeches. Speaking for ninety minutes, he hammered away at the point that the prosecution lacked a sliver of direct evidence connecting him to a crime. His voice was not on any of the tapes, and he was in prison during most of the time the Concrete Club felonies were committed.

Nearing the end of his speech, he pushed aside his notes, leaned over the rail of the jury box, and acknowledged that he had fled to evade arrest after the indictment. "Maybe I was afraid," he declared. "Maybe I was a little frightened. Not again. For what? What this time? What could I have done, being in jail so long? So many years? Maybe I was tired of going back and forth to jail, tired of being pulled into courtrooms and being tried on my name and reputation. When does it end? When does it stop? When do they leave you alone?" he asked the jury.

Disparaging the two principal witnesses against him—his cousin Fred DeChristopher and wannabe Joe Cantalupo—as untrustworthy and deceitful, he stressed that their testimony was insufficient to convict him. Following the defense's fundamental line, Persico blasted the prosecution for prejudicially smearing all of the defendants with the vile name of Mafia. Saying he had been punished sufficiently for his past crimes, he concluded with a plea for justice.

"How long do they want me to keep paying for that mistake I made years ago? They didn't come to try a case, they came to persecute people with the word Mafia. I can't say I never did anything wrong; you know I've been in jail. You can't send me back to jail 'cause I've been in jail; they have to prove I did something wrong, I did something else."

Lawyers for the remaining defendants were compelled in their summations to surmount three principal charges. They asked the jury to ignore the issue of the existence of the Commission, portraying it as no more dangerous to society than a Rotary Club. The government, they warned, was relying on anti-Italian bias to gain convictions. Calling the testimony about the history of the Mafia in Sicily and America outrageously prejudicial, they urged jurors to dismiss it as meaningless and irrelevant. Jim LaRossa noted sardonically that many of the historical events brought up by the prosecution occurred before most of the defendants were born.

The law team collectively challenged the validity of a second major charge—the formation and operations of the Concrete Club—by attacking the contractors. Again, they had to make a concession. Yes, the club existed and Scopo accepted payments. But the extortion charges were false. The rigged-bid scheme, in the defense's version, was conceived by avaricious businessmen, willing partners for their own primary benefit in order to make millions of dollars. The lawyers argued that the accused mobsters were simply mediators who were brought in to resolve competitive disputes among the contractors; the defendants were blameless referees, not extortionists.

Summing up, Anthony Cardinale, who took over as Salerno's lawyer after his first choice, Roy Cohn, died, scorched the contractors as the real criminals who should have been indicted. "It is a club of contractors, not of Commission members," Cardinale said. "The Commission had nothing to do with the concrete payments. Listen to the words that are actually being spoken, they do not contain any threats or pressure. The concrete companies gladly paid to gain an advantage in the industry."

Finally, on the Galante assassination charge, the lawyers demanded to know the prosecution's proof that Commission members were implicated in the killing. Bruno Indelicato's palm print in the getaway car, they said, had no bearing on the remaining defendants. Prosecutors had failed to show a fragment of evidence that any of the defendants knew Indelicato, associated with him, or ordered him to whack Galante.

In his summation, Michael Chertoff sought to demolish the defense's strategic theme that the crimes cited in the indictment were isolated, unproven accusations, lacking evidence of a coordinated conspiracy by the Mafia or any other group.

"Merely the fact that a person is a member of the Mafia does not make him guilty of the crimes," he told the jury, agreeing obliquely with the defense lawyers. "But, part of the crime charged here is being part of the Mafia and part of the Commission of La Cosa Nostra. That is one of the elements, that is one half of the crime, because the crime that is charged here is racketeering and what racketeering is about is setting up, joining, and associating with a criminal enterprise, organized crime activity, and using that organization to commit crimes like extortion and murder and loansharking."

The insulation that had served so effectively in the past to protect the Commission bosses from prosecution now was turned against them, as Chertoff cited the testimony of high-ranking Cleveland defector Angelo Lonardo and other Cosa Nostra turncoats, to underscore the Commission's supreme position in issuing commands to the Mafia's legions.

Chertoff's closing remarks were a barrage aimed at the defense's collective position. "So it is not true to say that this case has nothing to do with the Mafia or the Mafia is irrelevant. The Mafia is very relevant in this case. The Mafia is relevant because it is the Mafia that makes possible this kind of concerted criminal activity. The Mafia is relevant because what racketeering is, the evil that racketeering laws are designed to prevent, is people banding together in an organized and disciplined fashion for one purpose: to commit crimes."

The jury deliberated five full days, and the last exhibit it called for was a tape made at the Palma Boys Social Club in which Salerno and Corallo reviewed problems about recruiting talented soldiers. "If it wasn't for me," Salerno said, "there wouldn't be no Mob left. I made all the guys." Discussing the necessity for a contract hit on a disabled but traitorous soldier, Corallo philosophized to Salerno, "You pick 'em and ya kill 'em. He's in fucking bad shape. He's crippled. But we do it."

Jim LaRossa, the defense lawyer, realized that the jury's rehearing a tape relating to justifications for murder was an ominous sign. The outlook for guilty verdicts was so strong that he was surprised that Corallo, Santoro, Furnari, and Scopo, the only defendants free on bail, showed up every day and had not gone on the lam after the closing arguments. Privately, he concluded that the trial had been an "inquest" rather than a close adversarial contest.

On November 19, 1986, the sixth day of deliberations, the jury filed into the courtroom. The forewoman grew hoarse as she recited the verdicts for twenty-eight minutes. Sipping water from a blue plastic cup, she announced "guilty" on a total of 151 counts against the eight defendants. They were convicted of every charge. As the litany of guilty verdicts was read out in the hushed courtroom, only Indelicato showed any animation. He giggled and fidgeted at the defense table. The other newly coined convicts were stone-faced.

Two months later, the three accused bosses, Tony Salerno, Ducks Corallo, and Carmine Persico, and the other convicted leaders, Salvatore "Tom Mix" Santoro, Christie "Tick" Furnari, and Gerry Langella, returned to court for sentencing. The sentence was identical for each of them: the maximum for a RICO conviction, one hundred years without the possibility of parole. Scopo, the diligent Mob soldier and corrupt union leader, was hit with the same one-hundred-year penalty. Bruno Indelicato got a lighter term: forty years for carrying out the hits on Galante and the two men who were lunching with him.

Singling out Salerno for his harshest rebuke, Judge Owen said, "You have essentially spent a lifetime terrorizing this community to your financial advantage."

True to form, Persico, still representing himself, was the only defendant to rise and denounce the prosecution and the judge. "This case and the attitude of the prosecution and the court itself is in conformance with this mass hysteria, this Mafia mania, that was flying around and deprived every one of us in this courtroom of our rights to a fair trial and impartial trial."

The remaining mafiosi were impassive as they heard the sentences meted out to them. Appearing bored, Lucchese underboss Tom Mix Santoro sarcastically asked Judge Owen to hurry along. "Ah, give me the hundred years," he spoke up. "I'll go inside now." When the judge said he had pro forma requirements before imposing sentences, Santoro added bitterly, "You're in the driver's seat, Your Honor. And, you're doing a good job." (The mobster's flippancy was ignored by Owen, a federal judge for thirteen years, with extensive courtroom experience as a former prosecutor and trial lawyer. Owen sometimes referred to himself as "a musical judge" because he composed operas in his spare time.)

For Rudolph Giuliani, who spearheaded the Commission prosecution, the verdicts were a total vindication of his strategy and the extensive commitment of government resources. (Giuliani simultaneously triumphed in another significant trial that enhanced his national reputation: the conviction in November 1986 of Stanley Friedman, the Bronx Democratic party leader, for participating in a RICO enterprise to fix contracts in New York's Parking Violations Bureau.)

Michael Chertoff's flawless presentation in securing the multiple convictions was his springboard for advancement. He went on to become the U.S. Attorney for New Jersey, and in the administration of President George W. Bush obtained the same post that Giuliani once held—assistant attorney general overseeing the Justice Department's Criminal Division. In 2003, he was appointed a federal appeals court judge, one of the highest honors in the legal profession. Chertoff attained cabinet status in 2005 when Bush named him Homeland Security Secretary.

Several years after the Commission case ended, Tony Salerno was tried in a separate indictment involving another aspect of Mafia corruption in the concrete industry. A police sergeant at the trial mentioned to Salerno that Chertoff's career was flourishing. "Well, you give him a little message from Fat Tony," a smiling Salerno responded. "You tell that son-of-a-bitch he owes me a thank-you note."

27

"Far from Finished"

At first, the sweeping Commission verdicts seemingly resonated like a death knell for the Mob's most prominent families. A single trial had destroyed the Concrete Club. Embedded hierarchies were uprooted. And the Commission—organized crime's version of the United Nations Security Council—was apparently dissolved.

But as law-enforcement officials celebrated and assessed the unprecedented dethronement of Cosa Nostra giants Anthony Salerno, Antonio Corallo, and Carmine Persico, the infrastructures of New York's mafiosi brigades remained fundamentally sound and effective. The elimination of the $1.2 million shakedowns from the concrete industry was minuscule compared to the loot still collected daily from the Mob's traditional sources. Moreover, during the course of the trial and afterward, a new breed of mobsters—largely unknown to Mafia investigators—were enriching their families through novel schemes. Two of the freshest ideas were the theft of $100 million a year from gasoline excise taxes and stealing the remains of the dilapidated West Side Highway in Manhattan.

A typical player in the gasoline game was Mieczyslaw "Misha" Szczep-kowski, a Polish immigrant who was barely literate in English. After scratching out a living for two years as a house painter and handyman, Misha got an irresistible job offer. A group of Russian-Jewish immigrants in Brooklyn made him the salaried president of a new gasoline company that supplied millions of gallons of fuel to service stations. The Russians were not rewarding Misha for his executive talents. They were using him in a flimflam devised in the early 1980s to take advantage of a New York State law, which was intended to simplify the payment of gasoline taxes.

The new law shifted the responsibility for collecting and forwarding taxes to the government from the gas station proprietor to the wholesaler who delivered the fuel. Bureaucrats thought it would be easier and faster to gather taxes from a clutch of wholesalers rather than from thousands of gas stations. The catch in the law, however, was a provision that allowed wholesale distribution companies to trade or resell gasoline among themselves. Through that loophole, the Russians spotted a flaw in the tax process: only the last company that sold the gasoline to a retailer collected the taxes that were included in the total cost paid by the individual gasoline stations. The wholesaler was then required to pass along the revenue to the government.

In the mid-1980's, the excise and sales taxes amounted to about 30 cents on a gallon, a sizable revenue for federal, state, and local governments. The Russians devised a subterfuge to siphon the taxes from the pumps to themselves by setting up dummy or front wholesalers. They formed what became known as "daisy chains" of companies that supposedly transferred gasoline supplies to one another. There would be a sequence of paper transactions among five or six companies although no exchanges actually occurred. To escape detection when state or federal agents came looking for the overdue taxes, the Russians used resident or illegal aliens like Misha as fronts for scores of fictitious empty-shell companies that existed only on corporate papers. A dummy or "burn" company always was listed on the transfer records as the one making the final sale to retail stations and collecting the taxes. That company never existed; it was used just to bewilder the tax collectors when, months later, they noticed gaps in both the excise and sales revenues. The Russians actually delivered the gasoline and kept or stole the taxes paid by the retailers. The "front" immigrants were ignorant of the magnitude of the deals that had gone down and, like the unwitting Misha, usually were out of the country when finally traced by investigators.

It was a racket that became widely known as "gasoline bootlegging." The tax cheats who invented it were Jewish "Russian Mafia," immigrants from the Soviet Union who established a beachhead in New York, mainly in the Brighton Beach section of Brooklyn. The Russians were creative but they were no match for the original Mafia, especially the Colombo capo Michael Franzese, then in his early thirties. He had been efficiently indoctrinated in unrestrained law-breaking by his father, John "Sonny" Franzese, a former Colombo underboss.

In 1980 three Russian gangsters, Michael Markowitz, David Bogatin, and Lev Persits, solicited Michael Franzese's help in collecting a $70,000 debt stemming from one of their gasoline-tax swindles. Amazed at the largesse flowing from the gasoline pumps, and armed with the muscle power of his troops, Franzese gradually moved in on the Russians. His enforcers could guarantee the expeditious collecting of debts from gasoline stations. And through connections with state officials, the Colombos obtained licenses needed by the phony fuel dealers to pull off the "daisy chain" tax thefts.

Ever generous, Franzese allowed the Russians to continue their operations, handling all the paper work and taking most of the risks as long as they paid "tribute" to him. The Colombo end was 75 percent of the profits and the Russians', 25 percent. Franzese worked out a similar deal with a larcenous non-Russian wholesaler, Lawrence Iorizzo, who had also discovered the tax larceny loophole.

"To give you an idea how lucrative the gas tax business was, it was not unusual for me to receive $9 million in cash per week in paper bags from the Russians and Iorizzo," Franzese later confessed. At one point, the Colombos and their partners were stealing as much as 30 cents a gallon from the sale of about 500 million gallons a month, according to Franzese's figures. At their peak, the thefts generated $15 million monthly for Franzese and his Colombo partners.

By the mid-1980s, at the time of the Commission trial, the Gambino, Genovese, and Lucchese families wanted a share of the gasoline gusher. Following the lead of the Colombos, the other borgatas forged similar alliances with Russian hoodlums in the booming bootleg business in the city, Long Island, and New Jersey. Each family nominated a wiseguy as a "point man" to check the books and harvest payoffs of at least four or five cents on each gallon sold by the Russians. Investigators later estimated that in the 1980s and early 1990s, the Mob and their Russian collaborators fleeced the government of $80 million to $100 million a year in excise and sales taxes.

The immensely profitable gasoline-tax racket was a new Mafia venture, but the five families never relinquished their hold on the New York construction industry, their old sinecure. Seven years after the Commission trial ended, the saga of the West Side Highway unfolded to demonstrate how Mob families continued blending their talents to profit from their grip on the industry. The highway

A construction contractor who led a double life as a Mafia capo, the silver-haired Thomas Petrizzo was secretly photographed at a wake for a Colombo family member. One of Petrizzo's mob coups was pilfering a small fortune in steel when the West Side Highway in Manhattan was demolished. (*FBI Surveillance Photo*)

While a mob war raged in New York, Carmine Persico (far left) tried to influence events from a federal prison in Lompoc, California. Serving combined sentences of 139 years, "the Snake" was permitted by prison authorities to organize an Italian cultural club where he and inmate buddies could meet to reminisce about old times. (*Author's archive*)

The new boss of the Gambino family, John J. Gotti, (right), wearing an Oakland Raiders jacket on a walk-talk in 1986 with Anthony "Tony Lee" Guerrieri, a soldier, in front of the Bergin Hunt and Fish Club, Gotti's headquarters in Queens. Investigators overhead Gotti in a bugged conversation at the Bergin boast about creating an indestructible Mafia borgata. *(FBI Surveillance Photo)*

Frank DeCicco, a Gambino capo, who was instrumental in setting up the hit on Paul Castellano, was Gotti's first underboss. He was killed in a car explosion that failed to get Gotti, the main target, in revenge for Castellano's murder. *(Photo courtesy of the New York City Police Department)*

Bosko Radonjich, a gangster and Gambino ally, allegedly helped funnel a $60,000 bribe to a juror to fix Gotti's first RICO trial in 1986. Gotti's acquittal bolstered his reputation for invincibility. *(Photo courtesy of the New York City Police Department)*

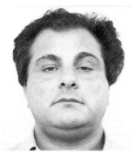

Gene Gotti (left), John's younger brother, was convicted on narcotics trafficking charges, largely on evidence the FBI obtained by bugging the home of Angelo "Fat Ange" Ruggiero (center). John Carneglia (right), a Gambino soldier and enforcer, was handpicked by Gotti for the assassination squad that ambushed Paul Castellano. *(Photos courtesy of the Federal Bureau of Investigation)*

Resplendtly dressed, a smiling, confident-looking John Gotti is photographed for mug shots upon his arrest on new RICO charges in December 1990. That same night, Underboss Salvatore "Sammy the Bull" Gravano (left) is visibly downcast. *(Photos courtesy of the Federal Bureau of Investigation)*

After his arrest, John J. Gotti designated his son, John Angelo Gotti, as acting Gambino boss. Known as "Junior," the son proved to be an unwise choice and a poor leader who was imprisoned for racketeering. He was indicted again in 2004 on a charge of ordering a botched hit on radio personality Curtis Sliwa. *(AP/Wide World Photos)*

Peter Gotti, lecturing an underling, became boss of the Gambino family after his nephew, "Junior," was convicted. Arrested soon after becoming boss and blind in one eye, he was imprisoned on racketeering charges and for plotting to murder Salvatore "Sammy the Bull" Gravano for betraying his brother. *(Photos courtesy of the Federal Bureau of Investigation)*

J. Bruce Mouw (left) devised the FBI's long-range game plan that ended John J. Gotti's reign as America's most notorious Mafia godfather. Despite Gotti's courtroom attempts to rattle him, a youthful John Gleeson (right) was the lead prosecutor who convicted the mob icon.
(Photo courtesy of U.S. Department of Justice)

Government officials in New York. (From left to right): Jim Fox, the head of the FBI's regional office; William Doran, the FBI's criminal division supervisor; and Andrew Maloney, the U.S. Attorney for the Eastern District, celebrate Gotti's guilty verdict. Maloney fought off attempts by federal and state prosecutors in Manhattan to wrest the Gotti case from his jurisdiction.
(Photo courtesy of U.S. Department of Justice)

Antonio "Ducks" Corallo was anointed boss of the Lucchese family in the late 1960s. A predecessor, Tommy "Three-Finger Brown" Lucchese pinned the nickname Ducks on Corallo for his finesse in evading prison sentences. *(Photo courtesy of the New York City Police Department)*

Vittorio "Little Vic" Amuso (in an early mug shot) succeeded Corallo as Lucchese boss, marking the first time the family's Brooklyn wing gained control. Amuso delegated wide powers to his sidekick and underboss, Anthony Casso. *(Photo courtesy of the New York City Police Department)*

Anthony Casso, aka "Gaspipe," outside La Donna Rosa Restaurant, a Lucchese hangout in Little Italy, across the street from a memorial to slain Mafia detective Joe Petrosino. As underboss and, in effect, the Lucchese's leader, Casso began dressing and living more elegantly, spending $30,000 on a one-day clothes shopping spree and $3,000 for a bottle of wine. *(FBI and NYPD Surveillance Photos)*

Peter "Fat Pete" Chiodo (right), once Casso's bosom pal, was marked for death by him in a purge of suspected disloyal mobsters. Although shot twelve times, Chiodo survived and doctors credited his obesity for saving his life. *(FBI Surveillance Photo)*

The classic Mafia success story, Anthony "Tumac" Accetturo became a multimillionaire overseeing the Lucchese family's rackets in New Jersey and Florida. Accetturo defected to the government's side in 1994, claiming that Casso and Amuso attempted to kill him and relatives over money disputes. *(Photo courtesy of William Sauro)*

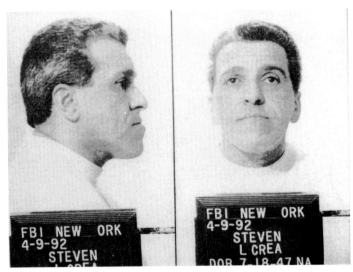

The next generation of Lucchese soldiers could be led by Steven "Wonder Boy" Crea, the family's underboss. A major Mafia overseer in the construction industry, Crea is completing a prison sentence for extorting companies that removed debris from the World Trade Center ruins. *(FBI Photos)*

plot involved the cooperation of three families, each trading favors and pulling strings with contractors and unions. It was another chapter in how mafiosi-inspired corruption inflated overall building costs in the city by at least 10 percent on each project.

In 1975 the disintegrating four-mile elevated section of Manhattan's West Side Highway, which paralleled the Hudson River from the Battery to 59th Street, was closed for safety reasons. A decade later, fearing the roadway would collapse, the state began dismantling the crumbling hulk in stages, awarding one demolition contract to the John P. Picone Company. Picone was paid $12 million to remove a one-mile section and was given the right to sell salvageable materials.

Another company, A. J. Ross Logistics, Inc., which was not involved in the razing, wanted to acquire the girders and other steel slabs before they could be dumped and discarded. At that time, Ross Logistics was a specialty company that reshaped and designed steel for multimillion-dollar construction projects, and was a major subcontractor in the New York construction field. In the mid- and late 1980s, the company was a significant player, keeping more than three hundred employees on its payroll and grossing about $50 million a year.

The head of the company, who had his eye on the highway's valuable 11,000 tons of steel, was Thomas J. Petrizzo, an executive well known in the construction business and without a hint of a criminal background. Years later, however, prosecutors would identify him as a capo in the Colombo family. Petrizzo had the important distinction of being his borgata's main representative on a Mafia-type commission that coordinated construction rackets for all New York families. He also had a direct social and family link to Carmine Persico, the Colombo boss, through the marriage of his daughter, Joanne, to Persico's younger son, Michael. For almost two decades, Petrizzo dealt with the city's leading contractors, developers, and architects, helping to shape New York's skyline. None of them seemingly suspected that he was a mafioso "sleeper," scheming to enrich crime families.

To get his hands on the West Side Highway's steel without paying for it, Petrizzo brewed a scheme that would benefit the Colombos and the Gambino and Lucchese families as well. Under existing union jurisdictional rules, the destruction of the highway was a job restricted to an ironworkers' local. Petrizzo lacked a connection to that union, but as part of his Mafia duties, he controlled a carpenters' local that normally worked only on dock construction and repairs. Through underworld alliances, Petrizzo knew that the Lucchese family was extorting the contractor dismantling the highway, the Picone Company, for labor peace. The Luccheses knew that the Picone Company was a powerhouse road-and-infrastructure builder with almost $600 million in state and city contracts in the 1980s.

Aware of the Lucchese influence at Picone, Petrizzo offered that family's construction coordinator, Anthony "Gaspipe" Casso, a nifty proposal. If the Lucchese leaders gave him the steel remnants, he would exert his power to get carpenters to work on the highway for Picone at much lower wages than iron-workers. The arrangement would increase Picone's profit and therefore guarantee a larger kickback share for Casso and the Lucchese family. In addition, Petrizzo was so confident of the profit he could extract from the steel that he gave Casso $800,000 for bringing the Picone company on board.

As a final segment of the Mob triangle, Petrizzo got Salvatore "Sammy the Bull" Gravano, then the Gambino underboss, to intervene with the ironworkers to prevent them from using their jurisdictional rights to disrupt the carpenter demolition crews hired by the Picone company. Gravano could head off labor problems since the Gambinos exercised control over the ironworkers' local. The payoff to the Gambinos was never disclosed, but Petrizzo's gift of $800,000 to Casso clearly indicated that big bucks were made by each crime family.

"It was a sweetheart deal," Alphonse D'Arco, the Lucchese's acting boss in the late 1980s, later confided. "The labor peace which ensued helped Picone and Petrizzo make a large sum of money from the scrap steel alone."

While their families continued to prosper from old and new enterprises, the three bosses convicted at the Commission trial awaited the outcome of their appeals. Traditional Mafia protocol enables a boss to retain his rank even while in prison, if he desires. As long as the appeals were pending, Salerno, Corallo, and Persico could cling to the faint hope that the convictions would be reversed, their life sentences voided, and that they might have the option of either returning to their previous posts or retiring tranquilly.

A blizzard of legal points was raised in appeals for the three identified bosses and their five lower-ranking codefendants. Challenging the constitutionality of the RICO law, the defense argued primarily that the statute unjustifiably allowed the prosecution to use irrelevant evidence and improper tactics, violating the defendants' basic rights to a fair trial.

None of the convictions was overturned by the United States Court of Appeals for the Second Circuit. The only count that created a troubling dissent was whether there had been sufficient evidence to convict the Commission members of conspiracy in the gangland rubout of Carmine Galante. All of the linkage to the slayings was circumstantial and the accusation was the weakest charge against Salerno, Corallo, and Persico. One judge, in a partial dissent, discounted the prosecution's theory that Bruno Indelicato's visit to the Ravenite Club shortly after Galante's murder implicated Commission members. The judge found the evidence insufficient, resting entirely on "speculation and inference."

But the overall thrust of the unanimous rulings verified the effectiveness of RICO. The judges declared that the prosecutors could introduce evidence of the history and customs of the Cosa Nostra and that these areas were neither prejudicial nor irrelevant. By allowing such testimony, the thick layers of insulation that had protected the bosses for half a century were stripped from them. Even if members of a Mafia hierarchy did not commit the actual crime, they could still be judged guilty as leaders of a racketeering "enterprise." Thus, in the Commission case, members of the Mafia's board of directors were guilty of extortion via the Concrete Club, even if they did not personally coerce any contractor. They were also guilty of Galante's murder, even if they did not pull the trigger. Upholding the convictions, the appeals court sustained the essential theory of RICO—that mobsters could be prosecuted at one trial for a diverse "pattern" of crimes.

Additionally, the judges found that one-hundred-year sentences for Mob leaders were not cruel and excessive. The Supreme Court then delivered the legal haymaker, declining to even review the appeals of the imprisoned dons and the lower-court decisions. The crux of the rulings established that the entire RICO statute was constitutional and enforceable. In short, the Commission case was enshrined as a legal milestone and breakthrough against the Mafia.

Ramifications were felt far beyond New York. With a clear signal from the courts, anti-Mafia prosecutors throughout the country could adopt the tactics used by Rudolph Giuliani's prosecutors to dismember Mob families in their jurisdictions. G. Robert Blakey hailed the courtroom victory against the Commission as a model and an incentive for attacking other Cosa Nostra strongholds. "It was a big win legally and psychologically," Blakey declared. He compared the seismic legal consequences of the Commission convictions and appeals decisions to the antimonopoly ruling by the Supreme Court in 1911, upholding the Sherman Antitrust Act. The 1911 case broke up the mammoth Standard Oil Company of New Jersey into a group of independent competitors. Blakey and other legal scholars saw the Commission case as a model for ending Cosa Nostra's infiltration of legitimate businesses and unions.

Agreeing with Blakey that the Commission case was without precedent, top Justice Department officials encouraged prosecutors to launch similar offensives. In November 1987, exactly one year after the New York convictions, William F. Weld, the assistant attorney general in charge of the department's criminal division, characterized RICO "as the backbone of our organized crime effort." Weld later governor of Massachusetts, observed in a progress report that the FBI and federal prosecutors no longer reacted only after crimes were committed by mafiosi. The new policy, he stated, "was the proactive targeting of specific OC [organized crime] figures who were responsible for large numbers of crimes."

In essence, the Justice Department had belatedly signed on in the late 1980s to an investigative and prosecutorial strategy that had been advanced almost a decade earlier by Blakey; one of his early supporters, Ronald Goldstock; and a handful of F.B.I agents, notably Jim Kossler, Jules Bonavolenta, Jim Kallstrom, and Neil Welch. "This concept of targeting entire criminal enterprises remains the current state-of-the-art method of attack in the evolution of the war on organized crime," Weld wrote, endorsing RICO as the government's most powerful weapon against Cosa Nostra fiefs.

RICO campaigns soon succeeded against top-echelon mobsters outside New York. Long-established Mob families were vanquished or severely undermined in Kansas City, St. Louis, Milwaukee, Detroit, St. Louis, New Orleans, Boston, Providence, Los Angles, Denver, and Buffalo. By 1990, more than two hundred high- and middle-ranking mafiosi were imprisoned for long stretches or were facing racketeering trials. All of these regions had been victimized for half a century, each by a single borgata. In most of the country, no understudies or substitute families waited in the wings to quickly fill the power gaps created by the imprisonment of top-dog mobsters.

New York was a different story. Investigators faced more complex obstacles in destroying the Mob's infrastructure than in any other part of the country. Metropolitan New York's vast size and the Mob's diversity of legal and illicit economic interests created extraordinary problems for law enforcement. The local Mafia was unique and more varied than its counterparts in other Mob realms. The existence of five clanlike families with a combined total of more than one thousand soldiers and at least five thousand associates meant that power vacuums brought about by RICO convictions were more easily filled than elsewhere. The large New York gangs had the in-house manpower reserves to take over rackets from fallen colleagues. And if one family relinquished an asset, a rival group always was available to grab the prize.

After the early euphoria of the Commission verdicts and the appeals court decisions, some investigators recognized that the Mob's recuperative powers were stronger than anticipated. Despite a spurt of convictions mainly involving the middle echelons of the Bonanno and Colombo families, New York's Mafia might not, after all, be living on borrowed time. By 1988, two years after the Commission case, federal and state officials conceded that one of the Mob's bottomless troughs—the construction industry—remained rampant with payoffs and rigged bids.

Before the Commission trial, Governor Mario Cuomo had disputed the notion that the Mafia even existed. Afterward, he agreed that the multibillion-dollar construction industry was "infested" by racketeers. He called on business executives to find the courage to drive out the Mob by cooperating with a reform campaign. Cuomo's blast came after a study by the state's Organized Crime Task Force found that high-level management and union groups had willingly accommodated themselves to the Mafia as a "necessary evil" that promoted stability, labor peace, and profits for everyone.

"By controlling the activities of disparate groups of racketeers preying on the industry," the report said, "syndicates can assure contractors that they will only have to pay off once for a specified result, that the amount to be paid will be 'reasonable,' and the 'services' paid for will be delivered." The report implied that as long as companies could pass along the price of kickbacks to their customers, they preferred living with a measure of Mob and union corruption rather than wrestling with honest, tenacious union leaders who could lawfully disrupt their completion schedules by exercising their collective-bargaining rights.

Construction delays are the bane of contractors and developers, and calculating mobsters counted on the threat of possible work stoppages to induce payoffs. On a $100 million project, the report estimated, each day of delay added $75,000 in interest costs alone.

"Nothing has changed, except that it's gotten worse," Governor Cuomo said glumly, discussing the Cosa Nostra's insidious presence. "After a while it becomes habitual. After a while if you don't cure it, the society takes it for granted—it is there and it grows."

Even before the report, the agent now leading the FBI's New York bureau,

Thomas Sheer, knew the war on many fronts was unending, and that greater efforts were needed to crack the Mafia's bear hug on unions and contractors. He highlighted greater use of RICO's civil provisions as a means of removing dishonest union administrations. "The next stage is an assault on the Cosa Nostra's main economic base of power, the money they make from corruption by taking over unions and legitimate businesses," Sheer told his agents in 1987.

One union immediately targeted for a purge was the District Council of Cement and Concrete Workers, a regional administrative body that had been headed by the convicted Ralph Scopo of Concrete Club infamy. Federal judges authorized the ouster of Scopo's deputies and appointed a monitor to supervise the union for four years, until honest elections could be held. Officials on the council and its main Mob-controlled subsidary, Local 6A, resigned their well-paid posts rather than answer prosecutors' questions and risk perjuring themselves in sworn pretrial depositions. The interrogatory they apparently most dreaded was: Did they know anyone who was a member of the "Colombo Crime Family of La Cosa Nostra and who in any way participated in or profited from the cement construction industry in the Metropolitan New York area?" Obviously, silence was the safest course.

Lieutenant Remo Franceschini, the New York detective toughened by twenty-five years of showdowns with mobsters, was certain the New York families had no intention of capitulating because of the Commission verdicts. He pointed out that historically the five borgatas were adept at adjusting to changing conditions. "All the recent cases showed that law enforcement could infiltrate the top leadership with informers and bugs. The new bosses probably will try to insulate themselves even more from us by having less contact with underlings, including capos. Despite what's happened, they're far from finished."

28

Turning Point

There was widespread agreement among Mafia prosecutors in the late 1980s that the permanent imprisonment of Fat Tony Salerno, Ducks Corallo, and Carmine the Snake Persico eliminated a vast reservoir of irreplaceable experience, contacts, and knowledge from the Mob's brain trust. Salerno's and Corallo's long-term relationships and corrupt manipulations of businessmen, politicians, and local police could not be swiftly duplicated by their successors. But they were in their seventies and probably close to stepping aside and relinquishing power, even if they hadn't been trapped in the Commission investigation. Both would die in prison, Salerno at age eighty in 1992, and Corallo at eighty-seven in 2000. Corallo's underboss, Salvatore "Tom Mix" Santoro, was also a ripe seventy-two when he went to prison for the rest of his life. The only relatively young boss receiving a life sentence, fifty-three-year-old Carmine Persico, was a more grievous casualty for the Colombo family. His conviction removed from the streets and from the Mafia's highest councils a promising Mob leader at the peak of his abilities.

As a sequel to the trial, and following more exacting interpretations of the one thousand hours of tapes obtained in the investigation, questions were raised by lawyers and scholars about the true dimensions of the Commission's authority and its genuine powers. James B. Jacobs, a professor at New York

University's Law School, and an authoritative Mafia researcher, said the extent of the Commission's national reach and its decision-making methods remained unclear from the evidence at the trial. Among the unresolved mysteries, Jacobs wrote, was how the Commission enforced its judgments, and on what basis it could intervene in internal family disputes.

Skeptical defense lawyers like Richard A. Rehbock, who represented members of the Gambino crime family, lambasted the prosecution for allegedly exaggerating the Commission's importance as the Mafia's controlling clique in the 1980s. "The government's theory that the Commission could dictate to families what could and could not be done was factually incorrect. It was a loose confederation, a meeting place to settle disputes and not a ruling body."

Compounding the frustrations of unraveling Mafia secrets was evidence that arose after the trial that contradicted the prosecution's labeling Fat Tony Salerno the head of the Genovese family, when he was arrested in 1985. Shortly after the Commission trial, Salerno's closest confidant, Vincent "Fish" Cafaro, "flipped"—became a prosecution witness after being indicted on racketeering charges. Although Salerno had represented the Genovese gang at Commission meetings, Cafaro revealed that Fat Tony had never been the family's godfather, and that he had been used as a figurehead by the real bosses to deflect law-enforcement attention from themselves. (Even if the prosecution's ranking of Salerno was wrong, it was still insufficient grounds to overturn his conviction. He had been found guilty of specific criminal acts and had not been tried on the accusation of being the Genovese godfather.)

Cafaro's disquieting revelation reflected the persistent fog that clouded much of the Mob's activities. Secrets remained that were difficult for FBI and other investigators to decipher from the veiled conversations overheard through electronic surveillance and from morsels provided by low-ranking informers. Mob soldiers and associates were often in the dark themselves about fundamental facts concerning their own families. Although mixed up with racketeers in the Bronx for decades, William Pellegrino Masselli, better known as "Butcher Boy", remained muddled into his mid-fifties about the accepted name of his borgata. An FBI bug had been placed in Masselli's office in an investigation of his links to hijacking, narcotics deals, and a possible rigged bid on a subway construction project. Listening in, agents heard Masselli, the reasonably intelligent owner of a trucking company, tell a Mob pal that he had read a newspaper story identifying a wiseguy who was his Mafia supervisor. "Geez, I didn't know we belong to the Genovese family," a surprised Masselli said. Another example of how little the street earners might know about their own organizations came from the lips of Vinnie DePenta, a small-time gambler and former Bonanno wannabe. In the early 1980s, the FBI set up a sting operation in Little Italy, opening a pasta-importing company. The spurious company was run by DePenta, who had switched sides to become a paid government informer after getting into life-threatening trouble with Bonanno loan sharks. Counting on DePenta's predatory Mob contacts to visit him in his D&M Pasta Company, the FBI concealed video cameras and bugs to record incriminating conversations. The sting failed to lure any big-time mafiosi but it entrapped a Colombo enforcer named Frankie "the Beast" Falanga, who informed DePenta that he would be "owned," protected by the Colombos from Bonanno barbarians in return for payoffs and the prospect of exploiting his pasta business.

Taking DePenta under his wing, Falanga felt dutybound to instruct him in the importance of Mafia history. Despite a misspent life mingling with made guys, DePenta was totally ignorant of Mafia genealogy. Frankie the Beast traced the roots of his crime family, which now controlled DePenta, to the renowned Joe Profaci, one of the five founding godfathers in 1931. Furthermore, Falanga boasted that he had been a driver and bodyguard for Joe Colombo. As part of the orientation, Falanga pointed out that the current acting boss of the Colombos was the aged capo Tommy DiBella, who was filling in for Carmine Persico. Professor Falanga's recital of borgata names and leaders left the student DePenta bewildered. The FBI recorded this Abbot-and-Costello "Who's on first"-type exchange.

FALANGA: "Now, everybody's got a family, right? DiBella's got a family, right?"

DEPENTA: "Right."

FALANGA: "He's got the Profaci family. And the Bonannos have got this guy. And the other guy has got that guy. Then there's another crew. You get it?"

DEPENTA: "I thought DiBella was Colombo."

FALANGA: "That's Colombo."

DEPENTA: "Profaci?"

FALANGA: "Right."

DEPENTA: "Profaci-Colombo are one and the same?"

FALANGA: "Profaci's all one, that's all one. It's all one."

Frankie the Beast, exasperated by the job of clarifying the borgata's background to his confused new associate, got to the heart of his plan to use the pasta company as a front for Mob activities.

FALANGA: "You know what the name of the game is here, right Vinnie?"

DEPENTA: "Yeah, what?"

FALANGA: "Make fucking money, that's what."

Comic moments were provided by Butcher Boy Masselli, the brutal enforcer Frankie Falanga, and FBI spy Vinnie DePenta, but the trio's activities showed that veils of secrecy and ignorance within the Mob's lower ranks were still in place to shield capos and leaders. Masselli and Falanga were far removed from Mafia power centers, and the information gained from investigating them did not enable the FBI to evaluate the strengths and weaknesses of their families.

Later information obtained by the bureau demonstrated that the Commission case had barely affected the diversified illicit operations of most New York mafiosi. Despite the murder of Paul Castellano and the convictions of Tony Salerno, Ducks Corallo, and Carmine Persico, business continued to hum in every gang, and replacements filled the gaps left by the stricken leaders and their cohorts. This continued prosperity could be credited to Lucky Luciano's ingenious organizational plan for the Cosa Nostra, devised in 1931. Fifty-five years later, Luciano's legacy kept each family's table of organization intact and functioning. As the 1980s ended, there seemed no end to the plundering by the five families.

The perennial cash cows for each borgata were gambling and loan-sharking. Bookmaking rings for sports betting and the numbers games also guaranteed huge profits. The exact "take" will never be accurately added up, but gambling researchers believe Mafia bookies netted a minimum of 15 percent of the gross wagered by bettors. Of course, there were overhead costs for employees and rental of places to handle telephone bets, but the profits—like all Mafia spoils—were tax free. The National Football League's Super Bowl game provides the clearest indication of the riches gambling can generate for the Mob. A study by the New York Police Department's Organized Crime Control Bureau in the early 1990's estimated that more than $1 billion was wagered on the Super Bowl every year with Mafia-controlled bookies in the city and suburbs, including New Jersey, Long Island, and Connecticut. On one game and in one day, the five families cleaned up with a profit of 15 percent—a "take" of $150 million. One of the most enterprising Gambino capos and bookies, John "Handsome Jack" Giordano, developed a network of forty sports-betting locations that alone grossed over $300 million a year, court records disclosed.

Loan-sharking is the symbiotic partner of gambling operations. Nobody with any sense welshes on a Mob bookie. Compulsive bettors in debt to a bookie frequently have recourse only to a loan shark for quick money. Most loan sharks offer two types of usurious loans: the "knockdown" and the "vigorish," "vig" or "juice." Howard M. Abadinsky, a professor of criminal justice and legal studies at St. John's University in New York, an expert on Mafia financial tactics, says that the knockdown, a variation of a type invented in the 1930s by Tommy "Three-Finger Brown" Lucchese, requires a specified schedule of repayment of the principal and interest—similar to a legitimate loan but at an astronomical cost. Every week the debtor must hand over six dollars for every five dollars borrowed; the one dollar interest is the vig or juice until the full principle is repaid. Abadinsky found that a $1,000 loan might be repaid in fourteen weekly installments of $100 for a total of $1,400.

There is no time limitation on a "straight vigorish" loan. Trouble mounts speedily if a debtor misses a weekly installment. For a late payment, the vig is compounded, and the weekly interest payments are increased without a reduction in the principal. The interest on an original loan of $100 is $20 for the first week. If vigorish payments are missed, the interest zooms sharply from $20 for the first week to $107 after four weeks—more in just one weekly interest payment than the value of the original loan.

Loan-shark interest rates in New York normally varied from a low of 2 to 5 percent a week to above 100 percent a year when late payments were factored in. The huge profits were illustrated by a Colombo crime family ring in the mid-1980s, which expanded its clientele from addicted gamblers and blue-collar workers to businessmen suddenly pressed for cash and unable to get legitimate loans. The Colombos employed the usual vig methods but on a loftier scale. The mobsters established a phony loan company with an impressive sounding name, the Resource Capital Group, and used their muscle and contacts to tap two teamster union locals to subsidize the company with $1.2 million as capital for the usurious loans. One borrower was forced to pay $14,000 a week in vigorish on a loan of $685,000. Another paid $50,000 in a three-month period on a $400,000 loan.

At the racket's peak, the Colombos were extorting about $40,000 a week from some fifteen businessmen who had fallen into their clutches. When the

FBI smashed the ring, agents termed it "a super Shylock operation." The borrowers said they were intimidated into making the excessive payments after learning the loan company was a Mafia front and after being apprised of the Mob's loan-sharking motto: "Your body is the collateral."

Family bosses, other hierarchy members, and capos traditionally profited from loan-sharking without the bother of doing any grunt work. They distributed $100,000 or more to soldiers and charged them one point—one percent— for an assured income of at least $1,000 a week. Any amount the soldiers imposed over the one percent lined their own pockets.

"The boss doesn't do anything," Police Detective Lieutenant Remo Franceschini, points out. "He puts $1 million in the street and gets half a million in interest every year, the money coming into him each week. If for some reason it doesn't come in, the soldier has a problem and he is going to get that money whatever way he has to. That's what makes the Mob rich. It's the ultimate pyramid scheme."

Heading into the 1990s, the FBI and state investigators had dossiers on about 1,200 made soldiers active in the New York area. Nearing the end of the century, the Mafia could field a combined army in New York totaling almost eight thousand made men and associates engaged in a melange of illegal adventures. Compared to some new sophisticated schemes, the old standbys, bookmaking and loan-sharking, were loose change for the bosses.

In 1990, each of the five families had its own characteristics and growth potential. Some of their activities were joint ventures.

The Gambinos, the nation's largest Mob family, with more than four hundred soldiers, were important players in crimes involving:

Corruption on the Brooklyn and Staten Island waterfronts with the aid of officials from the longshoremen's union; payoffs in the construction industry through direct ties to the teamsters' union; kickbacks from Key Foods and Waldbaum supermarket chains for soft union settlements; gasoline-tax rip-offs; and payments from companies in the Garment Center for labor peace and rapid trucking services.

Thomas Gambino, the son of the late Don Carlo and himself a Gambino capo, controlled much of the Garment Center's vital trucking network, and had accumulated a personal fortune of $75 million in bank accounts, stocks, and bonds. By inflating transportation and manufacturing costs, the Gambino family added $3.50 to consumers for every $100 purchase of clothing, according to an analysis by the Manhattan district attorney's office. One of the family's most productive operations, in conjunction with the Genovese borgata, was rigging prices for collecting nonresidential trash from office buildings, factories, and stores. The Mob-run private garbage-hauler associations were cartels with fixed prices, and customers were denied a choice in selecting a carter. The system inflated costs by $400 million a year, with a large part of the overcharges kept by Gambino and Genovese members and their associates.

In another construction sideline—also practiced by the Genoveses—Gambino soldiers gouged companies for protection from demonstrations and work stoppages by bogus civil-rights activist groups. The synthetic "community coalitions" collaborated with the Mafia by picketing and harassing contractors, demanding greater employment of blacks and Hispanics. Mobsters would then step in, promising the contractors that they had the muscle to end the protests, and thousands of dollars were paid them to head-off or end the demonstrations. For their services, coalition organizers were usually bribed by the contractors with no-show jobs for as much as $1,000 a week; the Gambinos' profit was much larger, up to $100,000 for a single project.

Organized prostitution was no longer a respectable trade for Mafia entrepreneurs, but the sex industry churned out profits for the Gambinos. A suave, impeccably dressed capo, Robert DiBernardo, owned Star Distributors, the largest pornography wholesaler in the New York area. In the 1980s, anti-smut laws—no longer on the books—made the illegal sales of porno magazines and photos a big underground business. DiBernardo was also a partner of Show World Center in Times Square, one of the city's most profitable video porn and striptease emporiums.

The Genoveses, with at least three hundred identified soldiers, were believed to be more affluent than the Gambinos. In addition to carving up the city's private waste-hauling racket with the Gambinos, the Genoveses' main interests focused on labor and industrial profiteering. Helped by officials in teamster and longshoremen's locals, the family extorted payoffs from shipping and stevedoring companies in New Jersey and Manhattan. Paying blackmail was the only way the companies could avoid costly work stoppages. The family's ties to the carpenters' union placed it in a linchpin position to extract payoffs from major dry-wall and construction contractors. In another ploy, connivance with the carpenters' union allowed the Genoveses to extract bribes from trade-show organizers, contractors, and exhibitors at the Javits Convention Center, in return for labor peace. The family also placed dozens of mobsters on payrolls at the center for no-show jobs. (The Gambinos had a smaller extortion racket, based on its control of a teamsters' local that worked there.)

Indicative of the Genovese borgata's range of influence in the construction industry was the hiring of a family associate, Michael J. Crimi, as primary labor consultant by the state's Battery Park City Authority when it was in the midst of a billion-dollar development program in the 1980s. Crimi was appointed in disregard of warnings from Mafia investigators that he was linked to Genovese soldiers and to the roofers' union, which had been cited by federal authorities as mobbed up. Crimi had a loan-sharking conviction, which was reversed on appeal, and he had been acquitted in an indictment for participating in the slaying of a loan shark.

At the city's bustling Fulton Fish Market, the Genovese gang had been the dominant force since the 1930s. Through strong-arm bullying and threats, the family enriched itself at the nation's largest wholesale fish market, which every year had gross sales of nearly $1 billion. Genovese thugs thrived by controlling the unloading and loading of fish and sea food, and granting parking privileges. Payoffs came from fishmongers, suppliers, and customers whose livelihoods depended on the prompt handling of food that was perishable and worthless unless sold quickly.

Although Fat Tony Salerno was confined to a prison cell, his brother Charles "Speed" Salerno was raking in illicit profits for the family from the city's 1,200 private parking lots and garages. As head of teamsters' Local 272, which represented garage employees, Speed Salerno was the bagman for payoffs from employers. (He was later charged with accepting about $300,000 in bribes for contracts that allowed lower wage scales.)

Without the necessity of risking a single bet at the Atlantic City, New Jersey, casinos, the Genovese family was a big winner. Allied with Philadelphia's Mafia family, New York's Genovese leaders dipped into the treasury of the union representing casino employees, Local 54 of the Hotel and Restaurant Employees and Bartenders Union. Strategically placed officials of the local were Mob associates, who conspired with the Philadelphia and Genovese groups in frauds that milked the local's dues and its pension and medical welfare plans.

Religion was another profitable area for the Genoveses. At a celebrated tourist attraction, the annual San Gennaro Feast in Little Italy, a Genovese crew was around to shake down vendors for the right to set up food and souvenir stands. The mobsters also operated illegal gambling games and unashamedly stole thousands of dollars in donations to a local church from festival visitors who pinned bills to a statue of Saint Gennaro.

The Luccheses, with close to two hundred wiseguys, excelled at labor racketeering. Manipulating teamsters' locals at the John F. Kennedy and Newark Airports, they got systemic payoffs from air freight companies for the right to employ cheaper nonunion labor, and delivered sweetheart collective-bargaining contracts at the expense of union employees. Similarly, the family's grip on several painters', plumbers', and carpenters' locals allowed it to collect under-the-table payments from construction companies. The usual payment was $100 for each nonunion employee allowed to be hired "off the books," which sharply lowered hourly wage scales and exempted contractors from required fringe-benefit contributions to union pension and medical funds.

Strategic jobs at the air-freight companies provided golden information for conventional crimes—cargo hijackings outside the airports and inside thefts in storage areas. More than $350 million worth of cargo moved in and out of the airports every year, tempting targets for Lucchese wiseguys. Supplied with inside information from a tipster employee at JFK Airport, a Lucchese crew in December 1978 pulled off one of the nation's largest cash heists. The gangsters overpowered guards and stole about $5 million in cash and $875,000 in jewels from an easily cracked vault in the Lufthansa Airline storage terminal.

A building-trades bonanza in the 1980s, which the Luccheses shared mainly with their Genovese partners, was rigging bids totaling almost $150 million for window replacements at the city's public housing projects. Prosecutors later said those deals significantly inflated costs and netted Mafia families "tens of millions of dollars" in kickbacks from companies that got the contracts. And in a mutual pact with the Gambinos, top Lucchese leaders created and operated the Garment Center's only trucking companies. The monopoly allowed the two families to control freight shipping costs and indirectly added to overhead and consumer prices for dresses, suits, and other apparel throughout the country.

An important racketeering sideline existed at two of the city's major newspapers, *The New York Times* and the *New York Daily News*—both of which prided themselves on their reporting of Mafia inroads elsewhere. Through influence in the Newspaper and Mail Deliverers Union, the family got no-show jobs, ran bookmaking and loan-sharking activities inside the newspaper plants, and stole and resold copies of the newspapers.

The Colombos, with 100 to 125 soldiers, relied mainly on gasoline-tax thefts and the traditional bookmaking and loan-sharking techniques for the bulk of their illicit income. They had a smaller stake than the Gambinos and Luccheses in protection payoffs from Garment Center companies resisting unionization attempts. The family, however, rivaled the Gambinos in getting a slice of easy money from transporting city schoolchildren. Both families were secret partners in ten Brooklyn school bus companies that mysteriously managed to obtain about $40 million in annual contracts without the nuisance of bidding competitively against other companies. One Mob outfit responsible for transporting children was run by a professional hit man, Robert Bering, who years later revealed that wiseguys and associates headed the two unions that represented drivers for all of the city's school buses.

The innovative capo Michael Franzese moved the family into another new arena, capitalizing on sports and entertainment activities. He became a secret partner in an agency that represented athletes and showbusiness personalities. Banking on the clients' inherent fear of resisting the Mafia, the agency used its Colombo connection to pressure them to sign up.

Narcotics trafficking—always a Colombo franchise—became an increasingly important resource for the family's leaders after the river of money from the Concrete Club dried up. Another innovation was the creation of a financial pipeline to Las Vegas. Through a crew led by a feared capo, Charles "Charlie Moose" Panarella, the regime profited from loan-sharking in Las Vegas, and ran brothels, a practice shunned by the other New York families.

The Bonannos, battered by decades of internal turmoil and its disastrous infiltration by FBI agent Joseph Pistone, were the smallest and weakest of the five families, mustering about 100 soldiers. Narcotics deals, run mainly by Zips, the family's Sicilian wing, along with bookmaking and loan-sharking, were the family's mainstays. Its labor-racketeering exploits had been reduced mainly to payoffs and no-show jobs derived from influence in the Newspaper Deliverers Union at the smallest of the city's three daily newspapers, the *New York Post*. A veteran Bonanno soldier and *Post* employee, Alfred "Al Walker" Embarrato, doled out phantom jobs to mafiosi and controlled loan-sharking and bookmaking in the composing room and on the loading bays. Embaratto also supervised the daily theft of ten thousand copies of the *Post*, priced at 50 cents, and sold them for 20 or 30 cents each to news dealers. (Overall, the Bonanno and Luchesse thefts and other operations at the city's three major newspapers, mainly from the *Post*, netted the Mob about $5 million a year.)

Another Bonanno innovation was installing illegal video poker machines in neighborhood stores in Brooklyn, Queens, and Staten Island. The enterprise was inspired by the family's imaginative consigliere, Anthony Spero, whose gorillas placed the gambling games in groceries, restaurants, and candy and bagel shops, and shared the proceeds fifty-fifty with the proprietors. Nevertheless, by 1990, the Bonanno borgata appeared to be a fading shadow of the expansive empire that Joe Bonanno, its first godfather, had created.

New York's most prominent district attorney, Manhattan's Robert Morgenthau, was frank in assessing the robust health of the combined Cosa Nostra families. Mobsters were skimming "multimillions" annually from the construction and garment industries alone, Morgenthau said in an informal "State of the Mob"–type review in 1990. "They have imposed an invisible tax on the region," he asserted. "What they do translates directly into high costs for such basic things as clothes, the cost of an apartment and an office, and discourages legitimate businesses from coming here or staying here."

As the last decade of the twentieth century began, new faces and a third generation of American mafiosi were in control or seeking to govern each of the five families. This latest batch of mobsters was acquainted with the pitfalls that had destroyed the previous generation of dons: Paul Castellano, Antonio Corallo, Anthony Salerno, Philip Rastelli, and Carmine Persico. The RICO arrests and trials of the old godfathers was a transitional round for the Cosa Nostra. Although that struggle ended with a jolting defeat for the Mob, the Commission trial had previewed for the new ruling generation the main law-enforcement tactics that would be employed against them.

FBI agents and prosecutors openly advertised that their blitz did not end with the Commission verdicts. They were committed to destroying the Mob's remaining power centers with the same weapons used against the previous generation. RICO would be the government's prime instrument to remove the latest coalition of bosses and their closest henchmen. Agents would count on tested methods—a rash of informers violating the *omertà* oath and electronic bugs and wire taps—to demolish the new regimes. "Our mission is to reduce the families to the level of street gangs that they were sixty or seventy years ago," William Y. Doran, supervisor of the FBI's New York Criminal Division, proclaimed confidently. "We have no intention of pulling out now and giving them a chance to revive."

In handing out life sentences at the Commission trial, Judge Richard Owen emphasized that the harsh terms were meant as a strong deterrent message to mobsters hoping to succeed the imprisoned leaders. If caught and convicted, the new dons surely knew the draconian consequences awaiting them. The future of the New York families and, in effect, the American Mafia, rested squarely in the hands of four ambitious mobsters heading their revamped gangs: John Gotti (Gambino); Vincent Gigante (Genovese); Anthony Casso (Lucchese); Joseph Massino (Bonanno); and oddly enough, one of the convicted Commission godfathers, Carmine Persico. Although imprisoned, Persico refused to relinquish power in the Colombo family. The modern-era Mafia was at a turning point and these five men would be its saviors or its ruination.

29

Snake Charmer

In the clandestine fraternity of La Cosa Nostra, Carmine Joseph Persico evoked either unqualified loyalty or enmity. His moody personality elicited contradictory nicknames: the affectionate "Junior" from his charmed supporters, and the derogatory "the Snake" from his detractors. Born on August 8, 1933, he grew up in Carroll Gardens and Red Hook, Brooklyn sections then populated mainly by working-class Italian and Irish families. Unlike most blossoming hoodlums of his generation, Persico was raised in comfortable circumstances. During the Depression years, almost every family in Persico's neighborhood barely scraped by as breadwinners desperately scrambled for backbreaking jobs on the nearby docks or in factories. Better educated than most of his neighbors, Persico's father, Carmine senior, was a legal stenographer for prestigious Manhattan law firms and brought home a weekly pay packet even in hard times. The boy's mother, the former Susan Plantamura, was a strong-willed woman who tried to keep a tight rein on Carmine and his siblings, the elder Alphonse, the younger Theodore, and a sister, Dolores.

The neighborhood was ideal territory for Mafia crews, notably Joe Profaci's organization. Youngsters were attracted to the wiseguys flashing big bankrolls, who idled away afternoons drinking coffee and playing cards at storefront Mob hangouts, misleadingly called "social" or "athletic" clubs. The Persico brothers, starting with Alphonse, followed by Carmine and Theodore, joined in the adulation of the neighborhood mafiosi.

At sixteen, over the objections of his parents, Carmine dropped out of high school. He was already known to the police as one of the leaders of the Garfield Boys, a street gang armed with knives, clubs, and zip guns—primitive single-round weapons often secretly constructed in high-school machine shops—for wild battles with rival gangs and for extorting money from defenseless classmates. In March 1951, at age seventeen, Carmine was arrested for the fatal beating of another youth during a brawl in Prospect Park. It was his first felony, and when the charges against him were dropped, his street reputation for boldness was enhanced. A Profaci capo, Frank "Frankie Shots" Abbatemarco, recognized Persico's underworld potential even though the skinny, five-feet six-inch tall teenager hardly resembled a tough enforcer. Abbatemarco put Persico to work in his bookmaking and loan-sharking rings, and later upgraded him to burglaries and truck hijackings. Persico advanced swiftly, and at an unusually early age, in his mid-twenties, got his "button" as a made man in the Profaci family.

In the 1950s Persico piled up more than a dozen arrests. His rap sheet encompassed almost every Mafia activity: numbers betting, running dice games, loan-sharking, burglary, assaults, hijackings, possession of an unregistered gun, and harassing a police officer. Through the assistance of the Profaci family's stable of politically connected lawyers, who knew how to manipulate Brooklyn's criminal court proceedings, the felony charges were dropped or reduced to misdemeanors. When Persico's cases came to trial, the complainants and witnesses often refused to testify or were out of town, a frequent occurrence in mobster trials. As a result, Persico never spent more than two weeks at a time in jail; most of his arrests ending with insignificant fines, the Mob's equivalent of routine business overhead costs.

Early on, Persico hooked up with three other young Brooklyn soldiers in the Profaci gang, the Gallo boys, Crazy Joey, Larry, and Albert. Persico's reputation for violent audacity rose sharply after the shocking 1957 murder of Mob boss Albert Anastasia in a Manhattan hotel barbershop. Together with the Gallo brothers, Persico was credited in the underworld with carrying out the big-time hit at the request of their boss, Joe Profaci, and other Mafia leaders who resented Anastasia's lust for power.

A conflict enveloped the Profaci family in 1959 after Frank Abbatemarco, Persico's crew leader, was murdered. The ambitious Persico and the Gallos expected Profaci to reward them for the Anastasia contract and other services by handing them a huge hunk of Frankie Shots' Brooklyn rackets. Instead, Profaci dispensed all of Abbatemarco's loan-sharking and numbers spoils to his older cronies. Infuriated, the Gallo brothers and Persico retaliated in commando-style lightning kidnappings of Profaci's brother-in-law and underboss, Joe Magliocco, plus four of his capos. Joe Valachi, the first Mafia soldier to publicly renounce *omertà*, said that at the time of the revolt Persico explained to him that he and other Young Turks believed that Profaci was taxing them more heavily on their illicit profits than the older wiseguys were levied. As an example of Profaci's greed, Persico griped to Valachi that the boss once forced him to turn over $1,800 from a $2,000 robbery.

To gain the release of his five lieutenants, Profaci quickly agreed to the insurgents' financial demands. Once the men were freed, Profaci reneged on his deal with the rebels and an internal battle erupted, the first time New York mafiosi had "gone to the mattresses" since the Castellammarese War of the 1930's. Between 1961 and 1963, at least nine combatants were killed, three others disappeared and were presumed murdered, and fifteen were wounded in the combat known as the "Gallo Wars."

The major defector and double-crosser in the Gallos' trenches was Carmine Persico. He returned to the Profaci fold soon after the fighting began. According to Valachi, Persico's decision was influenced by a heart-to-heart talk with the recently retired Mafia sage Frank Costello, who convinced the younger mobster that his Cosa Nostra loyalties should lie with his boss, Profaci.

Persico's importance in the war became evident on the morning of August 20, 1961. A police sergeant on a routine inspection walked into the darkened Sahara Club, a South Brooklyn bar, and came across two men strangling a third man with a rope. Bolting from the club, the two assailants ran past the sergeant and another cop. The intended victim, barely breathing, was Larry Gallo. Persico was identified by the police as one of the assailants. But true to the code of *omertà*, Gallo refused to utter a word against Persico, and the assault charges against him and the second hit man were dropped.

The attempted garroting of Larry Gallo solidified Persico's Mob reputation for duplicity and earned him the crude sobriquet "the Snake." He first double-crossed the Gallos by rejoining the Profaci forces, and then lured Larry Gallo to the bar on the pretext that he was switching sides again and reenlisting with the Gallos. Moreover, it was clear that Profaci had given Persico and his pals a contract to kill the brothers. The Gallos knew how to exact revenge, and on the morning of May 19, 1963, they struck back. Persico, a passenger in a car, was peppered by a burst of gunfire from a passing pickup truck. Bullets grazed his head and several slugs ripped into his left hand and arm. Wheeled into a hospital emergency room, his eyes were swollen, his face caked with blood. Asked by a detective to identify who shot him, Persico stared at the ceiling and shook his head negatively. He would never violate *omertà* and cooperate with the police, even if his own life was in danger.

Persico's troops were certain that the drive-by shooter was Larry Gallo, who had narrowly escaped being strangled by Carmine. The episode was magnified by Persico's supporters to bolster his reputation for toughness, claiming that a slug had punctured his jaw and that he had spat out the bullet. Although Persico minimized his wounds as mere paper cuts, he was an authentic casualty, never regaining the full use of his left hand.

Joe Profaci's death from cancer in 1962 gave Carlo Gambino and other dons the opportunity to intervene in the Gallo Wars. They imposed an armistice and ended the violence in 1963 by installing Joe Colombo as boss of the old Profaci gang. Persico's services in behalf of the Profaci-Colombo faction were rewarded with promotion to capo. The fighting over, good times and more loot beckoned. Persico was a rising star, heading a Colombo crew that included his two brothers. Detectives began hearing from informers that Carmine, who a few years earlier had been regarded as a thuggish hired gun, was now well-tailored, and hiring other gunmen to do his dirty work.

Only one unresolved matter from leaner times hung over Persico's head: a federal indictment that he participated in a 1959 truck-hijacking in Brooklyn of a $50,000 cargo of linen. Carmine's main codefendant was Hugh "Apples" McIntosh, his bodyguard and ace partner in crime. The physical contrast between the two gangsters was striking. Built like a tree trunk, McIntosh at 250 pounds and six-feet five-inches tall towered over the wiry, 150-pound Persico. Although McIntosh was Persico's loyal henchman, his Irish heritage precluded induction as a full-fledged made man.

The hijacking charge entangled Persico in courtrooms for a decade and became one of the longest federal cases recorded in New York's Eastern District jurisdiction. At the onset, prosecutors offered Persico a deal. A guilty plea would have been his first felony conviction, resulting in a light sentence of about three years, and probably parole in a year. Arrogantly confident, Persico rejected the offer, sure that with his Mob know-how and battery of expensive lawyers, he could again escape legal punishment. The first trial in 1961 ended in a hung jury. A year later, he and McIntosh were convicted, but the verdict was overturned on appeal. A third trial was halted when Persico was shot and wounded. In 1964 he was convicted for a second time, but that decision also was reversed on appeal. A jury at a fifth trial in 1968 found him and McIntosh guilty, and this conviction stuck. After three years of recondite arguments, the verdicts were finally sustained in 1971 by an appeals court. Instead of the one-year plea bargain Persico had spurned in 1960, he was hit with a maximum prison term of fourteen years; McIntosh got six years.

Before the federal appeals process was completed, Persico, free on bail, was back in court on another charge in 1971. The Manhattan district attorney's office brought state accusations that he had created a multimillion-dollar loan-sharking enterprise. Meanwhile, Persico's well-documented seamy past created a legal contretemps. In an extraordinary move that caused an uproar, a state judge closed the trial to the public and the press. Judge George Postel ruled that newspaper articles about Persico's Mafia background could unfairly influence the jury and jeopardize his right to a fair trial. Postel was later severely admonished by a higher court for violating the constitutional rights of the public and news organizations to view and report on the trial.

At the closed trial in December 1971, Persico's attorneys obtained his acquittal on all charges, ten counts of loan-sharking conspiracy. As in most of his arrests, an essential witness, whom the prosecution was relying on to implicate him in the loan-sharking business, vanished just as the trial started.

Six months before the loan-sharking trial, the Colombo family's overall tranquility was shattered when Joe Colombo was shot at his Italian-American civil-rights rally. Persico had already begun serving his hijacking conviction in January 1972, and with the paralyzed Joe Colombo incapacitated, the family's elders chose Tommy DiBella, a proficient capo, as interim boss. Prison did not hamper Persico's resolve to maintain influence in his crime family. Relaying instructions through his two brothers and the paroled Hugh McIntosh, he organized a powerful bloc in the borgata. By the late 1970s, although still behind bars, he was recognized as the family's leader, his formal anointing only awaiting his parole.

Joe Cantalupo, an admitted loan shark and Colombo family associate, who became an FBI informant in the mid-1970s, reported that Carmine and his brothers wrested control from Joe Colombo's sons and partisans in the confusion following the assassination attempt in Columbus Circle. "The wheel has turned," Cantalupo informed his FBI handlers. "The Colombo boys are on the bottom now and the Persicos are on the top."

Cantalupo specified that in Bensonhurst and other Brooklyn neighborhoods with heavy Italian-American populations, the Persico branch of the family was extorting protection money from almost every legitimate business—funeral parlors, restaurants, catering halls, garment manufacturers. "They shake people down, put fear in them," Cantalupo told the FBI.

Paroled in 1979 after serving twelve years, the forty-six-year-old Persico was the godfather of one of America's most prosperous and dangerous criminal organizations. Home again, he lived with his wife, Joyce, and their three sons and daughter in middle-class Hempstead, a Long Island suburb. His working headquarters was an old haunt, a storefront hangout in Carroll Gardens called the Nesta Social Club. Outside of Brooklyn and Long Island, he could usually be found in his nine-bedroom villa on a fifty-nine-acre spread in upstate Saugerties, New York, that he named the "Blue Mountain Manor Horse Farm." A police raid at the farm shortly after Persico went to prison for hijacking uncovered a stockpile of some 50 rifles and 40 bombs.

Unfortunately for the newly freed Don Carmine, his return coincided with the start of the FBI's proactive crusade against the five New York families. For the first time, the bureau was directly targeting and surveilling Mafia bosses and their administrations. Agents swooped down on Persico in November 1980 with a twenty-six-count indictment for a conspiracy he had engaged in from prison. His cohort, Hugh McIntosh, and his cousin Andrew "the Fat Man" Russo, a made man, tried to bribe an Internal Revenue Service agent in 1977 and 1978. The mobsters offered $250,000 for either Persico's early release on the hijacking sentence, or his transfer from the maximum-security federal penitentiary in Atlanta to a less restrictive prison near New York. They also wanted the IRS agent to fix income-tax cases for a select group of Colombo mafiosi. The agent was working a sting, and Persico's men not only trapped themselves but also implicated him in their secretly recorded conversations with the supposedly corrupt agent.

Freed on a $250,000 bond in the bribery and conspiracy case, Persico saw his legal problems multiplied, this time because of his older brother, Alphonse "Allie Boy." Looking for Allie Boy, who had jumped bail on a racketeering charge, federal marshals inadvertently crashed a meeting Carmine was holding in Brooklyn with other Mafia family leaders in May 1981. Allie Boy was not in attendance, but Carmine was slapped with another serious accusation: violating parole by associating with known criminals.

With no way to slip out of the double-barreled criminal complaints, Persico "copped" a plea bargain for the first time in his life. Wearing a modish three-piece black suit, white shirt, and patterned tie, he admitted to one count of conspiracy to commit bribery and obstruct justice in the IRS sting. By dropping five other counts, prosecutors spared him the fifteen-year sentence he would have been given if convicted at a trial. Instead, he got a maximum of five years, to run concurrently with a four-year term for parole violation.

It looked like a good bargain in March 1984, when he was released after serving less than three years for the IRS bribery and parole violations. What he had not anticipated was the government's next move. Even before his exit from prison, the FBI and federal prosecutors were closing in on him on two fronts: a RICO indictment, citing him as the head of the Colombo family, and his complicity in the Commission case. Seven months after his second release from prison, Persico got wind that his head was on the block again when a law-enforcement official leaked news of his pending arrest to the *New York Post*. Days before the first racketeering indictments charging Persico with being the Colombo boss were unsealed, he vanished, along with his underboss, Gennaro Gerry Lang Langella.

Damon Taylor, the supervisor of the FBI's Colombo Squad, soon picked up Langella in Brooklyn, disguised with a beard, after being alerted to his where-abouts by an informer. Persico was more slippery, and ended up with the rare distinction of being the only Mafia boss ever included in the FBI's list of Ten Most Wanted criminals. A four-month manhunt ended when Fred DeChristo-pher, Persico's relative and later a witness in the Commission case, disclosed his hideaway: DeChristopher's home in Wantagh, Long Island. An insurance salesman, DeChristopher was acquainted with the Colombo family through his marriage to Katherine Russo, Persico's cousin. His wife's brother, Andy "Fat Man" Russo, was not only Persico's cousin but a top-echelon Colombo capo.

DeChristopher told the FBI that early in his marriage he got a close-up, frightening view of his brother-in-law. One night, in a restaurant Russo sud-denly became irritated with a third man at their table. Grabbing a fork, he placed the tines on the white of the man's right eye, hissing, "Look, when I tell you to do something, you do it, okay, asshole?" As the terrified man frantically signaled his compliance, Russo snarled, "The next time you fuck up, I'll push this fork right into your fucking eye."

Later that night, Russo proudly explained his modus operandi to DeChristopher. "If they fear you, Freddie, they'll lick your hand or kiss your feet. They'll respect you. I'm a gangster, see, Freddie? I can lie, and I can cheat, and I can kill."

Fleeing from arrest in the Commission and Colombo family indictments, Persico hid out in DeChristopher's home for three months. He counted on his personal family's loyalty to shield him, but DeChristopher was the relative who betrayed him.

Outside DeChristopher's Long Island home, on the afternoon of February 15, 1985, Agent Taylor dialed DeChristopher's number on a mobile telephone. "I'd like to speak to Mr. Persico," the agent said when DeChristopher, who was expecting the call, answered the ring. Holding the phone, Persico growled, "Who is this?" The soft-spoken investigator replied, "This is the FBI. We have the house surrounded. Come out with your hands up."

Persico, who had been sleeping in the attic, marched out with his hands in the air. Another fugitive bagged with him was capo Dominic Donnie Shacks Montemarano. Through a tap on the DeChristopher phone, the FBI knew that Montemarano had been invited for a luncheon conference with the boss, and agents timed the raid to capture him, too. Both gangsters were unarmed. On the ride back to FBI headquarters in Manhattan for booking, Persico seemed unflustered, cracking lighthearted jokes with the agents. He even cordially autographed for Taylor an FBI Most Wanted poster with his photograph displayed prominently on it.

The Colombo family RICO trial in 1986 was a warm-up event for Persico's Commission trial later that year. The strongest evidence against him was testimony from Fred DeChristopher and former wannabe Joe Cantalupo, also principal witnesses at the Commission trial. DeChristopher's words were extremely damaging to Persico. He testified that the fugitive Mob boss appeared at his home without warning and simply settled in as an uninvited guest. In convivial moments Carmine delighted in preparing for DeChristopher and his wife one of his favorite dishes, pasta with a simple sauce of olive oil and garlic. To DeChristopher, Persico bragged that he had run the family from prison and that he had stashed away enough cash from his crimes to "last ten lifetimes."

On another occasion, while reminiscing about his accomplishments, Persico casually mentioned, "I killed Anastasia." It was a boast that he had belonged to Joey Gallo's "barbershop quintet."

Besides testimony from the informer Cantalupo and the reluctant host DeChristopher, the prosecution counted on electronic eavesdropping. Bugs at the Casa Storta Restaurant that recorded Gerry Langella's conspiratorial conversations about Colombo family rackets were crucial in securing convictions of Persico and eight codefendants.

Blood and loyalty ties, vital factors in solidifying and protecting Mafia borgatas, backfired this time, entangling Persico's relatives and his sturdiest friend in a RICO "family" trial. Hugh McIntosh was sentenced to ten years. The Snake's cousin Andy Russo got fourteen years. Persico, the boss, received a thirty-nine-year term. Probably the most difficult aspect of the trial for him was the involvement of his oldest son, Alphonse, known as "Little Allie Boy," so as not to be confused with his Uncle Alphonse, Carmine's brother. Little Allie Boy was convicted of being a capo, supervising family rackets, and trying to bribe prison officials for preferential treatment of his father.

The hard-boiled Carmine Persico declined to seek leniency for himself, but he implored the sentencing judge, John F. Keenan, to spare his thirty-three-year-old son. He contended that Little Allie Boy was innocent and that the turncoat witnesses against him were liars. "I'm not really concerned about myself," Carmine said as several relatives of the father and son wept in the courtroom.

Judge Keenan imposed a sentence of twelve years on the son. Recommending a stiffer sentence, Aaron A. Marcu, a prosecutor who had spent three years investigating the Colombo family, portrayed Little Allie Boy with these prophetic words: "He is his father's trusted lieutenant. He is the future of the Colombo family."

Except for the unlikely possibility of his busting out of a federal prison, even the brazen Carmine Persico realized that a combined 139-year term for the "family" and the Commission RICO convictions, was equivalent to a death sentence. He might be doomed, but he was determined to pass on his scepter to his son and heir. Little Allie Boy could expect parole in eight years at about age forty, still in his prime, ready to be crowned and to reap for many years the illicit wealth produced by the Colombo borgata. Until his son was freed, Persico intended to retain the title of boss and transmit important policy decisions to surrogates, as he had done during previous imprisonments. By maintaining his position, Persico could insure that a large percentage of the Colombo booty would still be funneled into the coffers of his relatives, just as if he himself were out on the streets. Ever the dutiful husband and father, he wanted to take care of his wife and their three children at home. And it was vital that cash and other assets should be waiting as an inheritance for Little Allie Boy when his prison term expired.

Shortly after the trials of her husband and son, Joyce Smoldono Persico openly expressed her affection for Carmine, insisting that he had been unfairly convicted on flimsy evidence by ambitious prosecutors. "I know the kind of man he is," she said of her husband in a letter in January 1987 to the newspaper *Newsday*. "The love that Carmine and I have for our family and home has helped us through the years of excessive punishment the government has inflicted upon us. We survived the ordeal, Carmine came home, and just when we thought it was safe to resume our lives again, along came RICO and Giuliani."

Persico also had U.S. Attorney Rudolph Giuliani on his mind. Seeking revenge for his life sentence and his son's conviction, he put out contracts for the murders of Giuliani; two prosecutors at the Colombo family trial, Aaron Marcu and Bruce A. Baird; the head of the FBI's Colombo Squad, Damon Taylor; and the case agent, Denis Maduro, who dug up evidence against him and his son. The multiple murder plans were disclosed by Michael Lloyd, a bank robber and thief, whom Persico thoroughly misjudged and took into his confidence while they were fellow inmates at federal prisons in Marion, Illinois, and in Lompoc, California.

Lloyd testified about details of the plots at his parole hearing in 1998, when he revealed that he had been a government informer in prison during the late 1980s and early 1990s. The godfather and the snitch met in 1987 at the federal penitentiary in Marion, one of the government's toughest maximum-security correctional institutions. Imprisoned with Lloyd for the next eight years in Marion and in Lompoc, Persico took a liking to him and increasingly trusted him. Keeping his ears open, Lloyd culled information about Persico's surreptitious maneuvers with mobsters on the outside, mainly from working as Persico's prison secretary.

Over the years, Persico recounted to Lloyd chapters of his lifetime in the Mob, claiming that he was responsible for slaying about twenty-five men, half of them killed by himself. Carmine confided that he used visiting lawyers and relatives to shuttle messages to New York, and that he sanctioned Mob hits by the same relay system. Another method Persico employed was sending letters typed by Lloyd to lawyers, which were passed along to Colombo mobsters.

Prison authorities were barred from opening and reading letters from inmates to lawyers. According to Lloyd, Persico also arranged bribes to prison guards for favors and was allowed to have sex with a woman attorney who visited him in the Lompoc prison.

Lloyd sent his own letters to Giuliani, warning him of Persico's intentions after he learned Persico had put out hit contracts on prosecutors. Lloyd was then recruited as a government informer under the code name "the Snake Charmer." His information helped foil Persico's plots to murder the government officials, but Persico apparently never suspected him.

Double-crossing Carmine Persico was a dangerous pastime, and Lloyd knew the risks he was taking. But ingratiating himself with federal prosecutors could procure an early parole for him. Whatever useful items Lloyd picked up he sent to the FBI through an attorney's address that was really a mail drop. Federal law-enforcement authorities in New York's Southern District decided against bringing a new murder conspiracy indictment against Persico because he was already confined behind bars for the remainder of his days. A more important reason for overlooking his homicidal revenge contracts was that additional charges would expose Lloyd as a spy and sever a wellspring of information about shifting fortunes inside the Colombo family. Although serving combined sentences of 139 years, Persico was manipulating events in his borgata on the East Coast from a prison cell in California. Capricious as ever, he had turned on a former deputy, a decision that would generate fateful consequences for his Mafia family. And through Michael Lloyd, the Snake Charmer, Carmine Persico, the Snake, was unwittingly providing insight into an internecine Mob war that he himself had launched.

30

Carmine's War

Driving alone in the mellowing light of a summery evening, Victor Orena was nearing the driveway of his home when his instincts sounded an alarm. Four men were seated in a parked car directly across the road from his elegant two-story home on Buckingham Road in Cedarhurst, Long Island. Slamming on the brakes, Orena spun into a quick U-turn and roared away from his placid suburban street. He had recognized the men in the parked car and instantly realized why they were staked out at his house. There was a contract on his life and the four men were a hit squad, with him in their crosshairs.

Victor John Orena was no ordinary businessman returning from a day at the office. He was an accomplished, wealthy mafioso eager to ascend to the rank of a mighty godfather. As Orena sped away from Cedarhurst in the twilight of June 20, 1991, he knew who was behind the ambush attempt. The orders must have originated 3,000 miles away, and could only have been issued by the perfidious Carmine the Snake Persico.

Known as "Little Vic," Orena had been abruptly thrust into a powerful position in the Colombo family in the wake of the racketeering convictions of Carmine Persico and Little Allie Boy. At the time of the guilty verdicts, Orena was merely a striving soldier in the younger Persico's crew. But when Little Allie

Boy went off to prison for racketeering in 1987, he picked Orena as his crew's replacement capo.

Sentenced to life imprisonment, Carmine's first choice as acting boss to supervise the family for him was his older brother, Alphonse, the original Allie Boy. But after a brief reign, Allie Boy became a fugitive, skipping out on a $250,000 bail bond to avoid a long sentence for a loan-sharking conviction. So, in 1988, with his brother and his son out of circulation, Persico by a method of elimination settled on Little Vic Orena as acting boss.

Viewing Orena as a trusted ally but at most a temporary second fiddle, the Snake delivered one primary directive to him: keep the throne secure for Little Allie Boy until he comes out of prison to take over as the family's godfather. Orena's other big task was to ensure that the imprisoned Persicos and their relatives on the outside continued receiving their share of the family's take. Kenneth McCabe, a federal Mafia investigator, later learned that Carmine displayed his exceptional faith in Orena's loyalty by extending to him two powers rarely given to temporary bosses: Little Vic could unilaterally order hits and induct soldiers.

Carmine and his son's confidence in the fifty-four-year-old Orena arose from his record as an exceptional earner and an obedient soldier. Short and chubby, with penetrating green eyes and gray-flecked hair, Orena was well regarded among the Colombo cognoscenti for his business acumen. A mobster with decades of unfailing service to the Persico wing of the family, Orena skillfully handled major loan-sharking and labor rackets, principally on Long Island. His "yellow sheet," his arrest record, was skimpy: minor busts for gambling and one for perjury, without any prison time. The most serious entry against him was a loan-sharking conviction, which cost him four months in a Long Island county jail.

As a soldier, the levelheaded Little Vic had ducked out of violent tasks, but he knew which "cowboys" to choose for dangerous work. In fact, after taking charge of Little Allie Boy's crew as a capo, he often instructed soldiers and wannabes assigned to murders that he preferred a traditional Sicilian method known as *lupara bianca* (literally, "white shotgun" but meaning "white death"), the euphemism for making certain the corpse is not found.

Orena had developed an invaluable asset for himself through a relationship with Dennis J. Pappas, a lawyer and fiscal consultant. Federal investigators eventually untangled a dizzying array of eleven companies and 165 bank accounts created by Pappas in the 1980s to launder at least $5 million dollars for Orena and his confederates. Untold millions more, prosecutors and FBI agents conceded, were untraceable. As Orena's banker and money man, Pappas, then in his late thirties, was known in the borgata as the "finance consigliere." In return for huge payoffs to himself, Pappas's primary function was moving the family's cash from loan-sharking, gambling and gasoline bootlegging into dummy corporations and bank accounts. The money was then cleansed by being paid out to relatives of the mobsters, who were given fake jobs at the sham companies.

Pappas further assisted Orena and his partners by siphoning about $1 million from pension funds in unions the Colombos controlled. The money was used for loan-sharking capital. An accountant working for Pappas got an alarming gift after he raised questions about some of the lawyer's bookkeeping legerdemain. He received a package containing a dead fish wrapped in newspaper—the customary Mafia warning that he would be murdered if he opened his mouth to law enforcement.

For two years Victor Orena served as a reliable caretaker, heeding Carmine Persico's decisions from prison regarding the family's most important policies, murders, inductions of new members, hierarchy appointments, and demotions. By the spring of 1991, Orena was tired of Persico's intrusions and told his hatchet men that Carmine was out of touch, obstructing the family's profits, and that he, rather than Little Allie Boy, deserved the title and recognition as boss. Orena was especially rankled by Persico's negotiations to have a version of his life broadcast on television shows. The acting boss feared that Persico's grandstanding would increase law-enforcement pressure on the family, just as Joe Bonanno's biography and television appearances had helped spark the disastrous Commission case.

Complying with Mafia custom, Orena decided to take absolute control by winning support from a majority of the family's dozen capos. He instructed Carmine Sessa, the family consigliere, to poll the captains to determine if they favored installing him as boss. Their firm endorsement would smooth Orena's path to acceptance as a godfather by the other New York families and end Carmine Persico's claim. Sessa, who had been elevated to consigliere, the family's third highest position, by Carmine Persico, never carried out Orena's request. He informed Persico of Orena's treachery, most likely through Carmine's brother Ted, a capo who had permission to visit Carmine in Lompoc. Persico's loyal troops had their own complaints about Orena to forward to the imprisoned boss. They were incensed that Little Vic was cutting them off from the family's most rewarding rackets and building an empire by favoring other crews.

The news about Orena's proposed referendum poll was conclusive for Carmine. His message to his soldiers was direct: whack Orena. And on the evening of June 20, 1991, they amateurishly attempted to carry out the boss's command. Four of the Snake's gunmen, led by consigliere Sessa, failed to eliminate Little Vic when he spotted them parked near his home.

Over the next three months, Orena and Persico representatives met for sitdowns to work out a peaceful compromise. The Orena forces numbered close to 100 and the Persico combatants 25 or 30. Neither side budged on the question of leadership, and in November 1991, bullets began flying. The war was on.

A bug in Camden, New Jersey, across the river from Philadelphia, provided the FBI in New York with the Orena battalion's casus belli. The bureau's Philadelphia office had concealed microphones in the office of a lawyer who allowed high-ranking Philadelphia mobster clients to meet there secretly. At noon on December 5, 1991, John Stanfa, the Philadelphia boss, and his underboss, Anthony Piccolo, were solicited in the lawyer's office for support in the newly started war by Salvatore Profaci, a pro-Orena capo. Salvatore was the son of Joe Profaci, the founder and first godfather of the family that eventually assumed the Colombo name. He was in charge of the family's activities in parts of New Jersey. Nicknamed "Sally Pro" and "Jersey Sal," Profaci had mutual deals with the Philadelphia Mob in Atlantic City and southern New Jersey.

"You know, to me La Cosa Nostra's very sacred," Sal Profaci said. "Okay, and my word is better than anything else that I got to offer." Explaining his reasons for siding with Orena as his choice for *representante*, Profaci pictured him as "a gentleman, beautiful person, very very capable, very very qualified, level-headed." The Snake was "crazy," igniting the war by trying to kill Orena. "Carmine Persico is losing his mind. Carmine Persico is calling press conferences . . . He wants to go on *60 Minutes*, Barbara Walters interview . . ."

Profaci claimed that a large majority of the family's 125 soldiers favored dethroning Persico because his long-distance rule and frequent hierarchy changes were creating chaos. "A hundred people say no we don't agree with what he's doing, and it's not right what he's doing, and he's got a hundred-year sentence, therefore we can't stay without a family," he intoned, his voice rising. "I mean, that's no way to live, you gotta have a family, you gotta have a share." Blaming Persico's relatives, his brothers, cousins, and nephews, for inciting the mayhem, Profaci lamented, "Now we started shooting and where's it gonna end? Where's it gonna end?"

That December, five Colombo mobsters were slain in Brooklyn, one of them while hanging a Christmas wreath on his front door. Innocent civilians were shot in the volleys of gunfire. One victim, eighteen-year-old Matteo Speranza, was brutally murdered in the bagel shop where he worked, mistaken by Orena gunmen for a Persico supporter.

Trying to prevent the Colombos from turning the city into a killing field, Brooklyn District Attorney Charles J. Hynes in late December subpoenaed forty-one suspected members and associates before a grand jury. Only twenty-eight showed up, their faces concealed in the collars of lumberjack shirts or leather jackets. None of them was a canary, and none would offer any information about the slayings. "They've turned this into a class-B movie," Hynes fumed. "We're not going to allow this county to become a shooting gallery where innocent people are being gunned down."

The ambushes and drive-by fusillades, however, continued.

Oddly, the FBI was getting blow-by-blow reports on the carnage and internal Colombo politics from a bizarre source—Gregory Scarpa Sr., a warhorse Persico capo, sociopathic killer, and longtime undercover government informer. A stylish dresser, Scarpa routinely carried $5,000 in cash as pocket money and for bribes if he were arrested. Starting in the 1960s, he ran auto theft, loan-sharking, narcotics, and extortion rackets for Joe Colombo and Carmine Persico. A classic underworld success story, Scarpa, at his prime in the late 1970s and early '80s, had homes in Manhattan's exclusive Sutton Place, Las Vegas, Staten Island, and Brooklyn. Compactly built at 200 pounds, he radiated power, and his guile and penchant for brutality earned him the nickname "the Grim Reaper." His confidants gleefully related that he so enjoyed whacking a hated rival that he told them he wanted to dig up the corpse and kill the victim again.

Scarpa's headquarters for thirty years was the storefront Wimpy Boys Social Club, in his home neighborhood of Bensonhurst in Brooklyn. Despite numerous arrests for loan-sharking, fencing hijacked goods, assault, carrying unlicensed guns, stock and bond thefts, distributing counterfeit credit cards, and attempting to bribe police officers, Scarpa somehow emerged from these scrapes with the charges dismissed or was freed on probation.

An explanation for Scarpa's good fortune finally surfaced in the mid-1990's. As a young soldier in the Colombo family, he had taken out an insurance policy in the 1960s by secretly working for the FBI. His most astonishing exploit was helping agents after the 1964 slaying of three civil rights workers, James Chaney, Andrew Goodman, and Michael Schwerner, in Philadelphia, Mississippi. The bureau, uncomfortable that it had employed a mobster for aid in a high-profile investigation that attracted international attention, has never officially credited Scarpa. But former law-enforcement officials, who asked for anonymity, and lawyers who are aware of the circumstances, verified that the Brooklyn mobster compelled a Ku Klux Klan member to disclose that the three missing bodies had been buried in an earthen dam.

"He went down to Mississippi for the FBI and kidnapped a KKK guy agents were sure was involved in disposing of the bodies," said a New York lawyer who has represented many mafiosi and who knew Scarpa. "The guy had an appliance store. Scarpa bought a TV and came back to the store to pick it up just as he was closing. The guy helps him carry the TV to his car parked in the back of the store. Scarpa knocks him out with a bop to the head, takes him off to the woods, beats him up, sticks a gun down his throat and says, 'I'm going to blow your head off.' The KKK guy realized he was Mafia and wasn't kidding and told him where to look for the bodies."

After the Mississippi mission, Scarpa continued his affiliation with the bureau, supplying information about the Colombo borgata for three decades. Like numerous criminals, his motive for ratting was to obtain behind-the-scenes intervention from the bureau, and leniency if he were confronted with arrest or conviction. Although spying for the FBI and violating *omertà*, he had no intention of abandoning his gangster spoils. Before and during the Orena-Persico conflict, FBI agent R. Lindley "Lynn" DeVecchio was Scarpa's contact and handler. DeVecchio filed dozens of "confidential informant" reports—called 209s by the bureau—describing events in the war based on information supplied by Scarpa. The agent met clandestinely with Scarpa and received telephone calls from the mobster on a supersecret telephone that no agent but DeVecchio could answer. Agents called it a "Hello phone."

During the war, while seemingly cooperating with the FBI, Scarpa was Persico's generalissimo, doing his utmost to wipe out Orena's shock troops. Scarpa's reports to DeVecchio were filled with incriminating leads about illegal operations run by the Orenas. He also betrayed his own gunmen by identifying them as participating in conspiracies to whack Orena's men. Although he killed at least three Orena soldiers and tried to murder others, Scarpa omitted those details in his tips to DeVecchio. He never reported that he was a willing participant in the deadly clashes. He did inform DeVecchio of attempts on his own life and that Orena gunman had sprayed his car with bullets while his daughter-in-law was behind the wheel.

Over the years, Scarpa was paid $158,000 by the FBI for his services. He had agreed to work for the bureau with the provisos that his identity would never be disclosed to anyone outside of the bureau—even to prosecutors—and that he would never be called as a trial witness. It is a type of agreement used by law-enforcement agencies with informants they consider extremely important.

Before the war, in 1988, when Scarpa was fifty-eight, he underwent emergency surgery for a bleeding ulcer and received a pint of blood from a member of his crew who later died of AIDS. Three years later, in the midst of the war, Scarpa was diagnosed as suffering from the illness. He lost fifty pounds, became emaciated and easily fatigued. But ignoring failing health, he supervised his crew with an iron hand, eagerly hunting for Orena foes. Although Orena's men were unable to clip Scarpa, his luck faded. On December 29, 1992, near his home in Brooklyn, he was shot in the left eye in a dispute over a narcotics transaction unrelated to the Colombo battles. By 1993, blind in one eye, bald, and emaciated, he was unrecognizable as the terrifying warlord he had once been.

At the outset of the conflict, the Colombo family was relatively secure. Indeed, the government knew little about the scope of the family's expanding illicit operations. Scarpa's information had mainly provided the FBI valuable intelligence about the borgata's chain of command, vague information about deals that were being engineered, and pejorative gossip about his Mafia enemies. But generally Scarpa withheld information that could lead to indictments on serious charges against anyone in the gang.

"We had very little on the Colombo family," admitted John Gleeson, the prosecutor in the U.S. Attorney's Office in the Eastern District who was then in charge of the organized-crime section. "We were struggling along, there was nothing big in the works."

Gleeson, like other federal lawyers in New York, was unaware of Scarpa's involvement with the FBI, when in 1990 he assigned another prosecutor in Brooklyn, George A. Stamboulidis, to start making inroads against the Colombos. Stamboulidis got a break when a Colombo wannabe, Michael Maffatore, desperate for leniency on narcotics charges, began talking about an unsolved murder in the family. Wearing a concealed tape recorder, Maffatore obtained small victories for prosecutors by implicating other wannabes in the homicide. It was a start, but it was more like a pinprick than a weighty blow to the Colombos' superstructure.

To stir up more action, Stamboulidis bombarded accountants, and other supposedly legitimate people known to be working for the family, with subpoenas to testify before a grand jury. Counting on the fear of perjury to loosen tongues of the family's civilian auxiliaries, Stamboulidis hoped the subpoenas would become building blocks for evidence against the main targets: Vic Orena; his two mobster sons, Victor junior and John; and Carmine Persico's son, Little Allie Boy, who, like his father, was believed to be playing a big hand in the gang while in prison.

The strategy paid off just as the internal fighting flared up. A subpoenaed accountant, Kenneth Geller, cooperated with inside information about the Orenas' loan-sharking rings and Little Allie Boy's seamy business ventures. Fear drove Geller into the welcoming arms of the prosecutors. He was paying the Colombo family $11,000 a week in vigorish for loans of more than $1 million. Seeking to strike it rich, he had borrowed the cash from loan sharks for investments that failed. To meet his weekly installments to the Mob, Geller dug himself into a deeper hole by embezzling money from legitimate clients. With subpoenas flying, Geller thought the Colombos would bump him off as a possible informer as soon as it became evident that indictments were imminent. His only option was moving quickly to help the government by wearing a wire to obtain evidence against the mobsters, and then seek anonymity and security in the Federal Witness Protection Program.

Between November 1991 and October 1993, twelve gangsters and an innocent teenaged employee in a bagel shop went to their graves. At least a dozen Colombo warriors and five passersby were wounded. Among the dead was Joseph Scopo, an Orena supporter, son of Ralph Scopo, the union leader convicted in the Commission case. The absurdity of the shoot-outs was highlighted by Persico gunmen apologizing to the Genovese borgata for mistakenly killing one of their inactive soldiers, seventy-eight-year-old Gaetano "Tommy Scars" Amato, who made the mistake of visiting an Orena social club when a Persico raiding party attacked.

The warfare simplified the government's efforts to decimate the family through convictions. Colombo members and associates flipped and became cooperating witnesses to avoid long sentences after being arrested on racketeering and murder conspiracy charges. Others defected out of fear they would be slain. At least twelve members became government witnesses, including Carmine Sessa, the consigliere, and two capos.

Aided by the accountant Geller's testimony and by Mob traitors, the government made its biggest catch by snaring Victor Orena, whose quest to become a godfather was his undoing. He was arrested on April Fool's Day in 1992, hiding in the home of his mistress, equipped with an arsenal of four loaded shotguns, two assault rifles, and six handguns. Before the year ended, Orena was found guilty on RICO charges, of murder, conspiracy to murder, and large-scale loan-sharking. The sentence for Little Vic, at age fifty-eight, was life imprisonment without the possibility of parole.

A total of sixty-eight capos, soldiers, and associates from both sides were rounded up and indicted as a result of the two years of gunfire, internal wrangles, and Stamboulidis's grand jury summonses. Like their leader, Little Vic, high-level Orena warriors and helpers were convicted, mainly for murder conspiracy, racketeering, and loan-sharking. Also imprisoned were Little Vic's sons, Victor junior and John, and Tom Petrizzo, the construction racketeer who pilfered a small fortune in steel from the West Side Highway. Dennis Pappas, Orena's financial guide, went to prison for his large-scale finaglings.

From the Persico camp, sentenced to long prison terms were Carmine's younger brother, Ted; his cousin Andy Russo; and his strongman, Hugh McIntosh. The oldest Persico brother, Alphonse "Allie Boy," died before the war at age sixty-one, in 1989, while serving a twenty-five-year sentence for extortion.

The most mysterious combatant finally convicted as a byproduct of the fighting was Gregory Scarpa, the Persicos' ruthless capo and FBI mole. Federal prosecutors, unaware of his double life as mobster and informer, brought racketeering charges against him for the first time in his life. The federal indictment came only after the Brooklyn DA's office grabbed him on a state gun-possession charge. Even after his indictments, Scarpa continued to provide information secretly to DeVecchio in the flickering hope of being spared yet one more time. But his double-dealing tricks were played out, and in 1993 he pleaded guilty to multiple federal counts of racketeering.

Scarpa's court sentencing was closed to the public. There was real fear by the prosecution and the defense that revelations about his undercover work would mark him as a high-level squealer and probably endanger his life in prison. At the secret hearing, he made a final pitch for leniency on the basis of his liaisons with the FBI. It failed. He was sentenced to ten years by Judge Jack B. Weinstein, who described his duplicity and violent acts "as worse than those of a wild animal." A year later, Scarpa died of complications from AIDS in a prison hospital. He was sixty-six.

Scarpa's tangled relations with the Mob and the government became a searing legal headache for prosecutors and created another casualty: his handler, FBI Agent Lynn DeVecchio, the Colombo Squad supervisor. News of Scarpa's extraordinary FBI alliance seeped out to lawyers representing the Orena faction. At a racketeering and murder trial in 1995 of seven Orena members, embarrassed prosecutors admitted that the relationship between Scarpa and DeVecchio had compromised their case. The government conceded there was circumstantial evidence that DeVecchio had disclosed confidential information to Scarpa. Prosecutors were compelled to turn over to defense lawyers internal complaints from other agents that DeVecchio presumedly provided highly sensitive information to the mobster about the identities of Colombo turncoats who were secretly aiding the FBI. DeVecchio's critics alleged that he had helped Scarpa evade arrests and had given him tips on how to track down Orena soldiers during the 1991–1993 struggle.

After reviewing classified FBI reports, some prosecutors suspected that DeVecchio had tipped Scarpa that his Wimpy Boys Club had been bugged by the Secret Service during a counterfeit-credit-card investigation, and also alerted him in 1987 that his son, Gregory junior, was about to be arrested on federal drug-trafficking charges.

Three FBI agents who worked under DeVecchio on the Colombo Squad testified about his behavior during the war. Their suspicions grew after he refused to arrest Scarpa in 1992, although two defectors implicated the mobster in the murder of an Orena partisan. Agent Christopher Favo asserted that DeVecchio was openly partial to the Persico band. On May 22, 1992, Favo walked into DeVecchio's office to report that two Orena members had been shot.

"As I started into that he slapped his hand on the desk and he said, 'We're going to win this thing,' and he seemed excited about it." Favo recalled. "He seemed like he didn't know who we were—the FBI. It seemed like a line had been blurred . . . I thought there was something wrong. He was compromised. He had lost track of who he was."

The accusations were unprecedented. No other FBI agent had previously been publicly accused of helping a mafioso commit crimes and covering up for him.

DeVecchio vehemently denied that he had spilled secrets to Scarpa or had undermined investigations of the Colombo family. An agent with a distinguished record, he resigned his $105,000-a-year job soon after the Justice Department found insufficient cause to prosecute him for misconduct. "The bottom line is that I never gave Scarpa any confidential information about the war or any other matter," DeVecchio insisted in an interview. He attributed the agitation over his relationship with Scarpa to agents and prosecutors inexperienced in organized-crime investigations, and who misinterpreted justified and legal techniques in dealing with informers.

As for his comment to Favo, "We are going to win this thing," DeVecchio added, "What I meant was that the fighting inside the Colombo family was going to help us—the FBI—win the war against the Colombos by providing us with tons of defectors and intelligence."

A defender of DeVecchio, Damon Taylor, the agent who preceded him as the head of the Colombo Squad and who was familiar with Gregory Scarpa's history, tersely summed up the gangster's value to the bureau: "He was the crown jewel, for all his faults. I would give credibility to anything he said."

Pouncing on the Scarpa revelations, defense lawyers for the Orena group tried turning the tables on the prosecution, accusing DeVecchio of inciting the war to manufacture evidence against Orena supporters. They contended that DeVecchio supplied Scarpa with information to help him kill opponents. In effect, the lawyers argued, Orena defendants, on trial for conspiring to kill their Persico enemies, had justifiably acted in self defense against the combined murderous plotting of Scarpa and DeVecchio. DeVecchio, according to the attorneys' theme, deliberately encouraged crimes rather than preventing them.

The defense arguments partially succeeded. In a setback for the U.S. Attorney's Office in the Eastern District, nineteen Orena faction defendants accused of gangland murder conspiracies were acquitted, or had their convictions reversed. Faced with spending the rest of his days in a cell, a desperate Vic Orena latched on belatedly to "the Scarpa Defense" theory in a bid for a new trial. The ploy did not work for him. His appeal to overturn his conviction was rejected and his one hundred-year sentence was affirmed by appeals judges.

For most Orena warriors the Scarpa imbroglio was a temporary courtroom victory. Plentiful evidence, and traitors, had been generated by the Colombo family war to convict them on other charges, and they eventually joined their leader, Little Vic, in prison.

Scarpa's double life ended with a judicial rebuke of the FBI and Lynn

DeVecchio. Federal District Court Judge Charles P. Sifton, examining evidence in several requests by Orena-faction defendants for new trials, chided the agent directly and, indirectly, the bureau. "Scarpa emerges as sinister and violent and at the same time manipulative and deceptive with everyone, including DeVecchio," the judge said. "DeVecchio emerges as arrogant, stupid, or easily manipulated but, at the same time, caught up in the complex and difficult task of trying to make the best use of Scarpa's information to bring the war to a close."

Scarpa's protégé Lawrence Mazza, forty years his junior, testifying as a defector against former companions in the Colombo family, sketched a complex portrait of his Mafia mentor. Mazza said that after contracting AIDS, Scarpa encouraged him to sleep with his young mistress, Linda, the mother of two of his children. "He told me he wouldn't take anything away from Linda that she wanted. He loved her too much and he knew how she felt about me and how I felt about her."

Describing how Scarpa trained him in the arts of loan-sharking, bookmaking, and murder, Mazza testified that the capo exulted in clipping Orena opponents. In a drive-by killing, Mazza said, he used a shotgun and Scarpa fired a revolver to bring down one of their prey. As Scarpa blasted rounds into the face of the dying victim, he shouted triumphantly, "This one's for Carmine."

31

Dynasty

The fierce Colombo dynastic struggle was the last New York Mob war of the twentieth century.

It had been a costly bloodbath for both sides, in casualties and convictions. Ultimately, forty-two Persico soldiers and associates, and sixteen from the Orena faction were convicted on an assortment of charges and packed off to prison. Ten turncoats undermined the family by defecting into the Witness Protection Program. Carmine Persico emerged as the seeming victor of the war of succession. The government indirectly decided the outcome in his favor by obtaining a life sentence for Victor Orena. With their leader gone, the Orena gunmen ended the revolt, and cleared the way for Carmine's son Alphonse to become boss when he was paroled after serving eight years for racketeering.

From an early age, Little Allie Boy, the eldest of Carmine's sons, was destined to follow in his father's footsteps. He was raised in South Brooklyn and Bensonhurst, the heartland of the Colombo family, where his father, in and out of prison, was looked upon by relatives and neighbors as a folk hero. Taller and more muscular than Carmine, the bespectacled son was a bright student. Favoring the Ivy League–look in tweed jackets, he toyed with the idea of becoming a lawyer, but dropped out of St. John's University after his sophomore year. By his mid-twenties, according to police intelligence files, he was a capo in his father's borgata. His first arrest in 1983 at age twenty-nine, on heroin trafficking charges, ended in a dismissal. Three years later, he was labeled a capo by prosecutors, convicted along with his father in the Colombo family RICO trial, and sentenced to twelve years.

"The kid wanted badly to get the same respect as his father," Aaron Marcu, a federal prosecutor at the trial, said afterward. "He had more education, style, and looks than the average mobster, but from tapes we got an image of him as the classic wannabe. He was taken by the life, bossing around people, barking orders." Scheduled for parole in 1993, Little Allie Boy's release was blocked by George Stamboulidis, the assistant U.S. Attorney and lead prosecutor in many of the Colombo family trials. Stamboulidis informed the parole board that Little Allie Boy was suspected of arranging from prison the murder of a man who had been dating his wife, Tori, mother of his three daughters. The victim, Michael Devine, a Staten Island bartender, was shot to death in 1992. Several of the slugs tore into Devine's genitals. Citing cooperating witnesses and Mob turncoats, Stamboulidis's letter to prison officials said, "When a murder victim's genitalia are mutilated, it is a sign to those who learn of his murder that he was imprudently intimate with the spouse of a member of La Cosa Nostra."

Although never formally charged with Devine's slaying, Little Allie Boy was tried in the summer of 1994 on federal accusations that he helped direct the Colombo family war from prison and had authorized plans to kill seven Orena partisans. Another homicide charge tagged on was the prewar murder of his brother-in-law, Steven Piazza. Prosecutors claimed that Carmine Persico wanted Piazza killed in 1985 because he was physically abusing Carmine's daughter, Barbara. Additionally, the Persicos believed Piazza was either using or selling drugs and might become dangerously talkative if picked up by the police. The murder was carried out by Little Allie Boy's crew with his specific blessings, according to an indictment.

In a legal twist at the 1994 trial, Little Allie Boy was found guilty of conspiring to kill Piazza; yet he was completely acquitted of racketeering charges because of a complex glitch in the RICO law. A jury found that yes, he had participated in Piazza's murder, but the slaying was not a count in the indictment; it was an underlying act or felony. A RICO conviction requires the commission of at least two underlying acts, and the jury failed to link him to any other underlying act. Observers felt that the prosecution was hoodwinked by a defector and former capo, John Pate, whom they expected to be the best witness against Persico. Instead, Pate, who had been a boon companion of Little Allie Boy, seemed to tailor his testimony to help rather than hurt him.

Nine other defendants in the RICO case were found guilty or plea bargained for reduced sentences. Little Allie Boy was the only one to walk out of the courtroom in 1995 a free man, his parole no longer thwarted.

The forty-year-old Alphonse Persico, crowned with the title of either boss or acting boss, was now in charge of rebuilding the divided crime family. On the other side of the continent, his father, Carmine, still the titular don, could look upon the war as an unqualified success. While the rival Colombo soldiers were killing each other in New York, Carmine had molded a comfortable niche for himself in the Lompoc penitentiary. Always a leader, the Snake founded an Italian cultural club in the prison where he and other Mob inmates, mainly killers, drug dealers, and extortionists, could meet to talk over old times. Prison authorities allowed the club members to prepare special banquets, birthday feasts, and entertain themselves as if they were in one of their storefront hangouts in South Brooklyn. Feared in the outside world for his cruelty, inside the sunny prison in central California, several miles from the Pacific Ocean, Carmine Persico whiled away his days cultivating a rose garden. Imprisoned for life, by the late 1990s the Snake could at last see his aspirations for a Mafia dynasty fulfilled through his son.

Following his narrow escape on RICO technicalities, Little Allie Boy tried to conceal his Mafia command position by posing as a businessman with investments in a Brooklyn limousine service, a restaurant, a wholesale coffee company, and two bagel shops. Evading investigators in New York, he spent much of his time over the next four years in Florida. It was there that his luck ran out. In February 1999, he was relaxing on a friend's yacht near Fort Lauderdale when the Coast Guard, acting on a tip from an informer, found him in possession of a 9-millimeter pistol and a shotgun. Because of his 1986 RICO conviction he was prohibited from carrying weapons.

Out on bail on the gun charges, Persico returned to New York, where bitter paybacks were still being exacted within the Colombo family for the 1991–1993 fighting. In an apparent compromise gesture to the old Orena faction, Little Allie Boy had allowed William "Wild Bill" Cutolo to be underboss. A huge loan-shark earner and labor-rackets extortionist, Cutolo had been booted out of an officer's position in the teamsters' union, only to take over an obscure "production workers" local representing city employees. The union post put him in a convenient spot to hand out no-show jobs to wiseguys and to steer contracts to mobbed-up vendors.

Cutolo, sporting a large cowboy hat as part of his Wild Bill character, had in the recent war survived numerous hit attempts, and had captained a crew in the Orena ranks that whacked several Persico soldiers. Little Allie Boy and his entourage obviously remembered Cutolo's disloyalty and bided their time. On May 26, 1999, eleven days short of his fiftieth birthday, Wild Bill vanished. His relatives knew the significance of a mafioso's abrupt disappearance. They were certain that Persico's men murdered him in revenge for his wartime activities. To inflict additional punishment on his kin, the Persicos arranged that Cutolo's body would never be found.

Whether or not the younger Persico had a hand in Wild Bill's removal, it would rebound against him. Cutolo's thirty-year-old son, William Junior, silently vowed to wreak havoc on the Persicos to avenge his father. Several weeks after his father's disappearance, the son contacted the FBI, volunteering to go undercover. A mini–voice recorder was taped to his chest and he mingled easily with Colombo soldiers who never suspected he was anything more than a compliant wannabe.

Dubbing his infiltration "Operation Payback," and using information supplied by young Cutolo, agents obtained a search warrant for the Brooklyn apartment of Little Allie Boy's daughter, where he often stayed. The warrant stated that agents were looking for a cellular phone that might contain evidence of calls linking Alphonse Persico to Wild Bill's slaying. The phone was found along with $25,000 in cash hidden in a shoebox and in a mattress. More damaging discoveries were computer disks and loan-sharking records stashed in a kitchen stove hood; they indicated that Little Allie Boy was collecting vigorish on $1 million in loan-shark business that Cutolo had been running before he vanished.

The evidence in the Florida gun arrest and Operation Payback was overwhelming. In February 2000, Little Allie Boy pleaded guilty in Florida; and in December 2001 he threw in the towel in New York, pleading guilty to RICO counts of racketeering, loan-sharking, and money-laundering. The undercover work of Cutolo's son—an epilogue to the Colombo war—helped convict young Persico and fifteen additional Colombo soldiers and associates.

The RICO sentence for young Persico was thirteen years and a forfeit of $1 million in cash or assets. If he had risked a trial and the thicket of evidence and defectors testifying against him, at age forty-seven he would have faced a possible term of seventy years. He cut a deal, but in doing so he violated *omertà*, dishonoring his father and uncles' code of honor by in effect admitting that the Mafia existed and that he was one of its leaders.

"You were not some errand boy," the sentencing federal judge Reena Raggi stated, asking him to acknowledge his status in the Colombo family. "You had a high-ranking role in the enterprise, you had the discretion of your actions?"

"Yes, I had," an abject Persico replied.

Calling Persico "a very dangerous man," Judge Raggi said she wished she had the authority to imprison him for life. Noting that through a technicality in the RICO law he had escaped punishment in 1994, even though a jury found that he had ordered his brother-in-law's murder, she added, "I think there's no crime he wouldn't commit."

Seventeen years earlier at Little Allie Boy's sentencing along with his father for his first racketeering conviction in the Colombo family trial, Judge John Keenan had urged him to change direction, emphasizing that he would be young enough to start a new life when he left prison. "You are a chump if you stay in the Colombo family," the judge warned. At the joint sentencing hearing, Judge Keenan also expressed admiration for Carmine Persico's able performance as his own lawyer in the Commission case. Sentencing the father to prison for life without the possibility of parole, the judge lectured him: "Mr. Persico, you're a tragedy. You are one of the most intelligent people I have ever seen in my life."

Keenan's analysis of father and son was cogent. Impelled by an oversized ego, Carmine the Snake fomented an internecine Mob war to retain control of a Mafia empire. He wanted a dynasty. His deceitful schemes culminated in a debacle. Besides a dozen known slayings, the final tally from the Colombo war included his son, and more than seventy hierarchy members, soldiers, and associates from both sides convicted and jailed. At the start of a new century, the Colombo borgata was reduced to roughly seventy-five experienced and unimprisoned surviving made members, much of their plunder gone, the family structure in shambles, its would-be leaders in prison, awaiting trial, or fugitives on the lam.

Wild Bill Cutolo's murder caught up with Little Allie Boy in late 2004 while he was behind bars. Describing him as still the acting boss, prosecutors indicted the younger Persico on charges of ordering Cutolo's execution. Once more, the evidence was based largely on the word of defectors, and this time a conviction would mean life imprisonment or the death penalty.

"The war helped us destroy the family from within," observed George Stamboulidis, the prosecutor in the most significant trials stemming from the family's endless vendettas. "Instead of pulling together in the face of government investigations, they were worrying about saving their lives, and that gave them incentives to become cooperating witnesses. The war had a snowball effect; it allowed us to pull the trigger faster than normal to develop big cases."

32

A Hell of a Legacy

John Gotti was in his private office, pondering his future. It was mid-January 1986, barely a month after he had seized control of the Gambino family in a murderous rebellion and crowned himself boss of the nation's largest Mafia borgata. Unbeknownst to Gotti and his unidentified companion, his ramblings were being recorded secretly by New York State investigators.

"The law's gonna be tough with us, okay," Gotti's rumbling voice was picked up by a concealed microphone. "But if I can get a year [sic] run without being interrupted. Get a year gonna put this thing together where they could never break it, never destroy it. Even if we die, be a good thing."

"It's a hell of a legacy to leave," the companion briefly interjected before Gotti continued his musings.

"Well you know why it would be, ah, because it would be right. Maybe after thirty years it would deteriorate but it would take that long to fuckin' succumb."

In the inner sanctum of his headquarters, the Bergin Hunt and Fish Club, the newly enthroned Gambino godfather had no compunction about expressing his ambitious plans to forge an even mightier Mafia empire from the already powerful Gambino family. For a decade, the storefront Bergin club in South Ozone Park, a blue-collar section of Queens, had served as Gotti's central command post. In his guarded sanctuary, a confident Gotti felt secure enough to express his innermost thoughts.

Four miles away in a utilitarian, tidy office on bustling Queens Boulevard, the specter of John Gotti preoccupied FBI agent J. Bruce Mouw, the supervisor of the bureau's Gambino Squad. Overnight, Gotti's ascension to the Cosa Nostra's top rung had elevated him to the head of Mouw's priority list. Almost the same age, the two men from starkly dissimilar cultural and social backgrounds were destined to be duelists. Gotti at forty-five, the product of a clamorous big-city environment: boisterous, garrulous, boastful, hard drinking, incorrigibly defiant of laws and the government to the point that one day he would wish for the defeat of America in war. The forty-two-year-old Mouw was an offspring of quintessential American small-town virtues; reared in the agricultural heartland, he was reserved, laconic, a virtual teetotaler, and a decorated naval officer who had volunteered for an extremely dangerous assignment during the Cold War.

From the day he became the Gambino boss, Gotti envisioned himself as a mythic Mafia leader who would inspire a new Cosa Nostra golden age. That same day, Mouw set himself the arduous task of unearthing every aspect of Gotti's life and destroying his criminal realm.

His baptismal name was John Joseph Gotti Jr. He was born on October 27, 1940, in the South Bronx, the fifth of thirteen children—two of whom died in infancy—raised by John and Fannie Gotti. Both parents, children of immigrants who arrived in steerage from the Naples region of Italy, had a hardscrabble life caring for their large brood, mainly because of the elder Gotti's difficulty in holding on to jobs as a construction worker and factory hand. Moving frequently from one working-class neighborhood to another multiplied the normal growing pains for young John Gotti and his siblings. He would retain painful memories of childhood, and among friends he disparaged his lackadaisical father's inability to care for his children. He told about being sent to school in unmatched shoes, and of bullies tormenting him for his ragged appearance. The incidents taught Gotti a lesson on retaliation. "I went in the school yard and fought them," he recalled proudly. "That's what people respected. The next day you see them, they salute you. I was tough when I was ten years old."

Gotti's nomadic parents finally brought a small measure of stability to the family by settling in Brooklyn's East New York section when he was twelve. The neighborhood was a blend of one- and two-family row houses, apartment build-ings, and factories for light industry. It was also a battleground for rival youth gangs and the perfect terrain for Gotti to exhibit his martial skills. A strapping teenager with fast fists, he organized the Fulton-Rockaway Boys, a gang named after a major neighborhood intersection.

During Gotti's adolescent years, East New York was thriving territory for the Cosa Nostra, with illegal bookmaking openly conducted in storefront clubs and pool rooms. Gotti's gang-war exploits and reputation were noticed by the local mafiosi and wannabes, and he eagerly ran errands for a Mob crew headed by Carmine Fatico, a capo in the crime borgata then headed by Albert Anastasia. By the time he was fourteen, Gotti and his pals developed a harder edge. They stole cars, mugged drunks, and pulled off two-bit burglaries. An attempt to steal equipment from a construction site ended disastrously when a portable cement mixer toppled onto Gotti's left foot, causing the amputation of a toe. The injury induced a permanent odd spring to Gotti's step that made him appear to bounce jauntily when he walked quickly.

Despite a respectable IQ of 110, Gotti was an inattentive student, his school records thick with complaints of his defying teachers and assaulting students. Formal schooling ended at sixteen when his obliging parents allowed him to drop out of Franklin K. Lane High School. For a year or two he held dead-end jobs as a trucker's helper and as a pants presser in a garment factory. His true calling was as an enforcer for Carmine Fatico's crew which, after the 1957 as-sassination of Albert Anastasia, became part of the renamed Carlo Gambino family.

Gotti relished the ambiance of Fatico's club. Here were rough, wisecrack-ing men with ready cash and large cars, at leisure all day. Unlike his father, they were treated with fulsome respect in the neighborhood. For the impressionable teenager, the club possessed the trappings of a select, privileged, revered society that young Gotti wanted to enter.

A police department intelligence report on the Fatico crew ranked seventeen-year-old Gotti as a low-level tyro. Over the next eight years, the rookie mobster's arrest sheet described a path of undistinguished crimes from street fighting, to intoxication, to possession of a gun, to petty burglaries in New York and Long Island. None of the arrests led to penalties of more than six months in a county jail. In one of the few extant records typifying Gotti's early escapades, a Suffolk County police officer, Edward Halverson, came across him using a crowbar to break into a tavern in Selden, Long Island, in the early morning of

March 31, 1965. When Gotti tried to flee, Halverson warned, "Don't move a muscle or I'll blow your head off." The twenty-four-year-old future don stopped dead in his tracks. "Don't worry about me," Gotti told the cop. "Just worry about that [trigger] finger."

Despite his tawdry crime record, Gotti, in his late teens, made an important Mob contact through an introduction to the Gambino underboss, Aniello Dellacroce. The highly placed mobster took an immediate shine to the cocky young hood who was astute enough to show him proper veneration whenever they met.

Several of Gotti's first nine recorded arrests were in company with Angelo Ruggiero, his boyhood gang mainstay and a constant companion at Fatico's club. A bit of a poseur, Ruggiero encouraged other wannabes to falsely believe that he was a nephew of Dellacroce, frequently referring to him as "Uncle Neil." Angelo, commonly known as "Fat Ange" for his rotund shape, hinted to others that his special relationship with the underboss had allowed Gotti to become acquainted with the Gambino's number-two leader. However, it was the other way around: through Gotti, Angelo had been permitted to meet Dellacroce.

Domestic life also was landing Gotti in court. After an on-again, off-again romance, he married the strong-willed teenager Victoria DiGeorgio in March 1962. He was twenty-two and she was nineteen. A daughter, Angela, had been born to them a year before their wedding vows. Vicky's parents—her father was an Italian-American and her mother of Russian descent—were divorced, and she took her stepfather's surname after her mother remarried. Beset by John's arrests, the birth of a second daughter, and money problems, the early years of the marriage were stormy, with several separations and Vicky hauling him into court for nonsupport.

The newly wed father was dodging another problem—military service. He had failed to show up for his induction into the army on November 22, 1963, the day President Kennedy was assassinated, and the FBI caught up with him two years later. "Gotti advised he did not realize he was delinquent with his draft board in as much as he is married and has two children," says an FBI memo dated January 7, 1966. "He further advised he felt because of this and the fact he had been previously arrested he was not eligible for the armed forces."

Eventually, Gotti's draft and domestic problems vanished. His arrest and conviction record for stolen cars and burglaries disqualified him as a soldier, and the wrangling with Vicky was eased by his advancement in Fatico's crew through involvement in more remunerative crimes: hijackings, bookmaking, and loan-sharking. Vicky's stepfather, a construction contractor, helped out with gifts of money and mortgage assistance. The reconciled couple and their expanding family of three sons and two daughters became prosperous enough to move out of a cramped apartment into a comfortable house of their own in Howard Beach, a leafy, middle-class Queens neighborhood.

Howard Beach was close to John F. Kennedy International Airport and also to the new headquarters of the Fatico crew. Distressed by the influx of African-Americans and Hispanics into East New York, Carmine Fatico, the Gambino capo, had moved his headquarters to a storefront in the predominantly white and Italian working-class neighborhood of South Ozone Park. The hangout was incorporated—sardonically—as a nonprofit association called the Bergin Hunt and Fish Club. The name apparently was a nostalgic misspelling of Bergen Street in East New York, the gang's roots.

Transferring the club to South Ozone Park, with its proximity to JFK airport, was a sensible tactical decision by Fatico. The airport, with its growing volume of cargo and passenger traffic, was replacing the Brooklyn waterfront as a prime Mafia target for pillaging. It was the world's largest air-cargo center in the 1960s, handling more than $200 million in freight every year. Thousands of employees were ripe for bookmaking and loan-sharking exploitation, and as a source of inside information for profitable felonies.

Capitalizing on the airport's riches, John Gotti, his younger brother, Gene, and their boyhood chum Angelo Ruggiero teamed up for a series of truck hijackings. During these hijacking capers, Ruggiero coined a private nickname, "Black John," for Gotti—as much a reflection of his menacing personality as his swarthy complexion. An older mobster, impressed by Gotti's take-charge characteristics, bestowed a more admirable nickname, "Crazy Horse," comparing the young hoodlum to the indomitable Sioux Indian warrior.

All went well for the hijacking trio until 1968 when, during an operation to stifle mounting thefts at the airport, FBI agents staked out at a cargo area observed the Gotti brothers and Ruggiero loading stolen dresses into a U-Haul truck. Through the JFK arrests and with the aid of witnesses identifying mug shots, the FBI implicated the trio in three cargo heists and two hijackings. John Gotti, then twenty-eight, pleaded guilty to his first major felony and was sentenced to three years in the maximum-security federal prison in Lewisburg, Pennsylvania. His brother Gene and Ruggerio got similar prison terms.

At Lewisburg, Gotti confronted Carmine Galante, the sinister Bonanno shark, who was serving a narcotics sentence, and in effect was the "warden" of the prison's Mafia wing. Although not a made man, Gotti had the nerve to complain to Galante that he was bribing guards to get steaks, other delicacies, and booze only for himself and nine or ten Bonanno wiseguys and associates. The upstart Gotti demanded that the don share the wealth with other imprisoned mobsters. Gotti's boldness and poise so impressed Galante that he expressed interest in enlisting him in his own family. Informers reported that Galante said, "I'd like to have him in my crew," and was disappointed to hear that John "belongs to Neil," a reference to Aniello Dellacroce.

Paroled in 1972, after three years in prison, Gotti was handed a promotion. His crew capo, Carmine Fatico, had been indicted for loan-sharking, and while awaiting trial had to stay clear of the denizens of the Bergin Hunt and Fish Club, a condition of his bail. When Gotti came home, with Dellacroce's endorsement, Fatico designated him as acting capo, his eyes and ears until his legal problems were resolved.

A grateful Gotti idolized Dellacroce, praising him to his confederates as "a man's man." Tall, broad-shouldered, and tough-talking, Neil Dellacroce had served as a hit man and capo for Albert Anastasia. On at least one kill, he was reputed to have masqueraded as a priest wearing a clerical collar, calling himself Father Timothy O'Neill. Dellacroce had been a strong Anastasia supporter, but Carlo Gambino in a deft political move chose him as underboss after arranging for Anastasia's assassination and then usurping control of the family.

Under Don Carlo, Dellacroce became the family's street viceroy, an exacting disciplinarian whose intimidating gaze kept capos and troops in line. Organized-crime detective Ralph Salerno said that the only mafiosi whose icy eyes propelled a shiver down his spine were Carmine Galante and Aniello Dellacroce. "You looked at Dellacroce's eyes and you could see how frightening they were," Salerno said. "The frigid glare of a killer."

Dellacroce was widely known as "Neil" an Americanization of his given Italian name. Because of his rugged Slavic peasant looks and square-shaped face, Gambino members among themselves nicknamed him "the Polack." But no one dared utter the name in his presence.

Little Italy was Dellacroce's home turf; he held court on Mulberry Street in a converted tenement store named the Ravenite Social Club. Windowless and fortified with a red-bricked facade, the Ravenite resembled a makeshift bunker. Long a hangout for criminals, it had earlier been a meeting place for the legendary Charlie Lucky Luciano in the 1920s and '30s. The inbred, suspicious nature of the neighborhood's residents provided a protective screen for Dellacroce. Tenants and merchants were ad hoc lookouts, hampering law-enforcement agents from surveilling Dellacroce and visitors to the club.

Because of the Commission's temporary ban on new soldiers, Gotti had not been inducted as a made man. But his designation in 1972 as the Bergin's acting crew chief marked him as a future star. His new post required frequent meetings at the Ravenite to fill in Dellacroce on the Queens gang's activities, and to deliver the weekly share of Bergin's loot to the Gambino administration. Dellacroce willingly assumed a mentor's role, captivating his new acolyte. Both men had much in common: they were heavy gamblers in dice and card games and loved to bet on sports, they were profane speakers, and calcified practitioners of violence to obtain results. Dellacroce's intriguing tales of past Mafia glories under Albert Anastasia—the Lord High Executioner and founder of Murder Incorporated—influenced Gotti to adopt Anastasia as his role model.

A huge opportunity came for Gotti in early 1973 when he carried out a high-priority assignment for the borgata's godfather, Carlo Gambino. A nephew of Gambino's had been abducted and murdered despite the payment of $100,000 ransom. The Gambino's intelligence network fingered a stickup man and small-time criminal, James McBratney, as the kidnappers' ringleader. Don Carlo wanted revenge.

On May 22, 1973, three men, impersonating detectives, accosted McBratney in Snoope's Bar and Grill in Staten Island. After a brief struggle, they fatally shot him. It was hardly a flawless crime; witnesses picked out two of the phony detectives, John Gotti and Angelo Ruggiero, from rogue's gallery photos. With the police hunting for him, Gotti left Vicky and their five children and hid out from the murder rap. A year later, he was arrested in a Queens bar after an informer from his own Bergin crew tipped off the FBI. A grateful Carlo Gambino hired the politically influential and expensive Mob lawyer Roy Cohn to represent Gotti and Ruggiero. The third suspect wanted for McBratney's murder vanished and was widely believed to have been whacked to prevent him from testifying for the prosecution.

Although the defendants were indicted for murder and had been identified by witnesses, Cohn manipulated a bargain-basement deal with the Staten Island district attorney's office. The artful lawyer persuaded the DA to drop the murder charges in exchange for guilty pleas by Gotti and Ruggiero to the lowest possible homicide count of attempted manslaughter. Cohn also procured lenient sentences for both men, a maximum of four years. The DA never explained why he compromised—or caved in to Cohn's blandishments.

Gotti whiled away his second felony sentence weightlifting and obtaining peculiar perquisites at a state prison. Seemingly in good health, he was taken on three 120-mile round trips from the Green Haven Correctional Facility in upstate New York to Brooklyn, ostensibly for examinations by a private physician. State investigators later discovered that, on each journey, guards were bribed to make private detours to his home in Howard Beach and to restaurants for meetings with fellow mobsters.

His godfather, Carlo Gambino, died in 1976, while Gotti was in prison. By normal rights of succession, Gotti believed that underboss Neil Dellacroce should have assumed the throne. But before his death Gambino had selected his brother-in-law and cousin, Paul Castellano, as heir. Dellacroce's consolation prize was remaining as the borgata's number-two leader and controlling ten of the family's twenty-odd crews.

When Gotti was paroled in 1977, he was a sturdily built two hundred-pound figure, five-feet ten-inches tall, his shoulders squared like a West Point plebe. For slaying McBratney he served little more than two years, a shorter stretch for murder than for his earlier hijacking conviction. At Green Haven he was the uncontested controller of the prison's Mafia row. His appreciative jailmates threw him a farewell party and presented him with an engraved plaque: "To a Great Guy, John Gotti. From the Boys at Green Haven."

Returning to his favored life, Gotti found that his younger brother, Gene, who had been the Bergin crew's caretaker during his prison stretch, had preceded him by becoming a made man in the Gambino family when the Commission reopened the books for all families. It was now John Gotti's turn to get his Mafia button, and there was no dispute that he had made his bones by murdering the kidnapper McBratney. The Gambino boss Castellano officiated at the induction ceremony, where Gotti swore his oath of fealty to Big Paul, his new godfather, and to Cosa Nostra. With Dellacroce's blessings Gotti was appointed a full-fledged capo in charge of a Mafia *decina*—the Bergin crew.

Back home, Gotti was reunited with Vicky and their five children in their white, split-level, eight-room house. It was an unpretentious home, similar to others in Howard Beach, with an attached garage and a tiny front yard. Apparently aware of her husband's true occupation and his distrust of strangers, Vicky herself did all the household cleaning. To ease her chores, Gotti placed television sets in every room so she could watch soap operas as she tidied the place.

Needing proof of legitimate employment to obtain parole, Gotti claimed he would be a roving salesman for a plumbing company. The firm was owned by his boyhood friend Anthony Gurino, who gave Gotti the phantom no-show job. Rather than meandering around Queens seeking plumbing contracts, Gotti established a private office in one of the two rooms at the Bergin Club, a short drive from his home.

For intelligence purposes, the FBI's hijack squad kept an occasional watch on the new capo, openly following him. "Most of the time, we were less sophisticated in those days with the LCN," says Stephen Morrill, the agent assigned to keep an eye on him. "They knew who we were when we were following them." Twice, in restaurants, Gotti, with a mischievous smile, sent over a bottle of wine to Morrill and another agent. Each time, Morrill sent the bottle back.

Morrill quickly learned that the plumbing salesman was not strapped for cash and was an avid gambler. A few paces behind Gotti at the Meadowlands Harness Race Track in New Jersey, Morrill saw him plunk down $8,000 on a single race. Suspecting that the mobster had "an inside tip," the agent placed a "more modest amount" on the same horse. The horse finished almost dead last.

"You're ruining me, John," Morrill said to Gotti in the grandstand when the race was over. "What do you want from me?" Gotti countered. "You know I'm a degenerate gambler."

Regardless of his good-natured bantering with agents, Gotti's inclination toward violence and his unquestioned authority were soon evident. A frightening example of his cruelty came after a personal tragedy. In March 1980, Gotti's second-youngest child, twelve-year-old Frank, darted into the road on a mini-motorbike and was killed by a car driven by a neighbor, John Favara. The death was ruled accidental and no charge was brought against Favara, whose children were playmates of Gotti's kids. When Favara tried to express his condolences to the Gottis, Vicky menaced him with a baseball bat. After death threats were left in his mail box and the word "murderer" was spray-painted on his car, Favara decided to move out of the neighborhood.

On an evening in July 1980, four months after the boy's death, Favara, fifty-one, was walking to his auto in a parking lot near the Castro Convertible furniture store in New Hyde Park, Long Island, where he worked as a service manager. Witnesses saw a man club Favara over the head and, with the assistance of other assailants, shove him into a van. Never seen again, Favara is presumed to have been murdered, and the disposal of his body remains a Mafia secret. His car was believed to have been destroyed, as if to erase all memory of the fatal accident of Gotti's son. At the time of Favara's disappearance, John and Victoria Gotti were in Florida; they both denied any knowledge of the incident. From the start, investigators suspected that Bergin crew members killed the unfortunate neighbor as a favor to the vengeful Gotti, and that the Florida trip was made to establish an alibi for him.

Annually for decades, on the date of their dead son's birthday, Vicky and John Gotti placed "In Memoriam" announcements in the *New York Daily News*, which read: "Dear Frank, even though you have gone away, you are never very far from us. Distance may separate us, but love holds us close. You are always here in our hearts. Loving you, Mom & Dad." And Gotti rarely let a week pass without visiting his son's crypt.

The tragic death of Gotti's son and the brutal murder of Anthony Favara occurred while the FBI and state and city law-enforcement agencies were reorganizing their campaigns against the Mafia's Commission and the leaders of the five families in New York. Outside of his home borough of Queens, Gotti was not high on the target list of Cosa Nostra investigators. One of a score of mid-level Gambino family capos, he was unknown to the media, his name never prominently mentioned in news accounts of the Gambino family's rackets. The official keeping the closest full-time watch on him was Remo Franceschini, the New York detective lieutenant who was one of the police department's few Mafia experts. In 1977, the year Gotti was paroled from state prison, Franceschini was put in charge of the Queens district attorney's detective squad. As a new commanding officer, Franceschini was primarily concerned with Mob encroachments in his jurisdiction. He soon discovered that Gotti was heading one of the most powerful gangs in the borough. As one measure of the growing respect accorded Gotti, other mobsters only used admiring nicknames for him: "Johnny Boy" or "the Good-looking Guy." The days of calling him "Black John" behind his back were over. It was too dangerous to be caught referring to him derogatorily.

Clues from an informer and from surveillance made it easy for Franceschini to conclude that Gotti was overseeing a large gambling and loan-sharking operation from the Bergin Hunt and Fish Club. Around the corner, Gotti widened his domain by setting up a younger brother, Richard, to preside over a bookmaking and gambling annex called the "Our Friends Social Club." (Insiders understood that "Our Friends" was code for made men.)

Obtaining a secret court order, the DA's office in 1981 planted a bug and tapped two telephones in the Bergin club. To their amusement, the DA's technicians found that the thrifty gangsters had rigged a pay phone to enable them to make free calls without the necessity of dropping money into the coin slot. More important, the eavesdropping unveiled a character sketch of Gotti as a brutish, tyrannical captain of a crew that included his brothers Gene and Peter, and their constant partner in crime, Angelo Ruggiero. Frequently, Gotti was taped launching profanity-drenched tirades, demanding respect and total obedience. On one telephone tap, he was recorded scorching one of his soldiers, Anthony Moscatiello, for failing to return his calls.

"Listen," Gotti bellowed, "I called your fuckin' house five times yesterday. Now if your wife thinks you're a fuckin' duskie, or she's a fuckin' duskie, and you're gonna disregard my motherfuckin' phone calls, I'll blow you and your fuckin' house up."

Even if Moscatiello was unfamiliar with the meaning of that obscure word, "duskie," he got the drift of Gotti's harangue, replying abjectly: "I never disregard anything you say . . ."

GOTTI: "Well you call your fuckin' wife up and you tell her before I get in the fuckin' car and I'll go over there and I'll fuckin tell her."

MOSCATIELLO: "All right."

GOTTI: "This is not a fuckin' game. I don't have to reach for you for three days and nights there. My fuckin' time is valuable. . . . You get your fuckin' ass down and see me tomorrow."

MOSCATIELLO: "I'm going to be there all day tomorrow."

GOTTI: "Yeah, never mind you'll be there all day tomorrow. And don't let me have to do this again, 'cause if I hear that anybody else calls you and you respond within five days I'll fuckin' kill you."

Franceshini's investigation broke up a high-stakes gambling den in Little Italy involving Gotti's crew, which provided grounds to raid the Bergin club in a search for evidence of bookmaking. Not one of the dozen men in the raided club could produce a driver's license or any form of identification.

But Gotti and his closest Bergin cronies were untouched by the raids and arrests. For the most part, Gotti appeared imperturbable when Franceschini notified him that his headquarters had been bugged and that his conversations could be used as possible evidence against him. What did roil Gotti, Franceschini recalls, was the news that detectives had heard him flippantly insulting Castellano and referring to Dellacroce as "the Polack," the forbidden nickname.

"I told him, 'Neil is not going to like this,' and it was the only time I ever saw him look remorseful," Franceschini said.

While the DA's investigation did little to crimp Gotti's gambling and loan-sharking rackets, the telephone taps exposed a personal weakness. They disclosed his brother Gene and Angelo Ruggiero grumbling behind Gotti's back about his huge gambling losses. The capo dropped $60,000 in one crap game, and his chronic bad bets with bookies from other families were draining the crew's profits. A losing streak in the 1982 college football bowl games cost Gotti $90,000. But neither Gene nor Ruggiero had the nerve to confront him directly with advice about his gambling addiction.

At FBI headquarters, Gotti remained a secondary quarry in the early 1980s. Determined to dismantle the Mafia's hierarchies, the Gambino Squad was concentrating on the family's talented leadership: the boss Paul Castellano, the underboss Neil Dellacroce, and longtime consigliere Joe N. Gallo (no relation to the Gallo brothers in the Colombo family). In the intermediate echelons, Gotti's stature was dwarfed by other capos with significantly more economic clout and influence in several of New York's multimillion-dollar industries. For starters, there was James "Jimmy Brown" Failla, who dominated much of the city's private garbage-carting system; Tommy Gambino, the son of Carlo, the Garment Center's trucking mogul; Pasquale Patsy Conte, a major narcotics distributor with corrupt business links to supermarkets; and Danny Marino, the behind-the-scenes controller of exhibition halls used for trade shows in Manhattan.

Nevertheless, Gotti's close ties to Dellacroce and the vicious bent of his crew merited attention, and the Gambino Squad was looking for a weak spot. Bugging Gotti's home was rejected because he never met in the house with mafiosi, and his home-phone records showed that calls were made only to "civilians," non-Mob friends and relatives. Instead of going directly after Gotti, the FBI in late 1981 obtained a court order to tap the home phones of his lieutenant, Angelo Ruggiero. It was one of many electronic intrusions then under way to penetrate the New York borgatas for evidence and intelligence purposes. Expectations were modest as to the value of leads that could be gained by eavesdropping on Ruggiero. A braggart, who exaggerated his supposed relationships to Mob chieftains, Fat Ange was mixed up mainly in gambling and loan-sharking for Gotti and was viewed as an old-style strong-arm type. The Ruggiero ploy, however, would unintentionally create a series of events with enormous ramifications for the entire Gambino family. The inspiration to zero in on Ruggiero came from the Gambino Squad's new leader—Supervisory Special Agent J. Bruce Mouw.

33

Quack-Quack

If the FBI needed a poster image for the prototypical G-Man, Bruce Mouw (rhymes with "Wow") was the model. Lean, six-feet three-inches tall, square-jawed, Mouw, in his late thirties, resembled a resolute Clint Eastwood–Gary Cooper screen lawman. His roots were concrete-solid Middle America; he was born in Iowa on a farm settled by his Dutch grandparents and was steeped in the virtues of hard work and loyalty to flag and country. There were no luxuries while growing up for John Bruce Mouw (he preferred being called Bruce to distinguish him from his father, whose given name was also John). When he was six, hard times forced Mouw's parents to leave the farm, and with their three children move to the nearby market town of Orange City (population 2,700), where his father found work and his mother was a librarian.

At fourteen, Mouw held two after-school and weekend jobs: a printer's devil or general assistant at the weekly newspaper, the *Sioux County Capital*, and night desk clerk at his grandmother's inn, the Village Hotel. Putting in a thirty-five-hour work week while in high school, Mouw found it convenient for studying to live in a tiny room at the hotel. Encouraged by his mother, he was a voracious reader, and although the nearest body of water was a small lake ten miles distant, he was captivated by seafaring tales. Dreaming of becoming a naval officer, and banking on his excellent grades and a stratospheric IQ, he applied to the Naval Academy at Annapolis, Maryland. While his admission chances were slim, the teenager understood that his family's economic straits meant that a scholarship, a stipend, and full room-and-board at Annapolis was his only hope of a college education.

His prospects seemingly were dashed when the local congressman nominated another applicant, coincidentally the son of his next-door neighbor. The congressman's candidate, however, flunked his eye examination and the midshipman's appointment was given to the first alternate—J. Bruce Mouw. Rail thin, the seventeen-year-old six-footer narrowly passed his physical with a weight of 152 pounds, the minimum requirement for his height. As graduation from Annapolis approached, Mouw had to decide in which branch of the navy to serve. His choices limited because he had been violently seasick as a midshipman training on surface vessels, the new ensign opted for nuclear-powered submarines. Cruising deep beneath the seas most of the time, the subs were as smooth as flying in an airliner for the queasy twenty-one-year-old officer.

At the peak of the Cold War and Vietnam War era, Mouw was assigned in 1966 as a navigator in the newly commissioned nuclear attack submarine USS *Lapon* (named for a rockfish native to the Pacific Ocean). Operating mainly under the equivalent of wartime conditions, the *Lapon*'s main objective was to trail and, if necessary, destroy Soviet subs that were armed with thermonuclear missiles capable of obliterating American cities. Other secret patrols were in the Barents Sea off the coast of Murmansk, a strategic Russian naval base. While Mouw served on the *Lapon*, the crew was awarded a rare Presidential Unit Citation in 1969 for obtaining intelligence data on an advanced class of Soviet nuclear strike submarine. The sub tracked one of the powerful Russian vessels at close range for forty days.

"I loved it; it was great, exciting duty, playing blind man's bluff," Mouw said afterward. But four grueling years' duty on tense seventy-day underwater missions were enough for him. A shortage of experienced submarine officers meant that he would most likely be permanently assigned to engineering duties that he disliked, and in 1970 Mouw resigned from the navy with the rank of lieutenant. "I don't know what I want to do, but I no longer want to be a career naval officer," he explained to friends.

Back home in Iowa, he was working on dreary construction jobs when an FBI recruiter, sifting through service records of newly discharged officers, spotted Mouw's. Out of the blue, Mouw decided after listening to the recruiter's pep talk that becoming an agent sounded enticing. In August 1971, at age twenty-seven, he joined the bureau. J. Edgar Hoover was still running the show, and Mouw's first posting was in St. Louis, where he cut his teeth for more than a year on the director's favorite investigative priorities: recovering stolen cars and arresting bank robbers and truck hijackers. A transfer to New York in December 1973 should have been a valued promotion, but it was blemished by culture shock. The agent from the vast plains of Iowa felt confined living in a pint-sized apartment, trapped in an untidy, raucous urban environment. Relaxing in a big city after a taxing workday was difficult. Opportunities to play golf or other outdoor sports were rare, and a drive into the countryside was impossible because it was too expensive to keep a car in Manhattan. "I wasn't crazy about New York," he admits.

Another disappointment was the prevailing atmosphere at the bureau, even after Hoover's death in 1972. "We had some tremendous, talented agents. But we were in the Dark Ages when it came to working complex criminal matters. Hoover's spirit was still alive and everything was numbers-oriented—better to close out thirty-five picayune cases than go after two quality ones."

Because of the engineering background he had gained in the Navy, he was reassigned to Washington as a desk-bound coordinator with contractors erecting the FBI's new headquarters, the J. Edgar Hoover Building. The last months of a five-year stint in Washington in 1979 were spent "doing some real work" in the organized-crime section, as the revamped bureau under its new director, Judge William Webster, began focusing on the Mafia. At the end of the year, Mouw was offered a promotion if he returned to New York. "I wanted a supervisor's job but I didn't want to go back to New York. Hell, no!" Swallowing his frustration, Mouw accepted the reassignment with a proviso: he would head the newly formed Gambino Squad, one of the five units that began functioning in 1980 under agent Jim Kossler's realignment plan for combating the major New York borgatas. "You bet I want the Gambino family," Mouw told Kossler. "It's the biggest family, the most challenging, and pretty much untouched."

Assuming command of a new squad, named C-16 in FBI patois, Mouw found the intelligence cupboard on the Gambinos almost totally bare. It consisted mainly of useless files dating back almost two decades to the 1960s, when Attorney General Robert Kennedy had compelled Hoover to use wiretaps, bugs, and other investigative tools. The stream of intelligence information, however, dried up in the 1970s when Hoover deemphasized Mafia investigations. There was not a single active case against a member of the Gambino hierarchy or capo in the New York office. "We start with literally nothing," the pipe-smoking Mouw informed his newly assembled squad. "We're up against guys who have been in the same business for fifty years, and they're way ahead of us."

Realizing it would take a year or two to develop essential intelligence dossiers on the Gambino's leading figures, Mouw assigned each of his agents to concentrate on one of the family's top-drawer leaders. The unit of at most fifteen agents was confronting an underworld powerhouse of approximately four hundred made gangsters and several thousand associates. An added obstacle was the bureau's shortage of experienced Mafia investigators. Mouw quickly recognized that several of his inherited agents were incapable of working Mob cases. "These investigations take years to develop, and one of the strong assets for organized-crime agents is patience. Some agents are not mentally suited; they want cops and robbers stuff, breaking down doors and making arrests quickly."

Sizing up his squad, he got rid of those who sat around the unit's Rego Park office waiting for tips to materialize, and began recruiting eager-beavers who understood his philosophy: "My motto is, you don't develop informants or cases sitting on your ass in the office." His rudimentary orders emphasized leg work and surveillance. Agents had to hit the bricks, reconnoiter Mob neighborhoods and hangouts, verify where the big-shot mobsters lived, what cars they drove, what businesses they were involved in, where they met and with whom.

Single, without friends or close relatives living nearby, Mouw put in long days and expected his troops to do the same. His culling of indolent, underachieving agents inspired those who stayed with the unit, and who admired his zeal, to tag him with a good-humored nickname, "Chairman Mouw."

Relying on the most fundamental element of police work, Mouw emphasized debriefing old informers and finding new ones as the surest method of getting results. "You won't have any problem getting money to pay informers," he promised. "These guys are putting their lives on the line. The information is priceless as far as saving us manpower and time and telling us where to put bugs." Like himself, most of the squad's agents were not native New Yorkers or familiar with the city's Italian-American culture and neighborhood mores. Mouw believed it was a myth that New York–bred agents were best suited to work Cosa Nostra cases. "If a wiseguy is jammed up in a criminal case or has a grudge against one of his bosses, he'll talk to you no matter where you come from," he lectured newcomers to the squad.

Practicing what Mouw preached, the C-16 agents began trolling for Gambino informers, cultivating them for intelligence nuggets that would produce an important case for the squad. Two years went by without a breakthrough against any of the family's big shots, but Mouw's patient tactics paid off in one Gambino outfit—John Gotti's crew. Several low-level associates of the Bergin club, none of whom were made soldiers, were regularly feeding agents tips about Gotti and his crew's activities. Gotti was far from the apex of the FBI's Mafia agenda, but convicting him and wrecking his crew were worthwhile objectives.

Under standard FBI security procedures, none of the squad's informers at the Bergin Hunt and Fish Club knew that other Gambino associates in the crew were working secretly for the bureau. Analyzing their separate reports Mouw concluded that the weakest component in Gotti's inner circle might be his longtime pal Angelo Ruggiero. Fat Ange, according to the helpful canaries, acted as Gotti's executive officer, checking the crew's loan-sharking and gambling books to certify that Gotti got the largest share of the loot. What made Ruggiero appear to be vulnerable was the informers' consensus that he was an uncontrollable gossip. Among Bergin regulars, his penchant for incessant chatter provoked the derogatory nickname "Quack Quack." One informer mentioned that the overconfident Ruggiero bragged that he had created a foolproof method to evade telephone taps; for Mob business he used a pink Princess phone listed in his daughter's name and which was on a separate line.

Based on the informers' assertions about Ruggiero's alleged criminal acts, a court order was obtained in November 1981 to tap phones—including his daughter's Princess model—at his home in Howard Beach, the same neighborhood where Gotti lived. At first, the eavesdropping failed to uncover incriminating evidence or a strong lead, and a gap occurred when Ruggiero moved to Cedarhurst, Long Island. FBI technicians had to get another court order and tap the new phones. This time, the bureau slipped into Ruggiero's new house and installed a concealed mike in a dinette, where informers reported Ruggiero liked to meet with other mobsters. It was the dinette bug and Ruggiero's garrulousness that would unexpectedly devastate the Gambino high command.

The first mafioso compromised by Ruggiero's loose talk was the godfather, Paul Castellano. Every other Sunday, Ruggiero ventured to Castellano's Staten Island mansion, and as soon as he returned to Cedarhurst, Quack-Quack was on the phone with Gotti and Bergin mobsters, recapping his conversations with Big Paul and narrating what he had heard Castellano discuss with other wiseguys. To the delight of agents recording the calls, Ruggiero blabbed about Mafia controversies that had to be resolved by the Commission. His obsessive chatter was an invaluable gift to the FBI and prosecutors, providing them with "probable cause" to bug and wiretap the home of Castellano, their number-one target. As an added gratuity to the government, Ruggiero presented enough incriminating information about Neil Dellacroce to justify a court order to bug the underboss's home in Staten Island. From one fruitful bug in Ruggiero's dinette, the two mightiest Gambino kingpins were for the first time placed under secret electronic surveillance. Eventually, the eavesdropping provided vivid evidence that implicated Castellano and Dellacroce in the groundbreaking Commission case and in other crimes.

Fat Ange also unwittingly expanded the FBI's insight into John Gotti's lifestyle and personal habits. Around noon on most mornings, it was Ruggiero's valet task to wake Gotti, whose night-owl partying, or card and dice games, rarely ended before 4:00 or 5:00 A.M. The calls fell into a typical pattern.

"Hey, John, it's eleven-thirty. You better get up. How you doin'?" "Okay, Ange, okay," followed by throat-clearing coughs, grunts, and yawns.

Gently rousing his capo, Ruggiero reminded him about priorities for the day. "John, we got this thing around two o'clock, remember?"

Fifteen or twenty minutes later, Ruggiero usually made a follow-up call. "You got your coffee?"

"Okay, okay, Ange. C'mon, okay." And so Gotti's day began.

A crisis for Ruggiero and another dramatic turn for FBI eavesdroppers occurred in the spring of 1982. On May 6, Angelo's brother Salvatore died in a private jet plane crash off the Georgia coast. A heavy heroin trafficker, Salvatore had been a fugitive for years, and his sudden death revealed Angelo's involvement in the narcotics trade. From bugged conversations in the Cedarhurst dinette and references to a Sicilian term, *babania*, a Mob code word for heroin, agents cobbled together evidence that Angelo had inherited his brother's drug network. The dinette talks also implicated Gene Gotti, John's brother, several other Bergin members, and a lawyer in a venture to obtain Salvatore's hidden heroin stockpile and to collect up to $2.5 million in profits from a recent drug deal.

Suspecting that he was now being trailed by agents, Ruggiero brought in a retired city detective to examine his home for taps and bugs. Alerted by informers, the FBI turned off their concealed mikes on the day that Ruggiero's home was swept for electronic listening devices. The former detective informed Ruggiero of the "good news"; he had no bugs to worry about. But, there was "bad news," too: his phones were tapped. Believing he was secure and that his house was free of electronic bugs, Ruggiero avoided compromising telephone calls, but inadvertently aided the FBI by talking even more freely with other mobsters about drugs and other crimes in his bugged dinette.

The former-detective-turned-technician for the Mob was put on the grill by Mouw's agents. They warned him about the consequences of performing future "cleaning jobs" for wiseguys. The intimidated man swore repeatedly that he had uncovered none of the bureau's devices at Ruggiero's home and, to justify his large $1,000 fee, had lied to him about finding a telephone tap.

In the FBI's war with the Mob, informers worked for both sides. Through a leak to the Mafia, Ruggiero learned several months later that mikes actually had been planted in his home. The news came to him obliquely. A Genovese soldier, Federico "Fritzy" Giovanelli, mysteriously obtained a draft copy of the FBI's court affidavit for the Title III eavesdropping and handed it to Ruggiero. Circumstantial evidence later pointed to a woman stenographer employed by the bureau as having supplied the confidential document to Giovanelli. Seething at the dire news that his home had been bugged, Ruggiero began making foul-mouthed threats against Donald McCormick, the agent who had signed the affidavit.

Ruggiero's menacing outbursts brought about the first face-to-face meeting between Bruce Mouw and John Gotti. One morning in 1983, at 10:00 A.M., Mouw and McCormick showed up at Gotti's Howard Beach front door and directed his wife to wake him.

"We have a problem with your crew," Mouw said caustically to a yawning Gotti, dressed in pajamas and slippers. "One of your guys is trashing my agent, Don McCormick. You know that's not allowed. Tell Angelo to cease and desist."

"I don't know what you're talking about, but thanks very much, agents," Gotti replied, ending the terse encounter between the two combatants.

Several days later, an informer divulged to a Mouw agent that an irate Aniello Dellacroce appeared at the Bergin to chew out Ruggiero for insulting Don McCormick and bringing the FBI to Gotti's home. The Gambinos' supreme leader, Big Paul Castellano, had a graver reason to be disturbed by Ruggiero's behavior. In August 1983, Fat Ange, Gene Gotti, and three accomplices in the Bergin crew were indicted by a federal organized-crime strike force on narcotics charges stemming from Salvatore Ruggiero's death and evidence derived from Angelo's gossiping and conferences in his dinette.

By 1985, serious legal troubles were exploding for Castellano and others in the Gambino power structure—partly because of the bug in Ruggiero's home and partly because of a festering dispute between the Castellano and

Dellacroce factions. After years of investigations by federal, state, and local agencies, grand juries were preparing a wave of RICO indictments: Castellano and Dellacroce in the Commission case; Castellano in the Gambino luxury-car theft ring; and in a separate inquiry, Dellacroce and John Gotti for gambling and loan-sharking.

Hints supplied by informers had given Mouw blurry snapshots of the increasing enmity between the rival Gambino camps. Clearer confirmation came in 1983, when agents listening to a bug at the Casa Storta Restaurant in Brooklyn heard Gerry Langella, the acting Colombo boss, and capo Dominic Donny Shacks Montemarano discuss the Gambino internal friction with dinner guest Angelo Ruggiero. An irate Ruggiero said Castellano had forbidden his militants any contact with Dellacroce, adding, "I think he's looking to whack Neil." Langella and Montemarano joined in, saying they believed Castellano also planned to kill "Johnny," a reference to Gotti.

Violating an ancient Cosa Nostra rule against criticizing a boss to members of another family, Ruggiero insulted Castellano, saying he "badmouths his own family." The remark prompted Langella to describe a recent meeting with Dellacroce. "I think I told Neil I know this cocksucker's [Castellano] badmouthing you. Let me tell you something, he ain't gonna get away with it no more, somebody's gonna . . ." Langella failed to finish the sentence but it was obvious to agents that he was suggesting that Castellano was inciting homicidal opposition inside his own borgata.

The loquacious Ruggiero's bugged dinette chats and telephone conversations were rife with contempt for Castellano's overbearing manners, mocking him as a "milk drinker" and "a pansy." He disparaged Castellano's sons who ran Dial Poultry as "chicken men." Agents listened avidly to the gravelly voiced Ruggiero rebuke the millionaire Castellano for hypocritically banning the lower ranks from drug deals under penalty of death, while he accepted sizable cash offerings from Gambino capos he knew were heroin dealers. Fat Ange and his narcotics partners were certain Big Paul had a financial stake in supporting the winning side in the Bonanno family's civil war in the early 1980s. Among themselves, the Bergin club gangsters speculated that their family boss was getting secret payments from the Bonannos' narcotics undertakings. What gave him the right, they groused, to deny them equal opportunities? Gotti's crew was echoing common knowledge within the New York Mafia: the prohibition against capitalizing from narcotics was broken more often than followed, even by the men who made the rules.

From informers at the Bergin Club and from Ruggiero's telephone calls, agents gleaned that the crew's martinet leader Gotti was terrified of Castellano. The normally fierce capo, the snitches said, shook like a leaf when Big Paul peremptorily demanded Gotti's presence at his mansion. "Why does he want to see me? What's going on?" agents heard Gotti moan on the phone to Ruggiero whenever Castellano summoned him for a must-attend session. Informers said he dreaded going there, knowing full well that Castellano commanded a brigade of stone-cold killers in the family and could also call upon the sadistic Irish gang, the Westies, to commit murders for him. The same FBI spies noted that Gotti was understandably "gloating" over Castellano's indictment headaches and the possibility of his being convicted and imprisoned for life.

Awaiting his own criminal trials, Castellano nevertheless displayed his wrath at Ruggiero and Gene Gotti for getting arrested on narcotics charges. If the accusations were true, it would be proof that both soldiers had violated his edict against trafficking—which was decreed a capital offense. The case hinged on bugged conversations in Ruggiero's dinette, and Castellano was incensed that his name had been bandied about by Fat Ange. When the evidence was turned over as discovery materials to Ruggiero's lawyers, Castellano demanded the tapes and transcripts for his personal inspection. Under Big Paul's rules, Gotti as the Bergin capo was responsible for the misdeeds of his crew members. In effect, the drug indictments and the revelatory tapes gave Castellano an opportunity to weaken Gotti and break up the strongest pro-Dellacroce crew.

Refusing to let Castellano get his hands on the tapes, Ruggiero urged Dellacroce to intervene on his behalf. Ruggiero's cover story was that he was overheard merely trying to straighten out the financial affairs of his dead brother, and that he had been uninvolved in the drug commerce. His brittle explanation for withholding the tapes from Castellano was his wish to spare relatives from hearing embarrassing personal details about the Ruggieros and to protect Mob friends.

It was an unconvincing excuse, and Castellano in the spring of 1985 kept pressing Dellacroce for the tapes. Battling cancer and undergoing chemotherapy, Dellacroce was largely confined to his home in Staten Island. On June 8, the ill underboss reviewed the problem in his bedroom with Gotti and Ruggiero; FBI agents secretly tuned in through a bug placed in the room. Ironically, authorization for the eavesdropping had come from evidence supplied by Ruggiero's dinette disclosures.

"I'm gonna tell you somethin'," Ruggiero argued, "if you two never bother with me again, again in the rest of my life, I ain't givin' them tapes up . . . I can't. I can't. There's some, some good friends of mine on them fuckin' tapes."

Lecturing Ruggiero about his obligation to obey Castellano and Mafia rules, Gotti admonished him for being caught on the tapes talking about the sacred Commission. "Angelo, what does Cosa Nostra mean? Cosa Nostra means, that the boss is your boss. You understand? Forget about all this nonsense."

An exasperated Dellacroce explained that he had delayed a showdown over the tapes for months, hoping Castellano would simmer down.

"I've been tryin' to make you get away with these tapes," he told Ruggiero. "But Jesus Christ almighty, I can't stop the guy from always bringin' it up. Unless I tell the guy, 'Hey, why don't you go fuck yourself, and stop bringin' these tapes up.' Then you, then we know what we gotta do then, we go and roll it up and go to war. I don't know if that's what you want."

Laying it on the line, Dellacroce warned that continued refusal to heed Castellano would ignite a devastating conflict between the Gambino factions. "Don't forget, don't only consider yourself. . . . And a lot of other fellas'll get hurt, too. Not only, not only you could get hurt. I could get hurt. He [Gotti] could get hurt. A lot of other fellas could get hurt. For what? For what? Over because you don't wanna show him the tape."

The meeting ended in stalemate, with Ruggiero adamantly refusing to surrender the tapes. The transcripts never reached Castellano.

It was Monday evening, December 16, 1985, and some 150 law-enforcement officials, FBI agents, detectives, prosecutors, lawyers, and professors were gathering for a conference at New York University's Law School in Greenwich Village. In town that night as principal speaker was Notre Dame professor G. Robert Blakey, the originator of the Racketeer Influenced and Corrupt Organizations Act. His topic, naturally enough, was "RICO and Organized Crime." The group was in a holiday mood, idly chatting over their predinner drinks when cellphone beepers began resounding through the conference room. By the time Blakey was ready to speak, more than half of his audience had rushed out of the chamber. Agents, detectives, prosecutors, federal and local officials had gotten the same jolting news: Paul Castellano had been assassinated. "I lost half of my audience in a flash," Blakey said. "Those who were left joked that I came to New York to arrange a hit."

On that first night of the murder investigation, knowledgeable Mafia prose-cutors and investigators like Bruce Mouw, who were clued in on the internal turmoil in the Gambino family, latched on to one prime theory: John Gotti was the most likely mobster to profit from the murder of Paul Castellano and his de-voted henchman, Tommy Bilotti.

Previously, John Gotti had been an obscure mobster. Suddenly he was prominently featured in the first accounts of the double murder in the city's ma-jor newspapers, *The New York Times*, the *Daily News*, and the *Post*. Overnight prosecutors, agents, and detectives thrust the Howard Beach capo into the na-tional limelight through speculation over who was behind the assassinations. The slaughter of a prominent godfather in midtown Manhattan was the most sensational gangland hit since the barbershop execution twenty-eight years ear-lier of Albert Anastasia. At the time of Anastasia's slaying, he was the boss of the Cosa Nostra family later renamed for Carlo Gambino, whose treachery led to the murder. Anastasia's demise occurred in 1957, when a teenager named John Gotti was beginning his Cosa Nostra apprenticeship in the backwaters of Brooklyn.

Theories by federal and local authorities about Gotti's involvement in Castellano's homicide were not admissible courtroom evidence. For half a cen-tury, *omertà* prevented Mafia murders from being solved through trials and convictions. On isolated occasions, solutions might be found through a canary like Abe Reles, who helped convict Louis Lepke Buchalter and other Murder Incorporated hirelings. Without a songbird, most Mob hits were dead-end in-vestigations. It would take Mouw's Gambino Squad six years to find a partici-pant who could unravel the enigmatic details of Big Paul Castellano's fatal dinner date.

The scenario for Paul Castellano's murder was conceived after Neil Del-lacroce became mortally ill in mid-1985. The main planner was John Gotti. Gotti knew Castellano would either demote or kill him once Dellacroce, his protector, was gone. Contemplating the murder of a Cosa Nostra godfather without secret approval from a majority of the Commission was an incredibly bold act. It violated the Mafia's First Commandment and Golden Rule (Thou shall not kill a boss without just cause and without consent by Commission members), promulgated by Lucky Luciano when the five families were formed.

Before 1985 Gotti's success rested on brute force and his reputation as the custodian of a hardened band of pea-brained hijackers, loan-shark collectors, gamblers, and robotic hit men. In organizing a rebellion, he demonstrated un-foreseen talents as a Mob strategist and diplomat.

From the onset, Gotti's three brothers, especially Gene, with whom he was most closely bonded, were excluded from roles in the conspiracy. A Mafia dictum discouraged brothers from participating in the same dangerous undertaking so that at least one would survive and take care of their relatives if disaster struck.

Gotti's first conspiratorial step was to dispatch Angelo Ruggiero as an envoy to sound out likely defectors from Castellano's own wing of the family. Fat Ange tested the waters in a blunt conversation with Salvatore Sammy the Bull Gravano, an ambitious mafioso of Gotti and Ruggiero's generation. Gotti correctly surmised that Gravano, an accomplished killer and a huge earner, was disenchanted with Castellano. Although only a soldier in a Brooklyn crew, Gravano accelerated Gotti's scheme because of his partnership with Frankie DeCicco, a popular capo presumably in Castellano's corner. Gravano could be used to approach DeCicco, who might be accommodating because he was friendly with Dellacroce and was an admirer of Neil's tough, old-school Mob style.

The convoluted strategy worked. It turned out that DeCicco and Gravano silently resented Castellano's demands for larger and larger cuts from rackets at the expense of themselves and rank-and-file soldiers. Both men were dismayed by Castellano's construction-industry extortion partnerships with the Genovese family, which enriched him personally while depriving other Gambino members of illicit profits. There was one more grievance. The two gangsters believed Big Paul had betrayed and dishonored his own borgata by authorizing the Genovese borgata to whack a Gambino capo in Connecticut over a money dispute. "He's selling out the family," Gravano confided to DeCicco.

DeCicco and Gravano worried that Big Paul's tactics were irrevocably dividing and damaging the family. Sammy used an anecdote to illustrate Castellano's rampant hostility to Neil Dellacroce, his trustworthy underboss. The previous year, 1984, Gravano delivered his mandatory Christmas envelope filled with cash to Castellano at his mansion. He mentioned that he was on his way to the Ravenite Club in Little Italy to pay his respects to Dellacroce. "He looked at me as if I had five heads. 'What are you going down there for? You're on my side,'" Castellano rebuked him. "What sides?" Gravano replied. "I thought we're all in one family. Neil's our underboss."

DeCicco had a personal gripe arising from a rumor. He understood that Castellano had decided, if he was imprisoned, that he would designate Tommy Bilotti as the acting street boss. The decision rankled DeCicco, who believed he was more deserving than Castellano's lapdog Bilotti of a top slot in the family.

Gotti's intuition was accurate about two other malcontents long in Castellano's corner. He persuaded Robert "DiB" DiBernardo and Joseph "Piney" Armone to secretly defect. Armone, a family elder and capo in his late sixties, was a pivotal player for Gotti. Once Castellano was removed, Armone's ties to old-timers in the Castellano crews could fend off a civil war, and his support would lend credibility to the Young Turk plotters who were in their forties. Jealousy appeared to be the main reason the stolid Armone welcomed Gotti's revolt. After years of suppressed envy of Castellano's wealth and position, Armone saw a last-chance opportunity to advance into the Mob's hierarchy. The nickname "Piney" had stuck to him from younger days, when he specialized in stealing and selling Christmas trees.

DiBernardo, a soldier without a crew who dealt directly with Castellano and was close to Gravano, was a financial asset. With a creative business mind, DiB had built up a multimillion-dollar pornography distribution network for the family, and he handled construction-industry payoffs for Big Paul through control of a vital teamsters' union local, 282, which delivered concrete and other materials to major building sites in the city.

Once they eliminated Castellano, the plotters counted on winning widespread internal support with a coordinated political theme: he had to be whacked to unify the borgata and to spread the wealth to everyone. Five conspirators—Gotti, DeCicco, Gravano, Armone, and DiBernardo—picked a symbolic name for their cabal as if they were reenacting a scene in an espionage novel or movie. Each would represent a finger of a lethal hand called "the Fist."

No attempt was made to directly solicit authorization from the godfathers of the other four borgatas. At the time, before the start of the Commission case trial, it was too dangerous to approach the established bosses, all of whom had long-standing relationships with Castellano. Instead, Gotti used a backdoor maneuver. His co-conspirators discreetly canvassed important figures in the Lucchese, Colombo, and Bonanno families—mobsters of Gotti's generation—to gauge their feelings about the possible removal of Castellano. Ange Ruggiero met with close friends Gerry Lang Langella and Donnie Shacks Montemarano of the Colombo family. "They say, 'What are you waiting for? Make the move,'" Ruggiero excitedly reported to Gotti. Approaching the fifth family, the Genovese, was too risky. Their leaders were friendly with Big Paul and the merest hint to a Genovese mobster could tip off Castellano to the impending danger. Later, Gotti would claim, through contorted Mafia logic, that the hit had been tacitly supported by "off-the-record contacts" with three families, who thereby comprised a majority of the five families.

The decision to move against Castellano was accelerated by Neil Dellacroce's death from cancer on December 2, 1985. Ever conscious of surveillance, the seventy-one-year-old underboss was vigilant even in his final days at a hospital. He registered as a patient under one of his assumed names, Timothy O'Neill. With Dellacroce gone, the collective reasoning of the plotters was that Gotti had to strike preemptively before Castellano could demote him, break up his crew, or whack him and Ruggiero for disobeying his narcotics prohibition and for Ruggiero's compromising tapes.

If the conspirators needed another emotional motive and rationale for killing Castellano, he handed it to them by refusing to appear at Dellacroce's funeral. Big Paul told intimates that law-enforcement agents would photograph him if he showed up, and the resulting publicity could hurt his chances of acquittal at his RICO trials. Nevertheless, his absence was viewed by Mafia traditionalists as both cowardice and disrespect for a venerated Gambino leader.

Frank DeCicco provided the essential information for ambushing Castellano and Bilotti. Frankie was one of three trusted capos Castellano invited for a dinner meeting in a Manhattan restaurant to begin at 5:00 P.M., on December 16. Armed with that insider's knowledge, Gotti assembled an eleven-member assassination squad to waylay their prey outside the restaurant. The murder team consisted mainly of proven killers from Gotti's Bergin crew. They were alerted the day before the event with vague instructions from Gotti: "We're going on a piece of work tomorrow. There's gonna be two guys killed. It's a huge hit and it has to be done."

To maintain secrecy, Gotti waited until almost the last hour before revealing the identities of the intended victims and the site of the attack—Sparks on East 46th Street between Second and Third Avenues. Shortly before 5:00 P.M., the assassins gathered for a final rundown in a park in Lower Manhattan. Two gunmen would be stationed on the sidewalk at the restaurant's entrance and two directly across the street. The four prime triggermen were given white trench coats, Russian-style fur hats, and walkie-talkie radios. Similar clothing, Gotti figured, would make identification by passersby on a normally crowded street difficult and confusing. Other shooters were placed on both sides of the entrance to the restaurant along 46th Street, to sandwich or encircle the victims. The additional hitters would finish off the job in case the four front-line gunmen missed Castellano and Bilotti when they arrived at the restaurant, and tried to flee on foot.

The two backup team members were Gotti and Gravano. Gotti was behind the wheel as they sat in a parked Lincoln Town Car with tinted windows at the corner of 46th Street and Third Avenue, half a block from Sparks. Shortly after five o'clock, another Lincoln Town Car stopped alongside them for a red light. Winter darkness had set in. But to Gravano's astonishment, the dome light in the other Lincoln was switched on and, from several feet away, he saw Castellano and Bilotti talking. On his walkie-talkie, Gravano radioed to the waiting assassins that their targets were "coming through."

From their vantage point, Gotti and Gravano saw Castellano's car halt in front of the restaurant. White-clad figures descended upon the auto, followed by flashes of gunfire. Gotti turned on the engine and drove eastward across Third Avenue toward Sparks. As part of the plot, Gravano was an emergency shooter to assist the principal killers if there was any resistance by Bilotti or trouble with the police or foolhardy pedestrians. When they pulled alongside of Castellano's Lincoln, Gravano saw Bilotti's body sprawled in the pavement. "He's gone," Gravano whispered to Gotti.

Sammy the Bull and Gotti drove off to Brooklyn for a celebratory meeting with other conspirators. All members of the hit team escaped untouched in cars parked on Second Avenue. On the way to Brooklyn, Gotti and Gravano heard a radio news bulletin: Paul Castellano had been shot to death. John Gotti's daring assassination plan had unfolded flawlessly.

Encountering no resistance from the now-leaderless Castellano partisans, Gotti went through the motions of democratically installing himself as boss. The only Gambino hierarchy leader left after Castellano's murder and Dellacroce's natural death was the consigliere, Joe N. Gallo. Powerless, without a tough crew behind him, and lacking the stomach for a fight, the seventy-five-year-old Gallo collaborated in arranging Gotti's formal coronation. Mafia protocol required the selection of a boss by a majority of a family's capos, and complying with Gotti's orders, Gallo presided at a meeting of most of the family's capos several days after the double murder. The conclave was held after closing hours at Caesar's East, a restaurant only a few blocks from Sparks, and partly owned by one of the arch conspirators, Sammy the Bull Gravano. Everyone in attendance knew that Gotti had engineered Castellano's slaying, but Gallo and the capos all pretended ignorance. Following Gotti's script, Gallo gravely announced that an internal investigation was under way to find and punish Castellano's killers. The other New York families, he continued, were being informed that the Gambinos were intact, strong, and united. Until a boss was formally designated, Gallo, Gotti, and Frankie DeCicco would run the family temporarily. The real news—understood by all the capos—was that Gotti was in charge, and that the plotters had agreed among themselves never to admit they had violated a cardinal Mafia rule by murdering a boss.

If investigators needed confirmation that Gotti was at the helm, they got it on Christmas Eve 1985. Concealed in a van in Little Italy, John Gurnee, a New York City organized-crime detective, witnessed a striking scene outside the Ravenite Club, Dellacroce's old hangout. "Numerous people bypassed others on the street and went directly to John Gotti and kissed him," Gurnee reported. Gambino capos and soldiers had gathered at the Ravenite to openly pay homage to the de facto boss. His formal investiture came at a meeting of some twenty capos on January 15, 1986. There was only one nominee, John Joseph Gotti, and at age forty-six he was unanimously elected the Gambinos' godfather.

34

"Shame on Them"

John Gotti's meteoric rise did not go unnoticed. At the start of the new year he was promoted to the top of Bruce Mouw's FBI "must-get" chart of the Gambino leadership. Other law-enforcement agencies had the same priority. Soon enough the bureau, federal prosecutors in Brooklyn and Manhattan, the Queens district attorney's office, and the State Organized Crime Task Force were stumbling over one another in separate quests to get the goods on Gotti. At the time it was unclear to investigators that Paul Castellano's murder had been a byproduct of the FBI's electronic eavesdropping on Ruggiero and Castellano's demands to hear the controversial tapes. Now, investigators were seeking authorization for more electronic intrusions. At one point, agents from the FBI, the Queens DA's office, and the state task force almost simultaneously had penetrated the Bergin Hunt and Fish Club to install mikes, unbeknownst to one another. These multiple electronic invasions were a continuation of the historic, sometimes comic jurisdictional rivalries that chronically plagued the vast array of investigative agencies operating in the New York area.

The first unit to bug the new Gambino boss was the state task force. Like the FBI and the Queens DA's detectives, state investigators had unearthed an informer—an arrested small-time narcotics dealer looking for leniency, Dominick Lofaro—whose information generated bugs at the Bergin Club. Lofaro, a Gambino associate, wore a wire and recorded a conversation with Gotti about gambling and loan-sharking by the Bergin crew. It was sufficient for court authorization to eavesdrop on Gotti's office. The electronic ears actually had sprouted in March 1985, nine months before Castellano's murder, and long before Gotti became a headline gangster. Microphones were secreted in two desk telephones, located in an unmarked storefront with a separate street entrance through a red door, next to the Bergin. Gotti had converted the space into his private quarters. Unattached to the club, it was the place where investigators believed Gotti conducted his confidential conversations, feeling more secure there than inside the Bergin's larger room. The busy, noisy club was otherwise a holding pen or reception area for people waiting to see him, not for sessions about Mob business. State investigators knew he was wary of telephone taps, but they counted on his not suspecting that two private phones in his office had been wired or bugged. Every conversation in his private chambers could be recorded by live microphones in the telephones when they were not being used for incoming or outgoing calls.

Gotti ranked as a capo when the devices were first turned on. His conversations failed to dredge up criminal evidence, and the mikes were shut off in October 1985. Two months later, citing the Sparks murders, Ronald Goldstock, the task force head, got court permission to reactivate the bugs hibernating in the phones. This time, there were interesting results. As boss, Gotti surprisingly dropped his guard, talking freely in his office with close comrades about his plans to reshape the Gambinos' organizational structure, reassigning soldiers, and prospective hierarchy appointments. One of the first pronouncements in January 1986 was his "hell of a legacy" goal: to construct an unconquerable Cosa Nostra family. The state tapes recorded Gotti ridiculing consigliere Joe N. Gallo as a nice old man, an ineffectual figurehead whom he intended to replace. However, he had no intention of appointing coconspirators Fat Ange Ruggiero or Sammy Gravano to the consigliere's post. Angelo, "he ain't bright enough," Gotti told a confidant; and Gravano at age forty-one, "he ain't old enough."

The state investigators learned that about this same time, in a meeting with Ruggiero, Gotti had selected Frank DeCicco as his number-two man, his underboss. Without specifying his reasons, the godfather had decided to temporarily prohibit the induction of new soldiers. "These guys are going to be in for a shock," Gotti chortled. "Look, fuckin' six months to a year we can't do none of them. We cannot do one," he was overheard telling Ruggiero.

As guidelines for the nation's largest borgata, Gotti directed Ruggiero to notify all lower ranks that he would be too busy to burden himself with routine problems and requests. "Forget about business here," he decreed, referring to himself. "Go see Angelo, go see your skipper, go see somebody else."

The whirling tapes provided the task force with news that Gotti was shifting his headquarters from the Bergin Club in Queens to the Ravenite in Little Italy. It was intended as a symbolic move, notifying his own family and the other clans of his rise from a provincial capo to a Mafia divinity. "Angelo," he declared, "I ain't comin here [Queens]. I'm going right to New York every fuckin' day. Right to New York. That's where I've been [inaudible word] since the day I [inaudible] live and I'll die there."

Befitting his lofty status, Gotti's personal mode of living underwent a sea change. As a capo, he had dressed neatly but in typical gaudy, wise-guy style, usually in turtleneck pullovers or open-collared shirts, a gold or silver pendant dangling on his chest. Sometimes he wore a black-and-silver Oakland Raiders jacket and loafers. Reinventing himself, he adopted a foppish color-coordinated appearance. Instead of windbreakers and sports jackets, he now appeared resplendent in custom-tailored double-breasted Brioni and DiLisi silk suits, accessorized by hand-painted floral ties. The once ragged, embarrassed school boy with unmatched shoes was swathed in cashmere overcoats and monogrammed silk socks. Almost every day, his silvery black hair was trimmed and his prominent widow's peak styled in a swept-back coiffure. Overnight, he became the Mob's Beau Brummell.

Where once he had spent most of his time at the Bergin Club and ate at simple neighborhood restaurants in Queens and Brooklyn, Gotti began frequenting Manhattan's trendy cafés and night spots. He was accompanied by a corps of brawny protectors, several resembling the massive Luca Brasi character in *The Godfather*, and was accorded effusive courtesies by his attendants; even his brothers Gene and Peter helped him don and doff his coat and held umbrellas over his head. One of two bodyguards accompanied him into restaurant and public washrooms, turning the water taps on and off for him, and obsequiously handing him fresh linen towels.

While redesigning the Gambino family and himself in early 1986, Gotti had to attend to two criminal accusations left over from his thuggish capo days. Two years earlier, he had double-parked near one of his bookmaking joints in Queens. Gotti's car had blocked a refrigeration mechanic named Romual Piecyk from driving through the street. A tall, beefy, hot-tempered individual, the thirty-five-year-old Piecyk blasted his horn and then approached Gotti on foot as if primed for a fight. The argument ended with Gotti and a Mob pal, Frank Colletti, smacking around Piecyk, who drove off and summoned the police. A search located Gotti and Colletti in the nearby Cozy Corner Bar and Grill, and Piecyk filed charges that they had assaulted him and lifted $325 in cash from his wallet.

Unaware of Gotti's underworld standing when he originally identified him, Piecyk then had wanted revenge. Ordinarily, charges involving a minor parking dispute without serious injuries would have stagnated in the city's clogged court system before being dismissed. The Queens DA's office, however, seizing upon the opportunity of reaping publicity by proving that the newly notorious John Gotti was a brutal hoodlum, insisted on prosecuting him. Far from ignoring the trivial case, the DA eagerly set a trial date for March 1986. Piecyk, the prosecution's only witness, now knew that Gotti was a kingpin mobster, and he was having nightmares about being murdered. Refusing to cooperate with prosecutors, the frightened mechanic had to be dragged into court by the DA's men. Looking like a zombie and wearing dark glasses, Piecyk recanted the identifications he had made before a grand jury. "To be perfectly honest," he testified, "it was so long ago, I don't remember. I don't remember who slapped me."

Without the necessity of jury deliberations, the presiding judge voided the charges. The New York Post characterized the proceedings in a cleverly apt headline: "I FORGOTTI."

A beaming Gotti left the courthouse with his newly retained lawyer, Bruce Cutler, a former Brooklyn assistant district attorney with the Homicide Bureau. A natty dresser, still retaining a husky build from his days as a high school champion wrestler and college football team captain, the thirty-eight-year-old Cutler physically resembled Gotti. At the brief trial, Gotti seemed pleased with Cutler's bellicose courtroom style; he had ripped into Piecyk as a deranged instigator who had flung himself on the innocent John Gotti in a drunken attack. The scrum of reporters besieging Gotti discovered he was an unorthodox godfather. Even while dodging questions, he smiled affably, not trying to hide or escape from the TV and photographers' lenses. The new Mafia don basked in the attention and respect enveloping him.

The nuisance assault case disposed of, a more serious and complex set of charges awaited Gotti in Federal District Court in Brooklyn. In March 1985, months before the Castellano murder, Gotti, his brother Gene, and a batch of

Bergin crew tough guys had been indicted on a RICO complaint. Gotti was only a secondary suspect in the original case; the lead defendant was Neil Dellacroce, who was then alive. As the principal subject of the investigation, Dellacroce had been accused of supervising two Gambino crews, one of which was Gotti's. Dellacroce's death, Castellano's murder, and Gotti's emergence as boss turned him into the lead defendant and catapulted the trial into a highly significant Mafia case for the government. The realignment of defendants meant that federal prosecutors had to hurriedly alter their strategy to focus mainly on Gotti instead of the deceased underboss.

While preparing in the spring of 1986 for the start of the RICO trial, Gotti warmed to his new duties as a don. An enjoyable part of his on-the-job training was discovering the copious wealth that would flow into his private coffers. Schooled in the more violent Mafia crimes, Gotti learned that he was entitled to shares of the borgata's sophisticated arts, most of which he had never practiced. Millions of dollars in kickbacks were now his largesse from an assortment of corruption and union rackets, including the waterfront, construction, and private garbage-carting industries. Besides getting slices from the borgata's traditional gambling and loan-sharking activities, he had become a partner in porno sales and in the forbidden fruits of narcotics traffickers. A bug at the Bergin Club heard his astonishment at a soldier's report that the Gambinos were getting a cut along with other Mob families from the theft of gasoline excise taxes through the daisy-chain system of phony wholesale fuel distributors devised by Russian gangsters. "I'm talking about two cents a gallon on 20, 30 million gallons a month," an underling pointed out. "That's six hundred thousand dollars," Gotti replied appreciatively.

Before getting bogged down in what loomed as a long RICO trial, Gotti began visiting crews that had been close to Castellano. He intended solidifying their loyalty to him by demonstrating that, unlike the reclusive Big Paul, he understood the ordinary trench soldier's needs. On the Sunday afternoon of April 13, 1986, the new don was scheduled along with his underboss Frank DeCicco to give a pep talk at the Veterans and Friends Club in Bensonhurst, Brooklyn. It was the storefront headquarters of James Failla, a capo who as the head of a Mob-dominated business-trade association controlled many of the city's major private trash-collecting companies.

Beefy and potbellied, Failla had grown up in Bensonhurst and still spent most of his time at his club in the neighborhood, although like many mobsters he lived across the bay in more suburban Staten Island. Failla was first noticed as a "comer" in the family when in his early thirties he was selected by Carlo Gambino, then the underboss, as a chauffeur-bodyguard. After assuming control of the family in 1957, Gambino placed Failla in charge of the borgata's new interests in garbage-carting. Without drawing much law-enforcement attention, Failla had been handling the carting rackets in the city and in Long Island for thirty years and running a crew out of Bensonhurst.

But Failla had been more than just a big moneymaker for the previous regime. His crew members had served Castellano as hardened "hitters," and Gotti wanted Failla and his soldiers to play the same roles for him: converting trash into cash and serving as efficient hit men.

Over the years, Failla became stuck with his underworld nickname "Jimmy Brown," because of his propensity to wear drab brown clothes. Unlike his new, flamboyant godfather, he had no interest in publicity. Approached once by a *New York Times* reporter for an interview about the garbage-hauling industry, he snarled, "Eat shit."

A loyal Castellano follower, Failla had been waiting inside Sparks Steak House for Big Paul on the murder night, the previous December. To greet their new boss, John Gotti, Failla assembled some thirty crew members and wannabes in his storefront base. The place symbolized Failla's prudence in warding off electronic eavesdropping. It had no telephone, and he had prominently displayed on a wall a large picture of a cockroach wearing a headset with the caption: "Our Bugs Have Ears."

At the last minute, Gotti canceled the visit to Failla's club, from which he was scheduled to ride in DeCicco's car to the Ravenite Club in Manhattan. The sudden change in plans may have saved Gotti's life. That afternoon, a remote-controlled bomb killed DeCicco when he entered his auto, parked across the street from Failla's club. Investigators learned from bugs and informers that an understandably perturbed Gotti was certain that the blast had been meant for him, but he was mystified as to who was behind the hit. Diehard Castellano supporters bent on revenge were the logical suspects, but Gotti thought he had assuaged all of Castellano's and Tom Bilotti's gangland relatives and potential avengers. The use of a remote-controlled explosive was baffling to both Gotti and lawmen. Traditionally, American mafiosi had never resorted to bombs because they could kill and injure innocent passersby and galvanize extraordinary law-enforcement pressure. Zips, Sicilian immigrant mobsters, or screwballs, like the Irish Westies, might attempt a bombing, but why would they be out to kill John Gotti? All that a puzzled Gotti could do was tighten security around himself and guard against an assassin getting close to him and his chauffeured limousines.

The bombing death incited a spate of headlines and stories about Gotti and the Gambino family; too many for Federal District Court Judge Eugene Nickerson, who had just begun picking a jury for Gotti's racketeering trial in Brooklyn. To avoid impaneling jurors tainted by adverse publicity about the lead defendant, Nickerson postponed the trial for four months. Appearing unruffled at the pretrial hearings, Gotti enthralled the press, especially television reporters. Unlike stereotyped, shadowy bosses, he was a radically different version of a violent mobster; he was graced with a mischievous smile, held doors open for women reporters, waved politician-like to spectators outside the courthouse, and responded to a barrage of questions about allegations of being a Mob godfather with a standard sound bite: "I'm the boss of my family—my wife and my kids."

Embellishing the public relations spin to news-hungry writers, lawyer Bruce Cutler portrayed his client as a hardworking plumbing salesman and a devoted father. If he had a son, Cutler said, he hoped the boy would model his character after the virtuous Gotti's. FBI agents, trailing Gotti on his extracurricular rounds, drew a much different diagram of Gotti's fidelity to hearth and home. From routine surveillance and from information volunteered by hotel detectives, the FBI watchdogs—without any prurient intent—knew that he was cheating on his wife. One of the longest affairs was with a daughter born out of wedlock to Neil Dellacroce. Philandering and entertaining a *goombata* mistress was a common practice among Cosa Nostra mainstays, an accepted symbol of virility. The assignations with Neil's daughter, however, violated the Mafia's code of honor because she was married to a Mafia gangster. Gotti therefore was cuckolding a fellow mafioso, an act punishable by death in the kingdom of Cosa Nostra.

Gotti's freedom and rakish night life were soon curtailed on a motion by Diane Giacalone, the lead prosecutor in the Brooklyn RICO case. She contended that the trial delay would increase the possibility that Gotti and his cohorts would intimidate witnesses. Cited as evidence in her motion was the previously undisclosed harassment and fear that befell Romual Piecyk, the refrigerator mechanic who got cold feet on the witness stand at Gotti's assault and robbery trial. Before the reluctant Piecyk testified, the brake linings on his van were cut, he received threatening telephone calls, and he was followed on the streets by menacing-looking men, one of whom kicked him in the behind.

Agreeing with the prosecution that Gotti was a potential danger to the community, Judge Nickerson revoked his bail in May and ordered him detained until the end of the trial.

Giacalone's request to remand Gotti was a jolt to the state's Organized Crime Task Force director Goldstock. He pleaded with her and the interim U.S. Attorney in the Eastern District, Reena Raggi, to allow Gotti to remain free. "We have a bug on him and we're picking up phenomenal stuff," Goldstock notified the federal prosecutors. He pledged that if Gotti continued using his private office adjacent to the Bergin Club, he would share the evidence from the active eavesdropping with federal prosecutors for additional cases against Gotti and other mobsters. Once more, overlapping law-enforcement jurisdictions were at loggerheads over tactics. The federal prosecutors decided that the state's tapes were of dubious value and that their own priority for a conviction trumped Goldstock's future possibilities. On the day Gotti was jailed to await trial, a judicial order required that the bug be shut down.

Pretrial detention meant Gotti would be off the streets for months and created administrative problems for him. His first consideration was establishing a system to keep the Gambino family running smoothly while he was locked up in the Metropolitan Correctional Center, the federal jail in Lower Manhattan. Before going behind bars, he arranged a method for being briefed in prison and transmitting orders. Messages would be relayed back and forth through authorized visitors, his brothers and Angelo Ruggiero. He placed control over nitty-gritty daily operations in the hands of a committee of three capos who had conspired with him to kill Paul Castellano. The panel consisted of his longtime crony Ruggiero, Joe Piney Armone, and a new deputy, Salvatore Sammy the Bull Gravano.

Gravano had been waiting inside the Veterans and Friends Club for Gotti when the explosion on that Sunday afternoon in April killed underboss Frank DeCicco. Since that mysterious, violent death, Gotti had brought Gravano into his small cabinet of advisers, consulting him on borgata business.

Before the plot against Castellano was spawned, the two relatively young mobsters, Gotti and Gravano, had been acquainted but had not worked together on a criminal venture. The forty-one-year-old Gravano, five years younger than Gotti, had grown up in Brooklyn but in less straitened circumstances than his future boss's indigent childhood. Gravano's Sicilian immigrant parents were sufficiently prosperous to own a small dress factory, a brick row home in Bensonhurst, and a vacation cottage in Long Island. An only son,

Sammy like so many other future mafiosi, took an early dislike to formal education and was an unrepentant disciplinary problem.

A slow learner, Gravano felt humiliated at school, and compensated for his inferiority complex by lashing out at children who laughed at him. After slugging two teachers, he was transferred to a strict "600" school for troublemakers, and at sixteen—like Gotti—he was a dropout. Later in life, Gravano faulted school authorities for contributing to his educational woes by failing to recognize that he was dyslexic, and not providing the remedial help he needed to learn to read.

Bensonhurst in the late 1950s, Gravano's neighborhood during his teenage years, was home to phalanxes of ambitious wiseguys and brawling wannabes. Slender, barely five-feet five-inches tall, Gravano took boxing lessons to protect himself from bullies. "You don't have to know how to read to learn how to box," he told friends. His Napoleonic-style pugnacity earned him a nickname. A local mobster, watching the enraged Gravano in a fist fight, observed, "He's like a little bull." After that, he was forever dubbed "Sammy the Bull" or "Sammy Bull."

While a teenager, he chalked up several years of experience as a burglar, a car thief, and a ski-masked stickup man. Caught trying to break into a lumberyard, Gravano was on the receiving end of a beating by cops. The arrest was long before the Supreme Court's Miranda ruling on a defendant's rights to remain silent, and the police worked him over in a vain attempt to identify his accomplices. Appearing in court with his nose broken and eyes blackened, Gravano agreed to a deal negotiated by his lawyer. The eighteen-year-old pleaded guilty to a reduced misdemeanor charge, and was released after promising the judge he would join the army.

Gravano lied about enlisting, but a year later, during the Vietnam War, he was drafted. Never shipped overseas, Gravano employed his mobster street training to make military life comfortable for himself. Paying off the military police, he ran barracks crap games, and matured into a GI loan shark. Home again after two years in the army, and unreformed, he resumed his occupation of petty rackets and muggings. Seeking bigger opportunities he went "on record," as an associate, working for a soldier in a Colombo family crew headed by Carmine the Snake Persico. As an obliging wannabe, Gravano was one of the scores of demonstrators dispatched by Joe Colombo to picket the FBI's offices in Manhattan during Colombo's civil rights protests in the late 1960s and early '70s.

Trying to make his bones and gain admission into the Colombo family, Gravano committed his first murder at age twenty-five, whacking another wannabe who had offended a made man. "I felt a surge of power," Gravano related years later. "It's just that killing came so easy to me." Gravano attended the victim's funeral, shamelessly offering his condolences to grieving relatives. About this same time, to impress Carmine Persico, who wanted a businessman worked over, Gravano brutally fulfilled the assignment. He proudly described using a blackjack to sever one of the man's fingers.

The homicide and the savage assault marked Gravano in the Colombo family as "a comer," a reliable, iron-nerved enforcer. But a feud with the relative of a Colombo capo could be peacefully resolved only through Gravano's departure from his chosen borgata. To avoid bloodshed, and acknowledging Sammy's competence, Colombo leaders authorized his switching allegiance to a Gambino crew in Bensonhurst. His new leader was Salvatore "Toddo" Aurello, a capo who became Sammy the Bull's Mafia instructor and benefactor.

The move enriched Gravano. Under Aurello's guidance, he established himself as a decent earner and a big-time loan shark. Before long, Gravano's rough tactics and the Gambino family's links with corrupt unions allowed him to diversify his criminal portfolio. He extorted construction companies for labor peace, and by having the muscle to arrange promanagement union deals, he started his own companies and operated as a semilegitimate building subcontractor. Flush with illicit profits, he invested as a partner in several restaurants and discothèques, convenient justification of high income on his IRS tax return.

Married to Debra Scibetta, a neighborhood sweetheart (whose uncle was a Bonanno soldier), and the father of a daughter and son, Gravano's personal life seemed smooth. In 1975, when the Mafia Commission reopened the books for the infusion of recruits, he was one of the first to be welcomed into the Gambino borgata.

Capo Toddo Aurello was Sammy's sponsor at the induction ceremony presided over by Big Paul Castellano in a Brooklyn basement. Afterward, what most persisted in Gravano's memory were Castellano's solemn words, "You are born as of today," and swearing an oath of absolute devotion and loyalty to Cosa Nostra, Our Thing. "In this secret society, there's one way in and there's only one way out," Castellano intoned. "You come in on your feet and you go out in a coffin. There is no return from this."

Aurello was a capo firmly committed to Castellano, and the boss often called upon his crew for "a piece of work," a murder. Gravano's turn came in

1977. Castellano's contract was carried out by Sammy, who never knew the victim's identity or the motive for his second Mob hit. Another contract from Castellano involved personal entanglements and demonstrated Gravano's unswerving dedication to his Mafia oath. Nicholas Scibetta, the brother of Gravano's wife, Debra, was an associate and minor player in another Gambino crew. A small-time cocaine hustler, Scibetta dipped into his own product and evolved into a quarrelsome addict. Reports reached Castellano about Scibetta's blatant violations of his no-drugs edict and of concerns that if "Nicky" got busted he would become "a rat," endangering the family. Wasting no time, Castellano ordered Scibetta rubbed out. The job was given to friends of Gravano who told him "off the record" that his brother-in-law was in imminent danger. Deciding that his allegiance to Castellano and *omertà* surpassed life and death obligations to a relative, Gravano remained silent instead of warning Nicky to flee from harm's way. Scibetta's body was never found, although a hand wearing his ring turned up. Again, Gravano comforted the victim's relatives, this time his wife and in-laws.

By the early 1980s, money was rolling in from Gravano's rackets and Mob-connected construction and nightclub businesses. Sammy's golden touch even extended to his wife, who won an $800,000 New York state lottery. Many of Gravano's Mob enterprises were in tandem with his brother-in-law Edward Garafola, also a Gambino made man. Gravano built a lavish $800,000 home in Staten Island, and acquired a thirty-acre farm in New Jersey for weekend jaunts and to raise harness racing horses. The financial successes brought him increasingly to Castellano's attention, and he was often selected for important acts of violence. Through Castellano he was given a contract in 1980 on John "Johnny Keys" Simone, a Philadelphia mobster who was opposing Nicodema Scarfo, the Commission's choice as boss of that city's Mafia family. Personally orchestrating the hit, Gravano abducted Simone and looked on coolly as an accomplice blew off the back of Simone's head.

Despite Castellano's praise of him, Gravano's loyalties to Big Paul gradually wavered, and he became an avid early recruit in Gotti's deadly conspiracy against their boss. His alliance with Gotti was rapidly and richly rewarded. One of Gotti's first moves was to promote Gravano to capo of the Toddo Aurello crew; the old captain, Sammy's tutor, was allowed to retire peacefully and unharmed. As a capo, Gravano rapidly built up a $1.5 million loan-sharking book enforced by his crew, which ensured him a steady yearly profit of $200,000 to $300,000.

Away from their gangster jobs, Gotti and Gravano found opposite ways of relaxing. Gotti, usually out with the boys gambling heavily and drinking, rarely spent a night with his wife and kids. Gravano profited from usurious loans to gamblers but never risked his own money on sports bets or cards. An early riser—unlike most mobsters—he could usually be found at home in the evenings. After his last prison stretch, Gotti gave up on heavy physical exercise, preferring less strenuous playboy recreation. Sammy the Bull, even with his increased borgata duties, was obsessed with keeping in tiptop shape and retaining his athletic image. To bulk up, he spent up to $3,000 a week on anabolic steroids, hired a professional trainer, and was a regular at a gym where he boxed younger men and sparred with professionals.

The revocation of Gotti's bail and his jailing before his RICO trial brought Gravano more deeply into the ruling council. In the first six months of 1986 he had soared from the rank of soldier to one of the family's three acting street bosses. Fully committed to the new regime, Gravano willingly carried out Gotti's directives—even if they required the murder of a friend and fellow conspirator in Castellano's murder. Using Angelo Ruggiero as a messenger, Gotti ordered Gravano to arrange the execution of Robert DiBernardo, the family's porno king and bagman for construction-industry shake-downs. Ruggiero explained that DiBernardo had to die because he was criticizing Gotti behind his back.

Years later, Gravano claimed that Gotti acted on false rumors spread by Ruggiero. Ange owed more than $250,000 in loan-shark debts to DiBernardo, who had disparaged Ange's leadership talents. According to Gravano, DiBernardo had insulted Ruggiero to his face: "You have the balls to be underboss, but not the brains." Maintaining that he could not contradict a command from Gotti, Gravano complied with his wishes. He invited DiBernardo to a meeting in his office on the pretense of discussing Mob construction-extortion matters. As the two men chatted, a Gravano triggerman shot DiBernardo twice in the back of the head. The body of the Mafia porno millionaire was never found.

Two months after being jailed, Gotti was in a courtroom facing his new antagonist, Diane F. Giacalone, an assistant U.S. Attorney in the federal Eastern District and the lead prosecutor in his RICO trial. Giacalone had a remote association from childhood with the Bergin Hunt and Fish Club, the vortex of the Mob crew on trial. She had grown up in South Ozone Park, and on her way to a Catholic parochial school passed near enough to see the disreputable characters milling outside the Bergin. Her indefatigable perseverance was largely responsible for the charges against Gotti, his brother Gene, and five other crew members. Over six years she had stitched together the case, largely as an outgrowth of an investigation of armored-car robbers who had paid cash tributes to Gotti to stay on good terms with him. Although Gotti was uninvolved in the heists, the inquiry expanded into RICO enterprise-accusations, including murder and loan-sharking by the Bergin crew.

But Giacalone encountered severe hurdles from the start. The original indictment had been tailored to convict Neil Dellacroce, and his death forced her to reshape the case with Gotti as the new prime defendant. When Gotti, then one of the lesser suspects, was arraigned on the charges in March 1985, he was so obscure that the judge and his clerk were uncertain how his name was spelled. A relatively inexperienced prosecutor, Giacalone had tried only one organized-crime case previously; it was against a low-ranking soldier and she lost. Her limited Mob-trial background, and her overall strategy for convicting the suddenly important Gotti, worried Mafia specialists. At that time, lawyers from the Justice Department's Organized Crime Strike Force handled most Mob trials in the Eastern District. The semiautonomous unit, which zealously guarded its preserve, opposed bringing the revised charges against Gotti. Ignoring standard protocol, Edward A. McDonald, the strike force's director, went so far as to advise Justice Department officials that Giacalone's evidence was weak. He cautioned that an acquittal would disallow future use of hard-gained evidence gathered against Gotti, immunizing him from all crimes he committed before 1985. The clash between Giacalone and McDonald had the earmarks of a prosecutorial race over who would be the first to bring down Gotti. Backed by her boss, Raymond J. Dearie, the U.S. Attorney in the Eastern District, Giacalone got the green light from Washington to go after the new Mafia celebrity.

Before a witness could be called, Giacalone was fighting another rancorous in-house battle, this one with the FBI. Preparing for the trial, Giacalone had discovered that one of the indicted Bergin crew defendants, Wilfred "Willie Boy" Johnson, was a paid FBI informer. She decided to expose Johnson's undercover acts and compel him to become a prosecution witness who could buttress essential points of the indictment. Johnson pleaded with Giacalone to maintain his secrecy, warning that he and his family would be slaughtered if Gotti learned what he had been up to. Under the code name "Wahoo," Johnson for fifteen years had been a valuable FBI source, and the bureau had promised that he would never be forced to testify. Supporting Willie Boy, the FBI argued vigorously that his secrecy had to be maintained. Agents knew that reneging on Johnson's agreement would discourage other potential informers and cause incalculable harm to ongoing and future investigations.

Giacalone was adamant. Despite Johnson's vehement denials that he was a rat, the prosecutor announced in open court that he had clandestinely cooperated with the FBI. She counted on the pressure of exposure as a sure means for changing Johnson's mind, and offered him security in the Witness Protection Program. The gambit failed. Johnson feared Gotti's powers of retaliation more than the government's, and he refused to cooperate. At the trial, he remained at the defense table sitting alongside Gotti and the other codefendants, repeatedly protesting to them that he had never been a squealer.

Most of the counts against Gotti stemmed from evidence dug up by agencies other than the FBI. When the Johnson controversy flared up, angry FBI officials retaliated against Giacalone by cooperating only marginally with her in the last stages of preparing the case. To add to the internal government feuding, another valuable informer, Billy Batista, a bookie and hijacker in the Bergin crew, was exposed by Giacalone, who also planned to use him as a trial witness. The FBI placed Batista in a hotel in New Jersey without constantly guarding him. After a month largely on his own, he vanished. In the empty hotel room, Batista's handler, Agent Patrick Colgan, found a note: "Thanks for everything, Pat. I'm out of here." Precipitated by Giacalone's decision to unveil him as a witness, Batista's flight severed another secret FBI source, further infuriating bureau officials.

Willie Boy Johnson's plight opened a window on the murky existence of Mob informers and their motives. He and Gotti had been teenaged terrors in the Fulton-Rockaway Boys gang, and both had worked as musclemen for Carmine Fatico's crew in East New York. Because Johnson's father was a Mohawk Indian iron worker and Willie Boy was only half Italian, he was prohibited from becoming a made man, even though he robbed and killed for Fatico, Gotti, and other wiseguys. Johnson grew resentful when Fatico failed to properly support his wife and children while he was in prison for armed robbery. Later, when Gotti led the Bergin crew, the 250-pound six-feet-tall Johnson was a loan-shark knee breaker for him. Gotti, however, contributed to Johnson's concealed anger, referring to him as the "Redskin" or "the half-breed."

Arrested by the FBI for gambling and extortion, Johnson saw a way out by becoming an informer. Upset at being derisively treated by mafiosi partners and seeking FBI intervention in case he got jammed up again, Johnson signed on with the bureau. The gambling-extortion crime was placed on the back burner so long as he produced information about the Gambinos and other families. Agents knew that he had to be involved in loan-sharking to remain in the Mob's good graces, but they winked at that so long as he was not arrested for other crimes. For the FBI it was a rational arrangement: letting a two-bit gangster—a minnow—off the hook in return for priceless tips on Mafia sharks was a reasonable bargain.

The competition between law-enforcement agencies was almost comically displayed through Johnson's activities. While aiding the FBI, he was picked up on a narcotics rap, carrying a $50,000 heroin payoff, by Lieutenant Remo Franceschini's detectives in the Queens DA's office. Grasping at an opportunity to penetrate Gotti's lair, the DA's men cut a deal with Johnson, turning him into an informer to betray the Gambinos. The $50,000 in drug money was confiscated. As a legal sword over Johnson's head to guarantee his cooperation, the DA held a sealed indictment against him for the attempted bribery of arresting detectives.

For over a decade, Johnson supplied similar tips and intelligence to the FBI and the DA's office, without either agency knowing he was serving two masters. One of his priceless gifts to the bureau was Angelo Ruggiero's boast that he had a "safe" means at his home of communicating with the crew—his daughter's Princess phone.

Gotti's RICO trial in Brooklyn lasted from August 1986 to March 1987. Giacalone and another young prosecutor, John Gleeson, depended on thirty hours of audiotapes and ninety witnesses to implicate Gotti and six codefendants in three murder conspiracies and on racketeering charges. The defense's aggressive, scorched-earth strategy and tone was set in the opening statements by Bruce Cutler. In a throbbing harangue, the lawyer attacked Diane Giacalone's integrity, accusing her of concocting a secret underworld organization, the Gambino family, that did not exist, in order to advance her own career. Holding a copy of the indictment above his bald dome, Cutler paced back and forth in the well of the courtroom. "It's rotten. It makes you retch and vomit," he fulminated, pointing to the document. "This is where it belongs," he concluded theatrically, slamming it noisily into a wastebasket.

The prosecution relied heavily on seven turncoat witnesses, all low-level gangsters, to reinforce the indictment. In a slashing counterattack, Cutler tore into the defectors, stressing that they were confessed murderers, kidnappers, or perjurers, who had evaded life sentences and obtained money and other favors from the government for testifying against Gotti. He tried to deprecate the taped conversations, insisting they were mere humdrum discussions by "knock-around guys," crude-talking gamblers and card players with unorthodox lifestyles, not mobsters or criminals.

The defense's insinuating attacks on Giacalone were extraordinary, bordering on being loathsome, with one defense witness calling her "a slut" during his testimony. At the opening of the trial, Giacalone, in her mid-thirties with shoulder-length raven black hair, wore a red dress to court, prompting Cutler to demean her as "the Lady in Red" when later addressing the jury, even when she wore another color.

Giacalone had intended to use an admitted bank robber, Matthew Traynor, to identify Gotti as a capo and crew chief, but he was dropped after prosecutors caught him lying. Instead, the defense called him as a witness to impugn the prosecutor, claiming that she had badgered him to frame Gotti. Traynor testified that Giacalone had offered him illegal drugs, and even tried to relieve his sexual frustrations in prison. "She gave me everything," he said. "Even her panties out of the bottom drawer, to facilitate myself when I wanted to jack off." (After the trial, Traynor was convicted of perjury arising from his incendiary testimony about Giacalone.)

Shortly after the trial began, a new U.S. Attorney, Andrew J. Maloney, was appointed to head the Eastern District office. Gregarious, with a ready smile for strangers, Maloney's exterior pose was deceptive. Underneath, he was an amalgam of an exacting drill sergeant and a case-hardened lawyer. A West Pointer, he had served as an officer in the Army's Ranger Corps before switching careers and graduating from Fordham University Law School. He then spent twelve years as a federal rackets prosecutor in Manhattan and head of a Justice Department anticorruption white-collar division. Maloney had not been involved in obtaining the Gotti indictment or in the trial preparations. But after looking in on the court proceedings, he was outraged by the enormous latitude Judge Nickerson was permitting the defense team. Gotti partisans in the courtroom were chortling over Cutler's corrosive cross-examinations, complimenting him for "Brucifying" prosecution witnesses. "Nickerson can't handle these guys," Maloney thought, observing the defense lawyers' tactics.

"The judge is a gentleman's gentleman and he's allowing them to turn the trial into a circus."

Maloney grew concerned about Giacalone's health. Rail thin, resembling the actress-comedienne, she appeared increasingly worn down during the stressful trial. "She's very tough, but she's knocking heads with the defense and even the FBI hates her over the Johnson controversy. She's very stretched out; she looks ready to go into a hospital."

Another concern for Maloney, which he withheld from Giacalone, were tips coming in to Bruce Mouw's Gambino Squad. "The FBI had unconfirmed reports that the wiseguys were making moves on the jury," Maloney said. "They were trying to reach two jurors."

The jury-fixing information turned out to be accurate, but five years would elapse before the accusations could be verified. Incredibly, a member of the anonymous jury, a middle-aged suburbanite named George Pape, volunteered, for a price, to hold out for an acquittal. At the start of the trial, Pape reached out to his friend Bosko Radonjich, who happened to be the new leader of the murderous and predominantly Irish Westies in Manhattan. (Bosko, a Serbian immigrant, took over the gang when most of the Irish leaders were jailed.) Beset by money problems, Pape wanted $120,000 to guarantee, at a minimum, a hung jury. Sammy the Bull, serving as Gotti's negotiator, whittled the bribe down to $60,000, and happily passed it along to Pape through Radonjich before the trial ended.

After listening to evidence and arguments for six months, the jury deliberated for a week before reaching verdicts. It was a Friday, the 13th of March 1986, and waiting apprehensively for the jury's return, U.S. Attorney Andrew Maloney sensed that it was an unlucky day for his staff. "I'd seen a lot of tough guys in my years as a prosecutor and there's always some anxiety," Maloney said. "But Gotti was sitting there as cool as a cucumber. It was unbelievable how relaxed he was. I knew he must have succeeded in fixing the jury."

Maloney's fears were accurate. A Cheshire cat smile on his face, Gotti heard the jury announce "Not guilty" verdicts on every count against him and his codefendants. A decade after the trial, *Daily News* reporters Jerry Capeci and Gene Mustain wrote that at first a majority of the jurors favored convictions. Pape, however, refused to budge, parroting Cutler's line that Giacalone hated Gotti and that she had failed to prove her case. Gradually, Pape's argument prevailed in arguing that there was sufficient reasonable doubt to acquit every defendant.

It was a stinging defeat for the government's campaign against the Mafia, the first time it had lost a significant RICO trial. And John Gotti, the godfather who had turned the tables on Justice Department lawyers, gloated with malicious satisfaction. "Shame on them," he snarled, shaking a fist contemptuously at Diane Giacalone and John Gleeson, the young prosecutors. "I'd like to see the verdict on them."

35

"He's Like Robin Hood"

John Gotti's trial in Brooklyn was one of two huge and simultaneous courtroom clashes between the government and the Mafia in 1986. Across the East River, in Manhattan, only two subway stations away, the Commission case had ended with one hundred-year sentences for three reputed bosses and their closest henchmen. "That has nothing to do with me," Gotti said to reporters, dismissing the Commission case as inconsequential. It was a lie and he knew it. In one blow, the Commission convictions had removed much of the Mob's Old Guard. In contrast, Gotti's stunning acquittal had turned him into the Cosa Nostra's most significant symbol of resistance to law enforcement since Al Capone had cavorted in Chicago a half century earlier. A repositioning of godfathers was under way and Gotti, the only boss to emerge victorious in court, had become the nation's preeminent Mafia outlaw. His national and international status was such that he was the first gangster since Capone to make the cover of *Time* magazine, his face portrayed by Andy Warhol. The prestigious Sunday *New York Times Magazine* also presented Gotti on its cover with an unflattering close-up photograph of his baleful, gimlet-eyed stare.

For the first time since ascending to power, Gotti was unencumbered by a pending trial or the threat of imminent jailing. Exultant, Gotti the Boss bragged to Sammy Gravano that he would change the face of Cosa Nostra, setting an example on how to defeat the government. A swashbuckler, he had no intention of cowering in the shadows even though he knew his movements would be under tight scrutiny by the FBI and other agencies. Indeed, his daily routine became familiar to a horde of investigators. At noon almost every day, he was picked up at his Howard Beach home by a bodyguard in a Mercedes-Benz, a more upscale auto than the Lincoln models he had previously favored. Wearing a jogging suit, he was driven to his office at the Bergin Hunt and Fish Club, which he had remodeled with multiple mirrors into a dressing salon containing a professional barber's chair and a curved sink for shampoos. A blown-up photograph of himself from the *Time* magazine cover and a picture of his dead son Frank were prominently displayed. One of the first orders of daily business was having his hair styled by a barber; his grooming routine often included a manicure and sun-lamp treatments to retain his tan. A complete wardrobe of suits, shirts, underwear, monogrammed socks, and shoes were kept there for him to change into before leaving in the late afternoon for the Ravenite Club on Mulberry Street in Little Italy. Every day his black Mercedes was washed and polished to a gleam before transporting him to Manhattan. Capos and other high-ranking members of the new regime were required to appear at the Ravenite at least once a week to report directly to Gotti. FBI agents sometimes got within earshot at the Ravenite to hear the Gambino entourage on the sidewalk entrance fawning over Gotti, telling him how wonderful he looked. Obviously aware of the government's electronic eavesdropping abilities, he was frequently seen with ranking mafiosi strolling the streets near the Ravenite in what investigators called "walk-talks," clearly out of earshot of interior bugs.

Seemingly enjoying the thrill of the chase, although he was the quarry, Gotti boldly displayed his contempt for the pursuers. Spotting detectives or agents on stakeouts, he taunted them by rubbing one finger against another, mouthing the words "Naughty, naughty." Seated one afternoon at an outdoor café on Mulberry Street, Gotti saw Rudolph Giuliani, the U.S. Attorney, eyeing him as he slowly drove by. Laughing at the prosecutor, Gotti gave him the naughty-naughty treatment, implying that Giuliani was spying on him. On other occasions, he turned toward detectives following him, mockingly formed his hand into the shape of a gun, and mouthed, "Bang, bang."

The night was party time for Gotti; he rarely missed an evening at Regines, Da Noi, or other voguish restaurants or supper clubs. His favorite drinks were invariably among the most expensive, often Remy Martin Louis XIII brandy or Roederer Cristal Rose champagne, each at $1,000 a bottle. His notoriety and his glamorous image always turned heads as people eagerly tried to get a look at him. Dining one night with Gotti, Sammy Gravano asked if he disliked people constantly staring at him. "No, no," Gotti exclaimed joyously. "This is my public, Sammy. They love me." Gravano thought Gotti had come to view himself as an heroic figure, genuinely admired by most New Yorkers.

At a period when celebrity gossip was a staple for many newspapers and TV news programs, Gotti's cavalier insouciance became an entertaining sidelight. News editors and TV producers relished fluffy yarns illuminating the social and private behavior of the smiling mobster. He was headlined by the tabloid press as "the Dapper Don" and "the Teflon Don," two appellations that he considered pleasing compliments. "Dapper" of course signified his near obsession with his high-style appearance. "Teflon" was a headline writer's transfer to Gotti of a title first widely applied to Ronald Reagon, the "Teflon President," because of his ability to avoid blame for blunders and scandals in his administration. Simply put, like food in a Teflon pan, no criminal charges stuck to the new godfather.

With Gotti's notoriety, every event in his life was grist for the media. How could editors ignore the extravagant wedding of his son, John A., more widely known as "Junior"? Held in the ornate Versailles Room at the Helmsley Palace, one of New York's most regal hotels, the nuptial reception cost nearly $100,000. The guest list of 200 included the top tier of the nation's Cosa Nostra. At the insistence of the bridegroom's father, the hotel flew the Italian flag over its main entrance, an honor normally extended only to visiting heads of state and foreign dignitaries.

Fed with items supplied by Bruce Cutler and other lawyers, reporters had ample yarns about Gotti's endearing, charitable personality. There were stories about his popularity in South Ozone Park; how he paid for July 4th block parties with free food, drinks, and fireworks, and appeared dressed in an immaculate white suit; how a local hospital, the Baptist Medical Center, honored him with a huge lobby plaque for donating $10,000; how he could quote Machiavelli.

Investigators knew that the amiable personality Gotti displayed in public was a fraudulent mask disguising a narcissistic tyrant with an incendiary temper. His lawyers claimed that he hated narcotics. Unlike Paul Castellano, however, Gotti never issued an edict that Mob execution awaited Gambino soldiers who were caught trafficking in narcotics. Castellano hypocritically accepted payoffs from soldiers secretly involved in drugs, but he never met openly with suspected big-time dealers. Gotti did. In addition to his brother Gene and Angelo Ruggiero, who were indicted in a major heroin transaction, he conferred and dined with international dealers. Two of them, the brothers John and Joseph Gambino, were distant cousins of Carlo Gambino, and ran a Sicilian-born crew in New Jersey and in New York for Gotti.

Additionally, one of Gotti's first moves as boss was to order a capo, Patsy Conte, to revive his heroin pipeline with the Sicilian Mafia. Gotti knew that Conte had regularly supplied Castellano with huge sums, and once, as a Christmas present, had presented him with a new Mercedes. A furious Gotti sent Gravano to lecture Conte. Terrified by the dressing down, the abject Conte said he had stopped trafficking only because he believed Gotti was opposed to it.

"I don't care what you have to do," Gravano warned. "You brought in tons of money under Paul, and in this administration you're bringing in nothing. I don't want to know anything about it [heroin deals]. What I want, what John Gotti wants, is money, the same situation that Paul had."

The fate of Willie Boy Johnson, the disgraced FBI informer, exemplified Gotti's implacable vengeance. At the RICO trial in Brooklyn, Gotti cast Johnson out of his Mob organization. But he swore to Johnson on the memory of his dead son that there would be no deadly retaliation for his treachery. Staying clear of the Bergin crew, Johnson got a legitimate job and moved to the Brighton Beach section of Brooklyn. On August 29, 1988, sixteen months after the trial, three men were waiting for him when he left for work. Ten shots were fired, with six striking Willie Boy at close range. Police and the FBI had no doubt that Gotti had bided his time and then exacted his revenge. Of course, Gotti had an alibi for the murder. Confronted by a *New York Post* reporter for his reaction to the slaying, Gotti was concise: "Well, we all gotta go sometime."

Through informers, investigators heard of the behavioral theme that Gotti wanted his capos to impart to soldiers. Even if arrested, his troops were not to skulk nor appear repentant like ordinary criminals. At trials, they were required to imitate his style: dress expensively, wear jewelry, and appear fearless. "Put it in their face," Gotti urged Sammy the Bull Gravano. "They want to see fucking lions and tigers and that's what we are."

Gotti's glamorization by the tabloid press and his truculent challenges to authority lay like sharp-edged bones in the throats of the city's top law-enforcement officials. Most were prohibited by internal agency rules from publicly condemning Gotti since he was not charged with a crime. The exception was Jules Bonavolonta, one of the first FBI agents to recognize the importance of the RICO law. Now supervising the bureau's organized-crime division in New York, Bonavolonta was affronted by Gotti's favorable press treatment. "He's a former two-bit hijacker and a degenerate gambler who rules right now because he is ruthless and vicious," Bonavolonta told reporters. (From informers' scuttlebutt, the FBI knew that even Gambino soldiers were astonished at some of Gotti's high-stakes losing sprees, including $300,000 in sports bets with non-Gambino bookies in one weekend.)

As the nation's largest investigative force, which had trumpeted its intention to demolish the Mafia, the FBI was under pressure to crush the arrogant Gotti. Within the bureau, responsibility for results fell on the Gambino Squad and its supervisor, Bruce Mouw. He refused to be stampeded into hastily assembling a rickety case that Gotti might again overcome. Despite the hoopla about Gotti, he was a newly installed boss, and Mouw understood that a new plan was needed to lasso him. Mouw's choice for the case agent who would work exclusively on digging up evidence against the Teflon Don was George Gabriel. Six-feet four-inches tall and athletically built, Gabriel had been working Mob investigations with the squad for only a year. The thirty-year-old agent had previously been assigned to hostage rescue and antiterrorist SWAT units, but Mouw considered him "one of the sharpest, most aggressive agents I ever met." Mouw also recognized that Gabriel's size and muscle would discourage any of Gotti's gorillas from trying to intimidate him in a tight spot.

"Agents fight for this kind of case, and I could see how excited George was for the challenge when I offered the job to him," Mouw recalled. His instructions to Gabriel were similar to his basic guidelines for the entire squad: "Be patient, focus on making a viable prosecution, don't go on endless, wild-goose white-collar crime chases. Concentrate on what Gotti knows best—murder, extortion, and shylocking."

While Mouw began searching for irrefutable evidence, federal and state prosecutors were maneuvering and jousting among themselves over future Gotti prosecutions. Andrew Maloney, the U.S. Attorney in the Eastern District, began the contest by taking the short subway ride from downtown Brooklyn to the Manhattan office of his counterpart in the Southern District, Rudolph Giuliani. Several years earlier, Maloney had been in the running for the esteemed Southern District post. Upon Giuliani's appointment, Senator Alfonse D'Amato offered Maloney a consolation prize, nomination to the Eastern District's top job. Disappointed and considering himself "a Southern District man," having been a prosecutor there for ten years, Maloney turned down D'Amato's first offer. Three years later he changed his mind, leaving a private law practice to accept the senator's endorsement and President Reagan's nomination for the Eastern District post.

The Southern District is viewed in the legal profession as the Justice Department's crown jewel. Maloney knew he was taking charge of a district overshadowed by its neighbor's reputation, and which many lawyers and prosecutors jokingly thought had a collective "inferiority complex." Gotti's RICO acquittal was a severe drubbing to the Eastern District's prestige, and Maloney, a canny litigator and a knowledgeable hand at Justice Department politics, was dedicated to quickly repairing his office's image. A welterweight boxing champion at West Point, Maloney knew the importance of landing the first solid punch.

When Giuliani and Maloney met in the spring of 1987 for a confidential tussle over who would get John Gotti, Maloney was a new U.S. Attorney without a distinguished record. In contrast, after three years of overseeing dozens of high-profile cases—the convictions of the Mob's Commission, billionaire Wall Street inside-traders, and corrupt politicians—Rudy Giuliani had been enshrined by his admirers as the country's super-prosecutor.

Unfazed by Giuliani's aura, Maloney brusquely got to the point: the Eastern District would prosecute the next RICO indictment against Gotti. Both prosecutors knew that each of their offices could claim rights to the case under the crazy-quilt jurisdictional map of the region. The Gambino family had extensive operations in Manhattan, the Bronx, and the suburban counties north of the city, all in the Southern District. Moreover, the Castellano-Bilotti murders eighteen months earlier, outside Sparks Steak House, had occurred in Manhattan, and Giuliani had impaneled a grand jury, which was hearing evidence about the slayings.

Maloney's jurisdiction included Brooklyn, Queens, Staten Island, and Long Island, which, he countered, was the Gambinos' "main power base."

"It's a matter of honor for my office," Maloney said firmly to Giuliani. "I want you to back off. I don't want the FBI going in three directions with different prosecutors and with your office and my office competing for information. I know you think no office can try a case as effectively as yours, but you're wrong; we can."

Besides the two federal prosecutors, the Manhattan district attorney's office also was involved, collaborating with Giuliani on the Sparks slayings. Homicide cases, even if they are Mafia-related, are normally the responsibility of local police and state authorities. But the importance of Castellano's murder had led to a combined FBI and police inquiry. Under a bill that agents dubbed "the Hit Man's Statute," Congress in 1984 empowered federal attorneys to prosecute mobsters for murders committed in aid of racketeering or for enhancing a position in a RICO enterprise, such as a Mafia family or a drug cartel. Saying he was committed to a joint investigation with the politically important Manhattan DA Robert Morgenthau, Giuliani refused to discontinue the murder probe or turn it over to Maloney.

The meeting, which Maloney referred to as "a sit-down," ended in a split agreement. Giuliani's office would handle and prosecute the Castellano-Bilotti murders with Morgenthau, and Maloney would be in charge of a initiating a RICO enterprise case. With Giuliani's strong connections to the Justice Department's highest officials, he almost assuredly would have prevailed in an internal political battle if he had asked Washington to resolve the RICO jurisdictional contest in his favor. But another political conflict might have affected Giuliani's decision. A New York election was near, and Giuliani was contemplating a run for mayor. A RICO case can take years to develop, leading to speculation by prosecutors about Giuliani's prime reason for quickly conceding the larger RICO inquiry to Maloney. The consensus was that Giuliani knew that by the time an indictment of Gotti was ready, he probably would no longer be a U.S. Attorney and get the applause for nailing him.

Another prosecutor in the race to indict Gotti was the state's Organized Crime Task Force director, Ronald Goldstock. His office had a valuable asset: audiotapes from the bugged conversations in Gotti's private offices adjacent to the Bergin club, recorded shortly after he became boss. Several days after Diane Giacalone's case went down the drain in Brooklyn, Giuliani wanted to hear the tapes of Gotti's incriminating remarks. According to Goldstock, he and Giuliani planned to pool their resources to investigate Gotti for a RICO indictment, including the murders of Castellano and Bilotti. "We both felt that Gotti was mocking law enforcement, and every day he was out there was bad for our credibility," Goldstock said. But Giuliani abruptly withdrew his offer, telling Goldstock, "I'd love to have this case but I can't do it. Maloney has drawn a line in the sand. I don't want to be seen stealing his case. You have to go to the Eastern District."

Confident that he had the foundation of a "great enterprise case" against Gotti from the tapes, Goldstock met with Maloney and Edward McDonald, from the Eastern District's Organized Crime Strike Force. All regional strike forces reported directly to the Justice Department in Washington, and there were often ill feelings between these units and their respective U.S. Attorneys. It was McDonald who had belittled Giacalone's evidence before she took on Gotti in her RICO indictment.

Goldstock now pitched his electronic-eavesdropping evidence at the two federal officials who ran separate prosecutorial units. The state's bug in Gotti's office had been reactivated immediately after Castellano's murder, picking up conversations between Gotti and some of his closest cronies for four months, until Giacalone jailed him for the duration of his trial. Goldstock enthusiastically reported to Maloney and McDonald that the eavesdropping had caught Gotti threatening a loan-shark victim, authorizing an assault on a union leader, boasting about bookmaking joints in his Queens domain, and discussing organizational changes he was making in the Gambino borgata. "It's really excellent material and evidence for RICO with Gotti as the head of an enterprise," Goldstock declared. "He's talking continually about how he was elected boss, where money is coming from, and who's going to control what."

Maloney and McDonald each had authority to use Goldstock's evidence for a RICO case. But they were unimpressed. Echoing each other, they thought the bugged remarks were too vague and circumstantial. The bugs, they agreed, were insufficient to convict Gotti on predicate counts—that he actually knew or participated in the crimes. "We need more evidence to back up the bugs," Maloney insisted. "Your evidence won't stand up against this guy. If we're going to bring him down, we have to make sure he's dead center in our sights. The evidence has to be more than just solid, it has to be overwhelming; otherwise we're going to make him look really invincible."

Maloney accepted Goldstock's tapes as a starting point, but he was far from ready to present their contents to a grand jury. Sizing up Gotti as an overconfident braggart, Maloney was relying on Mouw's FBI squad to find the "smoking gun" guaranteed to destroy the haughty Gambino godfather.

Free from jail and courtrooms, John Gotti rarely left the New York area. The fearless mobster abhorred flying. After Salvatore Ruggiero, the narcotics merchant, died in a private plane crash, Gotti vowed never to step aboard a plane and place his fate in the hands of a pilot. His longest holiday trips were to a hotel in Fort Lauderdale, Florida, where he traveled by train with a covey of card-playing bodyguards. The journeys were working vacations, giving him the opportunity to confer with Gambino members handling the family's extensive rackets in southern Florida. Boats were more to Gotti's liking, and he piloted cigarette speedboats off the Florida and New York coasts; his boat in Florida was named *Not Guilty*. The aquatic excursions paralleled his penchant for fast cars. Before becoming a boss, he was stopped four times for speeding and other violations, and once had his driver's license suspended for driving while impaired by alcohol. Closer to home, he took brief summer vacations in a private cottage at fashionable Gurney's Inn in Montauk, at the eastern tip of Long Island. For weekend getaways he bought a $300,000 house in Pennsylvania's Pocono Mountains, deeded in the name of his eldest son, John A. There was no nameplate or mailbox on the house. But a Pennsylvania Dutch hex sign affixed to a stone veranda, spelled out "LOVE."

Undaunted by the campaign he knew law-enforcement agencies were waging against him, Gotti had vast criminal businesses and organizational questions that demanded his attention. The FBI electronic eavesdropping in Angelo Ruggiero's Long Island home had not trapped Gotti. Fearful of telephone taps, Gotti had been circumspect in his telephone conversations with Fat Ange, and he had never ventured into Ruggiero's bugged dinette. The bugs and Fat Ange's incessant talking had been a godsend to the government. McDonald's Organized Crime Strike Force had used the recordings to indict Ruggiero and Gene Gotti on heroin-trafficking charges. Ruggiero's chatter also helped McDonald's prosecutors construct RICO cases against two Gambino veterans, Joe Piney Armone, Gotti's second underboss, and Joe N. Gallo, the elderly consigliere.

Two trials of Ruggiero and Gene Gotti on the narcotics accusations ended in mistrials as, each time, extra-vigilant prosecutors and FBI agents uncovered apparent jury-tampering attempts. Ruggiero became terminally ill with lung cancer and was severed from a third trial in the spring of 1989. This time, Gene Gotti was convicted and sentenced to a minimum term of twenty years.

Armone and Joe Gallo, both in their seventies, were found guilty of enterprise racketeering, which for them meant almost certain death in prison before completing their sentences. Citing Gallo's poor health and age, the judge allowed him to be released temporarily to spend a last Christmas with his relatives before going off permanently to prison. For Armone, the judge would only permit a Christmas leave if he admitted to a lifetime of crime and membership in the Gambino borgata. Upon taking control, one of Gotti's first rules was that capos and soldiers could never acknowledge the existence of the family, even if it meant a reduced sentence. Desperate for a last visit with his personal family, Armone sent a message to Gotti, asking for permission to accept the judge's conditions. "No, we can't do that," Gotti chided Armone's nephew, capo John Handsome Jack Giordano, who delivered the plea. "It would send out a wrong message."

Armone rejected the judge's offer. Gotti's cold refusal was intended as a directive to all Gambino members that the boss was pitiless, his rules unbreakable. Old friend Fat Ange Ruggiero received a dose of similar mean-spirited treatment. Infuriated by the damage caused by Ruggiero's careless talk, Gotti demoted him from capo to soldier at a time when Ruggiero, his 250-pound frame reduced to a weight of less than 150 pounds, lay fatally ill with cancer. Despite fervent requests from Ruggiero's friends and relatives, Gotti refused to visit or telephone his devoted follower in his final days. Ruggiero died in 1989 at age forty-nine.

The imprisonment of Gotti's underboss Armone and consigliere Gallo required a hierarchy realignment. Gotti's choice for the number-two post as underboss was Frank "Frankie Loc" Locascio, a capo who had been aligned with Neil Dellacroce before Gotti's takeover. An old-school gangster, Frankie Loc was an expert practitioner in gambling and loan-sharking, but untutored in sophisticated extortion and white-collar rackets. Now in his mid-fifties, his claims to Mafia fame were that he was one of the youngest wannabes ever made, inducted when he was in his early twenties, and that he ran the Bronx and Westchester County rackets for the family with an expert hand. To replace the imprisoned Gallo as consigliere, Gotti in 1987 named Sammy the Bull Gravano, the capo he had come increasingly to rely on. Reviewing management techniques with his new counselor, Gotti thought Gravano was overly generous in sharing the wealth with his closest lieutenants and helpmates. "Listen to me," advised Gotti, who before reaching the top had chafed at Paul Castellano's greed. "Keep them broke. Keep them hungry. Don't make them too fat."

When it came to dividing the family's lucre from the construction industry, Gotti had no compunction about accepting the meatiest portions. Gravano, the family's construction-rackets specialist, was delivering to Gotti about $2 million a year, 80 percent of his own shake-downs, and keeping the remaining $500,000 for himself.

Learning about the regime changes from informers and FBI surveillance intelligence reports, Bruce Mouw arrived at his own appraisals of the new regime.

"Locascio is as loyal as a sheep dog," the FBI supervisor concluded. "John will never have to worry that Frankie will do to him what he did to Castellano." Mouw thought Gotti wanted a stolid "Yes sir, no sir type" underboss, not an ambitious one with a large entourage of his own who might someday challenge him. Gravano, a big earner, had a loyal following from his old crew, and if he wished could gain additional adherents by cutting them in on his construction-industry largess. Puffing on his ubiquitous pipe and trying to plumb Gotti's state of mind, Mouw reckoned that Sammy the Bull, not Locascio, was the strong man next to the throne and the godfather's real right hand.

Because of a conversation in a toilet, Mouw soon had a valid reason for a second personal get-together with Gotti. In the summer of 1987, as part of an investigation of the Genovese family in New Jersey, the bureau's Newark office had placed a bug in a rest room at Cassella's Restaurant in Hoboken. The restaurant was owned by a Genovese soldier, and agents had figured out that the rest room was used for Mob conferences. Listening in one night, agents heard Louis "Bobby the Thin Man" Manna, the family's consigliere, discussing with other wiseguys possible methods of bumping off John Gotti and his brother Gene. The essence of the conversation was that the hit contract came from the Genovese boss, Vincent "Chin" Gigante.

Obligated by bureau policy to warn Gotti of the threat, Mouw and George Gabriel, the Gotti case agent, arrived at his Howard Beach home well past noon. Gotti was still in bed, and Mouw told Vicky Gotti that there was a good reason to wake him. A huge Rottweiler on the lawn began barking fiercely, leading Mouw to wonder how it would look in news stories if he were attacked by Gotti's dog and had to shoot the animal in self-defense. He could imagine the headline: "FBI Whacks Gotti's Pet."

Shuffling downstairs in a bathrobe, Gotti calmed the Rottweiler. "Great dog, I love him," Gotti said, seemingly undisturbed by the sight of two FBI agents on his doorstep. "What's up?"

"This is official," Mouw began. "We have information that your life is in danger. Another family is going to take you out."

"I got no problems," Gotti said, laughing. "I got nothing to worry about. Thanks, fellas." But his expression changed when Mouw added, "It's the West Side," a reference they all understood meant Vincent Gigante's turf, Manhattan's Greenwich Village.

Mouw later related, "He blinked when I said 'the West Side,' because that meant something to him." Mouw withheld from Gotti the specifics of how the FBI had unearthed the death threat and which gangsters were involved. Too many details, he worried, might trigger a war between two Mafia families. From informers and surveillance, agents immediately noted that Gotti took Mouw's warning seriously. The Gambino boss quickly altered his daily travel patterns and increased the number of bodyguards accompanying him on his business and social rounds. Gotti also mulled over the warning with Gravano and other confidants, according to informers. Was Mouw's message a trick by the FBI to incite friction with the Genovese family or was the warning accurate? For the first time, Gotti speculated that his first underboss, Frank DeCicco, might have been blown to bits on orders from Chin Gigante, in retaliation for the murder of his fellow boss and business partner, Paul Castellano. Gotti ordered that his Mercedes and all his cars be vigilantly inspected for bombs.

As an insurance policy, Gotti sent out signals through Gravano to the Genovese administration that he harbored no ill feelings toward Gigante. Indeed, within a year, the two bosses agreed to convene a truncated Commission meeting, signifying that neither of them was hostile to the other. It was the first formal gathering of godfathers since the Old Guard bosses had been convicted in the Commission case, two years previously. Besides Gotti, Gigante, and their deputies, the leaders of the Lucchese borgata took part in the conference. Excluded were the unsettled Colombos, because a permanent successor had yet to be chosen for Carmine Persico, that family's imprisoned boss, and the outcast Bonanno family, which remained under interdiction because of its past narcotics violations and infiltration by an FBI agent.

The representatives of the three largest borgatas met in the autumn of 1988 in the Greenwich Village home of a brother of a Gambino capo, Frankie D'Apolito. It was in a huge apartment complex called Washington Square Village, built by New York University mainly for its faculty. But the relatives of more than one mobster had managed to obtain apartments in the highly desirable neighborhood. In fact, Vincent Gigante's relatives had an apartment in the building where the gangsters met, and at the time of the Commission meeting he was occupying it while recuperating from open-heart surgery.

As Gotti and Gravano were escorted into the building through an underground garage by D'Apolito, they encountered the Lucchese boss, Vittorio "Little Vic" Amuso, and his underboss, Anthony "Gaspipe" Casso. "What a great place for a hit," Casso murmured to the others as the tempting targets moved en masse through the basement.

One issue discussed at the meeting was whether to approve a seat on the Commission for Vic Orena, at that time Persico's choice as acting boss of the Colombos. Gotti endorsed Orena, and he also wanted to restore the Bonannos to the Commission by permitting its new acting boss, Joseph Massino, to sit in and have a vote. Gravano knew that Orena and Massino were Gotti allies, and with them in his corner he would control a majority on the Commission and become the supreme leader of the nation's Cosa Nostra.

Gigante and the Luccheses had no objection to seating Orena as the Colombo representative to the Commission, but Gigante was cool to readmitting the Bonannos to the Mafia's ruling body. Before the meeting ended, the Gambino boss announced that his son Junior had recently been inducted as a made man. "I'm sorry to hear that," Gigante said, disappointing Gotti. Gotti had expected congratulations on his son's career choice, but Gigante commented that he would never bring his own sons into the perilous orbit of the Cosa Nostra.

On a wintry Wednesday evening two months after the Commission meeting, Gotti was engaged in a walk-talk with capo Handsome Jack Giordano. They were strolling on Prince Street, around the corner from the Ravenite Club, when a car screeched to a halt alongside them. Four men with drawn guns jumped out, shouting, "Stop right there! Police!" Gotti, shoved face forward against a wall, with legs spread apart and his hands raised above his head, was roughly frisked by an expert, Joe Coffey, a former New York detective working for the state Organized Crime Task Force. "Are you wearing a gun, you cocksucker?" Coffey, a brash, old-school cop growled, touching a metallic object on Gotti's waist. "It's only my belt buckle," Gotti said, as his hands were cuffed behind his back. He was hustled into a waiting car and driven a short distance to police headquarters in downtown Manhattan for booking.

Less than two years after being acquitted on federal RICO counts, Gotti was again under arrest. Confronting him this time were state felony accusations that he had ordered the shooting of a union official. "Three-to-one I beat this charge," Gotti quipped with a smirk when Coffey read the official complaint to him.

The new indictment for assault and conspiracy arose mainly from the persistence of the state task force's Ronald Goldstock, and a bug his investigators had planted in Gotti's office sanctum next to the Bergin Club. In February and May 1986, his first months as a boss, the electronic spying picked up discussions between Gotti and his men, apparently about a plan to punish a carpenters' union leader in Manhattan named John F. O'Connor. From the drift of the conversations, Goldstock believed that Gotti held O'Connor responsible for wrecking a new restaurant secretly owned by Philip Modica, a Gambino soldier. While constructing his Bankers and Brokers Restaurant in Battery Park City, Modica had refused to bribe O'Connor or hire union carpenters. O'Connor was connected to the Genovese family and later would be convicted on corruption charges, but he apparently was unaware that the new restaurant was "protected," and the Gambinos blamed him for vandalizing the place in retaliation for his not getting payoffs or union jobs.

One May morning in 1986, O'Connor, the business manager and top executive of Local 608, was waiting for an elevator in the lobby of his Midtown office building. Suddenly, he thought he heard thunder and felt searing pain throughout his body. Spinning around, he saw a man pointing a gun at him. As O'Connor slipped to the floor, more shots were fired at him. He was hit several times in the legs and buttocks. Based on clues from the bugged conversations in Gotti's office, Goldstock and his investigators were certain the attack on O'Connor had been arranged by Gotti; it was another example of the sordid Mob and union treachery plaguing New York's construction industry.

Andrew Maloney, the U.S. Attorney in the Eastern District, had reviewed the fragments from Goldstock's tapes and believed they were too weak and inconclusive to use in a trial against Gotti. Goldstock's interest in the case was revived in late 1988, when a killer from the Westies gang named James McElroy, searching for an escape hatch to wriggle out of a life prison term, reached out to the authorities. For a reduction in his sentence he could implicate the nation's most prominent mobster, John Gotti, in the O'Connor shooting. "I wouldn't rat out an Irish guy, but the Italians, who gives a shit?" McElroy candidly told a detective.

McElroy's testimony, Goldstock hoped, would bolster evidence his office had collected through audiotapes and would clinch Gotti's conviction. The turncoat's account of the shooting sounded accurate. He swore that he had met with Gotti, and that the Gambino boss had farmed out the O'Connor contract to the Westies. Federal prosecutors in Brooklyn, however, again rejected Goldstock's theory, viewing the sleazy McElroy's claims as too fragile for a conviction. After being rebuffed a second time by Eastern District prosecutors,

Goldstock brought the evidence to Manhattan District Attorney Robert Morgenthau. Because O'Connor had been shot in Manhattan, Morgenthau had state jurisdiction. A former U.S. Attorney in Manhattan and the son of Franklin D. Roosevelt's Secretary of the Treasury, Henry Morgenthau, he had one of the most impressive prosecutorial records in the country. His personal influence and the prestige of his office was on a par with that of U.S. Attorneys, and his decision to prosecute Gotti lent extraordinary weight to the indictment. Moreover, neither Morgenthau nor Goldstock could deny that sinking John Gotti would be a magnificent milestone for both of them. Framing the importance of the case, Morgenthau announced that if Gotti were convicted, he would seek to have him sentenced as a "persistent predicate felon," a three-time loser, subject to a harsh prison term. The two felony convictions on Gotti's record were for hijacking and the attempted manslaughter of James McBratney in Staten Island, performed as a favor for Carlo Gambino. Under New York law, a third felony could brand him as incorrigible, subjecting him to a minimum sentence of twenty-five years and a maximum of life.

A year after being arrested on his walk-talk, in January 1990 a beaming Gotti was center stage once more in a Manhattan courtroom. Originally, he was joined by two codefendants, Angelo Ruggiero, his former close confederate, and Anthony "Tony Lee" Guerrieri, a soldier, both of whom were caught on the tapes allegedly helping Gotti arrange the assault. Ruggiero's indictment was severed because of his terminal illness.

Maintaining his sartorial splendor for the duration of the trial, Gotti was appropriately elegant in one of his custom-tailored silk double-breasted suits, set off with floral ties and matching lapel handkerchiefs over his heart. The sixty-year-old Guerrieri, a bookmaking and loan-sharking lightweight, was an inconsequential, almost invisible extra at the defense table. The headline attraction was John Gotti. Unlike his well-tailored boss, Guerrieri appeared in wrinkled suits and checkered jackets, often in noisy hues of chartreuse and fire-engine red.

Before Gotti's RICO victory over Diane Giacalone's prosecution, his lawyer Bruce Cutler had been a minor figure in the criminal-defense bar. His widely publicized triumph in the RICO trial, combined with Cutler's histrionic courtroom tactics and his outspoken jibes against prosecutors, had turned him into a legal celebrity. Cutler's opening speech was an attempt to put the prosecutors in the dock. It was a rerun of the defense strategy at the earlier RICO trial in

Brooklyn, another scathing personal vilification of the prosecutors. His voice rising to theatrical levels, Gotti's counsel paced before the jury, at times pounding on a desk, a bible, or a lectern, as he derided the prosecution's case. He termed Ronald Goldstock a "publicity mad" official who had "peddled" the Gotti tapes for years, looking for a prosecutor who would do his bidding. Robert Morgenthau was characterized as "hungry for political power," willing to frame Gotti in a witch hunt fueled by "Mafia hysteria" and "a lust for headlines."

Dressed in imitation of his client in a double-breasted suit and flowery necktie, Cutler portrayed Gotti in softer tones as a rehabilitated ex-convict who had refocused his life to become a community leader and a model citizen. Twice he had been cleared of biased charges brought by unscrupulous prosecutors. Comparing his client's exemplary character to that of James McElroy's, Cutler accused the prosecution of contriving a case on the words of a "psychotic killer, a lying bum," who would say anything to get a lenient sentence for his own horrific crimes.

Lead prosecutor Michael G. Cherkasky, a battle-hardened trial lawyer, took eleven days to meticulously present his evidence. Cherkasky's strategy for conviction hinged primarily on six words said by Gotti on Goldstock's tape: "We're gonna, gonna bust him up." On February 7, 1986, shortly after the Gambino-controlled Bankers and Brokers Restaurant had been severely damaged, Gotti and Guerrieri were heard talking about locating O'Connor, the head of Carpenters' Local 608. According to the prosecution's interpretations of the bugged conversation, Gotti instructed Guerrieri before the assault was carried out to determine if O'Connor was associated with any crime family. Cherkasky played the salient excerpt for the jury.

GOTTI: "608, John O'Connor 608, er, at 16 something Broadway, 1694 Broadway somethin' like that, Broadway, Carpenters."

GUERRIERI: "In other words you want to see if . . ."

GOTTI: "Ah, he's a business agent."

GUERRIERI: "To talk, or somebody who could talk to him."

GOTTI: "No, we want to see who he's with."

GUERRIERI: "Oh, oh."

GOTTI: "We're gonna, gonna bust him up."

Those last six words, "We're gonna, gonna bust him up," comprised the marrow of the prosecution's indictment. Cherkasky also relied on segments from ten other tapes, which he contended showed Gotti ordering the attack. Another relevant conversation was recorded on May 7, 1986, several hours after

O'Connor was shot. In that one, Gene Gotti came in to interrupt Gotti and Ruggiero.

GENE GOTTI (WHISPERING): "John O'Connor's been shot four times. They hit him in the legs. I heard it on the news. Angelo, it went off just like that."

RUGGIERO: "Oh, yeah."

GENE GOTTI: "Heh, heh, heh (unintelligible). Heard it on the news."

After playing the tapes, Cherkasky argued that Gotti as a new boss had a motive for retaliating against O'Connor. He had to quickly demonstrate his authority and power to the entire Mafia underworld in New York.

Except for the tapes, the prosecution depended on a single turncoat, the Westie James Patrick McElroy. Before getting to his star witness's testimony against Gotti, Cherkasky had to acknowledge McElroy's gory catalogue of crimes and lies. Husky-voiced, his eyes panning the courtroom, McElroy said that starting at age fourteen, he participated in murders, assaults, knifings, armed robberies, drug deals, loan-sharking, and bookmaking—too many episodes to remember. Now forty-five and convicted on RICO charges, he was serving a minimum of sixty years before becoming eligible for parole. Despite having frequently lied in the past on the witness stand, McElroy said his testimony implicating Gotti was the truth.

McElroy's version began in April 1986, when he accompanied James Coonan, the Westies leader, to the wake in Brooklyn for Frank DeCicco, the Gambino underboss blown apart in the mysterious auto explosion. Years earlier, Coonan had made a handshake deal with Paul Castellano for the Westies to work as a farm team for the Gambinos. At the funeral home, Coonan introduced McElroy to Gotti, who asked, "Is this the kid?" Later, after he and Coonan met privately with Angelo Ruggiero, Coonan told McElroy that the Westies had an assignment from the Gambinos. "He said we want to break this carpenter guy's legs. John O'Connor, because he messed up some guy's restaurant."

"Did he tell you who you were going to do it for?" asked Cherkasky.

"Yes," replied McElroy. "John Gotti."

On the morning that O'Connor was wounded, McElroy said, he was one of four Westies who ambushed the union leader but he did not fire at him.

During four hours of cross-examination, Cutler and another defense lawyer, Gerald Shargel, tore into McElroy, trying to raise doubts about his account of having met Gotti. Calling him a "yellow dog," "a Benzedrine head," "an equal-opportunity killer," the lawyers got him to admit that his one slim chance of getting out of prison was helping the prosecution and being placed in the Witness Protection Program.

Ironically, the only defense witness was the victim of the Westies attack, John O'Connor. Under investigation at the time and later convicted for labor racketeering, O'Connor had refused to testify before the grand jury that indicted Gotti or to answer questions about his links to the Mafia. However, he aided the defense, saying he had never been warned by state investigators that his life might be in danger, thereby suggesting that the authorities had not considered Gotti's secretly recorded talks as a threat.

The rules of evidence prevented the prosecution from explaining or offering testimony as to why O'Connor had not been forewarned. Before the shooting, state investigators considered Gotti's words about O'Connor too vague to constitute a threat. "On the tapes Gotti was angry about many people," Goldstock said. "That doesn't mean he was trying to kill them."

O'Connor also testified that he was involved in rancorous union conflicts and had numerous enemies within the union. The statements provided the defense with a theory that rivals had motives to assault O'Connor.

Staring placidly at the jury, which had deliberated four days, John Gotti listened to the verdicts. "Not guilty," the jury foreman announced on the counts, two charges of assault and two charges of conspiracy. The forgotten defendant, Tony Lee Guerrieri, was also acquitted, but Gotti was the one who counted. It was Friday, February 9, 1990, and outside the courthouse, more than one thousand people cheered as Gotti emerged, raising his right arm in a gladiatorial victory salute. A maroon Cadillac idled at the curb, and Gotti, protected by his brawny brother Peter and a bodyguard, ducked into the car for the ride a few blocks away to his Mulberry Street redoubt. Another crowd roared, and fireworks were detonated as he strode into the Ravenite Social Club, where a grinning Sammy the Bull Gravano, and a throng of mobsters, waited to offer hosannas and congratulations.

In South Ozone Park, red balloons bedecked the Bergin Hunt and Fish Club. Pennants were strung from the club to a lamppost, and a sign in the window proclaimed: "Congratulations John and Tony. We love you." At Gotti's home in Howard Beach, yellow balloons, a symbol of remembrance of hostages and prisoners of war, were tied to a wrought-iron fence. People in passing cars honked their horns and shouted, "Terrific! Great!"

Among the cheering fans on the narrow street outside the Ravenite, a local resident, who gave his name to reporters as Louis D., summed up the adulatory views of many spectators who believed Gotti was being persecuted. "He's like Robin Hood," Louis exclaimed. "All the people cheered for him when he won."

Questioned by reporters, jurors discounted the prosecution's basic pillars. They critiqued the audio quality of the tapes as poor, and said that many of the conversations were difficult to hear and understand. Although Gotti's "bust him up" phrase was clearly heard, it was unconvincing proof to the skeptical jury of his intent to harm O'Connor. Equally important, none of the interviewed jurors found James McElroy, the prosecution's prize witness, credible.

The court triumph, his third acquittal in four years, magnified Gotti's reputation for invincibility and as the undisputed icon of organized crime. Lawyers wondered if law-enforcement agencies would risk prosecuting him again unless they could build an absolutely airtight case. Amid the uproar over Gotti's latest success, Jules Bonavolonta, commander of the FBI's organized-crime section in New York, pointed out an overlooked fact. "Listen," he told *The New York Times*. "The FBI hasn't brought a case against Gotti yet. When we do, he can take all the bets he wants, because he's going away to prison for a long time."

36

Mrs. Cirelli's Holiday

A jubilant John Gotti celebrated his latest judicial triumph in February 1990 by taking a winter vacation in Florida. Despite the dreary weather in New York, the FBI's Jules Bonavolonta also had reason to celebrate. He was sitting on a carefully guarded secret: after four frustrating years of scraping for evidence against Gotti, Bruce Mouw's Gambino Squad had finally struck a mother lode. At the start of the investigation in 1986, Mouw instructed George Gabriel, the case agent, to "figure out where Gotti is vulnerable." Strapped for manpower, Mouw depended primarily on Gabriel, backed up by one or two agents at most, to carry out the dogged pursuit of the evasive godfather and to cultivate informers in order to locate a weakness in Gotti's fortress. "Don't count on a task force helping you," Mouw cautioned Gabriel. What Mouw knew prosecutors wanted most of all was Gotti's own recorded voice providing irrefutable and damning evidence of his supreme role as the Gambino godfather. "Locate where he is talking business, the Bergin, the Ravenite, a safe house, a restaurant," Mouw emphasized.

Following in the footsteps of earlier city and state agency investigations, the FBI bugged the Bergin Hunt and Fish Club in South Ozone Park, the office Gotti continued to visit almost daily after seizing control. The Bergin eavesdropping failed to turn up significant evidence, and eventually Gotti's attentive soldiers found the bureau's secreted listening devices. By early 1988, Gabriel was convinced that the Bergin Club was of marginal interest since Gotti had moved his headquarters to the Ravenite Social Club in Little Italy, where his courtiers and capos visited him five nights a week. The windowless red-brick-faced club on the ground floor of a walk-up tenement on a grimy street became the command post for the nation's largest, most powerful Mafia family.

Scouting for a suitable observation post from which to monitor the steel door entrance to the Ravenite, Gabriel rented a sixth-floor apartment on the northeast corner of Mulberry and Houston Street. Two blocks north or uptown of the Ravenite, the apartment had a window with an unobstructed view of the sidewalk in front of the club. It was in an expensive new building on a street that was being gentrified by young professionals, tenants who were not on guard for law-enforcement snoops like the suspicious residents of the Ravenite block. Perched inside the window, agents, using long-lens and high-tech night video lenses and still cameras, began compiling a rogue's-gallery file of every-one entering and leaving the club and their auto license-plate numbers. Gotti's insistence that all of his capos and his important soldiers report to him at the Ravenite at least once a week provided the FBI with a Gambino family "Who's Who." Fifty or more of Gotti's vassals showed up almost every day, and the pho-tographs and videotapes elated Mouw. "It's a bonanza for us. They're supposed to be a secret society functioning in the underground and Gotti has all of them coming in daylight to the same location to talk to him, kiss his ass, and pass money to him." The hugging and adulation of Gotti, he knew, could be used as circumstantial evidence to support testimony that Gotti was a Mob godfather.

Although the squad had been investigating the Gambino family for almost a decade, Mouw was surprised at the huge gaps that had existed in the bureau's intelligence files before the Ravenite observation post was established. Agents discovered the existence of numerous previously unknown capos, soldiers, and corrupt union leaders only after their pictures were identified by turncoat in-formers. "We didn't know how big the family really was. Especially the Bronx guys; that was a foreign country to us."

The surveillance pictures were vital for the next phase of the investigation. Attached to statements from Mob informers, they gave prosecutors from An-drew Maloney's Eastern District documentation and "probable cause" for court-authorized electronic eavesdropping at the Ravenite Club, on grounds that crimes were being discussed there. It was now up to James Kallstrom's special-operations commandos to infiltrate the Ravenite. In the dead of a spring night in 1988, Kallstrom's lock pickers and technicians installed their first bug. Without any attack dogs or supersensitive burglar alarms to disturb them, the task was surprisingly easy. The bug and a transmitter were secreted in the rear of the club, near a huge round table that informers said was reserved for Gotti's use. Going about their work, the tech agents saw on the wall above the table a symbol of Gotti's past: a single framed photo of him and his late role model, Neil Dellacroce; both men were pictured in suits and ties, staring grimly at the world. Several hours later, about a mile away, agents at FBI headquarters in Lower Manhattan were ready to record Gotti's precious words.

The bug was a dismal failure. Most of his conversations in the club were drowned out by the roar of a soda machine and a booming television set. Even though Kallstrom's technicians returned surreptitiously several times to fiddle with the equipment and reposition the miniature mike, there was scant improvement. Conversations that were heard clearly usually were foul-mouthed personal chatter, meaningless as evidence of criminal wrongdoing. Mouw and his agents could only conclude that Gotti, increasingly wary about bugs, was apprehensive about speaking candidly in the Ravenite's main room. The only morsel of Mafia lifestyle gained from the bug was Gotti leading his button men in a chorus of complaints about devoting Saturday nights to their wives. Other nights could be spent with a *goombata*, but Mafia custom required Saturdays to be reserved for wives. Gotti's moans that Saturday evenings were his dullest nights were amusing but worthless gossip for agents.

Since Gotti routinely left the club for walk-talks in the neighborhood with Gravano and capos, Kallstrom's magicians resorted to other high-tech gadgetry. Planting listening devices in parked vehicles, FBI technicians tried to overhear his sidewalk conversations by activating tapes with remote controls. This gambit also failed.

It took an off-handed observation by an informer to pry open the sanctuaries where Gotti spoke freely and conducted his confidential meetings. During a debriefing, the FBI spy casually mentioned to agent George Gabriel that Gotti and his lieutenants sometimes left the Ravenite through a rear door that led to the apartment building's ground-floor hallway. Gotti and his companions always returned the same way, the informer recalled. The remark prompted Mouw and Gabriel to scrutinize transcripts of audiotapes and of time logs from the observation post two blocks away of persons entering and leaving the building. A startling fact emerged from the agents' analysis. Sometimes, for up to an hour Gotti's voice was curiously missing from the interior of the Ravenite. And, during these long spells, the observation logs showed he had not exited through the Ravenite's street door. Where did he go? Gabriel pressed informants for more details, any rumor or hunch about where Gotti went in the building. The possibilities: Gotti either talked with someone in the vestibule outside the Ravenite's rear door, or walked upstairs to an apartment for private meetings.

One informer was fairly certain. He assured Gabriel that Gotti used an apartment occupied by Nettie Cirelli, the widow of a Gambino soldier who had been the caretaker of the Ravenite in Neil Dellacroce's days. "Source C," Gabriel wrote in a confidential memo, "also stated that John Gotti would continue to use the Cirelli apartment for very secretive meetings when he has something very important to discuss with someone and does not want to be seen on the street with this individual."

With an amended Title III court order, Kallstrom's men returned to the Ravenite building in October 1989, this time to bug the tenement's rear hallway. The results were quickly gratifying for Mouw. There was no din from the interior club, and Gotti's voice was clearly heard discussing family criminal matters with capos. Especially captivating for Mouw and prosecutors was a whispered conversation in the vestibule between Gotti and capo Tommy Gambino about Garment Center rackets and Gambino's testimony before a federal grand jury in Brooklyn.

Buoyed by the hallway success, the next objective was Nettie Cirelli's apartment, number 10 on the building's third floor. According to an informer, when Gotti wanted to use the woman's home, he ordered the current Ravenite caretaker, her nephew Norman Dupont, to suggest she go shopping or visit with a nearby niece for several hours. Neil Dellacroce apparently had used the same technique for meets in the apartment. As the widow of a Mob soldier, Mrs. Cirelli recognized the codified meaning of her nephew's suggestion.

Planting a bug in the apartment would certainly yield results, but it was trickier than the hallway. Mrs. Cirelli rarely left the place, even in the daytime. Like many suspicious neighbors on the Ravenite block, she would probably not fall for the ruse of admitting technicians posing as utility company repairmen or insect exterminators into her home. Nor could Kallstrom's men risk entering the two-room flat at night, while Mrs. Cirelli slept; the shock of seeing her apartment invaded might cause a fatal heart attack for the seventy-two-year-old widow. And a failed break-in would certainly alert Gotti that the entire building was wired. Several bureau officials in New York thought Mouw should be content with exploiting the vestibule bug without endangering the whole operation by attempting an entry into the Cirelli apartment.

Mouw decided it was worth the risk and on November 19, 1989, a serendipitous opportunity arose. Agents in the observation post saw Mrs. Cirelli leave the building, carrying a suitcase, then being driven off by relatives. That night her telephone rang without being answered. More than likely, she had left for a Thanksgiving holiday and the apartment was temporarily vacant. Without waiting any longer, in the early morning hours Kallstrom's special-operations savants picked the door lock to Mrs. Cirelli's apartment. Her tiny living room contained a couch, two easy chairs, a wooden coffee table, two planters, and a TV set, and it was as neat as a pin. Kallstrom never revealed where the microphone was planted. "It was a small room, an easy job, and it went off perfectly," he confided.

The next ten days were torturous for Mouw and Gabriel. Gotti appeared at the Ravenite but he did not step into the Cirelli apartment. Had something gone wrong? Mouw wondered. Were the informers misinformed? Did a vigilant neighbor spot the FBI entry into the apartment? Did some sixth-sense warn Gotti that the apartment had become dangerous?

At 8:00 P.M., on November 30, 1989, the suspense ended. At the recording room at FBI headquarters, a bored agent was suddenly all ears. For the first time, sounds were coming from the Cirelli apartment. The apartment door creaked open and the voices of John Gotti, his consigliere Salvatore Gravano, and underboss Frank Locascio could be heard distinctly.

Listening to that evening's conversation through headphones the next day, Mouw's spirits soared. "As they started talking, Frankie Locascio turned on the radio in the apartment," Mouw recalled. "John said, 'It's too loud; turn it down.'" Locascio, taking a routine step used by mobsters to foil law-enforcement bugs, had turned the radio on full volume. But Gotti was hard of hearing in one ear, and Mouw realized that was the reason he wanted the radio off. "It was a big, lucky thing for us," Mouw added. "There was no background noise, no ambient sound, and John wanted everyone to talk loud."

Part of the discussion was Gotti's praise of himself, how his takeover of the Gambinos had been welcomed by the other Mob families. He related a conversation with Joseph "Jo Jo" Corozzo, a Gambino capo.

GOTTI: ". . . You know what Jo Jo told me outside in the car, today? We were standing about fifteen, twenty blocks from the other guy. He says to me, 'You know, John,' he says, 'let me tell you,' he says, 'I never was so proud, so happy in my whole life,' he says. 'I knew,' he said, 'I was talking with a few skippers [capos] from another family.' He says, 'Since youse are here, this is the first time that they could remember, in years, that the families ain't arguing.' Nobody's arguing." (clapping sound).

GRAVANO: "Right."

GOTTI: "None of the families are arguing with nobody. . . . Everybody's sedate."

The discussion then turned to Paul Castellano's murder. Gotti talked about Castellano's incessant demands to hear the government tapes that implicated Angelo Ruggiero and Gene Gotti in narcotics trafficking. Gotti's words seemingly supported the FBI theory of the motive behind Castellano's murder: that Gotti feared Big Paul planned to "hit" him because of Ruggiero's refusal to let Castellano hear the incriminating tapes.

GOTTI: "He [Castellano] couldn't succeed because, Sam, he felt, and you know what we heard, 'He felt he hadda hit me first.' But, if he hits me first, he blows the guy who really led the [narcotics trafficking] ring, Angelo and them. Supposedly. That's the guy on the tapes."

GRAVANO: "I think he would've hit Angelo and not you."

GOTTI: "Nah!"

Gotti's hatred of the dead boss was evident. He denounced Castellano as a "rat motherfucker" who had divided the family. His final comment about Castellano's murder mystified agents who were certain he had masterminded the assassination. "But, anyway, here's a guy, whoever done it, probably the cops done it to this fuckin' guy. Whoever killed this cocksucker, probably the cops killed this Paul. But whoever killed him . . . he deserved it."

On the evening of December 12, Gotti was alone in the apartment with Locascio. To agents Gotti's words that night were better than a signed confession. He described himself as a Mafia "boss," and reviewed some payoffs that he got as a godfather. And most damaging to himself, he admitted authorizing at least three murders.

The first murder that he discussed was that of Robert DiB DiBernardo, an original member of the Fist, the select group that had conspired to eliminate

Paul Castellano. Gotti outlined to Locascio that while he was in detention, awaiting trial in the Brooklyn RICO case in 1986, he was told "a story" that DiBernardo was criticizing him to other wiseguys. However, he was now dubious about his lieutenants' claims that DiBernardo was "subversive" and had bad-mouthed him.

"When DiB got whacked, they told me a story. I was in jail when they whacked him. I knew why it was being done. I allowed it to be done, anyway."

He attributed the second murder partly to his reliance on Sammy the Bull Gravano. The victim, a Gambino soldier named Louis DiBono, had a history of disputes with Gravano over the division of profits from construction rackets. Gotti suspected that Gravano had personal reasons for wanting DiBono killed. In retrospect, he believed that Sammy had lied about DiBono's cheating him and the Gambino administration. Even if he doubted Gravano, Gotti said, he wanted DiBono eliminated for another reason: he had defied Gotti's summons to appear for a showdown session.

"Louie DiBono," Gotti continued. "You know why he's dying? He's gonna die because he refused to come in when I called. He didn't do nothing else wrong."

For good measure, Gotti implicated himself in a third murder that he had approved. In a virtually unbroken monologue to Locascio, he dropped the name of the victim, a Gambino soldier from the Castellano faction named Liborio "Louie" Milito. A former partner of Gravano's on hits and in profitable construction projects, Milito had fallen out of favor and was seen by Gotti as a disobedient malcontent.

That night in the Cirelli apartment, Gotti also was peeved at Gravano's construction-industry deals. Expressing his concern that Gravano was using construction rackets to mold a private power base inside the family, Gotti raged, "You're creating an army inside an army. You know what I'm saying, Frankie?"

"End up creating another faction," Locascio chimed in.

"That's right," Gotti shouted back.

Ticking off his complaints about Gravano, Gotti implied that Sammy the Bull was fomenting unnecessary murders of his illicit business partners. "Every fucking time I turn around there's a new company popping up. And every time we got a partner that don't agree with us, we kill him." Obviously wound up about Gravano's plans, Gotti added, "And, I tell him a million times, 'Sammy, slow it down. Pull it in a fuckin' notch. Slow it down! You, you, you come up with fifteen companies, for Christ sake! You got rebars [metal rods]; you got concrete pouring; you got Italian floors now. You got construction; you got dry-wall; you got asbestos; you got rugs. What the fuck next?'"

Insisting that he was not acquisitive, Gotti nevertheless asked, "Where's my piece of these companies?" He said that while remanded to jail during Diane Giacalone's RICO case, he was delighted that Gravano and other earn-ers gave him ten percent of a new drywall construction scam they had origi-nated. "They sent me word in jail that you got ten percent. Guy did nothin' in his life; a fuckin' jerk like me. Best I ever did was go on a few hijackings. Never had nothing in my life. You're telling me, I got ten percent of a million-dollar business."

Relating details about his shares of the family's rackets, Gotti said he used his brother Peter to collect some of his payoffs, about $10,000 a month from one company. Without giving specific amounts, Gotti talked about booty he received from sources besides Gravano. "Well, let me put it this way, Frankie. I was getting X amount of moneys the day I became the boss when he [Gravano] had nothing to do with this." Another item that Gotti mentioned was a surprise contribution from his capos. "He turned in sixty-three thousand was my birth-day money. Youse gave that to me as a birthday present."

The tapes in Mrs. Cirelli's apartment began whirring as Gotti prepared to go on trial in state court for the shooting of the carpenters' union leader John O'Connor. Publicly Gotti glowed with confidence, telling reporters that he would escape unscathed on the assault charges. But on January 4, 1990, as the trial was about to start, he was evidently deeply worried. That night in the Cirelli apartment, the Teflon Don was planning for the future in the event he was convicted. His discussions gave the FBI a tape replete with evidence that he controlled a RICO enterprise with the authority to appoint the hierarchy and to induct members.

At first, Gotti was alone in the Cirelli apartment with Gravano, and Gotti was now full of admiration for him, contrary to the concerns he had expressed several weeks earlier to Frank Locascio. In fact, he was designating Sammy the Bull to replace him if he were imprisoned again.

GOTTI: "Hopefully, we got time. Tomorrow I wanna call all our skippers [capos] in. I'm gonna tell them: 'I'm the *representante* till I say different. Soon as anything happens to me, I'm off the streets, Sammy is the acting boss. He's our consigliere.' . . . So, I'm asking you how you feel. You wanna stay as con-sigliere? Or you want me to make you official underboss? Acting boss? How do you feel? What makes you feel better? Think about it tonight."

Without waiting for an answer, Gotti expressed doubts that Frankie Loc Locascio could handle the assignment as competently as Gravano. Saying, "I love Frankie," Gotti nonetheless wanted Gravano to succeed him as the head of the gang.

"I'm going to make our skippers understand that," Gotti went on. "This is my wishes that if, if I'm in the fucking can, this family is gonna be run by Sammy. I'm still the boss. If I get fifty years, I know what I gotta do. But when I'm in the can, Sammy's in charge."

A list of candidates for membership in the Gambino borgata was on Gotti's agenda that night. Looking over the wannabes, Gotti cited his priorities. "All right, let me tell you what, Sam. I wanna throw a few names out, five or six. I'm not. I'm trying not to make people (inaudible). I want guys that done more than killing."

Joined by Locascio (whose son was a mafioso), Gotti seemed discouraged by the difficulties of finding able new soldiers. Demographic changes were hampering the Mafia's traditional recruitment program. Solidly Italian-American neighborhoods were disappearing as residents moved to the widely scattered suburbs, and a better-educated generation of young men were opting for lives as legitimate professionals rather than swaggering mafiosi. The mobster talent pool was shrinking.

"And where are we gonna find them, these kinda guys?" Gotti asked rhetorically. "Frank, I'm not being a pessimist. It's gettin' tougher, not easier! We got everything that's any good. Look around, ask your son someday, forget who you are, what you are. Talk to your son like his age. Put yourself in his age bracket, and let him tell you what good kids in the neighborhood other than the kids that are with you. . . . You know what I'm trying to say? I told you a couple of weeks ago, we got the only few pockets of good kids left."

More proof that Gotti was an absolute ruler came from an admission that he had paid $300,000 to lawyers handling the appeals of his former underboss Joe Piney Armone and consigliere Joe N. Gallo. He was outraged at the fees paid to Bruce Cutler and Gerald Shargel, the lawyers in the O'Connor assault case. "Where does it end? Gambino crime family? This is the Shargel, Cutler, and whattya-call-it crime family. You wanna go steal? You and your fuckin' mother."

Gotti told Gravano and Locascio that in a talk with Cutler, the lawyer had complained that he was making him "an errand boy" by requiring him to find out if another "pinch" was coming down. "We're making you an errand boy," Gotti countered. "High-priced errand boy. Bruce, worse yet."

He concluded by belittling the lawyers for trying to butter him up with pledges of loyalty. "They got a routine now, the two lawyers. Muck and Fuck I call them. When I see Bruce, 'Hi, Gerry loves you,' he says. 'He's in your corner one hundred percent.' When I see Gerry, 'Hi, Bruce loves you. He's in your corner a hundred percent.' I know youse both love me? Both fuckin' (inaudible). I didn't think (laughter) dumb fucks, you know?"

On January 14, 1990, Gotti was upbeat, confident that if he were acquitted at the O'Connor trial he would never be prosecuted again. "They can't take no more punishment, Sammy," he said to Gravano. "Not if I win this one. If I lose this one, forget about it. But if I win this one, how the fuck could they, you know, they'd be punchy. This like you keep fighting the guy, he keeps knocking you out in the first round. What you kidding, he could last the second round? *Minchia!* (Gullible idiot)."

Even as his conversations were being secretly recorded, the threat of government wiretaps and bugs obsessed Gotti. Electronic surveillance was on his mind as he met on January 24 with Gravano and Locascio. He had to admit that he had been a prime offender, that his own words from bugs at the Bergin Club were the primary evidence against him in the O'Connor case. "I'm sick that we were so fucking naive. Me, number one."

To thwart the government, he wanted everyone in the family warned that loose lips would be severely punished. "And from now on," he said, "I'm telling you if a guy just so mentions 'La' or if wants to say, 'La, la, la, la.' He just says 'La,' the guy, I'm gonna strangle the cocksucker. You know what I mean? He don't have to say, 'Cosa Nostra,' just 'La,' and they go."

A few minutes later, Gotti seemed worried that his ongoing trial and possible conviction might encourage dissidents in the family. In fact, he had a report of one soldier's disloyalty. Without identifying the culprit, Gotti had a solution for anyone who defied him. "And he's gotta get whacked! Because he's getting the same, for the same reason that Jelly Belly's getting it. You wanna, you wanna challenge the administration? Well, we'll meet the challenge. And you're going, you motherfucker." (Jelly Belly was a reference to the 300-pound Gambino soldier Louis DiBono who was gunned down in his parked car in an underground garage at the World Trade Center.)

In winter months, conferring was measurably more comfortable and convenient fot Gotti in the Cirelli apartment than walk-talks in the frosty streets. But in mid-January, Gotti received a hint that the cozy apartment might have been detected by the government. The alert apparently stemmed from the overlapping and rival investigations of Gotti by prosecutors in the Southern and Eastern Districts. Walter Mack, a federal prosecutor in Manhattan's Southern District, was investigating the Castellano-Bilotti murders at Sparks Steak House. A reluctant witness before the grand jury was Jimmy Brown Failla, a Gambino capo who had been waiting for Castellano inside the restaurant on the murder night. After the grand jury session, Failla reported to Gotti that he had been questioned if he had ever met with Gotti, and where. That question about meeting places, though not specifically about an apartment, was an alarm signal that helped persuade Gotti to discontinue using the apartment.

The question about meeting sites displayed the lack of cooperation and communications between separate law-enforcement agencies investigating Gotti. Within the FBI and the Eastern District prosecutor's staff, only a small number of people knew about the breakthrough bug in the Cirelli apartment. Because the FBI and the Eastern District were withholding information from the Southern District, Walter Mack's questions to Failla might have inadvertently tipped off Gotti to the possibility the apartment was under surveillance.

Although Gotti was avoiding the Cirelli apartment, Andrew Maloney, the Eastern District U.S. Attorney, and Bruce Mouw, the Gambino Squad honcho, were certain Gotti had already talked himself into an ironclad conviction. After four years of seeking a smoking gun to get Gotti, Maloney believed he had been given a thundering cannon.

Maloney's choice for lead prosecutor to construct the courtroom case was John Gleeson, the assistant to Diane Giacalone in the 1986 RICO trial in which Gotti had been acquitted. Giacalone had left the office, but Gleeson had blossomed from an untried novice into a superb litigator. The quasi-independent federal Organized Crime Strike Forces had been phased out by 1990, and Maloney, with total oversight for all Mafia indictments, had put Gleeson in charge of the Cosa Nostra section. Thin, wearing tortoiseshell glasses, and cloaked in an academic demeanor, Gleeson had won a string of Mafia convictions that impressed the Mob's lawyers. Respectful of his quick mind, legal skills, and concise summations, opposition lawyers had nicknamed Gleeson "the Jesuit." The prospect of indicting and convicting Gotti offered the thirty-seven-year-old Gleeson a rare second chance to atone for the Eastern District's earlier courtroom debacle with Gotti and his fiercely combative lawyers.

Armed with tapes from five crucial meetings in the Cirelli apartment and from several bugged hallway conferences in the Ravenite building, Gleeson had to gather the FBI's video and still photos and witnesses to flesh out the evidence and put it into logical context. Meanwhile, in the summer and fall of 1990, Maloney was battling on another front: the perennial jurisdictional quagmire and rivalries with the U.S. Attorney's office in the Southern District. Maloney thought he had worked out an agreement in 1987 with Rudolph Giuliani that the Eastern District in Brooklyn would handle a Gotti RICO case and the Southern District in Manhattan would take on the Castellano-Bilotti assassinations. Under the Hit Man's Statute, the U.S. Attorney Otto Obermaier, who had succeeded Giuliani, was still seeking a federal indictment on the Sparks murders jointly with Manhattan DA Robert Morgenthau.

After preliminary feelers from Maloney about whether the murder or the RICO case should be tried first, Obermaier and Morgenthau offered another plan. They proposed to consolidate both cases into one broad RICO trial in Manhattan, in the Southern District. They contended that there was more valid jurisdiction in the Southern District since the Ravenite building tapes had been obtained in Manhattan and the most shocking crime—the gunning down of Castellano—occurred in that borough.

"After we had put together a strong RICO case," Maloney complained, "I outlined our facts to the Southern District. We didn't want the Castellano murder case in the RICO indictment; it wasn't that strong. But no good deed goes unpunished. Obermaier and Morgenthau suddenly wanted the whole enchilada. They wanted the headline part of the case—the RICO part."

The dispute could only be settled by the Justice Department's brass, and in November 1990, the warring districts debated the issue before their superiors in Washington. Obermaier was accompanied by the widely respected Morgenthau—a former U.S. Attorney in the Southern District for ten years—whose views could sway the Washington bureaucracy. Morgenthau supported Obermaier's main points that the Southern District judges were better qualified than those across the river in Brooklyn, and less likely to be bulldozed by the militant lawyers Gotti was certain to retain. Another weakness in the Eastern District, Morgenthau and Obermaier contended, was a vulnerable pool of jurors. Gotti and the Gambino family had a history of attempting to corrupt or intimidate juries.

In rebuttal, Maloney countered that the two courthouses were barely a mile apart. "Gotti can just as easily find a way to fix a case in Manhattan as in Brooklyn," Maloney told the Justice Department executives. Stressing that his office had prepared the entire RICO case—the heart of the pending indictment—he was irate. "What chutzpah these people have to come in and ask for someone else's work!"

Prepared for Obermaier and Morgenthau's criticisms of Eastern District juries, John Gleeson had a formula to forestall jury tampering. The scholarly prosecutor had composed an intensive questionnaire for potential jurors that would eliminate anyone remotely connected to the Mob or susceptible to its persuasion. Additionally, the prosecution would move to have the jury sequestered for the entire trial, guarded by U.S. Marshals, and therefore out of the reach of Gotti's hirelings.

Two weeks later, Maloney received an 8:00 A.M. call at his Westchester County home from Robert S. Mueller III, administrator of the Justice Department's Criminal Division. "We're going with you guys," Mueller said. It was a green light for the Eastern District although Mueller wanted Maloney to fold the Castellano-Bilotti murders into the indictment, extend a large measure of credit to the Southern District, and allow its prosecutors to participate in the trial.

Reflecting on the jurisdictional squabble, Maloney believes behind-the-scene endorsements from knowledgeable FBI agents influenced the Justice Department's decisions. Gleeson's strong presentation of his strategy for convicting Gotti and his plans for safeguarding the jury helped win the day. Privately, Maloney told aides that he would have resigned if the RICO trial had been turned over to the Southern District.

Maloney, however, looked askance at incorporating the Sparks murders in the indictment. Direct evidence against Gotti was thin at best, and Maloney evaluated the police department's investigation as full of gaping holes. The Southern District had counted primarily on circumstantial evidence and two witnesses. A passerby claimed he had seen Gotti on the sidewalk near the murder scene, looking at his watch and peering at the restaurant. It was a nighttime identification that Maloney feared would be shredded by defense lawyers. The second witness was Philip Leonetti, the turncoat Philadelphia Mob underboss, who would testify that Gotti had admitted to him that he had stage-managed Castellano's assassination. But Maloney doubted that uncorroborated evidence from Leonetti, who had obtained a leniency deal with the government, was sufficient to link Gotti to the crime.

Moreover, the defense would surely have a field day with Gotti's taped statement in the Cirelli apartment that the police had killed Castellano. Maloney viewed Gotti's cracks about the murders as an absurd joke, but they would give a jury a reason against convicting him on that count, and thereby soil the entire

RICO case. "The Castellano murder doesn't belong in the indictment. But we have to eat it for bureaucratic reasons. That's the price we have to pay to Washington for getting jurisdiction," Maloney reasoned.

The proud Southern District office rejected Maloney's offer of a junior partnership in the RICO trial in a Brooklyn courtroom. With the jurisdictional underbrush cleared away, Gleeson obtained a sealed indictment in November 1990 against the entire Gambino regime—John Gotti, Salvatore Gravano, and Frank Locascio. Although Gotti appeared composed and unruffled during his daytime business and nighttime social pursuits, by the autumn of 1990 he was aware of the imminent clash with the government. All he had to do was pick up a newspaper or turn on his television set to find out that the prosecutors' turf contests had been settled. News leaks warned that a plethora of new accusations would be aimed at him. Bruce Cutler boldly announced in November, "We're ready for them," acknowledging that another showdown loomed.

Bruce Mouw wanted the trio of Gambino leaders corralled in simultaneous raids as soon as they were indicted. Press reports, however, created a hitch in Mouw's plan. Uncertain who else might be accused along with him, Gotti ordered Gravano to go on the lam. Gotti had recently promoted Sammy the Bull to underboss and switched Locascio to consigliere. That way, whether or not Gravano was indicted, he would be free to supervise the family while Gotti almost assuredly would be locked up without bail awaiting trial. Following orders, Gravano grew a beard and hid out in his father-in-law's vacation house in the Pocono Mountains, and then in southern Florida. With weeks going by and nothing happening, a more relaxed Gotti lowered his guard and recalled Gravano for a summit meeting. It was scheduled for the night of Tuesday, December 11, at the Ravenite. After fruitlessly searching for a sign of Gravano, FBI agents in their observation post two blocks from the Ravenite saw him enter the club about 6 P.M. Frank Locascio also was there. Minutes later, Gotti arrived in his Mercedes, and over a walkie-talkie Mouw signaled George Gabriel, the Gotti case agent, to apprehend the indicted Gambino leaders in a single raid.

About thirty Gambino soldiers and wannabes were in the club and outside on the pavement when the agents rushed in, ready to snap handcuffs on Gotti and his two highest generals. There were murmurs and expletives from Gotti's bodyguards and stooges, but no resistance as Gabriel read the defendants their Miranda rights. Still exhibiting his authority and insouciance, Gotti ordered Norman Dupont, the club gofer, to pour cups of espresso laced with anisette for him and the other two arrested big shots. Mouw arrived as Gotti, seated at his usual table, nonchalantly sipped coffee. Picking up the club's phone, Mouw called Lewis Schiliro, the FBI's organized-crime supervisor at the bureau's New York headquarters. "I'm in the Ravenite," Mouw reported as calmly as he could. "We just arrested Gotti and his pals Gravano and Locascio. Everything's cool."

The three Gambino overlords, their hands cuffed behind them, were led separately into waiting cars by a detachment of agents and detectives for the short ride to FBI headquarters, where they would be booked and fingerprinted. As usual, Gotti dominated the fashion scene. Draped in a dark cashmere overcoat with a striking yellow scarf flapping around his neck, Gotti smiled serenely as he left for a jail cell. Bent over, the pudgy consigliere, Frankie Loc Locascio, exhibited his rage, cursing and scowling at the agents as he was taken away. Dressed in his customary austere work clothes of jeans, a white T-shirt, and a leather windbreaker, underboss Salvatore Gravano made no pretense of defiant resistance. Of the three, however, the only one who looked shocked, downcast, and disheartened was Sammy the Bull.

37

"I Want to Switch Governments"

The morning after their arrest, the big-three Gambino leaders, looking haggard and sleep-deprived, got their first inkling of the magnitude of the charges leveled against them. At a joint arraignment, Gotti and his codefendants Gravano and Locascio were indicted as leaders of a Mafia enterprise and on a gamut of thirteen RICO counts, including murder, conspiracy to commit three murders, illegal gambling, loan-sharking, obstruction of justice, and income-tax evasion. Gotti alone was indicted on the most sensational charge, participating in the Castellano-Bilotti homicides.

Ten days later, all three were hit with a real shocker: the disclosure that their private conversations in Nettie Cirelli's apartment had been recorded by the FBI. At a hearing closed to the public, John Gleeson moved to deny them bail as high-risk and dangerous defendants. To reinforce his point, Gleeson played portions of the tapes in which Gotti spoke about his reasons for authorizing hits on three Gambino members, Robert DiBernardo, Louis DiBono, and Liborio Milito. The sinister colloquies gave Federal District Court Judge I. Leo Glasser abundant grounds to order the three men detained without bail for the duration of the trial.

One tape was the long parley between Gotti and Locascio on December 12,

1989. It staggered Sammy the Bull. He heard Gotti heap scorn on him for prospering from construction-industry scams, and revile him for building his own rival Mob power bases. Even more ominous-sounding to Sammy's chances of acquittal were Gotti's remarks pinning the blame for a multitude of murders on him alone; supposedly the slayings were committed to resolve Sammy's financial disputes with Mafia business partners.

Another body blow to the defense soon followed when Judge Glasser disqualified Bruce Cutler as Gotti's trial lawyer, and Gerald Shargel as Gravano's. Bugged conversations between the attorneys and Gotti in the hallway behind the Ravenite Club gave Gleeson, a tenacious prosecutor, grounds for removing them on conflict-of-interest issues.

Other tapes indicated that Gotti had covertly paid the two lawyers fees for the defense of several Gambino family clients, thereby, in the prosecutor's words, making them "house lawyers" for the Mob. Gotti also was heard suggesting that he made under-the-table payments. "If they [the authorities] wanna really break Bruce Cutler's balls, what did he get paid off me," Gotti said to Frank Locascio. ". . . I paid tax on thirty-six thousand. What could I have paid him?"

Judge Glasser ruled that the transcribed conversations between Gotti and the lawyers, and references to Cutler and Shargel on the tapes, had turned them into potential witnesses. He declared that the attorneys had compromised themselves in the obstruction-of-justice charges that were part of the indictment. Glasser's elimination of the lawyers unsettled Gravano more than it did Gotti. In 1986, Shargel, a lawyer for numerous mobsters, had won an acquittal for Gravano in a million-dollar tax-evasion complaint. With deep faith in Shargel's skills, Gravano had counted heavily on his handpicked lawyer to extricate him from the RICO morass.

Believing that their chances of beating the charges were dismal, Gravano grew desperate enough to contemplate an escape from their cells on the eleventh floor of the federal Metropolitan Correction Center (the MCC) in Lower Manhattan. He reasoned that a jail breakout would be easier than busting out of a maximum-security penitentiary. His plan was to bribe guards to smuggle in ropes, and with help from accomplices on the outside, they would descend through a window. Gotti sneered at the idea as too reckless; he was leery of rappelling eleven stories on a rope. He had a different escape route. "Somewhere down the road," he told Gravano, "we'll put together $4 million or $5 million, bribe the president, and get a pardon." He reminded Gravano that Jimmy Hoffa, the corrupt and mobbed-up teamsters' union president, had pulled off a similar trick. In 1971 Hoffa's long sentence was commuted after he arranged contributions and political support for President Nixon's reelection campaign. Gravano thought "a window was a better shot" than counting on a presidential pardon or commutation, but he could not override Gotti's veto. In the same cell block, the two gangsters were drifting apart. Gravano had served in the army, and he was disgusted by Gotti's unpatriotic comments during the 1991 Gulf War. Watching television news at the MCC, Gotti said that in revenge for the government's campaign against him and the Mafia, he hoped America would be defeated by Iraq.

Gravano also brooded over Gotti's disparaging him behind his back in the taped meeting with Locascio. He had viewed himself as an unquestioning, loyal consigliere and underboss to Gotti. Although he had turned over about $2 million a year of his own illicit earnings to Gotti, the recordings exposed Gotti's resentment and jealousy of Gravano. Sammy's disenchantment mounted during their ten months in close quarters, listening to Gotti's daily bluster and self-admiration. He became convinced that Gotti was fashioning a strategy to save himself by directing the defense lawyers to imply at the trial that Gravano—not Gotti—was really the criminal brain behind the string of murders and other felonies. Gotti's edicts to the new legal team kept Gravano in the dark about the prosecution's most critical evidence. He refused to allow Gravano and Locascio to hear the prosecution's tapes, read the transcripts, or meet privately with their own lawyers. Finally, Gotti rejected Gravano's request for separate trials as the best hope that one of them might beat the rap and be liberated to preserve the Gambino family. According to Gravano's account, Gotti offered an egomaniacal reason for opposing a trial severance. "It's not about me now," Gotti told Gravano in a cell block tête-à-tête. "Everything has to be to save Cosa Nostra, which is John Gotti. Cosa Nostra needs John Gotti. You got a problem with that?"

Sammy did have a problem with that. He and Locascio both resented Gotti's demeaning treatment of them, and they conspired on steps they would take if, by some miracle, they beat the charges against them. "At one point, Frankie and I agreed to kill John," Gravano recounted. In the early fall of 1991, a jail visit by Gravano's brother-in-law, Edward Garafola, planted in Sammy the Bull's mind a radical solution. Garafola proposed that Gravano defect and become a cooperating witness for the government.

Betray or be betrayed were Sammy the Bull's alternatives. Gravano's self-interest was clear. He would desert the Mob. "I was disgusted with the whole thing," he later testified, saying he could no longer stomach Gotti's arrogance or abide by Cosa Nostra's strictures.

Through his wife, Debra, Gravano sent a message to Frank Spero and Matthew Tricorico, the FBI agents on the Gambino Squad who had been investigating him for several years. The startled agents learned from Debra that Sammy wanted to discuss a deal. One day in October, after a routine pretrial appearance at the courthouse in Brooklyn, Gravano was secreted through back corridors to a confidential meeting. Waiting for him were prosecutor John Gleeson and the FBI's Bruce Mouw. "I want to switch governments," Gravano said calmly.

Having sized up Gravano during eleven months of pretrial sessions, the prosecutors and agents had evaluated him as the least-likely mobster to crack. "He's the toughest guy in the courtroom," Gleeson thought. "He has a gangster's bearing about him. He looks more intimidating and menacing than anyone else." If Gleeson had bet on a defector, he would have chosen Frank Locascio as most vulnerable. Tears had welled in Locascio's eyes when a judge refused to temporarily release him on bail to visit with his gravely ill mother. "He's not acting like a wiseguy but like a regular person," Gleeson conceded.

A cooperation agreement proposed by Gleeson obligated Gravano to disclose his entire criminal history and all his knowledge of crimes committed by mobsters in the Gambino and other families. Most important, he would be cast as the main witness against his former hierarchy soul mates, Gotti and Locascio. His reward was Gleeson's promise that, in return for a guilty plea to a reduced RICO count and his aid in convicting Mob rulers, the government would recommend a maximum sentence of twenty years; he had been facing a RICO term of life without parole. Gravano wanted an even shorter sentence, but Gleeson would not budge. The turncoat negotiated one concession: his mandatory use as a Mafia trial witness was capped at indictments obtained within two years after his defection; after that deadline he could not be compelled to testify. He argued that the provision would allow him to lead a more normal life once he was released from prison.

Gravano also wanted exemptions from testifying against former friends in his old Brooklyn crew and against relatives. The government refused to make that concession in writing, but in effect granted it to him; he was never called as a prosecution witness against pals from that crew or any of his relatives.

News that John Gotti's right-hand man had defected was electrifying to the small number of prosecutors and agents let in on the secret. Sammy the Bull was the highest-ranking Mafia mobster ever to flip and to agree to testify. Inveterately suspicious of the devious Gotti, Andrew Maloney, the U.S. Attorney, and several agents wondered if Gravano's bid was genuine. "It's unheard of," Maloney cautioned his top aides. "The underboss of a major family testifying against his boss? Is he for real, or is this some kind of setup manipulated by Gotti?" Maloney's greatest concern was a double-cross: Gravano would step into the witness box, recant all his incriminating admissions, and undermine the prosecution's carefully wrought structure.

At midnight on November 8, 1991, Bruce Mouw, George Gabriel, and the two agents who had bird-dogged Gravano, Frank Spero and Matthew Tricorico, arrived unannounced at the MCC with documents authorizing the transfer of a prisoner into their custody. "You want us to bring down John Gotti?" asked a guard, misreading the court papers. "No. No," an alarmed Gabriel said forcefully. "Salvatore Gravano." Less than an hour after Gravano's departure, a guard, probably courting favors from Gotti, woke him in his cell. The news whispered into Gotti's ear was a thunderbolt: his underboss had been removed by the FBI. The midnight transfer, Gotti knew, meant only one thing: Sammy the Bull had become a rat.

That night, surrounded by a convoy of agents, Gravano was taken to an FBI "safe house," a motel in Long Island, for preliminary questioning. The next day, he was transported to the FBI training academy in Quantico, Virginia, for extensive debriefings. Gleeson, Maloney, and Mouw were quickly relieved to learn Gravano's defection was authentic, not a devilish Gotti trap. Retracing his underworld life, Gravano cleared up a miscellany of violent felonies that otherwise would have gone unsolved. He also alerted them to ongoing Mafia deals and activities. Indicted for three murders, Gravano stunned his questioners by confessing to participating in sixteen others, all unsolved. Maintaining that he had pulled the deadly trigger in only one of the nineteen Mob rubouts, Gravano rationalized that he had been an onlooker, not a serial killer. "Sometimes I was a shooter. Sometimes I was a backup guy. Sometimes I set the guy up. Sometimes I just talked about it."

The centerpiece of his revelations was the execution of Paul Castellano and Tommy Bilotti outside Sparks Steak House. Gravano had not been implicated in the double slaying, but he nevertheless provided inside details of the conspiracy, the planning, and the identity of the assassination team. His interrogators were astonished to learn that he and Gotti were at the scene, sitting in a parked car, watching the murder drama unfold. Moreover, he presented a radically different version of the slayings than the prosecution had pieced together for the trial.

"You guys had it all wrong," Gravano told Gleeson. "We never got out of the car." Standing in the street would have been too dangerous, Gravano added, because Castellano might have recognized them and fled before he was way-laid by the assassins. Gravano's portrayal of the murder scene disqualified a mys-tery witness who was ready to testify that he had spotted Gotti on the sidewalk outside of Sparks. Based on Gravano's evidence, the prosecutors speculated that the witness honestly misidentified one of the actual gunmen, Vincent "Vinnie" Artuso, who resembled Gotti physically.

In addition to the Sparks murders, Gravano gave a firsthand account of Gotti's takeover and actions as boss of the Gambino family for five years. His testimony solidified the cornerstone charge that Gotti was the emperor of a RICO enterprise. Another gift for the prosecution and the FBI was Gravano's disclosure of the jury-fixing in Brooklyn at Gotti's first RICO trial and acquittal in 1986. He provided the complete picture of how, with the help of the Westies gang, he had transmitted a $60,000 bribe to a juror in the case prosecuted by Diane Giacalone.

Sammy the Bull's incisive knowledge of previously unknown details required drastic changes in the prosecution's original trial scenario. As lead prosecutor, Gleeson spent two hectic months reconfiguring the game plan for convincing a jury to convict John Gotti. For relaxation during the countless debriefings at Quantico, the macho but hypertense Gravano jogged three to five miles daily and mixed it up in the boxing ring with younger and stronger FBI agents.

From day one—the outset of jury selection in January 1992—Gotti's persona dominated the courtroom atmosphere. His reputation, as America's premier gangster and the Justice Department's most-wanted mafioso, drew a cross sec-tion of the national and international press to the event. It was Gotti's fourth trial in five years. The stakes were high. An acquittal would be a demoralizing defeat for the government, fortifying the Teflon Don's reputation for invincibil-ity and possibly immunizing him forever from further prosecutions.

John Gotti, of course, flagrantly displayed his arrogance and contempt for his opponents. He glared defiantly at Judge Glasser, as if to mentally disquiet and bully him. Outside the presence of the jury, in audible stage whispers, he spewed profanities at the prosecutors. During one recess, Peter Bowles, a re-porter for the newspaper *Newsday*, heard him label the judge and the prosecu-tors "faggots" with "unwashed hair." Eyeing Gleeson, he stage-whispered that the prosecutor was conducting "a vendetta" against him, muttering to Locascio that Gleeson was obsessed with him and could concentrate on no other person. "I'm his only defendant. He wakes up in the morning and says to his wife, 'Hi ya, John.'" Often when Gleeson walked near the defense table, Gotti snarled, "Your wife's a junkie," an absurd allusion to Gleeson's wife, a nurse who presumedly had access to drugs in the course of her work.

Another prosecutor, James Orenstein, was tagged by Gotti as "that Christ killer," obviously because he was Jewish. On other occasions, Gotti openly called an FBI agent "a fucking scum bag," and Maloney "a fucking bum." In a totally inappropriate literary metaphor, he pointed to the well-built, muscular agent George Gabriel, mocking him as "Little Lord Fauntleroy."

Generally viewed as a fair-minded and firm judge, Glasser, the former dean of Brooklyn Law School, put a stop to the high-jinks that Gotti and his lawyers had pulled off in previous trials. Any more unruliness, the judge warned, and Gotti would be removed from the courtroom and forced to watch the proceedings over closed-circuit television. Gotti's courtroom antics ended.

Replacing Bruce Cutler in the courtroom was Albert Krieger, a highly respected trial attorney from Miami, a former president of the National Association of Criminal Defense Lawyers. The tall, bald Krieger, who resembled the actor Yul Brynner, was a masterful cross-examiner, but his gregariousness irritated Gotti. Observing Krieger chatting during a break with Maloney, Gotti motioned imperiously for his lawyer to stop talking with the enemy. "I better end this or I'll wind up in the trunk of a car," said Krieger, winking at Maloney.

Gotti also occasionally exhibited a light-hearted spirit. One afternoon Maloney informed Krieger that Thomas Gambino, the son of the late Don Carlo, had just worked out a deal with the Manhattan DA's prosecutors. In a plea-arrangement on charges that as one of Gotti's premier capos he illegally controlled much of the Garment Center's trucking business, Tommy agreed to pay a $12 million fine. He also agreed to relinquish his trucking routes in the center. The quid pro quo for Gambino was that he escaped serving a day in prison by pleading guilty to a reduced state racketeering complaint.

After Krieger whispered the news to Gotti, the lawyer returned to Maloney with a message: "Tell Maloney, I'll take the same deal for $20 million any time."

Fears that Gotti's leg breakers would again try to pressure the jury led to unprecedented measures. For the first time in the Eastern District, a jury was sequestered for a lengthy trial and lodged in hotels. Extraordinary security was imposed to shield the twelve jurors and four alternates, whose identities and addresses were withheld from both the prosecution and the defense. Guarded around the clock by marshals, the jurors were prohibited for the duration of the trial from seeing any visitors, even relatives, and all their telephone calls were monitored.

Every day a fan club of Gotti's relatives and acolytes packed one side of the walnut-paneled courtroom, gazing admiringly at him. On the opening trial date, outside the courthouse in downtown Brooklyn, Gotti's minions picketed, carrying placards, reading, "We Love You, John." Accompanying the demonstrators, a sound truck blared encomiums to him as if he were a candidate running for office. Hollywood's Anthony Quinn and Mickey Rourke, who often played fictional tough guys, and other show business personalities were invited by Gotti's retinue to join his rooting section as a subtle ploy to influence the jury. The actors waved at Gotti and wished him luck. "We better get Clint Eastwood to support our side," Maloney quipped, aware of the public relations program launched on Gotti's behalf.

Beginning with his opening statement, Gleeson unveiled a graphic canvas of crimes that, the prosecution alleged, proved Gotti's massive violations of the RICO law. The prosecutor traced the major elements of the case: Gotti's role as a capo; the daring preemptive plot to kill Castellano; Gotti's surfacing as Gambino boss; and the murders and other acts subsequently committed at his behest. Much of Gleeson's evidence was woven from eight years of electronic bugging by state investigators and the FBI. Carried back into time, the jury heard Gotti conversing in his private office next to the Bergin Club, in Aniello Dellacroce's home, and—most damaging to Gotti—in the hallway outside the Ravenite Club and in Mrs. Cirelli's apartment.

In the early stages of the trial, an impassive Gotti outwardly ignored the proceedings. He was forced to listen to six hours of incriminating tapes played over speakers in the courtroom, but he declined to don head phones to hear the conversations more clearly. To establish dates and to prove who was present when the eavesdropping occurred, the prosecution showed video and still photos of mobsters entering and leaving the Ravenite. Sometimes, when the pictures flashed on a huge screen, Gotti turned his back, as if to indicate that they were meaningless to him. Perhaps he finally realized the damage caused by his inflexible order that capos and important soldiers pay frequent homage to him at the Ravenite. Those visits had boomeranged and were now fortifying evidence that he was a Mafia boss.

The only time Gotti totally withdrew from his cocoon was for a caustic confrontation with the prosecution's most anticipated witness, Salvatore "Sammy the Bull" Gravano. Defecting had been a traumatic experience for Gravano. "He was a nervous wreck when he came in," Bruce Mouw noted, observing that the hard-edged Sammy needed constant reassurance that prosecutors and the FBI would support his leniency bid. "He told us, 'For years I hated you guys. How do I know you're going to back me and verify I was a good witness?'" Before Gravano testified, Mouw, Jim Fox, the bureau's New York commandant, and other agents met often with him to pledge their support. "We wanted him calm and on the beam, not to get cold feet on the stand," Mouw said.

On the days before Gravano's scheduled appearance, flyers showing a photo of Gravano's face superimposed on the body of a rat were distributed near the courthouse and fastened to trees and buildings. The caption said, "Epitome of a Rat Who Lies: Sammy the Liar Gravano." For his debut as a witness, Gravano shunned his customary casual workingman's dress style, and every day came to court clothed, almost in imitation of Gotti's high fashion, in well-tailored, conservative, double-breasted suits and matching accessories. Taking no chances with the welfare of their exceptional witness, the government ringed the courtroom with burly U.S. marshals. In the first row of public benches, directly in front of Gotti's cheerleaders, the FBI stationed a corps of muscular, crewcut agents from a SWAT team.

Testifying for nine days, Gravano was the predominant witness of the trial. Seated a dozen feet from the defense table, he and Gotti engaged in several stare-down duels without Gravano blinking or appearing unnerved. Responding to Gleeson's cordial questions, Gravano admitted a litany of heinous crimes, capped by his involvement in nineteen murders, ten of which occurred during Gotti's era as Gambino boss. His description of the planning and rationale for Paul Castellano's execution, and a compelling minute-by-minute reconstruction of the murders outside Sparks, were the firmest columns buttressing that specific charge.

Gotti's facetious speculation on one of the tapes made in the Cirelli apartment that the police must have killed Castellano was the defense's strongest point for exonerating him in Big Paul's murder. Present in the apartment when Gotti made the comment, Gravano dismissed the remark as a lie, an inside joke. "When he says the cops did it, probably the cops did it, he'll do an expression and move his hands, give a smirk," Gravano testified.

At most Mob trials, prosecutors use agents and detectives to interpret the significance of esoteric Mob expressions picked up on bugs. Sammy the Bull was a more convincing expert witness than any agent or cop when it came to deciphering Mafia argot and Gotti's bizarre remarks. Through Gravano, the prosecution offered the jury a priceless primer on Cosa Nostra customs and traditions. The Gambino family's chain of command, the movement of money to Gotti, the reasons for Gotti's actions, and the motives for five murders ordered by Gotti were minutely explained by Gravano.

As Sammy sat deadpan on the witness stand, the tension around him crackled. Two women tried to burst past guards at the court's entrance, shouting that he was covering up his own crimes. "Murderer! I want to spit in his face," one of them screamed, managing to get to the courtroom door. She later told reporters that Gravano had been responsible for the slaying of her two sons. Bomb scares became almost routine, forcing the evacuation of the entire courthouse three times. Nor was Judge Glasser immune from the vitriolic atmosphere. He was placed under twenty-four-hour protection after the receipt of death threats.

Over five days, Gravano was subjected to mordant, rapid-fire interrogation from Albert Krieger, Gotti's lawyer, and Anthony Cardinale, a nimble attorney representing Frank Locascio. Through barbed questions, they tried to undermine Gravano by implying that he was framing Gotti for crimes that he himself had committed without Gotti's knowledge. Krieger and Cardinale castigated Sammy the Bull as "a little man full of evil," "a snake" without a conscience. Krieger pounded at him to admit that the only way he could obtain amnesty for a lifetime of crimes was by delivering Gotti's "head on a silver platter to the government."

Not rattled, Gravano acknowledged that he wanted to avoid spending the rest of his life in jail. "I was looking to turn my life around and part of it was telling the truth about my entire lifestyle," he replied, repelling the defense's attack. Despite adroit efforts, the lawyers were unable to damage Gravano by exposing glaring inconsistencies or an outright lie in any phase of his testimony. A compelling witness, he added depth to what was already a powerful prosecution case, based on the tapes.

The longer Gravano testified, the more Gotti's composure dissolved. He smiled less often at his supporters and was visibly testy in whispered conversations with his own lawyers. Only one witness was called by the defense, a tax lawyer, who asserted that Gotti had been exempt from filing returns with the

Internal Revenue Service because he had been under investigation for alleged crimes. The lawyer's opinion was patently wrong, and under cross-examination his testimony was punctured as worthless. Otherwise, the defense relied on cross-examinations to refute the other counts. Judge Glasser refused to permit the defense to call several witnesses to challenge the auditory reliability of the Ravenite tapes and to question Gravano's mental stability. Glasser's rulings that the witnesses were unqualified as experts brought a vigorous protest from defense lawyer Cardinale. The attorney's barrage of fiery objections sparked a glow in Gotti's face. He warmly shook Cardinale's hand, gratified that at least one of his lawyers was battling and defying the judge's authority.

The summations by both sides centered on the twin pillars of the case—the tapes and Gravano. Krieger and Cardinale tried to minimize the recordings as conversations taken out of context, excusing Gotti's language as hyperbolic horseplay, exaggerated street talk to crude individuals and gamblers—not the comments of a Mob boss authorizing murders or talking about crimes. If actual murders had occurred, the lawyers contended, they had been committed by the prosecution's star witness, Sammy Gravano. In behalf of Locascio, Cardinale argued that his mere presence during conversations while uttering hardly a word, was insufficient to convict him for RICO crimes. Both lawyers railed at Gravano as a fabricator of tales to magnify his importance as a witness and purchase a pardon. To most observers, it appeared to be a feeble strategy. Try as they might, the lawyers had been unable to impugn Gravano, and Gotti's voice had come through crystal-clear on the recordings.

Gleeson's summation concentrated on his two contentions. The jury, he stated, could find overwhelming evidence to convict on every count based solely on Gravano's testimony or on the tapes alone. In effect, the prosecution had substantiated what Andrew Maloney had promised to prove in his opening statement: "This is a case of a Mafia boss brought down by his own words, his own right arm [Gravano]."

Having listened to recordings and witnesses for six weeks, the jury needed only fourteen hours over two days to arrive at verdicts. On April 2, 1992, Gotti was found guilty on all thirteen RICO counts, and Locascio was convicted on all except one minor charge of illegal gambling. Surrounded in the courthouse by prosecutors and agents who had labored for years to destroy Gotti, Jim Fox, the highest FBI official in New York, summarized the government's jubilance.

"The Teflon is gone. The don is covered with Velcro, and all the charges stuck."

Two months later, Gotti reappeared before Judge Glasser for the formality of sentencing. Arms folded and smirking, he passed up the opportunity to speak before sentence was pronounced. It was no surprise: life imprisonment without parole. Receiving the same sentence, Frank Locascio, the almost forgotten defendant at the trial, spoke up in praise of his fallen leader. "I am guilty of being a good friend of John Gotti. If there were more men like John Gotti on this earth, we would have a better country."

Ronald Kuby, then a twenty-seven-year-old lawyer who was assisting Gotti's legal retinue, thought the Dapper Don "a class act" that day. Moments after Gotti heard the sentence, Kuby and the other attorneys saw him in a holding pen, where he was changing from an expensive dark double-breasted suit, silk shirt, and yellow tie into a prisoner's plain jumpsuit. In addition to the life sentence, Judge Glasser, in a pro forma requirement, had assessed Gotti $50 for court paperwork costs.

"He was completely relaxed and had a big smile on his face," Kuby recalled. "The first words out of his mouth were, 'That judge, he sure knows how to hurt a guy with that $50 assessment.'"

Outside the courthouse a crowd, many from the Bergin Hunt and Fish Club crew, chanted, "Free John Gotti." Upon hearing the sentence, the protesters erupted into a mini-riot, overturning cars and scuffling with the police and court guards until reinforcements dispersed them.

Gotti was returned to his cell at the MCC, but not for long. He was awakened in the middle of the night, and before dawn transferred in a police motorcade to a small airport in Teterboro, New Jersey. John Joseph Gotti, who had previously refused to fly because of his fear of airplane crashes, was put aboard a small government jet plane. His hands and feet shackled in irons, and surrounded by U.S. marshals, he was flown to a maximum-security penitentiary in Marion, Illinois, then the harshest prison in the federal penal system. That morning of June 24, 1992, he was placed in a special isolation wing in which he was "locked-down," kept virtually in solitary confinement for the rest of his life.

38

Bitter Aftermath

The good guys won, but at a price.

The big winners were the vindicated Eastern District's prosecution team and Bruce Mouw's FBI Squad, the lawyers and agents whose strategy had unseated John Gotti. Placing the case in a larger framework, Justice Department and bureau officials pictured Gotti's defeat as a severe psychological shock not only to the Gambino family but to the entire Mafia. Jim Fox, the FBI head in New York, and U.S. Attorney Andrew Maloney happily pinpointed the reasons for the Mob's increased distress. Number one: the guilty verdicts demonstrated that the government could convict even the most formidable Cosa Nostra godfather. Perhaps even more important was reason number two: Sammy the Bull Gravano's betrayal, the officials were certain, had corroded the Mafia's strongest asset—*omertà*. By becoming the nation's top turncoat, he had publicized the effectiveness of the Witness Protection Program created in the RICO statute. He proved that mobsters anywhere in the country could save their hides and start anew by testifying against a higher-up. The widely respected Gravano's apostasy surely increased operational difficulties for bosses and capos, who now had to wonder about the loyalty of their troops and closest confederates should an indictment crisis occur.

While New York's law-enforcement aristocracy publicly expressed its unanimous delight at toppling Gotti, behind closed doors the acrimony stemming from the investigations had soured relationships between high-level officials. Underlying the resentment was the fallout from the sharply competitive race to convict Gotti, and the policies adopted by the FBI and Maloney.

The FBI bull's-eye in bugging Mrs. Cirelli's living room left a backwash of resentment in other agencies. Several of the most startling tapes were obtained in early 1990 during Gotti's trial in Manhattan on state charges that he had ordered the shooting of John O'Connor, the carpenters' union leader. FBI agents recorded Gotti talking about vital matters affecting the office of Manhattan DA Morgenthau and the state Organized Crime Task Force, led by Ronald Goldstock. The tapes revealed Gotti's possible scheme to fix the assault case by reaching a juror. Morgenthau and Goldstock's staffs were then jointly prosecuting the O'Connor case after years of intensive investigative digging. On one tape, Gotti was heard discussing an attempt to contact a juror named "Boyle" or "Hoyle" who was believed to be a utility company employee. Gotti's idea was to dispatch Irish members of the Westies to locate and influence the juror, who presumably had an ethnic Irish background.

Another tape contained the startling item that the Gambinos had a law-enforcement mole spying for them. From talk in the Cirelli apartment, it was clear that the spy had tipped the mobsters that Sammy Gravano's construction company office in Brooklyn was being bugged by the state task force. Gravano at that time had recently been promoted from consigliere to underboss, and the bug could have opened productive areas for investigation. Equally disturbing was information that in return for payoffs, the mole was providing confidential information about state investigations and pending indictments to the Mob.

With the concurrence of the FBI, Maloney, whose federal prosecutors were vetting the Cirelli apartment tapes, decided to withhold this new information from Morgenthau and Goldstock. The conversational fragments about jury tampering, Maloney decided, were "too vague" to be of value to the state prosecutors while they were trying Gotti. "There was nothing to tell them about tampering with a juror or obstruction of justice," asserted Maloney, who admittedly was influenced by the bureau's objections to unveiling the existence of the Ravenite bugs to other agencies. "The FBI didn't trust Goldstock's office because they thought there might be a leak," Maloney later confided.

Mouw agreed with Maloney that there was insufficient evidence of jury tampering. The FBI's main concerns, he said, were running the Ravenite wires successfully and tracking down the traitor burrowed in a law-enforcement agency. Federal officials were concerned about their own priorities, and the slightest hint during the O'Connor trial that Gotti was being overheard might have cut short the Cirelli apartment eavesdropping at an early stage, and ruined the RICO case being prepared by the Gambino squad and the Eastern District.

Months after suffering a humiliating defeat in the O'Connor case, Morgenthau was infuriated to learn that the FBI withheld from him their suspicions and evidence of a possible attempt to fix the jury. Bribing and intimidating jurors was a Gambino trademark, well known to prosecutors. Therefore, before the start of the assault trial, the DA had tried to prevent potential pitfalls. He and the second-in-command, Barbara Jones, exacted promises from Jim Fox to alert them if the FBI picked up any indication of a contaminated jury. Morgenthau went a step further, and asked William Webster, the bureau's director, for the same help. And Michael Cherkasky, the lead prosecutor, thought he had obtained a similar commitment from Mouw.

Evidence from the Cirelli apartment tapes about a discussion and plans to reach a juror could have led Morgenthau to ask for a mistrial. Additionally, the recordings would have strengthened the state's evidence, since Gotti talked about collaborating with the Westies—a major issue in the assault charges against him.

"The FBI lied to me," a seething Morgenthau complained to top aides. "They think they're a government unto themselves."

Goldstock, the state's ranking organized-crime prosecutor, felt doubly betrayed by the FBI and Maloney's silence. They had failed to alert him about the potential jury problem, and had not informed him that his office's expensive electronic eavesdropping in Gravano's office had been exposed by a mole. Compounding Goldstock's anger was the knowledge that he had gone all out to help Maloney and the FBI in their RICO investigation. His office had provided federal prosecutors with tapes of Gotti's incriminating remarks in the Bergin Club, obtained soon after Castellano's murder and Gotti's takeover of the family. One of Goldstock's prosecutors also had worked full-time for Maloney on the Eastern District's case against Gotti. "We're supposed to be part of a joint investigation, and they never tell us they have information from the Ravenite that affects our cases," Goldstock protested. "When I asked Maloney for an explanation, he told me, 'I don't apologize for anything. The FBI didn't want you to know about it and we didn't tell you.'"

After Gotti beat the O'Connor assault charges, Goldstock was embittered to learn of a conversation his investigator Joe Coffey had over drinks with an FBI agent. "He told Joe," Goldstock said, 'We're just drooling. We were waiting for you to lose so we could prosecute him,' " a candid Maloney agreed with Goldstock's assessment of the competitive squabbles over hooking Gotti. "The bureau was surely happy at the acquittal in the state's case," Maloney acknowledged. But the prosecutor and the FBI stuck to their guns, maintaining that no substantive evidence was ever turned up that Gotti's allies contacted or influenced a juror in the state assault trial.

Goldstock remains convinced that the Gotti tapes his investigators provided the Eastern District, supported by other available evidence, could have convicted the Teflon Don on RICO charges two or three years before the FBI came up with its Ravenite bugs. "It's not jealousies," Goldstock insists. "It's just the knowledge that the FBI had to do it by themselves and get all the glory. They didn't want another agency's evidence as the foundation for convicting Gotti."

For Mouw, unearthing the Gambino's law-enforcement spy was a consuming priority. With barely a clue from the tapes to help him, Andris Kurins, a resourceful agent on the Gambino Squad, tracked down the traitor. Kurins's skimpy leads from the tapes were that a Gambino associate, George Helbig, was somehow involved in the spying. A non-Italian, Helbig was an enforcer and loan shark for Joseph "Joe Butch" Corrao, a Gotti capo. Concentrating on Helbig's business links and records of his telephone calls, Kurins solved the mystery.

The informer was a detective named William Peist, assigned to the police department's Intelligence Division, the elite branch that coordinated complex Mafia investigations with the FBI and other agencies. Peist, nicknamed "the Baker" because he once worked as a chef, had a spotless police dossier. He was placed on light duty at the Intelligence Division after his left leg was amputated because of injuries suffered in an auto accident. An insurance company awarded Peist $1.345 million for the disability, but the police department rejected his claim to retire on a tax-free line-of-duty pension because the injuries were sustained when he was off-duty.

Apparently in revenge for being denied the pension and early retirement, Peist arranged with a cousin by marriage, Peter Mavis, to feed confidential information to the Gambinos. The detective knew that Mavis, beset by financial headaches, was a loan-shark client and occasional business partner of Helbig, the Gambino hood. Peist had access to classified information from police and state Mafia files and was willing to sell it. He never met with Gambino mobsters, transferring information to them through Pete Mavis. The secrets were passed on to Helbig, who relayed them to Joe Corrao, who then gave them to Gotti.

Because none of the mobsters knew his identity, Peist felt secure. And, although he had a million-dollar nest egg from his insurance settlement, the detective sold out to the Mob for a pittance of about $20,000 over several years. All of the conspirators were traced by the relentless Kurins, mainly by linking them through telephone records. In 1993 Peist pleaded guilty to a federal racketeering charge and was handed a prison term of seven and a half years.

Peist's conviction was a bittersweet finale to the O'Connor assault case. From Peist's admissions, Morgenthau and Goldstock somberly evaluated the full extent of the damage he had inflicted on their offices and the years of investigative efforts that he had wrecked. At the O'Connor assault trial, Peist had been assigned the sensitive job of guarding the anonymous jury and had slipped the Gambinos the name of at least one juror. He also was responsible for exposing the state's eavesdropping bug in Gravano's office and ruining any hope by state investigators of obtaining potential evidence and leads about Gambino operations. In toto, a single dirty cop may have prevented Morgenthau and Goldstock from being the prosecutors who defeated the Dapper Don.

Even the tightly disciplined FBI was roiled by dissension over the fame and financial gains generated by the high-profile investigation of the Gambino family. Agents Andris Kurins and Joseph O'Brien resigned amid a furor in 1991 over their book *Boss of Bosses*, an account of the investigations of Paul Castellano, John Gotti, and other Gambino movers and shakers. The agents wrote about investigative tactics and published excerpts from bugs that bureau officials said were unauthorized because the tapes had never been introduced as court evidence. Angry agents and officials blasted Kurins and O'Brien for allegedly inventing incidents, exaggerating their own exploits, and taking credit for the accomplishments of other investigators. There were details of Castellano's sex life in the book, which by law, should have been expunged from FBI files, further embarrassing the bureau's brass. A bedrock issue in the dispute was a sacrosanct FBI tenet: agents shall not profit from confidential evidence obtained while working for the government. Kurins and O'Brien reportedly expected to share $1 million in royalties and movie rights.

"What they have done is personally disgusting to me and virtually every agent on board," Jim Fox, said at the time. "It's a terrible precedent." According to Fox, the agents gave the Mafia "a textbook" on FBI undercover and surveillance methods.

The two agents in their mid-forties quit the bureau under pressure, only months before they would have qualified for pensions. O'Brien was the "tall" agent who, the state Organized Crime Task Force claimed, deliberately botched their attempt in June 1983 to videotape Mafia leaders arriving and leaving a Commission meeting on the Bowery. Before the book was published, both agents were highly praised, and O'Brien received the attorney general's Award for Distinguished Service, mainly for his work in the Castellano investigation.

Years later, defending the book's authenticity, O'Brien denied that it contained sensitive information that helped the Mob. Asked if his and Kurins's roles in indicting Castellano and other Gambino mobsters were exaggerated, he replied, "With some exceptions, it was the most accurate account ever written. Nothing is 100 percent accurate."

Sammy the Bull also became the hero of a book dealing with brutality and bravado in the Gambino family. Gravano's sterling performance at the Dapper Don's trial had lifted him from the role of second-banana mobster to star billing as a rehabilitated celebrity gangster. Eighteen months after the trial, he appeared in the same court before Judge Glasser to hear his own sentence for multiple murders and racketeering. The hearing resembled a testimonial dinner, with officials competing to outdo each other in extolling, with honeyed adulation, Gravano's contributions to law enforcement and society in general. Some ninety prosecutors and investigators wrote to Glasser, effusively commending Gravano.

John Gleeson, the lead prosecutor, while stating that the government recognized the "scope and seriousness of Gravano's criminal conduct," characterized him as "the most significant witness in the history of organized crime." Besides the downfall of Gotti, Gleeson credited Gravano's testimony, or just his threat of testifying, with bringing about convictions or guilty pleas from at least thirty-seven mobsters and helpers in the Gambino family and in other borgatas. As recognition of Gravano's exceptional services, the FBI's Jim Fox presented him with a private award that he handed out exclusively to agents for valor—a specially designed wristwatch with an American flag on its face.

Before pronouncing sentence, Glasser quoted the opinion of an FBI agent who characterized Gravano's decision to testify against Gotti as "the bravest thing I have ever seen." The judge seemingly agreed with the appraisal of Gravano's supporters that he had metamorphosed from an unprincipled mobster to a law-and-order advocate. "There has never been a defendant of his stature in organized crime who has made the leap he has made from one social planet to another," Glasser declared.

Gravano's pact with the government called for a maximum twenty years in prison. Citing Sammy the Bull's "invaluable" aid in the war against the Mafia, Glasser reduced the sentence to five years imprisonment and three years of supervised release. The lenient term meant that Gravano spent nine more months in pampered custody, occasionally testifying at Mob trials, before being permanently sprung. When the official custody period ended, Gravano, a free individual under a new name, Jimmy Moran, settled with his wife and two children in Arizona. At the time of his defection, Gravano's "shylock book," $1.5 million in loan-sharking money that he had on the streets, was gobbled up by the Gambinos. He had been pulling in at least $300,000 a year from that racket alone. The government allowed him to keep $90,000 of his multimillion-dollar assets in cash and property, and gave him $1,400 a month for startup living expenses.

Finding government financial aid and security regulations too restrictive, Gravano stayed in the Witness Protection Program only eight months before dropping out in December 1995, to fend for himself. In 1997 he negotiated a deal with writer Peter Mass for a biography centered on his Mob adventures. To promote the book, *Underboss*, Gravano appeared on television interviews, revealing that he had not substantially altered his appearance. The only change in his face was the straightening of his twice-fractured nose by plastic surgery. Although not disclosing his assumed name and new residence, Gravano said that he had no fear of being whacked in revenge by his former comrades. "I'm not running from the Mafia," he snapped defiantly.

A sanitized version of his odyssey from hoodlum to Cosa Nostra millionaire, *Underboss* either offered apologias for his appalling murders and misdeeds, or simply omitted them. Sammy blamed his dyslexia for forcing him to leave school at an early age. He blamed the overbearing Cosa Nostra atmosphere in his Bensonhurst neighborhood for enticing him to enroll as a mobster. (Gravano harped on the same misleading theme that he had been victimized as a youth when he testified against his former crime associates. At trials, he described himself as a "product of a ghetto environment," although the Bensonhurst of his boyhood was a viable middle- and working-class area of well-kept streets and tidy lawns, and his family was affluent enough to spend every summer in a vacation bungalow in Long Island. "It was a place where wiseguys taught kids how to steal, how to rob and congratulated them when they killed," Gravano asserted. "This is a ghetto as far as I'm concerned.")

He contended that his survival as a made man depended on obeying orders, even if they required killing and betraying relatives and friends. The repentant gangster portrayed himself as having been a semilegitimate construction contractor and restaurant owner, a Mafia reformer trying to discourage Gotti from murderous rampages and excesses. In Gravano's version of events, after five years of loyal service to Gotti, he defected upon realizing that his boss planned to betray him at their joint trial. After a quarter century of membership, he had a remarkable inspiration: the Mafia's respected codes of honor were fictitious. "It was all about greed and power," Gravano wrote of his unconvincing, belated discovery of the Mob's ethics and values. "In reality, it was a total joke."

The book netted him at least $250,000, enough capital to finance a swimming-pool construction company in Phoenix, called Marathon, the name he had used in Brooklyn for one of his mobbed-up concrete firms. Over the years, Sammy kept in touch with prosecutor Gleeson, who had prepped him for Gotti's trial. Appointed a Federal District Court Judge in 1994, Gleeson usually got a telephone call from Gravano around Christmas. Neither he nor the FBI agents who had befriended Gravano suspected that he was in any kind of trouble, but in February 2000, Sammy the Bull's life came full circle. Together with his wife, his son, his daughter, and her boyfriend, he was arrested in Arizona on state and federal drug charges. An indictment accused him of being the director and financier of a ring that grossed about $500,000 a week selling Ecstasy pills, an illegal stimulant favored by young people.

Narcotics had been an issue raised in cross-examinations of Gravano at the trials of Gotti and other mobsters. Defense lawyers tried vainly to discredit him by suggesting that he had engaged in drug deals. Both on the witness stand and later in his book, Gravano adamantly denied having the slightest links to trafficking, insisting that one of his underworld principles was a ban on narcotics. "I'm personally against them—drugs," he testified several times. "I was a gangster. I preferred not to be in the drug business."

Discussing another moral issue in Underboss, he excoriated Gotti for encouraging John Junior to become a made man. Gravano wrote that he would never allow his son, Gerard, or any relative to follow his path into the Mafia or any aspect of crime. "I was dead against it," he testified in 1996. "I want my kids to be legitimate kids, to have nothing to do with what I did and 'the life.'" Five years after being hailed as the government's model witness, he was a disgraced embarrassment, a drug merchant who had enlisted his closest relatives—not only his son, but his wife and daughter—in his schemes.

Sammy's deceit had fooled the FBI and he remained on good terms with agents until his narcotics bust by Arizona authorities. In September 1999, shortly before his arrest, he was a big-name lecturer at a national conference of bureau supervisors in Phoenix. His topic: How organized crime functions.

After pretrial hearings, in the same Brooklyn federal courthouse in which he had often testified as a prosecution witness, Gravano and his son pleaded guilty to conspiracy to sell dangerous drugs. The same type of evidence that had tripped up Gotti, secretly taped conversations and testimony from turncoats, now incriminated Gravano. On telephone taps, Gravano was heard discussing drug profits with his wife and daughter. Young, hero-worshiping members of his thirty-strong Ecstasy crew testified that Gravano liked being addressed as "Boss" and "Big Man." He tutored them on the best weapons and tactics to be used in hits, and in his raspy voice spoke of organizing a new kind of Mob in Arizona. "He couldn't sit in Arizona and be a pool salesman or run a construction company," Linda Lacewell, an assistant U.S. Attorney, said at a hearing. "He wanted the old days back; he wanted 'the life' back, the power back."

Following his arrest, Gravano, a dedicated bodybuilder, was diagnosed as suffering from Graves' disease, a progressive thyroid ailment that left him looking gaunt, with sunken eyes and large protruding ears on a hairless skull. As a result of the case, Arizona authorities seized $400,000 from Gravano's properties and book royalties, on the grounds that the proceeds of *Underboss* were traceable to his racketeering days. The state planned to distribute the money to families of Gravano's murder victims.

Assailing Gravano as incorrigible for violating the leniency and trust extended to him by the government and the judicial system, Federal Judge Allyne Ross sentenced him to twenty years. The term was four more years than recommended in sentencing guidelines, indicating the government's outrage at Gravano's betrayal. Combined with a guilty plea in Arizona on state narcotics charges, he is ineligible for parole until the ripe age of seventy-seven. Sammy's son, who called himself "Baby Bull," got nine and a half years.

The narcotics arrest may have saved Gravano's life. In July 1999, the *Ari-*

zona Republic newspaper reported that he was alive and well in that state, and expressing his disdain for the Mafia. Gravano claims that he tried to suppress the story but was "blackmailed" by the newspaper into an interview because it would otherwise have disclosed that his wife and children had joined him in the Phoenix area. The story was picked up nationally, and mobsters in New York were incensed at his living openly in Arizona and taunting his former compatriots to hunt him down. Gravano's effrontery was a raw insult to the Gambino hierarchy. According to investigators, other families goaded the Gambinos into whacking Gravano for his disrespect of Cosa Nostra, and to provide a vivid example of what happens when traitors brazenly defy the Mob.

An experienced killer himself, Gravano was ready for the hit team he knew sooner or later would be searching for him. He was always armed, wore a bullet-proof vest, moved frequently to different apartments which he rigged with extensive alarm systems, and kept a guard dog in his home.

One of the men entrusted to kill Gravano with a bomb or a gun was his brother-in-law, Edward Garafola, who would have had no difficulty recognizing him. The designated hit men tracked Gravano, but their efforts were frustrated by the Arizona police. Before the mobsters could lay a trap for Sammy, he was jailed on the Ecstasy rap.

Another mystery from Gravano's past arose in 2003, when professional underworld killer Richard Kukinski implicated him in the 1980 slaying of a rogue New York detective. Serving four life sentences in New Jersey, Kukinski claimed that Gravano gave him the contract and supplied him with the shotgun used to murder Detective Peter Calabro near his home in Saddle River, New Jersey. Gravano pled not guilty to that "cold case" crime, and Bergen County, New Jersey, prosecutors declined to specify a motive for the hit. But after Calabro was killed, he was suspected of having been on the payroll of a Gambino car-theft ring. A one-man Murder Incorporated, Kukinski bragged that he had committed more than one hundred hits for the Mafia and for other clients. His sobriquet was "the Iceman," a reference to his custom of freezing his victims' bodies before disposing of them.

In retrospect, government officials and Judge Glasser, who collectively were responsible for Gravano's gentle five-year sentence, were driven by their fixation: demolishing the myths of John Gotti's invincibility and his ability to outclass them in courtrooms. The federal authorities went overboard in extolling

Gravano's value, his aid in convicting Gotti, and his presumed character transformation. Gravano's testimony, prosecutors later conceded, was captivating but not decisive, except in convicting Gotti on the charge of programing Paul Castellano's slaying. The Ravenite tapes alone, implicating Gotti in three other murders, would have been sufficient to ensure guilty verdicts and an automatic life sentence. Defending their recommendations to extend maximum leniency to Sammy the Bull, prosecutors and agents exaggerated the ripple effect that he caused in inducing other Cosa Nostra defections. (RICO's harsh penalties and the government-financed Witness Protection Program had already produced a bumper crop of Mafia songbirds.) Rightly or wrongly, officials advertised Gravano as irreplaceable for convicting numerous killers and racketeers before they could cause more incalculable harm to the entire community.

Yet in weighing Gravano's contributions, the criminal-justice system lost sight of his selfish motives and submerged his sordid criminal *curriculum vitae*. He switched sides fully aware that a mountain of evidence against him from the Ravenite tapes was a guaranteed ticket to life imprisonment. He had no other option. Like all mafiosi impaled by RICO, he knew the prosecutors' mantra for a soft sentence to induce cooperating witnesses: "First in (to cooperate), first out (of prison)." Even a maximum of twenty years was a bargain price to pay for nineteen murders and his repugnant record as underboss. The contract that Gravano signed for testifying as a prosecution witness was the most successful steal of his criminal career—and he knew it.

"He got the deal of a lifetime," Bruce Mouw, the former head of the Gambino squad, said in assessing the difficulties of nurturing Mob turncoats. "Using some of these guys is like taming a wolf. You can feed them out of your hand but they're still wolves, and you can never trust them. Sammy was in that category."

39

Self-Worship

Confined deep inside the federal penal system, a thousand miles from his Cosa Nostra family and personal relatives in New York, John J. Gotti had no intention of relinquishing his title as boss of the Gambino borgata. It was a sacred rule, established in 1931 at the creation of the American Mafia, that a godfather could be removed only by death or abdication. And in 1992 John Gotti invoked that mandate. From bugs in Gambino clubs and intelligence reports from informers, the FBI knew that he was determined to hold on to a semblance of power and to maintain a voice in major policy decisions. The government was equally determined to foil his plans by making his prison conditions as onerous as possible. The Bureau of Prisons shipped him to what was then its most tightly guarded penitentiary, the super-security "correctional institution" at Marion, in southern Illinois. Opened in 1963 to replace the oppressive Alcatraz, Marion was reserved for 350 to 370 inmates who were classified as dangerous, or who had caused disciplinary problems in other prisons.

Designated as inmate number 182-053, Gotti was placed in Marion's most restrictive cell block for an indefinite period of solitary confinement. Most days he was locked in for twenty-one to twenty-three hours, in contact only with guards. His meals were passed to him on a metal tray through a slit in his cell door. The fastidious Dapper Don's sole change of clothes were identical jump suits, and his constant environment was a six-by-eight-foot concrete-walled cell, containing a stainless-steel toilet and wash basin, an eighteen-inch-wide concrete slab bed covered by a thin mattress, and a twelve-inch black-and-white television set. Every day, for recreation, he was permitted to walk, hands and legs shackled, for fifty minutes along a narrow thirty-six-foot-long tier inside the prison. Once or twice a month he briefly breathed fresh air with other prisoners in a small outdoor exercise yard. His only permitted visitors were lawyers and relatives, who could see him twice a month, separated from him by a glass wall, speaking with him on a telephone. All incoming and outgoing mail was screened by prison authorities.

During the first year of imprisonment, Gotti could harbor a glimmer of hope that attorneys would get his conviction overturned. Within eighteen months that hope was extinguished. His strongest appeal point—that Bruce Cutler's disqualification denied him his lawyer of choice and a fair trial—was unanimously rejected by the U.S. Court of Appeals for the Second Circuit. The court ruled that Cutler "had allegedly entangled himself to an extraordinary degree in the activities of the Gambino crime family," and he had been properly excluded from the trial. (Cutler's feistiness resulted in his being convicted in 1994 of criminal contempt for violating a pretrial gag order by Judge Glasser, prohibiting defense and prosecution lawyers from commenting to the media. For attacking the prosecution in interviews, Cutler was subjected to ninety days of house arrest and suspended from practicing in the Eastern District for six months. The extremely rare charge against a lawyer came under justifiable fire from civil libertarians and journalists as an abuse of Cutler's free-speech rights and as a biased attempt to stifle attorneys from vigorously representing organized-crime defendants.)

Gotti's defense also claimed that Gravano, the principal prosecution witness, had committed perjury at the trial, and that prosecutors had covered up evidence of his involvement in undisclosed murders and in cocaine trafficking. These assertions were denied as groundless. (The appeals decisions came down six years before Gravano's Arizona drug arrest.)

When the Supreme Court in 1994 refused to consider Gotti's appeal, the entire Gambino family knew that their boss was doomed. Though his fate was sealed, Gotti, following in the footsteps of Carmine Persico, the imprisoned Colombo boss, schemed to retain the top title for himself and establish a Cosa Nostra dynasty. The heir apparent was the elder of his two sons, John Angelo, widely known as "Junior." (Junior's middle name was bestowed in honor of his father's former bosom crime comrade, Angelo Ruggiero.) Another important motive was money. So long as Gotti was the undisputed boss, a huge portion of the family's illicit "take" would continue to flow to his son and to other relatives.

Long before his conviction, Gotti began grooming John Angelo as his successor. In many respects, Junior (a name he came to detest) was a carbon copy of his father in looks and attitude. Powerfully built, he became a weightlifting addict as a teenager and was a mediocre student. Lieutenant Remo Franceschini, the head of the Queens DA's Detective Squad, listened in to several tapped telephone conversations in the early 1980s between the father, then a capo, and his teenaged son. "It was clear he was instructing him how to behave as a wiseguy, telling him the do's and don'ts, how to behave with other made guys and when to keep his mouth shut," Franceshini said.

After attending New York Military Academy, a boarding school near West Point that stressed military-style discipline and accepted scholastic underachievers, Junior overnight became a prosperous businessman. By his early twenties, he owned trucking and real estate companies that never encountered union problems or competition in landing business. Much of his success was due to name recognition and the Gambino family's influence with teamster locals and with construction contractors.

Still in his early twenties, and like his father a habitual night owl, Junior and a clique of young toughs were embroiled in several brawls. Once he was charged with slugging an off-duty cop who tried to aid a patron being roughed up by the combustible Junior and his pals. None of the assault charges stuck, because victims were too frightened to testify or witnesses recanted original versions they had given to the police. Like fathers, like sons, two regulars in young Gotti's inner circle were sons of his father's Mafia buddies: Salvatore "Tore" Locascio, the son of Frank Locascio, the family's underboss-consigliere; and John Ruggiero, the son of the late Angelo Ruggiero.

At age twenty-four, two years after his father became a godfather, Junior was inducted as a Gambino made man, according to the FBI and New York Mafia detectives. "We know that his father gloated with pride," Franceschini noted. The son had gotten a waiver of the previously inviolable Mafia rule that both parents of a soldier had to be of full Italian heritage; Junior's mother was of Italian and Russian descent. The Gambinos, obliging the senior Gotti, had instituted a rule change that only a father's Italian family line was necessary for membership. Two years later, in 1990, shortly after Junior's marriage and lavish Helmsley Palace Hotel reception, Gotti gave him a unique Christmas present.

He promoted his son to capo, making him at twenty-six the youngest man in Gambino history to hold that title and to lead a crew.

From day one of Gotti senior's imprisonment in Marion, Junior was his primary ally and emissary to the rest of the borgata. Before his sentence was imposed, Gotti had deputized Junior as acting boss, with a panel of three capos, including his brother, Peter Gotti, to assist in daily operations and to offer advice on necessary quick decisions. The promotion was an exceptional act, making the twenty-eight-year-old one of the youngest mobsters in history to be nominally in charge of a Mafia family.

As a close relative, Junior was permitted to see his father twice a month and talk for several hours. Though all visits to Gotti were monitored on video and audiotape, the FBI was certain that the father and son used code words and subtle exchanges to discuss Mob family matters.

Back in New York, lessons learned from his father's slipups obviously guided Junior in relaying instructions from his father or mulling over pressing borgata problems with trusted Gambino professionals. Extremely wary of listening devices and wiretaps, he favored walk-talks in the streets—and these only with his Uncle Peter and senior capos. He avoided Peter's Queens encampment at the Bergin Hunt and Fish Club, and the government had closed his father's Ravenite Club in Little Italy. The five-story brick Ravenite building on Mulberry Street had been owned by Joseph "Joe the Cat" LaForte, who was identified by the FBI as a Gambino soldier. Under a 1993 court order declaring the club a hub of racketeering activities, the building was forfeited to the government and auctioned off to a new landlord. Symbolic of the gentrification of the neighborhood and changing demographics, the drab Ravenite, which had served as a Mafia lodge for seventy years, was gutted, and the interior remodeled into a shop selling women's accessories. The photo of John Gotti and Neil Dellacroce was gone, and Amy Chan, the boutique's proprietor, hung a spotlighted portrait of Mao Zedong in the now brightly lit entrance.

Realizing that he was under surveillance and investigation, Junior tried to modify his public image. His previous schedule of late nights in bars and discos ended. Evenings were spent at his fourteen-room, $1.3 million waterfront home on Long Island's North Shore, overlooking Oyster Bay, with his wife, Kim, and their four children. More conservatively dressed than in the past, he frequently showed up at PTA meetings and brought cookies to parties at his children's schools. Junior's lawyers, acting like spin doctors, forwarded to reporters news of his scholarly pursuits: he had become an avid collector of books and artifacts on American Indian life and was taking paralegal courses to obtain a better understanding of the legal system.

A shakeup of the family's table of command was urgently required in the swift undertow caused by Sammy Gravano's betrayal and the wholesale convictions of capos and soldiers. With reduced ranks, Junior set about consolidating crews and installing new capos. But his lightning-fast rise to surrogate boss was widely resented in the family as unmerited, and his leadership abilities were questioned by more experienced wiseguys. Disrespect is a cardinal sin in the Mafia, and older capos were offended by the young acting boss's haughty posturing. Reports from informers to the FBI's Gambino Squad highlighted appraisals within the family and from other families that the acting boss was clumsy and inept. Analyzing the younger Gotti's performance, Bruce Mouw noted in a report, "He loves the adulation, attention and most important the money that's coming in to him. It's gone to his head." Junior's bungling was costing Gambino capos and soldiers money in interfamily disputes over loan-sharking and extortion turfs. The Genovese gang thought so poorly of Junior that they refused to negotiate with him, and the Gambinos were on the losing end of most sit-downs with other borgatas. "He's a laughingstock," Mouw summarized.

Despite his stumbles, Junior reigned for five years, about the same length of time his father had been free on the street and boss, before his conviction. In 1998 Junior was in effect dethroned by RICO. A broad-based indictment accused him of succeeding his father and receiving payoffs from an array of extortion, gambling, loan-sharking, and labor-racket rip-offs. The most splashy counts centered on shake-downs by the family totaling $1 million over six years from Scores, a trendy topless club on Manhattan's Upper East Side, popular with celebrities and tourists. According to prosecutors, witnesses were ready to testify that the club's owners and employees were forced to pay protection money to Gambino family hoods for permission to operate, and that at least $100,000 had been passed on to John Gotti Jr. as his share.

Prosecutors added to Junior's humiliation by releasing evidence turned up in a raid on his business office in Queens to support their charges that he was a Mafia prince. Stashed in a wall safe were $358,000 in cash that Junior could not explain, and unregistered guns. The epitome of his carelessness was a list found in his office identifying scores of soldiers inducted in 1991 and 1992 into the New York borgatas. Investigators believed that the names had been given to the Gambino family for vetting, a traditional Mafia procedure. By allowing the authorities to find the registry, Junior had endangered dozens of mafiosi in other families and besmirched the Gambinos' reputation for reliability throughout the Cosa Nostra. Leaders in other mobs were dumbfounded by his holding on to the candidates' list for years; as a basic security measure it should have been destroyed immediately.

Junior seemingly had a penchant for maintaining lists. A second one found in his office files was another embarrassment for him and a bonus for law-enforcement intelligence dossiers. It was a record of $348,000 in cash gifts he had received from 173 selected guests at his 1990 wedding, many of the donors prominent mobsters in the five New York families. Tommy Gambino, one of his father's wealthiest capos, gave $70,000, and Sammy the Bull Gravano, $7,500. Prosecutors planned to use the nuptial offerings as circumstantial evidence to prove Junior's magnified position in the Mob and the recognition of his importance by other borgatas.

On the eve of his trial and after most of his codefendants had thrown in the towel and pleaded guilty to reduced charges, Junior Gotti copped a plea. The Scores extortion counts against him were dropped, but he admitted to loan-sharking, illegal gambling, and extortion, including the use of phony civil-rights activist groups to threaten construction work stoppages over the issue of minority-hiring quotas. For good measure, he was convicted of evading income taxes. At his sentencing in September 1999, Junior used one of his father's favorite aphorisms: "I'm a man's man. I'm here to take my medicine." His lawyers, Gerald Shargel and Serita Kedia, had negotiated a hard bargain, and, at age thirty-five, he was sentenced to six years and five months' imprisonment, and a $750,000 fine, a much lighter penalty than the twenty years in store for him if convicted at trial.

Possibly even more galling to both Gottis was the presentencing release of transcripts of taped conversations in the Marion prison between the father and relatives. In memos to the sentencing judge, prosecutors claimed the conversations verified Junior's high-ranking status in the Gambino family, and that his father had been aware of his son's criminal activities and had tried to guide him in running the gang.

The most candid tapes were obtained on January 29, 1998, when the imprisoned godfather was visited in Marion by his brother Peter, and his daughter Victoria Gotti Agnello, shortly after Junior was arrested. Though he knew his conversations were being recorded by prison authorities, Gotti's remarks about his son were laced with sarcasm and disappointment. He called Junior and his younger son, Peter, "assholes" for associating with untrustworthy associates, "garbage pails" in business deals. Gotti senior had read the indictment and lambasted Junior for getting involved with a codefendant known for "talking a lot . . . and getting people in trouble"—in other words, a mobster who might incriminate him.

Describing several codefendants in the indictment as "imbeciles," Gotti lamented, "If you stay in business with imbeciles you're going to get as wacked out as they are." He was upset that his son had delegated important assignments to low-level associates: "Why do you need all these butlers and waiters for," a coded suggestion that Junior had relied on unproven wannabes.

But most distressful to Gotti was his son's decision to store hundreds of thousands of dollars and lists of new mobsters in his basement office, alongside several guns. "Look what he gives them to hang their hat on," Gotti rattled on angrily. "Funny money in the basement. I'm not saying he gave them the list, whatever it was. Guns behind the wall. Insane asylum!"

Saying that his son had been "stupid" for allowing himself to get indicted, Gotti discounted statements by Junior's lawyers that he was being victimized because of his father's reputation. "And this you can't blame on names . . . well, you can't blame it on last names."

His son's misfortunes provoked a stunning statement: "Why do you think this group of people fell apart without me?" he asked his brother and daughter. "Everyone became their own boss, set their own moral codes, set their own reasons, their own rhyme, and that's the end of it. That's the end of the ball game."

At that 1998 prison visit, Victoria Gotti Agnello defended her brother Junior. An author of mystery novels, she vigorously professed his innocence and the government's bias against her relatives, including her husband, Carmine Agnello. Gotti had tried to scuttle Victoria's romance with Agnello, according to FBI agents. Mouw said that Gotti dispatched enforcers to work over Agnello with baseball bats soon after he started dating Victoria. Later, Gotti relented, allowed the marriage, and okayed the induction of his son-in-law—a "chop shop" specialist in cannibalizing stolen cars and valuable auto parts—into his own borgata. Gotti used the prison visit with his daughter to ridicule her husband, who suffered from manic depression. "Is he feeling good?" Gotti inquired. "Is he feeling good? Is his medication increased . . . Does he get in the back seat of the car and think someone has stolen the steering wheel?" Later, referring to Agnello's frequent brushes with the law in his auto-salvaging and towing businesses, Gotti stressed that his son-in-law needed his help. "He's gonna get indicted any day, this moron. He's built himself a gallows. He's bought the noose. There's no question of my love for him but he needs me out there."

Three years later, in 2001, Carmine Agnello was caught in a police sting, threatening to burn down competitors. Pleading guilty to racketeering and tax frauds from his scrap metal operations, he was sentenced to nine years and fined $11 million. His marriage to Victoria Gotti ended in divorce.

John Gotti Sr.'s tenuous hold over the family faded quickly in the new century. He was diagnosed with neck and head cancer in 1998, and his health gradually deteriorated after surgery in a prison hospital. He died at age sixty-one, on June 10, 2002, at the U.S. Medical Center for Federal Prisons in Springfield, Missouri. New York's tabloid newspapers and television stations, which had relished his activities for fifteen years, treated the news of his passing and funeral with the gravity accorded the death of a president or a royal princess. The *New York Daily News* filled fifteen pages of type and photographs to document his life, and the *New York Post* gave him a thirteen-page spread. Even the staid *New York Times*, which normally downplays villainous gangsters, ran a 2,500-word obituary on page one.

The end of Gotti's life was recorded in greater depth by the nation's journalists than all the eminent American Mafia dons who had preceded him, including Al Capone, Lucky Luciano, Carlo Gambino, Vito Genovese, Joe Bonanno, and Tommy Lucchese. Although he was denied a public requiem mass in church by the Brooklyn Roman Catholic Diocese, Gotti's departure was in keeping with his grandiose lifestyle: newspapers reported that his funeral cost about $200,000. After a wake at a Queens funeral chapel, his gold-encrusted bronze coffin, engraved with the dates of his birth and death, was transported through Queens. Following the hearse were twenty-two limousines, hundreds of private cars, and nineteen flower cars. The floral displays were artfully designed to reflect favorite aspects of his life: a martini glass, a racehorse, a royal flush in hearts, a cigar, and the New York Yankees logo. With thousands of onlookers, many grasping to touch the hearse, and with four television news helicopters hovering overhead, the cortège wound for ninety minutes through Queens, past his home in Howard Beach, and slowing in front of the Bergin Hunt and Fish Club in South Ozone Park. Near the Bergin and around Howard Beach, banners were strung reading "John Gotti Will Live Forever." At St. John Cemetery, his closest relatives, including his mother, Fannie, were in attendance for a brief prayer service conducted by a priest. Interred in a family mausoleum, John Gotti was placed next to his father and his son Frank, the twelve-year-old who died in an auto accident.

St. John Cemetery, dubbed by morbid punsters as the resting place for "Deadfellas," contains the graves of numerous significant mobsters. Buried near Gotti are his mentor Aniello Dellacroce, Carlo Gambino, Lucky Luciano, Joe Profaci, Joe Colombo, Carmine Galante, and Salvatore Maranzano.

In the beginning, John J. Gotti said that all he wanted was one year as boss to fulfill his legacy: the creation of a Mafia family that would never be destroyed. That was the "hell of a legacy" boast picked up on a law-enforcement bug in January 1986, only weeks after Gotti seized control of the Gambino family. As a nascent godfather, he inherited a criminal superstate, custom-designed over three previous decades by two innovative Mob entrepreneurs, Carlo Gambino and Paul Castellano. Gotti had five years of absolute power on the streets to complete his goal of forging an indestructible borgata. He began his reign overseeing the largest and probably the most powerful criminal organization in the nation's history. When he left, the Gambinos were a disintegrating, besieged clan. And, he was chiefly responsible for the whirlwind that tore apart both the borgata and his own personal family.

Early successes, his unopposed takeover of the family after the murder of Paul Castellano, followed by a string of courtroom acquittals, inflated his overconfidence. Flattering print and televisions stories about his opulent lifestyle, his unorthodox mannerisms, and his courtroom invincibility, magnified his opinion of himself. Gotti invented and epitomized gangster chic; he was a new type of openly fearless, flamboyant mobster, vicariously admired for his "come and get me if you can" defiance of authority.

"He was the first media don," says Bruce Mouw, the FBI agent chiefly responsible for the investigation that ultimately convicted Gotti. "He never tried to hide the fact that he was a superboss." Andrew Maloney, the U.S. Attorney who prosecuted Gotti, was angered by the media's obsession with their favorite gangster. "He was made to order for the press. The way he looked, dressed, his arrogance toward the law. The press was manipulated by him and turned him into a folk hero. Almost everyone forgot or downplayed the fact that he was a vicious murderer."

Wanted for the attempted assassination of Frank Costello, Vincent "Chin" Gigante surrendered after three months as a fugitive in 1957. Costello declined to identify Gigante as the gunman who grazed his head and he was acquitted.
(AP/Wide World Photos)

As Genovese boss in the 1980s and 1990s, Vincent Gigante's closest confidantes and trusted aides were (clockwise from top left) Venero "Benny Eggs" Mangano, the underboss; Dominick "Baldy" Canterino, a capo; and Dominick "Quiet Dom" Cirillo, a capo (on the left with unidentified man).
(FBI and NYPD Photos)

FBI agents discovered Vincent Gigante led a double romantic life and spent most evenings in a tony East Side town house. Investigators used a rooftop observation post at a nearby yeshiva to spy on Gigante's nocturnal mob meetings, observing him through the rear windows (below) of the town house. An attempt to bug the town house failed when agents drilled through the wrong wall. *(Photos from author's archive)*

Arrested on RICO charges, Vincent Gigante appeared for arraignment in his customary street garb: pajamas and a bathrobe. At the court hearing, "Chin," apparently feigning mental illness, appeared disoriented, insisting that he was at a wedding and wanted to see the bride. *(Photo courtesy of the Federal Bureau of Investigation)*

Liborio "Barney" Bellomo became street boss when Gigante was imprisoned; he is a strong contender to become the next Genovese godfather when his prison term for racketeering ends. *(Photo courtesy of the Federal Bureau of Investigation)*

Philip "Rusty" Rastelli emerged undisputed boss of the Bonanno family in 1979 after obtaining the Commission's approval to whack his archrival, Carmine Galante. *(Photo courtesy of the New York City Police Department)*

Joseph Massino, pictured around the time of Carmine Galante's murder in 1979, played a key role in arranging the hit, and was promoted into the Bonanno family's hiearchy. *((Photo courtesey of the New York City Police Department)*

Salvatore Vitale

Joseph Massino

Frank Lino

Accompanied by his brother-in-law and crime alter ego Salvatore "Good-Looking Sal" Vitale and capo Frank Lino, Joe Massino attended a wake for slain Gambino Underboss Frank DeCicco in 1986. To avoid law-enforcement surveillance, Massino later boycotted mob funerals. *(FBI Surveillance Photo)*

Joseph Massino

Gerlando Sciascia

On the morning of May 6, 1981, Joe Massino and Gerlando "George from Canada" Sciascia were seen outside the Capri Motor Lodge in Whitestone, Queens. The government claimed that Massino imported Sciascia and other Canadian triggermen to murder the rebellious "Three Capos" the previous night. In 2003, Massino was indicted for a hit on Sciascia. *(FBI Surveillance Photo)*

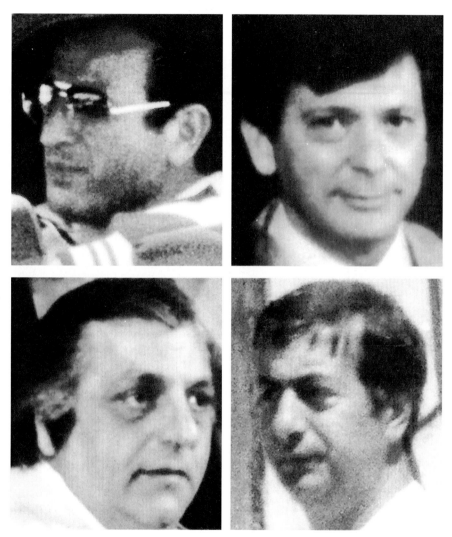

At the 1981 "peace conference," Joe Massino orchestreated the ambush-murders of three rival Bonanno capos: Alphonse "Sonny Red" Indelicato (top left), Philip "Phil Lucky" Giaconne (top right), and Dominick "Big Trin" Trinchera (lower left). Soon afterwards, Massino arranged the execution of his ally, Dominick "Sonny Black" Napolitano (lower right), for allowing an FBI agent to infiltrate the Bonanno family. *(Photos courtesy of the Federal Bureau of Investigation.)*

Joe Massino with his wife, Josephine, were in formal dress for the 1999 wedding of one of Sal Vitale's sons. Vitale's wife's face is blocked out because she is in the Witness Protection Program. (*Department of Justice Exhibit*)

Corpulent capo Frank Coppa picked up the tabs for Joe Massino and his wife on jaunts to France and Monte Carlo in 2000. Massino used overseas trips with capos to mull over family business out of range of FBI bugs and cameras. *(Department of Justice Exhibit)*

Joe Massino spotted leaving his doctor's office in Staten Island with Anthony "T. G." Graziano, a member of Massino's crime cabinet. The FBI suspected that Massino used the doctor's office in 2001 as a safe rendezvous for mob chitchats. *(FBI Surveillance Photo)*

After Joe Massino's arrest, relatives tied a yellow ribbon to a tree in front of his Howard Beach home, signifying that he was a heroic hostage and prisoner of war. Guarding against enemies and law-enforcement snoops, Massino installed closed-circuit cameras in his home that enabled him to spot anyone surveilling the house and street. *(Photo courtesy of Manny Suarez)*

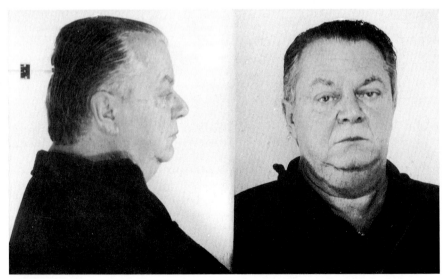

Dressed in a black velour jogging suit, Massino was prepared for arrest on RICO and murder charges when FBI agents came calling at dawn on January 9, 2003. *(Photos courtesy of the Federal Bureau of Investigation)*

The combination of Gotti's hubris and his complimentary media treatment only intensified the determination of frustrated agents and prosecutors to vanquish him. On bugs he was heard fulminating at the government's "vendetta" to convict him, and how "tough" the law would be on him if he were ensnared. Yet he repeatedly committed the fundamental mistakes that earlier had gotten him into difficulties, until they proved to be fatal. Aware of the government's wiretapping and bugging capabilities, he threatened to kill any underling trapped by electronic eavesdropping, including his longtime comrade Angelo Ruggiero. But Gotti disregarded his own directives. Figuring correctly that the Bergin Hunt and Fish Club would be a logical target, he evaded being caught by a bug inside the Bergin's main room. For Mafia business discussions, he retreated to an adjacent unmarked office, which he was confident was unknown to investigators and safe from electronic ears. Soon after becoming boss, he was enraged to learn that the state Organized Crime Task Force had planted mikes in his private den. Evidence from his office conversations was used to convict other Gambino mobsters, and taped conversations were the underlying element in his trial for the shooting of carpenters' union leader John O'Connor.

Yet three years after the Bergin bug fiasco, he repeated the same blunder at the Ravenite Club in Little Italy. Rather than being inconvenienced by walk-talks in cold weather or rotating his meeting places, he felt comfortable in the hallway at the rear of the Ravenite and upstairs in the homey Cirelli apartment. It apparently never dawned on him that informers would reveal his secret havens in the Ravenite building, just as they had his private office at the Bergin Club. Again, he was too lazy or overconfident to dodge investigators by alternating meeting places or sweeping them for bugs. His inability to hold his tongue continued in prison. At Marion, he made incriminating statements about his son, despite knowing his words were being recorded and could be damaging to his own flesh and blood.

Gotti's indifference to surveillance created extraordinary difficulties for himself and all of his capos. He continually ignored the basic principle that the Mafia presumably was a secret organization. The entire family knew that the FBI and detectives often videotaped and photographed everyone in the vicinity of the Ravenite. But Gotti disregarded the danger, demanding obsequious attendance and reports to him there by the hierarchy and capos. His decree delighted FBI agents at their observation post in an apartment two blocks from the club. Their pictorial records became part of the evidence against Gotti at his final RICO trial. Additionally, the compulsory gatherings at the Ravenite allowed the bureau to identify previously unknown Gambino members. Videotapes and still photographs of capos and soldiers showing up at the Ravenite were used as valuable circumstantial evidence against them at RICO enterprise trials.

His inability to judge loyalty and talent were pitfalls for Gotti. Following the murder of his original underboss, Frank DeCicco, Gotti depended heavily on Sammy the Bull Gravano, first as his consigliere and then as underboss. Gravano was an efficient choreographer for murders Gotti wanted, and a big earner who delivered more than $1 million a year to the boss. But his record for sacrificing others should have been a cautionary signal to Gotti. Previously, whenever Gravano became entangled in an internal dispute, his solution was to kill the rival and shift blame for the mishap onto someone else. Even among unprincipled mobsters, he had a reputation for unscrupulousness. If advancement required whacking his brother-in-law or a business partner, Sammy the Bull went along with it. Because Gravano, unlike many skilled mafiosi, had never been imprisoned, Gotti had no idea of how he would react in the crucible of prison. He misjudged Gravano's dedication to him and the myth of Cosa Nostra loyalty. According to Bruce Cutler, Gravano misrepresented himself to FBI agents and prosecutors as a strong-willed, tough-as-nails gangster who had confronted Gotti when he had disagreed with his Mob policies. The lawyer recalled that in Gotti's presence, "Gravano was always subservient, even obsequious around John."

And when the climactic test came, Sammy's self-preservation was more important to him than saving his boss and dozens of his crime colleagues.

Double-crossed by Gravano, Gotti next placed his faith in blood ties by designating his son as his surrogate and successor. Doing so, he disregarded Junior's inexperience and the resentment engendered in the family by this conspicuous nepotism. Mafia gangs traditionally had counted on merit, not the boss's kin, for picking competent leaders; sons were not granted the right of automatic succession and guaranteed wealth in the Cosa Nostra. Gotti knew from contemporary events in the Colombo family the danger of manufacturing a dynasty. Carmine Persico's promotion of his son without approval from a majority of capos had ignited a destructive civil war among Colombo factions. The Gottis averted a similar rebellion, but Junior's incompetent tenure culminated in his own conviction, and prison sentences for more than a dozen other capos, soldiers, and associates.

With his son imprisoned in 1999, Gotti's last hope for clinging to power and maintaining a dynasty was through brother Peter. As a close relative Peter, like John Jr., could visit him in prison and transmit news and receive advice in their private code. Long overshadowed by his more ambitious kid brothers, John and Gene, Peter had served them as a compliant assistant, a glorified gofer. John had appointed Peter capo of the Bergin crew, and after Junior's jailing, bestowed upon him the mantle of acting boss. Before matriculating as a full-time mobster, Peter had worked ten years for the New York Sanitation Department, and obtained a disability pension of about $2,000 a month for an on-the-job injury after falling off a garbage truck. The FBI's Gambino Squad had a low regard for Peter's underworld abilities. "He's not exactly a Rhodes scholar nor particularly aggressive," Mouw observed when it was learned that Peter was the new acting boss. "Does he have the capabilities of running a Mafia family? Absolutely not."

Trying to avoid the limelight that had been ruinous for his brother, Peter stayed close to his sanctuary in Queens, the Bergin Club. Like the rest of the Gambino family, the club had fallen on hard times; half its space was taken over by a butcher shop and a delicatessen. The new don's brief fling with glory evaporated a week before his brother died in prison. Arrested on a RICO indictment in June 2002, Peter was cited as being the acting Gambino boss and the head of the family. A year later, sixty-two-year-old Peter Gotti was convicted for the first time in his life, found guilty of extortion, money laundering, and corrupt control of a longshoremen's local.

Another brother, Richard V. Gotti, a Gambino capo, and his soldier son, Richard G. Gotti, codefendants with Peter, were brought down by similar racketeering charges. A theatrical sidelight to the trial of the three Gottis was a Hollywood foray by the family. The jury heard testimony that a Gambino crew tried to shake-down the martial-arts movie actor Steven Seagal for $3 million, to resolve a contract dispute with a Gambino associate.

Even after their initial convictions, there was no escape for Peter and Junior Gotti from deeds performed on behalf of John Gotti. In December 2004, Peter was convicted on separate charges of ordering at the behest of his brother the failed attempt to whack Sammy Gravano. Highlighting the prosecution's evidence were video-taped conversations in 1996 and 1997 of visits by Peter to John at the Marion prison, in which John railed that he was unable to sleep thinking of "rats" like Gravano enjoying freedom and profiting from having betrayed him.

"But that's a bill that's gotta be paid some day, just like every other bill, you know what I mean . . ." John ominously urged Peter. Still ranting about retaliating against Gravano, John vowed that if he ever again encountered Sammy the Bull, "I'll eat his fucking liver for him."

Grousing after his convictions and the probability of spending the rest of his life behind bars, Peter spoke up in court: "My name is Gotti. If my name wasn't Gotti, I wouldn't be here." It was an excuse of guilt-by-association, which Peter's brother John had once chastised his son for using to explain his legal woes.

And, as Junior Gotti prepared to leave prison in 2004 following his racketeering conviction, his parole was abruptly canceled by a new RICO indictment. The most startling revelation was an accusation that he had issued a contract in 1992 to kill Curtis Sliwa, a self-designated crime-fighter who had demeaned John Gotti on his radio talk show. Sliwa, founder of the Guardian Angels' civilian patrol group, was shot and severely wounded in an attack allegedly sanctioned by Junior to punish Sliwa for vilifying his father.

The verdicts and indictments in 2003 and 2004 meant that four Gotti brothers—John, Gene, Peter, and Richard—and two of their sons wound up in prison for RICO or for drug violations. (The Gotti name, however, may have benefitted a female relative, John's daughter Victoria. She has published novels under her maiden name and wrote a newspaper gossip column. Victoria also became the star of a popular cable television show, "Growing Up Gotti," which centered around her problems as a divorced, single mother bringing up three generally unruly teenaged sons in a luxurious Long Island estate.)

The prospects of the Gotti tribe wielding power again in the borgata appear slim. "The Gambino family is sick and tired of the Gotti family," Mouw believes.

However, Mouw and other Mafia watchers believe that John Gotti's relatives are in solid financial shape. "All they did was take the money," Mouw says of the Gotti wing. Reviewing the fifteen-year rule by the Gottis, Mouw is confident that they prospered at the expense of the rest of the crime family. He estimates that John Gotti alone was worth $20 million to $30 million in cash when he was packed off to prison. "Where it is? God only knows," Mouw admits. "Offshore? In suitcases? We'll probably never find it." The scope of illicit wealth reportedly obtained by Gotti and his relatives over a decade is based on information from Sammy the Bull Gravano and other defectors about systematic payoffs to the Gottis from rackets in the Garment Center, the construction and garbage-carting industries, and from waterfront companies. The Gottis also richly profited from the earnings of the family's gambling and loan-sharking rings.

An FBI forfeiture-seizure squad had limited success in the 1990s, trying to trace Gotti's buried treasure. "It's less than $100 million but in the multimillions," Jim Fox, the bureau's New York official, said of the vain search for Gotti's cache. Gravano told his FBI interrogators that Gotti's primary bagmen were his brother Peter and his son Junior. But Gotti never dropped a clue to Gravano of how and where he concealed the immense loot. "It was the biggest secret in the Mob," Mouw adds. "Even Sammy didn't know."

There was plenty of money to go around when Gotti became the Gambino godfather in 1986. From testimony at later Mob trials and from seized confidential records, federal and New York investigators estimated conservatively that in the mid-1980s the Gambino family grossed about $500 million a year. At the start, Gotti was handed profits from a galaxy of rackets run by twenty-one crews in New York, New Jersey, Connecticut, and Florida. By the time of his death, there were perhaps fifteen to eighteen functioning crews, the number of active soldiers not imprisoned was reduced to fewer than two hundred from a high of over four hundred, and several of their richest rackets had been smashed.

The damage to the Mafia caused by Gotti extended beyond his own borgata. New York's other Mob families, believing they had been directly harmed by the Dapper Don's excesses and the unwelcome notoriety his escapades brought upon the entire Mafia, expressed their disfavor of him in a symbolic manner. Not one important mafioso from another family showed up at Gotti's wake and funeral—a profound insult understood by all Cosa Nostra members.

Gotti's final bleak years in prison were darkened by estrangement from his wife of four decades. Prison authorities said Vicky stopped visiting him, and he was heard on a recorded conversation with Peter Gotti saying that one of his sons had pleaded with his father to prevent a divorce. FBI officials asserted that Mrs. Gotti, angered by her husband's bringing Junior into the crime family, blamed him for their son's arrest and conviction. "What father, if he had any love or compassion for his son, would encourage him to become a Mob boss or even a mobster," Mouw said, confirming the Gottis' dispute over their son's fate. The marriage may have been driven onto the rocks long before Gotti's conviction, when FBI surveillance reports of his affairs with other women were leaked to the news media.

During a recorded prison conversation with brother Peter in 1997, Gotti burst into a foul-mouthed condemnation of his wife. Denouncing Vicky as a traitor, comparable to Gravano, Gotti said he regretted having married her, and cursed her for blaming him for the impending imprisonment of their son Junior.

On the first anniversary of Gotti's death, his four children placed "In Memoriam" announcements in the *New York Daily News*. "Although your suffering was immense, you died the way you lived, proud and with honor," John Jr. said in his notice. The message from daughter Victoria was: "Dear Dad, not one day goes by without a thought of you, a tear from me—your strength, loyalty, dedication and love will live on forever inside." Significant by its absence that year was a tribute or remembrance from his wife. In later years, her name was included in the newspaper memorials.

Probably the largest flaw in Gotti's character and the underlying weakness that destroyed him and mauled the Gambino family was narcissism. Even in prison, his self-worship was unrestrained. Entombed in Marion, he could not resist boasting about his exploits and the difficulties he had created for the government before it could defeat him. "You know why I'm here?" he asked his daughter Victoria and his brother Peter, in a tape-recorded visit on January 29, 1998. "It took them $80 million and three lying cases, and seven rats that killed a hundred people in the Witness Protection Program, to finally frame me? You understand?"

Justifying his chosen Mafia path as predestined, he told Victoria and Peter, "My life dictated that I take each course I took. I didn't have any multiple choices. Listen to me carefully. You'll never see another guy like me if you live to be five thousand."

40

Gaspipe

is aptitude for violence developed at a tender age.

It was evident early on when, as a teenager, he delighted in brawling and in shooting hawks with a .22 caliber rifle. Careful to avoid attention and arrests—stealthy traits that later aided his criminal success—he killed birds from rooftops with silencer-equipped guns. Slaughtering hawks was his first taste of blood. Over three decades as a mobster, he participated or conspired in the murders of at least thirty-seven human victims. At a minimum, another twenty-five targets were on his must-kill list, including a judge and a prosecutor. Several of the intended victims were shot and wounded; most escaped unscathed when his plans went awry. Although his homicidal history far exceeded those of more conspicuous contemporary Mob leaders—the Gambino family's John J. Gotti and Salvatore Sammy the Bull Gravano—his reign of terror and his name were virtually unknown outside the Mafia's confines. It was a different story inside New York's Cosa Nostra. In the aftermath of the Commission case, he vaulted to the zenith of power in the Lucchese borgata. Among the five families, his fearsome passion for vengeance was universally recognized, and he operated under a dreaded nickname: "Gaspipe."

Gaspipe's baptismal name was Anthony Salvatore Casso. Born in 1942, he grew up in a gritty slice of Brooklyn's Park Slope and Carroll Gardens, a Mafia hatchery and environment that produced such renowned mobsters as the Persico and Gallo brothers. It was a neighborhood swarming with tough guys, and in the late 1950s young Casso was a swaggering member of the South Brooklyn Boys, a teenagers' gang that battled along the docks in Red Hook with fists, knives, clubs, and Molotov cocktails. Like many mafiosi, he was not physically imposing at five-feet six-inches and barely 150 pounds, but Casso nevertheless gained a macho reputation for his cast-iron demeanor, and especially for his marksmanship with a rifle and a handgun.

Using roofs as makeshift firing ranges with bull's-eye targets pinned to chimneys, he had developed into a crack shot with a pistol, able to hit a soda can at a distance of about one hundred feet. A former detective, who was reared in the same section of Brooklyn, says that Casso and his chums evaded police scrutiny by rigging up homemade gun silencers with cotton and cardboard wadding. Roofs served as recreational areas in the densely populated neighborhood, and a common hobby was tending pigeon flocks in rooftop coops. Young Casso's shooting skills were in great demand by pigeon-fanciers seeking to protect their birds from predatory hawks. "People used to call me all the time, 'Could you come over and get this hawk,'" he said in an interview. "I was like a doctor on call."

Despite New York's rigid gun-registration laws, gang members easily acquired illegal pistols and revolvers. "It was like buying a gun in a grocery store, everybody in my neighborhood had one in the house—if not ten."

The youngest of three children, Casso inherited his taste for weapons from his father, who took him on hunting trips starting at age nine. From his father he also acquired the bizarre name, "Gaspipe." Neighborhood gangsters jocularly branded the father with the moniker because he used a metal pipe as a bludgeon to intimidate victims on Mob assignments. The elder Casso never qualified as a made man, but in the 1920s and '30s, before becoming a longshoreman, he and his gas pipe were often dispatched by Vito Genovese to threaten and assault dissidents in a Mafia-controlled union that represented employees in New York's burlesque theaters. Casso the son detested the nickname, simmering with rage at anyone who used it, although he allowed a handful of close accomplices to refer to him as "Gas."

A high school dropout at sixteen, Casso followed his father to the docks, starting out as a longshoreman. On the Brooklyn piers, he showed a sadistic streak that would become his trademark. One day, Casso heard a stevedore boasting about his new metal-reinforced work boots. "Gaspipe took over a forklift and dropped about five hundred pounds of cargo on the guy's feet and broke most of his toes," the ex-detective who grew up in Park Slope recalled. "Afterwards, he laughed and said he wanted to see how good the new boots were."

Soon enough, Casso caught the eye of a Mafia capo in Brooklyn, Christie Tick Furnari, who one day would become the Lucchese consigliere. Furnari's apprenticeship program for his rookie gangster was the customary Mafia training schedule. Gaspipe became a loan-shark enforcer and a bookie. At age twenty, Casso chalked up his first arrest, for bookmaking, that landed him in jail for five days and cost him a $50 fine. It would be his only conviction for the next thirty-three years, despite five more collars between 1965 and 1977. Aided by the Mafia's formula of hiring sly lawyers and scaring witnesses, he won acquittals and dismissals for a variety of serious felonies: assault with a gun, fencing stolen merchandise, bribing a parole officer for the release of a gangster friend, bank burglary, and narcotics trafficking.

Gaspipe's first recorded murder occurred in the mid-1970s; the contract came from Furnari. The task: kill a drug dealer working for the Lucchese family, Lee Schleifer, who was thought to be cooperating with narcotics agents. Casso lured Schleifer to a Mob social club and finished him off with a volley in the head from a silencer-equipped .22 caliber pistol. The hit was proof positive that Gaspipe had made his bones and, with Furnari's blessings, he became a Lucchese made man at thirty-two.

"Soon after this killing took place," Casso wrote decades later in a letter to a judge, "Christie had then sponsored me to become a member in the Lucchese crime family, which was at that time one of the highest honors known among our own society."

Even before his induction into the Honorable Society, Casso was bonding with another wannabe in Furnari's crew, Vittorio Amuso, known (like the Colombo family's Victor Orena) by the familiar nicknames "Vic" and "Little Vic." Amuso was eleven years older than Casso, but their similar bully-boy mannerisms, stocky physical builds, oval faces, and pomaded black brush-cut hairstyles could allow them to pass as brothers or cousins.

Gaspipe and Vic paired off as an effective team and, despite the hypocritical Mafia ban on narcotics imposed by their Lucchese boss, Ducks Corallo, they plunged into drugs and marijuana trafficking. Arrested in one major transaction involving the Sicilian Mafia and heroin smuggled from Thailand, Casso and Amuso managed to get the charges against them dismissed for lack of evidence. Disregarding the hypocritical Mafia prohibition on peddling narcotics, the Lucchese regime gave Amuso his button as a made man, and he and Casso joined a select and sophisticated burglary ring. Dubbed by the police as "the Bypass Gang," a coalition of about fifteen skilled criminals—electronic experts, locksmiths, and safe crackers—disabled burglar alarm security systems, and over a decade in the 1970s and '80s broke into banks and jewelry stores in New York and Long Island. The loot from safe-deposit boxes and vaults was estimated at more than $100 million. Gaspipe and Vic were present at most of the larger heists as watchdogs, to ensure that the Lucchese leaders and other family bosses got their slices of the booty.

As teammates Gaspipe and Vic eagerly volunteered to carry out hit contracts in the 1970s for Furnari, then the capo of a Lucchese group known as "the 19th Hole Crew," named for a Brooklyn bar that was Furnari's headquarters. In addition to his solo debut murder of the narcotics dealer Lee Schleifer, Casso, accompanied by Amuso, carried out four other assignments. Wielding pistols, shotguns, and once a machine gun equipped with a silencer, they killed two victims, while two others miraculously escaped despite serious wounds.

Casso was so devoted to Furnari that he turned down an offer from him in 1980 to take over his old crew as capo, when Christie Tick became the Lucchese consigliere. Rather than a promotion for himself, Gaspipe successfully urged Furnari to reward his partner, Vic Amuso, with the capo's job—and the certain profits that would ensue. Portraying himself as a modest, loyal disciple of Furnari's, Casso preferred working directly for the new consigliere. The borgata's protocol allowed the counselor to retain one soldier by his side as an aide de camp; Furnari chose Casso.

Married to his childhood sweetheart, Lillian Delduca, and living in Brooklyn with her and their young daughter and son, Casso passed himself off as a trucker and as a sales representative for a construction company, while Lillian opened a lingerie boutique in their unpretentious Flatlands neighborhood. On the surface, they resembled many other hardworking, blue-collar families striving to move up in society.

After nearly getting arrested in a 1977 narcotics sting, Gaspipe disappeared from law-enforcement radar screens. As the FBI and New York's Organized Crime Task Force began besieging the five Mob families in the early 1980s, Anthony Salvatore Casso was relegated to the status of a Lucchese spear-carrier. The government's opening thrusts against the Mob were aimed at Mafia kings and barons. On the federal and state investigators' priority charts, Casso was a bottom-rung serf.

Gaspipe's hard-edged reputation, however, was recognized by the rebels in the Gambino family, John Gotti, Frankie DeCicco, and Sammy the Bull Gravano. Rating Casso a potential force to be reckoned with in the Lucchese borgota, DeCicco went so far as to sound him out for his views on their planned murder of Castellano. "Frankie said that Gaspipe told him he didn't give a fuck about Paul," Gravano reported.

Casso never told his immediate supervisor, Furnari, about this conversation. Keeping his mouth shut proved to be a wise decision.

One month after the December 1985 slaying of Castellano, Vincent Gigante, then the boss of the Genovese family, conferred with his Lucchese counterpart, Tony Ducks Corallo, in Furnari's Staten Island home. Although present in the house, Casso did not participate in the high-level meeting. The next night, Furnari filled in Casso and Amuso on the purpose of the huddle: a decision had been reached to avenge the slaying of fellow boss Big Paul Castellano.

The vindictive godfathers, Corallo and Gigante, dismissed as insulting the line put out by Gotti that the Gambinos were mystified by Castellano's murder and were themselves searching for his killers. They concurred that Gotti had violated a holy Mafia canon by assassinating a boss without the tacit authorization of a majority of the Commission. After putting their heads together, the two bosses agreed that Gotti and his second-in-command, Frank DeCicco, had to pay the supreme penalty. Chosen to handle the dangerous double-murder assignment were Casso and Amuso.

Several months earlier, Casso had expressed indifference about the plot to kill Castellano when he was approached by DeCicco. Now his most urgent chore was scheming with Amuso to retaliate for Big Paul's assassination by executing his successor, John Gotti, and Frankie DeCicco. The vendetta against Gotti would lead to DeCicco's brutal execution by a remote-controlled bomb, a crime that confounded Gotti and law-enforcement experts for seven years, until Gaspipe divulged the weird details.

Accompanying the operational orders to murder Gotti and DeCicco was an unorthodox tactical directive. The Genovese and Lucchese leaders wanted Casso and Amuso to wipe out both targets with a weapon traditionally outlawed by the American Mafia—a bomb. Previously, bombs had been banned by the Commission because innocent people might be killed, drawing too much attention to the Mob's internal bloodbaths. Using explosives in this instance, it was thought, would camouflage the Mafia involvement and deter Gotti's revenge seekers from fingering the Genovese and Lucchese families as being behind the murders. A big bang also would distract law-enforcement agents from zeroing in on American mobsters as suspects. Explosives would confuse everyone and, most likely, focus blame on Sicilian mafiosi Zips, who had a record in Italy for blowing up opponents.

A key participant lent to Casso by the Genovese family for the "Get Gotti" job was Herbie "Blue Eyes" Pate. An experienced hit man in the Genovese family, Pate had a rare Mafia talent: he was an ammunitions craftsman, trained while in the U.S. army. The resourceful Casso obtained a plastic explosive called C-4, resembling a long bar of soft clay, and Pate figured out how to detonate it by tinkering with the remote control of a toy car. At his upstate rural home, Pate demonstrated in a trial run for Casso and Amuso the effectiveness of the weapon and his remote-control zapper. All that was left for the conspirators to do was to find the right place to ambush Gotti and DeCicco.

As Gotti in the spring of 1986 tried to solidify his dominance within his own family, he had no inkling of the Genovese-Lucchese intrigue to avenge Castellano's death. Nor did he suspect that the Genovese hierarchs had cemented a pact with two of his own capos, Jimmy Brown Failla and Danny Marino, for help in assassinating him. A confidant and longtime friend of Castellano's, Failla resented Gotti's lightning coup. He also may have harbored the hope that the Genovese regime would help install him as the Gambino boss once Gotti was eliminated.

Gaspipe, responsible for drawing up a plan, found that Gotti was a hard quarry to isolate in a location that would be practical for the hit and would also allow the assassins a fair chance of escaping. Gotti, he complained, "bounced from one area to another," usually in congested spots, surrounded by a thick cordon of bodyguards. Through Failla, however, the C-4 bombers learned of a rare opportunity to knock off Gotti and DeCicco with one blow.

Trying to pacify crews that had been in the Castellano faction, Gotti was visiting their hangouts to rally their support. As one of these goodwill gestures, Gotti and DeCicco scheduled a joint visit to Failla's Veterans and Friends Club in Bensonhurst, Brooklyn. Tipped off by Failla, Casso and his conspirators went into action. Failla told them Gotti and DeCicco would be departing the storefront club together in DeCicco's car. It was a perfect setup for a double wipeout.

Early on Sunday afternoon, April 13, 1986, Casso, together with Amuso and Amuso's brother, Bobby, were staked out in a sedan about a block from Failla's club. The car's tinted windows prevented them from being observed. Herbie

Pate was nearby in his car. All of them saw DeCicco arrive and park his Buick Electra across the street from the club before entering. Pate had concealed the C-4 explosive in a brown paper bag and, carrying that bag and another bag filled with groceries and bread, he strolled toward DeCicco's car. Pretending he had dropped something, Pate bent down, placing the bag with the C-4 explosive under the Buick. He then sauntered back to his own auto.

Gotti probably saved his life that day by canceling his trip to Failla's headquarters at the last minute. Stationed in his car, Pate saw DeCicco walk from Failla's club to his Buick, accompanied by another man. Assuming the second man was Gotti, Herbie Blue Eyes turned on his ignition. With the passenger's side window rolled down, Pate drove slowly toward DeCicco's car, and when he was alongside pressed his remote-control switch. The detonation almost instantly killed DeCicco, who was inside his car, rummaging in the glove compartment for a lawyer's card and telephone number for the man who had accompanied him from the club. That second man, Frank "Frankie Heart" Bellino, slightly resembled Gotti. An undistinguished Lucchese soldier and friend of DeCicco's, Bellino survived, though suffering serious leg and feet wounds.

Metal and glass fragments from the explosion showered Pate's car, and his right ear and face were nicked with minor cuts. Casso and the Amuso brothers drove off unharmed. Christie Tick afterward instructed Casso, "Tell everyone to be on their toes and lay low for a while, but keep looking for an opportunity to get Gotti." The bomb plot, however, was the Lucchese family's only attempt to eradicate Gotti, who remained on good terms with Casso and Amuso, never suspecting that they had tried to blow him to bits.

Accustomed to killing, and never considering himself a target, Casso often traveled alone. Occasionally, the police shadowed him but, alert to surveillance, he was difficult to trail, zooming across lanes and flashing through red lights. On a bright September afternoon in 1986, alone in his car, Gaspipe headed for a restaurant near his home in Brooklyn. Stolen bonds were on his mind, according to an informer's report to federal prosecutors. A Gambino family associate had arranged to meet Casso, presumably to discuss fencing a sizable collection of stolen bearer bonds. The meeting was a ruse. As Casso parked his Cadillac on the street in front of a Carvel's ice cream store, another auto with at least three gunmen pulled alongside and he was raked with gunfire and a shotgun blast through the driver's window. Unarmed and hit in the back and left arm, he staggered across the street to a restaurant, grabbing a table cloth to staunch his bleeding. None of the startled employees or diners told the police who descended on the area that Casso was hiding in a basement freezer. He emerged shivering from the freezer to telephone Vic Amuso, who picked him up and drove him to a hospital.

Detectives traced Casso to the hospital, where he brushed aside questions about the murder attempt and possible links to the Mafia. "There's nobody who doesn't like me. I don't know nothing about organized crime." Casso could offer no explanation for a curious discovery in his car: a confidential Police Department list of the license-plate numbers of unmarked cars used by investigators for surveillance purposes. Except for loss of blood, he was in fairly good condition when he was discharged from the hospital.

Gaspipe quickly surmised who had set him up. He was feuding over the division of spoils from a heroin sale that he had cosponsored with a Gambino capo, Michael "Mickey Boy" Paradiso. The argument between members of two families had festered because the Commission case trial was under way, and the customary sit-down formula for resolving Mob disputes was suspended.

Even before his wounds had healed, Casso's intelligence operatives identified the leader of the hit team that tried to assassinate him. He obtained the gunman's name and police surveillance photos of him from two "dirty" NYPD detectives who were on his payroll for several thousand dollars a month. Both were in units investigating organized-crime cases and had access to sensitive information, including the identities of informants, evidence obtained by the authorities, and pending arrests. Through an associate in the Lucchese family, who was the intermediary in contacting the detectives, Casso earlier worked out a deal with them to inform him of police and FBI investigations of the Mob.

Casso was prepared to kill everyone on the hit team that had failed to get him, but his revenge had to take a back seat for more important consequences arising from the Commission case.

Since the creation of the five families in 1931, the Lucchese borgata had proved to be the most stable and least divisive of the New York families. For more than fifty years, power had been peacefully transferred from Gaetano Gagliano to Tommy Three-Finger Brown Lucchese, and then to Antonio Tony Ducks Corallo. Unlike the other four major families, there had never been an attempt on the life of a Lucchese godfather, and the family had never been riven by an internal war.

Tony Ducks wanted to continue that harmonious tradition. With the Commission trial winding down in the autumn of 1986, Corallo saw the grim writing on the wall. The Lucchese family leadership was about to be decimated, more seriously affected than any other borgata by the Commission case. Realizing that he was finished along with underboss Tom Mix Santoro and consigliere Christie Tick Furnari, Ducks prepared for an orderly transition of authority. Shortly before the guilty verdicts were handed down in November, he summoned Gaspipe Casso and Vic Amuso to Furnari's home in Staten Island. Swayed by Furnari's lobbying, Corallo chose Amuso or Casso as the best candidates to take over the helm of the family. Although neither mobster had lengthy Mob managerial experience, they had proven their loyalty to Corallo's organization and to Furnari. Both were exceptional earners, an optimistic sign that they would keep the family prosperous and competitive with rival Mafia outfits.

Corallo shunted aside the knowledge that both Casso and Amuso were accomplished narcotics traffickers. Vic Amuso had served a prison sentence for a heroin conviction, and Gaspipe had beaten narcotics charges. Corallo must have suspected that much of the riches they brought to him came from drug deals, a practice ostensibly prohibited by him under penalty of death. It no longer mattered.

At the conclusion of the Staten Island meeting, Amuso was designated as the heir to assume Corallo's post as soon as Tony Ducks was trucked off to a life sentence in prison. Only one account of that fateful session has emerged: Casso's version. According to Gaspipe, Corallo, heeding Furnari's advice, decided the leadership could be safely entrusted to either of the consigliere's protégés. "Corallo said, 'One of them has to come up [become boss]' and Christie took me and Amuso into the next room in order for us to decide." Claiming he had no ambition for the family's highest position, Casso says he determined the outcome by endorsing Amuso as the next godfather of the Lucchese family. Although he had once declined becoming a capo in favor of Amuso, Casso soon accepted promotions to consigliere and then underboss in the new setup.

As 1987 began, the old Lucchese hierarchy was imprisoned for life. Ducks Corallo's parting gift to his beloved borgata was a peaceful transfer of power that he was certain would ensure the family's future.

He was dead wrong.

41

Blood Purge

For decades, the Lucchese family was roughly divided into three parts, its main contingent based in Manhattan and the Bronx, and two strong battalions operating in Brooklyn and New Jersey. Before Vic Amuso's anointment, the three previous bosses came from the Manhattan-Bronx section, the family's birthplace, and stocked with the largest crews. The first leaders to emerge from the Brooklyn faction, Vic Amuso and Gaspipe Casso now controlled the third-largest Mafia dominion in New York, consisting of some 120 made men and nearly 1,000 associates and wannabes.

From bugs and informers, federal and state investigators pieced together the high-level changes in the Lucchese borgata. Gregory J. O'Connell, a federal prosecutor in Brooklyn assigned to the Lucchese unit, was tracking the new command structure. Early on, he concluded, "Amuso has the title of boss but the brains and driving force behind the family is Gaspipe." Amuso began almost every day working out by playing handball near his home in Howard Beach, and FBI agents picked up street gossip that Vic was more interested in his sport than the nuts-and-bolts tasks of running the family.

Amuso and Casso were strangers to the capos commanding the Manhattan-Bronx and New Jersey crews. Most of them were older, more experienced mafiosi, and more than likely puzzled by or resentful of the startling ascension of the two Brooklyn wiseguys. Distrustful of the loyalties of the entrenched capos, the new leaders were determined to impose their own dictatorial authority. Motivated by paranoia and unbounded avarice, their strategy unleashed an internal and external reign of terror that rivaled Murder Incorporated's. Before the purge ended, some forty victims—mainly Lucchese made men and associates—lay dead or had vanished and were presumed slain. Most were slaughtered after being labeled by Casso, rightly or wrongly, as disloyal or as informers.

One of the first capos to disappear was the Bronx's Anthony "Buddy" Luongo, who was clipped shortly before Amuso and Casso were officially installed. Luongo's sin: Corallo was believed to have briefly considered naming him as his successor. He might, therefore, be envious of the Brooklyn upstarts who were taking over the borgata. Casso explained to an underling, Alphonse D'Arco, that he and Amuso resolved the potential headache, admitting, "We killed Luongo and buried him."

For a decade, Michael Pappadio, a Bronx soldier, was Ducks Corallo's deputy in the Garment Center, having inherited the important job from his older brother, Andimo. Pappadio was a good earner, funneling to the hierarchy millions of dollars every year from companies he was shaking down for labor peace, and from his own loan-sharking business in the commercial heart of Manhattan. Pappadio's holdings included a secret partnership in a profitable Mob trucking company that had exclusive rights to operate in the Garment Center. Suspecting that Pappadio might be skimming profits for himself, Casso and Amuso abruptly replaced him with Sidney Lieberman, a more trustworthy lackey and associate who worked for them. Since Lieberman was Jewish, they felt he would know how to wring more money from the Jewish-owned companies that predominated in the clothing industry. Lieberman knew his way around the district, and had been the source of rumors that Pappadio was cheating the new administration out of $15 million a year from his rackets. A defiant Pappadio, citing his status as a made man and a former confidant of Ducks Corallo, balked at being ousted from a plum spot by a non-Mafia outsider, a "Jew bastard." He made a grievous mistake. Acting on orders from Casso, a hit team one Sunday morning drove Pappadio to Crown Bagels, a Queens bakery that was owned by a Lucchese soldier. Pappadio thought a routine Mob meeting was to take place. When he entered, one killer shouted, "Surprise!" as another thug battered him over the skull with a heavy copper cable. "What are you doing that for?" a staggering Pappadio moaned, trying to stay on his feet. A third hood finished the contract, firing several shots into Pappadio's head at point-blank range.

The new regime had an ideal method of disposing of bodies. Pappadio's corpse was cremated by a funeral home that provided favors for George Zappola, a made man and Casso's ally.

A second Bronx capo high on Casso's "house cleaning" list was Michael Salerno. He was found in the trunk of his car, shot in the head, his throat slashed from ear to ear. In charge of a large and prosperous crew, Salerno was viewed by Casso and Amuso as a potential challenger to their authority, who was piqued at their promotions over him. He posed another problem for the new leaders because he had been close to Christie "Tick" Furnari, and Casso and Amuso suspected that he knew too much about their pasts, their "dirty laundry." Casso's stated reason for killing Salerno was that he was "a rat," and had skimmed money from the family's hierarchs by secretly running a profitable garbage landfill in Pennsylvania. As a bonus for Casso and Amuso after Salerno's demise they acquired the income from his shylock book, totaling about $7 million in usurious loans.

A Bronx soldier, Anthony DiLapi, handled labor rackets for the family through his post as a corrupt teamsters' union business agent. Sensing the animosity of the new family leaders, DiLapi relocated to California and was swiftly declared disloyal and a plotter against the administration. DiLapi was the nephew of the imprisoned former underboss, Tom Mix Santoro, and Amuso and Casso spun a story that before the Commission case he had schemed with his uncle against Ducks Corallo. With the help of information from the paid-off New York detectives, Casso traced DiLapi to California, where he was gunned down by a four-man hit squad from New York. To get DiLapi, Casso authorized an unusually high expenditure of $10,000 to cover the cross-country expenses of the murderers.

John Petrocelli's error was bragging about his loyalty to a mobster friend, Gus Farace, a Bonanno associate, who had killed a federal narcotics enforcement agent named Everett Hatcher. The agent's murder sparked a wide manhunt and brought immense pressure on the New York families to give up the killer. A general order was issued by leaders of the five families that no help should be given to Farace. Petrocelli was hiding the fugitive, and Casso sent him word that Farace must be killed immediately, thereby ending the Mob's problem. When Petrocelli refused to knock off Farace, a Casso squad shot the disobedient mobster to death in the hallway of his Yonkers apartment building.

His attempt to protect his friend was fruitless. Determined to get the law off the Mafia's back, Bonanno gunmen found Farace's hideout and killed him.

Bruno Facciolo, a Lucchese soldier in Brooklyn, fell out of favor with Gaspipe by neglecting to visit him in 1986 while he was recuperating from the ambush attempt on his life. Casso's enmity was further fueled by Facciolo's socializing with Gambino members, and by a rumor that he had slipped information to the authorities about the DiLapi murder. The two rogue detectives helped out, reporting that they believed Facciolo was working for the FBI. Lured by fellow Lucchese soldiers to a meeting at a Brooklyn auto-body repair shop, Facciolo realized too late that he had been set up. Trying to flee on foot, he was tackled to the sidewalk and dragged inside the shop; passersby made no attempt to intervene or call the police. Aware of his fate, Facciolo begged a last favor—a telephone call to bid farewell to his daughter. The three killers refused. Shot and stabbed, Facciolo's body was found in a car trunk with a canary stuffed in his mouth, the traditional Mafia warning to squealers.

Facciolo's brutal death provoked the murders of two of his Mob partners to prevent them from retaliating. Al Visconti and Larry Taylor, Lucchese associates who specialized with Facciolo in jewel burglaries and holdups, were stalked and shot to death by Casso's assigned gunmen. Visconti was deliberately shot several times in the groin; the new leaders believed he was homosexual and had disgraced the family.

Corrupt union leaders paid a heavy price for conspiracies with Casso and Amuso. Starting in the late 1950s, the Lucchese borgata had forged alliances with union officials to extort millions in payoffs from painting contractors in return for preventing eleventh-hour construction headaches. (As the last construction workers on jobs, painters can create exceptionally costly delays for contractors and developers through slowdowns.) The corrupt painting contractors were further rewarded by mobsters with sweetheart collective-bargaining agreements and permission to hire cheaper, nonunion workers. Investigations by state and federal prosecutors in the late 1980s threatened the arrangements and alarmed the new Lucchese lions, who feared that they might be exposed to indictments. Casso saw James Bishop, a former top official of the six-hundred-member painters' union and a Democratic Party district leader, as a weak participant and the most likely individual to cooperate with prosecutors for a lenient sentence. If he defected, Bishop would have plenty to tell. Unscrupulous union leaders and their Mob partners were dividing with Casso and Amuso kickbacks of up to 10 percent of net profits on almost every large public and private painting contract in the city. On a huge subway job alone, they had split $4 million with the Luccheses.

Casso again called on the corrupt detectives, and they confirmed that Bishop was "singing" to the Manhattan DA's office. So, one May morning, as Bishop prepared to drive off after spending a night in his mistress's Queens apartment, two Casso gunmen made sure he would never testify. He was shot eight times in the head and chest with silencer-equipped automatics.

Along with Genovese, Colombo, and Gambino leaders, Casso and Amuso were reaping steady protection payoffs from companies allowed to participate in rigged inflated bids for the installation of windows at public housing projects. As the FBI closed in on the racket in 1989, the Lucchese bosses grew apprehensive about a linchpin in the conspiracy, John "Sonny" Morrissey, a shop steward in an ironworkers' local representing window installers. The union had long been a Lucchese fief, and Morrissey, a bagman for the borgata, knew a great deal about the mechanics of the shake-downs and the distribution of payoffs to his Mafia handlers. A burly ironworker and a crude scrapper, he proudly advertised himself as a gangster. "I'm a thief and a hoodlum," he often exclaimed after a few drinks. Taking no chances that the talkative Morrissey might sing to the authorities, Casso ordered his extermination with the proviso that his body should not be found; his disappearance would look as if he had fled, seeking to avoid prosecution. Persuading Morrisey to spend a carefree day in the country with them, Lucchese hit men made a detour, pulling up at a deserted housing development site in rural New Jersey. The first gunshot grazed the disbelieving Morrissey. "I'm not a rat," he moaned, crumpling to his knees. As the executioners advanced toward him, he implored them to finish him off quickly and painlessly. They hid his body under tons of landfill. Though his words had failed to save him, Morrisey had been truthful; he had not cooperated with the FBI.

Casso and Amuso exhibited rare moments of relative compassion for their perceived opponents. In his late seventies, and in poor health, Mariano "Mac" Macaluso, a former consigliere, was nevertheless added to Casso's "enemies list." Wealthy and widely respected as an elder by Lucchese mobsters, Macaluso had been a Lucchese soldier for fifty years and could become a threat if he joined a dissenting movement. Summoned to a restaurant meeting by Alphonse D'Arco, a courier from Casso and Amuso, Macaluso was ordered to give up his illicit interests. Macaluso sobbed, "I'm being thrown to the side. It's unfair." D'Arco's reply was blunt: the choices were mandatory retirement or death.

Casso now had the power and troops to settle personal scores. His first priority was identifying and hunting down the gunmen who had ambushed and wounded him in Brooklyn. Aware of Casso's unforgiving fury, the incompetent shooters had scattered to different hideouts after failing to kill him. Target number one for Casso was the principal member of the hit team, James Hydell, a small-time drug trafficker and hoodlum from Staten Island, a half-Italian associate in a Gambino crew. Hydell was the nephew of Gambino capo Danny Marino, a fact that did not earn him clemency from Casso.

"The kid knew he was in trouble," Casso related years later. "I didn't die and he became leery of everybody. Nobody could get near the kid."

Casso asserted in interviews in 2003 that he employed an FBI agent and two New York City detectives to find Hydell. The corrupt trio, he said, were contacted and paid off by Burton Kaplan, a Lucchese associate and his liaison with the lawmen. According to Casso, the FBI man located Hydell and notified the detectives, who picked him up when he ventured out to visit a Mob club in Brooklyn. Pretending they had a warrant for his arrest, the detectives handcuffed Hydell and drove him in a car given to them by Casso to a closed garage. (The green auto was an unmarked police car that Gaspipe had bought at an auction.) Removing their captive from the rear seat, they bound and jammed him into the car's trunk, and then met Casso at a prearranged spot in a Toys "Я" Us parking lot. It was the only time that Casso had personal contact with the detectives and he shook their hands for a job well done. He claimed that although he knew the identity of the FBI agent, he never met him, communicating only through Kaplan. Taking the wheel of the green car, Casso drove off with Hydell still in the trunk, and the detectives followed in Kaplan's car.

"The kid, a big guy, about six-two or three, was kicking the lid in the car and there were a lot of people around in the parking lot," Casso sneered. "But I was not concerned, I had the law on my side, two fucking detectives with me if there was any trouble."

For several hours in the basement of a house in Bergen Beach, a residential section of Brooklyn, the sharpshooter Casso used Hydell for target practice, firing bullets into his legs, arms, and body without delivering a mortal wound. Finally, after Hydell identified the rest of the hit squad that tried to kill him,

Casso ended the torture with a coup de grace slug in his brain. Like many of Casso's victims, Hydell's body was never found.

To locate and abduct Hydell, Casso said he paid a total of $75,000; $25,000 to each of the New York detectives and the FBI agent who assisted him. He claimed he routinely sent each venal lawman $1,000 to $1,500 a month to provide him with confidential information about Mob investigations, and they always got bonuses for special assignments like Hydell's abduction.

Hydell's wretched death did not satisfy Casso's mania for revenge or end the search for the other men who had ambushed him. His private execution squad thought they had bumped off one of Hydell's accomplices, a hood named Nicholas Guido. Tragically, they gunned down the wrong Nicholas Guido, killing a 26-year-old telephone installer outside his home on Christmas Day 1986. The innocent man died because of a slipup by the detective spies who were moonlighting for Casso. Asked to find the would-be assassin Nicholas Guido, they produced the address of a man with the identical name, who lived in Park Slope, Brooklyn. The victim was three years younger than the wannabe mobster Casso was determined to kill.

Casso shrugged off this murder.

"Hey, it's a mistake," he said in an interview. "No big deal." The real Nicholas Guido fled to Florida and surrendered to police on an assault charge; he knew that life in prison would be safer than being on the streets with Gaspipe Casso gunning for him.

The third member of the failed murder team, Robert Bering, escaped Casso's clutches by seeking safety in the Witness Protection Program. A former Transit Authority police officer, he turned himself in to the FBI, admitted that he had been a hired killer for the Mob, and testified about crimes unrelated to Casso, including covert Mafia ownership of city school-bus companies. Bering died in jail of a heart attack at the age of forty, perhaps from anxiety that Gaspipe's vengeance could penetrate prison walls.

Moving up in the underworld as an underboss, Casso decided to live well in the real world. He lavished $1.2 million on constructing and furnishing a new home in Mill Basin, an upscale waterfront enclave in Brooklyn. The architect overseeing the construction was Anthony Fava, a Lucchese associate who had designed and supervised the construction of expensive homes for other family members. Soon after the house was completed in 1991, Fava turned up dead in

Brooklyn. His mutilated, nude body, feet and hands trussed, was left inside a stolen auto. He had been sadistically slain, his body punctured by scores of bullet and knife wounds. While still alive, his face, chest, and arms had been scorched, probably with cigarette burns. The murder was committed on Casso's and Amuso's orders, ostensibly because Fava was suspected of being or becoming a stool pigeon.

From informers' reports, investigators theorized a second factor may have influenced Fava's fate. Casso was worried that, from paper work and records for the new home, the architect had picked up too much information about his financial affairs and money spent on the sumptuous house. Casso's retainers passed along the word that Fava deserved to die because he had overcharged Casso and was a government snitch. Fava had been stripped to his shorts before being killed, indicating that he had been searched for a hidden recording device. He was one more victim falsely smeared as a rat. Afterward, Gaspipe, in a rare suggestion of compassion, chastised the killers for torturing the architect without specific orders from him. The "piece of work," he believed, had warranted a routine murder without prolonged flourishes.

Simply as a friendly gesture for a Brooklyn neighbor whom he liked, Casso could decree death. The neighbor had complained that an overly romantic young man named Angelo Sigona refused to stop pestering his daughter for dates and might endanger her engagement to another suitor. A hit man shot and killed the lovelorn Sigona as he sat in his car. It is unclear if the neighbor only wanted Sigona slapped around, intimidated, not permanently removed. But Casso apparently liked posturing as an omniscient, old-country Mafia godfather who had a solution for every problem.

A more straightforward request came from capo Sal Avellino, the Lucchese family's controller of the garbage-carting industry on Long Island. In the backlash of the Commission case, several old scores needed settling. Avellino wanted to whack Robert Kubecka, the gutsy carter whose undercover work for the state Organized Crime Task Force had led to the bugging of Avellino's car. The Jaguar tapes were devastating evidence against Ducks Corrallo and other Mob aristocrats in the Commission trial. Avellino had escaped indictment in the Commission investigation, but feared that Kubecka might be initiating new criminal and civil cases that would endanger him and the Mafia's $400,000 a year profits from Long Island's carting business.

The Jaguar bug had undercut Avellino's Mob status and reputation for competence. He worried that his words on the tapes might be construed as evidence that he had extorted payoffs from contractors through influence in a teamsters' union and in the association representing garbage haulers. "Whoever controls the employees controls the bosses," Avellino was heard saying on the taped 1983 car conversations, outlining his tactics to two of his soldiers. "Because . . . if you got twenty people and they're not gonna come to work tomorrow [to] pick up that fuckin' garbage, who are you going to listen to?"

Avellino chortled over the Mafia's domination of the teamsters' and the carters' association. "Now when you got a guy that steps out of line and this and that, now you got the whip. A strong union makes money for everybody, including the wiseguys. The wiseguys make even more money with a strong union."

Still free and still running the Long Island rackets in 1989, Avellino feared that Kubecka and his relatives would be vital witnesses in a federal investigation. He wanted Kubecka killed immediately. Authorizing the hit, Gaspipe confirmed that the Long Island carter was indeed talking to the FBI and prosecutors, and therefore was a threat not only to Avellino but to his and Amuso's huge profits from garbage carting. "I have a hook into getting classified information from inside the FBI office," Casso assured underlings.

Casso okayed the murders of Robert Kubecka and his father, Jerry, who had founded their small independent waste-removal company. The Gambino family, which was sharing in the profits from the Long Island garbage rackets, agreed that the hit should be carried out by the Luccheses. At dawn on August 10, 1989, Robert Kubecka and his brother-in-law, Donald Barstow, who also was cooperating with the FBI, were alone in their tiny Long Island office, preparing the day's work schedules. Two Lucchese gunmen burst in and killed them. Jerry Kubecka was spared because he had stayed home that morning.

Although the two witnesses were eliminated, Casso and Amuso faulted the killers, Rocco Vitulli and Frank Frederico, for messing up the job, leaving behind a gym bag containing a gun, and leaving bloodstains from one of the gunmen who had grappled with Kubecka. Still, Gaspipe did not regret the executions. "The guy was an informer. In this life, there's only one way you deal with informers, you kill 'em. He was going from the state to the FBI, he was really pushing the envelope. There was no other option."

For fulfilling the assignment, Frederico got his button from Casso and Amuso and was inducted as a made man. (Indicted for the slayings, Vitulli in 1995 plea-bargained to lesser federal charges for a soft prison term of four years.

Tracked down after fourteen years in hiding, Frederico admitted his role in 2004 and at age seventy-six was sentenced to fifteen years.)

The murder of the two courageous businessmen attracted widespread news coverage. The stories displayed both the Mob's audacity and law-enforcement's weak spots, potentially discouraging other witnesses from whistle-blowing on the Cosa Nostra. The tragedy also embroiled law-enforcement agencies in a dispute over their obvious laxity in safeguarding Kubecka and Barstow. FBI agents and federal prosecutors blamed the state's Organized Crime Task Force for misleading the Kubeckas about the perils of working undercover, and for failing to respond to numerous protection requests by the victims—including Robert Kubecka's plea for assistance the night before the killings. Ronald Goldstock, then the task force's director, maintained that Kubecka had rejected offers to relocate or to enter the Witness Protection Program, saying he wanted to retain his business interests and remain in Long Island. Holding the FBI and federal prosecutors at fault, state investigators argued that Kubecka and Barstow had been working solely with the federal government in the period immediately before the murders, and that this was the Mob's primary motive for the slayings. Kubecka, forty, and Barstow, thirty-five, left behind their wives and five children.

A lawsuit by the widows laid the blame for the murders squarely on the state task force. In 1996, a judge found the unit had failed to alert Kubecka and Barstow that their lives were in danger and had been negligent in protecting them. Their families were awarded a settlement of $9.6 million.

"The state task force took no steps at all for the security of these two men," Robert Folks, the widows' lawyer, said angrily. "They didn't want much, security cameras outside their office and occasional posting of police cars as a warning to the bad guys." A former federal prosecutor in Manhattan, Folks said that state investigators and prosecutors neglected to employ a routine step taken by agencies to protect witnesses: "They should have contacted the Lucchese top guys and warned them about harming 'our witnesses.' That's what is usually done and it puts the heat on them to behave."

Casso's internal purge and the assassinations of dangerous outsiders like Kubecka appeared to be a tactical triumph for the Lucchese bosses. Early in their reign, Vic Amuso and Anthony Casso designated a new capo, Alphonse D'Arco, as the main bagman to collect and deliver payoffs due them from the family's various enterprises. D'Arco got clear instructions on the distribution of loot. "Vic told me, 'Al, we'll let Anthony take care of the cash. I'm more interested in Cosa Nostra things, you know, important things.'" Amuso relied on

Casso's business sense and his fearsome image to ensure that they would get the lion's share of payoffs. As boss, Amuso preferred attending to policy issues, hobnobbing with other dons, appointing capos, and selecting new button men.

Casso had a mania for details. He meticulously kept ledgers recording payments channeled to him from capos and soldiers, and their overhead expenses, including bribes to corrupt lawmen. Another quirk was keeping card files listing the criminal abilities of soldiers and associates. Explaining his filing system to capo George Zappola, Casso noted that he catalogued top-notch car thieves under the letter C. Gaspipe's sharp wit deflated Zappola when he asked for his classification. "Under U for useless."

Before taking charge of the family, Casso and Amuso's main source of income had been derived from narcotics deals. As hierarchs, their drug money was dwarfed by the leadership entitlements they suddenly shared: $15,000 to $20,000 a month from Long Island carting shake-downs; $75,000 a month in kickbacks for guaranteeing eight air-freight companies labor peace and allowing them to cheat employees out of union benefits; $20,000 a week in profits from illegal video gambling machines; and $245,000 annually from a major concrete supplier, the Quadrozzi Concrete Company, to shield it from tough union contracts. (Construction contractors were cautioned by Lucchese strong-arm thugs to use Quadrozzi's ready-mix concrete if they wanted to avoid "serious problems.")

Sidney Lieberman, their special envoy in the Garment Center, was extremely useful. He reportedly enriched them by some $200,000 a year through a subtle shake-down system. According to Department of Labor investigators, Lieberman would get a corrupt official from the International Ladies Garment Workers Union—the industry's largest union—to threaten unionization drives at targeted firms. After an ILGWU organizer showed up at the companies, Lieberman or a lawyer who assisted him would work out under-the-table cash deals to keep the union out of the shops, with more than half of the systemic payoffs destined for the two Lucchese hierarchs. (Years later, Lieberman pled guilty to a RICO labor-racketeering conspiracy and was sentenced to four years in prison.)

As family leaders, Casso and Amuso also got portions of all gambling and loan-sharking profits picked up by the lower ranks. There were also lush, single-shot payoffs. The Colombo family anted up $800,000 for Casso's aid in helping them pilfer steel from the demolished West Side Highway. For allowing the Gambino family to take over a Lucchese-protected general contractor for one project—a huge Coney Island housing complex—they were rewarded with $600,000.

Following the lead of the Colombo family, the Lucchese borgata branched into gasoline-tax thefts, forming a partnership with a Russian gangster, Marat Balagula. "He made millions off the gas-tax business and our family made a lot of money with him," Gaspipe disclosed years later. When another Russian tough guy demanded a $600,000 protection payment from Balagula, the Luccheses killed him. Casso could only recall the rival Russian's first name, "Vladimir." His full name was Vladimir Reznikov.

For himself, Casso was drawing more than $100,000 a year from his personal loan-sharking business. He also maintained an exclusive sinecure: control over George Kalikatas, a Greek-American gangster who in 1990 alone passed along $683,000 to him for permission to operate loan-sharking, bookmaking, and extortion rings in Queens. And every Christmas, there was a customary combined gift of more than $100,000 to the boss and underboss from the crews, a token of respect.

The onrush of wealth substantially altered Gaspipe Casso's lifestyle. In addition to his costly new house, he went on regal buying sprees, spending in one day $30,000 for clothes and more than $100,000 for a 10.5-carat diamond ring. His arrogant, roughneck character, however, never deserted him. Dining in a French restaurant in Miami, he ordered the most expensive wine available, a magnum costing $3,000. The sommelier performed an elaborate decanting ritual with a candle flame to remove sediment and to ensure the delicate bouquet of the grapes. Gaspipe tasted the wine, nodding approvingly to the hovering sommelier. Then as his companions roared, Casso poured a bottle of Seven-Up into the decanter. One Christmas season, Casso showed up with a large group of gangsters and their girlfriends at Rockefeller Center's Sea Grill Restaurant, popular for its picture windows facing the ice skating rink. Lacking a reservation, Casso was told by the maître d' that there was no hope of getting a table. Counting and placing $100 bills in the man's hands, Casso got a ringside table. The tip cost him $1,400.

In 1990, after almost four years at the pinnacle of the Lucchese family, Casso and Amuso felt secure. By inducting seventeen young members, they had fattened the ranks of loyal soldiers who could be relied upon to report any murmur of dissent. Their real or imagined internal borgata enemies were in their graves. Another asset was their obscure profiles. There were no media or government spotlights illuminating them as important mafiosi and Cosa Nostra monarchs. All signs were favorable for a long and successful run of their administration. Life was so comfortable and they were so close that Gas and Vic and their wives vacationed together without bodyguards in Disney World.

Best of all, millions of dollars were pouring into their coffers.

42

The Professor and Fat Pete

Even in the fading light, Al D'Arco could see the agitation roiling Anthony Gaspipe Casso. As they walked along the embankment in Brooklyn's Fort Hamilton Park, watching the sun sink over New York harbor, Casso delivered the unsettling news: he and Vic Amuso were going on the lam to escape imminent arrest on racketeering charges. Late that Saturday afternoon in May 1990, D'Arco had been summoned to an emergency meeting at "the Cannon," a spot in the park near an old artillery piece.

Casso had in the past dropped more than one hint that bribed federal and local law-enforcement agents were surreptitiously giving him valuable confidential information. He had coined the nickname "Crystal Ball" for the corrupt mole who had reported his own pending arrest.

Now, Casso hurriedly filled in D'Arco on the details. In two days, federal indictments would be unsealed against him, Vic Amuso, and high-ranking members of the Genovese, Gambino, and Colombo families. They had been reeled in on RICO enterprise charges stemming from the Mob's control of contracts to install windows in the city's housing projects through extortions and rigged bids; the investigation would be dubbed "the Windows case."

The Lucchese boss Vic Amuso was already holed up in a hideout. "What are you doing?" D'Arco asked. "You'd better get out of here too. How do you know you ain't going to go to your house and they're going to be laying there for you? You're going to be pinched."

Confident that his information—presumably from a dishonest FBI employee—was accurate, and that the arrests were set for the following Monday, Casso explained his reasons for becoming a fugitive. He and Amuso believed they would stand a better chance of beating the charges after the other defendants were tried. The first trials would be a preview of the prosecution's evidence and its strength. Tried at a later date, Amuso and Casso would come into court with lawyers better-armed for legal combat.

Casso delivered other important news. While Amuso and Casso were away, D'Arco would be acting boss, although not with the official title. Major policy decisions would still be in the hands of Amuso and Casso, and they had devised a circuitous system for contacting D'Arco from their hideouts. Handing D'Arco a list of public pay phones and their locations in New York City and in Long Island, Casso said he would call him at these numbers. A courier would tell him when and where he should take the calls It was a system intended to frustrate law-enforcement efforts to tap the mobsters' conversations and trace their calls.

"I'll see you," Casso said, winding up the rendezvous. "I'll be in touch. You're the boss. Don't worry. Do only the big things, don't bother with small things." Before parting, Casso locked D'Arco in a tight embrace and tears soaked the eyes of the callous killer.

Alphonse D'Arco was a relative newcomer to command. His career in the Lucchese family had been tedious and unpromising. Slightly built, balding, and generally soft-spoken, he was one of those mafiosi who passed more easily for an obsequious clerk than a strong-armed gangster. Most of his Mafia life had been spent as a scrambler, a low earner, a wannabe mixed up in crimes where a made man or a capo thought he might be useful as an accessory. A Brooklyn boy, with several Mob-connected relatives, he grew up in neighborhoods where the Cosa Nostra was looked upon as a natural part of the landscape. In D'Arco's words, "It was like a forest and all the trees around it were organized-crime guys."

Formal education was of secondary importance to D'Arco, and at fifteen he was working full-time at legitimate menial jobs while trying to ingratiate himself with a Lucchese crew in Canarsie, a middle-class section in Brooklyn. Never pulling off a big score, he made a hardscrabble living participating in a variety of crimes: robberies, burglaries, arsons, hijackings, bookmaking, running dice games, counterfeiting, and one armored-car robbery—any illegality where he could fit in as an accomplice. His one attempt to pull off a big solo stunt was a disaster. He was nabbed trying to fence $500,000 in stolen stock certificates, and at twenty-nine, was sentenced to five years in Sing-Sing (Ossining) Prison.

Returning to the streets in 1966 as an associate with the Canarsie crew, D'Arco resumed scratching out an illegal income from his old trades, primarily illegal gambling and loan-sharking. He also tried his hand at narcotics trafficking, the surest way of making big bucks quickly. Never eminently successful himself as a heroin and cocaine wholesaler, D'Arco made some important connections in the Lucchese family through attempted drug deals, and connected with a pair of comers, Vic Amuso and Anthony Casso.

D'Arco's long service to the Canarsie crew finally was rewarded when, in 1982, at the overly ripe age of fifty, he was inducted as a made man, with Ducks Corallo himself officiating. Plagued by hard luck, D'Arco barely had time to enjoy or cash in on his promotion to the rank of soldier. Several months after becoming an official wiseguy, he was sentenced to a prison term of almost four years. After an arrest on heroin trafficking, he plea-bargained for a reduced sentence. Paroled in late 1986, D'Arco returned amid tectonic changes in the Lucchese clan. Amuso and Casso had taken over the borgata.

The capo of D'Arco's Canarsie crew, Paul Vario, died of natural causes in 1988, providing Amuso and Casso an ideal opening to install their own man as captain of one of the family's wealthiest outfits. Despite his undistinguished Mafia resumé, paltry earnings, and limited time as a soldier (more than half of which had been spent in prison) Al D'Arco was chosen. He had the prime qualifications the bosses desired: gratitude, loyalty to them for his rapid promotion, a record of obediently following orders, and an unassertive background that virtually guaranteed he would never pose a threat to the bosses. Almost from the start of his association with the Lucchese family, D'Arco had been called "Little Al." Amuso and Casso thought he deserved a snappier nickname. His unthreatening persona and his bespectacled appearance—he favored tweed jackets, white shirts, and bland ties—prompted them to sarcastically tag him "the Professor."

Along with his promotion came an immense boost in D'Arco's finances. Previously, he operated a combined bookmaking and snack stand, the Hamburger Palace, near Manhattan's West Side docks, to supplement his meager Mob earnings from numbers and loan-sharking. Suddenly, thanks to Amuso and Casso, his pockets were bulging. One of his entitlements as capo was acquiring his predecessor's shylock book, which included an initial payment to him of $160,000, and a weekly income of about $10,000: Additionally, his share of the earnings of his crew—fourteen soldiers and some one hundred associates—netted him several thousand dollars a week. A good part of this treasure came from shake-downs of air-freight companies, bakeries, and funeral parlors.

Earlier, D'Arco had moved to Manhattan from Brooklyn, and his soaring wealth enabled him to open La Donna Rosa restaurant in Little Italy. The restaurant, which became the Luccheses' new meeting hall, was on the square named in memory of Lieutenant Joseph Petrosino, the New York detective killed by the Sicilian Mafia at the turn of the twentieth century. Through Mob and political influence, D'Arco wangled a prize sought by millions of New Yorkers from the state: an inexpensive rent-subsidized apartment. Ideal for D'Arco, the apartment was located in a desirable section of Little Italy and near La Donna Rosa. Staying clear of storefront Mafia clubs to avoid law-enforcement surveillance, D'Arco used the restaurant as a convenient and safe site for conferences with Casso and other Lucchese mobsters. Aware of the woes caused by Title III wiretaps and bugs, the Professor had his apartment and restaurant swept periodically for listening devices. As a sign of gratitude to his bosses, D'Arco sent his technicians to certify that Casso's home and the Walnut Bar, a Brooklyn hangout frequented by Amuso and Gaspipe, were free of secret mikes.

The new Lucchese bosses, Vic Amuso and Gaspipe Casso, had other uses for D'Arco. They appointed him their personal bagman, responsible for picking up systematic payoffs from various rackets, and at Christmas, it was D'Arco who gathered about $100,000 from crew captains as a holiday gift to Amuso and Casso.

D'Arco handed all the plunder, more than $1 million a year, to Casso, the hierarchy's treasurer. Aware of Casso's paranoia about being shortchanged and of his zeal for exactitude, D'Arco gave him a written record of every penny he received for the bosses and its source. For added insurance, D'Arco kept his own ledger of the payments.

Partly as a reward for D'Arco's services, the two bosses honored him by presiding at the induction of his son Joseph into the borgata and placed him in his father's crew. Following the ceremony in the basement of a Canarsie home, Casso nudged Amuso and announced gravely to D'Arco, "Your son belongs to us now, he doesn't belong to you anymore." Following his father's path, Joe

D'Arco became a drug dealer. He also began sampling his own wares, descending into heroin addiction.

Before D'Arco came under Casso's tutelage, there was no firm evidence of his involvement in any murders. But as Amuso and Casso's most dependable capo, he served as a conspirator in many of their reign-of-terror killings. The Lucchese family's Professor helped lure Mike Pappadio, the ousted Garment Center rackets supervisor, to his death in a bagel factory, where D'Arco bludgeoned him before he was fatally shot by another mobster. He participated in or knew the details of at least eleven executions. For the murder of Anthony DiLapi, he assigned his son to the team that hunted him down in California. The killers of a fellow capo from the Bronx, Mike Salerno, were personally selected by D'Arco. To facilitate one murder for Casso, D'Arco obtained a submachine gun with a silencer, test-firing it from a window in his apartment before transferring it to the designated hit man.

Amuso and Casso's flight in May 1990 failed to halt the internal purges. Many of the hits were arranged by D'Arco at Casso's orders. Murder instructions came from Casso, rarely from Amuso, via the prearranged calls to the public phones. Even as a fugitive, Casso managed to obtain confidential information from his law-enforcement spies, relaying the secrets to D'Arco. In the fall of 1990, he told D'Arco to warn John Gotti and Sammy Gravano that they would be arrested on federal indictments around Christmas. The information was accurate.

The fugitive Lucchese leaders were sufficiently confident to surface for occasional conferences with the Professor. He met them twice in the Scranton, Pennsylvania, area, once in a tavern and once in a supermarket parking lot. Affecting disguises, both men had grown beards and wore sunglasses and baseball caps. Apparently confident that they would not be recognized, or that D'Arco might have been tailed by agents, Amuso and Casso drove off together in a black Jeep at the end of the sessions. Taking even a greater risk, they slipped several times into New York for talks with D'Arco, usually in safe houses in Brooklyn. D'Arco found Casso undaunted by the problems of being a hunted fugitive, continually tossing him ideas for expanding the family's activities. Seizing upon the divisions in the Colombo family between the Carmine Persico and Vic Orena factions, Casso proposed a peace plan in a private conversation with D'Arco. The Luccheses, Casso said, could end the Colombos' incessant wars by absorbing them into their own gang. The judicious D'Arco had agreed to all of Casso's previous proposals, regardless of their danger, but now he ratcheted up his courage and objected to the merger idea. The Colombos, he argued, could not be trusted as partners, and the Gambino and Genovese families would be incensed if the Luccheses created a borgata larger and stronger than either of theirs. In his own mind, he reckoned that Casso's ulterior motive for uniting the two gangs was to establish himself as boss of the combined family and thereby become the country's most important Mafia don.

It was a rare display of candor by D'Arco. A moment later, he reverted to his usual submissiveness. An outburst by Casso about Lucchese wiseguys gave him a renewed warning of what happened to Mob members Casso distrusted. Ticking off the names of ten soldiers, Casso vowed that he would invite all of them to a victory party as soon as his legal problems were over. Before they ate, he continued, "I'm going to kill them all because they took advantage of me while I was on the lam."

Seven months after the bosses went into hiding, D'Arco was given the title of acting boss. On January 9, 1991, the family leadership met at the Canarsie home of a Lucchese soldier. "Al, you're the boss now," Amuso said, opening a bottle of wine to celebrate. "You're running the family." Though he had the title, D'Arco's actual authority remained severely limited. Amuso and Casso informed him that they would continue calling the shots, making all major policy decisions, and receiving the bulk of the regime's income. Moreover, Amuso forbade D'Arco to authorize murders or induct soldiers, a boss's unquestioned prerogatives. Indicative of D'Arco's subservient role, before the meeting broke up the new acting boss turned over to Casso $75,000, the latest cash pickup he had made for him.

Amuso and Casso's absence created bickering within the ranks over who actually had the authority to make snap decisions and resolve disagreements with other families. D'Arco increasingly perceived that Gaspipe, who talked with him frequently through the prearranged telephone system, distrusted him. Although designated as acting boss, D'Arco sensed he was getting "curved instructions" from Casso, who was transmitting the same information and directions he received to other Lucchese members. The curved instructions were designed to determine if D'Arco was faithfully carrying out his bosses' commands. It was evident they were questioning either his loyalty or his ability.

That spring of 1991, Casso ordered a hit that astonished D'Arco. The contract was for a capo who, D'Arco knew, had been Casso's right hand for years:

Peter "Fat Pete" Chiodo, a four-hundred-pound intimidator of balky contractors and tardy loan-shark clients. Together with Amuso and Casso, Chiodo had been indicted the year before on RICO charges linked to the Windows case. Compounding Chiodo's legal problems was a second indictment for corruption involving the Lucchese family's control of a New York painters' union. One of Casso's "Angels of Death," Fat Pete had led the team that whacked Sonny Morrissey, the ironworkers' union leader.

Fat Pete had not become a fugitive. Facing two trials, the forty-year-old mafioso decided to plead guilty to both indictments, hopeful that a reduced sentence might allow him to be paroled in ten years. Otherwise, the double-barreled racketeering convictions could mean his spending the rest of his life in prison. Before copping pleas, Chiodo committed an unpardonable sin by failing to ask permission from Amuso and Casso. His bosses both had vital stakes in his decision since they were also defendants in the two cases. Infuriated at not being consulted, and suspecting that Chiodo was cooperating with the prosecution for leniency, Casso telephoned D'Arco. "Kill Fat Pete" was his brisk order.

Having worked for and murdered for Casso, Chiodo realized that his guilty pleas might enrage Gaspipe. Protecting himself before his sentencing date, he kept close to his home in Staten Island, venturing out only when encircled by a swarm of relatives. To smoke out Chiodo, D'Arco recruited a member of his crew who knew his habits and the places he frequented, and used Mob technicians to tap Fat Pete's home phone for leads on where hitters could jump him. The mobsters learned from the taps that Chiodo was leaving the area for an undisclosed hideout until his sentencing date; before departing on the morning of May 8, 1991, he planned to drive his Cadillac to a Staten Island service station for an engine checkup. Three shooters, including Al D'Arco's son Joe, were waiting in two cars to waylay him. Opening the hood of his car, Chiodo spotted the assassins approaching. Drawing his gun, he fired first, retreating as bullets whistled around him. None of the shooters was nicked, but Chiodo collapsed in a heap, struck twelve times all over his body. Believing him dead, the gunmen and their wheel men sped away.

The shooters were wrong. Although he suffered grievous abdominal wounds and a disabled right arm, emergency surgery lasting eight hours saved Chiodo's life. Surgeons credited his enormous obesity for saving his life; his fat prevented the slugs from fatally penetrating a vital organ or artery.

Still trying to fulfill Casso's orders, D'Arco's hit squad looked for a second chance to finish him off in the hospital. A Lucchese gangster masquerading as a doctor, accompanied by a nurse who was friendly with one of the family's soldiers, tried to sneak into Chiodo's hospital room. But a screen of FBI agents and police officers guarding the wounded mobster prevented unauthorized persons from getting close to him.

Before the attempt on his life, Fat Pete Chiodo had spurned an offer from prosecutors for greater leniency if he testified against higher-ups and other mobsters. "I appreciate what you guys are trying to do but no thanks—goodbye and good luck," Chiodo told Charles Rose and Gregory O'Connell, the federal prosecutors handling the Windows case. Twelve bullet wounds finally convinced him that survival depended on his breaking his *omertà* vow and converted him into an informer. At bedside interrogations, he fleshed out for the two prosecutors details of numerous murders and other crimes committed by his former bosses, Amuso and Casso, and other Lucchese members.

Realizing the damage that Chiodo could inflict upon them, Amuso and Casso tried another tactic to dissuade him from ratting. Casso instructed D'Arco to get word to Chiodo's parents that they would be killed if their son testified or cooperated with the prosecution. The threat violated the Mafia's presumed code of honor that exempts innocent relatives from retaliation for a mobster's transgressions, but, once again, following orders, D'Arco's soldiers made sure the message was delivered. Chiodo took the threat seriously and his wife and children and other close relatives were whisked into the Witness Protection Program. The two Lucchese bosses did strike back at Fat Pete's family members who declined joining the parade into the protection program. The body of his uncle, Frank Signorino, was found stuffed into a car trunk, and his sister, Patricia Capozzalo, was seriously wounded when a masked gunman shot her in the back and neck with a silencer-equipped pistol.

The bungled hit on Chiodo further weakened D'Arco's reputation as an effective acting boss. In July 1991, he attended a priority meeting with the bosses in the Staten Island home of a girlfriend of Richard Pagliarulo, a Lucchese soldier. Amuso and Casso showed up clean-shaven, their beards gone, making no attempt to disguise themselves. They announced D'Arco's removal as acting boss and the establishment of a panel of four capos as a temporary hierarchy to conduct the family's business in their absence. Although D'Arco was one of the four, it was a humiliating demotion, indicating the leadership's displeasure with his handling of crucial assignments. He was particularly disturbed by Amuso's refusal to speak directly to him or look him in the eye.

Several days after the administrative shakeup, the borgata was rattled by the arrest of their titular boss, Vic Amuso. Alone at a shopping mall near Scranton, Amuso was pounced upon by FBI agents as he made a call from a public phone. His last hideout was never located. The FBI did learn that, registered under the surname "Ricci," Amuso had spent two of his fourteen months as a fugitive in The Inn at Nichols Village, a resort hotel in Clarks Summit, a town north of Scranton, where he had friends. The circumstances of his capture indicated that help from an informer, not investigative skills, had tipped off the feds. An anonymous telephone caller had "dropped a dime" on Amuso, informing the bureau of the approximate time he would appear at the mall. Someone close to Amuso in the Lucchese family knew about the prearranged telephone system and had betrayed him.

With Amuso in custody and facing a RICO trial, Casso's shadow over the family loomed larger. Totally in control of the borgata, he continued to communicate with D'Arco, getting updates from him about the family's business affairs and transmitting orders. But D'Arco sensed a growing frost, an estrangement, in the clandestine telephone conversations. Preying on the Professor's mind was Casso's attempt to terrorize Chiodo's relatives and a haunting conversation he had had with Fat Pete shortly before the contract was issued on his life. "These guys [Amuso and Casso] have a pattern of calling people rats and they are marking guys rats and killing them," Chiodo cautioned. "I got information that you and I are going to be killed and hurt."

Having assisted in the murders and attempted homicides of more than a dozen victims Casso had classified as stool pigeons, D'Arco fretted about his own fate. He knew that the mere whisper of disloyalty, without substantiation, would provoke Casso into whacking even the most faithful servant.

The four-man panel set up by Amuso and Casso to oversee routine matters gathered once a week, and on Thursday, September 19, 1991, D'Arco dutifully attended a meeting in the Kimberly, a Midtown Manhattan hotel. During the afternoon session, Mike DeSantis, a soldier, showed up although he was not part of the group. DeSantis worked for another panel member, capo Frank Lastorino, and was an efficient gunman frequently used by Casso. D'Arco spotted a pistol stuck in the small of DeSantis's back, under his shirt, and noticed that he was wearing a bullet-proof vest; the gunman looked as if he were preparing for a shoot-out.

"This is it. I'm going to be hit," D'Arco thought. Jumping to his feet, over the protests of Lastorino and the other panel gangsters, he scurried out the door.

Friday, the next morning, D'Arco's parole officer from his narcotics sentence telephoned him at home and told him that the FBI had learned there was a contract on his life. Now certain that Casso was out for his hide, D'Arco crossed his own Rubicon. Together with his wife, Dolores, his mobster son Joe, and other close relatives, he fled from the city. He had decided to defect but was too frightened to surrender at FBI headquarters in downtown Manhattan, fearing that Casso might reach "Crystal Ball" or another of his moles, and order his death. On Saturday night, the cautious Professor showed up unannounced at the FBI office in suburban New Rochelle, ready to confess to his own serious offenses and tell all he knew about the hideous crimes he had committed on behalf of Gaspipe Casso and Vic Amuso.

Called in for his questioning, federal prosecutors Rose and O'Connell met the jittery turncoat in an upstate hotel, an FBI cordon had been assigned to protect him. "Even though he was in a room with agents, he was so paranoid of Gaspipe that he was hiding in the bathroom when we came in," O'Connell recalled. "He told us, 'You have to understand how dangerous this guy is. He has sources, agents, he knows what's going on.'"

Looking back, trying to explain his reasons for deserting the Mafia, D'Arco was bitter about the way Amuso and Casso exploited him. "When a job needed to be done, whenever they needed to do something unpleasant to someone, I was the prick chosen by them," he told the prosecutors and agents. His sudden bolt, he acknowledged, had been costly, forcing him to abandon his Mob wealth, including $1.5 million in loan-sharking money circulating on the street. All of his illicit assets, he knew, would be confiscated by Casso and other capos, but he did hang on to $55,000 that he had kept as an emergency cache.

Before Fat Pete Chiodo was shot and Al D'Arco surrendered voluntarily, federal and state law-enforcement agencies were essentially ignorant of Amuso's and Casso's killing spree and the revamped Lucchese regime. Unexpectedly, two high-ranking capos were now providing them with chapter and verse on the family's most violent crimes and best-kept secrets. Hundreds of pages of debriefing reports by FBI agents, titled 302s, documented D'Arco's and Chiodo's firsthand accounts of murders and rackets, many previously unknown to the authorities. The defectors, reconstructing conversations and meetings with

Amuso, Casso, and other mobsters, gave the government a graphic inventory of slayings, attempted hits commissioned by Amuso and Casso, the killers' names, and the disposition of the victims' corpses. Amuso and Casso's operational methods, the Lucchese family's revised table of command, the telephone system used to communicate with the fugitive bosses, and the identities of new capos and soldiers were disclosed and gift-wrapped for the government. Professor D'Arco also produced the financial records he had squirreled away in his apartment, providing the agents with the full dimensions of the family's wealth. D'Arco and Chiodo unveiled the Lucchese mosaic of rackets; how through control of some twenty union locals, the family exacted millions of dollars in payoffs for protection and for rigged bids from dozens of construction, air-freight, and garbage-carting companies.

For added insight, the two turncoat capos explained how the borgata inflated the cost of buying a bunch of bananas or a head of lettuce in the city, by intimidating and shaking-down major wholesalers in the vast fruit and vegetable market in Hunts Point in the Bronx and in a smaller one in Brooklyn. It was common knowledge that the Luccheses had embedded interests in both produce markets, but the FBI had made little headway in cracking the Mob's control. D'Arco changed the bureau's prospects by identifying both the Bronx crew members and the union collaborators used to extract payoffs from merchants in the markets by threatening work stoppages and disruptions. The extortion costs, naturally, had been passed along to the public for decades in the form of higher consumer prices for fresh fruit and vegetables.

The detailed information about the Luccheses' violent and white-collar crimes was an evidentiary gold mine. Together, the Professor and Fat Pete sprung open the door to potential indictments of more than fifty Lucchese mafiosi and associates.

43

Tumac's Turn

As agents and prosecutors sifted through Al D'Arco and Pete Chiodo's evidence, a third and more important Lucchese capo was trying to extricate himself from the minefield laid by Gaspipe Casso.

He was Anthony Accetturo, the boy from Newark who obtained the nickname "Tumac," for his caveman ferocity, and who described his admission into Cosa Nostra by Ducks Corallo as "the greatest honor of my life."

A consummate mafioso and a fervent believer in the sanctity of the Mafia's code of honor, Accetturo represented the Mafia ideal. Loyal, absolutely trustworthy, he had profited beyond his wildest dreams from three decades of dedication to the Honorable Society. Tumac had risen from a lowly loan-shark muscleman and numbers runner in Newark to become a sophisticated capo, and eventually commander of the entire New Jersey branch of the Lucchese family. Corallo had been an indulgent godfather, allowing him wide latitude for more than twenty years as the Lucchese's most successful member in the Garden State and in Florida. "Unbelievably great," Accetturo replied to his soldiers when asked about his relationship with Ducks. Under Corallo's long tenure, Accetturo had grown enormously rich, netting about $500,000 yearly from his crew's traditional rackets—gambling, loan-sharking, narcotics, and protection extortions—and from its takeover of legitimate businesses.

Part of Accetturo's plunder was laundered through investments in real estate, insurance, asphalt, equipment-leasing, and garbage-carting companies. In the 1980s, Accetturo reported to the IRS average annual earnings of approximately $100,000. His criminal income was actually five times larger, but the investments provided reasonable cover for his affluent lifestyle in New Jersey and Florida.

Seeking criminal ventures beyond New Jersey, Accetturo in the 1970s established an outpost in South Florida, and bought a home in Hollywood, a resort town north of Miami. No single family exercised exclusive territorial rights in Florida, and the Miami area has always been wide open to Mafia entrepreneurs. When Accetturo set up shop in Florida, the state was experiencing an economic and population boom, and he took advantage of the opportunity to initiate drug deals, illicit gambling, and extortion shake-downs of various companies. Deputies safeguarded his New Jersey interests, and the Florida sojourns helped Accetturo avoid subpoenas from investigation committees in his native state. Tumac's New Jersey State Police intelligence file cited his frequent flights to and from Florida, under the alias "Anthony Anderson."

A file entry on April 10, 1975, wrongly characterized him as more powerful than any other organized-crime figure in South Florida. Although Accetturo's Mob status was then soaring, in retrospect he was never the most significant Mob manager in the Miami area. The only Cosa Nostra godfather in Florida from the 1950s through the '80s was Santo Trafficante, the uncontested boss in Tampa on the Gulf Coast, and a force to be reckoned with throughout the state. Accetturo never poached on Trafficante's territory or challenged him. He diplomatically exhibited the utmost deference to the Florida don, seeking his advise about racket innovations in the state, and personally chauffeuring Trafficante when he was conducting business from his second home in the Miami area.

One of the reasons why Accetturo admired Ducks Corallo was because the New York boss was undemanding when it came to money. When Ducks first took over in 1970, the New Jersey wing every year contributed hundreds of thousands of dollars to the New York hierarchy. By the 1980s, the annual payments had been substantially trimmed; Accetturo was transferring a paltry $10,000 to $50,000 without drawing flak from New York. Wealthy as Croesus and getting on in years, Corallo became less gluttonous and lowered his demands from the New Jersey crew. Duck's conviction in the Commission case and the ascension of Vic Amuso and Anthony Casso in the late 1980s ended Accetturo's idyllic era.

Now, for the first time, he was locked in a struggle with anointed Mob leaders. The new hierarchs considered a $50,000-a-year cut from New Jersey a base insult, and demanded that Accetturo fork over up to 50 percent of his crew's take. Simultaneously, the government's widening scrutiny added to Tumac's troubles. In early 1987, like his former boss, Corallo, Accetturo was indicted on RICO charges, with a life sentence looming if convicted. After thirty years of evading felony trials, he had been cited as the head of the Lucchese borgata's New Jersey crew, a criminal enterprise. The trial in Newark, New Jersey, delved into the gang's operations in that state and in Florida, including cocaine trafficking, credit-card frauds, gambling and loan-sharking. Federal prosecutors focused their case on evidence from low-level informers and bugged conversations, but the cautious Accetturo had never been caught on the tapes. He and nineteen soldiers and associates were defendants in a trial that lasted twenty-one months, the longest Mafia RICO trial ever held. Despite the length of the proceedings, the jury needed only fourteen hours to reach a decision in August 1988: all twenty defendants were found not guilty.

This was the first major RICO case to end in mass acquittals and a Mafia clean sweep. The bitter failure was a stinging rebuke to the Justice Department, and prompted it to avoid future "megatrials," involving a dozen or more Mafia defendants in complex, marathon proceedings. Federal prosecutors in the Accetturo trial, however, had been trumped by a tactic used frequently by the Mob: fixing the jury. In an extraordinarily lucky break, one juror turned out to be a nephew of an Accetturo crew member who had not been indicted. For a $100,000 bribe the nephew guaranteed at least a hung jury. As it turned out, his persuasiveness in the jury room was effective in obtaining blanket acquittals for Accetturo and his entire criminal entourage.

Having dodged a RICO bullet, Tumac Accetturo now faced Mafia justice as dispensed by Little Vic Amuso and Gaspipe Casso. Accetturo refused to turn over half of the crew's future earnings; nor would he come to New York to meet with the new leaders. By defying the regime, he knew he was violating a fundamental Mafia rule, but he was adamant, telling his lieutenants, "I won't kowtow or buckle under." His mafioso rationale was that Casso and Amuso's demands were insatiable, and they were breaking a financial tradition and pact established with him by their predecessor, Ducks Corallo.

Little Vic and Gaspipe had a ready solution for Tumac's recalcitrance. Stigmatizing him as a rat, they stripped him of his rank of capo and issued murder contracts on him and his son Anthony junior, a member of his New Jersey crew.

Casso also justified whacking Accetturo because he supposedly had violated a Cosa Nostra rule by using his wife, Geraldine, to transmit instructions to members of his crew. Casso claimed there was an inviolable prohibition against using women in Mafia activities.

In the fall of 1988, shortly after the acquittals in Newark, the entire New Jersey crew was summoned by Amuso and Casso to get the official word on restructuring their outfit. About ten members, half the crew's made wiseguys, showed up outside a home in Canarsie where the meeting was to be held in a basement. But in a comic-opera scenario, admitting to each other their fear of being set up for a mass execution inside the house, the New Jersey mobsters scattered to their cars and drove off. Later, the entire New Jersey faction boycotted a 1988 Brooklyn Christmas party thrown by Amuso and Casso, and refused in early 1989 to venture into Manhattan for another mandatory session. Casso exploded. "That's it! Kill them all," he commanded Al D'Arco.

Over the next year or so, most of Accetturo's band, were driven back to the fold by terror. They deserted him, aligning themselves with Amuso and Casso. Al D'Arco and Fat Pete Chiodo were delegated by Casso to arrange the executions of the disloyal remnants of the New Jersey crew: Accetturo, his son, and seven loyalists who stuck with their old skipper. Lecturing members of the New Jersey unit at a strategy sit-down in his La Donna Rosa restaurant, D'Arco read them the riot act. "Accetturo is an outlaw and you have to make all efforts to kill him and his son and whoever sticks by him." To home in on "the outlaws," two of Accetturo's former soldiers handed D'Arco photographs of Accetturo, his wife, their son Anthony junior, and several other soldiers and associates in his rebellious circle. Most of the photos had been taken at dinner parties in Accetturo's New Jersey home. Labeling Accetturo's photo as "Tu" for Tumac, and his son's as "Little Tu," D'Arco circulated the pictures to fourteen soldiers and wannabes on the lookout for the father and son in New Jersey and in Florida from late 1988 into 1990.

Emphasizing the urgency of the hits, Casso opened the administration's vault, doling out large sums for bumping off the Accetturos and their dwindling forces. Tommy Ricciardi, who stuck with Tumac, was located hunkering down in a rural home near Toms River, in southern New Jersey. Through a quirky coincidence, Ricciardi's hideout was adjacent to a farm owned by a friend of a Lucchese soldier from Brooklyn. Killers were sent to the farm to stalk Ricciardi, but he rarely left his hideout. One gunman proposed stocking the farm where they were encamped with horses, in the hope Ricciardi would be lured outside to get a close look at the animals. About $70,000 was spent bringing in horses, but the animals failed to entice the suspicious Ricciardi from his guarded niche. No one could get a clear shot at him.

Fat Pete Chiodo took a squad to Florida to hunt for Accetturo and his son, but Tony Accetturo Jr. turned the tables on his pursuers. The younger Accetturo became the hunter, tracked Chiodo's car, and called the police to alert them that a New York mobster was in the area. When the cops showed up and stopped Chiodo for questioning about his activities in Florida, "Casso blew his top" in D'Arco's presence.

Chiodo attempted to redeem himself by abducting Joseph LaMorte, an Accetturo soldier, and torturing him into disclosing Tumac's whereabouts. When LaMorte proved too evasive to pluck off the streets, Chiodo and his team tried to kill him, shooting him in the neck and shoulder as he sat in his car outside his Florida home. Fat Pete confidently reported to Casso that they had finished off LaMorte, but despite serious wounds, he survived. "Petey cost me twenty thousand dollars a bullet," Casso groused to D'Arco, saying he had laid out $40,000 for Chiodo's hit team's expenses in Florida.

The Florida trip was a misdirected expedition from the start. While Chiodo was scouring South Florida in 1988 and 1989, Accetturo was in a New Jersey jail. Following his acquittal on RICO racketeering charges, Tumac was held almost a year on a contempt order for refusing to testify before a state panel investigating organized crime. This fact inexplicably escaped the attention of the Lucchese hit team before they left for Florida.

Except for LaMorte, the other New Jersey dissidents evaded Casso's death squads. Tumac's long experience in the Mob had taught him how to spot assassins, but he no longer could escape the mounting law-enforcement pressure. Following the 1988 RICO acquittals, New Jersey state investigators began concentrating on Accetturo's past, and four years of dogged work got results. Aided by the dissension and disarray in the Luccheses' New Jersey operations, the state's attorney general's office unearthed evidence that the crew extorted a video-poker gambling-machine manufacturer in New Jersey, and boardwalk amusement arcades at New Jersey's beach towns. At a trial in 1993, Accetturo beat a murder-conspiracy count, but was convicted on racketeering charges that he was the leader of an organized-crime gang, and had shared the extortion payoffs. His longtime follower, Tommy Ricciardi, was found guilty of murdering a family associate who had refused to pay sufficient tribute to the Luccheses. Ricciardi beat him to death with a golf club. Most of the crimes had occurred in Accetturo's heyday, before Amuso and Casso took over his crew. Ironically, two of Tumac's ex-soldiers, who had aided the new regime's efforts to kill him, were found guilty as codefendants on the same racketeering and extortion accusations that tripped him up.

Overweight at 250 pounds, moonfaced, suffering from high blood pressure, the once robust Tumac Accetturo was in bad shape. At age fifty-three, he anticipated a sentence of thirty years without parole; the only way he would leave prison would be in a coffin. Searching for the roots of his downfall, he blamed the internal turmoil uncorked by Amuso and Casso for providing investigators with valuable leads and with testimony from turncoats. Al D'Arco, who defected to the government's side for fear of Gaspipe, had been turned into a vital witness against Accetturo. Brooding in his jail cell, Accetturo saw only one escape route. Painful as it would be, he was ready to renounce his lifelong devotion to the Mafia, the organization that had sheltered him for thirty-five years. He was now willing to testify against Men of Honor and to reveal Cosa Nostra secrets he had sworn to conceal.

The turning point for him was the revelation that his former lieutenants, on Casso's orders, had provided photographs of himself and his wife to the hit teams. "Me and my son accepted the life and what might happen to us," he emphasized angrily in an interview. "I can accept they were gonna kill me. But my wife? She used to treat them like her own and make dinner for them at our house. For me, that was the end."

Before converting, Accetturo reached out to the nemesis who had spearheaded the state's pursuit and conviction of him, an official named Robert Buccino. He and Buccino had been boyhood friends in their native city, Orange, and Buccino considered himself a wilder teenager than Tumac had been. While Accetturo nestled into the bosom of the Mafia, Buccino took the opposite road. A strapping six-footer with a steady smile, Bobby Buccino joined the New Jersey State Police. After seven years as a trooper, he was attached to the organized-crime division and began a watch on someone he knew well, Anthony Tumac Accetturo. They had a face-to-face collision in the early 1970s when Accetturo stormed out of his home in Livingston, New Jersey, demanding to know why Buccino was shadowing and hounding him. Trying to rattle the mobster, Buccino said the surveillance was a forerunner to subpoenaing him to testify before a state investigation committee. "It was a tactical lie," Buccino acknowledged, "but he believed me because other hoods were getting subpoenaed around that time, and that might have been the reason he hightailed it to Florida."

Decades later, as a high official and Mafia expert on the New Jersey attorney general's staff, Buccino supervised the investigation that brought about Accetturo's racketeering conviction. Desperate for a light sentence, Accetturo sat down with his boyhood chum and chronicled a multitude of Mafia crimes. For state, federal, and even Italian organized-crime authorities, Accetturo yielded a lode of untapped evidence and historical intelligence about the Lucchese family and other borgatas. Accetturo's narration of his life as a Mafia executive was the clearest picture investigators had ever obtained of the Luccheses' penetration and exploitation of legitimate businesses in New Jersey, and the borgata's corrupt compacts with municipal officials.

Among Accetturo's offerings was an explanation of the primary reason for a huge government setback. He revealed the jury-rigging that produced acquittals for himself and his crew at the federal racketeering trial in 1988. He provided a cornucopia of evidence about violent crimes during his nearly four decades as a mobster. His tips led to the seizure of forty weapons, including a machine gun, and the breakup of a Mob gambling ring that was grossing $40 million annually. Clearing up thirteen murders, Accetturo admitted knowledge of the conspiracies that led to them, although he insisted that he had never personally participated in a slaying. Always rationalizing his behavior, Accetturo compared his role in the borgata to that of any businessman. His objective, he claimed, was a fundamental American goal: to enrich himself and his pals, while keeping violence to a minimum.

Robert Buccino and the other interrogators were skeptical of Tumac's self-serving justifications. Nevertheless, Buccino allowed him to vent his frustrations without debate. Informers are an indispensable element in police work, and Accetturo was producing arrests and prosecutions. By renouncing the Mafia, he influenced his crony Tommy Ricciardi and two other Lucchese soldiers to follow him into the ranks of cooperating witnesses.

The detailed information coming from Accetturo and his band of turncoats persuaded twelve other Lucchese mobsters to plead guilty to an assortment of federal and state charges, including nine homicides. By the time Accetturo finished talking to the authorities, the state attorney general's office declared that the New Jersey affiliate of the Lucchese family was severely crippled.

Accetturo's unexpected contribution was historical data about the Mafia's origins in New Jersey that he had absorbed from conversations with mafiosi old-timers, information previously unknown to students of the Mob. At the creation of the American Mafia organization in 1931, Lucky Luciano had permitted the formation of only one independent New Jersey borgata, a small clan in Elizabeth that became known as the De Cavalcante family. Leaders of more powerful crews in the Newark area were offered a one-time opportunity to join one of the five newly defined New York families. Believing they would have little chance of upward mobility in the largest New York family, which Luciano controlled (later known as the Genovese), most Newark capos aligned themselves with the four other borgatas. Their decisions in 1931 established the strong and lasting presence of all the five major families in New Jersey.

Mysteries about the exact relationship between the American and Sicilian Mafias were clarified when Accetturo was debriefed by Italian organized-crime agents brought in to question him. He explained that dual membership in an American and a Sicilian family was prohibited; mafiosi could have allegiance to only one national group. Each New York family had links to the Sicilian Mafia, primarily to facilitate narcotics transactions. And, although most American mobsters resented the Zips, the Sicilian made men, because of their patronizing attitude, the Americans felt they were more dedicated and ruthless than their Yankee counterparts. Accetturo acknowledged that the Sicilians had the right to feel superior. Under strict control of their bosses in Sicily, they were better disciplined, more tightly knit, and more secretive than American gangsters, he thought. Younger American mobsters tended to disparage the Sicilians with uncomplimentary names like "greasers," and "grease balls," and with an expression once reserved for old-fashioned American mafiosi who spoke heavily accented English — "Mustache Petes."

Ducks Corallo had maintained a close relationship with the Sicilians, and Accetturo had often cooperated with Italian mafiosi sent on missions to the United States. Tumac found suitable lodging for them, and helped track down people they were looking for. To illustrate the Sicilians' merciless protocol, he spoke of two Zips who came to New Jersey "to do some work." Learning that their intended victim was dying of cancer, the Zips were undeterred. Under the Sicilian Mafia's system of justice, their target could not be allowed to perish of natural causes without being punished for his misdeed. Even on his death bed, the intended victim had to be murdered as an example to other violators, Accetturo related. And he was.

44

455 Years in Prison

In January 1993, Vic Amuso, the titular boss of the Luccheses, was in prison for life after being convicted at a RICO trial; and three important capos—Al D'Arco, Pete Chiodo, and Tumac Accetturo—were exposing all they knew about the family's operations. The defectors had opened the eyes of FBI agents and prosecutors to Anthony Gaspipe Casso's awesome power and to the violence that he had provoked inside and outside the family. Information from the former capos lifted Casso's capture to the highest priority status for the Lucchese Squad's prosecutors. "He is the most dangerous, cunning and ruthless Mafia leader left on the streets," Andrew Maloney, the U.S. Attorney in Brooklyn, declared. "He is number one on our hit parade of wanted criminals."

Two federal prosecutors in charge of Lucchese cases were so resolved to capture Casso that they postponed their plans to resign and set up a private law partnership. Assistant U.S. Attorneys Charles Rose and Gregory O'Connell were determined they would bring him to trial. "We consider him the most dangerous organized-crime figure in our scope," O'Connell told a reporter, "the one who is responsible for countless murders and could do the most damage to the public."

The prosecutors found that Gaspipe's reputation had even scared Sammy the Bull Gravano, who had defied the fearsome John Gotti. Gravano knew

Casso from interfamily construction rackets, and he begged off testifying against him should he be brought to court. Sammy feared that Casso would retaliate against his relatives, as he had against Pete Chiodo's.

Searching for Casso's secreted wealth, which might help him while he was on the run, the FBI and prosecutors located $684,458 in six bank accounts under various names. A safe deposit box in a Brooklyn bank, rented in Casso's wife's maiden name, Lillian Delduca, turned up an additional $200,000 hidden in a dog-food container.

Casso had eluded the FBI for twenty-two months. Disgusted, Jim Fox, the head of the bureau's New York office, stepped up efforts to smoke him out, warning, "He's a psychopath whose name should be 'Mad Dog.'" FBI agents and city detectives followed Casso's known henchmen and tapped their phones for leads. Clued in by Al D'Arco, the FBI tried to locate Casso's hideout by unraveling the intricate telephone-booth message system he used to contact his loyal coterie. On the lookout in Casso's home turf, investigators in the Brooklyn district attorney's office intercepted suspicious calls to the cellphone of Frank Lastorino, the new Lucchese consigliere. The calls were traced to a split-level home in the placid township of Mount Olive, New Jersey, fifty-five miles from Casso's turbulent haunts in Brooklyn. Real estate records were checked and the house was put under subtle surveillance. Located in a woodsy, sparsely populated section, the property was owned by one of Casso's girlfriends. On the morning of January 19, 1993, after the woman left, an FBI SWAT team used a battering ram to crash through the front door. Gaspipe emerged dripping wet from a shower, modestly draping a towel around himself. To alter his appearance he had sprouted a mustache, let his cropped hair grow long, and wore eyeglasses. The disguise was no longer of any value; the chase was over.

Casso was alone in the expensively furnished house. A search turned up a rifle, $340,000 in cash stuffed in briefcases, and photocopies of a large number of FBI agents' confidential 302 reports concerning Casso and other Lucchese members. More than likely, the documents had been furtively given to Casso's soldiers by defense lawyers, who had received them as discovery material for hearings and trials involving Lucchese mobsters.

While Casso was still underground, a more extensive, superseding RICO indictment had been handed up against him, derived largely from evidence supplied by defector capos Chiodo, D'Arco, and Accetturo. In addition to the original racketeering charges stemming from rigged bids for contracts in city housing projects, the Windows case, he now faced charges on a raft of felonies:

at least twenty-five murder and attempted murder accusations, plus numerous extortion and labor-racketeering counts.

After a judge pronounced him a danger to the community and ordered him jailed without bail, Casso's imaginative mind swirled with ideas to delay or prevent a trial. He manufactured two plans to escape from the high-security prison where he was held, the Metropolitan Correctional Center in Lower Manhattan, a short stroll from City Hall and FBI headquarters. Assisted from the outside by Lucchese members, Casso bribed a guard to help him escape. (Differing accounts estimate the bribe as either $80,000 or $200,000. Regardless of the exact amount, it was tempting to vulnerable guards whose annual salaries at the time were as low as $30,000.) The first plan called for Casso to walk boldly out of the MCC instead of attempting a more violent and dangerous breakout. Promised another $400,000 if the plan succeeded, the guard provided Casso with clothes to replace his prison uniform and helped him obtain duplicate keys to his cell and the cell block.

The escape was planned for 6:30 A.M., and Casso donned civilian clothes under his prisoner's jumpsuit. The corrupt guard, who was alone in the cell block, opened the electric-controlled doors that allowed Casso to enter an unguarded elevator that took him to the street level. Walking as calmly as he could, Casso headed toward an exit leading to a side street. He was a few feet from freedom when a guard stopped him. His cover story was that he had been summoned to the main floor for consultation with his lawyer. The suspicious guard found it hard to swallow that a lawyer's conference would be scheduled at daybreak. Escorting Casso back to his cell block, the vigilant guard apparently accepted the bribed guard's fishy tale that he had received a telephone call from the administrative office permitting Casso to go unattended to the ground-floor session with his lawyer.

Thwarted once, Casso worked out a more reckless escape scheme. For pretrial hearings in a downtown Brooklyn courthouse, he was normally transported in a van guarded by two U.S. marshals. He contrived a wild plan for his soldiers to bushwhack the marshals as they were returning him to Manhattan from court. Lucchese gunmen would use a crash car to block the van on a narrow Brooklyn street, and open fire on the marshals, compelling them to come out with their hands up.

Simultaneously, an alternative plan was conceived in a conspiracy with inmates from the Colombo crime family to kill Federal District Court Judge Eugene Nickerson, who had been assigned to preside at the separate trials of Casso and his Colombo jailmates. The judge's murder, Gaspipe hoped, would provoke a mistrial or at least delay the proceedings, giving him more a time to pull off an escape. His outside allies were instructed to follow the judge on his train ride home to Long Island, and to scout out a prime spot to shoot him, either on the train or after he reached his station.

All of Casso's schemes were abruptly canceled in late 1993 on an edict from his erstwhile boon companion, Vittorio Vic Amuso, still the titular Lucchese boss. Captured in 1991, Amuso was found guilty on fifty-four RICO and murder counts, and sentenced to life without parole. According to investigators and prosecutors, Amuso eventually concluded that Casso had double-crossed him, and that Gaspipe had been the anonymous tipster who steered the FBI to the Scranton mall where he was arrested. The reason for the betrayal? Amuso believed Casso wanted to seize the title of boss and gain absolute control of the family. From his prison cell, the avenging Amuso spread the news: Gaspipe was denounced, stripped of his rank and authority as underboss, and declared a pariah to be despised by all Lucchese mafiosi.

Bereft of escape help from the borgata, with devastating testimony from Al D'Arco and Pete Chiodo and a mountain of evidence looming against him, Casso played his last card. In February 1994, two weeks before the start of his RICO trial, a relative relayed important news to Richard Rudolph, the lead FBI agent in Casso's case. Anthony Gaspipe Casso wanted to cross over, to testify as a government witness against the Mafia. If the government granted him a lenient sentence, he promised he could match Sammy the Bull Gravano in revealing priceless information that would undermine the Luccheses and other families.

Before a cooperation agreement could be fashioned, prosecutors had to evaluate Casso's worth without alerting his prison mates to his deception. His cell block contained other Mafia defendants who watched every movement of fellow inmates in and out of the MCC, on the lookout for possible traitors. To protect him, a ruse was devised to get him to the courthouse in Brooklyn and into a secluded basement nook for a talk with prosecutors. On the pretext that he had to provide handwriting samples for possible evidence at his trial, he was summoned to appear at the courthouse alone, without the Lucchese codefendants who normally accompanied him to pretrial hearings.

Two weeks after Casso's secret courthouse meeting with prosecutors Rose and O'Connell, a deal materialized. On March 1, 1994, at a closed hearing before Judge Eugene Nickerson, whom he had conspired to kill, Casso pleaded guilty to fourteen murders and a medley of RICO racketeering and extortion charges. For the plea, Matthew Brief, a former federal organized-crime prosecutor, was brought in at the suggestion of Rose and O'Connell to represent Casso. (Prosecutors universally demand that defectors ditch their previous attorneys, many of whom have other Mafia-connected clients; they are distrusted by prosecutors as "Mob lawyers." In any event, most attorneys who defend Mafia clients refuse to represent defectors, believing it would compromise them with their clientele.)

There had always been the slim possibility, Rose and O'Connell worried, that without a single incriminating taped conversation as trial evidence, Casso might slip through their fingers. Now, without the necessity of a lengthy trial, and the possibility of an acquittal or a hung, jury, Casso was boxed in, with a guilty plea exposing him to fourteen life sentences.

"We now have him tied up six ways to Sunday," O'Connell told Rose after Casso signed a cooperation agreement pledging to disclose all the crimes and background intelligence information he possessed about organized crime. It was a nonnegotiable plea, with the provision that the prosecutors would advise a judge of the extent and depth of Casso's cooperation, thereby virtually insuring him a reduced sentence. Although repelled by Casso's record, Rose and O'Connell knew that a compromise with an infamous mafioso was always a balancing act. They would give him a break—but only if he measurably aided the government in dismantling the Mob. Any reduction from a life sentence depended entirely on the value of Casso's information. The prosecutors were confident that he could divulge a treasure house of evidence against other mobsters, corrupt unions, business executives, and possibly his law-enforcement moles, dishonest police and federal agents—if he were truthful with them.

Casso appeared content, believing that he had negotiated an eleventh-hour chance to begin a new life. In his mind, the prosecutors and FBI agents had strongly suggested to him, in an off-the-record unwritten accord, that they would seek a huge reduction in his sentence in exchange for testimony. He visualized himself being coddled in a "country club" prison environment for no more than five or six years, and then sheltered in the Witness Protection Program.

A highly valued defector, Casso was flown under heavy protection from the austere jail in Manhattan to the remote La Tuna federal prison, two thousand miles away in Texas, near El Paso and the Mexican border. There, he was installed in what passes for luxury prison accommodations reserved for conspicuous and endangered informers who needed a safe setting. Casso's cozy quarters, in a section of the prison isolated from other inmates, was called "the Valachi Suite." It had been constructed thirty years earlier for Joe Valachi, the Genovese soldier and the first made man to publicly violate *omertà*. Although locked in at night in a cell six feet long and nine feet wide, during the day Casso had access to an adjoining room, containing a sofa, a stereo, a television, a refrigerator, a microwave, and a hot plate for making coffee and tea. His rooms in the hot desert climate were made comfortable by a "swamp cooler," a local version of air conditioning through circulating water pipes.

At La Tuna, Rose, and O'Connell and FBI agents began prying out Casso's reservoir of Mafia confidences. Accustomed to the eccentricities of murderous mobsters, the prosecutors nevertheless were amused by Casso's housekeeping ardor and compulsive neatness. He was distressed at the lack of a shaving mirror. And at their long sessions, he served cakes and tea boiled on his single-burner hot plate, frequently wiping the table to remove stains and crumbs. His reading tastes also confounded them. He requested a subscription to the *Robb Report,* an expensive magazine catering to an audience "seeking the Luxury Lifestyle," a publication unknown to the prosecutors and agents.

Before Casso's capture, FBI investigations and informers had implicated him in fourteen murders that were listed in his guilty plea. At the debriefings he startled his interrogators with a catalogue of numerous whackings never linked to him. Overall, he confessed to ordering or having a hand in at least twenty-three other slayings—a grand total of thirty-seven victims—during thirty years as a Lucchese apprentice, made man, and underboss. There were an additional twenty-five victims he had marked for death, most during the recent reign of terror, who had escaped with wounds or were uninjured when the attempted murders went awry or were aborted. High on the list of Mafia mysteries that Casso resolved for the authorities was the car explosion that seven years earlier had killed Frank DeCicco, John Gotti's first underboss. From Casso they learned the astonishing fact that it was Gotti that the Genovese and Lucchese leaders were really out to get, but they had to be content with DeCicco's death as revenge for Paul Castellano's assassination.

Another murder target, Gaspipe admitted, had been one of his questioners—Charles Rose. While in hiding, Casso had put out a contract on him, directing his troops and two rogue New York detectives on his payroll to locate the prosecutor's Manhattan apartment, tap his phone to learn his movements, and kill him. Matter-of-factly, Casso explained that he had wanted Rose exterminated because he believed the prosecutor had leaked a false story to the *New*

York Post that the architect Anthony Favo had been tortured and murdered for having had an affair with Casso's wife.

Rose wryly replied to his would-be assassin, "I forgive you, Anthony. Let's continue."

It was at La Tuna that the agents and prosecutors learned about Casso's recent conspiracies and crimes while awaiting trial. They were riveted by his tales of his machinations to kill Judge Nickerson, his bold bribery of a guard, and his daredevil escape schemes.

Listening and recording Casso's gruesome accounts of gangland slaughters and the senseless murders of innocent victims, O'Connell tried to remain professionally cool. But one description unnerved him. In the late 1970s, Casso had profited along with other mobsters from smuggling drugs from South America to New York on *Terry's Dream*, a seventy-five-foot-long converted trawler. The vessel and its cargo of twenty-three tons of marijuana and a half million tablets of methaqualone or Quaaludes—a prescription depressant popular at the time—was seized by the Coast Guard in November 1978. Casso was not immediately implicated, but he decided to kill the boat captain's son to prevent him from caving in and informing.

The unsuspecting young man was invited on a fishing trip in the Florida Everglades with Casso and a confederate. Before the victim arrived at the meeting spot, Casso and his accomplice dug a grave. "When the kid showed up, I took my gun out and shot him," O'Connell recalled Casso saying. Casso became disturbed because the young man bled over the hood of his car. "Casso was laughing and his face was filled with mirth and merriment as he talked about the difficulties he had washing the blood from the car," O'Connell said. "As he was shoveling dirt into the grave, the kid, still alive, jumped up, and he struck him in the mouth with the shovel and continued to bury him alive."

Appalled, the prosecutor asked Casso if burying a man alive had distressed him. "'No,' he told us, 'it had to be done.'"

Over the next three and a half years, still awaiting sentencing, Casso was transferred to several prisons in New York and the Northeast. He was always housed in a protective-custody unit, reserved for cooperating Mafia defectors, segregated from the general prison population. Essentially, he was in a witness-protection program while imprisoned. Agents and prosecutors continued their debriefings, particularly interested in confirming his accounts of bribing two detectives to feed him confidential reports and to commit crimes on his behalf. One of his most shocking claims was his assigning the detectives as hit men for a Mob murder. As a favor to Vincent Gigante, the boss of the Genovese family, Casso said he gave the detectives the contract in 1990 to execute Eddie Lino, a Gambino capo.

Before they were fingered by Casso, the two detectives retired under a cloud, without murder or corruption charges lodged against them at that juncture. Casso had informed federal and police department investigators that he regularly communicated with the detectives through his go-between Burton Kaplan, a Lucchese associate who worked almost exclusively for him. Kaplan was instrumental in arranging the kidnaping and torture-murder of Jimmy Hydell, the gunman who tried to bump off Gaspipe. According to Casso, Kaplan also relayed the warning in 1990 that he and Vic Amuso were about to be indicted on RICO charges in the Widows case. Convicted for narcotics trafficking and tax evasion, Kaplan was hit with a twenty-seven-year prison sentence. At that time, in 1997, he refused a deal for a lighter term in return for corroborating Casso's story that investigators were selling secrets and committing crimes for the Mob. No other evidence was then available, and prosecutors felt it was impossible to build a case against the detectives on Casso's word alone.

In an interview in 2003, Casso said Lino's murder was committed because the Genovese family boss, Chin Gigante, wanted to weaken his hated Gambino rival John Gotti. Lino, a feared killer, was one of the triggermen who assassinated Paul Castellano and Tommy Bilotti outside Sparks Steak House. "He was one of John's strengths, a stronghold that we wanted to take down," Casso continued. "We were not that worried about Sammy [Gravano]."

Lino was found shot to death on November 6, 1990, in his black Mercedes-Benz, on the service road of the Belt Parkway, the main highway in Brooklyn. To trap the cautious forty-eight-year-old gangster, Casso believes the detectives activated a flashing dome-light on their car to pull him off the highway for a presumed traffic violation, then killed him. He remembered paying either $45,000 or $75,000 to the detectives for the slaying.

Corrupt cops have been a chronic sore point for police forces in the New York region since the birth of the modern Mafia. Errant officers and investigators are simply bought off or, as relatives or longtime neighborhood friends of mobsters, are susceptible to being corrupted. The Mob also hired former detectives and officers as private eyes who can easily obtain confidential information from their contacts in law-enforcement agencies. Rose and O'Connor knew about the Mob's ability to "reach" cops, and readily accepted Casso's version of purchasing information and deadly help from dishonest detectives.

An even more explosive corruption issue developed over Casso's account of an FBI mole on his payroll. FBI 302 reports reveal that after Al D'Arco defected in 1991, he informed his interrogators that Casso had spoken of getting leaks from the agent nicknamed "Crystal Ball". Years later, Casso's defense lawyers said that he had given them a similar version of a corrupt bureau agent in New York. As late as 2003, Casso said in an interview with the author that he had identified the FBI traitor to bureau agents who debriefed him. He asserted that the FBI was intent on covering up the tainted agent's involvement with a mobster, and his interrogators warned him that his leniency deal would be endangered if he stuck to his story and thereby tarnished the bureau's reputation. Casso insists that agents instructed him not to reveal the reputed agent's identity or existence when he was questioned by prosecutors. Rather than risk a sentencing problem, Casso claims, he kept quiet for years.

But the Justice Department, branding Casso an untrustworthy liar, repudiates his allegation. And Gregory O'Connell said that when he intensively questioned Casso shortly after the cooperation agreement in 1994, Gaspipe denied having an FBI agent on his payroll. "He called the mole story bullshit," O'Connell added. In defense of Casso, his lawyers stressed that he had been prevented from leveling with the prosecutors because of warnings from FBI agents that they would retaliate against him.

The end result was murky. Federal investigators accepted the tale of corrupt New York City detectives, and discounted the possibility that the Mafia had corrupted one of their own agents.

Immediately after his defection, the FBI advertised Casso as a prized catch, equal to Sammy the Bull Gravano in his ability to provide them with ammunition to defeat the Cosa Nostra. In fact, except for his appearance in May 1996 before a Senate subcommittee exploring the Mafia's alliance with Russian gangsters to steal gasoline excise taxes, Casso's potential testimony went unused. Prosecutors never called him as a witness before a grand jury to obtain a Mob indictment nor at a trial to help convict a single mobster.

Gradually, the cooperation deal unraveled. The ultimate blow to Casso's bargain came in August 1997, when prosecutors summarily rescinded the agreement and banished him from the Witness Protection Program. He has the unenviable distinction of being the only major Mafia defector thrown out of the program. The extraordinary step, prosecutors said, was brought about by Casso's duplicity, lies, and crimes committed after signing the cooperation agreement.

Citing a list of infractions occurring after his guilty plea, the government accused Casso of resorting to his old habit of bribing guards and prison employees for special treatment. He gave them cash, theater tickets, and new auto tires in exchange for their smuggling into his prison quarters assorted delicacies, including vodka, wine, sushi, steaks, turkey, veal cutlets, a disposable camera, radios, and toiletries. A second charge was an alleged assault on another Mob turncoat in the protective-custody unit, a former Colombo soldier with whom Casso was feuding.

The government's timing and decision to remove Casso, however, undoubtedly rested on a more contentious matter: his attempt to discredit two celebrated Cosa Nostra traitors, Sammy Gravano and Al D'Arco. Shortly before Casso was booted out of the program, he sent prosecutors a letter challenging testimony offered at important Mob trials by Gravano and D'Arco. Disputing the government's stellar witness at John Gotti's 1992 conviction, Casso claimed that Sammy the Bull lied when he swore to never having trafficked in narcotics. In the 1970s, Casso said, he had sold large amounts of marijuana to Gravano, and later Gravano offered to sell him a cache of heroin from China for $160,000.

Casso's letter also accused Gravano of ordering the stabbing of the Reverend Al Sharpton, a controversial political activist, in January 1991, while Sharpton was leading a protest march of mainly black youths through Bensonhurst, a white neighborhood with numerous Mob hangouts. At first, Casso insisted that on the day after the Sharpton stabbing, Gravano met with him in Brooklyn and told him about his involvement. Easily disproving this assertion, prosecutors pointed out that on the day of the assault and for months afterward, Sammy the Bull was locked up, awaiting trial as a codefendant in Gotti's RICO trial.

As for his former flunky Al D'Arco, Casso ripped into him, describing his testimony as replete with lies and exaggerations about crimes and events, including his claim that he had been appointed the family's acting boss. Casso wrote that prosecutors and the FBI allowed D'Arco to misrepresent his rank because it escalated his prestige and importance as a government witness. Dismissing Casso's assertions as "a litany of false accusations," prosecutors fired back that his misconduct spelled finus to the possibility of their submitting a recommendation, known in federal courts as a 5K1.1 application, for a reduced sentence in return for his cooperation. Almost from the start of his presumed "turning," prosecutors said, they believed Casso had been withholding information and misleading them about his participation in crimes. Two lie-detector tests administered to him in the early days of his defection indicated that he had been deceptive about the extent of his concealed money and about his attempts to kill Judge Nickerson and Charles Rose. (It was odd, however, that the prosecutors belatedly cited the lie-detector results after allowing Casso to remain in the protection program for almost four years.) Classifying Casso as a discredited outcast of no further value to them, the Justice Department wanted him finally sentenced on the full seventy-two-count indictment he had pleaded to in 1994.

Before the sentencing, Casso sent three more handwritten letters, totaling thirty-two pages, to Federal Judge Frederic Block, offering a minutely detailed rebuttal to the government's condemnation. Pleading for reinstatement in the protection program, Casso characterized himself as having been an honorable, decent mafioso. Adopting a Nuremburg-style defense, he attributed most of his crimes to the compulsion to follow Cosa Nostra orders. He saw himself wrongly impugned as a psychopathic killer, insisting that he had actually pulled the trigger and murdered only two men, not the vast numbers cited by the prosecution. One of these two acknowledged victims, Jimmy Hydell, had first tried to kill him in an ambush, he pointed out. Implying that Hydell deserved to die for an added reason, Casso wrote that Hydell had abducted, raped, and killed a young woman shortly before trying to murder him.

Casso conceded that he had wrongly implicated Sammy Gravano in the stabbing of Reverend Sharpton. But it was an honest mistake, a flawed memory of a long-ago conversation with other mobsters about the incident. Otherwise, he resolutely clung to the rest of his story that Gravano had engaged in drug deals, and that Gravano and Al D'Arco had committed perjury in several Mob trials.

Regarding allegations that he had bribed guards for special treatment, Casso asserted that he had been subjected to an unfair double standard. It was through him, he pointed out, that the government learned about widespread smuggling and other crimes committed by Mafia turncoats in prison special-protection units. FBI agents, he continued, cautioned him to keep quiet about these matters because they needed testimony from the defectors and were determined to keep their songbirds comfortable and happy.

Casso was certain he had been singled out for draconian punishment, after three and half years of cooperation, solely because of his allegations about Gravano. His letter to the judge suggested that prosecutors feared he could invoke a nightmare for the Justice Department by impugning Gravano and overturning John Gotti's conviction. To test his truthfulness, Casso asked for an independently administered lie-detector test before sentence was imposed.

His limited education, Casso wrote, made it difficult to explain himself. "I'm not denying my passed [sic] life of crime." Imploring the judge for a second chance in the Witness Protection Program, he offered a single motive for becoming a cooperating witness. "Only because I wanted the opportunity to experience a whole new lifestyle for myself."

Casso's petitions were no match for the combined credentials of prosecutors and FBI agents, who categorically refuted his assertions that they had unjustly revoked an agreement with him.

Yet a puzzling question arose from the blowup over the plea bargain. Why would Casso—an intelligent criminal—lie and disparage Gravano and D'Arco when he apparently had nothing to gain by defying the authorities who held the key to his own future? Prosecutors and agents offered several explanations for his turnabout. They theorized that he acted out of perverse jealousy, that unlike Gravano and D'Arco, he would not be a center-stage, headlined witness, glorified as a reformed mobster. He had expected to be used in at least one high-profile case, the potential trial of the Genovese godfather, Vincent Gigante. But the government decided Gaspipe's record was too blemished to qualify him as an effective witness in any trial. "Using him would be like putting Adolf Hitler on the witness stand," O'Connell commented. "It was impossible to overcome his history and make him sound credible."

At that point, according to the prosecutorial analysis, Casso realized his sentence would not be sharply reduced, and he declared war against the government. Lawyers and agents speculated that in order to guarantee his survival in prison, he decided to curry favor with the mafiosi by claiming that he had returned to the fold, and had attacked the two prominent Mafia traitors Gravano and D'Arco.

George Stamboulidis, the victorious prosecutor in the Colombo family trials, who was brought into Casso's case, pointed out that Gaspipe had been given a golden chance to turn over a new leaf, even though he had "more horrendous baggage than virtually any cooperating witness the government has ever signed up." The government acknowledged that Casso had provided valuable information. But the crimes he committed in protective custody automatically violated the cooperation agreement and destroyed his usefulness as a truthful witness, Stamboulidis argued in a court brief.

In July 1998, Judge Block accepted totally the prosecution's position, rejecting Casso's motion for a reduced sentence and a return to the Witness Protection Program. "Simply put," Block ruled, "criminal behavior by cooperators should be condemned, not condoned, and repudiation of the Government's obligations under a cooperation agreement is an effective means of delivering such an important message." The other message the judge gave the fifty-six-year-old Casso was a sentence of thirteen consecutive life sentences, a monumental 455 years in prison. Casso also forfeited $1.5 million in assets seized by the government as having been obtained through criminal acts.

"My original prosecutors told me not to worry," Casso grumbled as he was led away. "But they never had any intention of keeping their promises."

For years afterward, Casso's lawyers continued their battle for his sentence reduction and his restoration to the Witness Protection Program. The first appeal by attorney Matthew Brief condemned prosecutors for acting in bad faith and reneging on the plea-bargain solely because of Casso's narcotics allegations against Sammy Gravano.

When that tactic failed, a new lawyer, John D. B. Lewis, raised a claim that a conflict of interest had prevented Brief, the lawyer picked by prosecutors, from adequately representing Casso during the plea-bargaining period. Brief said in an affidavit that prosecutors Rose and O'Connell would brook no delay in getting Casso's guilty plea formalized before a judge, and contended that they threatened to bring ethical and disciplinary charges against him when he tried to withdraw from the case before Casso signed the cooperation deal. Brief stayed on, though troubled by the hasty arrangements, the lack of time to confer properly with Casso, and the absence of any tangible promises of leniency.

Despite voluminous motions by Lewis, the appeals courts denied Casso's numerous claims of prosecutorial misconduct, and that he had been railroaded primarily for denigrating Sammy the Bull Gravano as a narcotics profiteer. In 2002, four years after he was dismissed as an untrustworthy liar, his credibility was remarkably strengthened when Gravano pleaded guilty to engaging in large-scale Ecstasy drug sales. Suddenly, at least one aspect of Gravano's trial testimony for the government was suspect, and Casso's statements became more believable.

"From day one, Casso told the truth that Gravano had a long history of being involved in drugs, and it was rejected out-of-hand by the feds," Lewis said.

The lawyer stressed that after years of disbelieving and ridiculing Casso, the government eventually accused Gravano of being the number-one drug dealer in the Southwest. "Gravano obviously knew the ins and outs of the drug world, and it was just one of the many areas in which Casso was telling the truth and the government didn't want to hear it," Lewis added.

But there was a novel—and dramatic—twist in Casso's battle with the government.

After Casso's eleven years of trying to become a cooperating witness, an explosive indictment complicated his struggle for a shorter sentence. In March 2005, the two detectives he had pinpointed in 1994 as mercenaries were officially identified as Mob hit men.

Now retired, Louis Eppolito and Stephen Caracappa, were charged with personally committing one murder for Gaspipe and helping him track down and slay seven other enemies. A federal indictment in Brooklyn alleged that the detective partners happily worked for Casso from 1985 until his capture in 1993. They received as much as $4,000 a month, with bonuses for exceptional spying and homicide tasks, according to the accusations.

Details in the indictment differed in some degree from Casso's assertions in court documents and in interviews with the author of how the crimes were committed and his motives for carrying them out. Nevertheless, the indictment and prosecutors' statements in effect proclaimed that Casso had provided substantially accurate accounts about recruiting and corrupting the detectives.

The charges specified that the two detectives personally executed Frank Lino, the Gambino capo, who was gunned down after being stopped on a Brooklyn highway. They were also cited in another particularly heinous act: abducting James Hydell and delivering him in a car trunk to Casso, who proceeded to torture and kill him. Hydell was brutalized by Casso in revenge for his assassination attempt.

The arrests resulted from new witnesses coming forward and the reopening of the police-corruption case by the district attorney and the U.S. Attorneys' office in Brooklyn. Five investigators said they uncovered fresh evidence, including audio- and videotapes involving Eppolito. None of the new witnesses was immediately identified. But defense lawyers speculated that one of them was Burt Kaplan, the Mob associate named long ago by Casso as his intermediary to venal lawmen he classified as "my detectives." After eight hard years in a federal penitentiary, at age seventy, Kaplan reportedly had a change of heart about becoming a canary and testifying that he was Casso's contact man with the bribed cops.

Much-decorated detectives, Caracappa and Eppolito had each been on the police force for more than twenty years. Both were assigned to elite units investigating Mafia-related crimes, and Caracappa had access to the identities of undercover informants and sensitive FBI materials. Retiring from the NYPD in the 1990s on tax-free disability pensions of about $70,000 each, they were neighbors in Las Vegas at the time of their arrest. Prosecutors, in court documents, asserted that Eppolito lied when he applied for the police force in 1969. On his application, he swore that he was unrelated to organized-crime figures when, in fact, his father and uncle were both Gambino soldiers and he was acquainted with other mobsters.

In retirement, Eppolito co-authored *Mafia Cop: The Story of an Honest Cop Whose Family was the Mob*, and appeared in bit film roles, sometimes as a gangster, in eleven crime dramas.

Sammy the Bull Gravano's downfall and the break in the detectives' case apparently failed to aid Gaspipe's campaign for leniency. Evidence that Gravano was a drug trafficker did not erase complaints against Casso—lying, bribing guards for prison contraband, and assaulting an inmate—which were used to eject him from the witness-protection unit and to justify a life sentence. The charges against the ex-detectives were one of the sharpest scandals in the NYPD's history and on the surface fortified Casso's credibility in his dealings with the Justice Department. Investigators, however, declined to interview him after reopening their inquiries into the activities of Caracappa and Eppolito. As far as federal authorities were concerned, Gaspipe remained discredited. Prosecutors in 2005 said they had no intention of relying on his testimony or seeking a reduction in his harsh sentence.

Still protesting his unfair treatment as a turncoat witness, Casso was confined in the government's most oppressive prison, the "Alcatraz of the Rockies" in Florence, Colorado. Also dubbed "Super Max," the penitentiary is restricted to 575 inmates classified by the Bureau of Prisons as the nation's most dangerous federal convicts, including Islamic terrorists. Officially known as ADX–Florence, it opened in 1994 as a high-tech, escape-proof prison to replace the maximum-security institution in Marion, Illinois (where John Gotti was held), for inmates considered incorrigible. Like most prisoners in Florence, Casso is caged in an isolation cell up to twenty-three hours a day, with only a sliver of natural light filtering in through a tiny, meshed windowpane that allows no view of the sky or the nearby Rocky Mountains. Meals are delivered into his cell through double-entry doors, and he passes most of the time reading or watching television on a thirteen-inch black-and-white set. His hermetic cell contains a concrete slab bed with a three-inch-thick mattress, a concrete toilet stool, and a desk and bookcase anchored in place. Five days a week he is allowed out for one hour to walk in a small enclosed courtyard with several other prisoners, usually his only contact with other inmates.

Lamenting his decision to sign a cooperation agreement, Casso says that before his defection the prosecution offered him a deal that would have turned out infinitely better for him. He had been on the verge of accepting a plea bargain that would have made him eligible for parole after twenty-two years. "I help them and I get life without parole," he summed up in an interview. "This is really a fuckin' joke."

45

"Team America"

The Lucchese capos who switched sides, and in the words of prosecutor Gregory O'Connell, joined "Team America" were well rewarded. Unlike Gaspipe Casso, they got lenient sentences or none at all.

Fearing that he was on Casso's hit list, Alphonse the Professor D'Arco surrendered, pleaded guilty, and sought the government's protection for himself and Joe, his made-member son. (As part of the deal, the government granted Joe immunity from prosecution for his role in one killing and an attempted murder during the blood purge.) A cogent witness, D'Arco helped convict Lucchese boss Vic Amuso and more than fifty other hoods. On the witness stand, D'Arco admitted his complicity in ten murders and, in his words, "a bevy of crimes": shylocking, gambling, extortion, labor rackets, counterfeiting, arson, hijackings, and firebombing companies that resisted paying for protection. At one of his last court appearances, summarizing his metamorphosis, D'Arco told a judge, "I'm the same physical human being, but I'm not the same man." Prosecutors heaped praise on him for his cooperation, emphasizing that he broke away from the Cosa Nostra though no charges were pending against him. A federal judge accepted the government's 5K1.1 appraisal, and D'Arco disappeared with his nearest relatives into the Witness Protection Program. He did not serve a single day in prison.

Shot twelve times, partially paralyzed and confined to a wheelchair, Peter Fat Pete Chiodo survived to testify and help convict Vic Amuso, his former boss, and several other Lucchese mobsters. If Casso had gone to trial, Chiodo would have appeared as a principal prosecution witness. In his guilty plea, Fat Pete admitted to participating in five murders and numerous extortions. He was also embraced by the Witness Protection Program, given a new identity, and avoided prison time.

Tumac Accetturo emerged as the prosecution's most effective weapon in fracturing the New Jersey branch of the Lucchese family, which he had nurtured and led for more than two decades. His importance was magnified by his being the first Mafia leader in the state to defect, bringing with him a trove of high-level Cosa Nostra knowledge. He disclosed the New Jersey borgata's murders, infiltration of unions and businesses, loan-sharking, and jury tampering, providing state and federal prosecutors with a chart for wholesale indictments. Unbeknownst to mobsters implicated by Accetturo, it was unlikely that he would have appeared in court against them. Prosecutors were reluctant to use him as a witness because of his phony claim of "presenile dementia" in the 1980s to wriggle out of a racketeering conspiracy accusation in Florida. No jury in a Mafia case would bring in a guilty verdict if the prosecution's main witness had a record of mental instability. But the mere threat that he might testify worked for the government. A dozen of his former soldiers, faced with overwhelming documented evidence that Accetturo helped compile, capitulated and opted for plea-bargains rather than risk trials and life sentences.

Like all defectors, Accetturo felt entitled to a "pass," freedom from a prison term via a suspended sentence or probation on his state racketeering conviction. Investigators in the New Jersey attorney general's office, acknowledging that Tumac's help had paralyzed the Lucchese family's operations in the state, recommended a substantial reduction in the maximum sixty-year sentence he faced. At his sentencing in December 1994, Accetturo's lawyer, Robert G. Stevens, emphasized that Accetturo had a "uniquely nonviolent past" for a Mafia leader, and that as a prominent defector, his life would be endangered if he were imprisoned.

State Judge Manuel H. Greenberg saw Accetturo in a less sanguine light. Imposing a maximum term of twenty years and a $400,000 fine, Greenberg cited his extensive criminal record and found him to be "more than a spectator in the operations of a ruthless, violent organization." To protect Accetturo from Mob retaliation in a New Jersey prison where he would be easily recognized, the state arranged for him to serve his time in a North Carolina state penitentiary.

The New Jersey attorney general's office eventually helped rescue Accetturo. An internal report in July 1997 by the office's organized-crime investigators praised him for unveiling an enormous amount of intelligence information concerning the Mob in New Jersey, New York, and Florida that would not have been obtainable through other means. In December 2002, his sentence was reduced to time served, and he was released unconditionally after nine years and two months in prison, less than half his maximum term. The sixty-three-year-old Accetturo remained in the South, far from his past gangster habitat in New Jersey. After his admitted lifetime in big-time organized-crime, nine years was moderate punishment.

At the start of 1987, Vittorio Vic Amuso and Anthony Gaspipe Casso had inherited and commanded a tightly disciplined Mafia borgata—one of the nation's most affluent crime families. Although Ducks Corallo's old Lucchese hierarchy had been eliminated, the FBI and state agencies were rummaging for leads and scraps of evidence to close in on the masters of the new regime. Law-enforcement officials knew that Amuso and Casso were in control, but the two leaders and the family's fundamental structure were not in imminent danger from legal assault. Five years later, the Lucchese gang was in tatters, with more than sixty made men—about half of its membership—imprisoned, slain, or "turned."

Mafia investigators attribute the Lucchese shipwreck largely to the incessant intrigues Casso contrived to gain supreme power and riches for himself. Amuso wore the boss's crown, but Casso was the strategist behind the chaos that divided the borgata. Trial testimony, FBI interrogations, and acute observations by Lucchese apostates cast Casso in the role of arch manipulator, an Iago, steering a malleable Amuso. "Gaspipe was more dangerous than Amuso and more responsible for the mayhem that fortunately for us ruined the family," concluded Gregory O'Connell, who with Charles Rose, prosecuted Casso, Amuso, and other major Lucchese gangsters. The two prosecutors' knowledge of Casso's diabolical record—much of it gained listening to his admissions—spurred them to originate a private code name for him: "Lucifer." "He had boundless enthusiasm for conspiracies and for murder," O'Connell remarked. "I prosecuted drug dealers, organized-crime bosses, and terrorists, and the only one I feared who was clever and vindictive enough to reach out from prison and come after me was Gaspipe." (After Casso's capture and agreement to plead guilty and cooperate, Rose and O'Connell left the U.S. Attorney's Office to set up their postponed private practice. Rose died of a brain tumor in 1998 at age fifty-one.)

Of all the Lucchese veterans whom Casso drove into the government's arms, Tumac Accetturo probably was the most anguished. His thirty-five-year climb from being a $75-a-week apprentice to the highest rungs of the crime family and his ultimate desertion encapsulates the modern history of the American Mafia. Interviewed in a prison in Newton, New Jersey, shortly after his conversion, Accetturo sounded rhapsodic, reminiscing nostalgically about his glory years under Ducks Corallo's benevolent administration. He mythologized the Cosa Nostra as it functioned from the 1960s to the late 1980s as an authentic Honorable Society, populated by deserving men who otherwise would have been denied advancement and wealth because of their ethnicity and humble backgrounds. In Accetturo's romanticized flashbacks, his generation of mafiosi had resorted to murder and force as a last resort, and only for serious violations of Cosa Nostra rules. He refused to discuss reports from investigators that he had knowledge of at least thirteen gangland hits. He preferred to portray himself as a nonviolent capo dedicated to protecting a misunderstood but venerable organization. "There was no greater life," he said ruefully. "We were interested in money, but we didn't put money before honor. The old-time guys who taught me would never think of cheating somebody in a deal or in a dice or card game. They played by the old rules because they wanted the games and deals to go on forever."

Law-enforcement pressure finally confronted Accetturo with a tormenting dilemma: perish in prison or forsake his vows by becoming a rat. There was no question in his mind that under his previously esteemed bosses he would have borne a prison sentence and upheld until death the code of *omertà*. "It wasn't the all-American way. It was the life I chose and I considered myself a Man of Honor and would have stuck to it forever."

But by concocting fictitious reasons to murder him, Gaspipe Casso and Vic Amuso had destroyed Accetturo's faith in Cosa Nostra's sacred principles. He rationalized that they, not he, were the betrayers and defectors, and therefore his renunciation was justified.

Accetturo's Mafia life had been comfortable before federal and state agencies went on the offensive against the Mob. "Back then, we were disciplined, coordinated, and better-organized than they were and we took advantage of that." He smiled as he alluded to the halcyon years of feeble law enforcement. "Now, it's just the reverse. These guys are coordinated together and we're trying to kill one another."

With better leadership, he felt, the Lucchese family might have resisted and overcome the government's campaign. An intimate witness to the abrupt decay and decline of the borgata, Accetturo critiqued a cadre of made men inducted in the 1980s and 1990s as more devoted to greed and narcotics trafficking than to the Mafia's revered rules of conduct. He singled out Gaspipe Casso as the single major figure behind the internal anomie that generated the Luccheses' disintegration. "Casso and his people had no training, no honor," Tumac reflected mournfully. "Look at the trail he left behind. He'd sell his soul for money. He threw the old rules out the window. All he wanted to do is kill, kill, get what you can, even if you didn't earn it. That's the main reason why we fell apart."

46

The Pajama Game

Almost every day, a graying, shabbily dressed man emerged from a red-brick walkup tenement in Greenwich Village and gingerly crossed the street. Usually, one or two men were at his side, helping him cover a distance of two hundred feet on Sullivan Street. The stooped man's usual destination was a dingy storefront club where he whiled away hours, playing cards. Most days, he was dressed inconspicuously in baggy pants, work shoes, a windbreaker, a woolen cap. But there were times in gentle weather when he entered the street, seemingly disoriented, wearing pajamas, a bathrobe, and slippers. In street clothes or in pajamas, he sometimes was accompanied and aided by his brother, a Roman Catholic priest and community leader in New York City.

To passersby and nearby residents, the assistance offered the unshaved, middle-aged man on his brief saunters in the neighborhood appeared to be compassionate care by close kin and friends. His mother and brother characterized their tottering relative, who muttered to himself, drooled, and urinated openly on the sidewalks, as a mental and physical wreck.

The pajama-clad excursions were routine occurrences in the 1970s and 1980s by an ex–light heavyweight prize fighter, who a slew of doctors and psychiatrists attested was afflicted with a damaged heart and suffered from dementia rooted in organic brain damage by the time he reached his fifties. His relatives characterized him as a pitiful, punch-drunk ex-fighter with a sub par IQ of about 70.

There was an unseen dimension to the strange man from Sullivan Street. Late at night, he could be found residing in a million-dollar uptown town house, attired in a silk robe or a sport jacket, totally coherent and in control of his destiny. For three decades he faked mental illness. The improbable deception was designed to help him escape prosecution and imprisonment for his true calling. He was Vincent "Chin" Gigante, one of the nation's most enduring and tyrannical Mafia magnates.

Other mafiosi posed as legitimate businessmen; Frank Costello tried to pass as a gentleman; John Gotti and Al Capone as public benefactors. Chin Gigante was the only mobster who pretended to be a madman.

Rarely visible in public except for his brief strolls in Greenwich Village, the reclusive Gigante was the Cosa Nostra's version of the eccentric or half-mad Howard Hughes, the paranoid who, in his later years, ran a billion-dollar business conglomerate while cloistered in a Las Vegas hotel suite. Counting on his outlandish behavior to camouflage his real role as a Mob boss, Gigante controlled the Genovese family at the end of the twentieth century. He ruled over a diversified criminal corporation that became the nation's supreme Mafia borgata, its tentacles extending deeply into the Philadelphia, Buffalo, New England, and Midwest Mob families. With illicit profits topping $100 million a year, the Genovese gang under Gigante's administration was begrudgingly hailed in law-enforcement circles as "the Ivy League" and "Rolls-Royce" of the American Mafia.

Guileful, treacherous, and secretive, Gigante, at the slightest hint of betrayal, condoned the whacking of soldiers, associates, all perceived enemies. Just for uttering his name or nickname, wiseguys and wannabes were subject to summary execution. In his long tenure as boss, Gigante made only one exception to his rule of murdering anyone remotely suspected of having crossed over to the government. The exception was not a made man but an associate, a worker for the family, whom Gigante treated almost like a son. It was the only time he broke his iron rule about punishing potential traitors, and he would pay a heavy price for sparing this single individual. Eventually, it cost him his underworld empire.

Greenwich Village and the section near New York University and Washington Square Park in Lower Manhattan was Vincent Gigante's stamping ground as boy and man. His father, Salvatore, a jewelry engraver, and his mother, Yolanda, a seamstress, emigrated from Naples in 1921. They settled in the area around Sullivan, Thompson, and Bleecker Streets, which into the 1990s remained a colorful, slightly bohemian extension of adjacent Little Italy. The third of five sons, Vincent was born on March 29, 1928. Vincent was a common name in the neighborhood, and to distinguish him from his namesakes, early on Gigante's friends called him "Chin." The nickname was derived from his mother's habit of addressing him as "Cincenzo" (pronounced chin-CHEN-so), the Italian equivalent of Little Vincent or Vinny. His chums shortened that into Chin, his lifelong nickname.

A lackadaisical student, Gigante (pronounced gee-GAN-teh and meaning giant in Italian) completed the eighth grade but dropped out of a vocational school, Textile High, when he turned sixteen, the legal age for leaving school. The same year, still a juvenile, he acquired a "yellow sheet," an arrest record. Between the ages of sixteen and twenty-two, Gigante was pulled in by the police at least four times on an array of charges: fencing stolen goods, possession of an unlicensed gun, auto theft, arson, gambling, and bookmaking. Most of the accusations were dismissed or resolved with small fines. The only complaint that stuck to him was a collar for being a runner or collector of sports bets on the Brooklyn College campus for a large gambling operation that took wagers on college basketball and football games. Trying to look tough, the DA demanded jail time, not meaningless fines, for even the small fry in the case, and Gigante was hit with sixty days.

When arrested in his late teens and early twenties, Gigante listed his occupation as unemployed tailor. A strapping youth with a solid punch, he was better known as a professional boxer. He fought as a light heavyweight in clubs or small arenas around town, winning twenty-one of twenty-five bouts, and his accomplishments were recorded in *Nat Fleischer's Ring Record Book*, the boxing world's encyclopedia. At that time in the late 1940s, club boxers fought four- and six-round contests, usually getting a percentage of the tickets they themselves sold instead of receiving a fixed amount or purse. It was an era when most Mafia gangs were immersed in professional boxing, intent on fixing bouts and controlling money-making fighters. Although his boxing career petered out, Chin Gigante had the distinction of being managed by a big-time gangster, Thomas "Tommy Ryan" Eboli, a Greenwich Village neighbor. A member of the original Lucky Luciano family, Eboli was linked to prize-fighting rackets when the family was headed by Frank Costello.

Detectives assigned to organized-crime intelligence units in the early 1950s pictured Gigante as a wannabe, working his way up mainly as a gorilla for the family's loan-sharking and gambling enterprises on Manhattan's West Side. Three of his brothers, the older Pasquale and Mario, and the younger sibling, Ralph, also were budding mobsters. The youngest brother, Louis, was traveling along a different career highway; he was destined for the priesthood.

Of the four Gigante brothers mixed up with the Mob, Vincent was making the most headway, attracting the attention of Vito Genovese, the capo who had fled to Italy and supported Mussolini before World War II. Since his return to New York, Genovese was nominally subservient to Frank Costello, but, in fact, he was running a virtually independent faction in the family, and the four Gigante brothers were loyal to him. Genovese is believed to have endeared himself to the Gigantes by helping them pay for their mother's surgery. By the time Vincent was in his late twenties, he was a Genovese protégé, serving as a chauffeur and a bodyguard.

There is little doubt that Chin earned his spurs with Vito Genovese on the evening of May 2, 1957. That was the night a gunman saying, "This is for you, Frank," creased Frank Costello's skull with a single shot, a close call that prompted Costello to retire as boss and turn over the reins of the old Luciano borgata to Don Vito. The borgata thereafter was known as the Genovese family. The doorman in Costello's apartment building identified Vincent as the assailant, but when detectives came looking for him at his Greenwich Village apartment, the twenty-nine-year-old Chin was gone. While there was no immediate trace of Vincent, his brothers Mario and Ralph got embroiled with detectives staked out for him on Sullivan Street. In one tussle, Mario was arrested for assaulting an officer after detectives found a hatchet and a baseball bat in his car. The charges were later reduced to disorderly conduct, and both brothers got off with fines.

Three months after Costello was shot, Vincent walked into a Midtown police station house and asked, "Do you want me in the Costello case?" Chewing gum, the jaunty Gigante flashed smiles at the cameras as he was booked for attempted murder. For this contest, the former pugilist had in his corner Maurice Edelbaum, one of the most accomplished and expensive defense lawyers in the city. All Edelbaum would say about Gigante's abrupt disappearance after the Costello shooting was that he had been out of town, some five hundred miles away. Equally baffling was how Gigante raised $100,000 to be bailed out of the Tombs prison, and how he could afford to retain Edelbaum. At the time, the twenty-nine-year-old Gigante was married, had four children, and listed his occupation as a modestly salaried janitor for a federally financed housing-construction project in Greenwich Village. It was actually a no-show job that he obtained through the Mafia's influence in the construction industry. More than likely, Don Vito picked up the tab for Chin's costly legal fees.

At the attempted murder trial in the spring of 1958, only Costello's doorman fingered Gigante, even though he had trimmed thirty to forty pounds off his two hundred-pound-plus frame since the attack, and sported a crew cut instead of long, wavy hair. Edelbaum countered by contending that the prosecution's sole identifying witness was blind in one eye and had impaired sight in the other. Costello, true to the code of *omertà*, declined to identify Gigante as the gunman.

The all-male jury needed barely six hours to bring in a verdict: not guilty. Some forty relatives, including Gigante's wife, Olympia, and their four young children and friends burst into applause. Chin sighed with relief, sinking into his chair at the defense table. "I knew it had to be this way because I was innocent," he protested to reporters. "The cops picked on me." The only legal repercussion from the indictment was the police discovery that he had ignored dozens of parking tickets, costing him $500 in scofflaw fines.

Within three months, Gigante was in handcuffs again, this time alongside his godfather, Don Vito. They and thirty-five other defendants were arrested in July 1958 as participants in an international narcotics conspiracy. Genovese was described in the federal indictment as the ringleader, and Chin as his principal aide in a syndicate importing huge quantities of heroin and other narcotics from Europe, Cuba, Puerto Rico, and Mexico. It was part of the American and Sicilian Mafia's joint operation in the 1950s to develop drug markets in inner-city neighborhoods, mainly in traditional Mob spheres of influence, including New York, Chicago, Philadelphia, and Cleveland.

At their court arraignment, Genovese seemed placid behind his horn-rimmed glasses while Gigante looked downcast. The godfather's outward appearance signified success; he wore a conservative, well-tailored gray suit, a white-on-white shirt, dove-gray tie, and a white handkerchief peeking from his breast pocket. Looking bulky and rumpled with a plaid sports shirt flapping outside his trousers, Gigante perked up when a prosecutor got around to particulars about his importance to his Mafia boss. "He is a protégé of Genovese, a rising star in the underworld and the number-one boy of this man Genovese," Paul Williams, the U.S. Attorney in Manhattan, asserted. "Their participation in the conspiracy seems to be invariably together and simultaneous."

A year later, in 1959, both the boss and his disciple were convicted of violating narcotics laws. Don Vito, whose conviction was later questioned by law-enforcement experts as based on dubious evidence, got fifteen years. Genovese was packed off to the federal penitentiary in Atlanta, and Chin never saw his godfather again. He was separated from his boss and sentenced to seven years at the federal prison in Lewisburg, Pennsylvania. The presiding judge was planning a longer prison term for Gigante, but said he was swayed by an avalanche of letters from residents of Greenwich Village and Little Italy attesting to Chin's good character and work on behalf of juveniles. The judge's action came despite questions by prosecutors about the validity of the letters and Chin's previously unknown concern for underprivileged youths. At Lewisburg, Gigante was a model inmate, staying out of trouble, working as a maintenance man in the prison's boiler room. His good conduct earned him a parole, and in less than five years he was back in Greenwich Village.

Soon after his release, Chin Gigante became the capo of a crew based in Greenwich Village and Little Italy. His prospects were on the rise. He moved his wife and children from a congested apartment into a fine house in the upscale suburban New Jersey town of Old Tappan, about twenty-five miles from Lower Manhattan. It was here that the issue of Gigante's mental competency first arose. In 1969, he was indicted in New Jersey on a charge of bribing Old Tappan's police force to warn him of surveillance and possible investigations by other law-enforcement agencies. The entire force, the chief and four officers, was fired. Gigante never stood trial. Previously, there was no record of his being under psychiatric care, but he began seeking treatment after learning of the bribery investigation. His lawyers produced reports from psychiatrists that he was "psychotic, mute, schizophrenic" and a "candidate for electroshock treatment." His mind also was found to be "infantile and primitive," with his condition deteriorating, according to the diagnosis. It was an effective defense strategy. Ruling that Vincent Gigante was mentally unfit to stand trial and assist in his defense, a judge dismissed the bribery accusations. In effect, the judge determined that the Old Tappan officers were guilty of accepting payoffs from a paranoid resident who fantasized that he was being persecuted by the law.

When Vito Genovese departed for prison in 1959, he retained his title as boss, eventually leaving day-to day control in the hands of Philip Lombardo, a

New Jersey capo. Extremely myopic and forced to wear glasses with lenses almost as thick as a windshield, Lombardo bore the unflattering nickname of "Benny Squint." Don Vito never completed his prison sentence, dying of a heart attack in 1969. During the next decade, federal and local investigators, hampered by a lack of reliable informers, were never certain as to the exact makeup of the Genovese hierarchy. Mob families, naturally, never issue press releases about their internal chains of command, and investigators credited the Genoveses with being the most secretive branch of the American Mafia. There was clearly a power struggle in the early 1970s, and Tommy Ryan Eboli, Gigante's old boxing manager, was the prime loser; he was gunned down in Brooklyn in 1972. (Father Louis Gigante also knew Eboli and officiated at his funeral mass.) The boss's baton was officially seized by Lombardo, who was a role model for Gigante's later behavior. Vincent Fish Cafaro, a high-placed Genovese soldier, provided a portrait of Lombardo as an extremely self-protective man, who "wanted to stay in the background and keep the heat off of himself." Lombardo delegated a great deal of authority to a succession of underbosses, according to Cafaro, even allowing others to "front" for him and attend Commission meetings as the Genovese family's *representante*.

Chin Gigante came out a winner from the internal strife in the 1970s. He profited from the rubout of Eboli by taking over his huge gambling operations in Lower Manhattan and the West Side. Gigante's territory extended from the Battery at the southern tip of the borough to 14th Street; Mafia-controlled numbers and sports-betting bookies needed his permission to operate in his territory. The annual take for Gigante reportedly was in the multimillions; Fish Cafaro said that the most successful bookies were required to give Chin 50 percent of their profits.

Going Philip Lombardo one better on self-protection, Gigante began making short but frequent stopovers at psychiatric hospitals, especially when news seeped out that grand juries were investigating Genovese operations. His underworld confederates casually referred to these hospital examinations as "tune-ups." Chin's use of psychiatrists to ward off possible arrests and another prison stretch did not denigrate his reputation within the Cosa Nostra or diminish his power. By the mid-1970s, he was a capo whose word carried weight throughout the Genovese family.

A young truck driver from Little Italy got a firsthand lesson of Gigante's influence in those years. His New Jersey job was under the aegis of teamsters' Local 560, which was ruled by Anthony "Tony Pro" Provenzano, whose violent inclinations were well known. The local was arguably the most Mob-corrupted unit in teamster union history, and feared for its savage tactics. Provenzano, a Genovese capo, was suspected of helping to arrange Jimmy Hoffa's murder. The naive young truck driver, unaware of the local's reputation and its unwritten law about talking back to officials, got into an argument with a business agent about a grievance against his employer. The next day, as the driver was parking his truck, he saw three goons approaching him with the obvious intent of working him over. Faster afoot than the muscle men, he ran across the George Washington Bridge and got home safely.

"I'm in big trouble, and I'm going to get hurt," the driver told his father. Years later, in an affidavit to a government investigator, he described how his father escorted him to a Little Italy candy store, and instructed him to explain his predicament to a man sitting in a back room.

"I told him what had happened and he said to me, 'Kid, you're going to get a beating.'" The man laughed when the driver pleaded ignorance of the local being mobbed up. "He thought that was very funny. He said, 'All right, I'll take care of it.'" The upshot was that the man in the back room made a phone call. He then advised the driver to return to the union hall and, in front of all the business agents, kiss the official he had insulted on the cheek. "I had to swear that I would never challenge authority in Local 560."

After following instructions and redeeming himself with the union bosses, the grateful driver found out that the man who had intervened in his behalf was the neighborhood's Mafia headman, Chin Gigante.

Throughout the 1970s, Gigante was a shining light in his borgata and increasingly responsible for coordinating Mob rackets with other families. To insure that the Genovese-controlled carpenters' union would not hinder a Gambino construction project, Sammy the Bull Gravano paid a visit to Gigante in 1976. It was Sammy's first meeting with Chin, and a Gambino member introduced him as a capo. "Chin corrected him and said he was no longer a capo," Gravano remembered. "He was the consigliere."

At the sit-down in a Greenwich Village Mob club, Chin, in pajamas and robe and with a three or four days' stubble on his face, pledged to take care of Gravano's union problem. He sounded "perfectly clear and coherent" to Gravano. As a Gambino family expert on construction, Sammy the Bull accompanied his boss, Paul Castellano, and Tommy Bilotti in the late 1970s to a "mini-Commission" meeting with Gigante and other Mob big wigs in the basement of a Staten Island home. This time, Gigante was shaven, and dressed normally in pants, shirt, and a pea coat. "His pajamas must be in the laundry," Bilotti joked to Sammy. As in his previous discussion with Gravano, Gigante was articulate, never mumbling, stuttering, or at a loss for words.

"Chin took the lead basically. He felt that a Commission meeting should be strictly for Cosa Nostra reasons, not business, not money." Gravano remembered. Commission gatherings, Gigante chastised the group, should be about life-and-death issues, preventing Mob wars, and setting policies. Gravano noted that Chin said he was tired of attending meetings about union disputes and the distribution of spoils among the families. These matters, Gigante insisted, should be "straightened out at lower levels" by capos.

The frequent high-level conferences were too risky for Gigante. "I've put a lot of time into this crazy act, and I don't want to get caught in any of these meetings or picked up or bugged," Gravano quoted him.

Chin's strategy was more successful than he realized. He was unaware that his insanity charade had pulled the wool over the eyes of numerous FBI, state, and city investigators. They considered Vincent Chin Gigante a comical Mafia sideshow. Some were uncertain about his mental state; others thought he was legitimately loony. None recognized how much power the strange man from Sullivan Street actually wielded in the Genovese family.

47

Psychological Warfare

Gliding slowly, the car came to a halt in front of a cluster of men talking on the sidewalk outside a storefront. Two FBI agents, badges prominently pinned on their jackets, sat in the front of the car. Suddenly, the conversations halted, the eyes of the men milling on the sidewalk were drawn toward the passenger in the rear. His face was concealed by a paper bag cut with eye holes, and he was pointing to individuals on the sidewalk. As he whispered, both agents scribbled notes. In a flash, the knot of men anxiously dispersed in different directions, shouting to each other, "They got a rat."

The all-too-conspicuous appearance of the FBI and the man in the crude mask on Sullivan Street in Greenwich Village heralded a psychological phase in the government's investigation of the Genovese family. It was 1982, and the bureau's revamped Genovese Squad was trying novel tactics to kick-start a fruitful campaign against the redoubtable gang. Recently appointed the squad's supervisor, Donald Scott Richards found the unit in poor shape. "We have skimpy intelligence, morale is shot, and we're not going anywhere on a decent investigation," Richards glumly admitted to himself.

One of five units established in 1980 to concentrate on each of New York's Cosa Nostra borgatas, in its first two years the squad had failed to dig up indictable evidence against a significant Genovese soldier or to uproot a major family racket. The bureau was working on the assumption that Phil Benny Squint Lombardo had retired in poor health to Florida, leaving the family in the care of a new boss, Anthony Salerno. As the perceived godfather, Fat Tony was the squad's foremost objective, and his East Harlem headquarters in the Palma Boys Social Club was under intensive surveillance. But as yet no big case was brewing against him.

Expanding the range of targets, Richards decided to focus on the downtown Genoveses, particularly on a storefront hangout called "the Triangle Civic Improvement Association." The club, on Sullivan Street, between West Third and Bleecker Streets, was across the street from the apartment building where Vincent Gigante's mother lived and where he often stayed. The Triangle was a dimly lit hovel, stocked with worn chairs and tables, and with an espresso machine mounted on a small bar. Gigante spent most afternoons there. A white, gummy substance smeared on the club's plate-glass window blocked a view of the interior from the sidewalk. Inside, signs on the wall read: "Tough Guys Don't Squeal," "Don't Talk. This Place Is Bugged" and "The Enemy Is Listening."

Although the FBI was uncertain whether Gigante was mentally disturbed, officials were confident that in the Genovese pecking order he retained at least the rank of capo and headed a crew. There was another reason for homing in on the Triangle. It was a meeting place once a week for another recognized downtown Genovese capo, Matthew Ianniello. There was no question about his mental state. He was better known as "Matty the Horse," the gangster present in his brother's restaurant, Umberto's Clam House, when Crazy Joey Gallo was shot to death there in 1972.

Agent Richards reckoned that with two capos using the Triangle as a refuge, it was a prime site for surveillance. From an observation post in an apartment across the street from the club, FBI men saw Gigante talking with soldiers as they ambled with him along Sullivan Street. Richards's request for long-range parabolic microphones to eavesdrop on Gigante's walk-talk sidewalk conversations was vetoed by the Justice Department. Government lawyers cautioned that evidence gathered that way probably would be declared inadmissible; parabolic equipment intruded on the conversations of passersby and was not restricted to targeted suspects and a specific site.

Next, Richards placed miniature listening devices in the rearview mirrors of bureau cars parked on Sullivan Street. If Gigante stopped to talk near one of the rigged autos, agents in the observation post could activate a microphone through remote control. Technicians tinkered with the devices for a month but abandoned them after failing to clearly pick up any of Chin's conversations.

Bugging the Triangle was rejected as an unpromising venture. The small room, often packed, was so noisy that voices would be indistinguishable and worthless as evidence. The FBI's sparse information indicated that Gigante, when he did speak inside the club, whispered in the listener's ear. "There are too many guys talking in there at the same time for a bug to be of any value," Richards decided. He wanted to find quieter locations where Gigante and Ianniello felt more secure, and where mikes and telephone taps would be more productive. (What the FBI did not know was that, as a precaution, Gigante had the club swept once a month to detect electronic snooping.)

By employing "psychological warfare," Richards hoped Gigante and Ianniello would become wary of using the Triangle Club and lead agents to their private sanctuaries. "We want to drive them out of there," he urged his squad. On Richards's orders, agents camped openly in a restaurant directly across the street from the club and could be seen photographing everyone entering and leaving. Periodically, agents patrolled Sullivan Street, jotting down the license-plate numbers of every car parked near the club. A singular hoax was displaying the agent wearing a paper bag mask, posing as an informer. "There's no doubt that they think we have a rat-snitch fingering them," Richards rejoiced.

The obtrusive surveillance apparently failed to worry Gigante, who continued venturing into the club most afternoons. Agents believed he usually discussed important Mob matters at night, when it was more difficult to follow him in the South Village area near Sullivan Street and in nearby SoHo. On occasion, he entered il Bocconcino on Houston Street and Ruggiero's on Grand Street, neighborhood restaurants. The walk-talks and meets at the restaurants were largely restricted to a tiny knot of trusted, longtime lieutenants: Dominick "Quiet Dom" Cirillo, a soft-spoken gangster from the Bronx; Venero "Benny Eggs" Mangano, who obtained his nickname because his mother ran an egg store; and Dominick "Baldy Dom" Canterino, whose hair thinned at an early age, and who frequently chauffeured Gigante. Mangano and Canterino were old friends of Gigante.

Seven years older than Gigante, Mangano had spent his entire life near Chin in the Village and, when not at the Triangle, operated out of his own nearby club on Thompson Street. Short and paunchy, Mangano was a neighborhood character, particularly liked because he permitted old-timers—mostly non-mafiosi—to play cards and socialize in his club. The place was bedecked with American flags and photos of Frank Sinatra, Perry Como, and other Italian-American entertainers and celebrities. Although he had never served time for a felony, Mangano had a thick police record for gambling arrests, was listed in FBI files as active in bookmaking, loan-sharking, and labor extortions, and had been permanently banned as an "undesirable" from entering Atlantic City casinos because of gambling and shake-down allegations.

Besides his Mob deals, Mangano was successful in the wholesale clothing business. He founded M & J enterprises, a company that bought surplus designer jeans, shirts, and other garments at a discount and resold them in the country and overseas. For his bodyguard, Mangano selected John "Sausage" Barbata, a former gambling wire-room operator and a loan-shark enforcer on the New Jersey waterfront. The link between gangsters nicknamed for food—Benny Eggs and Johnny Sausage—prompted agents to refer to them as "Chin's Breakfast Club." (Gigante eventually rewarded Mangano by promoting him to underboss.)

In his day and nighttime wanderings, even in heavy rain, Gigante routinely dressed and acted abnormally. He would stop in his tracks, expose himself, and urinate in the street. Once, on a twilight meander, he spotted an FBI surveillance team. Abruptly, in front of St. Anthony of Padua Roman Catholic Church at Sullivan and Houston Streets, he dropped to his knees as if he were praying.

Normally, Chin appeared feeble, barely able to creep along without someone at his side. A New York detective, Gaetano Bruno, attached to an FBI task force, saw a different aspect of Gigante's physical agility. With a bodyguard holding him by the arm, Gigante was slowly crossing busy Houston Street, when the traffic light turned against them. Without difficulty, Gigante sprinted like a hare and beat his escort to the safety of the sidewalk. He then resumed his leaden-footed pace.

Gigante's bizarre behavior was also exhibited in his mother's fourth-floor apartment. A tactic, known as "tickling the wires," is employed by prosecutors and agents to encourage mobsters to exchange ideas and news on telephone taps and bugs. To get them worried and gabbing, subpoenas for possible evidence or grand jury testimony are simultaneously served to several members of a family or crew. One day, agents Pat Marshall and Pat Collins knocked on Yolanda Gigante's apartment with a subpoena for her son. Chin was standing in the bathtub, under a closed shower head, wearing a bathrobe. He had an open umbrella over his head, sported a wide smile on his face, and mumbled incoherently.

Turning to the agents, Gigante winked mischievously at them. Collins stuck the subpoena in Chin's bathrobe pocket. "He's nuts," Collins told Yolanda Gigante, and left.

Gigante's relatives, protesting that he was mentally ill and was being cruelly and unjustly harassed, hired lawyer Barry Slotnick to halt the FBI's pursuit of him. "He has been psychiatrically disabled for decades and it is inconceivable that he would be the leader of some organized-crime network," Slotnick said. "He couldn't run a candy store, much less a crime family." (In New Yorkese, "candy store" refers to a simple soda fountain, usually run by a man and wife, which also sells ice cream, candy, magazines, and newspapers.)

Relatives maintained that Gigante was so incompetent that he had to be assisted everywhere he went and that he often embarrassed them. The Gigantes' family dentist, Herbert Rubin, would only treat Vincent at night after other patients had left. Rubin explained that he could not allow a disheveled, deranged patient wearing a bathrobe and pajamas into his office during regular hours.

Chin's most ardent defender was the Reverend Louis Gigante, who frequently was at his brother's elbow on rambles in their old neighborhood. Known affectionately as "Father G," and as a "Ghetto Priest," he was renowned for his slum-clearance and housing-rehabilitation projects. Unlike his older brothers who were school dropouts and who early on became entangled in crime, Louis graduated on a scholarship from Georgetown University, where he was a basketball star. Ordained at twenty-seven, he became the pastor of St. Athanasius Roman Catholic Church in the South Bronx, an impoverished, crime-ravaged district. Almost single-handedly, in the late 1960s, Father Gigante organized the South East Bronx Corporation (SEBCO) to provide decent homes for thousands of residents at a time when the South Bronx housing stock was devastated by arson and decay. Overall, SEBCO built more than two thousand sorely needed new and renovated housing units, affordable apartments for low-income families and seniors. "Father G" was acclaimed as the driving force behind the stabilization of a huge swath of the Bronx. John Cardinal O'Connor, the Archbishop of New York, hailed him in the 1980s as the "Church's Master Builder."

In a move rarely undertaken by priests, Father Gigante used his prominence and success as an urban reformer to launch a political career. After a losing race for Congress, he was elected in 1973 and served one term as a representative from the Bronx's Hunts Point section to the City Council, New York's legislative body. Whenever given the opportunity as a clergyman and councilman, he refuted the existence of the Mafia, denouncing the media and law enforcement for inventing the concept of Italian organized-crime groups. Aligned with the Italian-American Civil Rights League, he was at the 1971 Columbus Circle rally when Joe Colombo, the Mob boss, was shot and paralyzed. Rushing to the speaker's platform, the priest helped restore order by leading the frenzied crowd in prayer.

Inevitably, the identification of his brothers Vincent, Mario, and Ralph as mafiosi, and his own personal associations with reputed mobsters led to controversies for Father Gigante. In 1979 he was called before a grand jury investigating his efforts to ease the rigors of prison for a convicted gangster James "Jimmy Nap" Napoli.

Jimmy Nap was no small-time neighborhood bookie or amateur gambler. A big-time Genovese earner, he had a lengthy yellow sheet for trying to fix boxing matches, for murder conspiracy, for felonious assault, for loan-sharking, and for heading a $35-million-a-year policy and horse-race-betting network in Manhattan. Prosecutors accused Father Gigante of dodging questions before a grand jury looking into attempts by the gangster and his pals to bribe prison officials for a Christmas furlough and early release from jail for Napoli. The bribes had enabled Jimmy Nap to have restaurant-catered meals and wine served in his cell.

Father Gigante contended that questions about his conversations and relations with Napoli, "an old and dear friend," infringed on his priestly duties. Defending himself against a charge of contempt of court, he cited the confidentiality of his "clerical privilege" and his First Amendment right to practice his religion without interference. The arguments and protest demonstrations in his behalf by other priests failed to impress the presiding judge. Found guilty of evading questions put to him before the grand jury, Father Gigante served seven days of a ten-day jail sentence.

Another Mafia-related issue popped up when Father Gigante issued a personal appeal for leniency in behalf of Steven Crea. Identified by the FBI as a Lucchese capo and a power in construction-industry rackets, Crea was convicted in 1985 of conspiracy in a murder plot. The priest, in a letter to the sentencing judge, called Crea a "special friend" who had aided him to resist the "onslaughts of crime and housing deterioration" in the South Bronx. (Crea's guilty verdict for murder conspiracy was overturned. Known to his Mob admirers as "Stevie Wonder," he later rose to the rank of Lucchese acting underboss, and was imprisoned in 2004 after pleading guilty to extorting a major construction company and to "enterprise corruption" involving contractors and unions.)

Despite his intervention on behalf of known mafiosi, law-enforcement authorities concur that there has never been a scintilla of evidence that Father Gigante was involved in a crime, let alone a Mafia activity. But newspapers raised questions about SEBCO, his housing corporation's affiliations with contractors identified as having strong ties to mobsters. *The New York Times* reported in 1981 about business relationships between SEBCO and Vincent DiNapoli, a Genovese soldier and construction-rackets specialist. Companies in which DiNapoli was a partner or an investor had obtained, without competitive bidding, a large share of drywall (interior walls and paneling) and carpentry contracts with SEBCO and with many other federally financed projects in the Bronx. DiNapoli's outfits raked in more than $25 million in public contracts in the late 1970s.

The Village Voice asserted in 1989 that drywall, carpentry, and construction-debris hauling firms allied with mobsters as officials, shareholders, or consultants, had obtained work totaling more than $50 million from SEBCO projects. Again, companies linked to DiNapoli, a convicted labor racketeer, and to Crea were profiting from SEBCO contracts.

Over the years, Father Gigante declined to discuss the propriety of the contracts obtained by the Mob-tainted companies. Other SEBCO officials stressed that none of the work had been directly awarded by SEBCO; instead, they were obtained through subcontracts with the general contractors in charge of the projects. The general contractors, however, must have known that SEBCO raised no objections to the Mafia-affiliated contractors, and that by employing these companies they would probably avert union problems and costly work stoppages. It was a convenient package for all concerned.

One Bronx mobster, Pellegrino Butcher Boy Masselli, a Genovese gangster, proudly exhibited his admiration for Reverend Gigante. On the front of his trucking company office and underworld headquarters in Hunts Point, Masselli placed a banner reading, "If You Can't Trust Father Gigante, Who Can You Trust?"

While Father Gigante was reluctant to discuss SEBCO's subcontractors, he often lashed out against what he termed law-enforcement authorities' "misuse and abuse of their power." He characterized the criminal records of his three brothers as nonviolent "gambling" arrests, and was particularly incensed in the mid-1980s at the "persecution" of Vincent.

In fact, the FBI was increasing its vigilance, trying to close in on Chin Gigante. As the FBI's Commission investigation wound down with the indictment of Anthony Salerno, naming him as the Genovese boss, some agents wondered if Gigante loomed as a possible successor.

A new Genovese Squad supervisor, John S. Pritchard III, was convinced that Gigante was sane and powerful. He ordered increased surveillance and a sharper eye kept on Gigante and the Triangle Club. One of his first steps was building a concealed observation post, a shed on the roof of a nearby New York University building, equipped with zoom-lens cameras to spy on everyone entering the club or appearing with Gigante on the sidewalk. Tailing Chin one night, Pritchard glimpsed his dual personality act. The agent saw him, wearing a bathrobe, shuffling slowly to a parked car with Baldy Dom Canterino. As Gigante ducked into the vehicle, he handed the ratty robe to Canterino and for a second exposed the well-tailored gray sharkskin suit and the necktie that he was wearing.

In 1985, agents finally turned up a meaningful discovery about Vincent Gigante's activities. "The enigma in a bathrobe," as FBI wags characterized him, had two homes, two love lifes, and two separate intimate families. Gigante and his wife, Olympia, raised two sons and three daughters in their New Jersey home in Old Tappan. His other home was in a town house on Manhattan's fashionable East Side, where he spent most nights with another woman. Her given name was also Olympia. (In affairs of the heart and voicing names in romantic moments, Chin was a prudent man.) Olympia "Mitzi" Esposito had borne him two daughters and a son.

Chin was conducting his daytime business affairs in the vicinity of Sullivan Street; he never left the New York–New Jersey area for even the briefest vacation or trip. After some difficulties, agents traced him to his posh nighttime nest. Charles Beaudoin and other agents spent hair-raising moments keeping up with Gigante once he left Lower Manhattan. Late at night, Vito Palmieri, a soldier and chauffeur with the skills of a racing-car driver, picked up Gigante in a Cadillac or other large-sized car for a pulsating trip. "He was hard to trail," Beaudoin marveled, as Palmieri defying speed limits and red lights, swerving the wrong way into one-way streets, weaved uptown. To determine if he were being followed, Palmieri engaged in "many risky maneuvers," Beaudoin reported.

Despite the evasive, high-octane tactics, Gigante was tracked to the hideaway, a town house on East 77th Street between Park and Madison Avenues.

It was a handsome building on an elegant block; a four-story white-bricked edifice with black trim, red doors framed by replicas of gas-flamed lanterns, and a tile frieze highlighting the top floor's brickwork. The stately dwelling was a virtual gift to Olympia Esposito from Morris Levy, the owner of recording companies and night clubs, who for decades had been mixed up in opaque financial transactions with top Genovese mobsters. According to real estate records, through a friend, Levy in 1983 transferred the town house, valued on the open market at close to $1 million, to Olympia for $16,000. Levy had acquired the property the year before for an estimated $525,000 but apparently was willing to absorb a huge loss on an extremely desirable building.

(In another real estate transfer with a Gigante relative, Levy in 1979 donated land on his sprawling two thousand-acre Sunnyside Farms, where he raised thoroughbreds in upstate Ghent, New York, to Father Gigante. A ranch-style house was built on the property, which Father Gigante claimed in court records was used almost exclusively for needy parishioners from his Bronx church. Nearby Ghent residents said in the 1980s that Father Gigante was frequently seen at the house with guests.)

The principal owner of Roulette Records, an independent record company, and the proprietor of nightclubs, including Manhattan's famed Birdland, Levy was dubbed by insiders as "Godfather of the Music Business." His thick FBI dossier, compiled over thirty years, described him as having been involved in loan-sharking, extortion, and money laundering for the Philadelphia crime family and for the Genoveses. Levy could never become a made man because he was Jewish, but FBI agents said he loved playing a tough-guy role and was a frequent visitor at the Triangle Club. "He never hid the fact that he was connected," John Pritchard recounted. "His associations with wiseguys made people afraid of him and helped his business." Levy, said to be worth $75 million in the mid-1980s, was a big earner for Genovese chiefs by cutting them in as discreet shareholders in his wholesale record-sales and music-publishing companies. The mobsters returned the favors by helping Levy's chain of Strawberry record shops and music companies in important ways: guaranteeing that he had no union problems and by "influencing" popular entertainers to cut records for him at favorable contract terms.

Levy's disreputable background was publicly exposed in 1988, when he was convicted on federal charges of extortion, spinning out of an attempt with mobsters to recoup $1.2 million from a record distributor. He died of liver cancer in 1990, at age sixty-two, before he could begin a ten-year prison sentence.

Convinced that Chin was using the town house as a retreat for Mob business meetings, Pritchard made it a priority objective for surveillance and bugging. A court-authorized Title III tap on the house's telephone lines ran sixty days in the autumn of 1985. Gigante's conversations produced no evidence or clues of crimes, but the tap provided substantial documentation that his deranged behavior was an act. On the telephone, Gigante chatted mainly with his children and Olympia Mitzi Esposito about mundane household matters—bringing home groceries, medical appointments, the weather—and his comments were invariably intelligent.

Calling Mitzi on October 17, 1985, Gigante inquired about her examination by a doctor for a severe cough. "Stop smoking," he scolded her. Before he rang off, there was a loud kissing sound, and he added, "I love you." On November 8, 1985, in one of the last recorded calls, he told Mitzi he was at "the barber's" and asked what items she wanted him to bring to the town house.

FBI teams tailing Gigante in his trips uptown saw him jump out of the car to randomly use telephone booths. There was no way to trace or monitor these sporadic calls. When the telephone tap at the town house failed to unearth clues to past or ongoing crimes, Pritchard tried other ploys. The bureau set up an observation post at night in the Ramaz Yeshiva, a Jewish parochial school on East 78th Street, whose rear windows and terrace overlooked the back windows of the East 77th Street town house. School officials gave the bureau a key to the front door and asked that they be notified whenever agents intended using the building for surveillance. Agents were told how to disengage a series of electronic burglar sensors upon entering the building.

Dr. Noam Shudolsky, the school administrator, was summoned to the building one midnight by a security service that reported a sensor had been tripped on the third-floor terrace. The FBI had not informed the school that agents would be there that night, and when Shudolsky—armed with a flashlight—

confronted a figure in the darkness on the terrace, he shouted: "Stand where you are. You're under arrest."

"Don't shoot, I'm with the FBI," was the instant reply.

Disturbed that agents felt "they could come and go" without alerting him, Dr. Shudolsky reclaimed the front-entrance key and barred the FBI from using the building. Pritchard blamed an overzealous agent for violating the agreement with the school.

Determined to spy on Chin while he was off-guard inside the town house, Pritchard tried another approach. An agent rented an apartment in a luxury building at 61 East 77th Street, next to the town house at number 67. Pritchard wanted the apartment because it directly abutted the third floor of Chin's uptown refuge.

The two-bedroom flat was leased for $4,500 a month in late 1985, and agent Charles Beaudoin drew the main observation assignment. Nightly, Beaudoin outfitted himself with green camouflage clothes, a small flashlight, a walkie-talkie, a notebook in a vinyl bag, and a lightweight waterproof canopy or tiny tent built by the FBI. From the apartment's rear terrace, the athletic, six-foot-tall Beaudoin scrambled across a distance of about eighteen inches onto the Ramaz terrace without triggering a sensor. The agent said he might have used the Ramaz terrace "unofficially" under the assumption that "we still had permission" from the school.

Prone, concealed, and sheltered from snow and rain by the canopy, Beaudoin was about fifty feet from the town house. He had an unobstructed view of the interior of the three-story building through its large rear windows. Agents on the street alerted Beaudoin on his walkie-talkie when Gigante arrived. Sprawled on concrete, and surrounded by planters, Beaudoin relied on his eyesight to record his observations without the help of binoculars or a camera. (At the time, a court ruling, which was later reversed, prohibited the introduction of evidence obtained with the aid of binoculars or a camera unless agents had obtained a search warrant for viewing the interior of a building.)

Beaudoin noted in his official 302 reports that Gigante's nocturnal visits fell into a pattern. Generally, he arrived before midnight, showered on the top floor where the bedrooms and a living room were located. Chin sometimes donned a bathrobe after showering, but wore it only briefly. Usually, he changed into a blazer, a sport jacket, or a sweater for a meal in the dining room with relatives and friends or for meetings with Genovese underlings. Chin always sat at the head of the table for conferences with other mobsters, and personally served drinks to his guests, Beaudoin wrote. He saw Gigante occasionally pull aside a visitor and whisper into his ear. At all times, in Beaudoin's view, he showed no sign of physical distress, moving easily around the three floors and using the elevator without assistance.

The agent often observed Chin on the third floor, wearing eyeglasses, reading a newspaper or perusing documents and ledgers that he removed from a bookcase and a file cabinet. In a 302 report, Beaudoin recorded that one night Angelo D'Acunto, a Genovese soldier, walked with Gigante out of the agent's sight into the kitchen. Returning alone from the kitchen, Gigante began counting "a large stack of American currency" on a table. To Beaudoin, whose medical records showed he had extraordinarily acute vision, "The amount appeared to be substantial."

Gigante normally left the town house between 9:00 A.M. and 10:00 A.M., in the same shabby clothes or bathrobe he had worn when he arrived, and was driven back to his mother's apartment on Sullivan Street. Later in the afternoon, he emerged, with bodyguards at his elbow, for the short stroll past the Children's Aid Society headquarters, a few doors away, and into the Triangle Club. His schedule was as predictable as the tides.

Almost every night for four months in the winter and early spring of 1986, Beaudoin lay on the Ramaz School terrace, peering into the town house. His observations and those of other agents and a police department detective who spelled him, gave Pritchard, and the FBI, the "probable cause" needed for the next attack on Chin Gigante—a bug in the town house.

A court order for hidden microphones was obtained in the spring. Rather than trying to break surreptitiously into the house, which was usually occupied and was guarded by a state-of-the-art burglar-alarm system, technicians decided to use the FBI apartment in the adjacent building as a means of entry. Relying on a makeshift blueprint prepared by Beaudoin of the layout of the town house, Jim Kallstrom's special-operations unit drilled through a common wall separating the buildings. They used a noiseless drill that sucked out debris and did not leave a telltale trail of plaster and wood dust on the town house floor. The eavesdroppers intended to install a bug in the wall behind a kitchen cabinet. Technicians were certain the powerful miniature microphone would be concealed and there would be an "air path" allowing voices to be recorded from the kitchen and the adjacent dining room, the two areas where Gigante often conferred with aides. But Kallstrom's eavesdroppers miscalculated. Their first try placed a microphone behind a refrigerator, instead of a cabinet, and the motor drone overwhelmed all other sounds. Next, they drilled through a wrong section of a wall, into a bathroom, penetrating too deeply. The hole burrowed through, knocked off a wall tile, and was clearly visible inside the town house before the frantic agents could patch it up.

"The floor plan we had was inaccurate, off by a few feet," Kallstrom sighed.

Unintentionally notified that the bureau was trying to penetrate the town house and that he was under watch there, Gigante stopped holding meetings in the dining room. Curtains were drawn at all times, covering the rear windows, preventing observations from the terrace.

There was one more huge disappointment for the Genovese Squad. One night, when Baldy Dom Canterino left his Cadillac for several hours in a parking lot, Kallstrom's break-in artists entered the car, removed a rear panel and replaced it with an identical one that contained a listening device. The objective was to duplicate the state task force's earlier success with the Jaguar bug on the Lucchese boss, Ducks Corallo. "We had seen Chin and Baldy Dom in conversations in the Caddy and we were sure we'd pick up important evidence or intelligence," Pritchard said. "But we had unbelievably bad luck. Almost on the very day the Caddy bug began operating, the news came out that Goldstock's office [the state task force] had bugged the Jaguar, and Chin stopped talking in the car."

Its campaign against Gigante was stalled, but the FBI was having much more success against two other Genovese garrisons. Mainly through electronic spying at the Palma Boys Social Club, Fat Tony Salerno was bagged in the Commission case investigation and in two separate labor-racketeering indictments. Salerno's career as a Mob leader ended with a life sentence.

Donald Richards's plan to drive Matty the Horse Ianniello out of the Triangle eventually paid dividends. Ianniello began relying on a Midtown office, where FBI bugs and concealed video cameras produced evidence for a series of indictments. Matty was found guilty in 1986 of skimming millions of dollars from topless bars and restaurants, shaking down construction companies, and extorting protection payoffs from food suppliers, including a company that provided hot dogs at Yankee Stadium.

When the trials were over, Ianniello was hit with more than twenty years in prison time. The government even moved in on his favorite restaurant, Umberto's Clam House in Little Italy. The popular trattoria's listed principal owner was Ianniello's brother Robert, but the Justice Department found that profits from the restaurant's zesty dishes of calamari, scungilli, and pasta were being fed to the Genovese family. For seven years, a federal manager was stationed at the restaurant to watch the books and the cash register. The monitor left in 1994 after a court suit by Robert Ianniello accused the government of bankrupting Umberto's through mismanagement.

With court triumphs over Fat Tony and Matty the Horse, only Chin Gigante remained from the FBI's designated Big-Three Genovese targets. Yet all gambits against him had failed. "We burnt a lot of manpower following Chin without getting a bang for our buck," the FBI's Don Richards conceded. "He was a real challenge, a mystery."

48

The Real Boss

". . . I'll leave this up to the boss."

Somehow the immense significance of those words casually spoken by Fat Tony Salerno was overlooked by FBI agents and prosecutors.

For more than five years, U.S. Attorney Rudolph Giuliani and FBI officials remained steadfast about one fundamental aspect of the Genovese crime family: until the Commission trial in 1986, Tony Salerno was the Genovese godfather. They were uncertain about Chin Gigante's sanity, but in court documents and news pronouncements, they never wavered from this certainty about Salerno's status.

Nevertheless, long before the 1986 Commission trial, investigators were missing clues that came directly from the mouths of wiseguys, speaking freely, unaware that they were being overheard on bugs and telephone taps.

As early as April 4, 1982, Bruce Mouw's Gambino squad intercepted a telephone conversation between Angelo Fat Ange Ruggiero and John Gotti that strongly suggested Gigante was then equal in rank to Paul Castellano. In his Long Island home, Ruggiero explained to Gotti, then his capo, that "Paul and Chin made a pact." He continued, "Any friend of ours that gets pinched for junk, they kill 'em. No administration meetings, no nothing, just go kill him. They're not warning nobody; not telling nobody because they feel the guy's going to rat." It was an obvious reference to Castellano and Gigante's imposing the death penalty on any mobster caught in narcotics trafficking. Only a godfather could unilaterally exercise that ultimate penalty, and it was proof that Chin Gigante was in command of the Genovese family.

From the Jaguar bug, State Organized Crime Task Force personnel heard Tony Ducks Corallo, the Lucchese boss, complaining on June 23, 1983, that "Chin" and "Paul" had made a Commission decision without consulting him. "What Commission?" Corallo griped. "The Commission was him [Gigante] when they okayed a guy to be killed and nobody come [sic] and told Tom [Santoro, the Lucchese underboss] and me a thing about it."

A brief segment of a bugged conversation at the Palma Boys Social Club between Tony Salerno and Matty the Horse Ianniello, on May 22, 1984, also failed to register properly with agents and prosecutors. Salerno and Ianniello were reviewing a list of candidates to be inducted as made men in another family. Upset that the nicknames of the proposed soldiers had not been included, which would have made it easier to identify them, Salerno said, "I don't know none of them. They don't put the nicknames down there. . . . But anyway, I'll leave this up to the boss." Salerno's remark was a blunt admission that he was not the final arbiter of decisions in the family.

On February 6, 1985, only days before the Commission indictments were unsealed, Fat Tony was dejectedly discussing with a soldier, Giuseppe Sabato, newspaper stories that arrests of Mafia godfathers were imminent. They wondered if Chin would be among the chieftains indicted. "Forget about the papers," Sabato said. "There's arrests next week. I'm pretty sure Paul and the other guy and Tony Ducks. I'm pretty sure I'll find out tonight. If they get Chin they're wrapped up."

Referring to Gigante's feigned mental illness, Sabato continued, "All, all the finagling, manipulating, manipulating and manipulating to fool the government, fuck it, it won't stick." Salerno responded, "He's got to worry if he gets pinched, all them years he spent in that fuckin' asylum. For nothing."

The FBI might have erred connecting the dots to compose an accurate picture of the Genovese chain of command, and agents were unsure for years of Gigante's true mental state and his role in the family. But mafiosi of all ranks in the New York families understood that the government had for years identified the wrong man, Tony Salerno, as the Genovese supreme leader. They knew that Chin Gigante was the godfather of a mighty Mafia family, his erratic behavior was a stunt to avoid prosecution, and Fat Tony Salerno just a straw man used by Gigante to deceive investigators.

Clearly, Angelo Ruggiero and John Gotti, two veteran wiseguys, were positive that Chin was the paramount leader of the Genoveses. In 1982 the FBI overheard them discussing the punishment for getting caught in drug deals, and that year even a neophyte like Alphonse D'Arco was clued in. At Little Al's induction into the Lucchese family as a made man, Ducks Corallo informed him that, among the bosses, Vincent Gigante led the Genovese family.

In the early 1980s, Sammy the Bull Gravano, then only a middle-ranking mobster, learned from Gambino higher-ups that Chin was a major Cosa Nostra force with lethal influence outside New York. Gravano was told that Gigante, in a power play to gain a larger portion of gambling and union rackets in Atlantic City, had authorized the murder of Angelo Bruno, the boss of the Philadelphia Cosa Nostra, which had territorial interests in Atlantic City. About that same time, Philip Leonetti, who became the underboss of the Philadelphia family, discovered that Gigante had approved six additional Philadelphia Mob slayings in the 1980s to resolve an internal feud.

The New England crime family, the Patriarca gang, active in Boston and Providence, was another borgata that deferred to Gigante. When Al D'Arco was the acting boss of the Lucchese family, Gigante's emissaries invited him to attend the installation of a new Mob hierarchy in Boston. "We picked the administration," Genovese soldier Jimmy Ida boasted at a sit-down in an Elizabeth Street bakery. "Vincent has selected the names."

Gigante's awesome reach and position was also evident to Anthony Gaspipe Casso before he moved up to a leadership spot. In the autumn of 1986, during the Commission trial, his Lucchese superiors informed him that Chin had issued a contract on John Gotti to avenge Paul Castellano's murder.

That Gigante had been the unchallenged Genovese boss for years was revealed conclusively to government investigators in the autumn of 1986, almost two years after the Commission indictments. The information came from a defector. Facing conviction and a long sentence on labor-racketeering and extortion charges, Vincent Fish Cafaro, began cooperating with the government. Agents said he flipped partly to save his son Thomas and a girlfriend from prosecution. (Tom Cafaro disowned his father, refused a plea-bargain, and remained an associate in the family.)

Fat Tony Salerno's closest confidant for decades, Cafaro dissolved the mists shrouding the family's hierarchy for almost ten years. He provided convincing first-hand evidence that Chin Gigante had orchestrated a double deception for years. Chin had playacted his madness and had set up Salerno to conceal his own omnipotence in the borgata.

"Straightened out," made in 1974, Cafaro was working under Salerno in 1981 when Philip Benny Squint Lombardo retired as boss, apparently because of failing health. Salerno, who had been consigliere and underboss—never the boss—suffered a stroke about the same time Lombardo left the scene. At that point, Cafaro said in FBI debriefings, Chin Gigante took over as godfather. There was no internal strife. One of Gigante's first moves was to "pull down," demote, Salerno to the lowest rank, soldier, and to leave him virtually powerless.

Recuperating from his stroke at his country home in upstate New York, Salerno became bored and wanted to resume his racketeering activities in the city. Gigante, adopting some of Lombardo's protective tactics, gave Cafaro these instructions: "Let Tony come down and you stay with him, watch him and see that he's all right." Salerno was ordered to resume attending Commission meetings as he had for Lombardo, but to withhold from other families as long as possible the identity of the real Genovese boss. "Chin wished the heat to remain uptown rather than on his downtown base of operation," Cafaro said, and he used Salerno as a decoy. Cafaro recalled Gigante attending only one Commission meeting. But before sit-downs with other borgatas, "Fat Tony conferred with Chin on any major matters affecting the family." All Fat Tony's decisions were first "put on the record with Chin," Cafaro added.

During the period when the FBI believed that Salerno was running the Genovese clan, according to Cafaro, two murders affecting important federal investigations were sanctioned by Gigante in 1982. In March, shortly before he was to go on trial with Genovese mobsters on bid-rigging and extortion charges, Theodore Maritas, president of the 25,000-member carpenters' union, "disappeared." Prosecutors believe he was killed because of Mob fears that he might become a government witness against the lead defendant, Vincent DiNapoli, a Genovese controller in the construction industry. After Maritas vanished, DiNapoli negotiated a plea deal for a lighter sentence.

Cafaro disclosed that a second highly publicized slaying ordered by Gigante was wrongly linked by law-enforcement agencies to an inquiry involving Raymond Donovan, first Secretary of Labor in President Ronald Reagan's cabinet. In 1982, a special federal prosecutor was looking into allegations that Donovan, while a construction-company executive, had met with organized-crime figures and knew about payoffs to mobsters. A prime suspect in the federal investigation was Pellegrino Butcher Boy Masselli, the Bronx-based Genovese gangster, who had a multimillion-dollar trucking contract with Donovan's former construction firm. In August 1982, Butcher Boy's son, Nat Masselli, was shot to death by Genovese mobsters. The younger Masselli was secretly assisting the special prosecutor, Leon Silverman, and the slaying touched off speculation that the Mafia was impeding the Donovan-Masselli investigation. Silverman later determined that there was "insufficient credible evidence" for a federal indictment of Donovan for associating with mobsters or knowing of illegal payoffs.

But the whacking of Nat Masselli and the uproar over his undercover work in the federal investigation triggered a probe by the Bronx DA's office that charged Donovan, Butcher Boy Masselli, and six others with defrauding $7.4 million from a subway-construction contract. After a nine-month trial, all eight defendants were acquitted on the state indictment.

The Bronx investigations ended with the conviction of two Genovese soldiers for Nat Masselli's murder. Cafaro said Gigante approved the hit because the younger Masselli knew about Genovese rackets and had become an informer. Although the Bronx DA's office alleged that the federal government covered up contacts between Donovan and organized crime, Cafaro insisted that Nat Masselli's murder was unrelated to Donovan and Special Prosecutor Silverman's inquiry. Contradicting the DA, Cafaro said the Genoveses were unaware of the young man's involvement with the special prosecutor and Chin wanted him killed simply because he was believed to be a rat.

Cafaro also tipped the FBI on how Chin had paid $175,000 to trim two years from the eight-year federal sentence of his brother Mario for loan-sharking and extortion. According to Cafaro, in 1984, Roy Cohn, the slick lawyer who represented numerous mobsters, told him that a three-year sentence reduction would cost $250,000, and two years, $175,000. Chin opted for two years, and Cafaro said he delivered the prescribed amount in cash to Cohn after the lawyer obtained the shorter term. How did Cohn manipulate the reduction? Fish assumed the money was "used for a 'reach' or a 'payoff,'" but he did not know to whom. On another occasion, Cafaro claimed that he "laundered" a $200,000 illegal bookmaking debt through Cohn's office. The debtor, a businessman, wrote a $200,000 check to Cohn's firm as a supposed legal fee, and Cohn passed along most of the money in cash to Cafaro and to Tony Salerno, after deducting a service fee. None of Cafaro's allegations against Cohn resulted in a criminal complaint against the attorney, who died in 1986, soon after Cafaro switched sides.

From the start of his regime, Gigante worried that his underlings' loose talk could be perilous and used against him. No bug, no telephone tap, and no wired informer would ever ensnare Chin by obtaining an incriminating remark from his own lips. To protect himself from being implicated through circumstantial evidence in a RICO or other criminal indictment, Gigante circulated a warning to the Genovese and the other borgatas that he would severely punish anyone who spoke his family name or his nickname in a direct or a telephone conversation. Top lieutenants Benny Eggs Mangano, Baldy Dom Canterino, and Quiet Dom Cirillo relayed the decree to all families: never mention Gigante's name in a conversation. Genovese soldiers could refer to him by pointing to or touching their chins, or by shaping a C with thumb and forefinger and saying, "That guy," "My aunt," or "Aunt Julia."

During a meeting over joint construction rackets, the Gambino's Sammy the Bull Gravano was admonished by his Genovese counterpart, Vincent DiNapoli, for using Gigante's name. Teasing DiNapoli, Gravano deliberately asked about Chin's views on an interfamily issue. "Sammy," DiNapoli said gravely, "you get caught on tape, or you get this guy in trouble, you're going to get hurt."

Anthony Tortorello, a Lucchese soldier, was overheard by a Genovese gangster in 1986, asking why Chin was upset by drug deals when he himself was profiting from trafficking by his men. A furious Gigante sent consigliere Louis Bobby Manna to the Lucchese hierarchs, demanding that Tortorello be killed. Gaspipe Casso, then the Lucchese underboss, agreed that Tortorello had sinned but considered him too valuable to be whacked. Appeasing Gigante, the Lucchese leaders pledged that Tortorello would be severely beaten for insulting Chin. A phony mauling was staged to satisfy Gigante that the violator of his edict had been punished.

A Colombo mobster, Joseph "Joe Black" Gorgone, was picked up on an FBI bug saying that Gigante was merely acting and was not crazy. A report reached Gigante that the bureau had taped Gorgone's remark. "I'll kill him if that statement ever makes it into a courtroom," Gigante threatened in a message to the Colombo consigliere, Carmine Sessa.

One medical condition Gigante was not faking was his coronary ailment. In 1988, he underwent an aortic valve replacement, and a pacemaker was inserted to regulate his heartbeat. Convalescing that autumn, he agreed to John Gotti's bid for a truncated Commission meeting. Gotti's people arranged the first face-to-face conclave between the two bosses in the apartment of Gambino capo Frankie D'Apolito's brother. The Gambinos figured that it would be a safe site for Gotti, in case the meeting was a setup by Gigante to ambush him. They were unaware that it was even safer for Chin; his relatives had an apartment in the Greenwich Village complex.

After Gotti arrived with the Lucchese representatives Vic Amuso and Gaspipe Casso, Gigante showed up, accompanied by his underboss, Benny Eggs Mangano. Wearing pajamas and a robe, he explained that he was recovering from his recent surgery in an apartment used by his mother and other relatives. To attend the meeting, all he had to do was step into the elevator.

The main topic was approval of seats on the Commission for the Colombo and Bonanno borgatas. Gigante had no objection to the reappearance of the strife-torn Colombos, but he rejected Gotti's proposal to allow the Bonannos to return from exile. Recognizing the Bonannos' Joe Massino as acting boss with full voting rights would allow Gotti to dominate the Mob's supreme council, with a sure three votes out of five; Massino was Gotti's ally and would be beholden to him in the event of any disagreements between the Genovese and Gambino families. More than likely, the Colombo delegate, Vic Orena, would also line up with the Gambinos. Chin could count on support from the Lucchese combination of boss Vic Amuso and underboss Gaspipe Casso, who disliked Gotti and had joined in Gigante's plot to kill him. Chin was taking no chances on relinquishing control of the Commission by giving Gotti two satellite votes.

Another item was replenishing the families' ranks. Chin complained that the Luccheses had recently made eleven men without vetting them with him. Moreover, he objected to one of the candidates, mocking him as "a good Samaritan" because he had helped the police arrest a mugger. "He's no longer a problem," Gaspipe chimed in. "We killed him."

Both the Gambino and Genovese families, the nation's two largest Mafia borgatas, were down from their maximum strength of roughly four hundred soldiers each. Seizing on the reduced-ranks situation, Gotti urged Gigante to reinforce his family with forty additional men. Sammy the Bull Gravano knew that Gotti was scheming to undercut Gigante and to court loyalty from the new Genovese cadre by informing them that he was responsible for their admission into Cosa Nostra.

Chin saw through Gotti's machinations and, according to Sammy, curtly rejected the idea. "Why would I have to make men for you to respect them? If they were with me, you would respect them, no? I appreciate your concern but I'll make those moves when I'm ready."

Gravano was impressed by a remark Chin made about surviving as a Cosa Nostra don. Mentioning that he had enough wealth from his own schemes, Gigante said he was not pressing his crews for huge cuts from their rackets. Sammy the Bull thought that was a smart strategy for insuring loyalty in a family that had plenty to go around—more than $100 million a year.

Before the meeting broke up, Gigante discussed his heart surgery and opened his pajama top to show a huge scar on his chest. As they left the apartment, Gotti remarked to Gravano how "clever" and security-conscious Gigante had been to arrange their first meeting in a building in which he was living. "He's smart as a fox, this guy," Gotti said grudgingly.

It was the only sit-down ever held between Gigante and Gotti. One thorny topic left off the agenda was the conviction of several New Jersey Genovese members, accused in a federal indictment of conspiring to kill Gotti and his brother Gene.

Although no criminal accusations were lodged against Gigante, the New Jersey charges generated a buzz inside the Mob that Chin had issued a contract on Gotti. Before their Commission session, Gigante had tried to smooth over the issue. Through a conciliatory message to Gotti, Chin assured him that the New Jersey gangsters, including his consigliere Bobby Manna, were "renegades" who had conspired without his knowledge.

Gigante's explanation was a patent lie and Gotti was not deceived. But Gotti was wary about taking on Gigante and his army. Listening to Gotti's bugged conversations, Bruce Mouw, the head of the Gambino Squad, sensed Gotti's concern about crossing swords with Chin. "We heard John trash everybody. He called the Colombos 'Cambodians.' Vic Amuso and Gaspipe were ridiculed as 'the Circus.' He even mocked his good friend Massino. But he never trashed Chin, never once. He always spoke of him with deep respect."

Gotti failed to grasp the extent of Gigante's hatred. He never realized that Chin schemed with two disloyal Gambino capos, Jimmy Brown Failla and Danny Marino, to whack him and thereby himself become the kingmaker in the Gambino family. To avenge the assassination of his ally Paul Castellano, Gigante told confidants, "somebody has to pay." Although he failed to eliminate Gotti, Chin exacted a heavy toll from his devoted entourage, killing three of them. He authorized contracts on Frank DeCicco, Gotti's first underboss; Eddie Lino, a Gambino capo, who was on the hit team that clipped Castellano outside Sparks Steak House; and Bartolomeo "Bobby" Borrelli, a Gotti chauffeur and bodyguard. The Lucchese's Gaspipe Casso, in an interview, claimed that he helped arrange the three "hits".

When Chin learned that the FBI had his town house under surveillance, and the Commission case revealed the effectiveness of the government's electronic eavesdropping, his obsession with insulating himself was further heightened. Simultaneously, he tried to beef up his medical record of incompetency. Under the care of his personal psychiatrist for treatment of "dementia rooted in organic brain damage," Gigante's stays in a mental health clinic at a Westchester County hospital became more frequent. Over two decades he checked into his favorite clinic twenty-eight times, for "tune-ups." Of course, he knew it would embarrass the FBI to drag him inhumanely out of a psychiatric ward to stand trial.

Within the Genovese family Gigante cultivated his penchant for constant vigilance and covertness. He instituted longer testing periods or apprenticeships before inducting members, and he instructed capos and soldiers to conceal as long as possible the identities of prospective soldiers from other families. The secrecy, he thought, would prevent investigators learning from informers about new and possibly vulnerable Genovese inductees. Concealing rookie soldiers from the other borgatas would also camouflage the actual Genovese strength in the event of a violent showdown. In another directive, capos were urged to keep a low profile, to avoid being seen in public with him, and to forward all messages through two trusted lieutenants, Quiet Dom Cirillo and Benny Eggs Mangano.

The main communications link to and from capos and soldiers in the field to the Genovese godfather was Quiet Dom, dubbed in the family *"il Messaggero,"* the messenger. Cirillo was a big moneymaker for Gigante, handling Chin's loan-sharking bank. Quiet Dom went back a long way with Gigante, to a time when they both had been club boxers in the late 1940s. Cirillo's prizefighting career ended in quick failure. A welterweight, he lost three bouts by knockouts and managed one draw before retiring ingloriously at age twenty from the ring. Investigators looking to connect Cirillo to Gigante found him to be a skilled dodger. Leaving his home in the Bronx, he drove onto a highway and at high speed abruptly pulled over to the side of the road while his tails zoomed past his car. In Manhattan Quiet Dom had innumerable escape routes. "He would go into an office building or a restaurant that had more than one exit and often lose us by darting out of one of them," John Pritchard, the FBI supervisor, said.

Before Chin's ascension, the New Jersey crews strutted around almost brazenly, greeting each other outside hangouts with traditional Mafia embraces and kisses. Robert Buccino, the New Jersey's Organized Crime Division official, soon noticed the mounting caution of the Genoveses under Chin's rigid command. Soldiers stopped greeting each other effusively in public, became more watchful, and took exceptional measures to deter surveillance. Sometimes, the gang's best efforts failed, as when the FBI uncovered meetings of a New Jersey crew in a Hoboken restaurant's toilet and bugged it. One soldier, Tino "the Blade" Fiumara, an important Genovese racketeer on the New Jersey waterfront, conceived a disappearing act that worked for a while. Buccino's investigators eventually deduced Fiumara's trick: he was traveling to meetings curled up on a car floor or in the trunk to avoid being tracked.

A recognized connoisseur of Mafia talent, Philadelphia underboss Phil Leonetti gave Gigante's administration the highest compliment. Known as "Crazy Phil," for his murderous rampages, Leonetti, the nephew and protégé of the imprisoned Philadelphia boss Nicodemo Scarfo, defected and became a government witness in 1989, after indictments for racketeering and murder. Debriefed by agents, he described Chin Gigante's administration "as the most sophisticated, cautious, secretive, and powerful Cosa Nostra family in the United States."

49

Chin's Millions

Providing a crash course in Mafia Economics 101, Fish Cafaro explained how the Genoveses prospered to a Senate committee in 1988. "My family made a lot of money from gambling and the numbers rackets. We got our money from gambling, but our real power, our real strength, came from the unions. With the unions behind us, we could shut down the city, or the country for that matter, if we needed to, to get our way."

Cafaro was right on the mark. The government's anti-Mafia crackdown in the mid-1980s had crushed Fat Tony Salerno and Matty the Horse Ianniello, and dismantled several of their construction and extortion rackets. Nevertheless, the Genovese family's Mob industries were practically unimpeded. Rivers of cash still cascaded from gambling and loan-sharking, and the family's most prized gold mine—labor rackets—flourished.

Chin Gigante's brigades counted on unending payoffs and well-paid "no-show" jobs from their under-the-table arrangements with corrupt union mandarins. The borgata also got willing assistance from unscrupulous management associations in four sizable industries: the Fulton Fish Market, conventions and trade shows, garbage collection, and waterfront services.

In the darkness before dawn, tractor trailers rumbled over the cobblestones of Lower Manhattan, and workers grappled with ice-coated crates to keep fresh fish moving through the nation's largest wholesale seafood-distribution center, the Fulton Fish Market. Operating since 1833, the market inspired colorful tales of gritty merchants and laborers toiling from midnight to dawn on the banks of the East River to supply the New York area with every species of salt- and fresh-water produce.

By the 1930s, the Mafia was entrenched in the market, largely due to the ruthlessness of Joseph "Socks" Lanza, a hands-on capo. Lanza organized a seafood workers' local and acquired his nickname for punching out merchants and suppliers who refused to pay him for permission to do business in the market. Largely through control of the union that Lanza had formed, fifty years later the Genovese family was still the dominant, invisible force in a $1 billion-a-year enterprise.

To survive, more than one hundred trucking companies and fifty wholesalers depended on the rapid unloading of quickly perishable seafood brought into New York five days a week. The Mob's iron grip derived from this movement of food in and out of the market. Six companies, called "unloaders," were the only ones authorized by the Genovese family to unpack refrigerated trucks arriving with their valuable catches from East Coast ports and fish hatcheries. The self-appointed, Mob-approved unloading companies operated without required municipal licenses in the market, on city-owned land. They granted themselves exclusive territorial rights to unload trucks, to set the order in which the vehicles were handled, and to dictate the prices for their services; supplies were not unloaded on a first-come, first-served basis. For prompt delivery to a wholesaler's stall, only a few feet away, the merchant or the trucking company had to bribe the unloaders; otherwise, the seafood was left to spoil on the pavement and become worthless.

A similar setup of unlicensed companies, known as "loaders" and endorsed by the Genovese borgata, handled all after-sale transfers by wholesalers to their customers. Only a handful of Mob-favored loading companies was allowed to transport the food on handcarts from wholesalers to the parked vans or trucks of customers, essentially hundreds of restaurateurs and suppliers to retail stores. No one who sold or bought fish or seafood had a choice in selecting an unloader or loader, dickering over the prices charged, or even choosing a parking space.

An intimidating frontier-style justice prevailed where the laws of the state could not reach. The Mafia's presence and its culture of suspicion intimidated honest merchants and workers, preventing them from cooperating with investigators or testifying. The rare rebel who objected to the established order would find his vehicle vandalized, his tires slashed, and himself threatened with being manhandled or worse. Since all vendors and customers were subject to the same conditions, the market functioned on the principle that the jacked-up costs were simply passed along to the consumers.

Over half a century, sporadic investigations would temporarily remove mafiosi, such as Socks Lanza and several of his successors, from the scene. The Genovese family simply brought in a replacement enforcer to continue its exploitation. City officials responsible for licensing merchants and monitoring business practices at the market privately admitted that the atmosphere was too dangerous and volatile for civil servants to supervise. Since few wholesale vendors and suppliers had the guts to complain publicly, the city government, in effect, decided to allow the Mafia to profit so long as a plentiful amount of seafood was available in restaurants and stores.

Chin Gigante appointed two capos, Rosario "Ross" Gangi Sr. and Alphonse Malangone, to control the market and funnel profits to the regime. Both captains, along with Carmine Romano, a former Genovese controller, had sons who owned wholesale seafood companies in the market. Gangi was listed as an employee of a fish company, and Malangone was often seen in the area, allowing his ominous countenance to be known. His nickname, "Allie Shades," came from dark lenses he wore because of an eye ailment.

The unloading and loading system alone netted $2 million to $3 million a year in "fees," more properly called shake-downs, for the Genovese. Each year about 150 million pounds of fish and seafood were sold, totaling $800 million to $1 billion in sales, salaries, and ancillary services, with a goodly portion siphoned off by mobsters as phantom partners in companies doing business there, or for "protection" from union problems. The market was a prime setting for other fundamental Cosa Nostra crimes: thefts of seafood from the arriving trucks, and fleecing the one thousand market employees through gambling and loan-sharking.

"The market is the most intractable organized-crime problem in the Northeast," Michael Cherkasky, a prosecutor and official in the Manhattan DA's office, observed in the early 1990s. "You remove one guy and a whole set of two-bit hoods are lined up to replace him."

In 1986 the glittering, glass-sheathed Jacob K. Javits Convention Center, stretching over five blocks, was completed by the state on Manhattan's West Side. Named after a U.S. senator, and built at a cost of $486 million, the modernistic, atrium-styled showplace was conceived to bolster the city's economy. Projected to host eighty topflight industrial trade shows and conventions annually, the facility was seen as a surefire way of creating jobs, aiding the hotel, restaurant, and transportation industries, and generating billions of dollars in sales and hotel-guest taxes for the city and the state.

Unforeseen by its planners were the opportunities the site offered to the Genovese family. From opening day, Chin Gigante's minions turned the soaring 185-foot-high "Crystal Palace" into a hiring hall for mafiosi and ex-convicts, and a choice arena for pillaging.

The abusive system rested on the borgata's control of the carpenters' union, which had a collective-bargaining agreement with the center that gave it the sole right to select one hundred carpenters to work there. These jobs, assembling and disassembling exhibits, were plums, paying the highest union wages, and considered recession-proof. More important, the Genovese family, through its sway over the union's top command, designated the chief shop steward at the center—the official who assigned carpenters to work there.

A steward's primary watchdog function is to guarantee that collective-bargaining agreements are fulfilled by employers. Under the Genovese plan, the steward at the center became an essential gear in bullying companies that built and assembled the displays and exhibits used at trade shows and conventions. It was the tried-and-true Mob tactic of threatening slowdowns or work stoppages unless payoffs were made through the steward. The official also had the muscle to overlook union contract violations in exchange for kickbacks. The principal favors given to display-construction companies in return for bribes were: "double breasting," permitting low-paid, nonunion workers on a job, and "lumping," paying wages below the hourly rate. These illegal practices enabled companies to avoid fringe-benefit contributions to the union's pension and welfare funds and added to company profits.

About 50 percent of the take arranged through the stewards was channeled to the Genovese administration. Understandably, the entire "pool list" of carpenters handpicked by the stewards eagerly complied with the corrupt deals.

Most were made men or associates in the borgata and many had criminal records. They somehow were given preference to Javits jobs over 25,000 other union carpenters.

Two of the first shop stewards had little experience as carpenters but nevertheless were approved by the union's highest officials for the post—with a starting salary of $100,000 a year. One was Ralph Coppola, a soldier in the Genovese family and a convicted arsonist. He was succeeded by Anthony Fiorino, brother-in-law of Liborio "Barney" Bellomo, a Genovese capo who replaced Fat Tony Salerno as the head of the family's East Harlem and Bronx crews. Fiorino had been a jeweler before being appointed a carpenters' shop steward. His main claim to fame was having won several professional paddleball tournaments.

As word of the extortion and union problems created by the Genovese gangsters filtered out, trade show and convention business at the Javits Center shriveled during its early years. The Javits management originally had anticipated attracting 5 to 10 percent of the $73 billion spent annually in the nation on major conventions and trade expositions. Instead, it was drawing 2 percent and bleeding red ink, losing about $1 million a year in operational costs.

Besides high-paying and no-show jobs and union shake-downs, there were other money-making opportunities at the center for the Genovese wiseguys. From 1986 to 1991, the value of stolen merchandise and equipment lifted from trade shows and conventions ranged between $500,000 and $1 million annually. Almost any movable item was apt to be stolen. At a trade show for vision products, a sealed package containing 525 artificial eyes was snatched; it was a theft that probably proved difficult to fence. But overall, the Jacob K. Javits Convention Center was a pleasant crime and corruption playground for Chin Gigante's borgata.

Garbage is always a messy business, and getting rid of it became too expensive for the City of New York. In 1957, to sharply cut costs, the city undertook a radical step: it stopped carting garbage from office buildings, factories, restaurants, hospitals, and all nonresidential enterprises, from the largest elegant department stores to the smallest mom-and-pop candy store. The goal was to reduce the Sanitation Department's budget by limiting its task to collecting residential trash. All commercial pickups were privatized, handled by companies licensed and regulated by the city. The city naively believed private carters would do the job more efficiently and cheaper than the Sanitation Department.

Within a decade, the Genovese and Gambino families were the ones cleaning up from the changeover. Just as the Luccheses and Gambinos manipulated a trade association and the teamsters' union to organize a refuse collection cartel on Long Island, the Genoveses teamed up with the Gambinos to duplicate that rich racket in the city's five boroughs. Domination of Teamsters' Local 813 and of management groups enabled the families to dictate terms throughout the garbage-hauling industry. Mobsters decided which customers, called "stops," companies could retain or seek, and the prices they charged.

Conditions for doing business in the city were arranged by two citywide trade and borough associations, run by the Genovese and Gambino families: the Waste Paper Association and the Association of Trade Waste Removers of Greater New York. Any maverick carter who defied the associations' rulings on carving up routes, selling "stops" to each other, and setting prices would be confronted by teamsters' union headaches and threats of violence and vandalism to equipment. An illegal but ironclad monopolistic regulation by the associations forbade companies from competing with other members for the same customer. All bids and prices for highly profitable "stops" were rigged.

About three hundred companies operated in the city in the 1980s and '90s, removing refuse from 250,000 businesses that paid out over $1 billion in fees annually. Businesses generally had no possibility of lowering costs, and only one choice of a carter—the company that the associations and removers determined was entitled to the "stop." The corrupt practices created an inefficient crazy-quilt pattern in which, in one instance, a dozen haulers operated on the same block in Midtown Manhattan.

Although New York was the richest prize in the country for carters, powerful national companies stayed away rather than wrestle with the Mafia. Soon after Browning-Ferris Industries, then the nation's second-largest waste-removal enterprise, dared to begin competing in 1992 for business in the city, it got a crude signal. The company's New York sales manager awoke one morning to find a dog's head on his lawn. Stuffed in the animal's mouth was a note: "Welcome to New York."

"We knew that was a traditional warning from the Mob not to get involved in New York," a top Browning-Ferris official, Philip Angell, remarked, vowing that the company would not surrender to Cosa Nostra threats.

Despite press accounts and allegations by investigators that the carting system was violent and sleazy, the city government was unable to overcome the lobbying and political pressure exerted by the carters' trade associations against imposing meaningful reform.

Genovese appointees dominated the leadership of the Waste Paper Association, and its offices on Canal Street in downtown Manhattan were a base for Vincent Esposito, Chin's son by Olympia Esposito, and Vito Palmieri, one of his father's chauffeurs and bodyguards. The son also was employed by Angelo Ponte, the owner of a large carting company and a popular downtown restaurant, Ponte's, who was an important member of the carters' associations.

The versatile Ally Shades Malangone, the feared Genovese capo from the Fulton Fish Market, was also responsible for managing the family's carting interests. He exercised much of his control through his role as "administrator" of the Kings County Trade Waste Association.

Malangone's counterpart in the Gambino family was capo Jimmy Brown Failla, a Mafia elder statesman, who, since the late 1950s, was the ranking executive of the Trade Waste Removers association. Every Tuesday, with unfailing punctuality, Failla arrived at noon at the association's office carrying a supply of succulent Italian pastry. The Tuesday cannoli klatches were the sitdown days reserved for carters who had problems or sought Failla's permission to clinch deals and rig bids for "stops."

Studies by the Rand Corporation, a private research group, and civic organizations in the late 1980s indicated that the two crime families shared a considerable fortune from overcharges. The analyses found that private garbage removal charges in New York were the highest in the country, twice as much as in Chicago, Boston, and Los Angeles. A typical bill for a grocery or a delicatessen ran to $15,000 a year; for a fast-food restaurant, $36,000; and for a medium-sized restaurant, $50,000. Macy's at Herald Square paid about $500,000, a skyscraper office building, $1 million, and Con Edison, the utility company, $2 million.

With average costs inflated by an estimated 40 percent, the carters, in the 1990s, collected fees every year in the range of $1.5 billion. When investigative auditors finally got a look at the cartel's books, they found that the Genovese and Gambino families and their main garbage-collector partners raked in a minimum of $600,000 every year in overcharges. And by capitalizing on lax city inspections, Mob-affiliated companies cheated customers of hundreds of thousands of dollars annually by falsifying the weight of rubbish removed from many buildings and stores.

Long before he portrayed the benevolent boss Don Corleone in *The Godfather*, Marlon Brando starred in a different Hollywood story of the Mob. In the 1954 movie *On the Waterfront*, Brando was Terry Malloy, a gruff longshoreman combating union racketeers. The film's graphic portrayal of mobster treachery, outrageous working conditions, and corruption on the Hoboken piers in New York harbor was part of a groundswell to counteract Mafia influence in the ILA, the International Longshoremen's Association. A cleanup campaign in the 1950s resulted in the establishment of a bistate Waterfront Commission empowered to regulate and license employees and companies and ban ex-cons with serious records from working on the New York–New Jersey piers.

The Waterfront Commission ended the "shape-up," a system in which employees did not have steady jobs but had to show up every day and usually fork over part of their wages to an ILA dock boss in order to be hired. Since the 1930s, the Genovese and Gambino borgatas had divided the waterfront loot, which was derived mainly from employee payoffs and from defrauding union welfare and benefit funds. The Gambinos controlled the ILA locals and chicaneries in Brooklyn and Staten Island, and the Genovese domain was the Manhattan and New Jersey piers.

The abolition of the shape-up forced the two families to switch tactics from primarily victimizing workers to taxing stevedoring and shipping businesses in the vast harbor. Containerization revolutionized shipping in the 1960s and made the freight companies easier prey for the Cosa Nostra. Instead of gangs of up to thirty longshoremen unloading "break-bulk" cargo piece by piece, goods stored in huge containers were lifted on and off vessels by cranes. The modernized system concentrated the shipping industry primarily in the ports of Newark and neighboring Elizabeth in New Jersey—an area under the jurisdiction of a Genovese colony, ILA Local 1804-1.

The new cargo-handling system created a demand for dockside companies needed to maintain and repair containers. Soon enough, the Genovese and Gambino borgatas controlled a trade organization, the Metropolitan Marine Maintenance Contractors Association (METRO), representing the two dozen firms that negotiated industry-wide with the ILA. Top administrative posts in the ILA local and in METRO were filled by Genovese lackeys. With the union and METRO in its pocket, the family had the New Jersey side of the harbor in bondage. The repair firms were extorted in exchange for sweetheart union contracts and to prevent featherbedding, the compulsory hiring of unneeded employees. On the union end, Mob-allied consultants were awarded hefty contracts for advice on investments of hundreds of millions of dollars in members' benefit funds. Kickbacks for these contracts were laundered for the private benefit of Genovese big shots.

An FBI probe in the late 1970s resulted in 117 convictions of ILA officials, businessmen, and several Genovese and Gambino soldiers for extortion and corruption in East Coast harbors. The intermittent pressure, however, failed to dislodge the Genovese hold on Local 1804-1 and on METRO at Port Newark and Elizabeth. Evaluating the Genovese successes in the harbor, Robert Buccino, the deputy chief of the New Jersey attorney general's organized crime division, considered Gigante's gang a frustrating opponent. "We've attempted to infiltrate them over the years and always struck out," Buccino commented in 1989, conceding that the Genoveses were the most powerful crime family in the state.

At their 1988 Commission meeting, Chin Gigante disparaged John Gotti's delight in his son's initiation into a Cosa Nostra life. While Chin's oldest son, Andrew Gigante, was not a made man, Chin had no objection to his enjoying the fruits of the family's harbor ventures. A prime example of "no show" largesse, Andrew landed executive jobs with two METRO companies, paying him $340,000 a year in combined salaries, and he was a stockholder in another container-repair company in New Jersey and a shipping company in Miami. Inside the Genovese family, savvy capos and soldiers were aware that Chin was opposed to his sons formally embracing a life in Cosa Nostra, but they recognized another aspect of the father-son relationship: Andrew was Chin's surrogate, guarding the regime's valuable interests in Port Newark and Elizabeth.

As the 1980s ended, the FBI and the Justice Department's best-informed Mafia experts had to admit they had been duped by Gigante's erratic behavior into designating the wrong man as the Genovese boss. "The Genovese were different from other families, who had clear lines of reporting," FBI squad supervisor Donald Richards discovered, adding that Chin's maneuvers to keep the FBI off balance had worked. "Based on surveillance and informers we thought Salerno was the boss. It turned out that Chin was more powerful than we originally suspected."

Michael Chertoff, the lead prosecutor who obtained the Commission case convictions which listed Fat Tony as a godfather, cited trial evidence that Salerno went to Commission meetings and "was treated and respected like a boss." Perhaps, Chertoff conceded, Gigante and Salerno should have been viewed as coequals with "Salerno, the chairman of the board, and Chin, the CEO."

The FBI's organized-crime supervisor in New York, Jim Kossler, had no regrets about the fairness of Salerno's conviction and branding him the family's top chief. "Even if he was a front, to all intents and purposes under the law he was the boss, making decisions, settling disputes, going to all the Commission meetings. You can't take away the fact that Fat Tony was acting as boss of the family."

Fish Cafaro's defection in 1986 and later testimony cleared the smoke screen covering the family's hierarchy and finally exposed Gigante's omnipotent position. After flipping, Cafaro wore a wire for a year, but he was unable to get close to Chin, let alone talk with him. Cafaro's undercover work produced one mid-level narcotics-trafficking case for prosecutors. Overall, he did not severely damage the family or obtain what the FBI wanted most of all: strong evidence to implicate Gigante in a crime. Unlike other borgata leaders, the resourceful Chin Gigante could not be trapped through bugs or telephone taps. Outside his select inner circle, no one was allowed to venture near him to gain his ear or his trust. And, he seemed to possess a dedicated following of soldiers and associates who would never betray him.

John Pritchard, the FBI's Genovese Squad supervisor, who went on to hold high city and state law-enforcement posts, tipped his hat to Gigante's evasive abilities. "Without a doubt, he was the smartest, most scheming Mafia figure to come down the pike in my time. There seemed to be no way to get him."

50

"I Know Where Bodies Are Buried"

Lying comfortably in bed with his girlfriend snuggled beside him, Bobby Farenga felt secure. He had a $20,000 stash from the sale a few days earlier of half a "K" of coke and good prospects for future drug scores as a middleman who was being supplied by a reliable importer. Dozing off, he heard a rustling at the front door of his Brooklyn apartment. "Open up—FBI—we have a warrant for your arrest, Bobby," a harsh voice commanded. Before he could get his brain clicking or a foot onto the floor, the door sprang open and a small army of men, guns drawn, invaded his bedroom. Bobby—Barclay was his given name, but it was too pretentious-sounding in his line of work and he never used it—had been busted for the half-kilo sale. It was an FBI sting and he had fallen for it, selling the cocaine to an undercover agent posing as a buyer.

The raid that November night in 1987 was routine, one of scores made by an FBI–NYPD narcotics task force trying to contain the irreversible torrent of drugs into the city. All the raiders knew about Bobby Farenga was that he was a low-level scrounger in the narcotics universe, with no tight connection to major drug dealers or to organized crime. But his arrest was about to prove the validity of the adage voiced by the old Cosa Nostra prophets about the pitfalls of narcotics trafficking: dealers, faced with long prison sentences, will squeal and endanger everyone, including the bosses.

Bobby Farenga had never even seen Vincent Chin Gigante, the Mafia enigma who had stymied the FBI. Yet his two-bit arrest would steer the FBI onto a serpentine road leading to the Genovese godfather.

The squad of eight agents and detectives that burst into Farenga's nondescript bachelor apartment in Bay Ridge was spearheaded by Lewis Schiliro, the FBI supervisor of the joint narcotics task force. Schiliro went directly from law school into the bureau, and was admired by fellow agents as a "brainy guy," who could grapple with the complicated nuances of criminal statutes and also devise tactics for the risky duties of disarming felons without anyone getting hurt. Most agents dreaded assignments to New York, but Schiliro had grown up in Long Island, understood the area's ambiance, and had volunteered for New York's two most dangerous units: narcotics and organized crime. His ability to unravel complex cases was quickly recognized, and within three years he was supervising an investigative squad, an impressive achievement for a relative newcomer in the starchy bureaucracy. (Before retiring, Schiliro went on to head the bureau's New York office.)

Quiet and reserved on the outside, he chafed at paper-pushing administrative duties, and whenever possible, was out on the street, tailing suspects, questioning witnesses, and nabbing "mutts," bad guys. Enjoying the detective work and the action that came with hunting mobsters and narcotics traffickers, Schiliro described his job as "like having the best seat at a Broadway show." Slightly built, bespectacled, and sporting a droopy mustache, he hardly typified the canonized image of a hardened G-Man. But in the mid-1980s, he was the lead agent and supervisor of the squad that dismantled "the Pizza Connection," a network of Sicilian heroin traffickers. At the time, it was the biggest drug-smuggling operation in the country run by the Sicilian Mafia.

Apprehending Bobby Farenga was a small part of a larger investigation involving a web of some twenty heroin and cocaine dealers. A stoolie, acting as an intermediary, ratted out Farenga, and introduced him to an undercover agent who made the $20,000 buy when Bobby happily sold him a half-kilogram, more than a pound of coke. Gaining sufficient evidence on Farenga through a wiretap, Schiliro decided to arrest him, and obtained a search warrant for his apartment. In Lew Schiliro's book, Farenga was relatively insignificant—"not a big dealer compared to what else we were doing." But there was always the possibility that he might know something about higher participants in the drug game, and notes in his home might provide clues to other traffickers. The thirty-five-year-old Schiliro had refined narcotics raids to a fine art, eliminating the need for battering rams and ferocious gun battles. He preferred staging the arrests shortly after midnight, when the suspect was usually vulnerable, befogged by sleep, too confused to discard a drug cache, unlikely to resist, and prone to blurt out an incriminating remark.

At Farenga's apartment, the raiders applied their usual break-in technique, issuing a loud official warning to open up as they wedged a specially designed tool, the Rabbit, between the door jamb and the lock. In five seconds the lock snapped open. Inside, the perplexed, fortyish Bobby Farenga, paunch protruding from his underwear, was handcuffed while his Miranda rights were read to him. Searching the one-bedroom apartment, a police detective spotted a loaded .25 caliber pistol resting on the night table next to Bobby's female companion's side of the bed. Schiliro ordered the woman arrested for possession of a gun. As she was being cuffed, Farenga's mind began to clear, and he realized that the agent with the conspicuous mustache was in charge of the show. After hearing the charge against him, Farenga asked to speak alone with Schiliro in another room. His first question was how much time he was facing for a half-"K" conviction. "Twenty to twenty-five," Schiliro informed him. Federal drug laws were tough, even for first offenders.

"Let her go," Farenga whispered. "Cut her a break. I can give you some pretty good stuff. I know where bodies are buried." Using a profanity or two, Schiliro cautioned Farenga that his tips would have to be valuable and accurate if he wanted to help himself and his girlfriend. "Don't waste our time, otherwise you'll be in bigger trouble."

Farenga said he could lead the raiders that very night to a building in the Williamsburg section of Brooklyn where two bodies were hidden. Farenga then startled Schiliro with another assertion: they were Mob hits. "If you let her go, I'll take you there right now." Wasting no time, Schiliro hurried Farenga into his pants, and Bobby and his captors completed the ten-mile drive to the other end of the borough in about twenty minutes.

At a one-story brick warehouse in a grimy industrial section on Scott Avenue, Farenga stopped on a ramp in front of a loading dock. "Here's where you'll find Shorty, his feet are pointing to the warehouse," Farenga said confidently. Using two sledge hammers stored in their car trunks, agents and detectives made little headway hacking at the concrete surface. They needed help.

By 3:00 A.M., the police department's Emergency Services Unit, a division used for rescue and hostage missions, was at the scene with huge generator-powered lights, drilling with jackhammers and using a backhoe to carve out a section of the ramp. Two or three feet below the surface, the diggers unearthed bones—but they were from a chicken, not a human. The discovery cheered Farenga. "When we buried him, we had a takeout order of fried chicken and someone must have tossed bones into the grave," Bobby reassured Schiliro. "It's the right spot." The wiseguys obviously had worked up an appetite digging the grave.

Another foot of digging turned up the body of Tommy "Shorty" Spero, a Colombo mafioso, wrapped in a sleeping bag. Then a second corpse was found inside a plastic sheath. It was the remains of Richard Scarcella, a Genovese associate. The second corpse was precisely where Farenga said it would be: beneath a urinal in the warehouse. "Every time we took a piss, we said it was on Richie," Farenga blithely told Schiliro.

Despite the mess he was in, Farengo grew more relaxed, almost jovial as the night wore on and his information about concealed bodies was proven accurate. Summoned in the middle of the night by the local police precinct, the owner of the warehouse arrived with his lawyer, an attractive woman in a red evening dress and high-heeled shoes. Maneuvering around the ogling policemen, the lawyer stumbled and was righted by Farenga. "Thank you, you're a real gentlemen," she said. "No, lady, I'm a criminal," he cracked. The warehouse owner was not amused. He had recently acquired the property, and now FBI agents and detectives were questioning him about two corpses. The questions were routine—he had no reason to worry. Farenga had already filled in Schiliro about the building's former owner, who was deeply implicated in both homicides.

With two bodies exhumed, Schiliro eagerly listened to Farenga's sketchy accounts of the murders as they sat in a car outside the warehouse. Farenga had dredged up two previously unknown Mafia hits carried out by the same team of killers working for the Genovese family. He also opened the door to a separate, more intriguing revelation. He had peripheral knowledge of an ongoing multimillion-dollar fraud and bid-rigging racket conducted by four Cosa Nostra families. Through the arrest of a minor narcotics hustler, the FBI had bumped into two entwined cases. Even though Bobby Farenga's ties to the Genovese family were remote, Schiliro knew his prisoner was more valuable to an organized-crime squad than to his narcotics task force. The Lucchese Squad had picked up signals about a new multifamily construction conspiracy, and Schiliro alerted the agent working the case, Richard Rudolph. Immediately,

Rudolph and federal prosecutors in Brooklyn, Charles Rose and Gregory O'-Connell, began the process of debriefing Bobby Farenga. (Rose and O'Connor were the same prosecutors involved in Gaspipe Casso's case.)

The background of the two murders was easy to assemble. Starting in the mid-1970's, Farenga had teamed up on drug deals with Gerard "Gerry" Pappa, a soldier in the Genovese family, and Peter Savino, like him a Genovese associate. Over the years, he had helped Pappa whack five victims. Pappa did the dirty work, and Farenga and Savino went along as accomplices or to help dispose of the corpses. The two stiffs in the Williamsburg warehouse had been hidden there when Savino owned the building.

Richard Scarcella was slain in 1978. A masonry contractor and an associate in the Genovese family, Scarcella made a fatal error on a renovation job at the home of Frank "Funzi" Tieri, a family hierarch: he asked Tieri to pay for the construction materials. Tieri assigned Pappa to "work over" Scarcella for his disrespect in seeking money from a Mob aristocrat. It was not a hit contract. But Scarcella was a tough egg, and fearing that he might seek revenge for a rough beating, Pappa decided it would be expedient to shoot him.

The second body in the warehouse was Shorty Spero, a Colombo capo missing for seven years. Spero was shaking down and robbing drug dealers in Brooklyn, and Pappa, Farenga, and Savino divvied up a $500,000 fee from narcotics merchants for disposing of Spero and his brother. It was Savino's idea to deposit the bodies at the warehouse while construction work was going on; the newly poured concrete would create ideal concealed tombs.

Bobby Farenga's information was solid and the slayings could be wrapped up as "solved." But Gerry Pappa, the shooter and arch villain was dead, blown apart seven years earlier by shotgun blasts. More compelling for Richard Rudolph and prosecutors was the Mafia interfamily bid-rigging plot that Farenga had described. His statement added substance to rumors heard by agents that the Mob was milking millions of dollars from contracts with the NYC Housing Authority, the agency that built and maintained vast public-housing projects. Farenga knew the outline of the scheme but lacked specifics. He had invested in a window-manufacturing company organized by Pete Savino that was an essential part of the scam, but had always been on the fringe of the conspiracy, his knowledge derived mainly from what Savino told him. Several years earlier, Savino had dumped him as a crime and business partner. Bobby's expertise was drug trafficking, not windows, and his information about the Housing Authority swindle was imprecise and dated. But he knew that Savino, with the muscle of the four families behind him, had dreamed up a surefire plan to rig bids for the installation of windows in Housing Authority projects. The key to unlocking what the prosecutors instantly code-named "the Windows case" was Pete Savino, an unknown Mob prodigy.

An untypical wannable without traces of wise-guy associations in his early history, Savino had conventional, prosperous, rock-solid middle-class parents. No Mafia relative influenced him with tales of the virtues of the Honorable Society. Growing up in Brooklyn's Bensonhurst section, he had been a good student, graduated from Catholic schools, and after a year of college went into the family business, working for his father's metal works factory. It was the mid-1960s, the Golden Age for the New York Mafia, and the bright twenty-year-old Savino saw that mobsters, through the takeover of one union, had their claws in several construction businesses. The union, Local 580 of the Architectural and Ornamental Iron Workers, which represented window installers for jobs at major residential and commercial buildings, was mobbed up, and its officials got systemic kickbacks for sweetheart contracts.

Over six-feet tall, with jet black hair, dark, handsome features, and an innate gift of charming everyone he met, Savino decided that the quickest route to big money was through corrupt Local 580 shop stewards and their Mob cronies.

After working for the union, Savino allied himself with neighborhood buddies from his teenage days, Bobby Farenga and Gerry Pappa, who had matured into eager borgata recruits. Pappa was in a Genovese crew run by Anthony "Dutchie" Tuzzo, and was clued in on hoodlum angles for making quick bucks. Pappa welcomed Savino as an underworld accomplice and taught him the basics of drug trafficking. They also devised a system of smuggling thousands of cases of cigarettes from southern states into the high-tax New York area. It brought them a profit of fifty cents for each carton. One transaction in New Jersey, however, flopped, and Savino was arrested in 1973 by the FBI on interstate smuggling and federal tax-evasion charges. An agent in the Newark office offered to spike the most serious accusations and get Savino a suspended sentence for a reduced charge—if he become an informer. It was a comfortable compromise for Savino. He avoided a conviction and for fourteen years was listed by the Newark FBI office as a "C.I.," confidential informant. However, he provided little information to the bureau about his pals or what he was really up to. "I never volunteered information," he later testified about that period. "I answered questions when they called but withheld important information."

There was plenty Savino could have told the FBI, had he wanted to. His Mafia business partnerships were making him rich. Then, too, there was the occasional murder. In addition to the two men interred in his Williamsburg factory and warehouse, he was an accomplice on four other hits with Gerry Pappa; a total of six, one more than Bobby Farenga had participated in. Through Pappa he met Gaspipe Casso and Vic Amuso of Lucchese family fame, and made hundreds of thousands of dollars by investing in their marijuana and Quaalude imports from Latin America.

Savino was also flush with money from his corrupt Local 580 contacts, which allowed him to operate window-manufacturing and installation companies under extremely favorable union terms. For selected bribes, the local gave him a competitive edge by allowing him to underpay and cheat his employees on welfare and medical benefits. Searching for larger and still easier payoffs, Savino spotted a windfall opportunity in the late 1970s from a new federally financed program. To conserve heating oil, the government's Department of Housing and Urban Development, HUD, began subsidizing the installation of double-glazed thermal windowpanes in public-housing units. New York's Housing Authority was in line to have 900,000 windows replaced, with the goal of saving $5 million a year in heating bills. It was a once-in-a-lifetime opportunity to steal a fortune, and Savino, with Pappa's assistance, convinced the Genovese regime that a cartel could reap enormous profits though rigged bids. It was almost a carbon copy of the Concrete Club, which the old Mafia Commission had successfully run for decades.

The window-installation program began in 1978. Savino organized two companies, Arista Windows and American Aluminum, to get his thick slice of the profits. Because the Luccheses controlled Local 580, the window workers' union, the family naturally had to be brought in. Since the Colombo and Gambino families had hidden ownership in several window manufacturers, they also were added. Thirteen Mob-connected companies, including Savino's, divided the work by determining among themselves who would submit the phony lowest "competitive" bid, and substantially inflate all contract prices. The mobsters doubled and tripled what should have been reasonable profits on honestly competitive work. Besides the money that rolled in to Mob-dominated companies through the exaggerated prices, non-Mafia firms were permitted to join the cartel and paid a tax of $2 for each window they installed, with the kickbacks parceled out to the four families. With the Housing Authority planning to replace nearly a million windows, the families could be assured of more than $1 million in payoffs from non-Mafia companies alone.

Contractors excluded from the cartel were prevented from competing through intimidation. Sonny Morrissey, the Local 580 steward and the Luccheses' strong-arm pawn, warned outside firms what to expect if they honestly obtained a Housing Authority job. Morrissey threatened them with work stoppages; every window they installed would be smashed; and their factories would be vandalized. His warnings and the power of his union were heeded throughout the industry.

Pete Savino was not made, but his relationship with the Genovese family seemed solid, especially after Gerry Pappa was inducted as a soldier in 1978, the year the cartel was created. Pappa, who had branched into loan-sharking, was a partner in Savino's two window companies and, more important, was his liaison with the Genovese administration. There was no hint of danger until July 1980, when Pappa was killed by a shotgun blast, an obvious Mob retaliatory hit for the slaying of the Colombo's Shorty Spero. After Spero disappeared and long before his body was found in the warehouse, the Colombos suspected Pappa had killed him because of disputes over money. Savino sweated out two months, worrying if, as Pappa's partner, he was next on a contract list. In September he got a call one afternoon to drop everything and report immediately to Ruggiero's Restaurant on Grand Street in Little Italy; someone in the Genovese family wanted to see him. It was the first time he had been summoned to a sit-down with unknown mobsters. One thought consumed him: he was being set up for a kill and it was futile to attempt to escape.

Ruggiero's was owned by a Genovese soldier, Joe Zito, who escorted Savino to a private room on the second floor. Seated around a table, with bodyguards nearby, were the Mafia moguls Fat Tony Salerno, Funzi Tieri, and Chin Gigante. Savino was unable to camouflage his fear; his nerves were on fire and he dabbed at slivers of perspiration creasing his face. This was it! He was sure the Genovese leaders were about to sentence him to an unpleasant death because he had dealt in drugs and had helped Gerry Pappa kill Shorty Spero.

"Calm down," Gigante spoke up. "You're not in any trouble. Just tell us the truth."

Gigante did most of the questioning. First off, he wanted to know if the acting capo of Pappa's crew had taken all of the dead man's assets, mainly his loan-sharking money. When Savino confirmed this, he was surprised by Chin's reaction. Spitting on the floor in disgust, Gigante asked rhetorically, "Are these the new rules? We take money from widows and orphans?"

Chin proceeded to tell him that Pappa, as he suspected, had been executed in retaliation for murdering Shorty Spero. Not only had he lacked permission for the hit, but he had whacked a capo—a protected mafioso—from another family. Savino did not volunteer that he had helped conceal Spero's body under a canopy of concrete and had profited from the drug dealers' reward for Shorty's murder.

In Savino's presence, the three leaders—he was unsure of their rankings—talked openly among themselves as to who would control him, now that Pappa was gone. "I'll take him," Gigante decided. Chin's first order to Savino was expensive: he had to shell out $1 million to the Lucchese family's Gaspipe Casso and Vic Amuso. At that time, the two future Lucchese despots were only soldiers and had given Pappa $500,000 as an "investment" to expand Savino's window companies. They intended to cash in on the Housing Authority racket and Savino's other quasi-legitimate window enterprises. But Savino felt Gaspipe and Vic lacked business sense and were too meddlesome as partners, and he and Pappa had dissolved the arrangement. Gaspipe had complained to Chin and was demanding $1 million, a $500,000 profit, from the Genovese clan because the up-front money had been given to Pappa, a soldier in that borgata. Under the Mafia code of honor, the Genoveses were responsible for Pappa's compact, even after his death. Chin told Savino to pay the $1 million on behalf of the family, and he pledged to cough up the money, even though Pappa had kept the $500,000 for himself. A lowly associate in the family, a slave to the hierarchy, Savino had no right to complain or protest its decisions.

Before dismissing Savino, Gigante instructed him to keep Benny Eggs Mangano apprised on all his window-contract arrangements and decisions with other families; Mangano would be Pete's main conduit to Chin on all Mob undertakings. Pete was obligated to report to Mangano three or four times a week at his club on Thompson Street in Greenwich Village. Chin also gave him permission to visit the Holy of Holies, his own hangout at the Triangle Civic Improvement Association.

The meeting at the restaurant had cost Savino $1 million, but he was relieved to walk out alive.

Chin and Mangano's clubs were opened to Savino for practical reasons. He was a big earner and, with Pappa gone, the Genoveses needed his expertise to continue the windows profiteering. At the outset, Benny Eggs gave Savino lessons in Genovese protocol. He was never to mention any of Gigante's names in conversations, and if he had to refer to him, Mangano cautioned Savino, "Point to your chin and say 'this guy.'" Another expression that could be used was "my aunt." Mangano and Baldy Dom Canterino stressed that whenever he was asked by curious outsiders about Gigante's mental condition, he should reply, "Vincent's crazy."

At the Triangle Club, Savino saw Gigante, sometimes dressed in pajamas and a robe, playing cards, and holding private, whispered conversations, often with Benny Eggs and Baldy Dom. He watched Gigante plod slowly along the streets, mumbling to himself, and once saw him pause on Sullivan Street to urinate on the sidewalk. But Savino understood that Gigante's behavior was "fake, a standing joke."

Gradually, Chin warmed up to Savino, but with his usual caution never talked about exact details of the Housing Authority windows racket. Savino found him to be coherent, even when he was wearing pajamas. One afternoon at the Triangle, Gigante took him into the toilet, turned on the water tap, and in a whisper asked if anyone in the family or union bosses was squeezing him for additional payoffs or badgering him for free window installations in their homes. When Savino assured him that no one was pressuring him, Gigante replied, "Okay, I just wanted to know if anybody was taking advantage of you." Motioning Savino to follow him outside the club, Gigante, with a wink, said, "You know you can tell your friends that I'm not right. I'm not okay." Savino nodded, trying not to laugh or appear embarrassed, realizing that Gigante was honoring him by taking him into his confidence about his erratic stunts.

Gigante showed his increasing regard for Savino by inviting him to meals in a private room at Ruggiero's Restaurant. On one occasion, Joe Zito, the restaurant proprietor, began disparaging Savino's appearance. "You dress too casually," Zito said. "I'm going to change the way you dress and make a real man out of you." Picking up an umbrella with a distinctive duck's head carved on the handle, Gigante hit Zito on the forehead, adding sternly, "He dresses okay for me."

Between 1980 and 1987, Gigante met numerous times with Savino, introducing him to his wife and his mistress. Chin objected to anyone else in the borgata getting free services from Savino, but he encouraged him to replace windows at the Gigante home in Old Tappan and in his mistress's East Side town house. After meeting several of Gigante's children, Savino asked Baldy Dom about the sons' occupations. "Vincent doesn't want to have his kids involved in the life," Canterino said, ending the discussion.

Savino was immersed in "the life," and it could be scary. Once at 3:00 A.M., he was awakened at home by a telephone call from Baldy Dom. "Get down here, right now," Canterino barked. "I'm not coming back," Savino thought. Unaware of what fatal mistake he had made, Savino left all his pocket cash and jewelry with his wife. To him it looked like he was being set up for a Mob "ride." No one would be seen leaving with him from his home, and he was to meet Canterino on a deserted Greenwich Village block before dawn; there would be no witnesses to his disappearance. On Sullivan Street, Canterino wordlessly escorted Savino to the rear of a barber shop near the Triangle Club. Gigante was waiting for him, holding a catalogue of men's clothing in his hand. Pointing to jogging suits, Chin asked Savino, "Can you get me one in red, blue, and green?"

Inwardly sighing with relief, Savino remembered having given a mail-order catalogue to Canterino, telling him that he would obtain whatever Chin wanted. "It's not for me. It's for my kids," Gigante said, handing the booklet to Savino. "You can go now." Pondering the events of the last few hours as he drove home, Savino fathomed that the late-night command appearance had been a test. Chin was gauging his unquestioning obedience and dependability at any hour, the hallmark of a made man.

51

Brought to Bay

Chin Gigante's first line of defense against the FBI was his insanity subterfuge. He also hit upon the queer notion that he could safely conduct his underworld affairs late at night. Pete Savino learned from Baldy Dom Canterino that their leader was unshakably convinced that FBI agents never worked after midnight. Gigante was certain that he would not be under the bureau's surveillance during predawn hours.

Savino grew accustomed to late-night summonses, usually to the Triangle Club. At one session, in another test of his reliability, Gigante asked if he could get "close"—a euphemism for a hit—to a man who had killed the son of a Genovese soldier. Savino was reluctant because the target was a neighborhood acquaintance, but it would have been foolhardy to disregard Chin's request. He suggested a plan for the murder. "Take him," Gigante directed. To Savino's relief, before he could carry out his assignment the intended victim was convicted of a crime and imprisoned.

Despite occasional tense moments, Pete Savino enjoyed his ties to Gigante and his assured profits from the Housing Authority fixed contracts. His cartel stratagem worked to perfection, enabling him to buy a maroon Rolls-Royce and a Jaguar, and to move from Bay Ridge in Brooklyn to a more luxurious house in Staten Island. His financial future was bright, and his new factory in

Brooklyn was humming to meet contracts obtained through his own business savvy and Mob affiliations. Easy money whetted his philandering eye and, although married three times, he had numerous paramours. His first two marriages, which produced five children, ended in divorce. At forty, Savino's once rugged physique became bloated and, rather than exercise and diet, when his weight reached almost 300 pounds he underwent liposuction surgery to trim down. His schooling (a year at a southern college) and early background set him apart from the mobsters he mixed with. They thought he was quirky; he read books and magazines. Even odder to them, he enjoyed collecting old Charlie Chan movies, the 1930s and '40s series about a brilliant Chinese detective.

By 1987, Savino had given up the dangerous business of merchandising narcotics. He far outclassed Bobby Farenga in underworld high finance and had severed all relationships with his unreliable ex-partner. But it was Farenga who led the FBI to his front door. Picked up for questioning but not arrested, Savino heard the grim tidings that Bobby had ratted on him. The government had unearthed two bodies buried in the Williamsburg warehouse when he owned the building, and Farenga had yoked him to five murders, dozens of drug transactions, and the huge Housing Authority windows scam.

Involving leaders in the Genovese, Gambino, Colombo and Lucchese families, the Windows investigation had all the earmarks of a career-making trial for ambitious prosecutors and agents. Charles Rose, Gregory O'Connell, and the lead agent in the developing case, Dick Rudolph, were at the starting gate for a multifamily Mafia trial. Centering on the new Mafia overlords, the investigation loomed as potentially just as devastating to the Cosa Nostra as the Commission trial had been.

Though only a Genovese associate, Savino was the brains and most likely would be the core witness against the Mafia at a trial. His role was important enough for him to be in direct contact with mafiosi in four families, and he knew the statistics on how much money was siphoned by each of the borgatas and by crooked union leaders. And there was yet one more riveting element to Savino's story. The mobster who had taken him under his wing, met with him frequently, and protected him for the last seven years, was supercautious Vincent Chin Gigante.

Only a little pressure from Rudolph and the prosecutors was needed for Savino to roll over, to confess all he knew about Gigante and other mafiosi. First, Rose met alone with Savino at a diner, and over coffee delivered an ultimatum: "You have twenty-four hours to agree to cooperate and help us or you're going to jail." The next night, Savino showed up for a follow-up session with Rose and agents in a motel room in Queens and heard the terms set by prosecutors and the FBI. Confessing to his own crimes was not enough to swing a soft sentence for him. The government could easily convict him for six murders and the multimillion-dollar swindle. To build a case against important mafiosi participating in the Windows scam, prosecutors needed more evidence than Savino's testimony. An admitted conspirator, profiteer, and murder accomplice, Savino's word alone would fall short of obtaining indictments, let alone guilty verdicts. Essential evidence could be obtained only if Savino worked undercover. Rudolph and the prosecutors wanted him to wear a wire and secretly record incriminating conversations about the ongoing bid-rigging with as many players as possible, especially Chin Gigante.

It was a risky proposition for Savino—sure death if wiseguys discovered the wire. The FBI could not protect him around the clock. Desperate for leniency, Pete Savino agreed to the terms. Otherwise, at forty-four, and looking ahead to a minimum of twenty years in prison, life seemed pointless to him.

News of Bobby Farenga's arrest and the uncovering of the warehouse bodies had filtered out to the Genovese hangouts. No formal charges against Savino were made public, and to deflect suspicions that he was in the clutches of the law, prosecutors and agents devised a disinformation tale. Rudolph informed Savino's lawyer that he wanted to speak with Pete about the two corpses in the warehouse. The attorney, according to Savino, cooperated with the Genovese family and would communicate information about the FBI's interest in Savino to the borgata's high command. Questioning Savino at the lawyer's office, Rudolph assured him that Pete was not a suspect in any crime. The agent's line was that the FBI was only interested in what Savino knew about the construction of the Williamsburg building and who had access to it. Rudolph's questions painted Savino as an innocent, victimized businessmen, and implied that the bureau had other suspects in mind for the murders. The ruse seemingly worked. The lawyer passed along the news to the Genovese rulers that Savino was in the clear and had not divulged any useful information.

The only snag in Rose and O'Connell's plan arose from the continual rivalries between the city's two federal Justice Department jurisdictions. A prosecutor in Rudolph Giuliani's Southern District learned of Farenga's arrest and began questioning him as a potential witness in an investigation of corrupt practices in the construction of a high school. Fearing that Giuliani's office might hijack the Windows case and get to Savino, the Eastern District's Andrew Maloney had another of what he termed sit-downs with Giuliani at FBI headquarters. "Rudy knew it was shaping up as a major organized-crime case and he wanted to grab it," O'Connell, who was at the meeting, asserted. "We told him that Farenga didn't want to work with the Southern District and Giuliani lost the argument."

Savino's agreement required him to plead guilty to participating in six murders and to RICO violations. He did so at a sealed hearing with the routine proviso that the maximum sentence of twenty years might be shortened, depending on his assistance in the investigation.

Savino's main handler was Dick Rudolph, a native New Yorker who grew up close to the Gambino family's Bergin Club in Queens, and was well acquainted with Mafia practices. A bored accountant, eager for a more adventurous life, he had joined the bureau a decade earlier, at twenty-six, and had spent most of his time in the Lucchese Squad. It was now Rudolph's job to advise and direct Savino on the day-to-day tactics of collecting evidence that would stand up in a courtroom. For almost two years, they talked daily about the progress Savino was making and the perils surrounding him, usually meeting at night in New York motels or out of town. "Regardless of the stress, Pete was a charmer and gregarious with a great sense of humor," Rudolph said. "Putting aside the murders and other crimes in his background, there was a flip side to him that made being with him enjoyable."

The undercover pursuit began in February 1988 with the wiring of Savino's Brooklyn office in Bay Ridge, where Mob conferences on window contracts were sometimes held. Savino's most hazardous task was wearing a concealed body mike at Mob clubs, in restaurants, in diners, and on walk-talks without arousing suspicion. To his amazement, he was never "tossed," patted down and searched, by a wiseguy. Chin Gigante was the ultimate objective, and FBI technicians devised miniature equipment that presumably would record Gigante's voice even if he whispered in Savino's ear. Savino never caught him on tape, but he recorded dozens of incriminating conversations with representatives of the four families that suggested Gigante's involvement.

On March 11, 1988, reviewing a contract with Mangano, Savino tried to interject Gigante's role in the conspiracy, saying, "Vincent had said when it comes time to . . ." Mangano cut him off. "Don't mention that guy." Trying again, Savino continued, "Okay. I won't mention him. All right, he had said to go out and bid the work." The only reply he got from Mangano was "Yeah."

During a walk-talk with Savino in front of the Empire State Building, Mangano reiterated that he must falsify records to cover up the frauds. "But make everything aboveboard, papers, everything. Everything legit. . . . Keep your nose straight because we're not looking to get caught in a trap here for no reason at all."

On another occasion, Savino explained the ABC's of the rigged-bid process to a newcomer, Vincent Ricciardo, a Colombo family enforcer who had obtained a piece of a windows company. "Let's say a bid came out tomorrow and we flipped a coin. Okay," Savino said. "This is 10,000 windows. All right, you won the toss. Now, you get that one, the next one I get. Whatever it is."

Ricciardo emphasized that the four families would prevent any maverick company from landing a contract; they would arrange for a Mob-controlled union to picket the building site. "We stop the job," he added. "It's that simple." Referring to a contractor who was balking at paying kickbacks of $2 for every window, Ricciardo had a solution. "I'm throwing him out that window. I'm telling you, he's getting it. He don't want to pay nobody. I'm telling you, Tuesday he's going out that window."

At a conference attended by made men from the four families, Sonny Morrissey, the Local 580 official who was bagman and enforcer for the Luccheses, angrily announced that a non-Mafia-controlled company in the cartel had won a contract without permission. After Morrissey threatened "to break every window on the project," the company withdrew its bid. As punishment for the owner, the families decided to tax him $14 a window on all future contracts.

At Ruggiero's Restaurant on June 5, 1989, Savino reported to Mangano that the Luccheses' Gaspipe Casso and the Gambinos' Peter Gotti wanted more loot from the contracts. Setting Savino straight, Mangano admonished him to remember that the Windows racket belonged primarily to the Genovese borgata. "It's all ours. Nobody's supposed to touch it," Mangano said firmly.

It was one of his last face-to-face meetings with Mangano and other mafiosi. For almost two years, Savino had been on thinner ice than he realized with Gambino and Lucchese leaders. After the warehouse bodies were found in November 1987, the Gambinos' Sammy the Bull Gravano told Mangano that the wisest course would be to kill Savino and not take a chance that he might betray them. "Sammy," Benny Eggs replied, "I don't like him myself but Chin loves him. We're not going to be able to do nothing."

The ever-suspicious Gaspipe Casso, alarmed by the warehouse discoveries, declared that Savino must be "a rat" and urged Gigante to whack him. "The robe said, 'No,'" Gaspipe confided to Al D'Arco, using his private, derogatory nickname for Gigante. (When news of the FBI's Windows case investigation surfaced in 1989, Casso had no qualms about killing a potential witness in his family, the associate Sonny Morrissey, although the union official had not turned and was himself under investigation.)

Paradoxically, the demands by the Gambino and Lucchese bigwigs for Savino's head might have protected him. Considering himself the supreme Mafia boss in the country, Gigante had no intention of heeding the advice of rivals, particularly the detested John Gotti, and Gaspipe Casso, a relative novice in high Mafia politics. It was Chin's judgment call; no one in his borgata had turned up a negative fact on Savino, and Pete had fulfilled every request asked of him. Greed might also have influenced Gigante. Early on, Savino had paid a $1 million Genovese family debt to the Luccheses, and he was a money-engine for the family. The Housing Authority rigged contracts totaled more than $151 million for the four families; although investigators were unable to put a precise pricetag on the fraud, prosecutor Gregory O'Connell reckoned that "multimillions" wound up in the pockets of Genovese gangsters.

Gigante's confidence in Savino finally wavered in the spring of 1989. Gaspipe Casso's law-enforcement moles reported that Savino was indeed spying for the government, and the Luccheses cut all contacts with him. Earlier, Benny Eggs Mangano became furious upon learning that Savino had failed to inform him about a meeting with Gambino and Colombo delegates. The discussion with other families sounded to Mangano like a double-cross, and Casso's warning rang more alarm bells for Benny Eggs.

Danger signals also were going off at the FBI. On the afternoon of June 21, 1989, Savino got an ominous telephone call in his office. The caller refused to identify himself, but Savino recognized the voice of a Brooklyn mobster, who said he had seen Savino with FBI agents and was spreading that news. Discussing the call that night with Dick Rudolph, Savino described it as a prank and wanted to continue the undercover project. The agent was more perturbed; Savino's cover might be blown. "He's a wild card," Rudolph said of the mysterious caller. "Even if he didn't see anything, he might go around telling everyone that you're cooperating." Savino had survived twenty months as an industrious informer, prosecutors had more than fifty hours of secretly taped conversations, and the evidence against high-echelon mafiosi from four families seemed strong. "We have a lot and we need you as a witness—alive," Rudolph declared.

That night, FBI agents drove Savino to his home in Staten Island, where he packed a suitcase, and then vanished into the Witness Protection Program. His third wife wanted to join him, but decided against it because she would have been unable to bring along her young son from another marriage without the father's permission.

Welcoming Pete Savino into his exclusive flock and later vouching for him after bodies were found in the Williamsburg factory had been Gigante's egregious blunder. Chin's trust in Savino had endangered himself and his closest lieutenants, and provoked a groundswell of enmity from other families now in deep trouble. Even more embarrassing, Savino had damaged Chin's reputation for infallibility. Chin put out a contract on Savino and uncharacteristically sought help from other borgatas. During a walk-talk in Little Italy with Al D'Arco of the Lucchese family, Jimmy Ida, the new Genovese consigliere, gave him a photograph of a bare-chested Savino, standing with another man. "Al, Vince needs a favor from you," Ida said. "We got reason to believe that Petey Savino and his partner are in Hawaii, and we understand that you got a guy in Hawaii. Vince would like to kill these guys."

Guarded twenty-four hours a day by U.S. marshals, Savino was never found by the Mob. Genovese wiseguys tried to intimidate him through a telephone threat to his wife, warning that she and her son were in danger if Savino testified. That day she found a Molotov cocktail gasoline bomb with an unlit fuse in the front seat of her car. Although she was not formally in the witness-protection system, the government began safeguarding her and her child.

Lead prosecutors Rose and O'Connell fine-tuned the evidence for eleven months, and in May 1990, based largely on Savino's grand jury testimony and his tapes, Chin Gigante and fourteen other mobsters and associates from four families were indicted on a RICO enterprise charge. They were accused of skimming "tens of millions" of dollars by controlling 75 percent of the window bids, $151 million from a total of $191 million in contracts awarded by the Housing Authority from 1978 to 1989. The thievery eclipsed by far that centerpiece of the Commission trial, the Concrete Club. Although multimillions apparently were ripped off by the Mafia from concrete contracts, prosecutors could substantiate only $1.2 million collected over four years in that caper.

Gigante was arrested in his pajamas at his mother's Sullivan Street apartment on the morning of May 30, the day the indictment was unsealed. Told to dress, he put on a belted black bathrobe, shoes, and a woolen cap. Before his hands were cuffed behind his back, he wordlessly handed a card containing the telephone number of his brother Father Louis Gigante to an agent. Fingerprinted and photographed at FBI headquarters in Lower Manhattan, Gigante was more talkative. Asked by an agent about his eldest brother, Pasquale, Gigante pulled out a mass card, indicating that Patsy was dead. "He's with God," Gigante said. Fingerprinting him, another agent made small talk, inquiring about his boxing days and how many bouts he had won. "I was a heavyweight, then I lost weight and became a light heavy. It was a long time ago, I don't remember."

At the arraignment, Chin was alongside his underboss Benny Eggs Mangano, and capo Baldy Dom Canterino. Others arrested that morning were the Colombo consigliere, Benedetto "Benny" Aloi; Gambino capo Peter Gotti, John's brother; and Lucchese capo Fat Pete Chiodo. Two major defendants, Gaspipe Casso and Vic Amuso, the Lucchese leaders, were missing, having gone on the lam after a corrupt investigator warned Casso of the imminent arrests. In court, seated in the jury box with the other defendants, Gigante appeared disoriented, mumbling that he wanted to know when the "wedding" would begin. "Where's the bride?" he asked several times.

Gigante's lawyer, Barry Slotnick, contending that Gigante was mentally ill and unable to assist in his defense, obtained Chin's release on a $1 million bond supplied by his relatives. The tabloid press had a field day with Gigante's arrest and deportment in court. Headlines proclaimed him "Oddfather" and the "Daffy Don." Submitting reports from psychiatrists that Gigante was deranged and maintaining that he was incoherent, defense lawyers won their first legal skirmish with the prosecution. Chin's case was severed from the trial of the other defendants until there was a ruling on his sanity and ability to assist in his defense.

With Savino's testimony and his damaging tapes as the principal evidence, most high-ranking mafiosi in the Windows case were convicted. The Genoveses' Benny Mangano and the Colombos' Benny Aloi were found guilty after a six-month trial in 1991. Baldy Dom Canterino died of natural causes before he could be tried. After being captured, Gaspipe Casso and Vic Amuso wound up with life sentences, imposed partly from the Windows indictment. The only big-time mobster acquitted was Peter Gotti, who was defended by his brother's lawyer, Bruce Cutler. Ripping into Savino's character, Cutler portrayed him as a serial murderer who had profited from a fraudulent scheme that he originated, and then tried to entrap others to save his own neck. "The corruption, the soiling, the contamination is over here," Cutler, in his usual fiery manner, exclaimed, slamming his fist on the prosecution table. There was no smoking-gun tape against Gotti; in fact, one recording indicated that he had lost money on an investment with a window company. "I've been in this already two years now," Gotti was heard griping. "I didn't make a quarter."

The Windows trial gave Chin's lawyers a vivid preview of the government's strengths and weaknesses in the bid-rigging case as they tried to prove he was mentally impaired. But delaying his trial inadvertently helped the prosecution to expand the charges against Gigante. As the complex legal battle over his competence dragged on, three important mobsters defected, each with new evidence against Chin. Sammy Gravano and Al D'Arco were ready to testify that Gigante was a godfather and to describe his relationship as a boss with the Gambino and Lucchese families. D'Arco and Phil Leonetti, the turncoat Philadelphia underboss, were set to implicate him for ordering six murders and several attempted murders. Still free on $1 million bond, Gigante was back in court in June 1993, this time the lone defendant on a superseding indictment. In addition to the Windows racket, he was accused of more serious charges: being the Genovese boss and having authorized a series of Mob slayings, including the bomb attempt on John Gotti's life that killed Frank DeCicco.

In the meantime, a battery of psychiatrists retained by the defense diagnosed Gigante as suffering from hallucinations, schizophrenia, and dementia possibly caused by Alzheimer's disease or organic brain damage from his days in the ring. At a climatic sanity hearing in the spring of 1996, federal prosecutors in Brooklyn presented rebuttal opinions from other psychiatrists that Gigante was sane, and testimony from Savino, Gravano, D'Arco, and Leonetti that Mafia leaders understood Chin's deranged behavior was an act. The defectors concurred that Gigante's Cosa Nostra counterparts would never have accepted him as a boss if they believed he was unstable.

A federal judge resolved six years of litigation by ruling that Gigante was mentally competent to stand trial, and that he had engaged in an "elaborate deception" with the help of relatives to feign mental illness. But more delay was in store. On the eve of the trial's opening, Gigante for the second time underwent open-heart surgery, a double coronary bypass, and the trial was postponed for six months while he recuperated. Finally, in the summer of 1997, Gigante was rolled into a courtroom in a wheelchair by Father Louis, and the proceedings began. The Gigante family cardiologist was in attendance daily, checking his patient's blood pressure and condition during every recess. For a month, a pallid Gigante sat at the defense table, staring blankly into space, moving his lips silently as though talking to himself, or apparently dozing off while deserters testified and the prosecution played bugs and wiretaps of mafiosi identifying him as a boss and incriminating him in money-making plots and for arranging murders. Gigante's voice was on none of the recordings. But the government had tapes and wiretaps of mobsters, including John Gotti, referring to "Chin" and "Vincent" as a boss. Chin's threats to kill anybody who mentioned his name hadn't worked.

At the close of the month-long trial, the prosecution presented its most dramatic witness, Peter Savino, in an obvious attempt to provide a compelling finale for the jury shortly before deliberations began. Robust and indefatigable when he went undercover for the government a decade earlier, Savino now looked weary and withered beyond his fifty-odd years. Propped up in a wheelchair, gravely ill from cancer and too weak to travel, he testified by closed-circuit television from an undisclosed location. Constantly wiping perspiration from his skeletal face, he was the only former collaborator who provided first-hand information about direct criminal deals with Chin. His recollections of Gigante discussing murders and racketeering schemes with him riveted the jurors and spectators as he appeared on seven television screens in the hushed courtroom. Wincing in pain, his head sometimes sagging to his chest, and shifting uncomfortably in his seat, Savino needed several recesses to compose himself. In a halting voice, he implored, "I got to take a break, please," and, "I need to stop a minute now, guys."

Without calling a single witness, defense lawyers counted on cross-examinations and summations to discredit the six defectors who sought leniency and a parade of FBI agents who swore that Gigante was a highly respected Mafia overlord. The defense hammered at the fact that the government had earlier convicted Fat Tony Salerno of being the Genovese boss at a time the prosecution now said Gigante had run the family. If the FBI had been wrong about Salerno, the lawyers argued, it was logical that the bureau could be equally mistaken about the mentally and physically frail defendant Gigante.

An anonymous jury (a practice which had become de rigueur for Mafia trials in New York) deliberated for three days. Perking up when the jurors returned, and looking more alert than he had at any time during the trial, Gigante rolled his eyes in apparent disbelief when the forewoman announced the verdicts. He was convicted on the most serious counts: serving as the

Genovese godfather, participating in the Windows plundering, and conspiring to kill John Gotti, his brother Gene, and Pete Savino. As a poor consolation for him, the jury acquitted or deadlocked on charges that he had ordered four gangland murders in Philadelphia.

Imposing a sentence of twelve years instead of a possible maximum of twenty-seven, and a $1.25 million fine, Judge Jack B. Weinstein, reflected on Chin's career. "He is a shadow of his former self—an old man finally brought to bay in his declining years after decades of vicious criminal tyranny."

The judge was mistaken. Prison walls could not contain the old man's cunning or "vicious criminal tyranny."

52

Chin's Last Hurrah

Imprisoned at age sixty-nine, Chin Gigante continued doing what he had done for decades: behind bars, he acted as if he were mentally ill, and he remained the unchallenged ringmaster of the Genovese family. It took federal prosecutors five more years to unmask his true power. In 2002 he was indicted again, accused of leading his borgata from prison. He also was charged with obstructing justice by pretending to be deranged, thereby delaying his previous trial for seven years.

This time, his son Andrew, a wealthy container-shipping executive, was a codefendant, identified as the courier who ferried his father's instructions on major policy decisions to mobsters in New York. The indictment alleged that Andrew, while not a made man, was a "a key player in the Genovese family" and "a powerful presence on the New York–New Jersey waterfront."

Brought from the federal prison in Fort Worth, Texas, for his arraignment in Brooklyn, Chin resumed his befuddled pose. "I don't know what you're talking about," he spluttered when a judge asked if he had discussed the charges with his lawyer and how he wanted to plead.

Fifteen months later, in April 2003, Gigante was miraculously cured of his brain damage/madness/senility/dementia/Alzheimer's disease/schizophrenia. On the first day of the trial, he was lucid, animated, and made a stunning confession: to avoid further prosecution he admitted he had conned a succession of psychiatrists evaluating his mental competency over three decades. In exchange for his admission and a guilty plea to having obstructed justice, the government dropped the racketeering charge that he had continued to run a crime family from prison. A potential prison sentence of another twenty years was reduced to three more years, and three years of supervised probation.

Following in his father's footsteps, forty-six-year-old Andrew, looking like a well-tailored executive, accepted a bargain, pleading guilty to racketeering and extorting $90,000 from a shipping company. He was sentenced to two years—a sharp drop from a possible twenty if convicted on all counts—and ordered to pay $2 million in fines.

If he survives, Chin's earliest hope of freedom will come in 2012, when he will be eighty-four.

Clearly, father and son had viewed and weighed the weight of evidence that would have been lodged against them if they risked trials. Like John Gotti and his son, Chin and Andrew had been videotaped in prison and their telephone conversations had been recorded. Prosecutors were ready to substantiate that Chin used code words and hand signals to transmit messages for Andrew to deliver to Genovese battalions.

A solid witness with a long memory, a seventy-nine-year-old waterfront mobster and reputed hit man, George Barone, was eager to testify about Chin and Andrew's involvement in extortions at New Jersey and Miami ports. Barone renounced his Mafia loyalty to omertà after being indicted for waterfront racketeering and discovering that he was on Chin's hit list because of a money dispute with Andrew.

Another scheduled prosecution witness, Michael "Cookie" D'Urso, a Genovese associate, had flipped after his arrest on a murder charge. Using a recording device secreted in a Rolex watch, D'Urso over two years had taped Genovese gangsters talking about Chin's supervising the family from his cell block and using his son as his intermediary.

"Don't let anyone tell you we're dead," capo Alan "Baldy" Longo said on a recording. "We're not because Vito [Genovese] ain't here no more. Vincent is." A soldier, Pasquale Falcetti, was heard telling D'Urso about his illegal waterfront enterprises with Andrew Gigante. "Whatever the kid Andrew says, it comes from him," Falcetti said, touching his chin. "Who's going to challenge that?"

Gigante's guilty plea was highly humiliating for the psychiatrists who had diagnosed his mental disintegration as irreversible. Dr. Louis D'Adamo, Chin's principal psychiatrist for seventeen years, in a court affidavit had described him as "suffering from schizophrenia. Schizophrenia is a disease of the mind manifested by delusions, hallucinations, a thought disorder, and what we call negative symptoms." At the time of Gigante's 1997 trial, Dr. Wilfred G. van Gorp, director of neuropsychology at Columbia University Medical School, said the patient was afflicted by "moderate to severe dementia which reflects significant underlying central nervous system dysfunction." In 2003, after Gigante acknowledged his charade, Dr. van Gorp concluded that he might be both mentally ill *and* a faker. "The guy on the [prison] tapes is not the one I examined."

(Gigante's trial and reviews of his medical records disclosed another method he had employed to bilk the government. It might have been chicken feed to a mafioso of his stature, but Gigante and his relatives used the psychiatric diagnosis to obtain $900 a month in Social Security disability payments for Chin, from 1990 until he was imprisoned in 1997, probably the easiest money Chin had ever scored.)

Copping a plea like a common criminal was an unprecedented capitulation for a prodigious Cosa Nostra don. Chin broke tradition by admitting guilt and negotiating a deal. Regardless of the sentence consequences, godfathers did not surrender and seek breaks from prosecutors. Such actions harmed Mafia morale. John Gotti, Carmine Persico, Ducks Corallo, and even the figurehead Tony Salerno had stuck to their guns. Gigante's rationale was obvious to prosecutors and investigators: he was helping his son Andrew and other relatives who had been compromised because of him. The plea deal with the government spared Andrew a long prison sentence for racketeering, although it shattered Chin's self-righteous posture that he had quarantined his children from involvement with the Mafia. He had set up Andrew in a nefarious business, made him wealthy through Mob muscle, and used him as a conduit to maintain control of the borgata.

Another hypocrisy spread by Gigante was that he insulated and excluded his immediate family from his Cosa Nostra affairs. In 2002, a prosecutor, Daniel Dorsky, seeking court permission to examine Gigante's medical records, indicated that his close kin had deliberately misled psychiatrists about his mental condition. The plea bargain specified that any relative who aided Gigante's deception would not be prosecuted for obstruction of justice. Immunizing his wife, mistress, children, and his brother Father Louis from indictments was a concession that Gigante wrung from the government.

Chin learned the hard way that the era had ended when tolerant prison authorities allowed Mafia bosses exceptional liberties, and mobsters ran entire wings of penitentiaries. Tight security and close electronic monitoring of visitors foiled attempts by John Gotti and Carmine Persico to dictate Gambino and Colombo policies from afar and to use relatives as messengers. Their attempts to maintain a semblance of control landed their sons in prison. Chin ran his family by remote control for five years before the government also caught up with him and Andrew.

The precipitous slide in the Genovese family's fortunes began with the only mistake Gigante made in judging criminal character and loyalty. During his reign he lowered his guard for one newcomer—Peter Savino. After the two bodies were found in Savino's old warehouse, Chin disregarded warnings from other mafiosi and allowed Savino to continue his usual family activities, although he had never previously hesitated whacking anyone who might endanger him. "Pete was absolutely the cornerstone for getting Chin convicted; before him there was almost nothing to build on," the FBI's Dick Rudolph pointed out.

Gregory O'Connell, the Windows case prosecutor, also credits Savino with unintentionally setting in motion the Genovese family's decline. At first, O'Connell dismissed Savino as a "rich, spoiled kid, accustomed to getting everything he wanted and desperate to avoid jail." His contempt changed to admiration for the courage Savino exhibited. "It took a lot of guts to go out on the street every day wearing a wire and meeting with wiseguys who were in the business of killing informers who committed the slightest error and gave themselves away."

Literally from his deathbed, Savino completed his work for the government. In unremitting pain from terminal cancer, he testified as the central witness against Gigante at the 1997 trial, and died six weeks later at age fifty-five.

When Chin was convicted the first time on RICO charges, the Genoveses overall were in good shape. With over three hundred made men, it was the largest borgata in the country, and its fourteen crews were prospering almost as well as they had in previous decades. To law-enforcement analysts it remained the nation's most impregnable crime family. Five years later, Gigante's long-distance reign ended in dismal failure, partly because his oldest and most capable lieutenants were no longer available to help on the outside. Benny Eggs Mangano was in prison; Baldy Dom Canterino and Chin's brother Ralph were dead; another brother and capo, Mario, was serving time for tax evasion; and Quiet Dom Cirillo, a likely candidate to fill in as acting Genovese boss, was temporarily incapacitated by a heart attack.

The absence of Chin and his seasoned commanders contributed to infiltration of the family and his second conviction. Two crews were penetrated by Michael Cookie D'Urso, the associate who became an informer to beat a murder-conspiracy rap, and by an undercover detective known as "Big Frankie." The combined evidence resulted in the convictions and guilty pleas in 2001 and 2002 of six capos and more than seventy soldiers, wannabes, and associates. Their criminal activities had extended along much of the East Coast from Little Italy to the Miami waterfront. The arrests were for a wide range of familiar Mafia specialties: labor-racketeering, extortion of businesses, loan-sharking, illegal gambling, gangland executions, and robberies, including a thwarted attempt to steal $2 million to $6 million from *The New York Times* employees' credit union. Rackets in two other significant family strongholds—the private garbage-collection associations and the Fulton Fish Market—were largely shattered through investigations by the Manhattan DA's office and long-overdue regulatory crackdowns by City Hall.

Imprisoning Gigante in 1997 was a breakthrough in law-enforcement's battle against the Genovese family. Without Chin's close supervision the borgata plunged into a tailspin from which it is trying to recover.

After his 2003 conviction, back in a correctional institution containing a hospital ward should he need treatment for his cardiac condition, Gigante's reign as a "mad" godfather was over. There was no need to babble incoherently and stare vacantly into space. He had no alternative but to adjust, behave rationally, and make the best of the remainder of his days in mainly Southern and Midwestern prisons, the farthest Gigante had ever ventured from his roots in New York. As a wiseguy and as a godfather, he had avoided night spots and chic restaurants, never took a normal vacation, and restricted his movements within a radius of fifty miles from his birthplace in Greenwich Village. "It's hard to understand what enjoyment he got out of being a Mob chieftain," Ronald Goldstock, former director of the New York State Organized Crime Task Force, remarked in analyzing Gigante's aspirations. "His only pleasure appeared to be the pure power he exercised."

In prison, an aged Gigante still exhibited the cockiness and the authoritative aura of a Mafia godfather. Asked by guard Christopher Sexton if other inmates were bothering him, Chin replied, "Nobody fucks with me."

53

Nothing Magical: Forensic Accounting

Among FBI agents, Jack Stubing was known for his tenacity. "He doesn't be come obsessed with a hard case and lose sleep over it," fellow agent Pat Marshall observed admiringly. "He's more like a watchdog; if he sinks his teeth into an investigation he doesn't let go until he gets results."

But in 1998, Stubing was almost ready to admit that he was stumped for a solution to his chief preoccupation: designing a plan of attack against the Bonanno crime family. A square-shouldered, medium-sized man, who grew up in New York's suburbs, Stubing knew as much as anyone else in the FBI about the history and the contemporary makeup of the Bonanno borgata. After several years as a clerk for the bureau, he became an agent in 1984. Three years later, he began working exclusively on Bonanno investigations, eventually earning a promotion to command the small squad assigned to uprooting that Mafia gang.

Stubing's twenty-second-floor office in Lower Manhattan was a quiet refuge to contemplate strategy for the "C-10 squad," bureau shorthand for Criminal Investigative Unit Number Ten. The windowless room had been designed for administering polygraph tests to suspects and witnesses; its thick walls provided Stubing with isolation from outside clatter and distractions. Alone, gnawing on a toothpick, lights dimmed, listening to Beethoven, Copland, and Prokofiev on his CD player—habits that helped the forty-five-year-old agent organize his thoughts—he spent days poring over intelligence files and agents' 302 reports. His appraisal was bleak: the squad's recent results were paltry.

Ever since the American Cosa Nostra's birth, the Bonanno family had been an integral part of the Mob's DNA. Its roots and its name date back to 1931, to the end of the Castellammarese War when Joe Bonanno was anointed boss. Three decades of prosperity followed under the reign of Bonanno (disparagingly labeled by tabloid writers as "Joe Bananas"), until his power-play to make himself Boss of Bosses by killing other venerable dons backfired. In 1966, the Commission forced him into early retirement, creating an unsettled and confusing interregnum for more than a decade. The borgata's command structure was so cloudy that law-enforcement analysts were at a loss to determine the makeup of the family hierarchy. The FBI and the New York Police Department's top intelligence authorities mistakenly believed that a Bonanno kingpin, Carmine Lilo Galante, had filled the vacuum as boss for several years until he was gunned down in 1979. They were grossly mistaken about his status and power. He had never been a godfather, and was executed in a battle with the real boss, Philip "Rusty" Rastelli.

Mafia watchers soon saw that Galante's murder had failed to resolve the internecine Bonanno battles for dominance. Instead of tranquility, Galante's death ignited violence that was exacerbated by a startling disclosure in 1981. The FBI agent Joseph Pistone, under the pseudonym "Donnie Brasco," had infiltrated a Bonanno crew. The first agent ever to worm his way into the Mafia, over six years Pistone gathered a cache of priceless information about the family's internal structure, and incriminating evidence that produced convictions of dozens of Bonannos and allied mafiosi in Florida and Milwaukee. Pistone's brilliant feat incensed big shots in other families. Although no major New York mobsters immediately landed in prison, they felt endangered by the chaos in the Bonanno clan. As a result, the family was kicked off the Commission and restricted in its collaboration with other mafiosi and associates.

By 1988, FBI officials thought so little of the Bonannos' capabilities and withered strength that they discontinued the Bonanno Squad as a separate entity, merging it with the Colombo Squad as a combined unit. The rationale was that in the wake of the Commission case and other investigations, both families were so wracked by criminal convictions and weakened by infighting that they were rudderless and moribund. At that time, the FBI spotlight shown more brightly on the three largest and most formidable Cosa Nostra groups, the Gambino, Genovese, and Lucchese gangs.

"The Bonannos were not in our focus," Stubing recalls. "Even the wiseguys in other families were laughing at them. They were written off as a joke. Nobody took them as a serious threat."

Defections in the 1990s of high-ranking stars from other families had contributed to the bureau's minimizing the Bonannos as an insignificant planet in the Mafia universe. Sammy Gravano and other celebrity turncoats had little information to offer about the Bonannos because the family was out of the Mob's mainstream, expelled from the Commission, and excluded from lucrative consortiums in construction fields and in other rackets.

When Stubing became supervisor of the Bonanno-Colombo Squad in 1995, he sensed, however, that the tide had turned for the Bonannos. From his earlier digging around as a case agent, he suspected the borgata was flourishing and that its exclusion from joint projects with other families had actually shielded it from intense scrutiny and indictments. He was convinced the Bonannos were carving out exclusive and original terrain and had not been compromised by the torrent of traitors from other families, whose tips and trial testimony were decimating rival borgatas.

Stubing's lobbying persuaded the bureau after an eight-year hiatus to restore the Bonanno Squad as an independent unit in 1996. Stubing was its first commander. But two years of surveillance, leg work, and searching for evidence by the squad's ten or so agents failed to find a vulnerable point in the Bonanno's edifice. Conventional techniques that had undermined other families—electronic eavesdropping and attempts to cultivate informants and cooperative witnesses—had been unproductive. Stubing could not point to a single valuable snitch or to a developing case against a Bonanno bigwig or major capo.

"We had employed all the traditional techniques that had been effective against the LCN and they weren't working this time," Stubing says. "I looked around for a new idea and it came gradually. It wasn't a sudden brainstorm and there was nothing magical about it."

The investigative tactic that he hit upon had not been applied previously against a New York Mob family. Stubing would gamble on an unorthodox paper-trail search, "forensic accounting," with the ultimate goal of getting the mobster he knew was responsible for reinventing the Bonanno family in the government's crosshairs. The squad's main target was an emerging Mafia titan named Joseph Charles Massino.

54

"You Did a Good Job, Louie"

Over a thirty-year span, every agent and prosecutor who matched wits with Joe Massino was impressed by his disarming politeness and photographic memory. Unlike many mafiosi, he never snarled defiantly at lawmen; when arrested, interrogated, or put on trial, Massino was soft-spoken, unruffled, often jovial. His retention of details was awesome. Years after agents questioned him, he recalled their names and even the license-plate numbers of the unmarked cars in which they trailed him. Once, he affably apologized to an agent for having eluded him during a surveillance. A lawyer who represented Massino was impressed by his grasp of complex legal issues and his recall of numerous points discussed weeks earlier. Wherever he went in the underworld and upperworld, he generated respect.

Massino grew up and operated most of his life in the distinctly unfashionable working-class neighborhood of Maspeth, a slice of Queens dominated by one- and two-family row houses, dilapidated factories, warehouses, clogged highways, and a glut of cemeteries. Born in 1943, he was the second of three sons of a second-generation Italian-American couple. His mother took care of the boys, and his father earned a living as a fruit vendor. Joe got as far as his sophomore year at Grover Cleveland High School before leaving, and soon enough came to the attention of police in Queens and Brooklyn as a rookie wiseguy. Through a teenage friend, who was a nephew of Philip Rusty Rastelli, Joe hooked up with the uncle, a Bonanno capo who lived and made his base in Maspeth. Guided by Rastelli, whom he affectionately called "Unc," Massino advanced incrementally as an associate and earner. By Massino's late twenties, he was in the intelligence dossiers of the New York Police Department and the FBI as a versatile truck-cargo hijacker, bookie, and loan shark. He ran numbers games and loan-sharking deals from a snack truck parked at construction sites and truck depots. The wagons, known as "roach coaches," sold sandwiches, hot dishes, pastries, and soft drinks, but were also covers for Massino's illegal gambling and shylock endeavors.

A burly, five-feet nine-inches tall, Massino's weight surged to over 250 pounds when he was in his early thirties. "He ate too many of his own sandwiches and donuts and his weight ballooned," says Patrick F. Colgan, one of the first FBI agents to track the mobster. Attached to the bureau's hijacking squad, Colgan learned that Massino was made and a protégé of Rastelli. By the mid-1970s, agents evaluated him as a hijacker "kingpin" in New York, specializing in liquor and ground-coffee hauls. "When these occurred, we knew it was probably Joey," Colgan notes.

In the 1970s, hijackers pulling off five to six major road robberies every week in the New York region were a bureau headache. Massino's team of thieves was ranked among the best. From informers' tips, Colgan suspected that at a minimum Massino had gotten away with $2 million worth of Kodak film, a $500,000 cargo of clothing en route to the department store Saks Fifth Avenue, and a $100,000 supply of coffee. The modus operandi for most heists was to block a truck, jump on the running board, and stick a gun in the driver's face. Massino preferred a more orderly method: prearranged "give ups" by teamsters. "Some drivers were into shylocks and the only way they could pay the vig was by going along with a theft," Colgan explains.

The key to Massino's success was his ability to find "a drop," a concealed parking lot or a warehouse, where stolen goods could be unloaded before the crime was reported. Massino paid crew members $1,500 to $2,000 to strip a stolen cargo and load the goods into smaller trucks and vans for delivery to fences and prearranged clients. He, of course, got the cream of the profit from the loot.

FBI agents credited Massino with having "hooks," connections, for available warehouses and lots, especially in industrial sections of Maspeth, and having exceptional contacts with fences who would take entire cargos of hot goods. Known in the hijacking fraternity and the FBI as "Fat Joey," he often served as a middleman arranging—for a cut—drops and fences for other thieves. His organization became an underworld clearinghouse for a wide variety of hijacked and fenced swag. The merchandise that passed through Massino's portals included lobsters, shrimp, air conditioners, television sets, and liquor.

Massino's expertise led to a comradeship with another young hijacker of his era, the Gambinos' John Gotti. They became neighbors when Massino moved with his wife and three daughters to Howard Beach. Colgan says Massino often helped out Gotti. "Joey had two valuable traits: he was good at hiding a load at an exchange drop, and could supply something that was not that easy to come by, a single fence to take the load off your hands."

Although the FBI's hijack squad bird-dogged Massino, he was difficult to corner. Agents thought they had him trapped in a warehouse crammed with stolen goods, but as they rushed in through a front door he disappeared through a rear escape route. On another occasion, agents discovered that Massino's crew stashed stolen expensive men's suits in a warehouse in the Corona section of Queens, and propelled the clothes on a rope line attached to a haberdashery across the street whenever customers showed up for a cut-rate sale. "He was brazen and got away with a lot," agent George Hanna concedes. "He was smart and feared and nobody would give him up."

Pat Colgan thought he had the slippery Massino caged after a dustup in 1975. Driving alone, the agent spotted a hijacked truck with a cargo of clothes exiting a parking lot outside a Maspeth diner. As Colgan tried to follow, he was blocked for several minutes by a car, which then sped after the truck. Picking up the pursuit, Colgan saw the driver who had interfered with him stop the truck, hop on the running board, return to his own car, and race away. Recognizing Massino as the driver who had cut him off in the parking lot, Colgan thought, "Joey must have told the driver of the rig to dump it and try to escape."

A half mile from the diner, Colgan caught up with the hijacked truck driver, fleeing on foot. "Don't move or I'll blow you away," Colgan commanded his captive, whom he recognized as Ray Wean, a six-feet-tall, 350-pound enforcer working for Massino. "Wean's so big, I can't handcuff him, and in a minute Joey drives back in his car and asks, 'What's going on?' 'Stay put, I got bad news for you, Joey, you're under arrest.'"

Seeing that Colgan was without backup support, Massino hurried back to his car, shouting, "I gotta go to the bathroom," and drove off.

Two days later, in the company of a lawyer, Massino surrendered to stand trial with Wean for theft from an interstate shipment. Wean was convicted and served less than a year in prison. It was Massino's first felony count and, without testifying, he relied on his lawyer's opening and closing arguments that he had innocently stopped his car to find out if Wean, a casual acquaintance whom he knew from the neighborhood, was in trouble. The strategy worked and the jury acquitted him.

Although Colgan's testimony failed to convict Massino, Wean's arrest provided dividends three years later. Facing a long sentence for another robbery, Wean reached out to Colgan for aid and become an undercover informer in exchange for avoiding prison time. Over several years, Wean, who was not Italian and not made, snitched about mobsters but was hesitant to implicate Massino. "Ray was a monster, a psycho, not afraid of anything," Colgan asserted. "Yet he was scared to death of Joey for good reasons. Massino seemed very gregarious; he could talk a dog off a meat wagon, only he would then kill the dog."

Carmine Lilo Galante's assassination was an important building block for Massino, and he appears to have been an essential participant in the murder of the ambitious Bonanno gangster. Sometime in the early 1970s, Philip Rusty Rastelli, assuming that he was the new Bonanno boss, had inducted Massino into the borgata while Galante was still in prison on a narcotics rap. By 1979, the situation was reversed: Galante, free on parole, was maneuvering to seize control of the borgata and Rastelli was locked up on an extortion conviction.

Loyal to Rastelli, Massino visited him at the federal prison in Lewisburg, Pennsylvania, serving as his main messenger to his forces in New York. Learning of Massino's trips, Galante summoned him for a dressing down and ordered him to cease being Rastelli's liaison. Refusing, Massino told Galante, "He's like my uncle. He raised me, baptized me [into the crime family]. I can't abandon him." Disclosing the conversation to his closest confederate, his brother-in-law Salvatore Vitale, Massino admitted that he feared that the volcanic Galante might whack him for sticking with Rastelli.

Before any harm came to Massino, he delivered a request from Rastelli to his troops and to the Commission for a contract on Galante. The Commission approved, and on July 12, 1979, Massino was stationed outside a Brooklyn restaurant in Bushwick, probably as a backup shooter or in a crash car to block any passing police units. In the private patio of the Joe and Mary

Italian-American Restaurant, a hit squad eliminated Galante as a threat to Rastelli and Massino.

At the time of Galante's demise, Massino purportedly was an experienced hand at Mob homicides. Decades later, prosecutors learned that he had participated in at least two previous murders. In fact, Paul Castellano, the Gambino boss and top Commission member in 1979, supposedly owed Massino a favor for one "piece of work." Through his partnerships with the Gambinos, Massino had been recruited along with John Gotti to kill and dismember Vito Borelli, a boyfriend of Castellano's daughter, according to court documents. The apparent motive for the slaying was vanity. The imperious Gambino chieftain became infuriated upon hearing that Borelli had disparaged his looks, saying he resembled Frank Perdue, the poultry purveyor whose face was well known as a TV pitchman for his products. Perdue once solicited Castellano's aid as a Mafia magnate to get his chickens into New York's supermarkets.

Massino's second reputed victim in the mid-1970s was Joseph "Do Do" Pastore, a cigarette smuggler and loan shark, to whom Massino owed $9,000. Wiping out the debt, Massino was said to have pumped two bullets into Pastore's head and deposited the body in a garbage dumpster.

Galante's execution was a vital crossroad in Massino's career path. In the realignment that followed, his gangland candidate Rusty Rastelli, with the Commission's blessing, became the official Bonanno boss, and one of his first moves was to elevate Massino to capo. Forced to rule long-distance from a prison cell, the new godfather technically appointed an older capo, Salvatore "Sally Fruits" Ferrugia as acting boss. But it was apparent to savvy Bonanno soldiers that Massino was the prime warlord, the only wiseguy with a direct link to Rastelli and the only one he regularly conferred with in Lewisburg. Agent Joe Pistone, still masquerading undercover as jewel thief Donnie Brasco, though not directly involved with Massino's activities, surmised his soaring status from conversations with well-informed Bonanno regulars who trusted him, Benjamin "Lefty Guns" Ruggiero, a soldier, and Dominick "Sonny Black" Napolitano, a capo. "Lefty and Sonny classify him [Massino] as one of the top capos, top people, in the family," the agent reported to his FBI superiors.

From Pistone's intelligence reports, the bureau sensed that another storm was approaching the rambunctious Bonanno family despite the enthronement of Rastelli and the Commission's "no bloodshed" edict to its feuding cliques.

The complete story of a Mafia bloodbath and Massino's central role in it was finally revealed two decades later through eyewitness testimony and FBI debriefings of turncoats.

By early 1981, factions had formed in renewed friction over leadership posts and retaining Rastelli as an absentee commander. Two high-level sit-downs between disputant capos failed to resolve the strife. At these conferences, known as "administration meetings," the Mafia code of honor prohibited participants from carrying weapons. The Commission had technically warned the divided parties to avoid violence as harmful to Cosa Nostra business generally, and to work out their problems by themselves. But in the treacherous Mafia world, three New York families were secretly lining up behind favorites. Rastelli's loyalists were endorsed by the Gambino and Colombo families, and the Genoveses were encouraging a mutiny by their main candidates: Alphonse "Sonny Red" Indelicato, Philip "Phil Lucky" Giaccone, and Dominick "Big Trin" Trinchera, three aligned renegade captains who wanted a larger hunk of the borgata's loot and power.

In the spring of 1981, a Colombo soldier, Carmine "Tutti" Franzese, a friend of Massino's, brought him alarming news: his opponents—the three capos—were "loading up," secretly arming themselves for a showdown. For guidance, Massino turned to allies on the Commission, Paul Castellano, the Gambino boss, and Carmine Persico, the Colombo godfather. "They told me, 'You have to defend yourself. Do what you have to do,'" Massino informed Sal Vitale, his brother-in-law and sounding board. "They're trying to rob the family from Rastelli."

Interpreting "defend yourself" as Commission permission to eradicate the three capos before they wiped out the Rastelli faction, Massino designed a preemptive assault. Outmaneuvering his enemies, he wooed the swing vote—the mercurial Sicilian Zips—to join him and thereby share in the anticipated spoils of the new and victorious hierarchy. The Sicilians came on board and agreed to import shooters from their Montreal wing, who would be unrecognized in New York and afterward quickly return to Canada, for an ambush of the three targeted capos.

Laying out plans for the triple murder, Sonny Black Napolitano, a chief conspirator and strong Rastelli adherent, wanted to burnish the Cosa Nostra reputation of an associate in his crew—Donnie Brasco—by using him in the whackings. "I want to straighten out Donnie and want him to play a significant role," Sonny suggested to Massino and Vitale, unknowingly praising the undercover FBI agent. Massino instantly vetoed the suggestion. Presciently, he had earlier advised his crew members to stay clear of Brasco, forbidding them to even sit at the same table with him at weddings and social gatherings. "He might be bad," said the suspicious Massino.

To entice the three captains into a cul-de-sac snare, Massino arranged a third administration sit-down, at a presumably neutral site, an after-hours club run by the Gambinos. (Aniello Dellacroce, the Gambino underboss, was apparently clued in on the trap and authorized John Gotti's crew to lend a hand.) Two uncommitted Bonanno capos, Joseph "Joe Bayonne" Zicarelli and Nicholas "Nicky the Battler" DiStefano, were invited to the powwow, a stratagem intended to allay suspicion that it might be a set up. The meeting was deliberately set on a Tuesday night to bolster an alibi for Massino and his henchmen. Tuesdays were a festive time for dinner and all-night card games at Massino's club and hangout in Maspeth; a large gathering there on the night of the planned hits could be explained afterward as a routine party if it provoked police suspicion.

Late in the afternoon of May 5, 1981, more than a dozen soldiers and wannabes from crews run by Massino and Sonny Black Napolitano assembled at the club. Most were unaware of the impending agenda. An important Zip, known as "George from Canada," showed up with members of his outfit from Montreal. He was Gerlando Sciascia, a capo and heavy narcotics dealer, who had handpicked killers from his crew for the night's work. "It's a go," Vitale heard Massino ring out after a whispered conversation with Sciascia. George had one reservation: he distrusted using a non-Italian associate Massino had assigned as a lookout against possible police interference. His name was Duane Leisenheimer, then twenty-four, universally known to Massino's crew as "Goldie" for his thick crop of bright blond hair. Growing up in Maspeth, Goldie had latched onto Massino as a teenager. Under Massino's tutoring, he matured into a member of Joe's hijacking troupe, a prized "wheel man," crafty at eluding law-enforcement surveillance, an unsurpassed auto thief, and a chop-shop specialist.

Although blue-eyed Goldie lacked Sicilian or Italian genes, Massino assured Sciascia, "He's a good kid. Don't worry about him." The principal players—Massino, Sciascia, Napolitano, Vitale, and Goldie—departed for their rendezvous in three cars and a van. Extolled by his crew as an electronics virtuoso, Massino had equipped Goldie and other participants with radio-scanners, a device to listen in on police and FBI radio bands, and walkie-talkies to sound warnings if police cruisers or suspicious-looking cars approached the Mob meeting site. As they headed for their vehicles, Goldie heard Massino declare, "Come on, let's go. We're going to take care of this, once and for all."

It was 5:40 in the afternoon when the mobsters drove away from the Maspeth club. At that precise moment, Vincent Savadell, an FBI agent, was alone in his car on routine surveillance of the street outside the club. He had spent the previous hour circling the area, jotting down the license-plate numbers of vehicles parked near the hangout, a monotonous task intended to identify wiseguys and accomplices and to locate their home and business addresses. Spotting Massino driving off in a burgundy Buick, with several men as passengers, Savadell memorized the license registration. He followed the Buick but quickly lost it and the other cars in Massino's caravan on the nearby Long Island Expressway.

Even through Savadell was in an unmarked Oldsmobile, Massino had detected him and radioed a description of a "bad car" over the walkie-talkies, his code for a law-enforcement tail and a signal to drive evasively. Savadell's futile attempt to pursue Massino would be the FBI's only observation of him on that eventful night.

The mobsters' rendezvous point was in Brooklyn; the "administration meeting" was to be held in a catering hall that the Gambinos had converted into an illegal after-hours bar and gambling casino. It was in a commercial section of Bensonhurst on 13th Avenue near 67th Street. Goldie's job was to park about two blocks from the conference site and use his walkie-talkie to warn Massino and the others if potential trouble developed outside: essentially the presence of police patrols, suspicious-appearing cars, or opposition gangsters in the vicinity. Sonny Black and four of his hoods were parked in a red van across the street from the entrance to the Gambino's club.

Inside, on the ground floor of the two-story building, Sciascia and Massino gave last-minute instructions to some ten men gathered around them. Four were assigned as shooters, armed with a sawed-off shot gun, pistols, and a submachine gun. Three were Canadian Zips: Vito Rizzuto, Emanuel Raguso, and a gangster who Vitale and Massino knew only by his nickname, "the old man."

A former paratrooper, Vitale got the tommy gun because Massino thought he had learned how to handle it during his army days. Checking the weapon, Vitale, who had never wielded a submachine- or rapid-fire grease gun, accidentally fired off five rounds into a wall. "I don't want bullets flying all over the place," Massino admonished him, adding that he was not to use the gun unless absolutely necessary.

Because the neutral capos, Joe Bayonne and Mike the Battler, were not intended victims at the peace parley, the shooters were given ski masks to prevent the two outsiders from identifying them. The gunmen were instructed to hide in a large coat closet, to peek out, and emerge only after a signal from Sciascia: he would run his hand through his hair. The murders would be called off if Sonny Red Indelicato failed to appear. He was the most feared and bellicose opposition capo, and he had to be eliminated for Massino's scheme to succeed.

The previous evening, May 4, 1981, several blocks from the catering hall, the trio of dissident capos had met for a tense strategy session of their own in a Bensonhurst bar owned by Frank Lino, a Bonanno soldier. Lino was in a crew headed by Indelicato's son, Anthony Bruno, who had been promoted to captain two years earlier as a reward for whacking Carmine Galante. As Massino had been forewarned, the rebels were stocking up with heavy weaponry and had concealed the arsenal in Lino's bar. Among themselves, the three captains agreed to abide by Cosa Nostra rules and go unarmed to the next night's meeting with Massino's group. Lino was commanded to accompany them, also unarmed. The capos stressed to Lino that if they failed to return from the "peace" conference, Bruno Indelicato had been delegated to use the stored firepower in the bar to retaliate against the Rastelli supporters.

At about 9:00 P.M., on May 5, the three capos and Lino left together for the showdown. Before setting out, Alphonse Indelicato indicated his apprehension with a grim advisory: "If there's any shooting, everybody is on their own."

As the four men approached the club's entrance, Goldie was seated in his lookout car, and Sonny Black Napolitano and his gunmen were in the van. "They're here. They're coming in now," Goldie heard someone from the van announce over a walkie-talkie. Inside the club, the front doorbell rang and Vitale, peeking through a crack in the closet, saw Sonny Red Indelicato, Phil Lucky Giaccone, Big Trin Trinchera, and Frank Lino enter. The four men in the closet donned their ski masks. Vito Rizzuto, pistol in hand, sprung out, shouting, "This is a holdup. Everybody against the wall." Three other gunmen spilled out after him. The plan called for Rizzuto and Raguso to mow down the intended victims, if possible by lining them against a wall. Vitale and the fourth gunman, "the old man," were assigned to cover the front door and shoot any target trying to flee.

Although Vitale did not pull the trigger of his tommy gun, a crescendo of gunfire reverberated. Frozen with fear, Frankie Lino saw hooded men leaping into the crowded room, and watched Massino, holding Sonny Red's arm, strike or punch him with "an object". In the melee Vitale was certain that he saw Massino slug a different capo, Phil Giaccone. Before Vitale reached his assigned post to prevent an escape through the front door, a terrified Lino, regaining his senses, bounded over the fallen body of Big Trin Trinchera, and sped through that door. Turning around, Vitale observed George-from-Canada Sciascia lean over the sprawled Sonny Red and blast him with a bullet to the head. The barrage barely over, Vitale suddenly found himself alone with Massino and three dead men. Everyone else—their fellow conspirators and the two neutral capos—had fled through a rear door which neither Vitale nor Massino knew existed. Looking at Massino and surveying the floor splattered in blood, Vitale thought Joe was silently saying to him, "It's a mess. Where did everybody go?"

Massino's Sicilian allies had left without a word, carrying off one of their own, Santo Giordano, who was accidentally shot in the back during the fusillade. That night, the Zips paid $500 to an obliging physician to operate on Giordano without reporting the gunshot wound to the police, as required by law. (The wound left Giordano a paraplegic until he later died in a plane crash.)

With the deed done, Massino summoned Sonny Black Napolitano and his soldiers from their van. Assigned as backup shooters, they had ineptly neglected to station a gunman outside to block the front door and had allowed Lino to flee through the darkened streets. Now, their task was to clean up the grisly scene and "package" the bodies for removal. Using painters' canvas drop cloths and rope, Napolitano's men wrapped up the dead capos and scoured the crimson-stained floor to remove evidence of the massacre.

Returning alone to Massino's club in Maspeth, Sal Vitale was greeted by hugs and kisses from other crew members, who knew without being specifically informed that a spectacular feat had been accomplished. With James "Big Louie" Tartaglione, another Massino flunky, Vitale drove back to assist in removing the corpses and clues. Tartaglione collected more than a dozen shotgun and pistol shells strewn on the floor. Rolled up in the canvas, the bodies were loaded into Sonny Black's red van. It was past midnight, the street was desolate, and Vitale and Goldie's cars were stationed at two intersections to stall and prevent any passing motorist from viewing the activity. Tartaglione drove the van to Howard Beach, followed in a car by Massino, Vitale, and Goldie. Waiting on a side street were three men Vitale recognized as John Gotti's brother Gene; Fat Ange Ruggiero, John's bosom companion; and John Carneglia, a ferocious muscleman in the Gotti crew. It was unnecessary for Vitale to question Massino about the Gambinos' presence. He fathomed that they were helpmates in the slayings, trying to insure that the remains of the three capos would never be found.

After turning over the van to Gotti's men in Howard Beach, Tartaglione wisely resisted inquiring where it was being taken. He next met Massino several weeks later. Massino offered one oblique reference to his assistance on the night of the butchery. "You did a good job, Louie."

55

"Good-Looking Sal"

The killers left one loose end.

Frank Lino, the soldier who had torn off in terror during the carnage, knew what had gone down; he could identify Massino and his accomplices; and could tip off Sonny Red's son, Bruno Indelicato, to the double-cross and slaughter of his father and two allies. Again, Massino used his Gambino nexus to solve the problem. Eddie Lino, Frank's cousin and a Gambino soldier, accompanied Frank to meetings where Massino and other Bonanno leaders assured him that his life was not in danger and that he had not been an intended victim. "Don't worry, you're not going to get killed," Massino promised.

Lino was given a bonus: he was appointed acting capo of Bruno Indelicato's crew with pledges from Massino, "Everything's over"; there would be no additional casualties. He was instructed to spread the triumphant party's justification for the triple homicide as a defensive measure for the benefit of the entire family that would ensure peace. (Fearing revenge from cocaine-addled Bruno Indelicato, who once had the guts to whack Carmine Galante, Massino and Sonny Black's legions hunted for his head for a month. The Commission then gave Bruno "a pass," returning him to the fold but demoted to soldier in his old crew under Frank Lino as capo.)

The day after the murders, Massino thought it best to lie low to avoid possible police investigations or retaliation from Bruno, whose whereabouts were unknown. He repaired to Atlantic City, but his beach and casino time was cut short by an emergency appendectomy. Brother-in-law Sal Vitale was dispatched to comfort and guard him in the hospital and to escort the patient back to New York.

Nineteen days after the peace-meeting executions, Alphonse Indelicato's body was found in a shallow grave in a vacant lot on the border of Ozone Park and East New York. A $2,000 Cartier watch was on his wrist, an obvious sign that he had not been a robbery victim. The site was less than a mile from Howard Beach, where the Gambino soldiers had taken charge of the van containing the corpses of the three victims. (The bodies of Philip Giaccone and Dominick Trinchera also were dumped in the same large muddy field, but their remains were recovered twenty-three years later, in 2004, only after a tip to the FBI.)

Sonny Black Napolitano, whose slick dark hair was the reason for his nickname, exchanged words with Massino over Indelicato's burial. Massino had been responsible for eliminating all traces of the bodies, and Napolitano faulted him for the fouled-up burial, which provided proof of a homicide for investigators. Two months later, Sonny Black disappeared and it was evident to the authorities that he, too, must have received the extreme Mafia sentence. On the day he vanished, a lugubrious Napolitano left his prized diamond pinkie ring, a wad of cash, and the keys to his apartment with Charlie, the bartender in the Motion Lounge, his crew's hangout in the hardscrabble Brooklyn neighborhood of Greenpoint. "I'm going to a meeting and don't know if I'm coming back," Napolitano said gravely.

There was a ready explanation for Napolitano's fate. That summer of 1981, an earthquake rocked the Bonanno family when Agent Pistone surfaced from his six-year undercover operation as Donny Brasco with the stunning disclosure that Sonny Black had welcomed him into his crew and was planning to sponsor his induction into the family. Indictments were certain to follow as a result of Napolitano's credulity.

Before Pistone's unprecedented infiltration became publicly known, Napolitano was visited at dawn one morning by three FBI agents at his Greenpoint apartment above the Motion Lounge. Positive that Napolitano's life would be forfeited as soon as the Mob bosses learned of Pistone's exploits, the bureau was informing him as early as possible that he had been duped. Douglas Fencl, an agent Napolitano knew from previous brushes, offered Napolitano his telephone number in case he wanted the bureau to protect him. "You know better than anybody that I can't take that," Napolitano replied, rejecting the proposal to defect. To prove that Pistone was an authentic agent and that he was not trying to trick Napolitano into cooperating, Fencl showed him a photograph of a smiling Pistone with himself and three other agents.

"He was a standup guy," Fencl remarked. "He had the most to lose in the family because he had brought an agent into the family but he had no intention of cooperating, even to save his life."

A year later, a body bag containing Napolitano's skeleton was found in a wooded and swampy area of west Staten Island. He was identified mainly by dental records and jewelry, which relatives confirmed belonged to him. The full account of Napolitano's death was cobbled together in 2004, twenty-three years after a Mafia bullet exploded in his brain. Witnesses testified that it was Sonny Black's erstwhile ally, Joe Massino, who sanctioned the contract. For this hit, Massino tested the loyalty of Frank Lino, the new acting capo, who had barely escaped being gunned down with the three renegade capos.

A concrete-hard thug, Lino had shown his mettle and defiance of the police when he was twenty-five. Picked up in 1962 for helping the flight of a stickup man who had shot and murdered two detectives in Brooklyn, he kept his mouth shut despite barbaric beatings over four days by the police. A leg and an arm were broken and repeated battering of his head gave him a permanent incessant blink. Finally, a broom handle was plunged into his rectum—the same torture tactic that generated a scandal in 1997 when police officers sodomized a Haitian immigrant in a Brooklyn station house. Not yet a mafioso, Lino unflinchingly adhered to the code of *omertà*.

Massino commanded Lino to find a secure location and provide hit men for Sonny Black's elimination. On the night of August 17, 1981, Lino picked up Napolitano and Stefano "Stevie Beef" Cannone, then the family consigliere, at the Hamilton House, a restaurant in Bay Ridge, Brooklyn, and drove them across the Verrazano Narrows Bridge to Staten Island for another supposed administration meeting. Cannone, apparently ignorant of the real purpose of the ride, was brought along so that his presence would lull Sonny Black and keep him off guard.

At a house in the blue-collar Eltingville section of Staten Island, the three men were greeted at the door by Frank Coppa, a soldier, who told them the conference was to be held in the basement. As Napolitano descended, Coppa held back Cannone, slamming shut the basement door, a signal for Lino to shove Napolitano down the stairs. Two killers were waiting at the foot of the stairwell. The first shot fired by Robert Lino Sr., Frank's cousin, apparently missed or grazed Napolitano and the gun jammed. Sprawled on his knees, Napolitano looked up and said, "Hit me one more time and make it good."

The second triggerman, Ronald "Monkey Man" Filocomo, fired several .38 caliber rounds to finish off Sonny Black. The murder site was the home of Filocomo's parents. Despite his services to the family, Filocomo, who garnered his nickname by keeping a monkey as a pet, was automatically disqualified from induction as a made man because of a Cosa Nostra rule: he had once worked in law enforcement as a prison guard. With Vitale driving, Massino and George-from-Canada Sciascia had followed Lino's car in a bakery van. They waited outside the Staten Island house as backup shooters should Napolitano have managed to get out of the cellar alive.

Lino had arranged for a separate unit to remove and bury Sonny Black's body. Their night's work done, Massino and Vitale returned to their homes while Lino and Coppa, close friends since childhood, drove to an Italian street festival in Brooklyn to unwind. Because of the darkness, Lino's amateur undertakers were unable to find the grave prepared for Napolitano. Worried about being found with a corpse in their car, the burial squad hurriedly deposited the slain capo in a quickly dug hole that was discovered a year later.

Napolitano was killed to impress upon Bonanno mafiosi the need for constant vigilance, and to warn them of the penalty for being gulled by undercover agents. "I had to leave Sonny a receipt for Donnie Brasco," Massino told Vitale. "Receipt" meant a whacking in Massino's lexicon. Massino went on to say that even if he were someday convicted of the three capos' murders, he would still enjoy the satisfaction of knowing that he had bumped off Napolitano in retaliation for a blunder that disgraced and endangered the entire family.

Also in Massino's sights for extreme punishment was Benjamin "Lefty Guns" Ruggiero, a wiseguy in Napolitano's crew, who had "bounced around" with Agent Pistone and allowed the agent to "go on record" with him as an associate. Ruggiero's unforgivable sins were having taken Pistone under his wing, introducing him to family leaders, and vouching for him as a reliable wannabe and potential big earner. The "earnings" that Pistone handed over to entice Ruggiero and Napolitano were actually provided by the FBI, overhead for the undercover operation.

Three days after Sonny Black's last ride, through wiretaps the FBI got wind that hit men working for Massino had summoned Ruggiero to the Holiday Bar, a grubby hangout on Madison Street in Lower Manhattan, a short stroll from Lefty Guns's apartment in the Knickerbocker Village complex. "They were going to whack him," says Pat Marshall, an agent staked out near the bar. "That was a joint where people walked in through the front door and were carried out in the back."

Racing to "snatch" Ruggiero off the streets as soon as left his apartment, a car carrying the supervising agent for the arrest collided with a bus. As Ruggiero headed toward Massino's gunsels, another agent, Louis Vernazzo, who was secretly surveilling Ruggiero, got an emergency radio call to intercept the gangster before he reached the bar. Ruggiero shuddered with fright as Vernazzo, a muscular man with Italianate facial features, suddenly jumped out of a Cadillac carrying a shotgun. "Lefty thought he was going to be whacked and it was all over for him until he heard those comforting words, 'FBI. Freeze!'" Vernazzo recounted to fellow agents. Ruggiero's abrupt arrest on racketeering and gun charges probably saved his life that day.

Another endangered mobster was the fiery-tempered soldier Anthony Mirra, the first Bonanno member to use Pistone as an associate. A hulking six-footer, weighing 240 pounds, Mirra was an intimidating shake-down artist and a "knife man" who settled arguments by "sticking" his opponent. No fool, Mirra vanished from his usual haunts as soon as news of Pistone's duplicity reached him, realizing that he was on the government's list for indictment. But more perilous was the certainty that Bonanno higher-ups wanted him dead as another object lesson of what happened to mafiosi who allowed the FBI to penetrate the borgata, and because he might morph into an FBI stool pigeon to obtain leniency.

Frequently changing dwellings, Mirra kept in touch with only one other Bonanno wiseguy, his cousin Joseph D'Amico. Older by twenty-eight years, Tony Mirra had coached Joey D'Amico, helping him to become made at twenty-two, thereby distinguishing him as one of the Mafia's youngest inductees. The news that he was eligible for membership came in a surprise telephone call one day, instructing him to "Get dressed." A beholden Joey tried to emulate Tony's Mob style and deportment, viewing him as a sagacious uncle rather than a cousin.

On February 18, 1982, Mirra telephoned D'Amico and arranged to meet him at the apartment of a girlfriend in Lower Manhattan, where he was holed up before going out for an evening of relaxation. The fifty-four-year-old Tony greeted Joey with a bear hug in the apartment on Harrison Street, near the Hudson River. D'Amico realized that his ever-suspicious cousin was patting him down to see if he was armed. A few minutes later, the cousins entered Mirra's Volvo in the building's garage. When Tony halted the car to use a key which opened the exit gate, from the passenger's side Joey pulled out a pistol that he had artfully concealed and shot Mirra several times point-blank in the head.

Waiting outside in a getaway car were Joey's great uncle, Alfred "Al Walker" Embarrato (a Bonanno mafioso and longtime racketeer at the *New York Post*) and Richard Cantarella, also a cousin of D'Amico and Mirra. Later, examining Mirra's body, the police found a large stack of cash he was using while on the run—$6,779 hidden in one of his boots.

D'Amico considered the murder an entwined family affair. He got the contract from Embarrato—the man he called "Uncle Al"—who was also Mirra and Cantarella's uncle. Upon receiving a .38 caliber gun from Uncle Al, D'Amico was told that the order came directly from Joe Massino. It had to be fulfilled even though D'Amico admired—and loved—Mirra. Uncle Al was rewarded for orchestrating the difficult hit of his nephew with a promotion to captain.

Several years later, D'Amico was stopped by Massino to discuss the pending induction of his cousin Richie Cantarella into the family. Praising Cantarella, D'Amico alluded to his participation in Mirra's homicide. The subject of a gangland murder had been casually raised by Massino while circulating among guests at the wedding reception of his daughter Adeline.

The killings and upheaval in the borgata swiftly transported Massino to a prime post as uncontested deputy for the imprisoned Rastelli and the family's "street boss." Accompanying Massino's swelling importance was a shift in his attention from orchestrating hijackings and holdups to the more genteel art of labor rackets, the Ph.D. degree for big-time mobsters. Meanwhile, he held on to his assured and profitable standbys: gambling and loan-sharking. Agent George Hanna, who was pursuing Massino in the 1980s, discovered that hijackings were being eclipsed as a desirable Bonanno activity by simpler and more lucrative crimes, especially narcotics. Increasingly squeezed by law-enforcement pressure, hijackings were becoming too dangerous, and an informer reported to the FBI that $2 million worth of stolen film netted Massino's crew chump change, a measly $60,000.

Massino's headquarters remained in Maspeth. It was there that he and his wife, Josephine, established the J&J (Joe and Josephine) Deli, to prepare sandwiches and delicacies for roach coaches, the presumably legitimate business that justified Massino's comfortable lifestyle. Agents were more interested in a storefront adjacent to the deli, alternately identified in real estate records as J&S (Joe and Sal) Cake and MVP Trucking, that served as Massino's shape-up hall for crime. The MVP initials stood for Massino, his brother-in-law, Sal Vitale, and a Bonanno associate, Carmine Peluso, the club's unofficial chef. Among the Bonanno cognoscenti, the hangout on a side street was referred to as the "Rust Street Club" after a nearby main thoroughfare. Joe and Sal ran high-stakes card games there, usually Continental, a version of gin rummy with four decks and jokers wild. "The House," meaning the brothers-in-law, got 10 percent of the winning pots.

Nicknamed "Good-Looking Sal," Salvatore Anthony Vitale, was Massino's acolyte since boyhood. Romance brought Massino into the Vitale household. Selling Christmas trees on a neighborhood sidewalk, Joe met and flirted with Josephine, Vitale's older sister, then dated, and soon married her while both were in their teens. Four years older than Vitale, Massino functioned as a big brother, teaching him how to swim when he was twelve and, more important, how to survive on the tough streets of Bushwick where the Vitales lived, and in nearby Queens neighborhoods like Maspeth.

Graduating from Grover Cleveland High School, Vitale spent half a year at a municipal college before a two-year stint in the army. After his honorable discharge, he got a legitimate job as a corrections officer in Queens at a state rehabilitation institution for defendants convicted of low-level narcotics offenses. Bored, he quit after one year to work for Massino, operating a roach coach, using it to take numbers at 500-to-1 odds while selling snacks. In his spare time, and without Joe's knowledge, Vitale and two pals were committing petty burglaries, mainly breaking into factories. Confronting his brother-in-law, Massino offered an irresistible deal: "Phil Rastelli sent me word that you're doing scores. If you're doing them, do them with me." The twenty-four-year-old proudly "went on record" under him. By the mid-1970s, Joe had schooled Vitale on the finer points of essential Mob economics, employing him in arsons for insurance rip-offs, bookmaking, hijacking, loan-sharking, and money-laundering.

Vitale marveled at his mentor's canniness in evading arrest. "He's aware of everything that goes on around him. You'll never catch him sleeping. He has his eyes on everything," he told other wannabes.

The younger criminal passed all his integrity tests with Massino, even abetting him in the July 1976 murder of the loan shark and cigarette smuggler Joseph Do Do Pastore. Admitting that he had shot Pastore to death in the apartment kitchen above the J&J Deli, Massino asked Sal to mop up the blood.

A day after the hit, Vitale used a bucket, a carpet brush, and a bottle of Lysol to clean the kitchen, even removing stains inside the refrigerator.

By the late 1970s, Vitale, much leaner and more careful of his waistline than his brother-in-law, had blossomed into Massino's closest confidant and alter ego. Displaying to Mafia brethren his reciprocated affection for Sal, Joe honored him by serving as best man at his wedding.

"They were inseparable," says Pat Colgan, the agent who spent a decade tracking both mobsters. "Joey was his mentor for loan-sharking, hijacking, everything. But in reality Sal was then just his gofer. If not for Joey, Sal would have been selling coffee from the back end of a truck."

The signs of Joe's ascendancy to de facto leader of the borgata while Rastelli was in prison were clear to Vitale. He saw the homage paid to Massino as other capos and Bonanno elders trekked to J&S Cake for walk-talk consultations with him. Taking stock of events—the disappearance and apparent murders of four Bonanno capos and the large gatherings at J&S—the FBI decided it was a strategic time to bug the club to hear what the Bonanno hierarchs were up to.

But the bureau's eavesdropping technicians were challenged by an intricate "three-tier" defense system installed by Massino in his bulwark, a large storefront with two blackened windows and log-patterned brick sidings. "The place was fortified," Colgan says with professional admiration. "He had the best locks, a first-class alarm system, and we knew if you got inside you had thirty seconds to use another key and then you had to punch in a code to cut off the alarms."

Additionally, Massino had buttered up neighborhood residents and merchants, inviting them to be amateur watchmen, to alert him if agents or detectives prowled around when the club was shuttered. Colgan had a hunch about an unorthodox method of breaking into Massino's inner sanctum. He knew that the mobster relied on a nearby resident to clean the club in the morning. The custodian had a set of keys, and the code numbers to disable the alarms were written on a scrap of paper in his wallet which he pulled out every time before entering. Upon completing his work at J&S, the cleaning man spent a good part of the afternoon ensconced at a nearby tavern. Settling down and getting comfortable, he always placed his keyring and wallet on the bar. An agent spent some time at the tavern chatting up the man and memorizing the look of the keyring and wallet perched on the bar. One day, when the cleaner went to the men's room, the agent transferred the keyring and wallet to another agent in the bar, replacing them with similar-looking items. In a nearby motel room, a locksmith duplicated the keys that would unlock the front door. As hoped, the code to silence the alarms was inscribed on the sheet of paper folded in the wallet.

About an hour after the keyring was pilfered, it and the wallet were switched again at the bar, and the tipsy cleaning man never noticed the exchange. Soon afterward, at three o'clock in the morning, FBI Special Operations agents were inside J&S installing a mini-microphone. But this time, the bureau's raiders were on the losing end. For two days the bug operated without picking up an incriminating conversation; then suddenly the entire transmission system went silent. The tech experts guessed that Massino's men had ripped out the equipment.

Sal Vitale had foiled the FBI with a primitive method for unearthing bugs. With the police radio scanner turned on, he routinely had an assistant stand in a distant corner of the club, speak loudly and make a racket, sometimes flushing the toilet. One day, the scanner picked up voices and a toilet flush being transmitted from the room. Tracing the sounds to a dropped ceiling above the main card table, Vitale dismantled the FBI microphone and transmitter lodged in the ceiling.

Scanners were only one aspect of Massino's counterbugging defenses. All his crew members were strictly warned never to discuss business in the club. Nevertheless, he instituted another backup barrier. Every two weeks, a technician, "Tommy Computer," well known to important mobsters, was brought in to electronically sweep J&S for law-enforcement eavesdropping devices.

Undaunted by the setback at Massino's club, James Kallstrom, the FBI's thrifty Special Ops Chief, wanted the pricey state-of-the-art gear returned. He ordered Colgan to retrieve it. "I'm not going to let them keep our equipment," Kallstrom said. "It's government property. Get it back." Looking for an opportunity to get inside the club, Colgan "bobtailed," dashed behind a hood buzzed in through the locked door. "The guy turns around, 'Who the fuck are you?' and he takes a poke at me. I duck and deck him and all the other guys are heading for me when a voice booms out, 'Everybody cool it. It's just Pat.'"

It was Joe Massino who came to the agent's rescue. Calming the scrappers circling Colgan, Massino gleefully guessed the purpose of the visit, explaining in a cat-and-mouse manner, "We found it the first day. Why didn't you just call, I'd have brought it to you." Fetching the microphone and two bricklike transmitters, Massino offered the agent a beer. "How'd you find it?" Colgan asked. "We have our ways," came the laughing reply.

56

The Mob's Horatio Alger

As anticipated, Agent Pistone's infiltration generated indictments of more than fifty mafiosi and associates in the Bonanno family and in other borgatas in Florida and Milwaukee. The ax landed first in November 1981 on five soldiers from Sonny Black Napolitano's old crew, who were charged with conspiracy to murder the three capos and with various racketeering counts. (Sonny Black was named as lead defendant in the case, but his disappearance was not cleared up until his body was identified in 1982.) Four months after Sonny Black's crew members were hauled in, Massino learned that his arrest was imminent on similar murder-conspiracy and racketeering accusations. "I got word that an indictment is coming down," he whispered to Vitale in March 1982. Without disclosing the source of his information, Massino had no intention of being tried simultaneously with other defendants. That very day he was going on the lam. His plan was to outwait the first round of trials, a gambit often used by Mob leaders to gauge the prosecution's evidence and to devise a sturdier defense. "I got a better chance of winning by myself," he told Vitale.

The Hamptons, a popular summer resort on Eastern Long Island, was his first choice for a hideout. Although it was late winter and off-season, Massino ran into people he knew, and after two weeks he reached out for Duane Goldie Leisenheimer to find him a safer refuge.

Goldie was eager to help the man he called "chief," grateful for the on-the-job education he had received at Massino's side. Fascinated by automobiles, Goldie had spent a year at Brooklyn Automotive, a high school that trained mechanics, before leaving and employing his knowledge to steal cars rather than repair them. At sixteen, he made about $2,000 a week "boosting" up to fifteen cars on orders for specific models from a chop shop, which then cannibalized and sold the valuable parts. Working in the chopshop, he picked up another $300 weekly as he learned the art of dismantling hot cars. Vouching for Goldie, as "a standup kid," the chop-shop owner introduced him to Massino, and at eighteen, the blond teenager joined Joe's hijacking outfit. Goldie's original duties were offloading stolen merchandise from rigs and delivering stolen goods in smaller trucks and vans to fences and obliging merchants.

Demonstrating that a Mafia leader could be an equal-opportunity employer, Massino took Goldie aside for survival lessons of the trade, even though he was not of Italian heritage. He forbade the young criminal to heist cars or sell drugs in their Maspeth area because it would bring unneeded "heat" from the law to the J&S Club and to his hijacking drops. Goldie was further advised to cease stealing cars near other Mob hangouts in Queens, especially one used by John Gotti. "If those guys catch you, you'll end up in a trunk," Massino cautioned.

Massino harped on constant vigilance. "Watch your mirrors," he hammered at him, a warning about law-enforcement car surveillance. Goldie saw close up how Massino's watchfulness stymied efforts to trap him, even countering the FBI by spying on agents before they could get a bead on him. Always on the alert, he had noticed agents using the parking lot of a Maspeth diner to switch unmarked cars when they were in the neighborhood. Thus, by furtively watching the lot, Massino's men knew the make and license-plate numbers of bureau cars and could identify lawmen pussyfooting in the area.

Before long, Goldie was an accepted associate in Massino's crew. Massino admired his skill at shaking off tails and frequently used him as a chauffeur for trips around town and visits to "the old man," the boss Phil Rastelli, at prisons in upstate New York and Pennsylvania.

Goldie's participation in the three capos murders solidified Massino's trust in him, and in the spring of 1982, when Massino asked for his help in hiding out, Goldie suggested a haven: his parents' vacation home in Milford, Pennsylvania, eighty miles northwest of New York in the Pocono Mountains. Goldie's father allowed both men to stay there indefinitely, except when the parents used the place. On those brief occasions, mainly weekends, Massino moved to a motel.

The leak to Massino about an arrest and indictment was accurate. In July 1982, a federal grand jury in Manhattan unveiled RICO charges, citing him as a conspirator but not as an actual participant in the murders of the three capos.

A year later Rusty Rastelli was paroled and free to assume control of the borgata as "official" boss. Yet it was clear to most Bonanno mobsters that Massino, even on the lam, functioned as the essential head of the family. He relayed orders to Vitale through prearranged telephone calls to public booths, a system similar to the one adopted later by Gaspipe Casso in the Lucchese family. Rastelli raised no objections as capos and important soldiers showed their allegiance and obeisance to his protégé by journeying to the Poconos for instructions and to report on Mob matters. A high-ranking visitor from another borgata, old hijacking buddy John Gotti, also showed up to bolster Massino's spirits and enhance his Cosa Nostra stature.

Avoiding FBI tails, visitors to the hideout were either picked up in New York by Goldie or met him on Pennsylvania side roads before they were brought to Milford. Confident about Goldie's ability "to watch his mirrors," Massino ventured with him into the city for high-level meetings to resolve issues that could not be handled via the telephone or couriers.

One piece of business that Massino did take care of from the Poconos was the whacking of Cesare Bonventre, one of the gunmen who had helped rub out Carmine Galante. A Zip capo, Bonventre, for an unclear reason, had offended Massino. The contract for knocking him off was given to Sal Vitale at a 1984 meeting in the Milford hideaway. From Massino's remarks, Vitale believed that Joe questioned Bonventre's loyalty because he had not helped or visited him while he was on the lam and, in his words, "sacrificing" himself "for the good of the family." Vitale speculated privately that there might be another reason for the hit: as head of a powerful Sicilian group Bonventre loomed as a rival to Massino. Goldie, who was included in the murder plan, got another explanation. Massino hinted to him that he was acting on a request from Rastelli without knowing the reason. "The old man wants Cesare to go," Joe said without amplification.

Vitale put little stock in the notion that Rastelli was responsible for the decision. From his vantage point, Vitale thought the paroled Rastelli was worn down by the chronic family turmoil and was on the verge of retiring. "He wanted to live out his life peacefully," Vitale recalled. "He wanted to step down the day he got home [from prison]."

Before Goldie left for the Bonventre killing, Massino cautioned him that the

Zip capo—reputedly involved in twenty-five slayings—might be a difficult quarry. "He's a very sharp guy. You have to be careful."

Carrying out the plot conceived by Massino, Vitale picked up Bonventre in Queens one night in April 1984, for a presumed meeting with Rastelli. Instead, with a Massino gunman, Louis "Ha Ha" Attanasio, seated in the rear of the car, Vitale headed for Goldie's chop shop, where Goldie was waiting. As they approached the garage, Attanasio shot Bonventre in the head, but only wounded him. Struggling with Vitale for the wheel, Bonventre tried to swerve the car into a parked vehicle or the side of the road. Fighting him off with one hand, Vitale steered into the garage where Attanasio fired several more shots into Bonventre's twitching body. "I had to shoot him again. This cocksucker didn't want to die," Attanasio grumbled to Goldie.

The Bonventre hit was a benchmark event for Vitale. As a reward and recognition for his services, his brother-in-law authorized his induction as a goodfellow—a made man. With Massino and consigliere Steve Cannone officiating, Vitale, at age thirty-seven and after fifteen years of service to Joe, joined the Honorable Society. Most of the ceremony was in Italian, and Vitale, a second-generation American, barely understood a word.

Two years elapsed without the FBI closing in on Massino. Periodically agents followed Vitale and other known crew members, hoping they might lead them to the fugitive. Acting on a suggestion from an informer, the agent in charge of the manhunt, Pat Marshall, did concentrate on the Poconos. His investigation produced a solid clue: Massino had sent dolls to his daughters from an antique shop in the region. But that single lead was insufficient to track down Massino's lair in the huge Poconos region.

What agents did not know was that Massino was using the alias "Joe Russo," and that he committed an incredible blunder. Inexplicably, he tried to shoplift a bottle of aspirin worth less than one dollar from a store in the Poconos and was caught. He managed to talk his way out of the petty theft, showing identification as Joe Russo. No fugitive by that name was wanted in any "All Points Bulletin" and the local police allowed him to go free.

Belatedly, the FBI learned that Massino had been romantically comforted in his hideout. A woman with whom he was having an affair was driven from New York by Goldie for weekend assignations in motels. They had met when Massino, on numerous prison trips to visit Rastelli, had provided rides for her in his Cadillac or Lincoln to visit her husband serving time in the same institution.

The manhunt ended on Massino's terms after twenty-eight months. He returned to New York and surrendered in July 1984. Before showing up, he and his lawyers had time to study the court proceedings of the first five Bonanno mobsters from Sonny Black's crew tried on charges stemming from Agent Pistone's undercover exploits. Three, including Lefty Guns Ruggiero, were found guilty on RICO violations that they knew of the plot to kill the three capos. In fact, unbeknownst to agents and prosecutors, they actually had been back-up shooters and helped remove the bodies from the ambush site. The trial evidence was based largely on Pistone's infiltration testimony and a taped recording incriminating them in the massacre. As Massino had anticipated, the trial charted the limited evidence then compiled by the FBI in the murder case and revealed the prosecution's fundamental courtroom strategy.

"Get used to my face, because you're going to see a lot of it for a long time," Pat Marshall, the agent who had been hunting Massino, forewarned when he was brought to FBI headquarters for fingerprinting and photographing. As the case or lead agent for Massino's trial, Marshall recognized that he was confronting an imperturbable foe. "He took my warning with a grain of salt and said calmly, 'No problem, do what you got to do.'"

Massino made bail, but Marshall and prosecutors were far from through with investigating him and Goldie Leisenheimer. Called before a grand jury and granted immunity from prosecution, Goldie refused to answer questions about his sojourn with Massino in the Poconos. He was cited for contempt and imprisoned for fifteen months, the length of a grand jury's inquiry into new charges against Massino and other Bonanno gangsters. The night before Goldie's incarceration, Massino and his crew toasted him at a party in the J&S Club. Congratulating and embracing him as a "standup guy," the boys handed him envelopes totaling $17,000 in cash as a reward for his protection of Joe.

Within a year of his return, Massino was hit with another RICO indictment; as a codefendant with Rusty Rastelli, he was accused of union racketeering and extortion. Picked up at his Howard Beach home, Massino politely asked to be cuffed outside, not in the presence of his wife and teenaged daughters, Adeline and Joanne. "Because he was always the gentleman and cordial with us," Marshall granted him that favor.

Soon afterward, in June 1985, Marshall pounced on him again in Howard Beach as he sat talking in Sal Vitale's parked Buick near Joe's home. This time, Marshall was after both men. An additional charge had been tagged against Massino in the three capos murder case: conspiracy to murder Joseph Do Do Pastore, the loan shark and cigarette bootlegger who had been gunned down in the apartment above the J&J Deli a decade earlier. The superseding indictment also named Vitale, not as a defendant in any of the four murders, but as an accomplice in alleged hijackings.

Handcuffed, the brothers-in-law were placed in separate FBI cars, with Marshall riding in the same auto with Massino and two other agents. Because of Massino's girth, Marshall needed two sets of cuffs to lock his hands behind his back. When the agents stopped for a nearby traffic light, another car screeched to a halt alongside them. The imposing figure of John Carneglia, one of John Gotti's goons who lived in the neighborhood and had assisted Massino in disposing of the three capos' bodies, approached. Slamming his hand on the roof of the FBI car, Carneglia, demanded: "Joey, are you all right?" The agents, aware of Carneglia's hatred of lawmen and reputation for hair-trigger violence, fingered their guns. "Get out of here before you get hurt," one agent warned Carneglia. After an exchange of icy stares, Carneglia backed off, saying he would call Massino's lawyer.

At the booking, Marshall noted that Massino was flush with funds, carrying $3,192 in his pockets. He quickly raised $1 million bail for the new accusations. Befitting his position as an important Mafia official, Massino seemed unfazed as he prepared for two pending RICO battles. He continued to show up at his customary haunts in Maspeth, supervising his semilegitimate roach coach and food businesses and his clandestine Mob enterprises. He even found time to frolic at Caesar's Palace Casino in Atlantic City, where he ran up a $15,000 debt on a credit line, losses which he never paid.

In a rare turnabout, the surveillance-conscious Massino threw caution to the wind when it came to public appearances with his longtime Mafia comrade John Gotti, then a Gambino capo. Flaunting their relationship, the two mobsters from different families were often spotted visiting each other at their respective clubs. Disregarding the Commission's ban on close affiliations with the ostracized Bonannos, Gotti displayed to Mafia lords his confidence in Massino. One ostentatious example of their close relationship was Massino's attendance at the wedding of Victoria Gotti in 1984. A year later, after the death of Gambino underboss Aniello Dellacroce, Massino arrived conspicuously at Dellacroce's wake in the same car as Gene Gotti. His appearance with the mourning Gotti brothers was a reciprocal sign of his support for them in their rancorous confrontation with Gambino boss Paul Castellano. (A short time later, FBI eavesdropping tapes would jolt Massino when he heard that Gotti, in conversations with cronies, had disparaged him as "the whale" and "a punk.")

The spring of 1986 finally brought Massino into Federal District Court in Brooklyn for the first trial, as a codefendant with Rusty Rastelli, the government's main target. The Bonanno godfather had been indicted a year earlier in Manhattan in the Commission case, but those charges were dropped in favor of a giant labor-racketeering case against him, Massino, and ten other defendants. Over two decades, Bonanno chiefs and officials of teamsters' Local 814 had teamed up for systemic, standardized shake-downs. The mobsters and corrupt union bosses milked more than $1 million yearly from New York's largest moving and storage companies by rigging contracts and extorting payoffs to prevent labor problems.

A chagrined Massino thought he had been hit with a bum rap. "I never made a penny," he griped to associates about charges that he had profited immensely from the conspiracy. The crucial testimony came from an admittedly corrupt teamsters' official, Anthony Giliberti, who cooperated with the government after surviving a botched hit. Massino confided to other mafiosi that he had slapped around Giliberti: "I gave him a crack." In the scale of Mafia misdeeds, he considered a mild beating as an unjust reason for indictment. Giliberti, who had been threatened by Massino, was certain that he had been behind the plot to murder him, but that accusation was not leveled against Massino.

Dressed daily in off-the-rack dark suits and sport jackets, Massino was more deferential and jovial with prosecutors and agents in the courtroom than his fellow suspects. Laura Brevetti, the lead prosecutor from the federal Organized Crime Strike Force, observed his lighthearted attitude during a recess in a nearly deserted courtroom. That day Brevetti was using a chart to illustrate rigged bids and overcharges gobbled up by a moving company accused of delivering 5 percent kickbacks to the Bonannos. Studying the chart, and referring to the excess profits made by the head of the firm, Massino snickered loud enough for the prosecutor to hear, "I think the son-of-a-bitch owes me money." (Ironically, one Mob-inflated contract was for moving the FBI's furniture and equipment into new downtown offices.)

Bumping into Pat Colgan in the courthouse hall, Massino had a friendly greeting for his longtime adversary. "Hey, Pat, I hear you've been promoted," Massino said, revealing that he knew of the FBI agent's appointment to a supervisory job. "I hear the same thing about you, Joey." A huge grin was Massino's silent reply.

Rastelli was an epileptic and Massino came to his aid several times during the trial. Once, Massino showed his exceptional strength, prying open a telephone booth door and lifting out the trapped Rastelli during a seizure. He also comforted Rastelli and made sure he would not bite his tongue when he collapsed at the defense table. During that seizure, Rastelli's loafers flew off, and when Massino picked them up, Brevetti heard another defendant, Nicholas "Nicky Glasses" Marangello, a former underboss, rasp, "Don't be too quick to fill those shoes, Joe."

Joe Pistone's undercover work provided damaging firsthand evidence against the Bonanno gangsters. Leaving the witness box, the agent was stunned by Marangello's naïveté. Referring to him by his pseudonym, Marangello blurted out, "Donnie, how could you do this? You're one of us." Testimony from Pistone and fifty prosecution witnesses convinced the jury to convict the dozen defendants. In January 1987, Rastelli was sentenced to twelve years, and Joe Massino, for the first time in his criminal life, was going to prison. The maximum sentence was ten years.

Shortly after the verdicts, Laura Brevetti, the main prosecutor, got disquieting news about Massino's hidden hostility toward her and of a possible death threat. One of the dozen defense lawyers revealed to her that Massino, resenting the aggressive prosecution, had said under his breath, "I hope she dies of AIDS."

When the verdicts came down, Gotti was the new Gambino boss, and an informer told the FBI that, in an attempt to ingratiate himself with his godfather, a Gambino capo had offered to place contracts on Brevetti and the presiding federal judge at the rackets trial, Eugene Nickerson. Their motive was to avenge the conviction of Gotti's prized friend Joe Massino, and it illustrated that the Gotti-Massino axis was keenly recognized by Gambino stalwarts.

Brevetti was "a little spooked" by the reported threat on her life because she had returned home one evening to find her air conditioners, which she had turned off that morning, were running full throttle. Someone had been in her apartment. Advised by agents to leave town while they investigated further, she vacationed uneasily in Hawaii. Brevetti understood that there was no evidence that Massino knew of the hit plan. The FBI learned that the only gunman willing to take the assignment was Jimmy Hydell. Before Hydell could even plan the hits, in a unrelated development he was tortured to death for trying to kill the Lucchese leader Anthony Casso. Gaspipe had unintentionally eliminated the threat to Brevetti and Judge Nickerson.

Next on the convicted Massino's court calendar was a RICO trial in Manhattan, along with his brother-in-law Sal Vitale. Both were accused of being players in a Mafia "enterprise." The most serious, substantive charges of conspiring in four homicides—the three Bonanno capos and Joseph Do Do Pastore—were leveled only against Massino. The underlying charges against Sal involved joining Massino in two hijackings and obstruction of justice. The chief prosecutor, Michael Chertoff, fresh from his triumph in the Commission case, offered leniency to Massino if he admitted at least one of the murders. Rejecting the deal—a sentence of about twelve years to run concurrently with his ten-year labor racketeering term—Massino decided to risk a trial. It was a gamble that could cost twenty years if he lost.

"He's the Horatio Alger of the Mafia," Chertoff dubbed Massino, attempting to rivet the jury's attention to Massino's importance. The prosecutor sketched Massino's rapid criminal rise, warning the jury that he was destined for Mob stardom unless a guilty verdict derailed him. The government's central witness was hulking muscleman Ray Wean, Massino's former hijacking assistant. Wean ratcheted up the courage to testify against his former capo as the only way to keep himself out of prison. The FBI's Joe Pistone, who was instrumental in convicting Massino in the Local 814 trial, was called upon again as an essential witness corroborating Massino's dominant position in the family.

Ever sociable, Massino found an occasion during a break in the trial to buttonhole Joe Pistone. He wanted to know which actor would portray him in *Donnie Brasco*, a forthcoming movie based on the agent's undercover exploits against the Bonannos. "That's the problem, Joey," Pistone answered. "We're having a hard time finding an actor as fat as you are." The unflappable Massino laughed along with Pistone.

Two RICO-experienced lawyers were at the defense table. Samuel Dawson, who had battled Chertoff in the Commission case, represented Massino. Serving as Vitale's counsel was Bruce Cutler, who had vaulted to legal prominence after obtaining an acquittal for John Gotti in his first jury-tainted racketeering trial. Well versed in the intricacies of the RICO statute, the lawyers counted on a "time-limit" aspect of the law to overcome the prosecution's evidence, regardless of the verdicts.

Their strategy worked. Massino was acquitted of the four murder-conspiracy counts, but the jury voted unanimously that the brothers-in-law were guilty of many of the other crimes. The jurors, however, found that some critical substantive acts (specific crimes) had occurred more than five years before the indictments or ten years apart from each other. Ruling in favor of defense motions, the presiding judge cited a Statute of Limitations requirement and immediately overturned the verdicts. He dismissed all charges on grounds that the crimes, spanning nineteen years, did not fall within RICO's required time period. A technical loophole had won the day for Massino and Vitale.

At the start of the trial, Cutler rhapsodized about Vitale's affection for Massino. "Not only did they grow up together in Brooklyn, not only does he love Joe Massino, not only is he related to Joe Massino through marriage, but he is proud of it, and will show it," he told the jury. The RICO dismissals in June 1987 allowed Sal to celebrate with his lawyers at a Manhattan steak house while Joey, continuing his sentence for labor racketeering, had to be content with prison grub.

Before Massino was shipped off to the federal penitentiary in Talladega, Alabama, to begin his labor-racketeering sentence, Vitale paid him a visit in the Metropolitan Correction Center in Lower Manhattan, the federal detention jail. Brooding over his RICO conviction in the Local 814 Teamsters' case, Massino laid the blame on capo Gabriel Infanti. While Rastelli was in prison in the 1970s and early 1980s, Massino had collected kickbacks that flowed through the local from moving companies. The conduit for the loot was Anthony Giliberti, a convicted stickup man and distant relative of Phil Rastelli, who emerged from prison totally inexperienced in labor affairs, and swiftly became a high-salaried union organizer and business agent. Believing that Giliberti was disobeying orders and might be blabbing to investigators, Massino decreed his death. The contract went to Infanti, and in a drive-by attack on July 14, 1982, Giliberti was shot nine times as he was entering his car. Recovered from his wounds, the union official became the pivotal witness four years later against Massino.

Massino complained to Vitale that Infanti had messed up the Giliberti hit by not requiring the shooters to get out of their car to finish off the victim. He had other grievances against Infanti. The capo had been responsible for disposing of Cesare Bonventre's body, but the dismembered corpse was found stuffed into two barrels and was identified. Finally, Infanti was seen talking and joking with FBI Agent Pat Marshall. In Massino's eyes, that was sufficient evidence that he was a traitor.

Outlining a contract to Vitale, Massino said sharply, "I want it done and I want it done now."

A week before Christmas 1987, Vitale and an accomplice lured Infanti to a Brooklyn warehouse for another of those "routine meetings." Before it began he was shot in the back of the head and killed. The triggerman kept $2,500 that Infanti was carrying. Infanti's body was better concealed than Bonventre's and was never located. In essence, Infanti paid with his life for allowing Giliberti to testify and to send Massino to prison.

Patting itself on the back, the FBI looked with pride at the convictions of the Bonannos' upper crust. The boss, Rastelli, and Massino, who had officially been appointed underboss, were behind bars, and the bureau classified the Bonanno family as crippled and of dwindling importance. Supervisors and agents prepared to move on to larger Mob priorities throughout the late 1980s and early '90s.

Most of Rusty Rastelli's undistinguished reign had been ruinous, producing murderous purges, losses of lucrative rackets, and prison terms for himself, Massino, and other veteran leaders. Earlier, before his long prison sentences, Rastelli had been feared in the Mafia for his deadly rages. His wife, Connie, angered over her husband's infidelities, volunteered information to the FBI about his criminal freebooting. In 1962, soon after talking to the bureau, Mrs. Rastelli disappeared, and investigators believed she was murdered at the behest of Rastelli, although killing a woman, rather than terrifying her into silence, violated the Mafia's code of honor.

In prison for a second lengthy term, and soon stricken with cancer, Rastelli held the titular rank of boss, but his authority in the borgata waned. Not so for Massino; for him prison time was a period for retaining control and planning ahead. He relied on Vitale, promoting him to capo and using him as a transmission belt to maintain command of the borgata's shriveled ranks.

At monthly visits in Talladega, Vitale urged Massino to accept the mantle of leadership, stressing that it was the wish of a majority of the remaining capos. Honoring Cosa Nostra tradition that a boss keeps his title for life, and out of respect for Rastelli's sponsorship of his career, Massino refused to become a godfather while Rusty was alive. Yet, despite his affection for Rastelli, Massino did drop a stinging remark about him in a chat with Vitale. "How smart can he be? He spent half his life in jail."

Vitale became the principal financial caretaker for his imprisoned brother-in-law. Before his conviction, Joe had cut him in on a potpourri of rackets: loan-sharking, bookmaking, video gambling machines—popularly known as Joker Poker—and the extortion of a large catering company that supplied food to roach coaches. Thousands more rolled in weekly from other loot, and Vitale made sure the correct amounts went to his sister, Joe's wife, and their daughters.

"He made me what I am," Vitale told fellow mobsters about his distribution of illegal profits. "It's only right to give him his 50 percent."

Among the reasons for which Vitale had to show his gratitude was a buried secret about his past. Massino had allowed him to be straightened out although he should have been automatically disqualified for Mafia membership for having worked one year as a corrections officer. When wiseguys asked about the rumor that Sal had been a prison guard, Massino had always assured them it was untrue. "I know him all my life," he lied. "He was never a C.O."

Massino counted on Good-Looking Sal and the new consigliere Anthony Spero, based in Brooklyn, to serve as his overseers and keep the remnants of the borgata intact. All his orders and advice were delivered by Sal, who qualified for his prison visitors' list because he was a relative. Massino's basic instructions were: no wiseguys could be made without his consent; no captains should be broken while he was away; and no soldiers could be transferred to different crews during his prison term.

"But never show any weakness to other families, or they'll take advantage of you," Massino lectured Vitale. Another point that he pressed was: "Defend yourselves at all costs." Confident he was doing everything Massino would have wanted, Vitale snapped commands to capos: "This is how Joe wants it done."

Massino also compelled Vitale to stay close to his influential Gambino ally John Gotti, to consult with him at least every two weeks, and take his advice. To retain Gotti's good will, Vitale ordered the murder of Bonanno associate Louis Tuzzio in 1990. Gotti was incensed that Tuzzio, while carrying out a hit for the Bonannos, had accidentally shot and wounded the son of a Gambino soldier. Gotti flexed his muscles and Vitale had to soothe him.

In 1991 and 1992, Vitale acted with greater latitude when his direct line to Massino was severed. Nearing parole eligibility, Massino dropped Vitale from his visitors' list, fearing that the authorities might deny him early release by claiming Sal's visits were used to discuss organized-crime matters. Vitale believed that Massino would still "communicate" important instructions to him, even if the messages were cryptic, through his sister, Josie, who, of course, continued to see her husband.

Cut off from Massino, Vitale decided that as his surrogate he held the power of life and death if an emergency endangered the welfare of the family. He continued collecting payoffs for himself and for Massino, and he exercised the supreme power normally reserved for a boss. He ordered three slayings without Massino's knowledge. On the street, no one questioned Sal's right to the administration's share of loot or to issue contracts for capital punishment. "Everybody knows Sal speaks for Joe," FBI Agent Jack Stubing noted at the time.

Inside his cell in Talladega, Massino could rest assured that his Mob family interests and his financial coffers were safeguarded by Good-Looking Sal. He was ready for a spectacular reign as soon as the prison gates were flung open for him.

57

The Genial Godfather
aka "The Ear"

Rusty Rastelli died of liver cancer at age seventy-three in June 1991. The next year, granted "supervised release" (parole), after serving six years, Joe Massino on his first day of freedom was greeted as a Mafia godfather. Before his parole, Massino instructed Vitale, "If Rastelli dies, make me boss," and Sal had complied. A few days after Rastelli's funeral, consigliere Anthony Spero, following Mafia protocol, convened a meeting of some ten capos in Staten Island at the Dawson Circle home of a captain, Charles "Crazy Charlie" Musillo. Joe Massino, the lone candidate, was elected unanimously.

Mulling over the tactics used by the government in high-echelon RICO cases, Massino returned from prison determined to avoid the mistakes that had struck down other dons. At forty-nine, there was a long tenure ahead of him if he could avoid the pitfalls of RICO. His first move to protect himself and to remodel the family was to close the gang's social clubs; he considered them an open invitation to law enforcement for electronic eavesdropping and surveillance. An incentive for banning the traditional hangouts came shortly before his release. During Massino's imprisonment, Vitale encouraged a central meeting place for members, a one-story building at the rear of an alley next to the Maspeth Public Library on Grand Avenue. Known as the "Grand Avenue Social

Club," it was headquarters for capo Michael "Mickey Bat" Cardello. Vitale frequented the club and began holding large-scale weekly Tuesday feasts there for soldiers from all crews. He was, in fact, imitating Massino's previous weekly get-togethers at the old J&S Club, where wiseguys had come to show their respect to Massino; now, they came to honor Vitale as Massino's highest representative.

The festivities on Grand Avenue were spotted by the FBI, and agents planted a video camera and three bugs in the main room. Although careful inside the club, Cardello and soldiers spoke freely in the alley outside. Their walk-talk conversations were picked up by two bugs ingeniously hidden in the exterior walls and from a tap in a street public telephone booth that the mobsters considered a secure line. To Massino's chagrin, the FBI operation, code-named "Grand Finale," culminated in racketeering convictions of Cardello and seven soldiers and associates shortly before his parole.

Vitale, the FBI's prime objective in Operation Grand Finale, escaped the FBI dragnet. Nevertheless, a fuming Massino excoriated Vitale for sponsoring mass gatherings at the Grand Avenue Club that encouraged FBI penetration and indictments.

Closing the clubs was the prelude to Massino's security program. To insulate himself from potential informants and to evade direct implication in the family's crimes, he decentralized the borgata's structure, creating more secretive cells. A tight cadre of senior capos would each oversee a major activity without knowledge of anyone else's affairs and reporting indirectly to him through Vitale. Despite the contretemps over the Grand Avenue Club debacle, he named Sal underboss, realizing that his help would be indispensable in running the borgata as long as he was himself on supervised release. Massino could be returned to prison anytime in the next two years to complete his sentence if he violated the conditions of his parole. One prohibition was consorting with known criminals and convicted mafiosi. Even though Vitale was suspected of being a made man, he had never been convicted of a Mob-related crime. As close relatives the two men could reasonably justify visiting each other at their homes and meeting at personal family dinners and social events without endangering Massino's freedom. It was a discreet way of conferring without raising the hackles of the parole authorities and would complicate an FBI attempt to establish proof there was an illicit aspect to their association.

Upon returning to Queens in November 1992, Massino did preside at one celebratory session with all his capos in a hotel suite near John F. Kennedy International Airport. He used the occasion to assure the captains of their reappointments and to inform them that while on parole he would transmit orders to them through Vitale. Furthermore, they would continue to funnel cash tributes to him through his brother-in-law.

For added security, he pulled a leaf out of Vincent Chin Gigante's play book, outlawing the use of his surname or his nicknames. Gigante's Genovese battalions tapped or pointed to their chins when referring to him. Massino directed his underlings to touch or point to their ears instead of mentioning his name. Eventually, investigators unearthed Massino's secret command and jokingly tagged him "the Ear." Respectful gangsters in other families nicknamed him "Big Joe," signifying his reputation as a Mafia luminary as well as his 350-pound weight.

Passing along the warning to capos about using Massino's proper name, Vitale was emphatic: "We're only as strong as our boss is to other bosses. We must protect Joe or the family will disintegrate."

Another change ordained by Massino hinted at a touch of vanity. He decided that wiseguys should no longer consider themselves the "Bonanno" clan, the name that had cleaved to the organization for more than sixty years. Henceforth, it would be known among themselves as the Massino borgata. Massino claimed that expunging Joe Bonanno's name was long overdue because his autobiography and television interviews had disgraced the family, exposed Cosa Nostra secrets, and helped convict Commission members in 1986. "Joe Bonanno disrespected the family by ratting," Massino told Vitale. Massino's ego allowed him to overlook the inconsistency of renaming the family in his honor while forbidding the use of his name in conversations.

The new don's fixation with safety prompted him to alter the ritual for inducting members. Concerned that an FBI raid on a ceremony might uncover props for the oath of *omertà*—a saint's card for burning and a knife or gun symbolizing loyalty to the family—he prohibited their use. Vitale, Spero, and capos were authorized to conduct a simplified ceremony after he approved the new member. Those officiating could "make" the recruit without drawing blood from a trigger finger or holding a flaming saint's card. If agents burst in, the mafiosi could claim they were a group of friends playing cards or just spending a social evening together.

Another rigorous security test enforced by Massino was the requirement that a candidate for membership had to have had a working relationship with a made man for at least eight years. He believed it would ensure the reliability of the new soldier and decrease the possibility of another infiltration by the likes of FBI Agent Joe Pistone.

Vitale supervised about twenty ceremonies in homes, stores, factories, and hotel rooms using a new procedure. All participants, the new and old soldiers, rose in a tie-in, a *ticada*, as Vitale intoned, "In the name of the Massino family, we are locked in a network, in secrecy. You're reborn today. Today, you start your new life." After his supervised release was lifted in 1995, Massino attended inductions and proudly informed the new soldiers of the family's unique record among all of the nation's borgatas as the only American clan that had never spawned a stool pigeon or cooperative government witness.

Massino tried to restrict the flow of information, even to capos, on "a need to know basis," to prevent wider leaks if agents recruited informers or eavesdropped electronically on soldiers. Believing that danger lurked in depending upon the reliability of other families, he virtually banned participating in joint projects with them. He pulled a new capo, James Big Louie Tartaglione, off a major Mob committee; "We really have nothing to do with construction unions," Massino said. Capo Anthony Graziano withdrew from the gasoline excise tax scams that generated millions of dollars. "Let's forget it," was Massino's terse explanation.

He entwined his capos in specific areas of the family's rackets to create loyal courtiers and security screens for himself. Each capo would have his own personal fortune at stake, an incentive for vigilance against investigative traps. He also pressured captains and soldiers to volunteer their sons as made men on the theory that they would be more knowledgeable about Cosa Nostra practices and steadfastly loyal. Massino thought by recruiting offspring and placing them in the fathers' crews, the capos' lips would be sealed to protect their sons—and himself. And crew commanders would know that if they became traitors, their sons would be endangered by internal retaliation, possibly death. Massino insured that a defector would have a lot to lose.

Meeting with other godfathers was another bugaboo for Massino. Photographs of dons entering and leaving conferences was excellent circumstantial evidence in the Commission case, and he had no intention of being trapped by cameras. After the Commission convictions, high-powered gatherings were held infrequently, and he sent Vitale or Spero as his understudies.

His long friendship and admiration for John Gotti deteriorated. Gotti's life term in prison began just as Massino's incarceration ended. The newly crowned boss had learned from the Gambino chief's downfall that notoriety only inflamed law enforcement. In a heart-to-heart talk with Vitale, he critiqued

Gotti's flaws, censuring him for violating Cosa Nostra codes and riveting public attention on their previously secret society. "He broke every rule in the book. John destroyed this life. John set us back one hundred years and what he did to Paulie [the murder of boss Paul Castellano] I would never have done." When Gotti died, Massino boycotted his wake and funeral.

Unlike Gotti, Joe Massino preferred anonymity. He wanted to be unknown, his face kept off television news shows and his identity and photograph never emblazoned in newspapers. For that reason, he shunned most Cosa Nostra social events, the wakes, funerals, weddings, and baptismal celebrations of members of his own borgata and hierarchs in other gangs. Avoiding the prying eyes and cameras of investigators, he sent deputies to these Mob events only when respect for Mafia traditions had to be observed.

Up to date on technology, Massino banned the use of mobile phones for Mob matters. He knew that such phones could be monitored as easily as landline telephones. Listening in, law enforcement might identify previously unknown soldiers and gauge the borgata's true strength. He also believed that tiny mobile phones had been employed by the FBI to conceal bugs carried by informers trying to infiltrate the families.

All members were advised to emulate his courtesy when encountering lawmen. From now on, they would act like charm-school graduates, even when badgered by agents and detectives. They could remain reticent, but he disliked belligerent back talk that might incite aggressive investigations.

If a member got into a legal scrape, Massino's regime was ready to lend support. He instituted a war chest, requiring each soldier and capo to kick in $100 a month, and he controlled the fund. As long as an arrest resulted from a borgata-related crime, the family would pay the member's full legal expenses. Collecting the compulsory tax from his crew, Frank Lino observed, "If you have a problem, the boss will help you." Over the years, Massino doled out as much as $150,000 in one criminal case alone.

The Bonannos had always cultivated international Mafia ties, and Massino reestablished a close relationship with the Zips, the Sicilian-born faction in the family, whose specialty was narcotics trafficking. He had brought important Zips from New York and Canada into the Rastelli camp in 1981 to help wipe out the three rebel capos, and he intended to use them again as a secret army, largely unknown to the New York law-enforcement authorities. The family's Zip crew of some twenty soldiers in Montreal, led by Gerlando George-from-Canada Sciascia and Vito Rizzuto, enthusiastically endorsed Massino's ascension.

Rumors that Massino had been installed as a boss were picked up by the FBI. In early 1993, shortly after Massino's exit from prison, Lynn DeVecchio, then the head of the bureau's Colombo-Bonanno Squad, and Jack Stubing, his Bonanno expert, paid an unannounced call on Massino at his two-story white colonnaded house in Howard Beach. Opening the front door, Massino kept the agents outside. Stubing knew Massino was too well schooled to allow them to subtly reconnoiter the interior for a spot to plant a bug.

DeVecchio liked to play "head games," chatting up mafiosi to personally evaluate them and see how they reacted to pressure. There was always the possibility that one of them might slip up and accidentally reveal valuable information. It was also a longshot method of establishing rapport that could pay off if a mobster got into trouble, wanted to cooperate, and needed an FBI contact.

Besides sizing up Massino, the agents' primary purpose for visiting him was to relay a warning to Lefty Guns Ruggiero, the wiseguy who, fifteen years earlier, had been duped by Joe Pistone. The bureau was sure Massino had once tried to whack Ruggiero for his incompetence, but that Lefty Guns had been forgiven and was about to be released from a prison stretch caused by Pistone's evidence. DeVecchio and Stubing advised Massino to warn Ruggiero against retaliating against Pistone or his kin when he returned to Mob life. "Nothing is going to happen, you can sleep on it," Massino said with assurance, in effect confirming that he was in control of the borgata.

Bantering with the agents, Massino apologized to Stubing for having shaken him during a recent car surveillance. It was accidental, he said, not a deliberate dodge, caused by an abrupt turn because he had driven past the spot where he wanted to drop off his wife.

Driving back to their office, the agents knew Massino's pride was at work in demonstrating that he was the equal of the elite FBI. "That guy has a fantastic, encyclopedic memory for cars, license-plate numbers, and anyone who has ever tailed him," DeVecchio commented to Stubing. "He may be cordial and from the old school, but he sure does enjoy showing off how smart and careful he is."

To qualify for parole, Massino had to show a source of legitimate income. He maintained that his chief employment was as a consultant for King Caterers, a Farmingdale, Long Island, company that prepared hot dishes and snacks for roach coach vendors, some of whom, of course, handled bookmaking and loan-sharking as sidelines. Sal Vitale also was listed as having similar employment at the suburban food-preparation plant.

The brothers-in-law had landed their jobs in 1984 when the owners, knowing of the mobster duo's reputation, secretly solicited their help. A Lucchese soldier, Carmine Avellino, owned a similar catering establishment nearby and wanted to take over their successful business. Joe and Sal intervened by putting King Caterers under "protection," preventing further harassment from Avellino, who was heavily outranked by the Bonanno bigwigs. Laundering the payoffs, Joe and Sal created a shell company, Queens Catering, which received one bonus of $300,000 in return for an investment of $50,000, and a monthly fee of $17,500 from King Caterers. While Massino was in prison, Vitale passed along Joe's share to his wife.

Massino appeared at the catering plant once a week, usually passing the time by playing cards. In the event of an investigation, the company's cover story was that in addition to advising on roach coach routes, he prepared a succulent sauce for their products. Scores of trucks, cars, and people meandered in and out of the place on work days, complicating investigators' attempts to keep tabs on men Massino actually met inside the vast one-story building.

Interviewed at the plant by *The New York Times*, a good-humored Massino brushed off allegations that he was the latest godfather. "I don't believe there is such a thing as the Mafia. A bunch of Italian guys go out to eat, and they say it's the Mafia." Protesting that he was "legitimate," Massino said that besides the catering job he earned a living managing real estate properties. "I did my time; I paid my dues," he replied to this author, then a *Times* reporter.

The job at King Caterers was part of Massino's plan to justify to the IRS that he had a legitimate income to support a home valued at $750,000, and the means to acquire real estate in Queens and in Florida and to invest in parking lots in New York. Most of the acquisitions were in his wife's name, and she drew between $9,000 and $17,000 yearly from the lots. Overall, his net worth eventually would top $10 million.

Listings on his tax returns failed to record Massino's illicit income from loan-sharking and gambling, and tribute from crews under his reign. He and Vitale operated a surefire "bank," compelling capos and soldiers to borrow at interest rates of 1.5 percent weekly, which they lent at even higher amounts to their victims. Capos stressed to soldiers in their loan-sharking rings the dire necessity to obtain money and interest owed them on time, because of the compulsory vig payments that went to the administration. No one ever defaulted. "They know better," said Vitale. "How can you not pay your boss and underboss." With

$600,000 on the streets, the weekly vigorish reached $9,000 for Joe and Sal.

All loans were approved by Massino but Vitale supervised the bookkeeping, listing the amounts and payments in a pocket-sized spiral notebook, his shy book. Steady client Frank Lino borrowed $500,000, and over the years repaid about $1 million, a sizable return for the hierarchs.

Sports gambling was handled for Massino by "controllers," professional bookies who split profits fifty-fifty with their leaders. A good week would produce $10,000 to $12,000 for the administration. Massino discontinued baseball wagers in the late 1990s, complaining that he was "getting killed by the Yankees," a team that won consistently for their betting fans in New York.

Easy money for the borgata and the administration poured in through illegal video gambling games, generally called Joker Poker. Placed in cafés, bars, restaurants, pizzerias, Mob social clubs, and even candy and bagel stores, the machines accepted coins and bills up to a $100 limit. Each machine metered winnings and losses, and when finished, a player collected the remaining credit from the proprietor, who split earnings fifty-fifty with the mobster who owned the video game.

The Bonannos and other families in the 1990s offered four types of gambling machines:

Joker Poker, where the player had to draw at least a pair to win;
Cherry Master, a device similar to slot machines in legal casinos;
Eight-Liner, a machine that offered different games of chance, including Black Jack; and
Quarter Horse, in which the player wagered on picking the winner of a race on the screen.

Capo Frank Lino, who was a distributor of dozens of Joker Poker machines, chalked up as much as $40,000 a week in profits. Massino's administration demanded 10 percent of all earnings from video gambling. Calling the payments a "tithe," Lino told a colleague, "I guess the Mafia takes after the church."

An unwritten law required monthly cash "tributes" from Massino family capos and a generous contribution at Christmas. A wealthy captain, Frank Coppa, usually gave $6,500 a month and $20,000 for Christmas; and capo Richard Cantarella forked over $1,500 a month and $25,000 at Yuletide. The Canadian crew sent $15,000 every Christmas. Another generous capo, James "Big Louie" Tartaglione, estimated that in two decades he passed along $150,000 to Massino. Even Vitale kicked in to the boss with $10,000 at Christmas.

It took Massino less than five years to establish himself as New York's and the nation's paramount don, benefiting from the mass convictions that beset the other families in the 1990s. John Gotti (of the Gambinos), Vincent Gigante (of the Genoveses), Vittorio Amuso and Anthony Casso (of the Luccheses), and Carmine Persico and Victor Orena (of the Colombos) had all been swept into prison. Their organizations were fractured, struggling to regroup in 1998. The Bonannos were the exception; their administration was untouched, and Massino filled power vacuums vacated by the imprisoned godfathers. Recovering from the "Donnie Brasco" undercover debacle, when the family's roster had dropped below 100 made men, Massino had brought it up to over 150 in 15 functioning crews. His strict discipline and security strictures appeared to be working. In contrast to the flood of defectors in other borgatas, not a single Bonanno/Massino made man had become a turncoat—a sign of unflinching loyalty to *omertà* and to Big Joe.

The only free full-fledged godfather in New York, Massino's influence enabled him to set general policies for all Mafia families. Confident of his own security and ability to evade surveillance, he called for a rare Commission meeting at an unknown date in late 1999 or early 2000, and agreed to be present. It was attended by the Gambinos' boss Peter Gotti and acting bosses from the three other families. The conference site, chosen with care by Massino, was at the home of a highly trusted Massino soldier, Louis Restivo, in Rego Park, a largely Jewish middle-class Queens neighborhood not frequented by mobsters.

An important agenda item for the Commission was finding a solution to the interminable internal battles for control of the Colombo family. Massino was unable to mediate that thorny issue, explaining afterward to Vitale that the dispute "was too far gone."

The other major topic was replenishing the dwindling borgatas, hard hit by RICO convictions. In addition to quickly replacing dead and retired members, each family would get a bonus every year of two soldiers at Christmas time. A New York Cosa Nostra law requires that the names of all proposed members be vetted by other families. A family has two weeks to raise an objection about the acceptability of another borgata's candidate before the admission ceremony was conducted.

Soon after the Commission meeting, Massino suspected that other families were cheating to pad their ranks more swiftly. They were reusing the names of dead soldiers to expedite inductions and to beef up their strength. The basic size of each family had been rigidly established by Lucky Luciano in the 1930s to prevent one family from becoming too large and sparking Mob rivalries and wars. Determined to abide by the old rules, Massino instructed Vitale to maintain a necrology list to block other borgatas from recycling the names of dead mobsters.

In keeping with his new status as the nation's most secure godfather, Massino became more modish. He filled a closet with hand-stitched, European-styled suits and other clothing crafted by a Bensonhurst tailor to fit his obese frame. Content with mid-sized Fords and Buicks and Cadillacs during his days as a hijacker and capo, he now opted for Mercedes-Benzes.

Always interested in food, he became the behind-the-scenes owner in 1996 of the Casa Blanca Restaurant in Maspeth. Dining there frequently (a light lunch was linguine with sautéed peppers) and in the most open display of his importance, he had no compunction about breaking breadsticks and enjoying heaping plates of veal and pasta with capos and soldiers. Since the restaurant— officially owned by a soldier, Louis Restivo—was a public place, it would be difficult for prosecutors to prove that it was a Mob hangout where criminal activities were discussed.

The Casa Blanca was a blue-collar contrast to the voguish Manhattan nightspots that had been frequented by his former neighbor John Gotti. Indicative of Massino's outer-borough focus, the restaurant was located on a drab commercial street next to a Pep Boys auto supply store. Seating eighty customers in a pseudo-art deco room, bathed in bright neon lights, its most conspicuous motif was adulation of the classic 1942 movie *Casablanca*. A life-size statue of Humphrey Bogart in a white dinner jacket dominated the bistro's entrance, and all its walls were bedecked with posters for the movie and photos of its cast. The door to the men's room bore a picture of Bogart, and the women's room door was graced with the image of the film's costar, Ingrid Bergman. Featuring Sicilian and southern Italian dishes, the menu included a "Bogey Special" brick-oven pizza and, capturing a famous slice of dialogue by Bogart, a "Here's Looking at You, Kid" pizza.

A compulsory dining spot for Massino's mobsters, the restaurant's success allowed him to skim $750 a week from its receipts. To stay in Massino's good graces, soldiers and associates were importuned to hold their parties in the restaurant's adjacent catering hall. "It's the boss's place. Why give your money to anyone else?" capo Richard Cantarella strongly suggested to his crew members when they were planning social events.

Clearly, Massino won the opening skirmishes against the FBI's C-10 Bonanno Squad, which was even unaware of the borgata's name change. Reviewing the campaign in 1998 with other agents, the squad's supervisor, Jack Stubing, estimated that in five years "the Ear" had revived the family through standard Mafia rackets and was opening new frontiers in the 1990s booming stock market. Intelligence reports suggested that some of Massino's capos were Mob pioneers in corrupting brokerage firms, mainly by loan-sharking to high-living employees in financial straits. "They get a victim on the hook and put his talents to use in pump-and-dump and other schemes," Stubing told a new squad agent, Nora Conley. "They're getting stronger rather than weaker."

Stubing had tried every trick in his bag to crack Massino's defenses. Searching for an unorthodox approach, Stubing floated an idea to Kevin Donovan, the agent in charge of the entire Organized Crime Division in New York. He wanted to borrow forensic accountants, agents used for white-collar business and stock-fraud cases, whom the bureau had never considered particularly useful for initiating Mob investigations. Instead of "facing him head-on," Stubing thought accountants might get to Massino through a flanking maneuver: scrutinizing records of Massino's and Vitale's underlings, who were minting money for them. Stubing's plan was to pinpoint associates and others suspected of arranging the family's money-laundering schemes, or who were themselves extortion victims. All were potential weak links and likely to fear long prison terms if they were nabbed on financial crimes. A little pressure from threatened tax-evasion or RICO indictments might persuade these moneymakers and victims to cooperate, wear wires, and allow their phones to be tapped for incriminating evidence against Massino and his top commanders. It was a long-range gamble to construct a case methodically, inch by inch, tracing how loot flowed to Joe and Sal.

"It's impossible to change records in the banking system," Stubing told Donovan. "If we had someone who knows what to look for, where the money is going, and how it got there, we might unlock Massino's empire."

Stubing knew that regular Mafia agents had no training to decipher financial records, and he was counting on a relatively new species of forensic accountant to duplicate for his squad the successes they were achieving in embezzlement and fraud investigations. "The wiseguys can lie and cheat but bank records don't change," Stubing stressed to Donovan.

Stubing got his reinforcements, two young agents who were tyros when it came to pursuing Cosa Nostra despots but were qualified certified public accountants. The first was Jeffrey Sallet, a cheerful twenty-nine-year-old with a photographic memory for details, who had been with the bureau less than two years before plunging into the Massino investigation in mid-1998. Raised in a Boston suburb, Sallet had been inspired to become a G-Man by his uncle's compelling stories about his adventures as a Treasury Department investigator.

Next on board in March 1999, was raven-haired Kimberly McCaffrey, barely five-feet tall yet seemingly indefatigable at age twenty-six, with a year's experience as an agent. A Junior Olympics medal holder, she won a gymnastic scholarship at Towsend University in Maryland. Joining the Bonanno Squad, her knowledge about the Mafia was limited to her reading as a teenager in northern New Jersey about John Gotti's career and his ability to beat convictions. "I couldn't understand why he was on the street and not in jail," she later told friends. "It gave me the idea that someday I'd use my skills to combat the Mob."

Quickly pleased with his two forensic accountant agents, Stubing reported to Donovan, "They can look at a box of checks and records and instantly recognize patterns of laundering and tax evasion. It's something none of the rest of us can do."

Across the East River from FBI headquarters, where the two accountants were toiling to construct a paper trail to Massino, a more conventional police effort was enveloping the borgata's "Old Man," consigliere Anthony Spero. Unrelated to Stubing's master plan, a three-year police and federal Drug Enforcement Administration (DEA) investigation in Brooklyn had pinned murder and racketeering charges on Spero in 1999. The counselor's troubles arose from the Mafia's chronic pitfall: associating with narcotics dealers.

Spero had long operated out of a south Brooklyn Italian-American section, Bath Beach and Bensonhurst, where he ran the Big Apple Car Service as a cover. He was famous in the neighborhood for his skill at tending pigeon flocks from a rooftop and cashing in on the Joker Poker craze by manufacturing and distributing the illicit video gambling games in Brooklyn and Queens. Out of respect for Spero's loyalty, experience, and age, Massino had granted him an exemption to the social club ban, allowing him to maintain a neighborhood hangout, the West End Social Club, next to his livery company. A gang of young trigger-happy wannabes, "the Bath Avenue Boys," admirers of the legendary Spero, made the club their second home, carrying out assignments—

robberies, assaults, and murders—on orders from the consigliere's henchmen, never directly from him. One homicide victim was a junkie who made the mistake of burgling Spero's daughter's home.

Deeply immersed in the narcotics trade, ranging from sales of kilos to pushing "dime" ($10) bags of cocaine on the streets, nineteen Bath Avenue Boys were caught by the police and the Drug Enforcement Administration. A thuggish bunch, the boys relied on blowtorches and baseball bats to discipline anyone suspected of cheating them. Once in custody, many of the tough guys were stricken with loose lips, implicating Spero and his chief dispenser of orders, Joseph "J.B." Benanti, a made man. A decade earlier, when William Vanderland, an FBI agent, promised Spero, who had never served a long prison stretch, that he would get him, the veteran mobster replied crisply, "I can handle it." Listening in 2001 to the guilty verdict for heading a RICO enterprise, Spero's face reddened at the unimaginable news of a life sentence at age seventy-two, a conviction based entirely on circumstantial evidence, without direct testimony that he specifically had ordered the commission of any crime.

Afterward James Walden, the lead federal prosecutor at Spero's trial, acknowledged that investigators "searched and hoped for evidence to entangle Massino" but were unable to find a shred against him. "The other families were in mass confusion but it looked as if Massino had shored up his internal structure," Walden said.

Spero's difficulties heightened Massino's dread of being implicated by loose talk picked up by a wired informer or through a telephone tap. Previously, he had felt safe in walk-talks on streets and hushed conversations with Vitale and a handful of capos in the Casa Blanca. Before the start of Spero's trial in 2001, he stepped up vigilance by leaving the country for supersensitive discussions with trusted capos. He appointed them to temporarily take over the consigliere's duties by serving on a panel, his version of an executive committee. Massino was confident American law-enforcement agents could not pursue him abroad. In a relaxed atmosphere away from the threat of surveillance, he educated his warlords on their new responsibilities. The mobsters usually were accompanied by their wives, a ploy which helped camouflage the excursions as innocent tourist vacations. Capo Frank Coppa, who previously had lavished jewelry and a fur coat on his godfather, picked up the entire tab for a jaunt to France and Monte Carlo with Massino and their wives. Massino reciprocated in Paris by giving a gift of rosary beads to Coppa.

Another capo, widely considered in the family as the acting consigliere, Anthony Graziano traveled with his wife, Ronnie, and the Massinos to Mexico. Known as "T.G.," Graziano, in his early sixties, was a cash cow for the administration; heading a crew in Staten Island and Brooklyn that was a prolific distributor of cocaine; conducting a loan-sharking business with $500,000 on the streets; and operating a vast stock of illegal Joker Poker videos. T.G.'s crew was notorious for its savagery, singeing victims with cigarette lighters and dragging a slow-paying loan-shark client by a noose around his neck. Widening his horizons, Graziano opened a boiler-room shop in Florida to exploit the 1990s economic upswing by engaging in stock and telemarketing swindles. Returning from Mexico after a private interlude with his godfather, a nostalgic Graziano lined the walls of his Staten Island game room with photos of the smiling Massino and Graziano couples touring Mexico. The pictures were placed next to his prized collection of stuffed animal heads.

Airline records and videotapes of Massino and Graziano arriving at Newark Liberty International Airport from Mexico confirmed for the FBI the cozy relationship between Massino and Graziano. Agents suspected that Graziano had been promoted to replace Spero and that he was being briefed on his new duties during the overseas trips. They also observed Graziano emerging with Massino from the office of a doctor treating Massino for diabetes, another place the two men might feel secure to review mutual Mob enterprises.

Learning from an informer that at least three of Graziano's associates would deliver Christmas "tributes" to him, agents obtained a warrant to frisk him upon leaving the Bistro, a Staten Island restaurant, in December 2001. Disregarding Massino's edict on courtesy, Graziano growled at the agents, Joseph Bonavolonta (the son of retired FBI Mafia investigations supervisor Jules Bonavolonta) and Gregory Massa: "Why the fuck are you bothering me? Why aren't you out looking for bin Laden?" Rather than argue with the irate gangster, the agents confiscated as possible evidence of illegal payoffs more than $5,000 packed into a bulging envelope which was marked *"Buono Natale"* [sic]—Merry Christmas in Italian. Another $1,292 was found in his pockets. Reporting the harassment to Vitale, T.G. was relieved that he was not carrying twenty-five other envelopes containing thousands of dollars from soldiers and associates.

Massino's regard for Graziano was so strong that he was willing to protect him by killing a former ally and a highly respected capo, Gerlando "George-from-Canada" Sciascia. Sciascia, had played a vital role in Massino's extermination of the three rival capos in 1981, and had supported his takeover of the family when he came out of prison a decade later. A wealthy Sicilian-born international heroin trafficker, Sciascia operated in the United States and Canada and headed the family's Montreal crew. After being acquitted in Brooklyn on federal charges of conspiring with the Gambinos' Gene Gotti in a drug deal, Sciascia returned to Canada but was soon deported as an undesirable alien. Allowed to enter America in 1997, he moved into a fashionable apartment on Manhattan's East Side, remaining the long-distance manager of the Montreal faction and continuing to oversee drug deals.

Obviously trusted by Massino, he was put on a committee to undertake some of the duties consigliere Anthony Spero had to give up after his indictment. Working with Graziano, Sciascia grew concerned that T.G. was unreliable, often dipping into his own cocaine supplies. "Every time I see this guy he's stoned," Sciascia complained, urging Sal Vitale to report the situation to Massino. Swearing "on my children's eyes," Graziano denied to Massino that he was snorting coke, insisting that the only drug he took was "stomach medicine."

Massino settled the dispute between the two capos in March 1999. At the twenty-fifth wedding anniversary party of Vitale's nephew, Massino pulled aside his underboss. "George has got to go," Vitale recalls Massino telling him as they sat alone at a table in the Amici Restaurant in Hempstead, Long Island. Leaving the next morning for a holiday week in Cancun, Mexico, to establish an alibi, Massino wanted Sciascia whacked while he was away.

Following instructions, Vitale placed the contract with capo Patrick "Patty-from-the-Bronx" DeFilippo and soldier John "Johnny Joe" Spirito. Vitale supplied DeFilippo with a pistol and a silencer for the job, and Patty later gave him the details of the hit. In Vitale's account, DeFilippo had an "ongoing beef" with the sixty-five-year-old Sciascia and arranged to meet him on the evening of March 18, 1999, for a sit-down. To set up Sciascia, DeFillippo lied that they would rendezvous with another mobster who would referee their quarrel. With Spirito at the wheel, DeFilippo picked up Sciascia near his Manhattan apartment. During the ride, DeFilippo, sitting next to Sciascia, allegedly riddled him with bullets in the head and torso, and dumped the body on a dead-end street in the Bronx. Vitale circulated a story among capos that the crime was unsanctioned and unrelated to the Massino administration, and appeared to be a hit relating to a private narcotics deal. The smoke screen was intended to prevent Sciascia's Canadian crew of Zips from retaliating against Massino.

To mislead the Canadians and the rest of the family, Massino spread the word to his capos that the administration was searching for the killers. He ordered a huge turnout of more than forty wiseguys at Sciascia's wake to flaunt his pretended grief and respect for the slain capo. DeFilippo, the reputed assassin, attended, but Massino maintained his policy of avoiding gatherings that attracted law-enforcement photographers. Soon afterward Massino apparently expressed to two favored captains his true feeling that Sciascia deserved to die. "It served him right for telling me how to run the family," he remarked to Richie Cantarella. "That'll teach him to talk about my capos." Another clue about the motive for Sciacia's slaying came from Frank Coppa, to whom Massino admitted his displeasure that George-from-Canada "wanted to get rid of T.G." or "hurt him."

At a meeting in a Howard Beach diner, Vitale informed Massino that the car in which Sciascia had been shot had to be destroyed because the bloodstains could not be removed from the upholstery. "Poor George, he must have bled to death," Massino said lightly, adding that the family treasury would reimburse Johnny Joe Spirito for the loss of the vehicle. As a personal reward for Spirito, Massino cited the hit on George sufficient reason for straightening him out, inducting him, according to Vitale. The godfather considered it "a piece of work" well done.

58

Mafia Groupies

Joe Massino became a frequent world traveler—for security reasons. His overseas journeys, however, failed to secure his carefully constructed protective walls. Three years of poring over financial records were gradually producing dividends for Jack Stubing's forensic accounting sleuths, Jeffrey Sallet and Kimberly McCaffrey. Early on, they had singled out Sal Vitale as a "key guy" because of his long service as Massino's indispensable right hand, and in 2001, he was in their net. Having grown rich as the family's number-two man, Vitale had moved from modest Howard Beach—where Massino still lived—to tony Dix Hills in Long Island. Separating from his wife, Diana, he moved again in 1998 to a $400,000 town house in Syosset, another upscale Long Island town. The Long Island suburbs served both as his home and as a fertile ground for an unusual gambling and loan-sharking syndicate that converted a bank into a Mob annex and launderette.

With help from Suffolk County detectives investigating illegal gambling and a tip from an informer in an unrelated case, McCaffrey and Sallet discovered that Vitale and several associates in a makeshift crew were exceptionally well treated at a branch of the European American Bank in Melville, Long Island. Examining the bank's records, the agents noticed numerous convoluted deposits, withdrawals, and transfers slightly below $10,000. Banks are required to submit detailed forms—Currency Transaction Reports—to the Treasury Department for transfers over $10,000. It is a means of uncovering patterns of money laundering and tax evasion, known as "structuring." The two agents traced a spate of transactions just below the $10,000 cutoff to Vitale and his Long Island accomplices. Over five years, the underboss and henchmen filtered a sizable amount through that one branch bank.

The investigation picked up steam when loan-sharking and gambling victims, tracked down by the FBI and Suffolk County detectives, agreed to cooperate. They told of meetings with Vitale's enforcers in a conference room at the bank, where Vitale's goons were transacting loan-sharking business. While regular bank customers dealt with tellers, mobsters were in a back room threatening their own clients. Gambino associate Vincent "Vinny D" DeCongilio, who also laundered money through the bank, was particularly feared for punishing delinquent debtors by bashing them with his cane.

Vitale and six associates, including the bank's manager, were corralled in November 2001, on racketeering-enterprise charges. Earlier, another employee who had been paid off for turning the branch into a Mob mall, cooperated in exposing the mobsters' grip on the branch. Released on $500,000 bail and facing twenty years for racketeering, loan-sharking, and money laundering, Vitale, who had never spent a single hour in jail, began negotiating. His guilty plea and admission to collecting one-quarter of the crew's profits, resulted in the probability of a sharply reduced sentence of forty-five months. Awaiting formal sentencing, he was placed under house arrest through electronic monitoring of his movements. The sentence delay was caused partly by Vitale's request to be placed in a prison substance-abuse program, claiming he was an alcoholic. There is no evidence that he had ever been a heavy drinker, but the program would make prison life easier and shorten his incarceration by one full year. Following Vitale's lead, the bank manager and four other crew members "copped out," to wangle shorter sentences.

Ironically, the investigation of Vitale occurred as his relationship to Massino was withering. Beginning in the mid-1990s, Massino gradually stripped Sal of authority, relying more on the capos he had placed on panels to oversee the borgata's daily operations and channel his loot to him. Vitale was allowed to retain his underboss title and participate with Massino in their old projects, mainly loan-sharking, gambling, and shake-downs of King Catering. Massino's cold explanation to Vitale for the demotion was that rank-and-file capos and soldiers "detest you." Virtually banished, Vitale was even prohibited from appearing at the Casa Blanca, where every capo was welcomed at Massino's table in the restaurant.

Indignant at being shelved and turned into an outcast, Vitale was powerless to resist. Seething, he complained that Massino had sharply cut his illegal revenues by driving a wedge between him and the rest of the family. "There was nothing I wouldn't have done for the man," Vitale whined to a capo who still talked to him. "He's taken the captains away from me; they aren't allowed to call me; they aren't allowed to give me Christmas presents."

Massino gave Richard Cantarella and Frank Coppa his reasons for ostracizing Vitale: he was incensed at "the way Sal carried himself," acting "like a big shot." Over the years, Massino said, his underboss had become too haughty and vain, encouraging the use of the nicknames "Good-Looking" and "Handsome Sal." Massino thought his brother-in-law was cloning John Gotti's expansive personality, trying to dress modishly, and having his hair coifed by stylists. A sign that Massino saw as incipient disloyalty was Vitale's refusal to encourage any of his four sons to join the crime family. The sons of Frank Coppa, Frank Lino, Richard Cantarella, and other capos had enlisted as soldiers.

Vitale continued to deliver plunder to Massino from their long-established mutual enterprises and saw him at social events involving their personal families. Denied financial support from the borgata's capos, the underboss struck out on his own, developing new rackets in Long Island. Distance failed to assuage Massino's hostility toward him. "Watch yourself, Joe's not too pleased with you," Jimmy Galante, a soldier and nephew of the slain Carmine Galante, warned the pariah underboss. Frank Coppa, who was in Massino's inner circle, advised Sal of the boss's continued animosity: "Be careful, stay in Long Island, and make yourself scarce."

Vitale believed he had redeemed himself when Massino gave him the contract on George-from-Canada. "When he needs a shooter, he calls on me," Vitale thought to himself. That hope was short-lived, and his guilty plea in the Long Island RICO case only heightened Massino's distrust of him. Massino unlocked the family's war chest to pay $50,000 of Vitale's legal fees, but he wondered if a relatively short sentence of less than four years meant that he might be squealing. Discussing Vitale's situation with Coppa, Massino said, "We did seven pieces of work together," an acknowledgment that Vitale could implicate him in seven gangland murders. Shaping his hand as if it were a gun, Massino added that he was sparing Sal because he was his brother-in-law. "Otherwise, I'd take him out."

Equally bitter, Vitale believed he had been abandoned by Massino and the family after his arrest. He lamented that, except for one soldier, no one from the borgata had visited or called him when he was hospitalized with a mild heart attack. "I didn't get no support from the men," he grumbled to a friend as he waited to begin his sentence. "My wife and kids are going to be left in the street." It was an odd complaint since he had almost $500,000 in hidden cash, several million dollars in real estate holdings, and was estranged from his wife.

The next major trophy collected by the Bonanno Squad was Anthony T.G. Graziano. He was accused in 2002, on twin New York and Florida indictments for racketeering, murder conspiracy, extortion, fraud, drug trafficking, and an $11 million swindle. Facing insurmountable evidence, Graziano threw in the towel, pleaded guilty, and received an eleven-year sentence. Convicted with him was most of his crew, a dozen soldiers and associates. The agent accountants had a marginal part in capturing Graziano; much of the evidence had been spawned by the Bath Avenue Boys, the plug-uglies and narcotics peddlers who helped sink the consigliere Anthony Spero. The garrulous boys had worked as musclemen on drug deals for Graziano and Spero's crews. After implicating Spero, they gave the FBI leads to Graziano's criminal escapades and were willing to testify against him, dickering for lenient sentences.

The stock market bubble in the 1990s was a golden opportunity for Mafia pillaging, and Massino's capos were among the early buccaneers. Like Graziano, Frank Coppa and Frank Lino saw that the public's feverish greed offered pickings just as easy as loan-sharking and illegal gambling. Coppa, the first to branch out into high finance, had been profiting as a mobster since he was made by Carmine Galante in 1977. Under the illusion that Lilo was the Bonanno boss, Coppa was startled to learn differently after his assassination. Considering himself "an earner, a con man, not a killer," Coppa nevertheless participated in two murders and ingratiated himself with Massino by assisting Lino in whacking Sonny Black Napolitano.

A loan shark with clients in small brokerage firms, Coppa comprehended that "Wall Street likes muscle and wants to do deals with the Mafia." His Mob status gave him ground-floor entry to pump-and-dump swindles engineered at two brokerage houses. "Buy cheap and create demand" was his formula for churning out hundreds of thousands of dollars of easy money. With $2 million in cash and gold, much of it hidden in safe deposit boxes, he was proud of his underworld reputation as a "high liver," owner of luxurious homes in New Jersey and in Florida. By his mid-fifties, Coppa's extravagant lifestyle, including cocaine sprees and trencherman meals, had altered his once solid six-foot-two soldier's frame into that of an aging, potbellied mobster.

Caught for tax evasion in 1992, Coppa had a hard time adjusting to prison; it was his first felony conviction. He burst into tears at the start of a two-year sentence in a minimum-security institution. Released from prison in 1994, he reverted to his old ways as a prodigious money producer for Massino, who spurred his success by making him a captain and, at one point, giving him four crews to supervise.

The combined efforts of the Bonanno Squad and stepped-up government vigilance against Mafia intrusions in the financial markets ended Coppa's Wall Street gambols. In the spring of 2002, he was again convicted, this time for stock frauds, and sentenced to three years.

Coppa's early success in red-hot Wall Street motivated his long-time Mob colleague Frank Lino to emulate him. The two men had palled around and committed crimes together since they were teenagers in Brooklyn's Bensonhurst and Gravesend sections. Lino auditioned as a wannabe with the Genovese, Colombo, and Gambino families before Coppa informed him that the Bonannos were eager for recruits. Recognized in Mafia environs for having withstood a savage police beating rather than rat out a cop-killer fugitive, Lino was accepted by the Bonanno faction headed by Sonny Red Indelicato. Nicknamed "Blinkie" because of the eye disorder caused by police bashings, Lino was straightened out on a date he always remembered: October 30, 1977, his thirty-ninth birthday.

A committed Massino supporter after the three capos' murders, Lino made millions for himself and the administration through loan-sharking, credit card thefts, bookmaking, and Joker Poker. A rapid blink, a pixiesh smile, and a soft voice belied Lino's feral persona. On behalf of the administration, he participated in six murders, including hits on capos Sonny Black Napolitano and Gabe Infanti, although he was never known to have squeezed the trigger. Before Massino closed down the family's street clubs, Lino sponsored one in Gravesend with a title that was something of an oxymoron for a Cosa Nostra hangout—the Mother Cabrini Social Club, named for a nun who aided Italian immigrants and was the first United States citizen to be canonized.

Lino's record for escaping prison sentences despite four convictions over a forty-year period was shattered in 1997 by the government's crackdown on stock manipulations. Massino paid $75,000 for legal bills, but Lino was convicted of pumping-and-dumping frauds, plus extortion, and sentenced to fifty-seven months in a federal penitentiary. Almost totally ignorant of the basic stock market vocabulary, like "Initial Public Offerings" or "selling long or short," Lino was incapable of originating financial trickery by himself. He relied on Coppa's advice and his intimidation of brokers to cash in. A defense lawyer's comment that Lino was a stock market dunce was truthful: "My client doesn't know where Wall Street is."

The removal of Lino, Coppa, Graziano, and even the downgraded Vitale created gaps in Massino's chain of command, but his defenses against indictment seemed as impervious as ever. None of the charges against his underboss and capos implicated him, and he had a candidate ready to temporarily fill in as acting underboss. His choice as prime liaison to captains and important soldiers, and his continued bulwark against dreaded arrest, was Richard Cantarella.

Cantarella got an early start in the Mafia through Al Walker Embarrato who was his uncle. The soldier-capo Embarrato introduced his nephew, while in his teens, to wiseguy society and culture by taking him to social activities at storefront hangouts, and to wakes and funerals. These were opportunities for a bright wannabe to pick up pointers on Cosa Nostra protocol and to learn from his uncle how crooked compacts were arranged.

Mobsters are quick to apply nicknames, and the newcomer got stuck with a crude one, "Shellackhead," for his heavily pomaded hair, but it did not impede his progress. Through his Bonanno connections, Richie learned that by bribing a city official in the NYC Department of Marine and Aviation, Enrico "Rick" Mazzeo, he could lease news and snack stands at the Staten Island Ferry terminals. The concessions were guaranteed moneymakers, and Cantarella increased his take by using them for bookmaking purposes. Uncle Al, the borgata's powerhouse at the *New York Post*, also supplied him with a no-show union job as a "tail man," a helper on a newspaper delivery truck. The phony employment at the *Post* was an organized-crime entitlement for knowing the right people. Cantarella got a weekly pay check of $800, plus medical and welfare benefits, while he paid a substitute $300 to haul around and drop off bundles of newspapers.

An obedient Mob protégé of Uncle Al, Cantarella was the getaway driver for the hit in 1982 on his cousin Tony Mirra, who suffered the extreme penalty for vouching for FBI agent Joe Pistone. Four years later, Cantarella supervised a homicide in his own behalf. Caught on corruption charges, Rick Mazzeo, the former city official, was home from prison but jobless and frequently high on drugs. Taking no chances that Mazzeo might turn into a songbird, Cantarella invited him out one evening, and shot him in the back of the head as they walked through a deserted garage. Cantarella's cousin, Joey D'Amico, who had been the triggerman in the hit on their cousin Tony Mirra, was along for the homicide, and also plugged Mazzeo in the head. Joey collaborated in the gunplay as a sign of underworld camaraderie and solidarity with Richie, even though it was a hit unauthorized by the administration.

Advancing along the usual mobster highway of loan-sharking and gambling, Cantarella fell into disfavor with Uncle Al, who blocked his induction as a mafioso. A capo with influence, Embarrato thought Cantarella was engaged in too many deals with a Gambino soldier, Joseph Joe Butch Corrao, to the detriment of the Bonanno borgata. The ill will became so heated that Richie contemplated killing his uncle. Joe Massino solved the problem, intervening from prison in Talladega, ordering Cantarella's acceptance into the Honorable Society.

The new button man was straightened out in July 1990, just as the Manhattan district attorney's office began looking into the Bonanno cesspool at the *Post*. At the time, the *Post*'s plant was in Lower Manhattan on South Street, near Bonanno country, where many of them lived, congregated in social clubs, and drank at the infamous Holiday Bar. The Bonannos' control of delivery jobs and their associated rackets at the newspaper had been an open secret among union reformers for years.

By brute force in the newspaper drivers' union, and with Embarrato on duty as a foreman, the Bonannos dispensed no-show sinecures through the newspaper's delivery system. The perks were handed out to Cantarella, D'Amico, one of Vitale's sons, and a dozen other wiseguys and their relatives. On the newspaper's management side, Bonanno associate Robert Perrino, the *Post*'s superintendent of delivery, worked in tandem with the borgata. Perrino, the son-in-law of Nicky Marangello, the family's former underboss, got a cut from loan-sharking, drug sales, and gun-running activities that thrived on the loading docks under the protection of the Bonannos. He profited sufficiently to kick back $500 to $600 a month to Massino and Vitale.

By 1992 the DA's investigation was hot enough for Vitale and Cantarella to learn about grand jury subpoenas of the *Post*'s employment records and more ominous news that conversations in Perrino's office had been bugged and videotaped. Goldie Leisenheimer, who also had a *Post* delivery job, heard that Perrino "is knocking and badmouthing a lot of people," and muttering, "I'm not taking the fall by myself."

Labeling Perrino weak and untrustworthy, and without consulting Massino, who was still in prison, Sal Vitale issued the contract to end Perrino's life. "He's going bad and can do a lot of damage to the family," Vitale explained to Cantarella and other mafiosi who were accessories in the planned hit.

Cantarella's son Paul helped scout out places where Perrino could be abducted for a fatal ride. Changing plans, Vitale and Cantarella duped Perrino into attending a strategy meeting at a family club in Bensonhurst on the night of May 5, 1992. He was never again seen alive. Frank Lino provided part of the hit team that finished off Perrino and buried him. (The body was found eleven years later, under a layer of concrete in an abandoned Staten Island auto-repair shop. He had been shot several times in the head.) To establish an alibi in case anything went wrong on the night of the murder, Cantarella and his son and their wives made certain they were conspicuous at a lengthy dinner in Staten Island's Marina Restaurant.

Perrino's death and the loss of testimony he might have offered hampered the DA's investigation into the Bonanno rackets. Nevertheless, the inquiry turned up evidence to prove that with the help of mobsters, *Post* officials were dumping newspapers into the East River, incorporating them into the paper's circulation statistics, and thereby boosting advertising rates. A month after Perrino disappeared, he was indicted in Manhattan on state racketeering charges. Two other *Post* officials pleaded guilty to having falsified circulation figures and were placed on probation in lieu of imprisonment.

Only one mobster got jail time—Richard Cantarella. He was tripped up by payroll records and surveillance proving he was never at work. Getting off easy, he pleaded to grand larceny, in effect admitting the no-show job, and spent nine months close to home in a Rikers Island dormitory prison on the East River. Uncle Al Embarrato, then in his mid-eighties, also copped a plea; because of his age he got probation instead of jail time.

His prison term over, Cantarella resumed his soldier's life more vigorously under the aegis of Joe Massino, who also had completed his sentence. Teaming with his capo, Frank Coppa, Cantarella became a force and big-time earner from gambling, loan-sharking, and extortions. In the early 1980s, Cantarella widened his Mafia and financial horizons by carving out a new racket: the parking lot business. He answered an advertisement, acquired a lease on a Manhattan lot, and met a future business partner and sycophant, Barry Weinberg.

Weinberg had been in the parking business since he was a teenager and it had made him rich. He operated several lots, but his wealth was based essentially on brokering, obtaining leases on properties and then transferring the leases at sizable profits. Raised in a Jewish family in Brooklyn's middle-class Sheepshead Bay neighborhood, Weinberg was consumed with myths about the Mafia, longing to be accepted as a friend by organized-crime tough guys. A heavy gambler as well as a sharp businessman, Weinberg, in his mid-thirties when he met Cantarella, was immediately drawn to him. Delighted at being allowed into the select society and criminal ambiance of an authentic gangster, Weinberg taught Cantarella the basic steps for mining gold from parking lots. For decades, unscrupulous lot owners in New York found numerous ways to enlarge profits by "skimming" taxes added to parking fees. Since customers paid cash on the barrelhead when they retrieved their vehicles, and record-keeping was spotty, it was difficult for city and state tax collectors to accurately determine the volume of business and the revenues due the government. The parking-lot industry frauds mounted into millions of dollars in the 1980s and '90s, according to later analyses by state auditors.

Aided by Weinberg, Cantarella began operating lots in Manhattan, some in Little Italy. Whenever troubled by nearby competitors, Cantarella called on his thugs to intimidate them into paying for protection to stay open or forcing them to close. One tactic against recalcitrant rivals was to burn down the attendants' flimsy outdoor office and vandalize their lots. "This is the Mafia, I don't care," Cantarella once snapped when a wannabe asked about his reliance on beatings and arson.

By going "on record" under Cantarella, Weinberg saw financial benefits for himself. He believed associating with a mobster increased his prestige and power in negotiating deals because other businessmen feared that the Mafia was behind him. A chain-smoker and machine-gun-style talker, Weinberg saw another asset from his obsequious alliance with Cantarella. Twice-married, the father of four, balding, round-shouldered, and middle-aged, he was certain that the Mafia aura extended to him and attracted women.

An ostentatious spender, Weinberg drove prestigious autos—a convertible red Rolls-Royce, a Bentley, and Mercedez-Benzes. The wiseguys knew that he kept pocket money and ready cash of as much as $60,000 in the trunk of his car. By the late 1990s, Cantarella made his daily headquarters at a Little Italy restaurant, Da Nico, on Mulberry Street, which was owned by reputed Bonanno soldier Perry Criscitelli. Also attracted to Little Italy, Weinberg met frequently in the neighborhood with Cantarella and with mafiosi from the Bonanno and Gambino borgatas. An investor in restaurants, Weinberg became a partner in Dixie Rose, a Mulberry Street café, but spent more time a block away at Da Nico.

The relationship with mafiosi must have been titillating for Weinberg although there was a price to be paid for the adventure. Considering himself entitled to a share of Weinberg's businesses, Cantarella demanded a stream of payoffs, and he eventually siphoned $800,000 from Weinberg. Oddly, Weinberg supplied much of what the criminal code classifies as extortion by writing checks, sometimes laundered through a third party who passed the money along to Cantarella. Trying to conceal the reason for the extortion or tribute, Weinberg labeled the checks as "loans," in the naive belief that the practice made them appear legal.

Showing off his Mob connections, Weinberg in 1999 brought another businessman and Mafia devotee, Augustino Scozzari, into Cantarella's orbit. A native Italian, Scozzari immigrated to the United States after his construction company failed in Germany, where he had grown up. A heavyset, portly man in his mid-forties, Scozzari was steered by New York relatives to the purchase of Theresa's, a Little Italy restaurant. He changed the name of the restaurant on Mulberry Street to Due Amici (Two Friends), and he met Weinberg while he was looking for similar investments in the restaurant field. Weinberg unofficially brokered the sale to him of Cuccina Bene (Good Kitchen), a small Italian takeout-style restaurant on Exchange Place in New York's financial district. Having studied numerous books about the Mafia, Scozzari was captivated by the subject and overwhelmed by Weinberg's offer to bring him into Cantarella's sphere. Before long, Scozzari was used by Cantarella as an intermediary to help launder payoffs from his financial pigeon, Weinberg. Gradually, Cantarella built up trust in Scozzari, holding private conversations with him about the nuances of the Honorable Society, and introducing him to Joe Massino at a party. Seemingly grateful to be enveloped in Cantarella's roguish lifestyle, both Weinberg and Scozzari could be classified as "Mafia groupies," never balking at bending the law on his behalf.

While the two semilegitimate business associates were endearing themselves to Cantarella, he was looking out for Massino's interests. As part of his contributions to the administration, in the early 1990s he cut Massino and Vitale (before Sal's break with Massino) into the parking-lot bonanza. The arrangements listed Josephine Massino and Sal Vitale as partners in three properties, and the boss and underboss cited the investments as proof of legitimate income in joint tax filings with their wives.

Complying with Massino's plan to strengthen the family by inducting sons, Cantarella enhanced his relationship with the boss by sponsoring his son Paul as a soldier. Massino honored the Cantarellas by officiating at Paul's induction and explaining the traditional do's and don'ts to the newcomer. Showing his growing regard for Cantarella, starting in 1996 Massino invited him to dine weekly at the Casa Blanca. Their intimacy included exchanging license-plate numbers of law-enforcement cars that might be tailing them.

Cantarella became more indebted to Massino when he named him a captain with his, own crew in 1999, and appointed him to the select committees that supervised the borgata. Confident of Cantarella's fealty, Massino gave him details of top-secret communications with the heads of other families and insight into memorable murders. He also reminisced about his numerous accomplishments for Rastelli, advertising himself as having been a "one-man army" for the previous boss. Reviewing the massacre of the three capos, Massino told Cantarella that the hits occurred in "close quarters," an implied admission that he had been present. Raising the subject of Vitale's demotion, Massino explained that his displeasure with Sal began during his imprisonment in Talladega. He was particularly upset by Sal's decision to kill Perrino during the *Post* investigation, and would have vetoed it had he been consulted.

As a capo, Cantarella's coffers filled more quickly. He kept a larger share of his own booty and collected a portion of his crew's take. Under Massino's reign, as soldier and capo, he became a multimillionaire, possibly the family's richest racketeer after Massino. His take from loan-sharking—he charged 2 percent in vigorish—and assorted racketeering was a minimum of $500,000 a year. The riches pouring in enabled Cantarella to acquire thirteen parking lots in Manhattan and a small mansion, valued at more than $2 million, in the exclusive Ocean Gates Estate in Staten Island. Much flashier than his prudent godfather, Cantarella's extravagant tastes extended to collecting Jaguars, Mercedes-Benzes, Cadillacs, and vintage cars.

Vitale's arrest in late 2001 brought Cantarella even closer to Massino. He was appointed acting underboss, the family's official number-two leader. Selecting Cantarella as his main aide-de-camp, Massino was unaware of a vital development: the Bonanno Squad had explosive investigations under way of his new field commander, Richie Cantarella, and the groupie Barry Weinberg.

59

Divide and Conquer

Mapping out their strategy in 1999, the FBI's forensic accountants Jeffrey Sallet and Kimberly McCaffrey's first step was to examine the income-tax returns of Joe Massino and Sal Vitale and their wives. IRS records listed the names of the accountants who had prepared the annual tax returns for the two couples, and the firms were subpoenaed to hand over their records. That initial move turned into a lucky strike for the agents; the firms had saved memoranda dating back more than a decade, although not legally required to do so.

One eyebrow-raising item was the incredible gambling successes enjoyed by Joe and Josie Massino. On their joint income tax statements (only Mrs. Massino's occupation was noted: "HW" for housewife) they showed lottery winnings totaling almost $500,000 over four years in the 1990s. Agents doubted that any couple could be so inordinately lucky year after year, but never conclusively determined whether the lottery lucre was due to pure luck or Mafia chicanery. A consensus speculated that Joe used his borgata minions to obtain winning lottery tickets, offering a premium to the legitimate holders who turned them over to him. The actual winners got cash that was unreported to the IRS, and Massino, if audited, could cite the lottery prizes as legitimate income to account for his comfortable standard of living.

From 1996, the year the Massinos presumably began their run of lottery successes, until 2001, their reported annual gross income ranged from $373,052 to $590,789. Sifting through piles of tax minutiae, the forensic sleuths spotted a pattern more engrossing to CPA's than lottery gambling. They were drawn to faxes exchanged between separate accounting firms used by Massino and Vitale, concerning overlapping investments. What intrigued the agents were documents, known as K-1 reports, listing partnership interests and earnings. Attempting to substantiate their legitimate incomes, Massino and Vitale, in their tax filings, had included payments from three parking lots. The K-1s documented a connection to Richard Cantarella, because his wife, Lauretta Castelli, was a third investor and officer in the parking lot companies.

By fine-tooth-combing partnership records, the agents discovered the name of another player in the deals. They found checks which Joe and Sal's wives had written to Barry Weinberg for initial investments in the lots. Sallet and McCaffrey considered the previously unknown Weinberg's middleman involvement in the parking lots their most promising find. Who was the mysterious Weinberg? The agents decided to focus on him as a moneymaker for the Bonannos—and a potential soft spot for penetrating the family.

With Sallet and McCaffrey leading the way, the C-10 squad in 2000 placed Weinberg under an FBI microscope, tailing him and locating his bank and financial records. Surveillance squads watched him meet and party frequently with Richard Cantarella and his Mob crew, and with Augustino Scozzari. They became familiar with Weinberg's routine schedule, his morning departures from his posh Northern New Jersey home in Closter, and his rounds of meetings in Manhattan parking lots, restaurants, and sites in Little Italy.

The paper chase of Weinberg took a year, and the forensic accountants' instincts were right: he had evaded at least $1 million in taxes over a decade in which he neglected to file tax returns and to report estimated profits totaling a staggering $14 million. On the morning of January 9, 2001, driving in a new $90,000 Mercedes to one of his parking lots in Midtown Manhattan, Weinberg was pulled over by a police cruiser for a traffic violation. It was a ruse. Alighting from his car, he was hustled into an unmarked van where Sallet and McCaffrey waited. "You have fifteen minutes to make a life decision," Sallet began. The agents informed the now jittery Weinberg that he was accused of income tax evasion and that he had only one option to avoid prison: he would have to work undercover, secretly record conversations with Cantarella and other mobsters, and eventually be placed in the Witness Protection Program. Otherwise, he would be processed immediately on tax charges, thereby losing all his value as a confidential witness because Cantarella and his crew would shun him, fearful that he might have made a deal with the government.

Needing less than fifteen minutes, Weinberg chose the avenue of cooperation. That day he began "proffering," the process before a formal plea agreement can be signed, in which a defendant discloses to prosecutors and agents all of his own crimes and all illegal acts of which he is aware. Prosecutors could then evaluate Weinberg's value as an informant and potential witness, and determine the degree of leniency that might be offered to him.

Weinberg had plenty to tell. He described a decade or more of frauds and payoffs not only with Cantarella but also with another capo, Frank Coppa, who was involved in parking lot deals and had independently shaken him down for about $85,000. Details of parking-lot partnerships, money laundering, and extortion by both capos were illuminated. Weinberg's payoffs to Cantarella alone reached $800,000 and he revealed how he had shelled out another $250,000 six months earlier, after being beaten by Cantarella. Angered because he believed that Weinberg had complained about him to other mobsters, Cantarella confronted him in front of the popular Caffe Roma in Little Italy. Yelling, "Why are you talking about me," Richie punched him in the face, knocking him to the sidewalk. The capo demanded a peace offering of $500,000 before he would permit Weinberg to continue associating with him. Cantarella settled for $250,000 but with a threat: "You owe me for everything."

Turning Weinberg into an undercover operative was an unprecedented achievement for the C-10 Squad. Except for Agent Joe Pistone, the FBI had never infiltrated the Bonannos with an informer who would be secretly taping made members and who had access to capos. Their success with Weinberg created a double undercover triumph. During the debriefing with Sallet and McCaffrey, Weinberg implicated in money-laundering practices Augustino Scozzari, the businessman he had brought into Cantarella's web. A brusque conversation with the two agents about the legal consequences of conspiring with gangsters persuaded Scozzari to abandon his romanticized concept of the Mafia, and to join the undercover campaign. He, too, secretly began taping meetings with Cantarella. "It wasn't difficult to turn him," Sallet said. "Money guys like to live well and have a lot to lose."

The groupies were quickly converted into stellar FBI informers, ultimately producing more than one hundred tapes incriminating Cantarella and his crew. Eventually, Cantarella grew nervous that Weinberg might be a stool pigeon. He discussed his doubts about Weinberg with Massino, and the godfather shaped his hand into a gun, asking if he needed help to solve the problem. Before the mobsters could harm Weinberg, McCaffrey and Sallet sensed from Cantarella's secretly taped remarks that Weinberg was endangered. After a year of undercover service, Weinberg was pulled out in December 2001 and bundled into the Witness Protection Program. (The reformed groupie survived two years, dying of cancer at age fifty-eight.)

Perhaps because of Augustino Scozzari's Italian ancestry, Cantarella trusted him, even after he knew that Weinberg was singing to the authorities. Relying on his ability to detect double-dealers, Cantarella was confident that the lightning bolt of an informer would never strike him twice, and continued speaking freely and recklessly with Scozzari into the summer of 2002.

Six months after Weinberg's defection, Scozzari was still in Cantarella's good graces and succeeded in taping Cantarella talking about C-10's top target, Joe Massino. Moreover, Cantarella forgot or disregarded Massino's caveats against dropping his name, even obliquely, in conversations. After John Gotti's death in June 2002, Cantarella was troubled by newspaper reports and publicity that Massino's stock was soaring in the Mafia. "What the paper is saying is that Joe is the big guy now," the capo related to Scozzari. "That's not good. You know what I mean? That's not good."

That same summer, Cantarella was at it again, boasting to Scozzari that Massino, while in prison in 1990, had intervened to get him his button as a made man. "Actually the guy who did it was Joe. He was in jail. And he sent the word. . . . He did 10 years. . . . He said I want justification why Al [Embarrato] is holding Richie [Cantarella] back. Because somebody sent a whisper in Joe's ear."

Time was running out for Cantarella, and in August agents raided and searched his luxurious $1.7 million home. They located a safe containing a roster of his crew members and the unlisted telephone numbers of Massino, Vitale (under the heading, "Handsome Sal"), and Bonanno capos. Making a pitch to Cantarella to cooperate, Sallet said, "You're facing serious charges very soon. We're not bullshitting you. You know what you've done and so do we."

Stonewalling the agents, Cantarella rejected the offer to switch sides. Instead, complying with Mafia rules, he notified Joe Massino about the raid and the agents' pressure. He realized that Weinberg and Scozzari—who had also been whisked off the streets—were in the prosecution's pocket. But he was satisfied that while he might be indicted for economic crimes, government prosecutors could not fasten on him what he most feared—murder raps.

Less than two months later, he was proved wrong. On October 2, 2002, Sallet and McCaffrey were pounding on his door before dawn, rousing the sleeping Richie and his wife, Lauretta. The acting underboss was indicted on twenty-four racketeering counts, specifying every conceivable Mafia crime, including murder. At age fifty-eight, he faced life imprisonment for a homicide committed ten years earlier and which he assumed the FBI and police had forgotten: the slaying of the Bonannos' corrupt accomplice at the *New York Post*, Robert Perrino. There was no way he could have anticipated the diligence of Sallet and McCaffrey in reexamining moldering cases connected to him and other Bonanno rajahs. Working for three years with New York State Police detectives who had originally investigated Perrino's disappearance, they stitched together sufficient evidence from old wiretaps and a newly cultivated informer connected to the Bath Avenue Boys to link Cantarella to the murder conspiracy.

Handcuffed along with Cantarella was his fifty-five-year-old wife, accused of hiding and laundering his spoils through bank accounts and transactions in her name. Their thirty-one-year-old son Paul was simultaneously grabbed as an enforcer for his father and for participating in robberies and abductions.

Along with the three Cantarellas, twenty other Bonanno mafiosi and associates were indicted in the FBI roundup. Capo Frank Coppa, four months into a five-year sentence on his second stock frauds conviction, was hit with new charges of extorting Barry Weinberg. Traumatized by his first prison stretch, when he burst into tears in front of other inmates, Coppa at sixty-one knew that a RICO conviction of up to twenty additional years was a death knell, and that his concealed $2 million nest egg would be worthless. Before a month elapsed, Coppa took a fateful step that no made man in the seventy-year history of the Bonanno/Massino borgata had ever dared. He became a government witness. Through his lawyer, he notified the FBI that he would cooperate with the prosecution and testify against Massino, Vitale, Cantarella, and all his Mob brethren, in the hope of a sharply reduced sentence. "I don't want to do any more time," he appealed to agents and prosecutors.

Previously, when a multitude of "rats" in other families proffered deals with prosecutors, the Bonanno/Massino family had remained a bedrock of loyalty to *omertà*. Even during the trying times and long sentences meted out in the wake of Agent Pistone's infiltration, not a single soldier or capo had sought a favor from prosecutors or had violated the *omertà* oath. Coppa's defection in November 2002, provided the FBI and prosecutors with a gigantic breakthrough in the investigation of Joe Massino. Associated with Massino for a quarter of a century, Coppa could delineate Massino's rise to power and catalogue the boss's multitude of crimes. He could also corroborate Massino's involvement in gangland hits through the incriminating statements the boss had made to him in convivial moments.

Coppa's most startling revelation was his eyewitness description of the murder of Sonny Black Napolitano in the basement of a Staten Island home. It was the first account ever obtained of the hit, and Coppa identified the main participants, including Massino. Since boyhood, Coppa had been a partner with Frank Lino in violent and white-collar crimes, and had frolicked with him at cocaine parties and other social events. Now Coppa turned in his lifelong comrade, fingering him as another key performer in Sonny Black's murder.

Far from finished with his murder disclosures, Coppa bolstered evidence against Richie Cantarella in the Perrino murder, and implicated an even more important figure—Sal Vitale. In his early days as a soldier, Cantarella had been in Coppa's crew, and Richie bragged to him about helping Vitale lure Perrino to a deadly meeting and getting rid of the body. In another talkative mood, Cantarella gave details to Coppa about having been the getaway driver in the murder of his cousin, Tony Mirra.

From his lawyers and from jailhouse scuttlebutt, Cantarella heard that Coppa had flipped. Held without bail as a danger to the community and stewing in a cell, Cantarella realized that Coppa's treason would heap more murder charges against him and bury him for life in prison. A month after Coppa crossed the defectors' Rubicon, the three Cantarellas negotiated plea-bargains and also were absorbed into the Witness Protection Program. The only prospect Cantarella had for reducing a life sentence required him to betray Mafia superiors. That meant helping to convict Sal Vitale and the Mafia's foremost godfather, Joe Massino.

The tiny cracks in Massino's security facade were widening, and by January 2003, it was clear that his carefully wrought protective walls had disintegrated. He knew that Coppa and Richard Cantarella and his son Paul had been spirited away in the dead of night from their cells. Free on bail, Mrs. Cantarella had vanished from her Staten Island home, obviously joining her husband and their son in protective custody at a federal prison wing or military base, where high-level informers are usually housed. Conclusive proof that the two captains were cooperating with the government came when their lawyers were summarily replaced by attorneys friendly with the U.S. Attorney's office.

A master at sniffing out the most subtle tails, Massino saw that he was under siege. He had installed video cameras in the his Howard Beach home for panoramic views of the placid street, and the cameras confirmed that agents were staked out near his front door. At the start of the New Year, George Hanna, the new Bonanno Squad supervisor, had ordered a twenty-four-hour vigil. Recalling Massino's flight in 1982 from a pending RICO indictment, and suspecting that he might have established hideaways on his overseas trips, Hanna made sure he would not slither away this time.

At 6:00 A.M., on January 9, 2003—a day before his sixtieth birthday—Joe Massino was up and dressed when the doorbell rang at his home. There to arrest him were three C-10 squad members, wearing blue raid jackets with yellow FBI lettering on the back; an IRS agent; and a state police detective who had worked on the investigation. "It's no surprise to him," Seamus McElearney, a strapping six-foot-tall FBI agent, inferred as Massino, looking unperturbed, extended his wrists for handcuffs. "He knew we were coming. It was just a matter of when." At a kitchen table, Josie Massino, wrapped in a bathrobe, looked on silently as the agents intoned the Miranda rights against self-incrimination to her husband. From the hallway, before Massino was led to a waiting car, the agents got a narrow peek at expensive furniture and a crystal chandelier in an adjacent dining room.

Kim McCaffrey and Jeff Sallet, who launched the paper chase that had sprung the trap on Massino, had never spoken to him, but he recognized them. "You must be Kimberly and you must be Jeffrey," he said, singling them out in the arrest team. McCaffrey asked why he was up and dressed so early? "I was on my way to the pastry shop," he replied, jesting. "I thought you were coming yesterday. I saw surveillance cars in the area."

Wearing a pocketless black velour jogging suit, Massino had no possessions on him, not a wristwatch nor a penny. "He knows what to expect in jail," McElearney mused. Once inside a federal detention lockup, all expensive trinkets and money would be taken away and he would be issued prison garb.

On the ride to Manhattan for fingerprint and photograph processing at FBI headquarters, Massino opened the conversation, predicting he would be held without bail. "Frankie Coppa got to work quick," he continued, showing his awareness of the first Mafioso to double-cross him. Told that he would be charged as a planner and backup shooter in the murder of Sonny Black Napolitano, Massino shot back, "That was a long time ago. I had nothing to do with it."

Sallet and McCaffrey asked how he had identified them by name without any previous meeting. "You wired up Barry a lot," he replied, referring to the tapes Weinberg had recorded. Indicating his knowledge of the agents' backgrounds, he mentioned that McCaffrey had been recruited by the bureau shortly after college. She wondered where he had picked up the personal information. "You do your homework, I do mine." He grinned.

The godfather had a lot of help with his "homework." Cantarella had spoken with Sallet and McCaffrey during the raid at his home and he must have described them to Massino. Before Cantarella became a cooperative witness, discovery evidence, including details of Weinberg's wiring, had been turned over to Cantarella's lawyer, an attorney who represented many Bonanno defendants. The agents presumed that someone in the attorney's office relayed the discovery information or copies of the documents listing their names to Massino.

While Massino was being processed at the FBI's offices, he was introduced to Nora Conley, C-10's second-in-command. "That's similar to the underboss," he quipped.

Another big catch that morning was the titular underboss, Sal Vitale. On bail and under house arrest, he had been awaiting formal sentencing for his loan-sharking and money-laundering ventures at the European American Bank. For that plea arrangement, he had been assured a sentence of less than four years. Conviction on new RICO counts would be far graver, translating almost certainly into life imprisonment for fifty-five-year-old Good-Looking Sal.

Upon completion of Vitale's processing on the FBI's twenty-sixth floor, McCaffrey and Sallet played a divide-and-conquer card. They showed him the legal memorandum for an order to detain Joe Massino without bail as a danger to the community and a flight risk, which prosecutors would present to a judge that afternoon at Massino's arraignment. Of particular interest to Vitale, the agents pointed out, was a statement in the court papers that severely affected him. On the record, prosecutors stated they had evidence that Massino believed that Vitale might be a deserter-informer—and was ready to kill him.

"You have to make a decision," Sallet said after Vitale read the court document. "There are a couple of ways to go." Vitale was silent as a stone. But to McCaffrey, his dour eyes signified whirling emotions about loyalty to a brother-in-law who intended to whack him. "Sal," she thought, "knows it's the end of the line."

The Domino Syndrome

With his waddling walk, his copious size exaggerated by his black warm-up suit, Joe Massino cut an odd figure in a courtroom on the afternoon of his arrest. Crowing over his indictment, FBI and prosecution officials at news conferences hailed the apprehension of "the last Don" from the five families still at liberty. As Massino had anticipated, the prosecution won its motion to detain him indefinitely as a "danger to the community" until his trial. At the arraignment, Sal Vitale was automatically remanded to a cell because he was awaiting sentence for his earlier racketeering conviction.

Massino seemed unruffled, his composure probably founded on his quick appraisal of the specifics in the indictment. Most of the charges were boilerplate enterprise allegations of profiting from gambling and loan-sharking that are hurled in almost every RICO trial. The headline charge was his having orchestrated and participated in the murder twenty-two years earlier of Sonny Black Napolitano. At the hearing, prosecutors revealed that they had two unidentified made men and thirteen others lined up to testify against him on all the counts. It was obvious from prosecutorial claims that Frank Coppa and Richard Cantarella were the *omertà* violators, and probably the only witnesses who might seriously endanger Massino. Coppa had been present at the Napolitano hit and Cantarella had inside knowledge about Joe's activities as boss. Since there were no tapes in Joe's own voice to implicate him, the prosecution's strategy would depend heavily on the reliability of two career-criminal witnesses with a history of deception and lying. An experienced lawyer worth his salt probably could demolish them on cross-examination by pounding at their selfish motives to save their own necks by sacrificing Massino's. From first impressions, the other government witnesses apparently lacked firsthand evidence against him and appeared to pose no major threat.

"This guy can't hurt me," was Massino's standard refrain at strategy meetings with his lawyers and those representing Sal Vitale and another codefendant, Frank Lino, who was indicted for Napolitano's murder and other broad racketeering acts. The critical charge against Vitale—the decade-old disappearance and presumed murder of the *New York Post*'s delivery official, Robert Perrino, also was wobbly, even if Cantarella admitted his role and testified against the underboss.

Outwardly, Massino and Vitale, each charged with separate murders, appeared to be in lockstep, presenting a unified defense on the same racketeering counts. A month after their arrest, the brothers-in-law sat side by side at a pretrial hearing when Greg Andres, the chief prosecutor, detonated a blockbuster. Explaining why Massino was jailed in Brooklyn and Vitale in Manhattan, and why they were kept apart when not in a courtroom, Andres said the government had reliable information that Massino had considered "hurting" Vitale. "Hurting" was the lawyer's euphemism for murder. Andres did not reveal that the information came from debriefings of Coppa and Cantarella. Both turncoats had heard Joe's harsh opinion that Sal probably won a soft sentence in Long Island only by secretly cooperating and spying on him for the government.

Talking with his lawyer, John Mitchell, who had also represented him in the Long Island plea-bargain, Vitale brushed off the prosecutor's assertion that his life was endangered as a "ploy, bullshit to get me to cooperate." But Massino still remained dubious of Vitale's reliability. At the Metropolitan Detention Center in Brooklyn, he told fellow inmate Frank Lino that he was "very upset" with Sal and was planning to "give him a receipt," his Mob lingo for killing. Massino's coterie of Bonanno defendants at the jail joined in the chorus, referring to Vitale as "Fredo," the traitorous Corleone brother in *The Godfather: Part II*.

Two weeks after the court hearing, Massino's suspicions became a reality. Through a son's lawyer friend, Vitale secretly notified the prosecution that he wanted to bolt. Quickly transferred from a Manhattan cell to a more secure government setting, he began uncoiling the secrets of three decades of crime partnerships with Massino and other mafiosi. An astonished John Mitchell got a hand-delivered letter signed by Vitale, stating that he had been peremptorily fired as his lawyer. "He gets the Academy Award for his performance," Mitchell observed as the news of Vitale's defection sank in. "I saw him in jail on a Friday, and he was his usual charming, affable, self-effacing self. A few days later he was gone. He even sent me part of the fee, $25,000; that's not the kind of thing you do if you're considering to go over. I'm flabbergasted."

A seed sown by Agents McCaffrey and Sallet on the day of Vitale's arrest had borne fruit. They had shown him the prosecution's court memorandum that Massino had talked with other mobsters about eliminating him. The threat took hold quickly. On the very day of their joint arraignment, Vitale decided to desert Massino as soon as it could be safely arranged. "That's when I thought my thoughts and said, 'He doesn't deserve the respect and honor with me sitting next to him,'" Vitale related at a debriefing to agents and prosecutors. Displaying his new helpful spirit, Vitale turned over his rackets' ready cash, $481,000 hidden at his home and in a bank safe deposit box under an alias. Another item of interest at his home was his shy book, a catalogue of his and Massino's loan-shark clients and their arrears.

Like all witnesses angling for a reduced sentence, Vitale was required to chart the details of all his crimes and his knowledge of those committed by other mobsters. He pleaded guilty to having participated in eleven murders and a bevy of RICO violations over thirty years. His quest for leniency instead of life imprisonment hinged on a 5K1.1 document, a letter to the sentencing judge from prosecutors outlining his value to the government and recommending a reduction in sentence. Vitale did extract one concession from the prosecutors: none of his admissions or information could be used to prosecute Josie Massino, his sister and Massino's wife. In effect, he immunized her from complicity in receiving Mob payoffs while Massino was imprisoned and knowingly relaying Mafia messages between him and her husband.

Confirmation of Vitale's defection was delivered by defense lawyers at a conference with Massino and Frank Lino at the Brooklyn jail. Although Massino knew that Vitale's emergence as the prosecution's most sensational witness was a shattering setback, to his lawyers he appeared stolid, absorbing the news without indicating that it troubled him. Lino tried to appear equally calm and undisturbed, but inwardly he was desolated. The lone witness who had previously tied him to Sonny Black's murder was Frank Coppa, and without strong corroboration his testimony might be discredited as a self-serving attempt to curry favor in exchange for early release from prison. Sal Vitale would be a more threatening witness. He could corroborate Lino's role in three additional homicides and compromise him in the notorious massacre of the three capos. "This meeting is a funeral and I'm dead," Lino reckoned, not daring to speak up and show weakness in Massino's presence.

Lino, whose son Joseph was a soldier in the family, was in a quandary. He feared Massino would retaliate against his children and grandchildren if he suspected that his loyalty was buckling. Nevertheless, he wanted a deal to avoid a lifetime in prison, and he slipped a message to the prosecution that he might cooperate. Placed in solitary confinement for his own protection, Lino refused to attend strategy meetings with Massino and their lawyers while he haggled with the U.S. Attorney's staff. He even refused to speak with the new attorney retained by his son Joseph. Lino had no complaint about eighty-one days in solitary confinement, which he called "the Hole" and "the Shoe," considering it far safer than living with the general prison population once it was whispered that he was a canary. Proffering with the prosecution took almost three months before Lino signed on to become "a cooperative witness." Obligated to identify everyone whom he knew was a mafioso or an associate, Lino included his son's name in the Bonanno/Massino corps of soldiers. "You already know he's a made member. What's the big deal?" he rationalized to FBI agents.

By the spring of 2003, Massino and his lawyers knew that four self-confessed, highly placed mobsters were primed to testify against him, but they did not know that there were additional converts abandoning him.

Richie Cantarella's arrest the previous autumn had required Massino to appoint an acting capo for his crew, and his choice was Joey D'Amico. A made man since he was twenty-two D'Amico was sufficiently calloused at an early age to kill his cousin Tony Mirra on Massino's orders to avenge the Donny Brasco fiasco. Showing his fortitude, D'Amico took an eighteen-month rap for perjury in the wake of the grand jury investigation of the three capos murders. Later, in the 1990s, he gained a reputation as "a party guy," who enjoyed coke and marijuana interludes. Finally settling down as a member of his cousin Richie Cantarella's crew, D'Amico concentrated on family rackets and gained Massino's respect.

Several days before Massino's January arrest, two new solders from Cantarella's crew, Gino Galestro and Joseph Sabella, requested an urgent meeting with their acting captain. At Radio Mexico, an unpretentious restaurant near the Fulton Fish Market, unlikely to be on the FBI's surveillance screen as a Mob hangout, the two soldiers reported that Cantarella's Staten Island home was suddenly vacant, the driveway packed with uncleared snow; Cantarella's wife, free on bail, had disappeared; and their grandchildren had been abruptly removed from their schools. The signs were clear: the Cantarellas were in the Witness Protection Program.

"Go home, hug your kids, you're probably going to jail," D'Amico dejectedly told Galestro and Sabella. His cousin Richie was probably ratting out everyone in the crew and would incriminate him in hits they had done on Tony Mirra and Enrico Mazzeo. "He's going to bury me," was the thought dominating D'Amico for days until he made a telephone call to George Hanna, then the supervisor of the FBI's C-10 Bonanno Squad. Secretly pleading guilty to four murders and a parcel of other crimes, D'Amico agreed to work undercover against the family. In another FBI breakthrough, Joey D'Amico became the first made man in the Bonanno/Massino borgata to wear a wire and stealthily record evidence to capsize the gang he had sworn to protect.

On a Florida holiday in 2002, before his arrest, Joe Massino stopped in Boca Raton to chat with and welcome back from prison James Big Louie Tartaglione. A million-dollar earner for himself and the family, Big Louie had been an immensely successful loan shark (he always had ten to fifteen suckers on his hook) until he was nailed in 1997 for extortion and imprisoned for five years. Well off financially at sixty-five, Tartaglione was ready for sunny retirement, although Massino wanted him to return to New York and again serve on his executive committees. Still on supervised release (parole) and aware of the FBI crackdowns against Graziano and Cantarella, Tartaglione stalled until the news of Vitale's defection struck like a lightning bolt. Instead of heading north to help out Massino, Tartaglione contacted Ruth Nordenbrook, the federal prosecutor in Brooklyn who had obtained his guilty plea to loan-sharking. Although she had convicted him, Tartaglione was grateful to Nordenbrook for having helped his daughter with a medical problem during the court proceedings. From Tartaglione's comments, Nordenbrook, a seasoned Mafia prosecutor, understood that he was finished as a mafioso and eager to jump ship, but she cautioned him that there was no guarantee of a lighter sentence. Meeting in Florida with her and C-10 Agents Joseph Bonavolonta and Gregory Massa, Tartaglione admitted, "If Sal tells the truth, I'm in trouble. I have a lot of mortal sins that Sal knows about." Among his worst sins were participating in two hits and helping dispose of the bodies of the three capos killed in 1981.

Tartaglione's request for leniency required him to do more than testify; he had to wear a wire and work undercover. Early in May 2003, he returned to New York, notifying the jailed Massino through the family's grapevine that he would help run the borgata in its hour of need. The deception went smoothly, and he even introduced to Massino's surrogate leaders a female FBI agent, pretending that she could obtain confidential law-enforcement files from a court employee friend. Over nine months, Big Louie produced forty-five incriminating tape recordings and a miscellany of raw intelligence pinpointing the family's temporary hierarchy. The new top man appointed by Massino was the acting boss, Anthony "Tony Green" Urso, and Tartaglione's tapes caught Urso lamenting the consequences of Vitale's betrayal. "Sal is going to rat on every fucking body." On another occasion, discussing Vitale's duplicity and anticipated testimony, Urso added, "How would Sal feel if I killed one of his kids?" Totally hoodwinked, Urso trusted Tartaglione sufficiently to let him review confidential lists of proposed new members in other families.

Remembering Massino's edict about mentioning his proper name, capos and soldiers on Tartaglione's tapes usually made cryptic remarks about "our friend" and "the other guy." A videotape rigged by the FBI of Tartaglione meeting with his crew in a warehouse included shots of wiseguys touching their ears when saying "our friend." There were slipups, however, and agents heard "the Massino family" from the lips of a careless mobster.

The past also crept up on Duane Goldie Leisenheimer, who as a teenager Massino had taken under his wing. Vitale and other turncoats were generating evidence about Goldie's involvement in the three capos massacre, the slaying and mutilation of Cesare Bonventre, and numerous crimes sufficient for a RICO conviction and twenty years in prison. Still a newspaper truck driver, the now-married forty-six-year-old Goldie got a surprise visit in June 2003, from the case agents, Sallet and McCaffrey. "You went to jail once for this guy. You don't have to do it again," Sallet bluntly advised, referring to Goldie's fifteen-months' contempt conviction for refusing to testify about helping Massino hide out in the early 1980s. Considering himself "a standup guy," Goldie was mum, saying he would consult a lawyer. He also got a stern message from Greg Andres, the lead prosecutor: "You have a lot more to worry about than contempt this time."

Soon after the government's warnings, Goldie's lawyer was visited by a private investigator from Massino's defense, probing to see if Leisenheimer intended to snitch on his onetime patron. That visit backfired. Convinced his life was in danger, Goldie sprinted into the government's arms, supplying the prosecution with another witness to buttress its contention that Massino had been a Mafia Goliath for twenty-five years.

By summer's end in 2003, prosecutors possessed a bumper crop of unanticipated evidence from seven defectors, and a vastly different trial was in preparation against Massino. The original two main codefendants, Vitale and Lino, were in the prosecution's corner, and superseding indictments placed Massino in a vortex as the lone defendant in a tangled RICO conspiracy: eleven counts and sixteen specific racketeering acts. A case involving one murder, Sonny Black Napolitano's death, had ballooned into seven homicides and added accusations of attempted murder, arson, loan-sharking, illegal gambling, extortion, and money laundering. The bulk of the new charges, based on Vitale's confession and his long association with Massino, allowed the prosecution under the RICO law to plumb allegations of "enterprise" crimes dating back more than thirty years. Prominent in the enlarged indictment was the slaughter of the three capos in 1981. Massino had been acquitted in 1987 of "conspiracy" to murder the trio; the new charge did not subject him to double jeopardy because the charge had been altered to a substantive act of having directly participated in the shootings.

An eighth murder charge in the welter of indictments carried the extreme sentence—capital punishment. Largely through Vitale's grand jury testimony, Massino was accused of placing the contract on Gerlando George-from-Canada Sciascia because he had dared to criticize one of Joe's favorite mobsters, Anthony T.G. Graziano. The seven other murders had been committed before 1994, the year Congress enacted a statute that allowed the death penalty for conviction on a homicide in "aid of racketeering." Sciascia was shot to death in 1999, and his murder fell under the provisions giving the government the option of seeking execution upon conviction. The law was aimed principally at leaders of drug cartels and violent street gangs; Massino had the distinction of being the first godfather to possibly face execution for his crimes. Because of evidentiary technicalities in a capital punishment case, the Sciascia murder charge was severed from Massino's omnibus RICO trial and would be tried separately.

A plethora of criminal defense lawyers ached to represent the accused celebrity godfather Massino, and courthouse gossip suggested that some thirty attorneys offered themselves as candidates. Massino's choice was David Breitbart, who facetiously and proudly represents himself to reporters as a "fast-gun lawyer for hire."

Breitbart said Massino singled him out from the pack "because he wants a fighter who will not be intimidated by government agencies or prosecutors."

Athletic and brainy as a youngster, Breitbart made the basketball team at the city's academically rigorous Bronx High School of Science, earned black belt honors in jujitsu, and was a school psychologist, teacher, and reading specialist before becoming a lawyer. After two years as a prosecutor in the Bronx DA's office, he moved to the defense table, and his first notable client was Leroy "Nicky" Barnes, a major narcotics merchant known as "Mr. Untouchable." He won acquittals for the drug baron on state murder, drug, and gun charges until federal prosecutors convicted Barnes of heading "the most venal drug ring" in New York in the mid-1970s.

Besides run-of-the-mill civil-suit clients, Breitbart's regulars included Genovese, Lucchese, and Colombo defendants, and he won a relished acquittal for John "Boobsie" Cerasani in a memorable organized-crime trial. Cerasani was the only accused Bonanno soldier found not guilty in 1982 on racketeering charges stemming from Joe Pistone's infiltration of the family. Priding himself on his ability to demolish prosecution witness, Breitbart proclaimed his scalding cross-examinations were "the blast furnace of truth." Barbara Jones, a former prosecutor who became a federal judge, was so impressed by trial battles with Breitbart that she invited him every year to demonstrate cross-examination techniques to her students at Fordham University's Law School.

Facing off in court as lead prosecutor against Massino was Greg (his given name, not an abbreviation) Andres. An Assistant U.S. Attorney in Brooklyn, he was born in Alexandria, Virginia, thirty-six years earlier—about the same time Breit-bart began his law career. On the fast track as a premier prosecutor, Andres had a distinguished academic record. He was sufficiently scrappy to qualify for the Notre Dame boxing team and to survive two bouts of malaria while in the Peace Corps in Benin, West Africa. A quick learner about the Mob's tenets, in less than five years he had helped imprison more than one hundred defendants, most of whom pled guilty. His biggest victories came serving on the prosecutorial team that convicted the Bonanno consigliere Anthony Spero, and he obtained a guilty plea from the next consigliere, T.G. Graziano.

Acrimony ruled as soon as Breitbart and Andres met in pretrial skirmishes over routine motions and the defense's demands for quick release of discovery materials. Andres won most of the crucial legal disputes. Of particular importance for the prosecution, he was allowed to elicit testimony about George-from-Canada Sciascia's rubout, even though that case would be tried separately. Additionally, the prosecution was permitted to cite through witnesses other uncharged murders and crimes linking Massino to the overall RICO enterprise conspiracy. Although the jury would not decide Massino's complicity in the uncharged crimes, evidence about them added credibility to the prosecution's portrayal of him as a long-established, vicious criminal. A sore point for Breitbart was the Sciascia murder accusation, with the specter of execution. "They're raising the stakes to coerce a plea," Breitbart asserted. "He's sixty years old and a plea is the same as capital punishment for him. It means dying in jail."

For once in his life, Joe Massino was the underdog, and no one understood that better than Breitbart and his associate counsel, Flora Edwards, as trial testimony began in May 2004 in a downtown Brooklyn courtroom. Before the first witness was called, the lawyers were clued-in on the prosecution's basic attack plan, and it seemed overwhelming. One, perhaps two, turncoats were almost standard props as witnesses in RICO dramas. But never before at a godfather trial had the prosecution presented as its cornerstone theme a coven of seven formidable wiseguys, starring a confessed underboss, Sal Vitale.

Massino had personally picked Flora Edwards to "second seat," back up, Breitbart, aware of her reputation in organized-crime cases as "the princess of paper." She could expeditiously produce cogent, well-researched motions and briefs in the midst of hectic trials. And Massino's trial promised to be a fierce contest in which a seemingly minor legal point could affect the jury or prove decisive in a later appeal.

The two attorneys from the onset of jury selection faced another extraordinary task: diminishing the notoriety clinging to Massino. A panel of twelve jurors and eight alternates had been screened by the judge for their presumed lack of bias concerning Mafia allegations. Yet they surely scented a whiff of danger in the way they were treated. For their protection, jurors' names were withheld from the defense and prosecution, and they were forbidden from revealing their surnames or addresses to each other. As another measure to protect their anonymity and prevent jury tampering, federal marshals escorted them back and forth from home to court every day.

Breitbart's counterstroke was a Commission trial–type defense. Acknowledging that it was foolhardy to deny the Mafia's existence, he tried to turn the concession to Massino's advantage. "Whether or not Joe Massino is the boss is not sufficient to prove the underlying acts," Breitbart addressed the jury, stressing that the prosecution lacked direct evidence that Massino had committed a single crime. "You can vote not guilty even if you find he's a boss."

The defense's toughest challenge was undercutting Sal Vitale. Both sides knew that Vitale's relationship with Massino overlapped all the major charges, and that his evidence glued together the testimony of the other defectors. The courtroom's two hundred seats were packed with spectators, many of them prosecutors and defense lawyers professionally interested in the bout between the elite witness and the masterly cross-examiner.

A surreal melodrama also was under way between Vitale and his sister, Josie Massino, seated in the first gallery row, twenty feet from her husband. Always professing Joe's innocence to reporters, she sat stoically on the numbingly hard wooden benches every day of the trial—but never so attentively as during Sal's five days in the witness stand. Vitale avoided looking at her and her daughters, Adeline and Joanne, seated alongside her, even when his testimony concerned claims that he had comforted them with loving attention and money while Massino was in prison. Josie's eyes bore in at Vitale, the man she once doted on as her "baby brother," with the intensity of heat-seeking missiles. "He's my flesh and blood, but how could you forgive what he has done not only to me but to my husband and the father of my children?" she told John Marzulli, a *Daily News* reporter, during a recess.

Breitbart's acerbic questions and deft attempts to extract admissions from Vitale that jealousy and envy had led him to cover up his own crimes by framing Massino failed. The lawyer was unable to expose any glaring inconsistencies or flat-out lies, managing only once to crack Vitale's deadpan, low-voiced aplomb. Asked to point out Massino in the courtroom, Vitale's contempt was palpable. "Yeah, the gentleman right there with the glasses. The guy who's staring at me. That's him."

His testimony over, a relieved Vitale sprang up as if expelled from a fighter pilot's ejection seat, darting out a side door without a backward glance at his sister and brother-in-law.

Every day, Josie dressed in well-tailored suits and brought two large bags of home-cooked and takeout food for her husband's lunch, exchanging whispered words and affectionate glances with him. She listened impassively to accounts of hideous atrocities attributed to Massino and the revelations of his romantic peccadilloes while on the lam. Massino's uniform was a boxy blue or gray suit and open-collared white shirt. Scribbling notes and passing them to his lawyers at the defense table, he chewed gum or snacked incessantly on luncheon leftovers or candy. A diabetic, during breaks in the testimony he used medical equipment to test his blood-sugar level and blood pressure.

The court sessions, usually lasting up to eight hours, seemed to weigh on Massino; his face became more chalky and haggard as turncoat witnesses and former FBI agents replayed conversations and incidents recounting his activities over a thirty-year period. It was a courtroom version of *This Is Your Life*, with the prosecution displaying a huge board with some sixty mug shots and dozens of surveillance photos of dead and living mobsters assertedly linked to his underworld ascension. Instead of hearing proper names, the jury had to adjust to the Mob's preference for identifying each other by arcane nicknames: Marty Bopalone, Louis Ha Ha, Tommy Karate, Joe Beans, Louie Bagels, and Peter Rabbit.

Possessing almost identical *curricula vitae*, the prosecution's seven main defectors presented a composite chronicle of late-twentieth-century Mafia culture. All were children of working-class urban families, had little formal education, were early and eager recruits, and all became successful and wealthy mafiosi. Their histories demonstrated that ignorance was not an impediment to advancement in the Mob. Exemplifying that trend, James Tartaglione testified that he had difficulty comprehending what he read, could not recall pertinent dates, and was unaware that Cosa Nostra was Italian for "Our Thing." He thought it meant "friends." Only one of the seven showed a glimmer of remorse for the murders and other gory events that encompassed their lives. Frank Lino broke down, crying softly, while reliving the ambush of the three capos. In that episode, however, he was himself almost a victim rather than a hit man. All of them agreed with Tartaglione about carrying out a gangland whacking: "It's either him or me. If I disobey an order, I'm the one who's going to get killed."

Breitbart's thrusts to puncture and impeach the defectors' accounts of Massino's history erupted into testy duels with Andres. At the start, presiding U.S. District Court Judge Nicholas Garaufis reined in the adversaries with his gift for witty, ego-cutting admonishments. As the cross-examinations became more heated, so did the bickering between Breitbart and Andres. The prosecutor complained that Breitbart misstated facts and uttered improper, stage-whispered asides to the jury, demeaning and falsely characterizing answers by witnesses. In return, Breitbart protested that Andres besmirched his reputation, and at one point, sought a mistrial, saying the judge's restrictions on his questions and court conduct created "an impossible climate for my client."

An even-tempered jurist with a ready smile who sometimes sat on the judge's elevated bench without his formal black robe, Garaufis rebuked both adversaries, "Hold your tongues or there will be fines." His sharpest censure was aimed at Breitbart. The judge once abruptly halted a cross-examination and sent the jury out of the court because Breitbart ignored his instructions about improper questions. "Your sarcasm oozes out of your lips," said Garaufis, ordering Breitbart to sit down and cease complaining that his rulings were biased against Massino.

A parade of seventy-eight witnesses and over three hundred exhibits, photographs, and audiotapes were presented by the prosecution during nine weeks of testimony. The defense's lone witness was an FBI agent called in a feeble move to discredit Vitale by showing a minor inconsistency between Vitale's testimony and information he had earlier provided in a debriefing. Outside the court, Breitbart, who turned sixty-five during the trial, confidently pronounced that his cross-examinations had won the day, without the necessity of rebuttal testimony.

Breitbart's last chance was the summation to the jury, and his heaviest obstacle was deflating the seven turncoats' aggregate testimony. He accused the FBI and the prosecutors of inventing and embellishing indictments through disreputable informers to justify a string of costly, failed investigations of Massino over three decades. Despite numerous electronic eavesdropping attempts, he noted, the FBI had never obtained an incriminating word from Massino's lips, nor was there a fingerprint or other physical evidence implicating him in a crime. To get Massino, Breitbart asserted, the government had corrupted justice by promising freedom or light sentences to sociopaths responsible for a total of eighteen murders. "This group of individuals is the most selfish, most arrogant, and most corrupt who have ever been put together in the history of the courtroom," he told the jury. "Give us Joe Massino and you can go home."

Barely looking at his notes in a five-hour recitation, frequently seeking eye contact with jurors, the lawyer's greatest venom was reserved for Vitale, calling him a "crazy madman, despised by his people," and who "hated Joe Massino." Tacitly admitting that Massino was a Mob boss, Breitbart tried to use the concession to turn the tables on the prosecution's own expert testimony that only a godfather could order hits. Since the seven murders Massino was charged with at this trial occurred before he became boss in 1992, the lawyer insisted that fact alone proved his innocence. Citing the Cosa Nostra's power structure and its table-of-command rules, Breitbart contended that Massino, a capo before 1992, had lacked the authority to order the killings. He tried to deflect blame and responsibility for the crimes onto the previous ruler, Phil Rastelli, and other Bonanno bigshots. In a paradoxical interpretation of evidence, he characterized Massino's reign as benign and without bloodshed. "He showed a love of life, not a love of death," Breitbart declared.

Throughout the trial, Andres and two other government prosecutors, Robert Henoch and Mitra Hormozi, obtained testimony from the turncoats that Massino had been the de facto boss long before he was officially installed. Anticipating the defense's contention, Henoch in opening remarks to the jury asserted that under Massino's rule, "If you messed up, you didn't get a bad report card; failure was punished by death."

Delivering part of the prosecution's summation, Hormozi placed the onus for the contract hits on Massino. "Some might say the person who gives the orders, or decides whether someone lives or dies, is more responsible than the person who pulled the trigger."

It fell to Andres, in an energetic rebuttal of Breitbart's arguments, to tie together all the strands of the prosecution's mammoth case. Defending the use of defectors as a necessary evil to uproot Mafia bosses, he ticked off the murders and felonies that had been unsolvable without their admissions. The deserters, he acknowledged, were selfish and looking to get out of prison, but he pledged that all would be sentenced. "They're criminals, murderers, part of a criminal enterprise—that man's enterprise," he concluded, pointing at Massino, "the one person yet to be held accountable—the highest-ranking man in the enterprise."

Eleven reporters covering the trial followed a pressroom tradition by establishing a pool bet on the length of jury deliberations and the verdict. They disagreed on how long the panel of ten women and two men would be out, but were unanimous about the outcome: guilty. Five days later, on July 30, 2004, the jury forewoman needed almost fifteen minutes to announce the unanimous verdicts on eleven counts and fifty specific racketeering acts. "Oh, God," Massino's daughter Adeline moaned, her head bowed in her hands, as the forewoman pronounced "Guilty" or "Proven" sixty-one times. The jury also required Massino to forfeit almost $10.4 million, the estimated amount of his criminal haul over one decade. The judgment included the seizure of the Casa Blanca, his favorite restaurant.

When it was all over, Massino turned to his wife, gesturing with open palms as if silently asking, "What are you going to do?"

Despite numerous and crafty precautions to avoid the fate that befell other god-fathers, Joe Massino never anticipated the confluence of events that swamped him. He had thwarted conventional FBI tactics for more than a decade and had faith in his invulnerability. How could he have foreseen that the two forensic accountants, Agents Sallet and McCaffrey, would launch an unparalleled examination of the entire family? They brought about his downfall through a labyrinthian paper chase that stemmed from one of his rare law-abiding acts, filing income tax returns.

By using capos to run the family's financial engines, Massino devised insulated walls that worked efficiently for ten years to ward off routine FBI scrutiny. By enriching captains and their sons, he felt assured they had too much at stake to incriminate him. He visualized the decentralization system as a rock-solid barrier to indictments; it became an Achilles' heel when the capos turned on him as their only chance for leniency.

Massino's biggest blunder was his mistreatment of Sal Vitale. Even so, the humiliated brother-in-law apparently was prepared at first to ride out their joint RICO storm. All evidence indicates that Vitale had no intention of betraying Massino until Sallet and McCaffrey warned him about the plot on his life. If Vitale had remained steadfast, Massino would have stood a strong chance of beating the original indictment and again frustrating the FBI's best efforts to bring him to justice. A traditionalist, Massino broke a Cosa Nostra cardinal rule by blatantly "disrespecting" Vitale, his most dedicated supporter for thirty years. It was a fatal error. Vitale's decision to become "a C.W.," a cooperative witness, was the decisive factor in accelerating the domino syndrome of defections that cinched Massino's conviction.

His judgment mistake about Vitale had enormous ramifications beyond Massino's own plight. Returning from prison in 1992, he had invigorated a fading borgata into a sturdy clan of more than 150 soldiers in 15 crews prospering from family rackets. Much of Massino's illicit army, however, was erased by the sudden spate of important indictments aided immensely by Vitale's encyclopedic knowledge of the family's crimes and incriminating remarks obtained through Big Louie Tartaglione's undercover tapes. The new evidence sparked mass arrests of the family's second tier of leaders along with thirty-two capos and soldiers. Over two years, almost half of the gang's cadre—some sixty members and most veteran commanders—were imprisoned or awaiting trial.

Heading the newly arrested list was Vincent "Vinny Gorgeous" Basciano, Massino's latest handpicked acting boss. Denied bail on a RICO-murder indictment, Basciano in November 2004 found himself alongside Massino in Brooklyn's Metropolitan Detention Center. A beauty salon owner, whose rackets were mainly in the Bronx, Basciano, 45, was nicknamed as much for his profession as for his supposed good looks.

Vinny Gorgeous had a lot to discuss with Massino concerning their mutual problems, and the boss, aka Joe the Ear, was suddenly an attentive listener. He realized that Basciano could be the key to his future. Betrayed by a nest of Mob "rats," Massino, soon after his conviction decided to convert. Astonishing law-enforcement officials, he volunteered to become an informant. And, he was using the unsuspecting Basciano as his ace-in-the hole for cutting a deal with the government for leniency. He claimed that he could implicate Basciano in a parcel of unsolved, serious felonies and get the acting boss to talk about a spectacular crime that he was planning—the murder of a prosecutor.

In early January 2005, Massino recorded two jailhouse meets with Basciano; the topics ranged from continued Bonanno operations to unsolved murders. The most explosive item supposedly proposed by Basciano was a hit on Greg Andres, the federal attorney in charge of Bonanno family prosecutions.

Based largely on Basciano's alleged remarks, in late January he was charged with conspiring to kill Andres. Moreover, the superseding indictment disclosed a bombshell: Massino was cooperating with his former arch enemies, the government team that had long pursued him. His reasons for joining "Team America," were easy to fathom. Law-enforcement officials and defense lawyers knew that he wanted his relatives to retain some of his $10 million loot, and hoped to spare his wife and his eighty-nine-year-old mother from eviction from their homes. (The government planned to seize the houses as having been acquired through criminal proceeds.)

Another compelling factor for betraying his Mob family was the mandatory life imprisonment awaiting him for his 2004 RICO conviction. And looming over him was a possible sentence of execution by legal injection if convicted at a second trial for ordering the 1999 Mob murder of Gerlando Sciascia.

Besides taping Basciano, Massino reportedly tipped off agents to the gangland graveyard where they dug up the remains of Philip Giaccone and Dominick Trinchera, the capos massacred two decades earlier on his orders.

Law-enforcement officials also were eager to unlock Massino's secrets about his forty years as a major mobster and his knowledge of recent crimes committed by higher-ups in the other four families. (In an ironic turnabout, Massino retained a former foe, Edward McDonald, to negotiate a deal with prosecutors for sentence breaks. McDonald had headed the Eastern District's Organized Crime Strike Force when it convicted and imprisoned Massino as a Mob racketeer for the first time in 1986. With McDonald pitching for Massino, at least one notable compromise was reached with prosecutors. Massino pleaded guilty to the hit on Sciascia and the government withdrew its request for the maximum penalty—death.) Spared the death sentence, Massino, in June 2005, was ordered by Judge Nicholas Garaufis to serve two consecutive life terms.

For his cooperation, Massino obtained a $1 million financial break, which allowed his wife to keep their faux-Georgian home. Josephine Massino turned over to the government about $9 million, including $7.6 million in cash, gold bars, and real estate properties. In relinquishing the criminally acquired nest egg, Mrs. Massino indicated that a marital rift had developed over her husband's abandonment of *omertà*. The long-devoted wife informed reporters that she disapproved of Joe's apostasy and was uncertain about visiting him in prison.

Massino, the Mafia's highest-ranking canary, can still harbor a hope for freedom. His double life sentence could be shortened if prosecutors find that his testimony and disclosures prove effective in a raft of high-profile Cosa Nostra cases.

Once viewed as a pillar of the Mafia's old-world morals and *omertà*, Massino is the first New York-area boss to become a turncoat. (The only other Cosa Nostra chieftain to testify against his family was Philadelphia's Ralph Natale, who turned in 2000 after being convicted on RICO charges.) Long portrayed by law enforcement and mobsters as the last major twentieth-century don, Massino was looked upon as the Mafia's savior. His final handiwork at age sixty-two, however, left the Bonnano borgata in shambles and his conversion threatened other Mafia families.

"Like everyone he had previously condemned and tried to kill for cooperating, he too cracked," said a veteran lawyer who defended Bonnano wiseguys, and who asked to be quoted anonymously. Summing up the views of other attorneys who represent mafiosi defendants, he added: "At the end, after a lifetime of crime, Joe was just another hypocrite. He desperately wanted 'a pass,' a chance to walk the streets again."

Afterword

Back to the Caves

At the dawn of a new century, the American Mafia was portrayed as a crushed Colossus. With numbing frequency, prosecutors and FBI officials were unsealing indictments that seemingly decimated the Mob's sacred stronghold in New York. The message from the gleeful authorities was clear: the once-invincible five families, together with borgatas in the rest of the country, were nearing extinction. Some enthusiasts rhapsodized that it was the "Twilight of the Godfathers". The combined federal and state campaigns were arguably the most successful anticrime expedition in American history. Over a span of two decades, twenty-four Mob families, once the best-organized and most affluent criminal associations in the nation, were virtually eliminated or seriously undermined. (By comparison, a more costly half-century campaign against the narcotics scourge remains a Sisyphean failure.)

September 11, 2001, however, radically transformed that rosy scenario.

The terrorist attacks on the World Trade Center and the Pentagon endowed the Cosa Nostra with an undeserved bequest: renewed hope for survival.

The events of 9/11 have been a decisive factor in altering the Mob's prospects. The hijacked planes that destroyed the Twin Towers and ripped into the Pentagon, killing nearly three thousand innocent people, indirectly provided a reprieve for the Mafia. Since those kamikaze raids by Al Qaeda, the FBI and regional police forces justifiably have been dedicated to one paramount mission: guarding against terrorist attacks.

But even before 9/11, federal and local investigations of the Mafia were slowing down, official logic having concluded that the Mob, a terminally ill enemy, required less attention. Most indictments and convictions garnered in the first years of the millennium had been generated by investigations long in the pipeline, begun during the apogee of the FBI and state efforts in the 1990s. The first years of the new century saw fewer resources committed against wiseguys throughout the country, and 9/11 accelerated that trend. For three months after the World Trade Center carnage, almost all Mafia squad agents in New York were pulled off active investigations to pitch in on counterterrorism work. Some agents were reassigned for as long as seven months, and some never returned to Cosa Nostra duties. "There's no question that major operational plans were postponed for a time after 9/11," James Margolin, an FBI spokesman, concedes.

Counterespionage and the Mafia had been the two uppermost FBI concerns for over a quarter of a century. Abruptly, the Mob was reduced to a backseat status. Announcing the bureau's revised agenda in May 2002, FBI Director Robert S. Mueller III significantly excluded the Mafia in evaluating the agency's most pressing challenges. "Protect the United States from terrorist attack" headed the list; preventing violent and major white-collar crimes and combating public corruption had displaced the Cosa Nostra, which was relegated to the lower end of the priority table.

Other examples of the downgrading were evident. Even bureau-speak was symbolically altered at the FBI's Washington headquarters where the Organized Crime Section, which had overseen all "LCN" investigations, was renamed the "Transnational Criminal Enterprise Section."

For over two decades, every FBI assistant director placed at the helm of the New York office, the largest of fifty-six field branches, always came with extensive experience in supervising Mafia investigations. Indicative of the changing times, Mueller revised that pattern in 2003, selecting an expert on counterterrorism, Pasquale D'Amuro, to New York's top post. The five family squads were reduced in size, remaining under the umbrella of the bureau's Criminal Division while a substantially enlarged "Counter Terrorism Division" was created as an independent unit.

Overall, in the nation, the FBI repositioned more than five hundred of its eleven thousand agents from traditional crime-fighting duties to the struggle against Al Qaeda and its terrorist offshoots. Officials acknowledged that full-time organized-crime squads were cut or eliminated, but the precise numbers are secret.

In New York City, the linchpin in the FBI's crusade against the American Mafia, a sizable portion of its eleven hundred agents were moved to antiterrorism operations. At the high point of the FBI's war against New York's borgatas in the 1990s, as many as 350 agents and 100 police investigators worked full- or part-time on Mafia task forces. By 2005, that contingent of 450 was trimmed by roughly two-thirds. Some one hundred agents were assigned permanently or temporarily, aided by a handful of New York Police Department officers, instead of the one hundred police officers that once reinforced the bureau's Mob squads. Meanwhile, the Counter Terrorism Division was beefed up to more than three hundred permanent agents, plus four hundred investigators from other federal agencies and the NYPD.

Defending the personnel transfers, the FBI brass found abundant grounds for minimizing the Mafia as a threat. Many believed that the government had achieved its prime goal of dismembering the Mob to the status it held at the beginning of the twentieth century: a clutch of loose-knit, quarrelsome street gangs lacking competent leadership. "Their future is dim and fraught with peril," WK Williams, the FBI official in Washington directing the bureau's nationwide efforts against the Mafia, predicted in a 2004 interview. (Williams uses initials for his given names without periods.)

Confident that the Mafia's glory days were over, optimists were convinced that a few final nails would seal its coffin. To support that contention, current and former law-enforcement officials could cite a lengthy tableau of defeats inflicted on La Cosa Nostra.

1. Only families in New York and Chicago, the largest traditional bases, retained a semblance of organizational frameworks. Elsewhere in the nation, the twenty-odd borgatas were in disarray or practically defunct, except in areas where the New York and Chicago families had branches, especially in Florida. The remaining strength of the Mob was largely concentrated in New York and the Northeast Corridor, according to Williams.

2. Almost all established leaders in the New York and the nation's important families were in prison.

3. *Omertà*—the protective code of manhood and silence—had crumbled.

An endless exodus of turncoats was seeking shelter from RICO punishment by cooperating for lenient sentences. Even big shots were "turning" after a half century in which not a single leader or capo had switched sides.

4. Former Italian-American neighborhoods, transformed by demographic and sociological changes, no longer served as sanctuaries and as hubs for enlisting generations of reliable recruits. Discipline was unraveling and wannabes— like the Bath Avenue Boys in the Bonanno family—were increasingly addicted to drugs, vulnerable to arrests, and tattling to save their skins.

5. Racketeering alliances with core unions, most notably the teamsters' and construction trades' locals, had been weakened or severed through wholesale convictions of corrupt labor leaders and the appointment of internal watchdogs.

6. Money trees in Las Vegas for the most powerful families had been chopped down by government oversight of the teamsters' union, preventing union loans to Mob-tarnished hotels, and through acquisitions of the largest casinos by legitimate multinational corporations. The days of skimming gambling profits had apparently ended, and tighter licensing supervision by Nevada regulators had blocked casino takeovers by mobsters.

7. Domination of New York's invaluable resources—the wholesale food markets, the Garment Center, the garbage-carting industry, and the Javits Convention Center—had been curtailed, if not totally eliminated, by blacklisting scores of tarred companies, followed by tough licensing laws introduced in Mayor Rudolph Giuliani's administration. These regulatory steps were seen as firewalls preventing wiseguys from regaining influence at these commercial prizes. (The storied Fulton Fish Market, long beleaguered by mobsters, will be essentially shut down in 2005. Transplanting its businesses to a modern, enclosed facility in the Bronx was expected to strengthen the city's enforcement of rules aimed at barring future Mafia takeovers.)

8. Convictions had shattered the Mafia's Commission, and there was little likelihood that another supreme body could regain authority to resolve disputes, enforce traditions, and maintain the Mafia's institutional codes.

"There is no resemblance to the power they exerted in the '80s and '90s," says James Kallstrom, the former head of the bureau's New York office and a pivotal player in the FBI's maneuvers against the Mob. "They still have thugs and thieves out there but they have zero influence and no major impact anymore on controlling unions like the teamsters and major industries."

Echoing Kallstrom, Ronald Goldstock, the former New York prosecutor who was instrumental in generating the Commission case, portrays the remaining borgatas as disorganized rabble. "The Mob has been so weakened that it can't supply the services it once did to its members. Nobody obeys the rules anymore. They may be continuing criminal activities, but they're acting as individuals, not as a viable organization."

Shortly before he died in 2003, former New York detective Ralph Salerno, an early warrior against the Cosa Nostra, visualized it as a fading anachronism. A major reason for its defeat, he thought, was the "dumbing down" of recruits. "At one time, not so long ago, there was a supply of young Italian-Americans who wanted to be in the families. Now, they want to be CEO's of legitimate corporations. The families no longer attract young men with brains."

From their vantage point, defense lawyers offered an additional explanation for the succession of courtroom debacles suffered by godfathers and high-ranking loyalists. The attorneys contend that the harsh prison penalties imposed for RICO convictions spurred the deluge of deserters that demolished the Mafia's long-range survival plans. Expressing the views of lawyers who have represented major organized-crime suspects, Gerald Shargel says, "The prospect of getting a sentence of twenty to forty years or life without parole is a strong motivation to get people to cooperate." Shargel, who defended John J. Gotti, several of his relatives, and Sammy Gravano, contends that juries have become "more conservative" and likely to bring in guilty verdicts in Mob-related cases. "In the '70s and '80s, we got a lot of acquittals. Today, there is a stronger presumption of guilt if jurors hear the word 'Mafia.' What it means is that there are very few old-fashioned types left who are willing to risk a trial and draconian punishment."

The prevailing officialdom consensus holds that the Cosa Nostra entered the twenty-first century battered and reeling, with obituaries being prepared by thoughtful analysts. Nevertheless, there are cautionary markers, at least in New York, suggesting that the patient is not ready for the graveyard. Consider the following manifestations in the first years of the millennium:

Gambling and loan-sharking—the Mafia's symbiotic bread-and-butter staples—appear to be unstoppable. A Gambino capo was uncovered supervising bookie joints in Queens grossing $30 million a year. The Bonannos were profiting from similar setups, netting $20 million and $10 million annually from two sports betting rings in suburban Long Island. A crackdown by the Queens DA's office broke up a Bonanno-controlled high-tech international enterprise that allegedly handled a staggering $360 million in sports bets between 2002 and 2005. Sensible gamblers will always prefer wagering with the Mob rather than with state-authorized Off-Track Betting parlors and lotteries. Bets on baseball, football, and basketball games placed with a bookie have a 50 percent chance of winning, without the penalty of being taxed, while the typical state lottery is considered a pipe dream because the chance of winning is infinitesimal.

Additionally, Mob gambling networks are almost always tied into loan-sharking for compulsive gamblers who need instant credit, regardless of the staggering vigorish rates. Twenty soldiers and associates of a Genovese crew in New Jersey were arrested for operating a gambling and loan-sharking branch that charged up to an astronomical 156 percent interest.

Despite endless attempts to reform the construction industry and building trades unions, Mob families are still up to their old tricks. One outrageous example was hiking the cost of a $400 million skyscraper office building-renovation in Manhattan for the Metropolitan Transportation Authority, the main public transit agency in the New York region. A federal indictment charged that the project developer—a longtime Gambino associate—conspired with the family's Mob-affiliated contractors and corrupt union officials to siphon more than $10 million through inflated bills and violation of union hiring regulations. The developer admitted paying weekly tribute of $12,500 for years to a Gambino soldier as part of the family's share of the overcharges.

In another ripoff, before being convicted, a troupe of Genovese and Gambino soldiers plucked $2 million from "no show" jobs handed out by a union that operated temporary elevators at construction sites. Similarly, twenty-two Colombo and Genovese members were in a select group that obtained $3.5 million from phony jobs with a union that handled heavy equipment and from a painters' local. Work sites exploited by the Mob included the new Museum of Modern Art and baseball stadiums built for the Yankees' and the Mets' minor league teams. The recipients of the largesse included a son of imprisoned Colombo boss Carmine the Snake Persico and the sons of other Colombo stars. A déjà vu aspect of these interfamily scams was the creation of a "panel," reminiscent of the "clubs" set up decades earlier by the Mafia to apportion loot among the various gangs.

A federal grand jury also accused two sons of the late Joe Colombo of resorting to a familiar ploy in a "comeback" attempt to gain support in the Colombo family. They were indicted for allegedly extorting and bilking companies of hundreds of thousands of dollars in contracts for remodeling buildings and offices.

And far from finished with construction payoffs, the Genovese family has persisted in exploiting New York's drywall-carpentry industry. A decade after federal and state authorities boasted that they had broken the borgata's grip on the industry and its captive union locals, a capo and twenty-one underlings were indicted for fraud and labor racketeering involving multimillions of dollars.

All of these construction industry crimes were uncovered as products of investigations begun before 9/11, when the Cosa Nostra was still a priority target for the government.

Disputes over the Mob's retention of power in a pivotal national union—the International Brotherhood of Teamsters—resurfaced in 2004. A group of twenty investigators and lawyers resigned in mass protest, complaining that teamsters' president James P. Hoffa, son of the vanished Jimmy Hoffa, was stifling their efforts to uproot Cosa Nostra connections. The head of the cleanup effort, Edward Stier, a highly respected former federal prosecutor, asserted that Hoffa had interfered with probes into "pockets of organized crime" and corruption by teamster managers. Following numerous investigations and convictions of its highest leaders, the union in 1989 was placed under a federal monitoring system empowered to eliminate Mafia influence. Seeking to end government oversight, the younger Hoffa chose Stier in 1999 to lead a self-policing experiment known as RISE—Respect, Integrity, Strength, and Ethics—staffed with former FBI agents. Dismissing Stier's documented allegations as "reckless and false," Hoffa pledged his commitment to eradicating any remaining Mob influence. The resignations of his own appointed investigators, however, highlighted a chronic problem: the hazards of permanently reforming unions with histories of endemic Mafia penetration.

Even Mayor Rudolph Giuliani's wary anti-Mafia administration was embarrassed by a project at Giuliani's front door. Shortly before his term ended, companies supplying concrete for a $22 million restoration of City Hall Park were swiftly dropped after *The New York Times* reported that under previous corporate names the outfits had been implicated in labor-peace deals with mobster families.

Through their persistent presence in the construction industry, mafiosi even tried to profit directly from 9/11. Lucchese underboss Steven Wonder Boy Crea pleaded guilty to extorting payoffs from a company engaged in the removal of the World Trade Center debris. And the Bonannos tried unsuccessfully to steal and sell scrap metal from the Twin Towers ruins.

In the aftermath of concentrated crackdowns in the 1980s and '90s, New York's billion-dollar construction industry appears nearly as vulnerable as ever to determined gangsters. The obstacles blocking fundamental reforms in the industry were illustrated by a singular setback suffered by Giuliani. His administration imposed regulatory and licensing rules designed to weed out wiseguys and Mafia-linked companies from major wholesale food markets and the garbage-carting industry. When Giuliani tried to enact similar legislation to scrutinize building projects, he was blocked by an intractable combo of high-voltage developers, contractors, and unions who bottled up the proposed bill in the City Council. Since then, no politician has dared to raise the issue of strict oversight of that corruption-prone industry, and its unions, always heavy contributors to election campaigns.

Often, the Mafia seems determined to retain a semblance of historic ties. A sidelight in Joe Massino's 2004 trial revealed that Perry Criscitelli, a reputed Bonanno soldier and Little Italy restaurateur, was the president of the Feast of San Gennaro Committee, which presumably had been cleansed of Mob control by Mayor Giuliani's administration. Criscitelli was forced to resign from the panel overseeing the celebrated tourist attraction, but not before his Mulberry Street restaurant, Da Nico, topped Giuliani's recommended list for Republican Party convention delegates that year as his favorite dining spot in New York.

Other Cosa Nostra standbys rediscovered in the new century were Garment Center "protection" payoffs for labor peace, practices dating back to Lucky Luciano's heyday. The extortion artists came from Sammy Gravano's old Gambino crew in Brooklyn, which thrived long after his defection.

Auto "chop shops," another favorite Mob pastime, are said by the police to be still going strong, earning a Genovese faction in Brooklyn $2.5 million a year by reselling stolen car parts and air bags.

While time-tested crimes continue to support the five families, they have been simultaneously exploring new multimillion-dollar enterprises. Their imaginative innovations covered a wide spectrum of enterprises:

Telephone bill frauds: Capo Salvatore Tore Locascio, the son and heir of convicted Gambino underboss Frank Locascio, and nine other soldiers and associates were accused of filching over $200 million in five years from thousands of unwitting customers. A gimmick dreamed up by the mobsters was enticing thousands of victims to sample adult entertainment such as sex-chat lines, dating services, and psychic readings. The thefts were based on "cramming," a trap in which callers were clipped for up to $40 a month on their phone bills after being deceived by "free trial" advertisements. Investigators said tech-savvy mobsters devised a maze of shell companies that billed the callers indirectly through local telephone utilities. Assessing the swindle as one of the largest ever pulled off by the Mafia, Philip Scala, the head of the FBI's Gambino Squad, remarked, "The profit from that fraud alone makes the Gambinos look like a Fortune 500 company."

Bootlegged CDs: A Genovese group in Long Island counterfeited 10,000 compact disks a week for years, netting $2.5 million annually in profits before the scheme was thwarted.

Credit cards: In Queens, Genovese soldiers teamed up with store cashiers and clerks to copy credit card numbers, which were then used to manufacture fakes. The dishonest employees were paid $50 for each swiped number, while the bogus credit cards were sold for $1,000 apiece to clients who quickly purchased thousands of dollars worth of goods before the victims were alerted. Computer hackers working for a Bonanno crew pulled off a similar operation, obtaining credit card numbers issued by Mexican banks. The fraud was masterminded by capo William "Big Willie" Riviello, who camouflaged the operation by working out of a Bronx mushroom-packaging warehouse.

Health care: A New Jersey Genovese crew took over a company that arranged and managed group medical, dental, and eye-care programs for employers and unions. Administrators were strong-armed into approving excessive fees for spurious medical services, which the Mafia pocketed. The New Jersey attorney general's office stumbled onto the scheme while eavesdropping on the crew's bookmaking activities, but was unable to obtain an accurate estimate of the amount swindled.

Phone cards: The Gambinos stole several million dollars by setting up companies providing prepaid phone cards. The mobsters distributed the cards through retail stores, mainly in neighborhoods populated by immigrants who use them to call overseas. Each card supplied by the Gambinos was typically sold for $20, but most were worthless after $2 or $3 in calls because they had not been programmed for the listed amount. No one was arrested for the flim-flam of low-income victims, many of whom were illegal aliens fearful of complaining to the police. And guess who snared the illegal profits?

The Mafia's continued activities in New York demonstrate that holdouts can survive and still prosper from gambling, loan-sharking, and protection rackets. But a wider resurgence rests heavily on the ability of a new crop of mafiosi to shift into modern avenues of crime. A revival would not surprise G. Robert Blakey, the principal author of the RICO law. He views the recent incursions of the five families into financial and health industry crimes as the latest chapter of the Cosa Nostra's Darwinian survival adaptability. Characterizing the Mafia as "a mirror image of capitalism and a recurring capitalist disease," Blakey notes that it has always fed off technological innovations and subverted laws intended to govern industries, unions, and drug usage. "We don't win the war against the Mob," he advises, "all we can do is contain or control it."

Blakey and other experienced anti-Mafia campaigners fret that the government's devaluation of its perennial enemy will boomerang. "Keeping a boxer down is easier than knocking him down a second time," Blakey says. "By withdrawing resources, we'll just have to go back and complete the job at a larger cost."

Despite pronouncements of unabated vigilance, law enforcement's roller-coaster efforts against the traditional crime families are unmistakably in a downward cycle. FBI Director Mueller said as much in a National Public Radio radio interview in September 2003. In light of 9/11, he asked the public to "recognize that we can't do everything," and urged local authorities to pick up the slack left by the bureau's emphasis on counterterrorism and newer priorities.

State prosecutors and police forces, confronting terrorism as well as violent crime pressures and budget restraints, show less zeal than previously to engage the Mob. In New York, the state Organized Crime Task Force, which was established to coordinate cases and tackle Mob-infested industries, had 140 investigators, lawyers, and backup personnel in the 1990s. The staff was gradually cut to about 60. A Republican administration stripped the agency of its independence, folded it into the state attorney general's office, denied it a separate budget, and sometimes sidetracked it into investigations unrelated to organized crime. A new attorney general, Eliot Spitzer, a Democrat, maintains that he is trying to revitalize the unit but is hamstrung by budget restraints. Spitzer vaulted into national prominence by unearthing large-scale Wall Street, corporate, and insurance industry scandals. On the Cosa Nostra front, however, he made scant headlines in his first seven years in office. Spitzer considers the families "atrophied and much weaker" than in the 1990s but recognizes that "they are morphing into different areas." Regardless of budget slashes, he vows that his "leaner, meaner" task force can still help throttle the mob—a pledge that might be hard to fulfill with reduced personnel and priority commitments to other areas.

Similar organized-crime and intelligence-gathering divisions in other states long plagued by the Cosa Nostra were eliminated or downsized. Officials in New Jersey, Pennsylvania, California, and Florida have minimized the Mafia's contemporary importance and danger. Short on money, states are reluctant to pay for specialist training of organized-crime investigators and for undercover operations requiring extensive surveillance without guaranteed success. Phone taps and bugs, almost always essential for convictions, can tie up six agents daily for months—a staggering outlay for strapped local police and district attorneys faced with persistent violent crime problems.

Daniel Castleman, the prosecutor in charge of the Manhattan DA's organized-crime division, wants more, not less, manpower committed against the Mob. "Anyone who thinks the Mafia is dead is engaged in wishful thinking," he emphasizes. "There are still functioning crews ready, willing, and able to take advantage of human foibles. And there are still young hoods who want to emulate and perpetuate the gangster lifestyle."

Unless the FBI vigorously reasserts itself, law-enforcement aspirations for quickly finishing off the Mafia appear dim. Frederick Martens, the former executive director of the Pennsylvania Crime Commission, and former chief of organized-crime intelligence for the New Jersey State Police, warns that federal and local authorities have been "deluded" into believing that the flood of convictions at the turn of the century signaled the Mafia's doom. "I can't help being reminded of the generals in Vietnam who used body counts, fictitious as they were, to claim victory," he says.

While Mafia infrastructures appear to have been substantially damaged, Martens fears that the relaxed law-enforcement posture will rejuvenate the families. "Flexibility and durability are hallmarks of the LCN. Given a window of opportunity, they will take full advantage of it."

The FBI's overconfident assessment that the Bonanno and Colombo families were rudderless and moribund led to a painful setback at the end of the twentieth century. For eight years, the FBI saved manpower by using one squad to bird-dog both borgatas. The main result of this economy was a dramatic revival of the Bonannos under Joe Massino's leadership. "The lesson we learned is that you cannot deemphasize vigilance on any of the families," comments Bruce Mouw, who was temporarily in charge of the combined squad. "All are capable of comebacks."

Renewed energy is even evident in the shell-shocked Colombo family. Through Bonanno defector James Big Louie Tartaglione, the FBI learned that the Colombos, in the 2000s, asked other families to appraise a list of ten applicants selected for induction as made men. The ability to replenish its shattered ranks shows that the Colombo Mob still can count on a steady supply of recruits.

Another cautioner about a federal pullback is Andrew Maloney, the former U.S. Attorney on whose watch John Gotti was finally convicted. "If the government lays off, they'll be back," Maloney forecasts. "They [the Mafia] resemble a vampire; you have to put a stake through their heart and that has not been done."

Throughout the onslaughts against their families, America's wiseguys have retained a precious asset that contributes to their survival. It is the media's romanticization of mobsters, subtly encouraging acceptance of the Mafia as just another aspect of the nation's culture. The Oscar-winning *Godfather* movies in the 1970s set the stage for the public perception that a biased Wasp-run society had compelled a tiny segment of Italian-American immigrants to form criminal bands and resort to violence and stealth as their only means of acceptance and advancement. A raft of novels and films spiced with empathetic and comedic touches, such as *Prizzi's Honor, Analyze This, The Gang that Couldn't Shoot Straight,* and *Bugsy,* cast some mobsters as high-living, lovable rogues. These films present them as dedicated criminals; yet, too often, they are given redeeming qualities, a revered code of honor, loyalty, and obedience. Their quest is simply the American ideal of obtaining wealth and respect, even if an occasional homicide and betrayal is required.

Prospective jurors in organized-crime trials are frequently asked if their judgments might be influenced by movies or television programs dealing with the Mafia. Many fictional scenarios view the Cosa Nostra as comprised of both honorable and evil participants, in a profession that oddly parallels large, legitimate corporations, with a subtext that mobsters lead nonconformist, adventurous lives. In real life, no mafiosi are "good guys."

A prototype of show business's vicarious flirtation with the Mafia is *The Sopranos,* HBO's prize-winning television series, which is to television what *The Godfather* was to films—a super hit. The underlying humanizing theme of the series is that, except for his occupation as the boss of a New Jersey crew, Tony Soprano is a quintessential suburbanite, searching for the meaning of life, happiness, and security. He lives in a small mansion and is rolling in dough; yet he is afflicted by the common turmoil of middle-aged bourgeois fathers. His marriage to Carmela is on the rocks; she, tuned-in to womens rights, is seeking to liberate herself from a humdrum existence; his spoiled teenaged children are rebellious; and despite a harem of girlfriends, he agonizes over being unloved and unappreciated. The ambitious gangster-executive is constantly confronted by nuisances at his "office"—a workplace peopled by menacing types, where minor errors result in death or imprisonment.

Genuine capos and wiseguys would never emulate Tony's behavior. He stalks and kills victims, chores normally shunned by a capo or boss; murder is the task of soldiers and wannabes. No top-tier mobster would last long if he behaved like Tony Soprano, who defies basic mafioso caution by exposing himself as a ripe target, to be easily mowed down by rivals. He drives without a bodyguard; sips espresso in daylight at a sidewalk café; and begins his days in a bathrobe, sluggishly strolling down his driveway to pick up his newspaper near an open road.

Sex and psychiatry are prominent in *The Sopranos'* story line. Confiding in a psychiatrist, however, would be a radioactive mistake for a boss or capo, who can never display symptoms of weakness or mental instability. Seeing a shrink is guaranteed to incite dissension and doubts about a hierarch's reliability to head a borgata. Tony Soprano ignores the caveat by consulting a woman psychiatrist who, naturally, is fetchingly attractive as she counsels him on his nagging insecurities and interprets the Freudian symbols, fears, and sexual frustrations revealed in his dreams. No self-respecting mobster would confide intimate secrets to a stranger, let alone a female psychiatrist. An increased business-world role for women might be politically correct, but the Mob has resisted that trend.

There are aspects of *The Sopranos* that do accurately capture the Mob's crude lifestyle. The profanity-laced dialogue is much like bugged vitriolic conversations that have been featured at actual trials. Tony and his cronies vividly display the casual savagery that is trademark Mafia behavior. And Tony's compulsive whoring could have been modeled on the escapades of countless wiseguys.

Despite the cruelty, depravity, and sex, the presentation creates an undercurrent of sympathy for Tony, a mobster who yearns nostalgically for an earlier era when Men of Honor were Spartan and trustworthy. As the series antihero, he suffers the same angst as any law-abiding, average American striving to enjoy material success. He is generous, worries about his children, grieves over the death of a discarded lover, has compassion for a cancer-stricken friend and for a boyhood buddy who attempts suicide. Essentially a beguiling soap opera about a dysfunctional suburban household, *The Sopranos* contributes yet another deceptive image of a genuine Mafia family.

"They are displayed having a twisted sense of honor, 'taking no crap' from anyone, with easy access to women and money," Howard Abadinsky, an organized-crime historian, says of *The Sopranos'* cast of thugs. "Such displays romanticize organized crime and, as an unintended consequence, serve to perpetuate the phenomenon and create alluring myths about the Mafia."

For more meaningful pointers on the resurgent powers of authentic borgatas, America's law-enforcement planners might well look to the Mafia's birthplace—Sicily. After World War II, Italy's weak central governments tolerated a Mafia renaissance, allowing the clans to coerce legitimate businesses and to pollute the political system, principally through alliances with leaders in the since-discredited Christian Democratic Party.

A courageous prosecutor, Giovanni Falcone, launched the first sustained postwar assault against the island's Cosa Nostra in the 1980s, imprisoning bosses and some three hundred soldiers. Falcone and another prosecutor, Paolo Borsellino, won mass convictions partly by employing American tactics—fracturing *omertà* through plea bargaining with *pentiti,* penitents or turncoats, and following incriminating paper trails linking gangsters to extortion payoffs. Although heavily guarded and working in bunkerlike quarters, both prosecutors were killed by bombs in 1992, in a spectacular Mafia message of uncompromising defiance. Their murders galvanized Italy for several years into breakthroughs against the Sicilian chieftains by increasing the powers of prosecutors and by safeguarding *pentiti* and their relatives in the first effective Italian witness-protection program.

After a decade of stringent enforcement, the drive was hobbled when the government of Prime Minister Silvio Berlusconi promoted legislation in 2002 and 2004 that makes the climate less favorable for Mafia convictions. New laws limit the use of testimony from defectors, restrict the use of bookkeeping evidence to implicate mobsters in frauds and shake-downs, and hamper recruitment of *pentiti.*

Using public-relations finesse, Sicily's modern godfathers adopted low-profile policies known as *Pax Mafiosi,* Mafia Peace. Fearful of rekindling public outrage against their organizations, the new bosses avoid violent confrontations with law enforcement and prefer invisibility. They have imposed stricter discipline on soldiers, tamped down internecine feuds, and ceased murdering so-called "excellent cadavers," prosecutors, judges, police, and outspoken opponents. "Nowadays, the Mafia is stronger than before because its leaders have changed their strategy," Sergio Barbiera, the deputy director of the Anti-Mafia Public Attorney's office in Palermo, acknowledges. "No one can commit a serious crime which can attract the attention of the mass media."

Palermo's chief prosecutor, Pietro Grasso, adds, "The silence of the Mafia is a strategy, not an absence."

Law-enforcement authorities concede that the reconstituted Sicilian gangs have resumed their classical "protection" schemes in all types of businesses and public projects. The redesigned clans jolted prosecutors in 2003 by planting moles in their office in Palermo, the center of anti-Mafia activities. Two officials, working on cases involving Cosa Nostra's linkage to corrupt politicians, were arrested on charges of being double-agents and sabotaging the inquiries.

Alexander Stille, an American journalist who has written extensively about the Sicilian Mafia, says it has regained ominous political vitality, seeking the kind of supremacy that it enjoyed in the past. "Even if Cosa Nostra can deliver only five percent of the vote—the low end of most estimates—that can make the difference in many elections."

And, as so often was true in the past, eruptions in the Sicilian Mafia reverberate in America. Astute Mafia-watchers are aware that the Sicilians have the means to fortify the U.S. families through an infusion of new Zips. A defector from the DeCavalcante family in New Jersey, Frank "Frankie the Beast" Scarabino, disclosed that his leaders planned to hire "ghost soldiers" to rub out informers and to assassinate judges and FBI agents. "They were going to start importing Sicilian shooters," he testified at a Mob trial. DeCavalcante leaders referred to the Sicilians as ghost soldiers because they would be unknown to American police and could "do a piece of work [murder] and get out of the country with no problem," Scarabino said. A federal prosecutor in Manhattan, Miriam Rocah, described the plan as "no idle chitchat." Because the tiny DeCavalcante crew has often functioned as an auxiliary of the Gambino family and was close to Joe Massino, Scarabino's talk of ghost solders indicates that it might be an idea under consideration by the larger New York borgatas.

Sicily also beckons as a conscription area for the American Mafia's depleted battalions. The Bonannos and Gambinos have a history of sponsoring Sicilian branches in New York; and talk by the DeCavalcantes suggests more budding alliances with Sicilian mafiosi. In the aftermath of the rash of defections that roiled the American Mafia, Sicilians not formally inducted into an Italian gang could be made and welcomed as reinforcements by the U.S. borgatas. Zips are respected by the Americans for their steely discipline, and more vitally, their allegiance to the code of *omertà*.

A decade of defeats might embolden the next wave of American dons to apply a survival tactic long practiced by the Sicilian Mafia—slaughtering relatives of informers to stiffen the code of *omertà*. One rarely violated Commission rule is a ban on injuring "civilians," innocent relatives. In September 2003, however, the FBI secretly recorded Anthony Tony Green Urso, then the Bonanno acting boss and consigliere, talking about murdering children and relatives of cooperative witnesses. He proposed it as the surest way of stemming the tide of traitors. ". . . You gotta throw somebody in the streets—this has got to stop," Urso urged other Bonanno honchos in a discussion about muzzling informers following the arrest of Joe Massino. "You turned, we wipe your family out. . . . Why should the rats' kids be happy, where my kids or your kids should suffer because I'm away for life. . . . See, Louie, Louie, if you take one kid, I hate to say it, but you do what you gotta do, they're going to fucking think twice." (Unbeknownst to Urso, his words were captured on tape by Big Louie Tartaglione, a wired turncoat.)

Borrowing a page from the past, the five families now view proper blood lines as indispensable character references. Fixated on insuring loyalty and greater security, hierarchs restored a binding requirement that both parents, not just the father, must be of Italian lineage as a fundamental requirement to become a made man. At Joe Massino's trial in 2004, Sal Vitale disclosed that Massino and other leaders reimposed the rigid rule at a Commission meeting. Vitale also reported another step to weed out weaklings. In 2000 the godfathers decreed that any wannabe arrested on drug charges would have to wait at least five years after release from prison before being straightened out. The rule was intended to finally eliminate from membership vulnerable drug dealers, who often become informers to escape harsh prison sentences.

The extreme steps advocated by Mafia insiders should be a beacon warning against an easy surrender. "Backed into a corner, they might become desperate and lash out in ways they haven't before," Matthew Heron, a former supervisor of the FBI's Organized Crime Branch in New York, believes. Pointing to the Mafia's penchant for violence. Heren says that an FBI analysis attributed at least 912 murders in the New York area to the Mob from 1970 through 2003, an average of almost thirty a year.

Heren and two agents in front-line trenches—Philip Scala of the Gambino Squad and Michele Campanella, the chief of the Genovese Squad—confirm that additional agents are needed. "Despite the tremendous successes we have had, we need more resources and funding to get a real shot at wiping them out in three to five years," says Scala.

After the misfortunes of Joe Massino and his Bonanno compatriots, FBI officials believe the Gambino and Genovese gangs returned to the peak of the five families' pyramid. Scala and Campanella estimated in 2004 that they each had managed to raise their ranks to at least two hundred active soldiers and several thousand compliant associates. The Gambinos, under the direction of street bosses and capos, have become much more secretive in the wake of John Gotti's flashy reign. "They are trying to keep their big earners off our radar screens," Scala says. To shield the identities of money men and insulate them from investigations, the street bosses have instructed them to stay away from hangouts and from Mob social events where they could be spotted by agents.

Campanella credits the Genoveses, the other large borgata, with trying to reconstruct the widespread business structure it developed under Vincent Chin Gigante's direction. In prison, the aging Gigante retained his godfather title while senior capos ran the family in his absence. "The boss is incarcerated but there is somebody ready to step up to the plate for him and take care of the money-making possibilities," Campanella explains.

A thorny question is whether eased law-enforcement pressure can whittle away the Cosa Nostra's remaining strength. Institutional memories about the Mafia's potency might fade; investigative fervor and proactive policies might further lessen as fewer battle-hardened agents and prosecutors are assigned to combat the Mob. Most federal attorneys arrive as fledglings directly from law school, untrained in prosecuting mafiosi and unaware of Mob stratagems. Many leave within ten years for lucrative private practices, just as they have honed the skills to master complex RICO cases. For two decades, the Justice Department's fourteen Organized Crime Strike Forces relied on a corps of prosecutors who stayed longer and concentrated exclusively on the Mafia. Although many law-enforcement researchers believe the independent strike forces proved their effectiveness, they were eliminated in a 1989 political decision to mollify the regional U.S. Attorneys who viewed them more as rivals than as colleagues.

If the federal government continues its cutbacks, local officials wonder if the

FBI will pass along the intelligence it obtains from informers, particularly those relating to gambling and loan-sharking operations. The bureau reputedly still shares evidence and intelligence leads grudgingly with state prosecutors and police departments, which often breeds resentment and confusion within other agencies.

The emergence in New York and other urban regions of vicious Russian, Asian, and Latin American gangs may further deflect local and federal law-enforcement attention from the Mafia. These marauders, most of them recently arrived immigrants, rarely engage in sophisticated crimes, resorting mainly to drug trafficking and leg breaking to terrorize neighborhood merchants for "street taxes." Since the five families eagerly exploited the Russian mafia in huge gasoline-tax scams, and used the Irish Westies as hit men, it is conceivable that they could benefit through alliances with new ethnic hoodlums. Some Asian and Russian criminals are adept at high-tech frauds and money laundering, and Asians have been a major source of narcotics for mafiosi who disregard the Cosa Nostra's frequently violated prohibition on drug transactions.

A sign of another troublesome international collaboration is the Mob's flirtation with Albanian organized-crime groups. The FBI's WK Williams says the Mafia's ties to Albanian gangsters are expanding, and that the Albanians, once used primarily as musclemen, have moved up to equal status in mutually run narcotics, gambling, and prostitution ventures.

Vital to the Mafia's future is the durability of New York City's Business Integrity Commission and similar regulatory units, established in the 1990s to prevent the Mob from regaining footholds in the wholesale food markets and the private rubbish-carting industry. At least one banned Genovese-connected garbage carter was discovered back in business in the New York area. Counting on coercion, the mobster used two "front" companies to cheat customers out of more than $2 million. He was exposed when honest carters raised a cry to authorities that wiseguys were again using muscle to steal customers.

Further confirmation that the Mob continues to infiltrate the carting business came from defectors' testimony that the Bonanno/Massino family had helped a Mob-connected company grab the waste-paper removal contract at the *New York Post*. Until Joe Massino's arrest in 2003, the contractor rewarded the family with $2,500 a month, most of it going to Massino.

Former prosecutor Ronald Goldstock, who has analyzed regulatory agencies, is dubious about their long-range tenacity to battle mobsters. These licensing bodies are usually effective at the outset in disqualifying "bad actors," he says. But historically they have evolved into dumping grounds for civil-service hacks and corruptible, self-sustaining bureaucracies. Goldstock believes that vigilant law enforcement and basic operational changes in industries susceptible to infiltration are more essential for permanent reforms than political supervision. He and other critics wonder whether officials, after instituting minimal cosmetic changes, have the political stamina to alter vulnerable industries and giant wholesale markets when confronted by well-heeled lobbies opposed to government oversight.

Joe Massino's career is a template for evaluating the Cosa Nostra's prospects. Joe the Ear was eventually brought down, but his ability to resuscitate the Bonanno borgata into a booming conglomerate for over a decade was a scathing lesson to law enforcement. More than likely, Massino clones in the five families are biding their time, counting on investigative lassitude to aid their comebacks. "They want everyone to believe, 'We're done, leave us alone,'" the FBI's Philip Scala cautions. These gangsters undoubtedly will attempt novel strategies to escape the fates of their predecessors. A strategic shift could be exploiting new territories. Although big cities continue to be glittering attractions, there are signs that the Mafia, following demographic trends, is deploying more vigorously in suburbs. There, the families might encounter police less prepared to resist them than federal and big-city investigators.

"Organized crime goes where the money is, and there's money and increasing opportunities in the suburbs," Howard Abadinsky, the historian, observes. Strong suburban fiefs have already been established by the New York, Chicago, and Detroit families, and Abadinksy anticipates a continued expansion. "As long as the Mafia has a critical core of people functioning, they will see greedy opportunities and they can always bring in new people."

A vivid display of Mafia inroads into the suburbs surfaced in March 2005. After an unimpeded ten-year run, a Gambino crew with headquarters in upscale Westchester County was put out of business through the arrests of seven reputed made men and twenty-five associates. According to the federal indictment, the crew's illegal profits totaled $30 million, flowing mainly from illegal gambling, highlighted by Super Bowl betting. A goodly portion of the crew's total take came from "protection" shake-downs of suburban construction and trucking companies and a restaurant in Greenwich, Connecticut. Imitating the customary practices of big-city colleagues, the mobsters also were accused of embezzling a union's pension and welfare fund.

The impetus for the investigation was a reincarnation of "Donnie Brasco." An FBI agent penetrated the crew for almost three years, and his undercover work entangled the reputed new leaders of the Gambinos' post-Gotti era in racketeering charges. The indictment identified Arnold Squitieri as acting boss, and Anthony Megale as acting underboss. Possibly a sign of the Mafia's geographical shifts, the two men live in New Jersey and in Connecticut, not in Manhattan or other boroughs previously favored by Gambino grandees.

Another drastic alteration in the Mafia's future could be mergers among the beleaguered families. Robert Buccino, a New Jersey law-enforcement official and Mafia authority, says the consolidation idea was raised by crews in his state in the 1990s. At that same period, a similar idea struck Anthony "Gaspipe" Casso, the Lucchese kingpin, when he considered combining with the strife-torn Colombo family. Precedents exist. Out of chaos, the farsighted Lucky Luciano radically reorganized the disparate factions in 1931 into five stabilized families. The time may come when his twenty-first-century descendants overcome their internal disputes and realign into fewer yet stronger gangs to enhance their survival chances.

Before being nailed again on narcotics charges, the arch defector Sammy "the Bull" Gravano discounted predictions that the Mafia was finished. "Don't kid yourself. Cosa Nostra could come back," he wrote. "I hear the Chinese, the Russians are going to move in. Believe me, they can't put together what took us fifty, sixty, whatever years to do."

A longtime Mob adversary, former New York police lieutenant Remo Franceschini, holds the same opinion. He doubts that the Mafia, with its expertise in gambling, loan-sharking, and other crimes, will die quickly or quietly. "In the old days, back in Sicily, they would say, 'We're going back to the caves.' They would go back to the caves to protect themselves and regroup. That's what I expect the Mob will do."

These two sagacious judgments, from antagonistic sides of the conflict, should be a sobering reminder to law enforcement and to the nation: the Mafia is grievously wounded—but not mortally.

Appendix A

Family Trees

GENOVESE FAMILY

1931–1937: Charles "Lucky" Luciano, founder of the family and the Mafia's governing body, the Commission; convicted in 1937 of being a prostitution overlord, sentenced to thirty years: deported to Italy, 1946.

1937–1957: Frank "Prime Minister" Costello hastily retires in 1957 after bullet grazes his head in assassination attempt ordered by rival, Vito Genovese.

1957–1969: Vito Genovese replaces Costello but is convicted of narcotics trafficking in 1959; still in charge until he dies in prison in 1969. His name remains as family's title.

1970–1980s: Philip "Benny Squint" Lombardo; retires as leader because of failing health in early 1980s. Uses Anthony "Fat Tony" Salerno to pose as boss to deflect attention and deceive law enforcement.

1982 to present: Vincent "Chin" Gigante also uses Salerno as "front" boss until Fat Tony is convicted of racketeering and sentenced to life imprisonment in 1986. Gigante fakes mental illness for decades until convicted of racketeering in 1997 and 2003. Scheduled for release from prison in 2012, when he will be eighty-four.

BONANNO/MASSINO FAMILY

1931–1964: Joseph Bonanno, founder and original Commission member; forced to retire in 1964 after failed plot to kill rival godfathers and become Mafia's Boss of Bosses.

1964–1975: Interregnum and internal battles over control of family.

1975–1979: Carmine "Lilo" Galante schemes to become a godfather, expands narcotics deals, and imports Sicilian mobsters to bolster his faction; killed on orders of the Commission in 1979 to stop him from becoming too powerful.

1980–1991: Philip "Rusty" Rastelli; spends most of his reign in prison on racketeering convictions; dies of cancer in 1991.

1991–2003: Joseph "the Ear" Massino, rebuilds organization into the nation's top Mob family and changes gang's name to honor himself. Convicted on RICO charges in 2004, Massino becomes first New York boss to cooperate with government. Family's future leadership is unclear

LUCCHESE FAMILY

1931–1951: Gaetano Gagliano, an original godfather at the birth of the modern Mafia, maintains low profile and no arrests for two decades. Fatally ill, Gagliano retires in 1951.

1951–1967: Gaetano "Tommy Three-Finger Brown" Lucchese, former underboss, rules without opposition and family is named in his honor. Dies of cancer in 1967.

1970–1986: Antonio "Ducks" Corallo; becomes boss after three years of interim acting leaders while he is in prison. Powerful and effective godfather until he is convicted in Commission case trial in 1986.

1986–present: Vittorio "Little Vic" Amuso is appointed boss with underboss Anthony "Gaspipe" Casso as an equal, if not stronger, commander. Their bloody purge of suspected internal enemies produces numerous defections and convictions. Amuso sentenced to life imprisonment in 1992, and Casso gets life in 1998. Amuso remains nominal boss.

GAMBINO FAMILY

1931–1951: Vincent Mangano, secretive, virtually unknown to federal and local police, heads one of the original five families until he disappears in 1951.

1951–1957: Albert "Lord High Executioner" Anastasia, a key figure in "Murder Incorporated" is widely assumed to have killed Mangano in a coup to take over the family.

1957–1976: Carlo Gambino becomes boss after arranging the barber-shop hit on Anastasia. Gambino dies from a heart attack in 1976, at the height of power as the Mob's supreme godfather. Family adopts his name.

1976–1985: Paul "Big Paul" Castellano, Gambino's brother-in-law, ascends to the family throne. Castellano is gunned down outside Sparks Steak House in a preemptive strike orchestrated by a younger rival, John Gotti.

1986–2002: John "Johnny Boy" Gotti becomes the most publicized boss since Al Capone. Following three trial acquittals, he is convicted in 1992 on racketeering and murder charges, including Castellano's. Sentenced to life without parole, he dies of cancer in prison in 2002.

2002–2003: Peter Gotti, John's older brother, runs the family until he is found guilty of racketeering in 2003 and receives a minimum sentence of nine years. In 2004 is convicted of conspiring to kill Sammy the Bull Gravano, and faces life sentence.

2005: Acting boss Arnold Squitieri indicted on RICO charges.

COLOMBO FAMILY

1931–1962: Joseph "Olive Oil King" Profaci creates one of the original families. He becomes a multimillionaire but the last years of his life are plagued by younger members' rebellion, led by "Crazy Joey" Gallo, and he dies of cancer in 1962.

1963–1971: Joseph Colombo is appointed boss, mainly through the support of Carlo Gambino. His tenure is cut short when he is shot and paralyzed in 1971 at a rally protesting supposed bias by law-enforcement agencies against Italian-Americans. Colombo becomes the signature name for the family.

1972–1986: Carmine "the Snake" Persico is in firm control until he is convicted in the Commission case and at another rackets trial in 1986.

1987–present: Although sentenced to life without parole, Persico tries to maintain control from prison until his son Alphonse "Little Allie Boy" is ready to succeed him. Persico's attempt to create a Mob dynasty provokes an internal war. Alphonse is convicted of racketeering in 2001, creating a power vacuum and a fractured family. He is indicted in 2004 on new charges of murder.

Mafia Boss Succession

LUCCHESE FAMILY

1931—Gaetano Gagliano, Bronx gangster, becomes boss of one of five new families.

1951—Gagliano, fatally ill, turns over leadership to Gaetano "Tommy Three-Finger Brown" Lucchese and family adopts his name.

1967—Lucchese dies of cancer, creating brief leadership vacuum.

1970—Antonio "Ducks" Corallo is appointed boss.

1986—Corallo convicted in Commission case and sentenced to life.

1987—Vittorio "Little Vic" Amuso wins control of family with help of Anthony "Gaspipe" Casso. Amuso has title of boss but real power apparently wielded by underboss Casso.

1992—Amuso convicted of racketeering and gets life term.

1998—Casso sentenced to life imprisonment after pleading guilty to racketeering and multiple murder charges.

2004—Acting Boss Louis "Louie Bagels" Daidone found guilty of murder. Possible successor: Steven "Stevie Wonder" Crea.

BONANNO/MASSINO FAMILY

1931—Joseph Bonanno authorized by Lucky Luciano to head new family.

1964–1966—Bonanno vanishes after failed attempt to become supreme boss on the Commission. Reappears after two years, later claims he had been abducted by rival.

1966–1980—Power struggles roil family as factions form without a strong boss firmly in control.

1981—Philip "Rusty" Rastelli named boss.

1981–1991—Rastelli titular boss but real power is in hands of underboss Joseph Massino.

1991—Rastelli dies of cancer and Massino installed as boss.

1992–2002—Massino reinvigorates family, transforming it into the most powerful in the county, and changes its name to Massino Family.

2003–2004—Massino arrested and convicted of racketeering and murders on testimony by numerous defectors.

2004–2005: Massino becomes informer and leadership in flux.

GAMBINO FAMILY

1931—Vincent Mangano becomes first boss of new family.

1951—Mangano disappears, presumed to have been murdered by Albert "Lord High Executioner" Anastasia.

1951—Anastasia assumes title.

1957—Anastasia killed by gunmen in hotel barber shop.

1957—Carlo Gambino, underboss who plotted Anastasia's murder, becomes godfather and family is named in his honor.

1976—Gambino, America's most powerful Mafia leader, dies of natural causes.

1976—Paul "Big Paul" Castellano, Gambino's brother-in-law is crowned boss.

1985—Castellano gunned down outside Manhattan restaurant in murder engineered by John Gotti.

1986—Gotti takes control without opposition.

1992—After three acquittals, Gotti is convicted of racketeering and sentenced to life in prison.

2002—Gotti, still boss, dies of cancer in prison.

2002—Gotti's brother Peter succeeds him.

2003–2004—Peter Gotti convicted on racketeering charges.

2005– Acting boss Arnold Squitieri indicted. Possible successor: Nicholas "Nicky" Corozzo or Joseph "Joe Joe" Corozzo.

LUCIANO/GENOVESE FAMILY

1931—Salvatore "Charlie Lucky" Luciano organizes family under his name as first boss.

1937—Luciano convicted of heading "compulsory prostitution" ring.

1937—Frank "Prime Minister" Costello replaces Luciano.

1957—Costello "retires" after assassination attempt.

1957—Vito Genovese takes control.

1959—Genovese convicted on drug trafficking charges.

1969—Genovese dies in prison with title of boss.

1970s—Philip "Benny Squint" Lombardo appointed boss after interregnum.

1980s—Lombardo retires and Vincent "Chin" Gigante becomes godfather.

1997–2004—Gigante convicted of racketeering and remains titular boss in prison.

Release date: 2012.

Possible successor: Liborio "Barney" Bellomo.

PROFACI/COLOMBO FAMILY

1931—Joseph "Olive Oil King" Profaci, named boss and Commission member.

1962—Profaci dies of cancer during civil war with Joseph "Crazy Joey" Gallo.

1964—Joseph Colombo, with support of Carlo Gambino, is appointed boss and family name changed to Colombo.

1971—Colombo shot and paralyzed at rally he organized for Italian-American civil rights.

1972–79—Carmine "The Snake" Persico's forces take control of the family and he becomes full-fledged godfather after release from prison in 1979.

1986—Persico is convicted in two separate cases of racketeering and sentenced to life.

1986–2004—Persico attempts to run the family from prison until his son, Alphonse "Little Allie Boy" Persico, can assume title of boss. Gang war over leadership in early 1990s devastates the family and generates mass convictions, including Persico's son.

2004—Joel "Joe Waverly" Cacace, acting boss, convicted of murder and racketeering.

Family leadership unsettled.

Principal Sources and References

CHAPTER 1: A FIERY SAINT

Details of Anthony Accetturo's Mafia experiences are based on an interview with him and on his statements to investigators with the New Jersey Attorney General's office. Additional information on Mafia induction ceremonies was obtained from trial testimony and FBI reports of debriefings of Alphonse D'Arco, a former Lucchese family acting boss and Frank Coppa and Frank Lino, Bonanno family capos. Other materials regarding Mafia practices and induction rites were obtained in interviews with Pellegrino Masselli, a Genovese family associate; reports by the New Jersey Attorney General's office on interrogations of Thomas Ricciardi, a former Lucchese soldier; and a transcript of a Mafia induction ceremony held by the Patriarca family on October 29, 1989, in Medford, Massachusetts, and secretly recorded by the FBI

CHAPTER 2: TUMAC'S TALE

The criminal history of Anthony Accetturo was compiled through interviews with him and with Robert Buccino, former Deputy Director of New Jersey Attorney General's Organized Crime Division, who knew Accetturo since they were boys. Additional background information was obtained from New Jersey State Police Intelligence Division files on Accetturo's criminal activities; a pre-sentencing report on Accetturo by the Case Management Office for the New Jersey Superior Court; New Jersey Superior Court documents; reports by the New Jersey Attorney General's office on debriefings of Accetturo; and FBI reports of debriefings of Alphonse D'Arco concerning Lucchese family operations involving Accetturo.

CHAPTER 3: ROOTS

The early history of Sicily is based on the works of numerous historians, scholars, and cultural writers, particularly Eric J. Hobsbawm, Luigi Barzini, and Alexander Stille. Additional information was obtained from a confidential monograph prepared in 1958 for FBI Director J. Edgar Hoover on the history of Sicilian and American Mafia families. Details of the Mafia's origins in New York and the career and murder of NYPD Lieutenant Joseph Petrosino were obtained from contemporaneous newspaper accounts and interviews with Ralph Salerno, a former NYPD detective sergeant, an expert and author on the Mafia in America, and consultant to congressional investigation committees, and *Organized Crime* (Fifth Edition) by Howard Abadinsky, a Mafia historian.

CHAPTER 4: THE CASTELLAMMARESE WAR

Accounts of Italian immigration and criminal activities in the early decades of the 20th Century were derived largely from census records and contemporaneous reporting in New York newspapers. Benito Mussolini's campaign in Sicily was documented through numerous biographies of Mussolini; the FBI monograph in 1958; and *Man of Honor*, Joseph Bonanno's autobiography of his Mafia experiences in Sicily and in America. Details of the Castellammarese War, the murders of gang leaders, and the formation of the Commission were obtained from contemporaneous newspaper accounts of crimes; interviews and writings by Ralph Salerno and Howard Abadinsky. Additional information on the Castellammarese War was compiled by Richard McDermott, an organized-crime researcher. Bonanno's views on the Castellammarese War and the formation of the Commission were published in *Man of Honor*.

CHAPTER 5: DIRTY THIRTIES

Information on the ventures, crimes, and customs of New York's Mafia families and Jewish and Irish organized-crime gangsters in the early 1930s was compiled from contemporaneous reporting in New York newspapers; Thomas E. Dewey's recorded memoirs for the Oral History Project at Columbia University; the FBI's 1958 monograph on the Mafia; *Man of Honor*; NYPD records; trial testimony by Angelo Lonardo, the former underboss of the Cleveland Mafia family; and interviews with Salerno and Abadinsky.

CHAPTER 6: RUNAWAY JURY

The chronology of the Runaway Jury and the aftermath is based largely on contemporaneous accounts in New York newspapers; Dewey's recorded memoirs for the Oral History Project at Columbia University; *Thomas E. Dewey and His Times* by Richard Norton Smith; NYPD files on Dutch Schultz; New York newspaper accounts of Dewey's investigations and Schultz's murder; the memoirs of J. Richard "Dixie" Davis, Schultz's lawyer; and *Man of Honor*.

CHAPTER 7: UNLUCKY LUCKY

Lucky Luciano's influence in Tammany Hall is based on interviews with Ralph Salerno and Norton Mockridge, former city editor of the *New York World-Telegram and Sun*, co-author of two books on Frank Costello; *Tigers of Tammany*, a history of Tammany Hall by Alfred Connable and Edward Silverfarb. Dewey's investigation, arrest, and trial of Luciano is based on contemporaneous newspaper accounts; the biography, *Thomas E. Dewey and His Times*; Dewey's recorded memoirs for the Columbia University Oral History Project; court records of Luciano's trial; FBI and NYPD reports on Luciano's background; and interviews with Salerno.

CHAPTER 8: PRIME MINISTER

Costello's background was obtained from NYPD records, interviews with Mockridge and Salerno; *Fiorello H. LaGuardia And the Making of Modern New York*, by Thomas Kessner; testimony, statements and reports from the U.S. Senate investigation of gambling and organized crime (The Kefauver Committee 1950–1951); and *Tigers of Tammany*. Vito Genovese's criminal record and background were obtained from court and NYPD documents and reports by congressional investigation committees. Details of the disbarment hearing for New York Judge Thomas Aurelio were compiled from *Tigers of Tammany* and accounts in New York newspapers regarding Costello's contacts with Aurelio. William O'Dwyer's affiliations with Costello are based on testimony at the Kefauver Committee hearings, contemporaneous newspaper stories, and *Tigers of Tammany*.

CHAPTER 9: MURDER INC.

Frank Costello's relationship with Willie Moretti is based on NYPD intelligence files and interviews with Salerno. Lepke's criminal and personal histories and information about Murder Inc. were derived from newspaper accounts in the 1930s and 1940s, and from Kings County (Brooklyn) District Attorney's office records concerning the Murder Inc. investigations and trials that were obtained by Richard McDermott, an organized-crime researcher. Additional information on Lepke and his attempt to escape the electric chair were based on newspaper accounts and references by Dewey in the Columbia University's Oral History project. Details of Abraham Reles's death were derived mainly from a report issued by a Brooklyn grand jury that reinvestigated the case in 1951; New York newspaper stories on Murder Inc.; and interviews with McDermott and Salerno.

CHAPTER 10: A PROFITABLE WAR

Background materials concerning Carlo Gambino, his criminal roles and black market operations, were obtained from NYPD and FBI intelligence files; court documents; and testimony by Joseph Valachi, the first Mafia member to defect, before a Senate Investigation Committee in 1963. Additional information about Gambino was provided by Ralph Salerno and Paul Meskill, author of *Don Carlo: Boss of Bosses*. Details of Joseph "Socks" Lanza's influence on the waterfront and Mafia background were derived from court documents, NYPD intelligence files, and interviews with former prosecutors in the Manhattan District Attorney's office. The accounts of Luciano's aid to the government in World War II and Governor Dewey's granting him executive clemency were based mainly on a New York State Commission of Investigation report in 1954, and from interviews with former prosecutors in the Manhattan DA's office. Dewey's comments about Luciano's sentence were noted in *Thomas E. Dewey and His Times*.

CHAPTER 11: SERENE TIMES

Vito Genovese's background and activities in Italy and New York are based on NYPD reports; his indictment for murder in Brooklyn; extradition requests; U.S. Army Intelligence reports; newspaper accounts of his return to the U.S.; FBI debriefings of Joe Valachi; the FBI's 1958 monograph; testimony before the Senate Investigations Committee; and interviews with Ralph Salerno. Details on Meyer Lansky and Benjamin "Bugsy" Siegel and the Mob's emergence in Nevada were obtained from newspaper accounts; the FBI monograph; *Little Man*, a biography of Meyer Lansky by Robert Lacey; *The Black Book and the Mob*, a history of the rise of casino gambling in Nevada, by Ronald A. Farrell and Carole Case; and testimony before the Kefauver Committee hearings in 1950 and 1951. J. Edgar Hoover's administration and policies are documented by numerous internal reports disclosed after his death, and from interviews with former FBI agents—who asked for anonymity. Harry J. Anslinger's record at the Narcotics Bureau was obtained from newspaper and magazine accounts of his career. The post-World War II estimates of Mafia strength and activities were based on analyses by Ralph Salerno and Remo Franceschini, NYPD Mafia experts; interviews with newspaper reporters who covered organized crime; personal observations; and *Man of Honor*.

CHAPTER 12 "WAKE UP, AMERICA!"

The origins of and controversy over establishing the Kefauver Committee were obtained from newspaper accounts and interviews with organized-crime authorities, including G. Robert Blakey and Ralph Salerno. Details of the hearings in New York are from transcripts and the committee's report. Albert Anastasia's emergence as a boss is based on Joe Valachi's testimony and FBI and NYPD records. Tommy Lucchese's background was obtained from FBI, NYPD, and Manhattan DA intelligence files, and interviews with Salerno and other former detectives. Frankie Carbo's history and role in the boxing world was obtained from newspaper and magazine accounts, and from former prosecutors in the Manhattan DA's office. Lucchese's social meetings with Santo Trafficante were verified by Trafficante's lawyer, Frank Ragano, and his wife, Nancy. Information about the political machinations of Costello and Lucchese in the 1950s was obtained from Salerno, newspaper stories, and *Tigers of Tammany*.

CHAPTER 13: HEROIN AND APALACHIN

NYPD reports, trial testimony, and *New York Times* stories were used in the account of the wounding of Costello. Additional information about Costello's background and the assault were obtained from Norton Mockridge. New York newspaper stories and interviews with Salerno and other detectives provided details of the trial of Vincent "Chin" Gigante for the attempted murder of Costello. Information concerning the American and Sicilian Mafia's 1957 meeting in Palermo on the heroin compact came principally from reports in the 1980s by the Drug Enforcement Administration, the FBI, and the Italian government. Additional details were obtained from Joseph Bonanno's version of the meeting in *A Man of Honor*, and from an interview with Claire Sterling, an author and an expert on the Sicilian Mafia. NYPD reports and New York newspaper reports were used for a description of the assassination of Albert Anastasia. Frank Ragano was interviewed on his discussions with Santo Trafficante about meetings with Anastasia and suspicions of Trafficante's involvement in Anastasia's murder. The most comprehensive accounts of the Apalachin raid were obtained from a New York State Commission of Investigation confidential report to Governor Averill Harriman in 1958, and a New York State Joint Legislative Committee on Government Operations report on the raid. Additional details are based on FBI transcripts of bugged conversation between Sam Giancana and Stefano Magaddino; interviews with Ralph Salerno, G. Robert Blakey, and other organized-crime experts; NYPD and FBI intelligence reports on the purposes of the meeting; and a U.S. Select Senate Committee report in 1958. The accounts of Vito Genovese's arrest and conviction for narcotics violations were based on court records and *New York Times* stories.

CHAPTER 14: DEATH OF A PRESIDENT

Frank Ragano and his wife, Nancy Ragano, provided firsthand descriptions of Santo Trafficante's celebration after President Kennedy's assassination. Details of Kennedy's assassination and the aftermath investigations are based largely on the final reports and testimony by the Warren Commission (1964), and the U.S. House of Representatives Select Committee on Assassinations (1979). G. Robert Blakey and William G. Hundley, a former Justice Department official, were interviewed extensively regarding Attorney General Robert F. Kennedy's campaign against the Mafia from 1961 to 1963. Ragano, who was present at social occasions with Mafia leaders, described their reactions and comments about Kennedy before and after his assassination. Background on Carlos Marcello is based on Bureau of Narcotics and FBI reports on his suspected illegal activities. Accounts of Marcello's deportation and his anger against Robert Kennedy were derived from Marcello's testimony before the Select Committee on Assassinations (1979) and interviews with Ragano, who frequently met Marcello and gave him legal advice. Joseph Valachi's Mafia background was obtained from NYPD and FBI records; his testimony before the Senate Permanent Subcommittee on Investigations Committee (1963); and *The Valachi Papers*, by Peter Maas. Details on Valachi's recruitment and the preparation of his testimony before the Senate Subcommittee in 1963 were given in interviews by Hundley, Blakey, and Ralph Salerno.

CHAPTER 15: "THE RING OF TRUTH"

Accounts of President Kennedy's assassination are based on the Warren Commission report (1964); the Select Senate Committee on Intelligence (1978) testimony and its findings regarding recruitment of Mafia leaders in attempts to kill Cuban President Fidel Castro; and the House of Representatives Select Committee on Assassinations (1979) report and testimony on possible Mafia complicity in Kennedy's assassination. Additional information about the attitudes of Mafia leaders to Kennedy was provided by FBI reports on bugged and wiretapped conversations of important mafiosi before and after Kennedy's assassination. Frank Ragano was the primary source concerning Trafficante's hatred of Kennedy, and Trafficante's deathbed statements about Kennedy's assassination. Ragano's conversations with Jimmy Hoffa about the assassination were based on Ragano's recollection, supported by his contemporary notes, and hotel and airline receipts confirming his presence in cities on the dates he said the conversations took place.

CHAPTER 16: A SPLENDID BAND: THE MOB

An FBI report on bugged conversations of Meyer Lansky include his statement about the Mob and U.S. Steel. FBI reports on Cointelpro disclosed the surveillance of political and show business figures. Interviews with Ralph Salerno and Remo Franceschini and personal reporting at the time are the basis for the NYPD's strategy and investigations of the Mafia in 1960s and 1970s. Henry Hill's accounts of Mafia life are included in *Wise Guy* by Nicholas Pileggi. Incidents and theories about the Gallo Wars were obtained from intelligence files compiled by Brooklyn District Attorney Office investigators and NYPD reports. Analysis of Bonanno's failed plot to become Boss of Bosses is based on NYPD intelligence reports; Bonanno's version in *Man of Honor* of the internal Mob feud and his disappearance; FBI reports on bugged conversations of mafiosi concerning Bonanno's absence; and interviews with Salerno, who participated in the NYPD investigation. Salerno also was the source for the NYPD's main theories on the reasons for Bonanno's exile from New York. Salerno and Frank Ragano provided details on the arrests and aftermath of the Little Apalachin conference. Both men also offered theories for the reason of the meeting. Queens DA Nat Hentel's reactions after the raid on the Mafia meeting are based on contemporaneous interviews with him and on New York newspaper stories.

CHAPTER 17: THE BIRTH OF RICO

Extensive interviews were conducted with G. Robert Blakey concerning his upbringing, education, roles in the Justice Department, the Katzenbach Commission, and his work as counsel to congressional committees. *New York Times* and *Washington Post* stories and Blakey provided details on Senator John McClellan's background and activities in Congress. Blakey's confrontation with Whitney North Seymour on the RICO law was based on interviews with Blakey, Seymour, a former U.S. Attorney in the Southern District of New York, and Edward M. Shea, a former assistant U.S. Attorney in SDNY. David G. Trager's views concerning the effectiveness of the FBI and the Justice Department in the 1970s are based on published interviews in *The New York Times* and personal reporting.

CHAPTER 18: UNITY DAY

The accounts of demonstrations against the FBI and the shooting of Joseph Colombo at the 1971 rally are based on personal reporting and stories in *The New York Times* and the *New York Daily News*. An FBI report on a wiretap included a description of comments about Colombo by Sam "The Plumber" DeCavalcante. Details about the backgrounds and careers of Colombo and Joey Gallo, and Carlo Gambino's opposition to the second Unity Day rally, were obtained from FBI and NYPD intelligence files and an interview with Albert Seedman, former NYPD Chief of Detectives. Unpublished interviews with NYPD Detectives Douglas LeVien and Edward Clark provided further historical information about the Colombo family.

CHAPTER 19: UBAZZE AND LILO

Brooklyn DA and NYPD intelligence reports and arrest records were used to document the origins of the Gallo Wars against Mob godfather Joseph Profaci. Accounts in the *The New York Times* and interviews with Albert Seedman and other detectives are the main sources for Joey Gallo's associations with actors and writers. Information about the investigation of Gallo's murder was provided by Seedman; NYPD Detective Bureau records; Manhattan District Attorney Office reports on Joseph Luparelli's description of Gallo's murder and the aftermath; and contemporaneous personal reporting. Salvatore "Sammy the Bull" Gravano's praise of the movie, *The Godfather*, was contained in *Underboss* and told to FBI agents during debriefings. Carlo Gambino's history is based on FBI intelligence reports; interviews with J. Bruce Mouw, former supervisor of the FBI's Gambino Squad, Ralph Salerno and Edward Clark, and Paul Meskill, author of a biography of Gambino. Salerno and former NYPD Detectives Joseph Coffey and Remo Franceschini contributed information regarding the backgrounds and activities of Paul Castellano and Aniello Dellacroce. Details on Carmine Galante's history were derived from FBI and NYPD intelligence reports; arrest records; and reporting in New York newspapers of Galante's narcotics-trafficking trials. The account of Galante's attempts to gain control of the Bonanno family is based mainly on testimony by admitted members of the Bonanno family at the 2004 RICO trial of Joseph Massino. The description of Galante's murder and motives are based on personal contemporaneous reporting; testimony at the 1986 Commission trial; and interviews with Michael Chertoff and J. Gilmore Childres, former federal prosecutors; Mark Feldman, a federal prosecutor; and Pat Marshall, the FBI case agent for the Commission investigation and trial.

CHAPTER 20: THE FBI WISES UP

Interviews with Neil Welch, former head of the FBI's New York office, and former agents James Kossler and Jules Bonavolonta were used to describe the RICO seminar at Cornell University and the agents' reasons for implementing the RICO law. Background and personal information on Welch, Kossler, and Bonavolonta were obtained through interviews with them and with agents and officials who dealt with them. G. Robert Blakey and Ronald Goldstock, who conducted the Cornell seminars, provided information about the techniques and purpose of the project.

CHAPTER 21: THE BIG BOYS

Anthony "Fat Tony" Salerno's conversations are contained in FBI transcripts of bugs at the Palma Boys Social Club. Salerno's background and life style were obtained from police records; from FBI and NYPD intelligence files; from trial transcripts; and from confidential statements to the FBI by Vincent "Fish" Cafaro, a top aide to Salerno. Former FBI agents Pat Marshall and Brian Taylor provided details of their conversations with Salerno before his arrest. Conditions and policies at the New York State Organized Crime Task Force are based on personal reporting, and contemporaneous interviews with its former director, Ronald Goldstock, and its former chief of investigations, Fred Rayano. Statements by Benjamin "Lefty Guns" Ruggiero, were secretly recorded by Joseph Pistone, an FBI undercover agent, and used as evidence at trials of alleged Mafia members. Details of Rudolph Giuliani's strategy against the Mafia are based on contemporaneous interviews with him and later interviews with FBI agents, including James Kossler, Thomas Sheer, Pat Marshall, Jules Bonavolonta, William Horan, and former Assistant U.S. Attorney Walter Mack.

CHAPTER 22: OPERATION JAGUAR

The account of installing a bug in Salvatore Avellino's Jaguar was obtained primarily from interviews with Jack Breheny and Fred Rayano, former investigators with the N.Y. State Organized Crime Task Force, and with its former director, Ronald Goldstock. Background data on Antonio "Ducks" Corallo was found in FBI, NYPD and OCTF intelligence reports and his arrest and trial records. Information on Corallo's involvement in carting corruption in Long Island came from indictments, court documents, trial testimony, and civil suits brought by the New York State Attorney General's office and federal prosecutors. The courageous involvement of Robert Kubecka in the OCTF investigation of carting was documented by trial testimony, and interviews with his family's lawyer, Robert Folks; federal prosecutors; and FBI agents.

CHAPTER 23: PLANTING SEASON

Details on bugging the Casa Storta were obtained from James Kallstrom, the FBI agent in charge of Special Operations, and from agents James Kossler and Jules Bonavolonta. Paul Castellano's history and role as the Gambino boss is based on FBI and NYPD intelligence files; court records; and interviews with Bruce Mouw, former supervisor of the FBI's Gambino squad, and other agents; testimony given to the President's Commission on Organized Crimes (1983–1986); commission reports; transcripts of bugs and wiretaps of conversations by Gambino soldiers; and personal reporting. Information about the bugging of Castellano's home was pieced together through interviews with Kallstrom and Mouw, and other agents who asked for anonymity. Kallstrom and other agents provided information on installing listening devices at Anthony Salerno's headquarters, the Palma Boys Social Club.

CHAPTER 24: "THIS IS IT!"

Decisions to initiate the Commission case are based on contemporaneous interviews and statements by Rudolph Giuliani; extensive contemporaneous and later interviews with Ronald Goldstock and Fred Rayano, OCTF's former chief of investigations; former federal prosecutors Walter Mack and Michael Chertoff; former FBI agents Thomas Sheer, James Kossler, Pat Marshall, and Joseph O'Brien; and G. Robert Blakey. Statistics on the number of FBI agents and NYPD detectives assigned to the five Mafia family squads were obtained from supervising agents. Estimates of Mafia strength were based on FBI analysis and from testimony and a court affidavit by Kenneth McCabe, an investigator for the U.S. Attorney's Office in Manhattan.

CHAPTER 25: THE CURTAIN RISES

James LaRossa, Paul Castellano's lawyer, described Castellano's activities and conversations shortly before his assassination. Backgrounds on Roy DeMeo and Thomas Bilotti come from court records; FBI and NYPD reports; and interviews with F.B.I agent Bruce Mouw. Rudolph Giuliani's selection of Michael Chertoff as lead prosecutor in the Commission Case is based on contemporaneous interviews with Giuliani, other prosecutors, and later interviews with Chertoff. The texts of Commission trial testimony and tapes are from the trial record.

CHAPTER 26: THE CONCRETE CLUB

Information about defense strategy at the Commission trial came mainly from interviews with James LaRossa, a key defense lawyer, and Michael Chertoff, the lead prosecutor. Trial details were obtained from personal reporting, and transcripts of testimony and tapes introduced as evidence. Estimates of inflated concrete costs caused by the Mafia's rigged bids were cited in an analysis by *The New York Times* and in testimony by Salvatore Gravano.

CHAPTER 27: "FAR FROM FINISHED"

The gasoline-tax frauds are based on stories and personal reporting in *The New York Times*; trial transcripts; testimony by Michael Franzese, former Colombo family capo; and interviews with Laura Brevetti and Edward McDonald, former heads of the federal Organized Crime Strike Force in the Eastern District of New York. The theft of the West Side Highway materials was described in statements to the FBI and in court affidavits by Salvatore Gravano, former Gambino underboss, and Alphonse D'Arco, former Lucchese acting boss.

CHAPTER 28: TURNING POINT

Questions about the impact of the Commission trial on the Mafia are based on interviews and statements by James B. Jacobs, NYU School of Law professor; Richard Rhebock, defense lawyer; and Vincent Cafaro's debriefings by the FBI. The Mafia's loan-sharking profits and techniques were obtained through personal reporting, and interviews with law-enforcement and organized-crime experts, including Remo Franceschini and Howard Abadinsky. Data on the strength and rackets of the five families were derived from contemporaneous interviews with law-enforcement investigators and officials, and from court records.

CHAPTER 29: SNAKE CHARMER

Carmine Persico's background was obtained from court and arrest records; intelligence files compiled by the NYPD, the Brooklyn DA's office, and the FBI; and interviews with Edward McDonald, former chief of the federal Organized Crime Strike Force in the Eastern District, George Stamboulidis, a former federal prosecutor, and NYPD detectives, including Albert Seedman and Remo Franceschini; testimony in 1963 by Joe Valachi concerning Persico and the Gallo Wars; and summaries of FBI debriefings of Joe Cantalupo, a Colombo associate and informer. A description of Persico's arrest was provided mainly from testimony by Fred DeChristopher and from interviews with Damon Taylor, the FBI supervisor of the Colombo Squad in 1985. Information about Persico's attempts to place contracts on the lives of Rudolph Giuliani and other prosecutors is based on statements at Michael Lloyd's parole hearing, and interviews with Aaron Marcu, a former federal prosecutor in Manhattan, Lynn DeVecchio, the former head of the Colombo Squad, and other FBI agents.

CHAPTER 30: CARMINE'S WAR

The criminal background of Victor Orena and the origins of the Colombo family war were compiled from court records, trial transcripts, FBI and NYPD intelligence reports, and summaries of information supplied to the FBI by an informer, Gregory Scarpa. The government's strategy and tactics in prosecuting Colombo defendants were obtained from court documents and interviews with John Gleeson and George Stamboulidis, the main federal prosecutors involved in scores of indictments and convictions. Additional materials on the investigations and internal FBI controversies concerning Scarpa came from court documents; trial testimony; and interviews with Damon Taylor and Lynn DeVecchio, former Colombo Family Squad supervisors, and with federal prosecutors and defense lawyers who asked to be unidentified.

CHAPTER 31: DYNASTY

Alphonse "Little Allie Boy" Persico's history was documented from court records; FBI and NYPD reports; and interviews with FBI Colombo Squad agents, federal prosecutors, and organized-crime investigators in the Brooklyn and Manhattan District Attorneys' staff. The strength of the Colombo family in 2004 was based on data supplied by the FBI

CHAPTER 32: A HELL OF A LEGACY

A transcript of the tape of John Gotti discussing his plans for the Gambino family was introduced in court hearings and was obtained from a bug secreted in Gotti's office by the N.Y. State Organized Crime Task Force. Gotti's early background was derived from New York and federal court and probation records; intelligence files compiled by the FBI and the Manhattan, Brooklyn, and Queens DA's offices; interviews with FBI agents, including Bruce Mouw, Stephen Morrill, Pat Colgan, George Hanna; interviews with NYPD detectives, including Remo Franceschini, Joseph Coffey, Edward Clark, and Edward Wright. Details about Aniello Dellacroce were supplied by Ralph Salerno. John Favara's abduction was reported by witnesses to the Nassau County Police Department, and theories about his presumed murder and disposal of his body are based on informers' tips to the FBI and the NYPD. Gotti's telephone conversation with Anthony Moscatiello was recorded in a wiretap by the Queens DA's office and used as evidence to deny Gotti bail in 1986.

CHAPTER 33: QUACK-QUACK

Mouw's background, work style, and investigative methods were compiled from extensive interviews with him and with FBI officials and agents and prosecutors involved in Gambino Squad investigations. Portions of the Angelo Ruggiero wiretaps and his reactions were obtained from court documents and from interviews with Mouw, other FBI agents, and prosecutors. Paul Castellano's demands to obtain the Ruggiero tapes are based on informers' reports to the FBI and from secretly recorded discussions used as evidence in Gambino family trials. Details on the planning of Castellano's assassination and Gotti's installation as boss were derived largely from trial testimony by Sammy the Bull Gravano and from his debriefings by FBI agents and prosecutors.

CHAPTER 34: "SHAME ON THEM"

The accounts of the multiple electronic eavesdropping attempts on Gotti and the transcripts were obtained from court records and follow-up interviews with investigators and officials from the FBI, the N.Y. State OCTF, and the Queens DA's office. Information on Gotti's lifestyle was based on interviews with state and federal investigators who tracked him; from transcripts of wiretapped conversations principally between Gotti and Angelo Ruggiero; and from personal observations. Details of the Piecyk case came from arrest and trial records and contemporaneous interviews with Remo Franceshini. Gotti's behavior and activities as the Gambino boss were provided by Sammy Gravano's testimony; Gravano's debriefings by the FBI and federal prosecutors; and from conversations picked up on bugs in Gotti's office at the Bergin Social Club. Background on James Failla was obtained from court records; NYPD and FBI intelligence files; interviews with detectives, including Ralph Salerno and Remo Franceschini; and interviews with garbage carters who had dealings with him. Gravano's history was derived from court and probation records; his version in *Underboss*; from debriefings by FBI agents and prosecutors; and accounts he gave to his lawyers. The disagreements over strategy in the first RICO prosecution of Gotti in 1986 were confirmed in interviews with Edward McDonald, the former chief of the federal Organized Crime Strike Force in Brooklyn; Andrew Maloney, the former U.S. Attorney in Brooklyn; other federal prosecutors; and FBI agents who asked for anonymity. The role of Willie Boy Johnson in the Gambino family was obtained from court records and interviews with Franceschini and Mouw, and with other FBI agents. Events and comments by Gotti and other participants at the RICO trial are based on personal reporting and the reporting of Leonard Buder of *The New York Times*.

CHAPTER 35: "HE'S LIKE ROBIN HOOD"

Details of John Gotti's daily routine and Gambino family policies were obtained principally from interviews with Bruce Mouw; surveillance records; and reports by informers. Remo Franceschini, who visited Gotti's Bergin Club periodically, provided information from his observations and surveillance of Gotti. Salvatore Gravano corroborated many details of Gotti's private life and Mafia attitudes in debriefings by the FBI, in court testimony, and in *Underboss*. The agreement among prosecutors on seeking indictments of Gotti is based on contemporaneous and later interviews with federal and state prosecutors, including Rudolph Giuliani, Andrew Maloney, Ronald Goldstock, and Edward McDonald. Material on Gotti's trips and his properties outside of New York were compiled from surveillance reports disclosed by federal and state agents and from real-estate records. Gotti's refusal to allow Joe Armone to acknowledge membership in a crime family was reported to the FBI by informers and cited in *Underboss*. Additional information regarding Gotti's views on running the Gambino family was based on Gravano's testimony and his FBI debriefings. The proceedings of the Commission meeting attended by Gotti were obtained from separate debriefings and trial testimony of Salvatore Gravano and Anthony Casso of the Lucchese family by the FBI and federal prosecutors. The circumstances of Gotti's arrest in 1989 on state charges of assault were based on interviews with Joseph Coffey, an investigator for the New York Organized Crime Task Force, and Ronald Goldstock and Fred Rayano of the OCTF. Details of the shooting of John O'Connor and events at Gotti's assault trial are based on court records, trial testimony, and personal coverage of the trial and its aftermath.

CHAPTER 36: MRS. CIRELLI'S HOLIDAY

Facts about the FBI's bugging of the Ravenite Club and Nettie Cirelli's apartment were obtained mainly from interviews with James Kallstrom, the head of the FBI unit that installed the equipment; with Agents Bruce Mouw and James Kossler; and with Andrew Maloney, the U.S. Attorney in Brooklyn; and from reports by other FBI agents. Descriptions of the building and the club are based on personal observations. Transcripts of the recorded conversations in the Cirelli apartment and elsewhere are part of the court record of Gotti's 1992 RICO trial in Brooklyn. Gravano's testimony at the trial provided additional information about the circumstances of the conversations. Details of the contest among federal jurisdictions to prosecute Gotti were based on contemporaneous and later interviews, principally with Maloney; John Gleeson, the lead prosecutor in the case; Ronald Goldstock; and FBI agents and prosecutors in the Manhattan District Attorney's office who asked to be unidentified. A portrait of the arrest of Gotti and his codefendants was obtained from Mouw, Lewis Schiliro, then the FBI's Organized Crime supervisor in New York, and FBI reports.

CHAPTER 37: "I WANT TO SWITCH GOVERNMENTS"

Information on pretrial activities in Gotti's trial was derived from court records and personal observations. Gravano's accounts of his discussions and disagreements with John Gotti, and plan to escape from the MCC jail while awaiting trial are based on post-trial testimony by Gravano and statements in *Underboss*. Details of Gravano's defection, and plea arrangements, his removal from the Metropolitan Correctional Center, and his debriefings were obtained from contemporaneous and later interviews with Bruce Mouw, John Gleeson, Andrew Maloney, and Jim Fox, then the head of the FBI Office in New York, and court records concerning the plea. The description of the trial is based on transcripts; personal observations; the reporting of Arnold Lubasch of *The New York Times*; the reporting of Peter Bowles of *Newsday*; and interviews with Gleeson, Maloney and Albert Krieger, the chief defense lawyer. Details of Gotti's reactions to his sentencing and his transfer from the Metropolitan Correction Center were provided by defense lawyers Bruce Cutler and Ronald Kuby.

CHAPTER 38: BITTER AFTERMATH

The reactions of law-enforcement officials to Gotti's conviction were based on public statements and interviews with Joseph Fried, a *New York Times* reporter, and with prosecutors and FBI agents, including Jim Fox, and with U.S. Attorney Andrew Maloney. The discord over the withholding of information about a possible attempt to tamper with the Gotti jury in the 1990 state assault trial was obtained from interviews with Robert Morgenthau, the Manhattan District Attorney; Michael Cherkasky, the assistant D.A., and lead prosecutor in the trial; Ronald Goldstock; Maloney; and Bruce Mouw. The tracing and arrest of William Peist is based on court records, and interviews with Mouw and other FBI agents. The dispute over FBI authorization to publish *Boss of Bosses* was based on interviews with Fox and former FBI agent Joseph O'Brien. Salvatore Gravano's sentencing and details of his life afterwards, and his indictments on narcotics and murder conspiracy charges, were derived from court records in Arizona, New York, and New Jersey; Gravano's statements in *Underboss*; Gravano's testimony in 2003 at a federal trial in Brooklyn; and interviews with John Gleeson, the federal prosecutor, and with Mouw and other FBI agents.

CHAPTER 39: SELF-WORSHIP

Gotti's living conditions at the federal prison in Marion, Illinois, were based on statements by Bureau of Prisons officials and interviews with Gotti's lawyers, Bruce Cutler and Richard Rhebock. Information on Gotti's criminal and personal activities were obtained from court records and from interviews with FBI agents, including Mouw, and NYPD Detective Lieutenant Remo Franceschini. Additional information about Gotti was derived from FBI debriefings of Gravano, his testimony, and his accounts in *Underboss*. Evidence and materials found in John A. Gotti's office were noted in affidavits by New York State Organized Crime Task Force investigators, and in federal and New York State court documents. John J. Gotti's prison conversations with relatives were included in court documents submitted by federal prosecutors in the Southern District of New York concerning the pre-sentencing of his son, John A. and the trials of his brother Peter. Details of Gotti's funeral are based on personal reporting and accounts in New York newspapers. Details of the trial and sentencing of Peter Gotti and his relatives are based on personal reporting and court records. Estimates of John J. Gotti's illicit wealth were derived from interviews with FBI officials, principally Jim Fox when he was the head of the bureau's New York office, and with Mouw.

CHAPTER 40: GASPIPE

The description of Anthony Casso's boyhood in Brooklyn, his nickname, his crimes, and his associations with Mafia members were compiled from multiple sources: telephones interviews with Casso in 2003, in the presence of his lawyer, John D.B. Lewis, from the federal penitentiary in Florence, Colorado; Casso's NYPD arrest record; interviews with a former NYPD detective and boyhood acquaintance of Casso, who asked to be unidentified; interviews with federal prosecutors Gregory O'Connell and Charles Rose; FBI reports on debriefings of Casso; a pre-sentence investigation report by federal probation officers in 1998; and a letter from Casso to Federal District Court Judge Frederic Block. Information on Casso's involvement in murders was contained in his pre-sentencing report and his debriefings by the FBI. His associations with Christie Furnari and Vittorio Amuso were obtained from his letter to Judge Block, FBI debriefings, and interviews with O'Connell. Details of the murder plot against John Gotti and Frank DeCicco were based principally on debriefings of Casso by the FBI and interviews with O'Connell, who also interrogated Casso. Additional information about the plot was included in statements made to the FBI by Alphonse D'Arco, the former acting boss of the Lucchese family. Conversations between the Gambino family conspirators and Casso concerning the planned murder of Paul Castellano were obtained from FBI debriefings of Gravano and his statements in *Underboss*. Details of Gotti's escape from the bomb plot was derived from FBI debriefings of Gravano and his statements in *Underboss*. The account of the attempted assassination of Casso is based on NYPD records and a telephone interview with Casso from prison. Antonio Corallo's designation of Amuso to be his successor as Lucchese boss was obtained principally from Casso's letter to Judge Block; Casso's statements to FBI agents and to federal prosecutors; and a telephone interview with him.

CHAPTER 41: BLOOD PURGE

Information about the Lucchese's family history and its factional composition was based on FBI debriefing reports of former Lucchese members, including Alphonse D'Arco, Anthony Casso, Anthony Accetturo, and Peter Chiodo. Additional details were obtained in interviews with Accetturo, Ralph Salerno, Gregory O'Connell, and Richard Rudolph, a former FBI agent on the Lucchese Squad. Descriptions of the murders that occurred after Casso and Amuso gained control of the Lucchese family and the motives for the slayings were cited in FBI reports on debriefings of D'Arco and Chiodo; testimony by D'Arco and Chiodo at several trials; reports by the FBI on debriefings of Casso; a pre-sentencing report on Casso in 1998 by federal probation officers; a telephone interview with Casso in 2003; Casso's guilty plea in 1994, and NYPD reports on the murders. The background to the murders of Robert Kubecka and Donald Barstow was obtained mainly from FBI debriefings of D'Arco; court records; and a telephone interview with Casso. The dispute over negligence in protecting Kubecka and Barstow was based on allegations and testimony in a civil suit by relatives of the two victims and interviews with federal prosecutors and officials in the New York State Organized Crime Task Force. Information about the financial arrangements, wealth, and policies of the Lucchese family's Casso-Amuso administration were based on statements to the FBI and trial testimony by D'Arco and Chiodo; a suit by the Justice Department to seize the assets of Casso and his wife; Casso's testimony before a Senate Committee examining Russian organized-crime activities; and U.S. Labor Department investigations of racketeering in the Garment Center. Descriptions of Casso's spending sprees were obtained in interviews with federal prosecutors Gregory O'Connell and Charles Rose and FBI agent Richard Rudolph.

CHAPTER 42: THE PROFESSOR AND FAT PETE

Details of D'Arco's meetings with Casso were contained in FBI debriefings and D'Arco's testimony in trials of Lucchese family members. Information on D'Arco's background and criminal record were obtained from NYPD and from court documents of his arrests and convictions and from his statements to the FBI about his activities in the Lucchese family. The background on Peter Chiodo was based on details in his 1991 indictments on RICO charges; statements he made in FBI debriefings; and from interviews with prosecutors Charles Rose and Gregory O'Connell; and interviews with Richard Rudolph, a former member of the FBI's Lucchese Squad. The accounts of the attempts to kill Chiodo and his relatives and his defection are based on statements to the FBI and testimony by D'Arco and Chiodo at trials. Additional information was provided by O'Connell in interviews. The circumstances leading to D'Arco's defection were obtained from his interrogations by FBI agents; interviews with Rose and O'Connell; and D'Arco's trial testimony.

CHAPTER 43: TUMAC'S TURN

Information about Anthony Accetturo's criminal activities in New Jersey and Florida and his relationships with Lucchese leaders Ducks Corralo, Vic Amuso, and Anthony Casso were obtained in an interview with Accetturo. Additional details of his crime career were provided by Robert Buccino, a New Jersey law-enforcement official and boyhood friend of Accetturo's, and New Jersey State Police intelligence files. Accounts of Accetturo's disputes with Amuso and Casso and attempts to kill Accetturo were derived from interviewing Accetturo; trial testimony by Al D'Arco; and FBI debriefings of D'Arco and Casso. Accetturo's explanation for becoming a cooperative witness was spelled out by him in a lengthy interview with the author. The historical information about the formation of the New Jersey Mafia crews was obtained from reports by investigators in the New Jersey Attorney General's office who interrogated Accetturo. Accetturo's description of the American Mafia's contacts with Sicilian mafiosi is contained in a report by Italian government investigators who questioned him in New Jersey.

CHAPTER 44: 455 YEARS IN PRISON

The discovery of Casso's secreted cash was included in a court affidavit by federal prosecutors. Details of the search for Casso and his capture were obtained from FBI agents, particularly Joseph Valiquette. Information about Casso's plans to escape from the Metropolitan Correctional Center and discussions about killing Judge Eugene Nickerson are included in a pre-sentencing report for Casso prepared by federal probation department officers. Additional details about the escape, assassination plot, and Vic Amuso's renunciation of Casso were provided by Gregory O'Connell and FBI agents. Casso's conduct and conditions at La Tuna Prison were based on interviews with O'Connell, Agent Richard Rudolph, and La Tuna officials. Casso's assertions that two NYPD detectives were on his payroll and carried out murder assignments for the Mafia were made in a telephone interview with him and in interviews with FBI agents, federal prosecutors and his lawyer, John D.B. Lewis. Casso's claim that an FBI mole supplied him with confidential information was reiterated by him in a telephone interview in 2003 with the author and Lewis. Additional evidence about Casso's relationships with the accused detectives was contained in the March 2005 indictments of former detectives Louis Eppolito and Stephen Caracappa.

CHAPTER 45: "TEAM AMERICA"

Facts and statements concerning the sentences of D'Arco, Chiodo, and Accetturo were obtained from court hearings and trial testimony. Additional information about Accetturo's sentence, his value to law enforcement, and his views concerning his prison sentence and the decline of the Lucchese family are based on an interview with him and interviews with his lawyer, Robert G. Stevens, and Robert Buccino, a New Jersey law-enforcement official who investigated Accetturo; and internal reports by the New Jersey State Attorney General's Office. The evaluation of Anthony Casso's importance in the Lucchese family were compiled from interviews with O'Connell, former FBI agents, and Accetturo.

CHAPTER 46: THE PAJAMA GAME

Material on Vincent Gigante's strolls and his appearance on Greenwich Village streets were based on personal observations in the 1980s; from interviews with neighborhood residents and merchants; and interviews with FBI agents, particularly John Pritchard III, former head of the Genovese Squad. Information about the East Side town house occupied by Gigante was obtained from New York real estate records. Details about Gigante's attire and behavior inside the town house were compiled from testimony at court hearings and trials, and from an interview with Charles Beaudoin, the FBI agent in charge of surveilling the town house. Gigante's personal and early criminal background were assembled from NYPD arrest records, court proceedings and interviews with former NYPD detectives who investigated Gigante. The origin of the nickname, "Chin," was obtained in an interview with Gigante's brother the Reverend Louis Gigante. Details about Gigante's surrender in 1957 for the attempted murder of Frank Costello and his trial came from court records and accounts in *The New York Times*. Court records and the *Times* were the principal sources for Gigante's arrest and conviction along with Vito Genovese on narcotics charges. Statements by psychiatrists and physicians concerning Gigante's mental competence were obtained from court records. Gigante's rise in the Genovese family following his release from prison in the 1970s is based largely on statements to the FBI by Vincent Fish Cafaro, a soldier and confidant of Anthony Fat Tony Salerno. Cafaro's statements to the FBI are the main source for details about Philip Lombardo's leadership of the Genovese family in the 1970s. The incident involving a frightened truck driver seeking Gigante's intervention with a mobster-controlled union local is contained in a report on organized-crime influence, published by the International Brotherhood of Teamsters in 2002. Salvatore Gravano's meetings with Gigante were described in his testimony at hearings on Gigante's competence to stand trial. Additional background material on Gigante was obtained in interviews with Pritchard, Donald S. Richards, a former head of the Genovese Squad, and other squad agents and supervisors.

CHAPTER 47: PSYCHOLOGICAL WARFARE

Details of the FBI's psychological warfare tactics against Gigante and attempts to bug cars and the Triangle Club were obtained mainly from interviews with Richards and Pritchard. The description of the Triangle Club and Venero Mangano's club were based on personal observations. Mangano's background was derived from court and FBI records. Information on Gigante's odd behavior in public came from court hearings and trial testimony, and from interviews with Agents John Pritchard, Charles Beaudoin, and Pat Marshall. The comments from Barry Slotnick, Gigante's lawyer, were made in contemporaneous interviews. Father Louis Gigante's background was obtained from accounts published in *The New York Times*. Information about Vincent Gigante's two households and children were obtained from court records, probation reports, and FBI surveillance reports. The background on Morris Levy was based on real estate records, indictments, trial records, and accounts in the *Village Voice*. Additional information about Levy was provided by Pritchard, who was involved in FBI investigations of Levy's relationships with the Genovese family. Telephone-tap recordings of Gigante's conversations regarding the East Side town house were included in court hearings. Details of the FBI's attempts to secretly observe Gigante in the town house from the Ramaz School were obtained in interviews with Dr. Noam Shudolsky, a school official, and Pritchard. Additional information about the surveillance was contained in trial testimony by Beaudoin and follow-up interviews with him. Former FBI supervisors James Kallstrom and Pritchard supplied information about the attempts to plant bugs in the town house and in Dominick Canterino's car.

CHAPTER 48: THE REAL BOSS

Remarks made by various Mafia members regarding Gigante's position as Genovese boss before he was formally identified as a godfather by law-enforcement authorities were obtained from transcripts of bugged conversations and telephone taps. The conversations were used as evidence at the Commission trial and trials involving John Gotti and other Gambino and Genovese members. Additional information about Gigante's role came from FBI debriefing reports of defectors Alphonse D'Arco, Salvatore Gravano, and Anthony Casso. D'Arco and Gravano also testified about Gigante's activities at court hearings regarding his mental competency. The most comprehensive picture of Gigante's early years as boss were described by another defector, Vincent Cafaro, in debriefings and statements given to the FBI. Cafaro's statements are the principal source of Gigante's payments to get a sentence reduction for his brother Mario. Gigante's warnings about using his name in conversations is based on testimony and FBI debriefings of defectors, including Cafaro, Casso, D'Arco, and Gravano. Details about the Commission meeting attended by Gigante and Gotti were obtained from trial testimony by Gravano; statements by Casso to prosecutors and the FBI; and a telephone interview with Casso. Agent Bruce Mouw provided further insight about Gotti's relationship with Gigante. Information about Gigante's psychiatric treatment was contained in medical records at court hearings on his mental competency. Dominick Cirillo's background was obtained from NYPD and FBI intelligence files; New York State Boxing Commission records; and interviews with FBI agents, particularly Pritchard. Robert Buccino, a New Jersey law-enforcement official, provided details on tactics used by Gigante and the Genovese family members to avoid detection.

CHAPTER 49: CHIN'S MILLIONS

Vincent Cafaro's statements about the Genovese Family's profiteering from labor racketeering was made before a Senate investigation committee in 1988. Details about Joseph Socks Lanza's control of the Fulton Fish Market from the 1930s to the 1950s are based on accounts in *The New York Times* and NYPD intelligence files. Facts about operations at the market were obtained from personal reporting and interviews in the 1980s and 1990s with market merchants, employees, and suppliers. Data about Mob influence in the 1980s and earlier at the market was provided from testimony at a civil RICO suit brought by the Justice Department and reports issued by Frank Wohl, a court-appointed administrator of the market in the late 1980s and early 1990s. Additional information about Mafia influence at the market was obtained through interviews with Wohl; his chief investigator, Bryan Carroll; Randy Mastro, a former federal prosecutor and Mayor Giuliani's Chief of Staff; and market wholesalers and employees who asked for anonymity. Another valuable source about market conditions was testimony about assaults and harassment of suppliers and merchants at a 1992 hearing by a New York City Council committee. Material about the Genovese Family's sway at the Javits Convention Center was based on affidavits and allegations made in a 1990 civil RICO suit brought by the Justice Department against the District Council of New York City and Vicinity of the United Brotherhood of Carpenters and Joiners. Vital data about Genovese influence was supplied in reports issued by Kenneth Conboy, a former U.S. District Court Judge, who in the early 1990s was a court-appointed investigator of the carpenters' union. Conboy and his chief assistant, Geoffrey S. Berman, provided additional details in interviews of the Genovese family's power at the center. Interviews with officials of companies using the center provided facts about conditions there and widespread thefts reported to the NYPD. Data about the Genovese and Gambino families' control of New York City's private garbage-carting industry was based mainly on testimony against sixteen accused mobsters and associates convicted by the Manhattan District Attorney's office in 1997 on charges of participating in a cartel and racketeering. Additional information was obtained in interviews with Manhattan DA Robert Morgenthau and the two main prosecutors in the case, Daniel Castleman and Patrick Dugan. Details about abuses and overcharges were provided in interviews with Mark Green, the city's former Consumer Affairs Commissioner and Public Advocate; Randy Mastro; Philip Angel of Browning-Ferris Industries; and numerous customers of carting companies. Intelligence information about the Genovese family's influence on the New Jersey waterfront was obtained principally in interviews with Robert Buccino, and with other officials in the state's Attorney General's office; and testimony and evidence used in federal racketeering indictments and trials of Vincent Gigante, his son Andrew, and other defendants in the late 1990s and early 2000s

CHAPTER 50: "I KNOW WHERE BODIES ARE BURIED"

The circumstances of Bobby Farenga's arrest and the discovery of the bodies of two gangland victims were obtained mainly from interviews with FBI Agent Lewis Schiliro and prosecutor Gregory O'Connell; and FBI reports on debriefings of Farenga. Peter Savino's personal history, his business and union involvement, and his dealings with Gigante and other mobsters were compiled from these sources: Savino's testimony at court hearings and a trial involving Gigante; FBI reports on his debriefings; interviews with O'Connell and FBI agents, particularly Richard Rudolph.

CHAPTER 51: BROUGHT TO BAY

Gigante's nocturnal practices are based on testimony by Savino, and testimony by and interviews about surveillance with FBI Agents Beaudoin and Pritchard. Background information about Savino was obtained from his testimony at a hearing and a trial, with additional materials provided by Richard Rudolph and Gregory O'Connell. Rudolph and O'Connell were the principal sources on Savino's agreement to work undercover, the methods used to protect him from being discovered, and the techniques he used to gather information. O'Connell and former U.S. Attorney Andrew Maloney provided details on their jurisdictional encounter with Rudolph Giuliani, regarding the use of Bobby Farenga as a witness. Savino's secretly recorded conversations with mobsters were used as evidence, mainly in the "Windows Case" trial. Testimony and FBI debriefing reports concerning Gravano, D'Arco, and Casso were the basis for mafiosi suspicions that Savino was an informer. Rudolph in an interview described the reasons for ending Savino's undercover operation; and other agents and prosecutors were sources for the threats made to Savino's wife. The circumstances of Gigante's arrest were obtained from testimony by FBI agents at Gigante's pretrial hearings. Gigante's demeanor at his trial was based on personal observations and reporting by Joseph Fried, a *New York Times* reporter.

CHAPTER 52: CHIN'S LAST HURRAH

Gigante's attempts to supervise the Genovese family from prison are based on allegations in his second indictment in 2002, and court motions and applications and statements by prosecutors. The diagnoses of his mental condition by psychiatrists were included in court documents concerning his indictment and plea. The roles of cooperating witnesses George Barone and Michael D'Urso, and "Big Frankie," an undercover detective, were obtained from indictments, court testimony, motions, and statements by prosecutors in Gigante's case and in trials of other accused mobsters. The size and influence of the Genovese family was based on trial testimony and debriefings of family defectors and interviews with FBI agents and prosecutors. Gigante's behavior and comments in prison were obtained from court documents and video and audio tapings in prison.

CHAPTER 53: NOTHING MAGICAL: FORENSIC ACCOUNTING

Jack Stubing's background and work habits were compiled from interviews with him and FBI agents. The bureau's downgrading of the Bonanno family was based on interviews in the 1980s and 1990s with numerous FBI officials and agents.

CHAPTER 54: "YOU DID A GOOD JOB, LOUIE"

Joseph Massino's personal and criminal history and his dealings with law-enforcement personnel was obtained from the following sources: arrest and court records; an interview with his brother John; interviews with defense lawyers who asked for anonymity because of lawyer-client relationships; and interviews with former and current FBI agents, including Patrick Colgan, Pat Marshall, George Hanna, Jack Stubing, Lynn DeVecchio, Stephen Morrill, Jeffrey Sallet, and Kimberly McCaffrey; and interviews with former federal prosecutor Laura Brevetti. Valuable information about Massino's style, activities, and policies was obtained from trial testimony by co-operative Mafia defectors, particularly Salvatore Vitale. Details of the three capos' murders and the aftermath were compiled from trial testimony by cooperative government witnesses, especially Vitale, Frank Lino, Duane Leisenheimer, and James Tartaglione. Additional information about the murders was contained in court documents filed by federal prosecutors and in their statements at hearings.

CHAPTER 55: "GOOD-LOOKING SAL"

Frank Lino's alignment with Massino's faction was described by him in FBI debriefings and trial testimony, with additional information from testimony by Frank Coppa. Accounts of the search for Bruno Indelicato came primarily from Lino's trial testimony. Details of Massino's trip to Atlantic City and his dispute with Sonny Black Napolitano were obtained from Salvatore Vitale's testimony and FBI debriefings of Vitale. Napolitano's activities before his murder were based on interviews with former FBI agents Joseph Pistone and Douglas Fencl. The description of Napolitano's murder was compiled mainly from trial testimony of Vitale, Lino, and Coppa. Additional details came from FBI debriefings of the three defectors and the autopsy report. Lino's background was compiled from NYPD and FBI intelligence reports and his testimony. Information about the attempt on Benjamin Ruggiero's life was provided by former agents Marshall and Fencl. Details of Tony Mirra's murder were disclosed in trial testimony by Joseph D'Amico and Richard Cantarella, and an autopsy report. Vitale's background and criminal career was obtained from his trial testimony, NYPD and FBI intelligence files, and interviews with numerous agents. Information about Massino's club in Maspeth was compiled from testimony by Vitale and other cooperative government witness and from interviews with former agents Marshall and Colgan. The unsuccessful attempt to bug the J & S Club was obtained from interviews with Colgan, former agents Kallstrom and Pritchard, and testimony from Vitale and Leisenheimer.

CHAPTER 56: THE MOB'S HORATIO ALGER

The leaking of information to Joe Massino about a pending indictment in 1982 and his reason for fleeing was based on testimony by Vitale and his FBI debriefings. Leisenheimer's background and his relationship with Massino were obtained from Leisenheimer's testimony, interviews with FBI agents who debriefed him, and testimony by Vitale. Massino's flight to the Hamptons and the Poconos, and his experiences and comments while hiding out, were obtained principally from testimony by Vitale, Leisenheimer, and Lino. Details of Cesare Bonventre's murder came from testimony by Vitale and Leisenheimer, and FBI reports. Vitale's Mafia induction was described in his testimony. Facts about the FBI's search for Massino were obtained in interviews with Agent Marshall. Massino's shoplifting incident in the Poconos was contained in a statement by prosecutors after his 2003 arrest. The accounts of

Massino's trysts while hiding out in the Poconos were based on the woman's 1985 grand jury testimony, disclosed at Massino's 2004 trial, and Leisenheimer's testimony. Details of Massino's surrender in 1984 and the arrest incident with John Carneglia were obtained in interviews with Marshall and from Vitale's testimony. Massino's gambling debt in Atlantic City was cited by the New Jersey Division of Gaming Enforcement. Massino's appearances at the wedding of Victoria Gotti and the wake and funeral of Aniello Dellacroce were based on FBI and NYPD surveillance reports. Massino's complaints about his 1985 indictment for labor racketeering were included in testimony by James Tartaglione and Vitale. Massino's demeanor and his assistance to Philip Rastelli at the 1986 trial were obtained from interviews with the lead prosecutor, Laura Brevetti, his lawyer, Ronald Fischetti, and Agent Pistone. The reported attempt on the lives of Brevetti and Judge Nickerson were confirmed in interviews with Brevetti and Edward McDonald, former head of the Justice Department's Organized Crime Strike Force in Brooklyn. Details of Massino and Vitale's RICO 1987 trial in Manhattan were derived from court records; the reporting of Arnold Lubasch in *The New York Times*; and interviews with Pistone and Bruce Cutler. The circumstances of the attempted murder of Anthony Giliberti were based on his testimony at Massino's 2004 trial and NYPD records. Vitale's testimony was the main source for the account of Gabriel Infanti's murder. The disappearance of Rastelli's wife was obtained from NYPD records and interviews with former FBI agents and NYPD detectives. Vitale's testimony was the source for Rastelli's lack of interest in Bonanno affairs after his 1986 conviction. Massino's views and advice about running the family while he was in prison were based on Vitale's testimony and his admissions in FBI debriefings, and interviews with FBI agents.

CHAPTER 57: THE GENIAL GODFATHER AKA "THE EAR"

Details of Joe Massino's formal election as the Bonanno boss were based primarily on testimony at his 2004 trial by Vitale, and on FBI debriefings of Vitale. Massino's tactics and policies as boss were described at his 2004 trial by Vitale, Frank Lino, and James Tartaglione. The FBI's electronic eavesdropping at the Grand Avenue Social Club was outlined in testimony by Agent Stephen Silvern at Massino's 2004 trial. Additional information about the surveillance of the club was obtained in interviews with Agents William Vanderland, Pat Marshall, and Jack Stubing. Massino's directive to mafiosi about never mentioning his name was cited in testimony by Vitale, Lino, and Frank Coppa. References to Massino's nickname, "the Ear" were contained in intelligence reports compiled by the Brooklyn District Attorney's office. Vitale, Lino, and Coppa testified in 2004 about the reasons that Massino changed the name of the family from Bonanno to Massino. Federal prosecutors also referred to the name change in their 2003 application for a court order to detain Massino without bail pending his trial. Lynn DeVecchio, former head of the FBI's Bonanno Squad, and Stubing in interviews described their meeting in 1993 with Massino after his release from prison, and their thoughts afterward about his behavior. Massino and Vitale's connections to King Caterers and payments to the company were based on Vitale's testimony and records of the payments introduced as evidence by the prosecution at Massino's 2004 trial. The real estate holdings of Massino and his wife are based on public and income-tax records, cited at the trial. The operations of a loan-shark "bank" by Massino and Vitale were described in testimony at the trial by Vitale, Lino, Coppa, and Tartaglione. Additional evidence came from Vitale's "shy book," listing the amounts of loans to clients, which was used as evidence at the trial. Vitale described in his testimony the operations of Massino's sports-gambling methods. Details of Joker Poker video machines and the illegal profits were based on testimony by Vitale, Lino, and Agent Vanderland. Tribute payments to Massino were contained in testimony by Vitale, Lino, Coppa, and Richard Cantarella. Data on the strength of the Bonanno family under Massino was obtained from testimony by Vitale and Coppa and interviews with Agent Stubing. Vitale's testimony was the source for the Commission meeting called by Massino, its agenda, and Massino's suspicions about the improper induction of members in other families. Massino's dining habits and his relationship to the Casa Blanca restaurant were obtained from testimony by Vitale and Cantarella; interviews with waiters at the restaurant; and personal observations of the restaurant's food and decor. The strategy behind the FBI's forensic accounting investigation was described in interviews by Stubing and Agents Jeffrey Sallet, Kimberly McCaffrey, and George Hanna. The account of Anthony Spero's trial and conviction was based on court records, newspaper accounts, and an interview with James Walden, the lead federal prosecutor in the case. Details of Massino's overseas trips were obtained from detention memos and other court motions by federal prosecutors; testimony by Coppa; and from interviews with Agents Joseph Bonavolonta and Gregory Massa. Bonavolonta and Massa were the main sources for the description of Anthony Graziano's trophy room and their search and seizure of money found on Graziano. Vitale's testimony provided additional details about the FBI's search of Graziano. The description of Gerlando Sciascia's murder and the motive were based on testimony by Vitale, Coppa, and Cantarella; the grand jury indictment of Massino for the murder; prosecutors' motions for pretrial detentions of Massino's two codefendants in the case; and the government's motion to admit evidence about the murder in Massino's 2004 trial. Sciascia's background was obtained from FBI intelligence reports. Massino's conversations concerning Sciascia's murder came from testimony by Vitale, Coppa, and Cantarella.

CHAPTER 58: MAFIA GROUPIES

The FBI's strategy to concentrate on Vitale and the gathering of evidence against him were obtained from indictment and court records and interviews with the case agents, Sallet and McCaffrey, the Bonanno Squad chief, Jack Stubing; and with Vitale's defense lawyer John Mitchell. Massino's rift with Vitale is based mainly on Vitale's testimony at Massino's 2004 trial, with additional materials obtained from Vitale's

FBI debriefings and testimony by Frank Coppa and Richard Cantarella at the 2004 trial. Anthony Graziano's convictions are based on indictments and court records. The Massino/Bonanno family's involvement in financial market crimes was obtained from indictments and court documents; testimony by Coppa and Lino; and interviews with Stubing, other FBI agents, and federal and state prosecutors in the Manhattan DA's office. Lino's history was based on his testimony at the 2004 trial; NYPD and FBI intelligence files; and newspaper accounts of his arrests and convictions. Details of Cantarella's criminal career came from his 2004 trial testimony; court statements by federal prosecutors; FBI and NYPD intelligence files; and testimony by Coppa and Joseph D'Amico. Details about the Manhattan D.A.'s investigation at the *New York Post* were obtained from indictments; other court documents; and pleas and contemporaneous and follow-up interviews with Manhattan D.A. Robert Morgenthau and prosecutors in the case, Daniel Castleman and Michael Cherkasky. Information about the murder of Robert Perrino came from the indictment of Cantarella; an application in 2002 by prosecutors for Cantarella's pretrial detention; and testimony in 2004 by Cantarella and Leisenheimer. Cantarella's involvement with Barry Weinberg and parking-lot deals is based on the pretrial detention memo; Cantarella's trial testimony; and interviews with FBI Agents Sallet and McCaffrey. Details about parking-lot profits were derived from personal reporting; interviews with parking-lot company executives and New York Department of Taxation and Finance officials; and testimony by Cantarella and Coppa. Weinberg's background was provided primarily from interviews with Sallet, McCaffrey and Ruth Nordenbrook, a federal prosecutor in several Bonanno cases. Augustino Scozzari's background and role in the investigation was obtained from Cantarella's pretrial detention memo and testimony; secretly recorded tapes used as evidence against Massino; interviews with Sallet, McCaffrey, and Nordenbrook, and merchants in Little Italy. Vitale and Cantarella testified about Massino and Vitale's financial interests in parking lots, and additional information came from tax documents concerning their partnerships and earnings which were used as evidence in the 2004 trial. Cantarella's relationship with Massino and his criminal wealth were based on Cantarella's testimony and a pretrial detention application by prosecutors.

CHAPTER 59: DIVIDE AND CONQUER

FBI Agents McCaffrey and Sallet, in interviews, were the main sources for the information about Massino and Vitale's tax documents, their earnings, and lottery winnings. McCaffrey testified about the financial matters at Massino's 2004 trial. Details of the investigations, arrests, and turning of Barry Weinberg and Augustino Scozzari into undercover witnesses were obtained in interviews with McCaffrey and Sallet. Cantarella testified in 2004 about his suspicions of Weinberg and his discussion about Weinberg with Massino. Cantarella's comments about Massino were recorded by Scozzari and cited in a pretrial application by federal prosecutors to detain Massino without bail. Descriptions of the search of Cantarella's house and his later arrest were provided by McCaffrey and Sallet in interviews. Additional details were obtained from Cantarella's testimony. Coppa and Cantarella's reasons for defecting were included in their testimonies at Massino's 2004 trial. Further information about their decisions was obtained in interviews with FBI agents. The video cameras outside Massino's home were personally observed, and confirmed in interviews with FBI agents. Descriptions of the arrests and processing of Massino and Vitale were obtained in interviews with McCaffrey, Sallet, and Agents Sean McElearney and Nora Conley. McCaffrey also testified at the 2004 trial about Massino's behavior and conversations.

CHAPTER 60: THE DOMINO SYNDROME

The description of Massino's appearance and composure during his pretrial hearings was based on personal observations and from interviews with defense lawyers who asked for anonymity. Vitale's comments to his lawyer, John Mitchell, refuting the prosecution's claims that Massino wanted to harm him, were obtained in interviews with Mitchell. At Massino's 2004 trial, Lino testified about Massino's jailhouse threats against Vitale. References by Bonanno family defendants to Vitale as "Fredo" was mentioned in an interview with a defense lawyer who asked for anonymity. Vitale's reasons for defecting and seeking a plea agreement were given in his testimony at the 2004 trial. Massino and Lino's reactions to Vitale's decision to help the prosecution were based on Lino's trial testimony and his debriefings by FBI agents. Lino and D'Amico gave their reasons for becoming cooperative witnesses in trial testimony. Tartaglione testified at the trial about his meeting with Massino in Florida; his decision to become a cooperative witness; and his undercover work. Additional information about his defection was obtained in interviews with Nordenbrook and Agents Bonavolonta and Massa. Details of Leisenheimer's becoming a cooperative witness were based on his trial testimony and interviews with Agents Sallet and McCaffrey. Attempts by lawyers to represent Massino was cited by attorneys who were interviewed. The account of David Breitbart's background and courtroom style was obtained in interviews with him, his wife, other lawyers, and prosecutors who tried cases against him, Federal District Court Judge Barbara Jones, and New York newspaper accounts of his cases. Greg Andres's background was based on his curriculum vitae and interviews with other prosecutors and lawyers. Details of the strategy, tactics and atmosphere at Massino's 2004 trial were obtained through personal reporting; transcripts of testimony; and interviews with Breitbart, his co-counsel Flora Edwards, Andres and other prosecutors, and lawyers who observed the trial. The apparent reasons for Massino's defection are based on interviews with FBI agents and lawyers familiar with the case who spoke on the condition of anonymity.

AFTERWORD: BACK TO THE CAVES

This chapter is based on personal reporting and analysis, court documents, and interviews with law-enforcement officials and experts whose opinions are cited.

Selected Bibliography

Abadinsky, Howard. *Organized Crime, Fifth Edition*. Chicago: Nelson-Hall, 1997.

Aleandra, Emelise. *Little Italy*. Mt. Pleasant, S. Carolina: Arcadia, 2002.

Anastasia, George. *Blood and Honor: Inside the Scarfo Mob—The Mafia's Most Violent Family*. New York: William Morrow, 1991.

Asbury, Herbert. *Gangs of New York*. New York: Knopf, 1928.

Barrett, Wayne. *Rudy*. New York: Basic Books, 2000.

Barzini, Luigi. *The Italians*. New York: Atheneum, 1965.

Blakey, G. Robert and Billings, Richard N. *The Plot to Kill the President*. New York: Times Books, 1981.

Blum, Howard. *Gangland: How the FBI Broke the Mob*. New York: Simon and Schuster, 1993.

Blumenthal, Ralph. *Last Days of the Sicilians: At War with the Mafia: The FBI Assault on the Pizza Connection*. New York: Times Books, 1988.

Bonanno, Joseph (with Sergio Lalli). *A Man of Honor: The Autobiography of Joseph Bonanno*. New York: Simon and Schuster, 1985.

Bonavolonta, Jules, and Duffy, Brian. *The Good Guys: How We Turned the FBI 'Round— and Finally Broke the Mob*. New York: Simon and Schuster, 1996.

Brashler, William. *The Don: The Life and Death of Sam Giancana*. New York: Harper & Row, 1977.

Brill, Steven. *The Teamsters*. New York: Simon and Schuster, 1978.

Capeci, Jerry, and Mustain, Gene. *Gotti: Rise and Fall*. New York: Onxy/Penguin, 1996.

Caro, Robert A. *The Power Broker: Robert Moses and the Fall of New York*. New York: Vintage Books, 1975.

Coffey, Joseph, and Schmetterer, Jerry. *The Coffey Files: One Cop's War Against the Mob*. New York: St. Martin's Press, 1991.

Cressey, Donald R. *Theft of a Nation*. New York: Harper & Row, 1969.

Cutler, Bruce (with Lionel R. Saporta). *Closing Argument*. New York: Crown, 2003.

Dannen, Fredric. *Hit Men: Power Brokers and Fast Money Inside the Music Business*. New York: Vintage Books, 1991.

Demaris, Ovid. *The Boardwalk Jungle*. New York: Bantam, 1986.

——. *The Last Mafiosi: The Treacherous World of Jimmy Fratianano*. New York: Bantam, 1981.

Downey, Patrick. *Gangster City: The History of the New York Underworld 1900–1938*. Fort Lee, NJ: Barricade, 2004.

English, T. J. *The Westies: Inside the Hell's Kitchen Irish Mob*. New York: G.P. Putnam's, 1990.

Exner, Judith Campbell (with Ovid Demaris). *My Story*. New York: Grove Press, 1977.

Falcone, Giovanni (with Marcelle Padovani. Translated by Edward Farrelly). *Men of Honour: The Truth about the Mafia*. London: Fourth Estate Ltd, 1992.

Farrell, Ronald A., and Case, Carole. *The Black Book and the Mob: The Untold Story of the Control of Nevada's Casinos*. Wisconsin: University of Wisconsin Press, 1995.

Feder, Sid, and Joesten, Joachim. *The Luciano Story*. New York: David McKay, 1954.

Fox, Stephen. *Blood and Power: Organized Crime in Twentieth-Century America*. New York: William Morrow and Co., 1989.

Franceschini, Remo. *A Matter of Honor: One Cop's Lifelong Pursuit of John Gotti and the Mob*. New York: Simon and Schuster, 1993.

Franzese, Michael, and Matera, Dary. *Quitting the Mob*. New York: Harper Paperbacks, 1992.

Fried, Albert: *The Rise and Fall of the Jewish Gangster in America*. New York: Holt, Reinhart and Winston, 1980.

Friedman, Robert I. *Red Mafiya: How the Russian Mob Has Invaded America*. Boston: Little Brown, 2000.

Gosh, Martin A., and Hammer, Richard. *The Last Testament of Lucky Luciano*. New York: Little Brown, 1974.

Guiliani, Rudolph (with Ken Kurson). *Leadership*. New York: Hyperion, 2000.

Hobsbawm, Eric J. *On History*. New York: New Press, 1997.

Hoffa, James R. (as told to Oscar Fraley). *Hoffa: The Real Story*. New York: Stein and Day, 1975.

Ianni, Francis A., and Reuss-Ianni, Elizabeth. *The Crime Society*. New York: New American Library, 1976.

Iannuzi, Joseph. *"Joe Dogs": The Life and Crimes of a Mobster*. New York: Simon and Schuster, 1993.

Jacobs, James B. (with Christoher Panarella and Jay Worthington). *Busting the Mob: United States v. Cosa Nostra*. New York: New York University Press, 1994.

——. *Gotham Unbound: How New York City was Liberated from the Grip of Organized Crime*. New York: New York University Press, 1999.

Katcher, Leo. *The Big Bankroll: The Life and Times of Arnold Rothstein*. New York: Harper and Brothers, 1959.

Katz, Leonard. *Uncle Frank: The Biography of Frank Costello*. New York: Drake Publications, 1973.

Kessner, Thomas. *Fiorello H. LaGuardia and the Making of Modern New York*. New York: Penguin Books, 1989.

Kleinknecht, William. *The New Ethnic Mobs: The Changing Face of Organized Crime in America*. New York: Free Press, 1996.

Koskoff, David E. *Joseph P. Kennedy: A Life and Times*. New York: Prentice-Hall, 1974.

Kurland, Michael. *A Gallery of Rogues: Portraits in True Crime*. New York: Prentice-Hall, 1994.

Kwitny, Jonathan. *Vicious Circles: The Mafia in the Marketplace*. New York: Norton, 1979.

Lacey, Robert. *Little Man: Meyer Lansky and the Gangster Life*. London: Century, 1991.

Lardner, James, and Reppetto, Thomas. *NYPD: A City and Its Police*. New York: Henry Holt, 2000.

Lehr, Dick, and O'Neill, Gerard. *Black Mass: The Irish Mob, the FBI, and a Devil's Deal*. New York: Public Affairs, 2000.

LeVien, Douglas, and Papa, Juliet. *The Mafia Handbook: Everything You Always Wanted to Know about the Mob but were Really Afraid to Ask*. New York: Penguin Books, 1993.

Lunde, Paul. *Organized Crime: An Inside Guide to the World's Most Successful Industry*. New York: DK, 2004.

Maas, Peter. *Underboss: Sammy the Bull Gravano's Story of Life in the Mafia*. New York: HarperCollins, 1997.

——. *The Valachi Papers*. New York: Pocket Books, 1986.

Mandelman, Stephen. *Comrade Criminal: Russia's New Mafiya*. New Haven: Yale University Press, 1995.

Martin, Raymond V. *Revolt in the Mafia*. New York: Duell, Sloan and Pearce, 1963.

McClellan, John L. *Crime Without Punishment*. New York: Duell, Sloan and Pearce, 1962.

Meskill, Paul. *Don Carlo: Boss of Bosses*. New York: Popular Library, 1973.

Messick, Hank. *Lansky*. New York: G.P. Putnam's Sons, 1971.

Moldea, Dan E. *The Hoffa Wars: Teamsters, Rebels, Politicians, and the Mob*. New York: Charter Books, 1978.

Mustain, Gene, and Capeci, Jerry. *Murder Machine: A True Story of Murder, Madness, and the Mafia*. New York: Dutton, 1992.

Nelli, Humbert S. *The Business of Crime: Italians and Syndicate Crime in the United States*. New York: Oxford University Press, 1976.

O'Brien, Joseph F., and Kurins, Andris. *Boss of Bosses: The Fall of the Godfather: The FBI and Paul Castellano*. New York: Simon and Schuster, 1991.

Peterson, Virgil. *The Mob: 200 Years of Organized Crime in New York*. Ottawa, IL: Green Hill Publishers, 1983.

Pileggi, Nicholas. *Wiseguy: Life in a Mafia Family*. New York: Simon and Schuster, 1985.

Pistone, Joseph P. (with Richard Woodley). *My Undercover Life in the Mafia*. New York: New American Library, 1987.

Prall, Robert H., and Mockridge, Norton: *This is Costello*. New York: Gold Medal, 1951.

Puzo, Mario. *The Godfather*. New York: G. P. Putnam's Sons, 1969.

Ragano, Frank, and Raab, Selwyn. *Mob Lawyer*. New York: Scribners, 1994.

Reid, Ed, and Demaris, Ovid: *The Green Felt Jungle*. New York: Cardinal Paperbacks, 1964.

———. *The Grim Reapers: The Anatomy of Organized Crime in America*. Chicago: Henry Regnery Co., 1969.

Remnick, David. *King of the World: Muhammad Ali and the Rise of an American Hero*. New York: Random House, 1998.

Repetto, Thomas A. *The Blue Parade*. New York: Free Press, 1978.

Robinson, Ray, and Anderson, Dave. *Sugar Ray: The Sugar Ray Robinson Story*. Reading, MA: Perseus Books, 1994.

Salerno, Ralph, and Tompkins, John S. *The Crime Confederation*. Garden City, NY: Doubleday, 1969.

Sann, Paul. *Kill the Dutchman: The Story of Dutch Schultz*. New York: Popular Library, 1971.

Schoenberg, Robert J. *Mr. Capone: The Real—and Complete—Story of Al Capone*. New York: William Morrow, 1992.

Seedman, Albert A., and Hellman, Peter. *Chief*. New York: Arthur Fields Books, 1974.

Smith, Dennis Mack: *Mussolini*. London: Granada, 1983.

Smith, Richard Norton. *Thomas E. Dewey and His Times*. New York: Simon and Schuster, 1982.

Sondern, Frederic Jr. *Brotherhood of Evil: The Mafia*. New York: Farrar, Straus and Cudahy, 1959.

Sterling, Claire: *Octopus: The Long Reach of the International Sicilian Mafia*. New York: W.W. Norton, 1990.

———. *Thieves' World: The Threat of the New Global Network of Organized Crime*. New York: Simon and Schuster, 1994.

Stier, Anderston, and Malone, LLC. *The Teamsters: Perception and Reality: An Investigative Study of Organized Crime Influence in the Union*. (Prepared for the International Brotherhood of Teamsters), 2002.

Stille, Alexander. *Excellent Cadavers: The Mafia and the Death of the First Italian Republic*. New York: Vintage Books, 1996.

Sullivan, William C. (with Bill Brown). *The Bureau: My Thirty Years in Hoover's F.B.I.* New York: W.W. Norton & Co, 1979.

Talese, Gay. *Honor Thy Father*. New York: World Publishing, 1971.

Turkus, Burton, and Feder, Sid. *Murder, Inc: The Story of the Syndicate*. New York: Farrar, Straus and Young, 1951.

———. *Murder, Inc.* Manor Books Inc., 1974.

Zuckerman, Michael J. *Vengeance is Mine: Jimmy "The Weasel" Fratianno Tells How He Brought the Kiss of Death to the Mafia*. New York: Macmillan, 1987.

Index